Each card in a Tarot spread presents a unique set of circumstances that enables the inquirer to stand aside and view their own psychological processes in a way few other methods allow. This use of the Tarot is brilliantly explored by Michael Owen in *The Maya Book of Life* which offers endless insights into the human psyche. As the painter of *The Xultun Tarot* and a Tarot author, I recommend it highly.

—**Peter Balin**
creator of *The Xultun Tarot,* author of *The Flight of Feathered Serpent*

A brilliant, eye-opening synthesis of post-Jungian tarot and the shamanic genius of the classic Mayan civilization. Michael Owen shows a remarkable command of this important and original material. His psychological sophistication and savvy interpretations of the archetypes illuminate a more universal cosmos for the emerging 21st century tarot. A fascinating and inspiring journey of natural wisdom, Jungian depth, and timeless spirituality.

—**Arthur Rosengarten**, PhD
psychologist, author of *Tarot and Psychology: Spectrums of Possibility*

This book is more than an impressive analysis of Peter Balin's artistic creation of the Mayan Tarot. It has warmth. It is to be in touch with Michael Owen's sensitivity to Nature and to his understanding of a world in which all living things are inwardly and outwardly connected.

—**Ian McCallum**, psychiatrist, Jungian Analyst
former rugby Springbok, bush guide, author of *Ecological Intelligence*

Out of the Xultun Tarot, Michael Owen has created both a memory device and a philosophical machine that twists together the threads of spiritual alchemy, Jungian psychology, indigenous medicine teachings and DNA coding. Owen shows that, in Peter Balin's single painting of the twenty-two Major Arcana of the Tarot, we have a multi-textured tapestry that depicts the Self from a shamanic perspective. This is a profound book of wisdom that will richly reward the reader who has an affinity for these teachings. It offers a fresh look at the tarot and its myths and symbols that can take your personal work with any tarot deck to a new level.

—**Mary K Greer**, author of *21 Ways to Read a Tarot Card*

The new edition of the Xultun Tarot is cause for celebration. The Xultun was the first "cultural" tarot, adapting the European images and structures to a very artistic and spiritual tradition. This has become standard but it was Peter Balin's deck that showed the way. It is fitting, therefore, that we now have Michael Owen's deep study, using the insights and wide-ranging knowledge of Jungian studies to open the deck up further and re-connect the Mayan images and teachings to traditional tarot, psychology, alchemy, and ancient wisdom teachings.

        — **Rachel Pollack**, author of *Tarot Wisdom*

In writing this book, Michael Owen has performed a dual service. First, he has brought the Xultun Tarot deck to the level of prominence it has deserved since first being revealed in 1976. Second, he has added a significant work to the corpus of Tarot literature. This book not only amplifies and illuminates the Xultun deck, but also provides a welcome reminder about how the Tarot enriches consciousness.

        — **Kenneth James**, PhD, Jungian Analyst

An inspirational book that uncovers not only an unknown part of New Zealand tarot history but reveals many mysteries about tarot itself. Together Peter Balin's original artistic genius and Michael Owen's depth analysis interweave many strands — Mayan mythology and culture meets European Western Mystery tradition; Jungian psychology blends with indigenous wisdom. The Maya Book of Life becomes a new World card in itself, where the past marries a multi-cultural present to dance the birth of our future.

    — **Fern Mercier**, tarot reader and educator, www.tarot.net.nz

I have been very excited and inspired by your impressive and sensitive integration of shamanism, alchemy and earth consciousness.

        — **Renee Ramsden**, Jungian Analyst

THE
MAYA BOOK OF LIFE

Understanding the Xultun Tarot

Michael Owen

KAHURANGI PRESS

Tauranga

Published in 2010 by
Kahurangi Press
RD 3, Tauranga
New Zealand 3173
www.xultun.com

Cover art by Peter Balin. Reprinted by kind permission.

National Library of New Zealand Cataloguing-in-Publication Data
Owen, Michael.
The Maya Book of Life : understanding the Xultun Tarot / Michael Owen.
Includes bibliographical references and index.
ISBN 978-0-473-11989-8
1. Divination. 2. Tarot. 3. Maya mythology.
I. Title.
133.32424—dc 22

Book design and typography by Michael Owen.
Printing History:
Version 1.0 March 2011
Version 1.1 December 2012 (minor edits, links to colour .pdfs in Appendix, references moved to end)

Also by Michael Owen
Jung and the Native American Moon Cycles, Nicolas-Hays, 2002
The 27 Club: Why Age 27 Is Important, Kahurangi Press, 2012

CONTENTS

Figures

Preface

I've waited almost thirty years for this book to show its face. I was first introduced to the Xultun Tarot in 1981. I didn't know much about tarot cards then and wasn't too interested in knowing more. Over the years (it's a long story, too long for here) I became increasingly drawn to the Xultun deck. It returned this attention by giving me glimpses of the wisdom it held and I began to realise that it was different from other tarot decks. Like all seeds, this one was small and hungry and so compressed as to be unrecognisable as the ancestor of what it would become. It bedded itself in a corner and waited for spring. It was a long wait.

Finally, it has shown its several faces. This book is an exploration, sort of an extended meditation, on the archetypes of the major arcana using the analytical psychology of C. G. Jung and indigenous medicine teachings. Indigenous knowledge is the extroverted, objective counterpart to the introverted subjectivity of analytical psychology. Both honour the worlds of matter and spirit and each supplies what the other lacks.

The book is also an outline of emotional and spiritual development throughout the lifespan. In other words, the journey of the soul. It compensates somewhat, I hope, for the current cognitive and behavioural fevers that make much of modern psychology unwell and render it incapable of depth perception. Finally, it is an exploration of the richness of pattern and meaning hidden within a unique tarot deck, the Xultun Tarot.

The major arcana tell us about our subjective inner life that has the rhythm of trees and seasons while the minor arcana tell us about our outer daily circumstances. Due to limitations of space I have omitted any discussion of the minor arcana and other matters related to the tarot such as divination, synchronicity, readings and layouts.

There are four levels of attention for a tarot reader. The first attention is learning the archetypal meanings of the cards and committing them to memory. At the second attention, the story, symbols and teachings held by each card can be used in the reading. At the third attention, the cards begin to breathe and the web of associations between them awakens. The reader can then start to weave a coherent narrative that relates to the querent's issues—spoken and unspoken. At the fourth attention, the cards begin to walk, talk and dance. The reader is able to speak the unknown as well as the unspoken and the unconscious. This book will help the reader develop the first and second attentions and some chapters will assist in developing the third attention. Further training and experience is necessary to develop the fourth attention.

What you are reading is the fruit of four Flowering Trees of creativity. The first is the work and inspiration of Peter Balin who created the Xultun Tarot in 1976. Generously giving of his creation, I am deeply indebted to him for allowing me to use the Xultun images and for his continuing interest in where this all leads.

The patterns in the cards would not have been visible without the medicine teachings of Harley SwiftDeer Reagan. The breath and body of these teachings have fed and sustained me for many years. I am enduringly grateful to SwiftDeer for making these shields of knowledge available to the collective. My thanks also go to him for his comments on the manuscript.

The third tall totara I acknowledge is the spirit and work of Carl Jung. As a teenager with a hungry mind, I remember watching John Freeman's interview with Jung on TV. I recall little of the content but it left a deep impression on me that was reawakened many years later. Jung's ability to bridge inner and outer, nature and spirit, remains unique and his wisdom adds psychological breadth and depth to the tarot.

The fourth tree is the Xultun Tarot itself. Over the years the cards have taught me that they have consciousness and intent. But, like morning dew on a spider's web, they only show themselves when the conditions are right. Even though I have taken from these three *ketes* or baskets of knowledge above, this book would not have come into being unless the cards had been willing to teach me. Much of the pattern, the weaving and the body of this book, although clothed with the inspiration of Balin's art, the beauty of SwiftDeer's medicine teachings, and the wisdom of Jung, was shown to me by the cards themselves as I wrote about them. The tarot is a way of remembering the world of spirit, of regaining spiritual memory. The cards would not let me finish until they had recapitulated themselves. So credit should go to the Book of Life, the double 11, the 22, the archetype of the tarot. It had its way with me, I was just the one with opposable thumbs, some words and a laptop.

I thank those friends, colleagues and teachers who have helped me (intentionally or otherwise) to find the solid ground within myself. To name but a few: I thank Daryl Sharp for his skill in staying out of my way so I could find a way. Thanks also go to my colleague from many years ago, Oriah House, for her dreaming. I remember with gratitude the conversations at the C. G. Jung Institute in Zurich. And I do not forget Martín Prechtel for the beauty of his speech and writing. He inspired me to find something I lost in high school out by the bicycle sheds between Mr Yates's English class and the Green Lane cross-country course, the one with the brambles. *Oxlajuj matioxiil* to him and to the Maya people and their ancestors who have not forgotten the old ways.

My warm thanks go to Sharon Parker and Teddy Rauhina for their friendship and to them and Therese McLachlan for their comments and discussions which were always vibrant and useful.

I thank Tania Jenkins, Marie-Claire Lionnet, Therese McLachlan and Sharon Parker for reading drafts of this book and to Curt Leeson and Monique Vajifdar for reading earlier versions.

In ways that go underneath the words and make me find the unspoken places, I say thirteen thankyous to Therese McLachlan for her dreaming and noticings and always-surprising gifts with the animals. I am deeply grateful for the blessing of your companionship (in the truest sense). May you "walk slow" all your days.

Finally, I thank Tui for his hysterical sense of humour when things occasionally got too serious. And I offer up a thousand thankyous to those who shall remain unnamed. You followed me from earlier than I ever knew and have showed yourselves in surprising ways. May we dream your Dream onwards.

Michael Owen
—Koh Libong, September 2010

1

Xultun

Concepts are coined and negotiable values; images are life.

—C. G. Jung

Tarot is a dream that stands still.

—Joanna Young

The Xultun Tarot was created by Peter Balin in 1976. It is also known as the Maya Tarot or the Maya Book of Life. It consists of twenty-two cards of the major arcana plus two cards representing the masculine and the feminine principles (Figure 109) and fifty-six cards of the minor arcana. I shall use the noun "Maya" to refer to the people and adjective "Mayan" to refer to the language, however "Mayan" is commonly used for both. The Maya "x" is pronounced "sh" so Xultun is pronounced "shool-tun."

Origins

Tarot cards first appeared in Renaissance Italy in the 14th century and were known as tarocchi cards. In the 17th and 18th century the tarot fell into disrepute but was revived by late 19th century esoteric movements such as the Order of the Golden Dawn. However, with this esotericism the cards and their interpretations tended to become more arcane as with, for example, the Rider-Waite or Crowley decks. The Hermetic Order of the Golden Dawn was a magical order active in Great Britain during the late 19th and early 20th centuries. Members included Algernon Blackwood, Aleister Crowley, Bram Stoker, Evelyn Underhill, A. E. Waite and W. B. Yeats. The Rider-Waite Tarot was painted by Pamela Colman Smith from the instructions of Arthur Edward Waite, a member of the Order of the Golden Dawn. In the early 1900s, he commissioned Smith to illustrate a set of cards for him. They were first published in 1909 by the Rider company. The Thoth Tarot was painted by Lady Frieda Harris between 1938 and 1943 according to instructions from Aleister Crowley. After Crowley's death, a follower published the work in 1969.

For want of a better term, I shall refer to the historical and modern tarot of this lineage as the "European" tarot. In the last twenty or thirty years there has been an explosion of New Age tarot decks. Unfortunately, most of these have little or no connection to the underlying archetypal structure of the tarot and are often a collection of pictures that only reflect the author's conscious intent.

However, early European decks such as the Marseilles Tarot give us a less clouded view of the tarot. Unlike many later tarot they are not burdened with self-conscious symbolism nor do they attempt to make the cards conform to a particular metaphysical or psychological theory. I shall take the Marseilles deck as representative of European and modern tarot in general and refer to its more familiar images alongside the images of the Xultun Tarot.[1]

So what is the tarot? The tarot is an aide-mémoire for the soul. It is an archetype in itself as well as a series of archetypal images that tell the story of the stages of spiritual and psychological development that are possible over a lifetime. It is the story of the flowering of the soul and how it participates in the great cycles of creation. It is a symbolic depiction of the soul's journey from spirit to substance and back to spirit, from heaven to earth and earth to heaven, and finding heaven on earth and earth in heaven. If we look at the major arcana in Figure 109 we see the Great Light at the top of the deck above the Fool and the Sorcerer. At the bottom of the deck we see the zigzag design symbolising the earth. All the human action happens in between and in the process both spirit and substance are changed.

The tarot embodies two principal archetypes. First, the archetype of the Self and how it manifests over a lifetime. Jung defined the Self as the organising centre of the psyche or the "God-image within." Shortly before his death, he said to the soldier and writer Sir Laurens van der Post, "I cannot define for human beings what God is, but what I can say is that my scientific work has proved the pattern of God exists in every human being. And that this pattern has at its disposal the greatest transforming energies of which life is capable."[2] Second, the archetype of number which Jung said was the archetype of order become conscious.

Although the tarot is generally thought to have originated in Europe we should bear in mind that when an archetype emerges from the collective unconscious it arises in different places and cultures and historical times. The form of the archetype may be different but the essence is the same. We see the same archetype that underlies the tarot in the Cabala with its 22 Sephiroth, alchemical manuscripts like the *Rosarium Philosophorum* with 20 woodcuts and *Splendor Solis* with 22 paintings, the biological structure of

DNA and the 20 or 22 amino acids, the Maya vigesimal system based on the number 20, and the teachings of the Twenty Count.

The practice of divination, the opening of discussions between the visible and non-visible worlds, is an archetype. All cultures have had divinatory tools: the cracks in the heated tortoise shell that became the I Ching; the bones of the Xhosa sangoma; the haruspication of entrails by the Roman augurer; or the seeds of the Maya daykeeper. Some indigenous medicine people in the Americas carried a medicine item similar to the Xultun Tarot in their medicine bundles. These "cards" were made of sandpaintings on thin wood and covered with animal glue and contained something from each of the Mineral, Plant, Animal and Human Worlds. It was known as the Book of Life or the Children's Fire.

The Maya say that in hard times what needs to be preserved has to be "driven into seeds." Seeds are small places where big things can hide and their spiritual DNA can be saved to feed a time beyond our own. The seed flowers when the conditions are right or when their beauty is most needed. I use the term beauty here not in its aesthetic sense but in its indigenous sense of what nourishes the soul and feeds the holy. The soul cannot live without beauty.

The tarot is a gift, not from any individual, culture, or time but from spirit or, in psychological terms, the collective unconscious. This book does not agree with the widely-held, Western-centric notion that the tarot belongs to one geographical place and one historical period, although the modern form did emerge in 14th and 15th century Italy. The tarot was not invented but emerged at different times and places in response to a need for balance and beauty. Not balance between humans but for humans to be able to hold the balance between nature and spirit within themselves. An oracle not only helps us see ourselves through spirit's eyes but also allows spirit to see itself through our eyes. Thus the tarot allows those two great opposites, spirit and nature, to come into balance through the intercession of humans, a theme we shall return to throughout the book. Rilke wrote:

Take your well-disciplined strengths
and stretch them between two
opposing poles. Because inside human beings
is where God learns.[3]

Although Western culture emerged from the last physical Ice Age over 10,000 years ago it has gradually succumbed to a spiritual Ice Age over the last 2,000 years. The tarot first appeared when Europe was being ground under the glacier of Christianity and had been almost completely severed from its indigenous and instinctual roots by 5,000 years of "progress" and "civilisation." When spirit and nature become estranged within a rationalist culture, as was the case in medieval Europe, the result is that divination and other non-rational pursuits have to live in the shadows. At the same time they become increasingly needed, not to foretell the future but to bring about a balance between spirit and nature, this world and the other world, head and heart.

Jung said, "The ideal of spirituality striving for the heights was doomed to clash with the materialistic earth-bound passion to conquer matter and master the world. This change became visible at the time of the 'Renaissance.'"[4] It was a time when scholars had returned to the only roots they could find that they thought were "civilised" enough and happened to be in the neighbourhood—classical Greek and Roman culture. Their desire was to be reborn into an age of light out of the ignorance and superstition of what they called the "Dark Ages."

The brilliant but highly specialised consciousness of the Renaissance later became the "Age of Enlightenment" of the 17th and 18th centuries. This philosophical and cultural movement, seen in the writings of John Locke, Rene Descartes and Thomas Hobbes, for example, had an abiding faith in the power of reason to engender progress and enlightenment. However, this enlightenment came at a price. What was of the earth, the feminine and nature fell into the collective shadow. Just as a dream compensates for the one-sidedness of personal consciousness so archetypes compensate for the one-sidedness of cultural consciousness. The tarot emerged from the collective unconscious during the Renaissance as a compensation for the historical excesses of what was to become "Western" culture.

Differences

The Xultun Tarot is similar to other tarot decks in that there are twenty-two major arcana and fifty-six minor arcana. However, it differs in several important ways.

The names and numbering of the Xultun cards differ from the European tarot. The equivalent names are shown in Figure 101. Rather than Roman numerals, the Xultun cards are numbered at the bottom of each card using the Maya notation where a "dot" is one and a "bar" is five.

The Xultun is the only tarot where the major arcana, when laid out, form a picture. This is not an artistic convenience but a reflection of the fact that the tarot is an interconnected whole with multiple cross-connections between the cards. Although the illustrations in this book show a two-dimensional picture, the Xultun Tarot is actually a spherical, 3D hologram. Each card resonates with all the other cards in specific patterns that we shall explore further in the Loom of Time chapter.

As well as a richly cross-connected web, the cards also form a linear sequence that tells the story of the transformation of the soul. Many interpretations of the tarot lean towards considering the cards individually in isolation from each other rather than as part of a coherent and connected developmental sequence. Because the European tarot do not emphasise the developmental sequence of the cards they have blurred the difference between the first and second halves of the deck. The cards in the first half, from the Priestess (2) to the Balance (11), have more to do with personal and collective processes whereas the cards in the second half of the deck, from the Hanged Man (12) to Planet Earth (21), are more concerned with impersonal, archetypal processes.

The Xultun Tarot was the first tarot not based on traditional images derived from the medieval European tarot or the Western occult tradition. The imagery and teachings of the Xultun Tarot are indigenous to the Americas so the cards are less encrusted with the layers of European tarot interpretation that have accrued over the centuries.

Finally, because of its imagery the Xultun Tarot reveals more clearly the archetypal pattern that underlies all tarot decks (see Chapter 8).

Beginnings

Peter Balin was born near New Plymouth, New Zealand. A self-taught artist, he travelled widely and by the mid-1970s was living in Los Angeles. In a talk he gave in 1977 he relates how, on the evening of December 21, 1975, some friends came to his house and one of them had a tarot deck. It was the first tarot deck he had ever seen and Balin thought it was sort of medieval and uninteresting. Later in the evening one of his friends suggested that he should draw a tarot deck but Balin thought it was a silly idea and said so. Right in the middle of his protestation:

> Something occurred which had never happened to me before in my life, and which is extremely difficult for me to explain. The only way that I can do so is to say that it approximated a colour slide going on in my brain. That is all of a sudden, I was telling her how crazy I thought she was, and the next minute... Voom! I should say about like that, it's very difficult to describe because it was not quite like that either. But this large thing appeared in my head it seemed, or somewhere inside of me, I just really don't quite know where.[5]

The image was of the twenty-two cards of the major arcana assembled to make one picture and all the figures were in Maya dress. The next morning Balin had a tremendous urge to paint. He took a sleeping bag to the art gallery where he worked and slept on the floor. He painted almost day and night for three months. Balin said, "Apparently I had a lot of the qualifications necessary to be able to make this deck. One of [which] was that I knew

Figure 1. Box lid, Xultun Tarot (first edition) 1976

nothing about the Tarot. Because if I did, obviously I would be tripped up by what I knew. There would be a great battle in my head.... Within a year of the time that the original cards were painted, they were printed and out on the market. Obviously something somewhere felt that it was very important to get these cards out."

The first edition of the Xultun Tarot was printed by the George Banta Printing Company in Menasha, Wisconsin in 1976. The cards were larger (136 x 89 mm, 5.5 by 3.5 ins) than most other tarot decks. During that year Balin had travelled to Mexico on a bus and ended up sitting next to Frank Waters, novelist and author of *Book of The Hopi* (1963) and *Mexico Mystique: The Coming Sixth World of Consciousness* (1975), for the six hours of the journey. After he returned to Los Angeles to finish painting the cards he received a postcard from Mexico. It was from Waters and had rounded corners and the single word "Hola!" (Hello! in Spanish) written on it. Balin realised that this postcard would be the ideal size and proportion for the Xultun cards.

The deck came as a boxed set with the major arcana of twenty-two cards, the minor arcana of fifty-six cards, two feathered serpent cards representing the feminine and the masculine, and a text insert briefly describing the cards and layouts. The box (Figure 1) was in brown with the Ruler in white and lettering in black. The back of the cards were also brown with two feathered serpents facing in opposite directions (Figure 2). Balin flew to Menasha to proof the cards prior to printing and ensure the colours were true to his original paintings. (The major arcana was one single painting and the minor arcana were painted in sets of four). But, having been preoccupied with the painting of the cards during the year, he had given little thought to the box. As a result, the design of box in Figure 1 was done at the last moment. Balin was dissatisfied with it and redesigned it in green with a gold feathered serpent winding around the box. He then hand-covered the re-

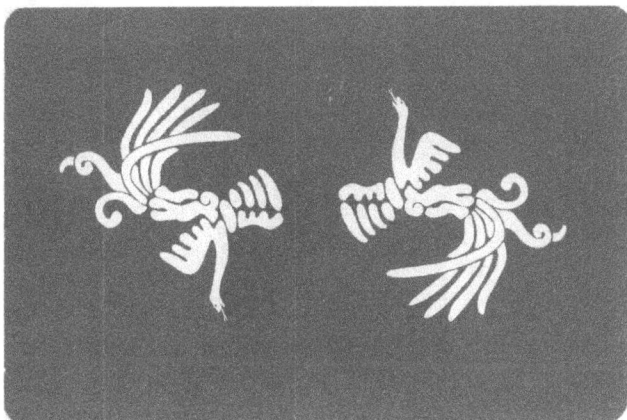

Figure 2. Card back, Xultun Tarot (first edition) 1976

maining brown boxes of the original print run with the new design. Subsequently, these decks were given *gratis* to the new publisher in Los Angeles, Wisdom Garden Books. The original cards in the brown box are now hard-to-find and a collector's item. No decks with the re-covered boxes have ever been found.

For the 2010 edition Kahurangi Press has recreated the cards in their original size and vivid colours. And, in cooperation with Peter Balin, the back of the cards has been redesigned in cinnabar red with a new feathered serpent design (Figure 3) as well as the box in green with a blue feathered serpent encircling it (Figure 4).

Historically, almost all tarot decks were named after their creator but Balin did not want the deck named after him. So he made a list of Maya place names and selected Xultun, the name of a Maya site near Tikal in north-eastern Guatemala. Tikal, occupied for about a thousand years but abandoned by the 9th century, was first discovered by Europeans in the mid-1800s. Xultun is a large Early Classic Maya site about 45 kilometres northeast of Tikal. The site contains a thirty-five metre tall pyramid, two ballcourts, twenty-four stelae and several plazas. It is the largest Classic Maya site that has not yet been fully investigated.

Xultun is a 12-square-mile site where tens of thousands once lived, Monument construction began in the first centuries BC and was inhabited until the late 800s AD when the Classic Maya culture collapsed. It was discovered by a *chiclero* (tree gum collector) in 1918. Between 1920–1923 the Carnegie Institution of Washington organised three visits to Xultun.[6] On the first visit Sylvanus Morley, the archaeologist, gave the site its name which can be translated as "end stone" or "closing stone" in reference to a late date (889 AD) found on one of the stelae. Until recently the site has been unexplored with the exception of the visits by Barbara Fash of the Peabody Museum in 1974–1975.

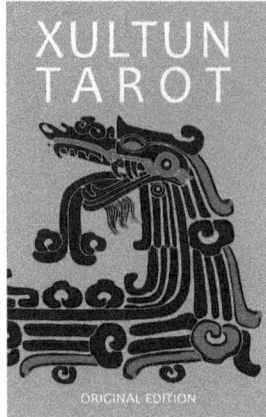

Figure 3. Box, Xultun Tarot (Kahurangi edition) 2010

Since the first printing of this book wall paintings were discovered at Xultun by William Saturno of Boston University and the findings were published in 2012.[7] The paintings, dated around the mid- to late 800s, were of a kind not seen anywhere else in the Maya world. Some appear to represent the various calendrical cycles charted by the Maya--the 260-day ceremonial calendar, the 365-day solar calendar, the 584-day cycle of the planet Venus and the 780-day cycle of Mars.

Sometime after painting the cards, Balin discovered that the word *xultun* also means "a storage place" where the Maya stored water or maize.[8] The limestone of the Yucatan peninsula is so porous that no water collects on the surface. The only sources of water are a few cenotes—deep, steep-walled sinkholes with water at the bottom. So the Maya had to dig bottle-shaped cisterns or xultun beneath the ground. These had broad, sloping surrounds, plastered with limestone, to funnel rainwater into the cistern. The bodies of human sacrifices were thrown into abandoned xultun and in shamanic healing ceremonies the conjured evil spirit was cast into a xultun. So the Xultun Tarot is a storage place, a container for the light and the dark, and a repository for seeds of knowledge.

Another use for the xultun was as a star-tube. The Maya created a sophisticated astronomical calendar for marking the progression of time. For them, time was alive and events were conducted on dates that were most charged with *ch'ulel* or life force. To make their calendrical calculations they observed the movement of the stars during the day as well as at night. The Maya priest sat at the bottom of a xultun looking up at the sky through its narrow neck. Here, even at midday, he could see the stars quite clearly overhead (Figure 5). In the early 1600s the Italian astronomer Galileo used a similar method for observing stars during daylight by sitting at the bottom of a deep well. So when we open the Xultun Tarot we are looking through the

Figure 4. Card back, Xultun Tarot (Kahurangi edition) 2010

star-tube of the tarot, in the daylight of consciousness, at our stars — the patterns of our soul's movement in time.

Many of the images in the cards are adapted from the Codex Nuttall which had just been re-published in 1975. This codex, known formally as the Codex Zouche-Nuttall, was made in the 14th century and is one of a small number of known pre-Hispanic codices. It is made of deer skin and comprises forty-seven leaves. The codex contains two narratives: one side of the document relates the history of important centres in the Mixtec region of the Oaxaca highlands, while the other, starting at the opposite end, records the genealogies, alliances and conquests of the Mixtec ruler, Eight Deer Jaguar-Claw who died in the early 12th century at the age of fifty-two. The codex probably reached Spain in the 16th century. It was first identified at the Dominican Monastery of San Marco, Florence, in 1854. Later, Sir Robert Curzon, 14th Baron Zouche of Haryngworth (1810–73), loaned it to the British Museum. After his death his family donated it to the Museum in 1917. The Peabody Museum of Archaeology and Ethnology first published it in 1902 with an introduction by Zelia Nuttall (1857–1933). Interestingly, ninety-nine images of the Codex Nuttall are painted on the exterior walls of the Edward R. Roybal Health Centre, Los Angeles.

Balin had lived for some months in a small Maya village with many ruins close by. He became familiar with how the local people dressed and the particular way they tied their sashes. He spent the summer of 1972 sketching images at Tikal. The first six figures in the cards (Fool, Sorcerer, Priestess, Consort, Ruler and Priest) are all drawn from wooden lintels in Temple III at Tikal as are the glyphs running across the base of the platform that the last three figures stand on. The glyphs between the second and third rows come from Stela 26 at Tikal. Additional designs are taken from Stelae 1 and 31.[9] A stela (Latin for standing stone) was an upright stone slab or pillar often carved with glyphs. Maya called them *tetun*, or "tree-stones."

Figure 5. Maya priest star-gazing in a xultun (Madrid Codex)

Indigenous

The English word indigenous comes from the Latin, *indigenus*, meaning born of a land or to a group of people who have ancestral connections to a geographical place. Worldwide, there are over 5,000 distinct indigenous cultures in over seventy countries. Generically, indigenous peoples are referred to as Aboriginal, Native, or First Nations. Maori are the indigenous people of New Zealand who came here in seven great *wakas* (ocean canoes) from Hawai'iki. All Maori can trace their ancestry (*whakapapa*) back to one of these wakas. In *te reo Maori* (the Maori language) the word maori means normal, natural or ordinary. Maori refer to themselves as *tangata whenua,* meaning People of the Land.

Up to about 1,000 years ago most of the world had an indigenous consciousness and lived an indigenous way of life. These were farming or hunting and gathering cultures which were self-supporting. They were non-urban, either settled in a region or nomadic, and community-oriented rather than individualistic. Now, indigenous peoples living a mostly traditional lifestyle comprise only about five percent of the earth's population. The European "discovery" of the Americas was the beginning of the colonisation and decimation of indigenous cultures world-wide. In colonial times, indigenous peoples were referred to as "savages," "primitive," "backward" or "uncivilised."

I will use the term indigenous to indicate not a race, people or culture but a particular consciousness or world-view. The characteristics of this worldview include the interrelatedness and livingness of all creation, a close relationship to the natural and the spirit world, and the attachment to a particular place, land or territory. I shall use the term "Western" to refer to the Judeo-Christian-Islamic economic, scientific and religious tradition that has lost its indigenosity and has now become globalised. The opposite of Western however is not Eastern but indigenous. Western culture has long had a fascination with Eastern cultures on account of their different "civilisations." Japan, China or India, for example. Japan and China were long closed to the West but India became the "jewel in the crown" of the British Empire because of its "advanced" culture. One could not imagine, say, Bushman or Aboriginal culture being held in the same regard by Queen Victoria. Both East and West are estranged from their indigenous roots however the East has retained more of a connection.

The creation of the Xultun Tarot and the recent resurgence of interest in tarot in general, is a similar compensation to that which occurred during the Renaissance. But this time the compensation is not just a local European affair. The spiritual DNA that is contained in the seeds of the European Tarot is needed for the planet itself. Beginning in the 1970s, around the same time as the creation of the Xultun, many indigenous elders around the world began to respond to the increasingly dangerous state of imbalance on the planet by sharing knowledge that had been previously kept hidden. In Aotearoa/New Zealand[10] the Waitaha elders say:

> We are Waitaha. Until now we have hidden our beginnings, and all that followed, in the shadows. In this way we protected our knowledge in the silence of the Whare Wananga, the School of Learning of Waitaha. Tuatara, the Keeper of the Knowledge, guards the trails of the mind and spirit that gave us life. We lead you past Tuatara, our ever vigilant kaitiaki [guardian], and invite you to share the words and the wisdom of our ancestors. For it has been decided it is time for our treasures to be brought in to the light.... We kept safe this knowledge of the Tides of Life that flow from Marama, the Moon. Our Star Walkers joined the stars to the land. These kete [baskets] are the treasures of the peoples of the Nation of Waitaha. We have kept them safe through sixty-seven generations, for they are the sacred songs of our ancestors. Now we share them with all born of these mountains, and all who call this land home, for you are of this land as we are of this land.[11]

The tuatara is a lizard-like reptile that is a "living fossil" found only on a few islands off the coast of New Zealand. The species is the sole survivor of an order that became extinct about 200 million years ago even before the dinosaurs disappeared. It has a highly developed third or pineal eye on top of the head.

Vusamazulu Credo Mutwa, a Zulu sangoma or shaman, says, "Ultimately I saw that the lore of my people was destined to die with those of us who knew it, and that it would then die forever. I felt I gradually recognised that by breaking my oath—something originally made to protect the sacred lore in times that were very different from these times—I was doing something for my own people, preserving the eternal wisdom that has been carried on for centuries; and also doing something for mankind as a whole. For there are people of many lands and many races who share in this wisdom and learn the wonder of these stories — they existed for the good of our people, but also now for all people."[12]

Lorraine Mafi Williams, an Aboriginal elder says, "In 1975 our elders prophesied a shift, and have been preparing our people for it... the ancient teachings are being revived by the elders around the Earth."[13]

Twisted Hairs

Beginning in the early 1970s, with the publication of Carlos Castaneda's books, a loosely-connected body of teachings which had previously been an oral tradition became accessible to the public. Since the mid-1970s they have been taught by Harley SwiftDeer Reagan and written about by various authors such as Teisha Abelar, Lynn Andrews, David Carson, Florinda Donner, Jamie Sams and Hyemeyohsts Storm.

The source of this knowledge was a teacher or teachers to whom the author apprenticed or a tradition or lineage from which the teachings came. For Andrews it was Agnes Whistling Elk and Ruby Morning Star from Saskatchewan, for Castaneda it was Don Juan and Don Genaro from Mexico, for Storm it was Estchimah and the Zero Chiefs, and for Reagan, who studied with Storm, it was the Navajo medicine man Tom Two Bears Wilson and the Twisted Hairs Medicine Council of Elders.

Traditionally, Twisted Hairs were medicine people, shamans and storytellers who travelled throughout the Americas (Turtle Island). What differentiates a Twisted Hair from a traditional medicine person is their ability and desire to seek knowledge from outside their tradition. These men and women gather knowledge from every direction of the wheel of life in order to find their own centre and come into alignment with the Creator. Hair symbolises knowledge and a Twisted Hair is one who braids knowledge from all traditions and ways into his or her Path with Heart and makes it their own knowledge. Their purpose, their dream, is to preserve the beauty and integrity of the web of life that has been dreamed by the consciousness of this planet. They hold the breath and the blood of this first dream, so that we can feed it, remember it and dream their dream onwards. The Xultun Tarot holds many of the Twisted Hairs teachings in symbolic form.

The name Xultun has Twisted Hairs associations. The site of Tikal near the border with Belize was settled as early as 800 BCE but the city itself was not founded until six centuries later. It grew to become the largest Maya city with a population of 90,000 people at its height but was abandoned around 900 CE. Tikal was the name used by the local Itzá Maya people and means "Place of Voices" or "City of Echoes."

Figure 6. Twisted hair name glyph of Tikal

But this is not the original name of the city. The name glyph of Tikal (Figure 6) was recently deciphered by epigrapher David Stuart as Mutul.[14] The glyph appears in the Sorcerer card (Figure 28). A name glyph was like a national flag or coat of arms for a Maya city-state. The central part of Tikal was called Yax Mutul which means "Great Green Bundle." The surrounding area over which Tikal ruled, which likely included Xultun, was referred to as Mutul which means "knot of hair," "hair bundle," or "hair twisted or coiled and tied into a bun."[15] The Temperate Man, the number 14 card, is one of the most important cards in the Xultun Tarot and he is a Twisted Hair. For those who remember The Band, listen to Robbie Robertson's *Twisted Hair*, on his *Music for the Native Americans*, Capitol, 1994, lyrics by David Carson.

Maya

The Maya are the predominant indigenous people of Central America. They live in Belize, the Yucatan of southern Mexico, the western areas of El Salvador and Honduras, and in Guatemala where they make up two-thirds of the population. The Maya are, in fact, many different peoples (for example, Quiche Maya, Tzjutzil Maya) and speak many different languages such as Yucatec, Cakchiquel, Chol and Chorti.

Archaeological evidence of the Maya goes back to 1500 BCE but the height of historical Maya culture was from 300 BCE to 900 CE, the so-called Classic period (Figure 7). Great ceremonial centres such as Palenque, Copan, Tikal, and Uaxactun were built without the use of the modern wheel or metal tools. Their temples, pyramids and platforms were built of a rubble core, bonded with cement and faced with limestone plaster painted in bright colours. Thatch-roofed temples stood at the top. The Maya did not build great cities like Teotihuacan in Mexico of the same period but their

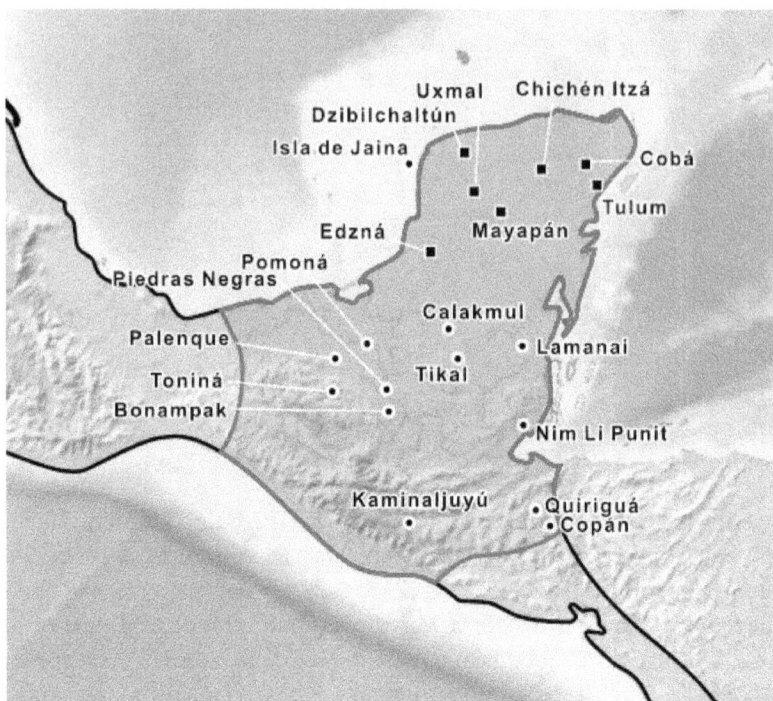

Figure 7. Historical Maya sites

temple sites included large plazas, courts for ball games, and stone carvings. The people lived in simple thatched dwellings near their temples.

At the height of the Classic period the temple cities may have had populations of 5,000 to as much as 100,000 in the case of Tikal and El Mirador. Each large city had one ruler (lord or *ahau*) who usually ruled over the city and the surrounding region for life. Upon his death, a son or brother took over. In some cases, the ruler's wife might be next in line. The accession of rulers, and each twenty years of their reign, were commemorated with stelae bearing their image and describing their lineage, and the events and achievements of their reign.

The Maya developed a very accurate calendar that arose out of their understanding of the numinous nature of time. They created a mathematical system based on the number 20 and were the first culture to develop the concept of the zero.[16] Maya calendars used a 20-day month and a 360-day year. They measured time in periods of 20 years, 400 years (20 x 20 years) or larger multiples up to millions of years. Using some of their temples as observatories, like the one at Chichen Itza, they tracked eclipses and the movements of Venus with great accuracy. The passages of Venus were used in the timing of battles and warfare. They also developed a hieroglyphic (Greek, *hieros*, sacred; *glyph*, carving) system of writing that has been decoded only in the last few decades.[17] The hieroglyphs were carved on stelae or written in folded books called codices.

The images in the Xultun Tarot show what the historical Maya wore. Cloth woven on a backstrap loom was used for loincloths as in the Temperate Man card. Women wore a *huipil*, a roomy dress worn over a long underskirt. In hot weather the women went bare-breasted in the underskirt as in the Lovers card. Hair was often tied in a scalp lock as in the Sage card. Ceremonial costumes were elaborate with jaguar skins, ornamental backracks, woven headbands, high-backed sandals, capes, and jade ornaments. The Consort has a headdress made of shell or jade plaques mounted on a wooden or mat frame with long feathers on the crown and a Jester God at the front. The animal headdresses often lacked a lower jaw thus making the wearer's face visible as in the Priest card. Ceremonial bundles containing sacred objects and double-headed serpent bars were carried by rulers, as in the Ruler card. Thrones were covered with jaguar skins as in the Warrior card.

About 900 CE the great Maya centres were abruptly abandoned, probably as a result of the worst drought for 7,000 years following centuries of warfare, overpopulation and deforestation.[18] Some Maya migrated into the Yucatan and during the Post-Classic period, from the 10th century to the arrival of the Spanish in the 16th century, the Yucatan cities of Uxmal, Mayapan and Chichen Itza flourished. A Toltec migration or invasion from the valley of Mexico to the north strongly influenced their art styles.

In 1519 Hernan Cortes with eleven ships, five hundred soldiers (or "Conquistadors" as they became known) and twenty horses, landed at Cozumel in the Yucatan. Within a few years they had conquered Central America and subjugated both the Maya and the Aztec. In 1549 Diego de Landa, a Spanish Franciscan friar, was sent to the Yucatan. In his zealous attempts to catholicise the Maya and eradicate all heathen practices de Landa set about destroying their religious artefacts and killed and tortured many of the Maya. He is the main reason that so few Maya codices exist today. On one occasion in July 1562 de Landa burned 5,000 idols and 27 codices at Mani in the Yucatan. He wrote, "We found a large number of these books and as they contained nothing in which there was not to be seen superstition and lies of the devil, we burned them all, which they regretted to an amazing degree and which caused them great affliction." The Maya response to the attempted Christianisation of their culture was to simply continue what they had been doing for centuries but clothing it differently. Over the centuries Catholicism has been seamlessly and colourfully assimilated into many Maya religious ceremonies.

For centuries after Spanish colonisation the Maya continued to be increasingly marginalised peasants in their own lands. In the 1980s over 150,000 Maya were killed by death squads from both sides of the Guatemalan civil war between the right-wing military government and left-wing guerrillas. In 1992 the Nobel peace prize was awarded to Rigoberta Menchu, a Maya rights activist from Guatemala. On the 500th anniversary of Christopher Columbus' "discovery" of the Americas, she was the first indigenous person to be awarded a Nobel prize. Since the signing of a peace accord in 1996 there has been a renaissance in Maya cultural identity.

2

Jung

Through scientific understanding, our world has become dehumanised. Man feels himself isolated in the cosmos. He is no longer involved in nature and has lost his emotional participation in natural events, which hitherto had a symbolic meaning for him. Thunder is no longer the voice of a god, nor is lightning his avenging missile. No river contains a spirit, no tree means a man's life, no snake is the embodiment of wisdom, and no mountain still harbours a great demon. Neither do things speak to him nor can he speak to things, like stones, springs, plants, and animals. He no longer has a bush-soul identifying him with a wild animal. His immediate communication with nature is gone forever, and the emotional energy it generated has sunk into the unconscious. This enormous loss is compensated by the symbols of our dreams. They bring up our original nature, its instincts and its peculiar thinking. Unfortunately, one would say, they express their contents in the language of nature, which is strange and incomprehensible to us.

—C. G. Jung

By the end of the 19th century extroverted European colonisation had spread around the globe and the scramble for colonies was almost over. The league table had Britain well in the lead (Canada, Australia, South Africa, India and New Zealand). Spain, a fading second (Central and South America, the Philippines). France, a disgruntled third (North and Saharan Africa, French Indo-China, Quebec and scattered islands such as Mauritius, Réunion, Martinique, Saint Pierre et Miquelon, and French Polynesia). These were followed by the colonial also-rans—Portugal (Brazil, Mozambique, Goa, Macao), the Netherlands (South Africa, Dutch East Indies, Dutch Antilles), Germany (South West Africa), Belgium (the Belgian Congo), and Italy (Abyssinia and Somalia). The USA colonised itself. It spread westwards bringing with it George Washington's "civilising" process for Native Americans to prepare them for "citizenship."

By 1900 a large portion of the globe had been occupied or controlled by non-indigenous people in a way never before seen in history. Queen Victoria ruled half the world and Western civilisation was secure in its belief in the superiority of scientific progress and rationalism. Indigenous cultures in the Americas, Australia and elsewhere had been annihilated. Even today the words genocide and holocaust are terms largely reserved for European or non-indigenous atrocities.

In 1900 Lord Kelvin famously stated, "There is nothing new to be discovered in physics now. All that remains is more and more precise measurement." Kelvin (1824–1907) was a Scottish mathematician and physicist and the leading scientist of his generation. He opined that X-rays were a hoax and heavier-than-air flying machines were an impossibility. In 1895 he headed the International Niagara Falls Commission and on visiting the falls he declaimed, "I look forward to the time when the whole water from Lake Erie will find its way to the lower level of Lake Ontario, through machinery.... I do not hope that our children's children will ever see the Niagara cataract."

Unfortunately for Kelvin's mechanical world-view and the comfort of the Victorian era, the Curies discovered X-rays in 1898, the Wright Brothers flew in 1903, Einstein published his paper on relativity in 1905, and the Great War began in 1914.

The intellectual inflation of the Age of Enlightenment fuelled the geographical expansion of colonialism. Consciousness was colonised by reason and as a result the irrational was railroaded out of town and forced to find accommodation in out-of-the-way places. One of the places it showed up was in Vienna in 1899 in Sigmund Freud's first book, *Interpretation of Dreams*. Freud (1856–1939) was an Austrian neurologist who was the founder of psychoanalysis. Carl Jung (1875–1961) was a Swiss psychiatrist who was a colleague of Freud's from 1904–1912 until they parted ways. Jung went on to develop what he called analytical psychology including concepts such as archetypes, the collective unconscious, shadow, and the Self, as well as writing extensively on alchemy.

Jung pointed out that the modern "discovery" of the unconscious was the culmination of thousands of years of estrangement from the world of spirit as it revealed itself in nature.[1] Because the collective unconscious is nature itself and the Xultun Tarot is a product of nature, Jung can be helpful to us in understanding the tarot.[2] I will outline some of his basic ideas that we shall use throughout this book.[3]

I shall also use the terms "unconscious" and "spirit" interchangeably. Although there are differences in meaning, with one used in the realm of psychology and the other in the realm of spirituality, I shall use them to refer to the "other world" that lies outside our conscious, collective experience. This world of spirit is invisible to the five senses (and so it does not show up on the rationalist radar) but can be experienced and interacted with. It has its own ways and means while remaining intensely interested in this phenomenal world. I shall also refer to the *nagual* which is the world of spirit, the unconscious or the fifth dimension, and the *tonal* which is the secular, physical world of matter or the third dimension. Time is the fourth dimension.

Ego

In everyday speech I refer to myself as "I" or "me." Our conscious awareness thinks that it knows all there is to know about itself and sees itself as a whole, undivided and obvious. But there is more to the personality than the common-or-garden "I." The total psyche is made up of many different parts of which the "I" we are aware of is only one. When the psyche is undeveloped, the person doesn't know about the whole personality and doesn't know they don't know. Accordingly, the individual is largely under the influence of the unconscious, though they will think they are in control and behaving "rationally." The unconscious is like the body in that it functions beneath the level of consciousness and goes about its business whether or not we know anything about its biochemistry, physiology or anatomy.[4] So I shall use the term ego (Latin for I) to refer to the everyday "I" we are familiar with which is but a part (but an important part nonetheless) of the whole psyche.

The ego arises in childhood when the demands and limits of the outer world collide with the desires and impulses of the inner world. If we develop a healthy ego then we have a sense of identity, we can tolerate a degree of stress without collapsing, we can tolerate painful and pleasurable feelings without losing ourselves, we know what is inside and what is outside, we can tolerate ambivalence and contradiction, and we can be separate and connected at the same time. The process of becoming conscious and developing an ego is the hero or heroine's journey that is told in many myths and legends.[5]

In the first part of life one develops a career, a social position and an ego that can function in the world. This inevitably leads to a psychological lopsidedness because we rely heavily on what Jung called the superior function, the one that works best for us. But our other functions are neglected, so the academic has no time for feeling, the artist cannot balance the books, and the property developer does not know he has an inner life. Rarely do we take the path of individuation (the process of developing the whole personality) willingly but have to be dragged, kicking and screaming. Often it is only crisis, illness, loss, or failure that forces us to realise that something about our attitude is not right, that we are out of balance. Later in life, we can let go of being in charge, acknowledge our dependence on the Self and develop our inferior function. If individuation proceeds then the ego slowly becomes relativised, meaning it realises it is not the centre of the personality and is only one part of the whole psyche. Gradually, the ego learns to behave itself.

Collective Unconscious

Like an island in the ocean, ego consciousness rests on the deeper levels of the psyche, the personal and collective unconscious. The personal unconscious is the uppermost layer. It contains all the mental events that we are not consciously aware of: feelings, thoughts, desires, fantasies, longings, forgotten memories, repressed traumas, and subliminal perceptions. The top of this first layer consists of those things that with effort or attention we can become aware of such as momentary sensory perceptions, or thoughts and fantasies that are normally pushed aside. At a deeper level, there are longings or memories that we have forgotten or unconsciously repressed.[6] At the bottom of this first layer, are our own unique potentials that have not yet (or may never) come into consciousness as well as those things that will never come to consciousness except under special or rare conditions. These are what Jung called "psychoid" processes, the unknown but experienceable connection between psyche and matter.[7] They are "the chthonic portion of the psyche... through which the psyche is attached to nature."[8]

In the warm Cretaceous seas millions of years ago, when tiny diatoms (single-celled organisms with a chalky shell) died they sank to the bottom. Over millions and millions of years, the layers became compressed into limestone. Like limestone, the collective unconscious is the accumulation and sedimentation of the collective intent, desires and longings (*dreaming*) and actions (*stalking*) of humans since always. It contains our spiritual and psychological heritage "born anew in the brain structure of every individual."[9] Jung distinguished the personal unconscious from the collective unconscious:

> The collective unconscious is a part of the psyche which can be negatively distinguished from a personal unconscious by the fact that it does not, like the latter, owe its existence to personal experiences and consequently is not a personal acquisition. While the personal unconscious is made up eventually of contents which have at one time been conscious but which have disappeared from consciousness through having been forgotten or repressed, the contents of the collective unconscious have never been in consciousness, and therefore have never been individually acquired, but owe their existence exclusively to heredity. Whereas the personal unconscious consists for the most part of complexes, the content of the collective unconscious is made up essentially of archetypes.[10]

We can become aware of the contents of our personal unconscious through some effort. The more we are conscious of ourselves the less we are at the mercy of our instincts, personal complexes and cultural pressures. We have true freedom and life goes better. The more we become aware of our personal unconscious, the more the collective unconscious reveals itself. This has the effect of enlarging the personality and freeing us to relate to the world in a truly objective way. But an awareness of the collective unconscious and its archetypes is much more difficult because it is impersonal and shared by all of humankind. It is much more distant from consciousness than the personal unconscious and so has a greater but less consciously recognised influence over our thoughts, feelings and behaviours. We are fish and don't know about water. To become aware of something means that we step outside of it to a degree. So to become conscious of the way one is affected by the archetypes means that we must sacrifice some of our shared identity with the mass of humanity. This, we shall see, is part of the journey of the tarot.

The collective unconscious of Humans in turn rests on even deeper layers of the dreaming and stalking of the other Children of Grandmother Earth: the Stone Peoples, the Plant Nations, and the Animals. And yes, they do dream. We are the product of a long physical and spiritual lineage. Evolution, in the Darwinian sense, is an expression of life's desire to individuate — to become what it dreams, to create and re-create itself in all its potentials in space and time. The Minerals are the dreaming of the elements, the first bacteria and algae are the dreaming of the Minerals. The Animals are the dreaming of the Plants. We are the dreaming of the Animals. Darwin was correct, life does evolve, but not only through the natural selection of chance mutations. The notion of matter itself having its own intelligence and desire to evolve was so unthinkable that science had to invoke the Goddess of Chance.

Indigenous consciousness is closer to the collective unconscious and when we draw close to the collective unconscious our indigenosity comes out of hiding. Indigenous peoples do not forget the ancestors that have dreamed them. What some anthropological literature condescendingly calls "ancestor worship," "nature worship" or "animism" is a continuing dialogue with those ancestors, human and non-human, who have gone before. These are All Our Relations in space and time. We are physically born from the bodies of our parents and spiritually born from the dreams of our ancestors. All our ancestors have dreamed a dream, light or dark. The sum total of all those wishes, hopes, plans, desires and visions our forebears have had is the reality that we are living now. Likewise, we have a dream that those who come seven generations after us will live out. The ancestors are drawn to the living because we are repairing what they have damaged, are completing what has been left incomplete, or are damaging what has been whole. We reflect their self-image and we are each an image in the dream of our ancestors. We are their dream in physical form and we dream their dream onward.

Archetypes

The particular forms and shapes within the collective unconscious are called archetypes. The word archetype comes from the Greek *arche-* meaning "first" or "original," and *typos* meaning "form" or "impression." So it is the original pattern from which copies are derived. Jung said, "An archetype is like an old watercourse along which the water of life has flowed for centuries, digging a deep channel for itself."[11]

Just as the laws of physics and chemistry order the material world so the archetypes are the psyche's natural laws. Like physical laws, they are impersonal and are not limited to any particular time, place, culture or race, any more than the law of gravity is. These archetypal patterns and deep structures of the psyche manifest themselves in images, symbols, dreams, mythology, fairytales, religions and repetitive patterns of behaviour. All humans are born with potentials for sexuality, love, spirituality, violence, work, compassion, or exploration, to name a few. In animals, we call these inner laws instincts.

Archetypal forces can remain dormant until cultural conditions allow, like dry river-beds that fill when it rains. The expression of the archetype changes with the culture but the drive behind it remains the same. The desire for sexual pleasure—insatiable, raunchy, tender or sanctified—was the same for the Scythian nomad as it is for the Chicago street kid. Falling in love was the same in the Shang dynasty three thousand years ago as it is in Argentina today. The Pitanjara mother who walked the Australian bush 40,000 years ago loved her child in the same way as does the Muslim mother living in south London. The warring of Maori *iwi* (tribes) with one another five hundred years ago was the same warring as the Serb-Croat conflicts in the Balkans. The urge to pray was the same for a Maya *ajk'ij* (priest) 1,500 years ago as it is for a modern Afrikaans *dominie* (pastor). Love, motherhood, war and spirit—all are archetypes and we are in their thrall.

An archetype is the spiritual equivalent, multiplied, of whatever collective culture is dominant in our material world. Just as you can't fight City Hall, an archetype cannot be experienced directly, it is too powerful. The closer we get to its power the more we lose our individuality and our humanness. Only if we are as equally organised within ourselves (that is, we have a functional connection with the Self) can we hope to keep our head above water when we are swamped by archetypal passions or beliefs.

There are as many archetypes as there are typical human situations — mother, father, lover, hero, wise man, paradise, the perilous journey, the helpful animal, or the crucified and resurrected god. When we experience an archetype it is altered by being perceived and it will take its colour and form from the individual or cultural consciousness in which it appears.[12] For example, the archetype of the sun is expressed by images of the lion, the king, the gold guarded by the dragon, or the power that gives life and health. Each card in the Xultun Tarot is an expression of an archetype not the archetype itself. But for convenience we shall refer to them as archetypes.

When we experience an archetype directly it produces what religions call a spiritual experience, and what Jung called a numinous experience of the archetype. This can lead to the ego identifying with the archetype and losing its identity. The person thinks that the experience is special and something that they have, rather than something that has them. This possession leads to either a positive inflation such as believing we are the next Messiah or we have the one and only secret to wealth, weight loss or enlightenment, or a negative inflation such as debasing ourselves as "a poor, miserable, hell-deserving sinner conceived in lust, delivered in evil and slave to every loathsome appetite the flesh is heir to."[13] Both are puffed-up. On the other hand, the ego may disidentify with the archetype and project it onto someone or something else that is then worshipped as the saviour or hated as the devil.

The ego must neither cut itself off from the blessings of the archetypal forces nor lose itself in their numinosity. It must try to develop a relationship with the archetype, a personal standpoint from which it can treaty with these impersonal powers. Then, Jung said, something unique happens — both the ego and archetype become transformed in a profound way. Human descriptions of gods and goddesses are an attempt to speak about these forces by personifying them, giving them names, and telling stories about them. The attributes of a god or goddess always describe archetypal forces such as birth and death, law and order, art, fertility, or the movement of the heavens. The monotheistic brother-religions of Judaism, Christianity and Islam have gathered up the archetypal functions of the many earlier gods into one God who is in charge of everything. Intense competition for top spot has been the result.

Jung called mythology the "textbook" of the archetypes. In myths the unconscious presents itself as a story not as a didactic lecture or infomercial. Myth and fairytale are the native languages of the psyche and no intellectual formulation comes close. The story of Cinderella, for example, is a household tale on every continent and takes different forms according to the culture. The name Cinderella means stars in the cinders.[14] The story is about the light of the soul almost extinguished in the darkness of matter, its exile because it has forgotten its divine origin, and its transformation from a sooty drudge to a radiant bride.[15] After descending into the material world, the soul journeys to find herself and regain her relationship to the divine world from which she came, so she may return with the knowledge of who she really is.

The tarot tells the same story. Cinderella's fairy godmother is actually Sophia, or divine wisdom, who guides the soul in her quest. In the Xultun Tarot, the Temperate Man is the card of divine wisdom. At the end of the Cinderella story, the masculine and feminine potentials of the soul unite in a sacred marriage. In the tarot this is the Bound Man and the more cosmic Planet Venus, the planet of love and bonding.

Persona

> The persona is a complicated system of relations between individual consciousness and society, fittingly enough a kind of mask, designed on the one hand to make a definite impression upon others, and, on the other, to conceal the true nature of the individual.[16]

The persona was the name given to the mask worn by actors in ancient Greece, with a hole at the mouth through which they spoke (Latin: *per*, through; *sonare*, to make sound or speak). It is the part of us that adapts to society by fulfilling its expectations about how to behave. The persona is what we think we are and what we would like others to think we are. Because it is adapted to the collective norms, the persona is the opposite of the shadow.

Its function is to act as a buffer between our internal world and the external world. It is a useful social skill to know when to hold one's tongue and when to speak plainly. It mediates between the ego and the outer world effecting a compromise between the demands of the culture and the needs of the ego. This allows us to adapt to society but at the expense of our individuality. The persona also acts as a buffer between the individual and the culture, protecting the individual from the collective's pathology and the collective from the individual's pathology. As the extroverted cards in the top row, the Ruler and the Consort represent the masculine and feminine aspects of the persona.

If the ego is not sufficiently developed, is too rigid, or is too fragile then the persona by default has to take its place. If we do not develop an adequate persona we remain socially inept, we are blind to our impact on others and how they perceive us. But this is less frequent a problem than when it is overdeveloped and we identify with our persona. Then we imagine that our social face is all we are or could be, our reactions are determined by collective expectations and "shoulds" and our personality has the depth of a coat of paint. And we tend to be reluctant to let go of our persona because it is, as Jung said, "rewarded in cash."[17]

Shadow

> If you imagine someone who is brave enough to withdraw all his projections, then you get an individual who is conscious of a pretty thick shadow. Such a man has saddled himself with new problems and conflicts. He has become a serious problem to himself, as he is now unable to say that *they* do this or that, *they* are wrong, and *they* must be fought against. He lives in the "House of the Gathering." Such a man knows that whatever is wrong in the world is in himself, and if he only learns to deal with his own shadow he has done something real for the world. He has succeeded in shouldering at least an infinitesimal part of the gigantic, unsolved social problems of our day.
>
> —C. G. Jung[18]

The shadow is the dark side of the personality, the parts of oneself that are unpleasant, shameful, or unacceptable to the ego. But the shadow is not what we consciously like or dislike about ourselves. It is what the ego is unconscious of and will fiercely disavow—"I'm not like that!" or "I could never, would never, do that!" It often appears in dreams as a same sex person behaving badly or behaving goodly—doing things we could not imagine ourselves doing in waking life. Confrontation with the personal shadow is painful but crucial for self-knowledge.

The shadow is compensatory to the persona (our social mask) and the more we identify with a bright persona, the darker becomes the shadow.[19] However, the reverse is also true—the more we identify with a dark persona, the lighter the shadow. Murderers dream of angels, angels dream of murderers. For example, a person with low self-esteem who is really a good person but cannot recognise it, or the criminal who does not live out his good side which remains as his shadow.

The persona, which aligns itself with the collective norm, influences the form and content of the personal shadow. In communal, indigenous cultures the shadow will show itself as individual deviancy but in individualistic, Western-style cultures there will be a tendency toward collective, group deviancy. Nick Hornby gives a vivid description of his experiences as a soccer hooligan:

> But those who mumble about the loss of identity football fans must endure miss the point: this loss of identity can be a paradoxically enriching process. Who wants to be stuck with who they are the whole time? I for one wanted time out from being a jug-eared, bespectacled, suburban

twerp once in a while; I loved being able to frighten the shoppers in Derby or Norwich... My opportunities for intimidating people had been limited hitherto, though I knew it wasn't *me* that made people hurry to the other side of the road, hauling their children after them; it was us, and I was a part of us, an organ in the hooligan body. The fact that I was an appendix — small, useless, hidden out of the way somewhere in the middle — didn't matter in the slightest.[20]

As awareness of the shadow grows, the ego is humbled by the realisation that what it thought was repulsive, alien, impossible or unachievable could be present so close by in the same psyche without its knowledge. If the conscious attitude is "goody two-shoes" then the ego may have difficulty acknowledging anything other than being sweet and mild. If the conscious attitude is staunch and tough, the ego may be terrified of any softer or more vulnerable feelings. We become humbled by the realisation that we are not as good (or as bad) as we thought. Compassion is born, not by striving for goodness, but from knowing our own darkness. "One does not become enlightened by imagining figures of light," Jung said, "but by making the darkness conscious. The latter procedure, however, is disagreeable, and therefore not popular."[21]

The initial skirmish with the shadow is often a stand-off, or a paralysis of doubt resulting from equally powerful but contradictory feelings.[22] The shadow is a moral problem in that it confronts the ego, which up to now has spent considerable time and energy in accommodating to the established norm, with all the impulses that conflict with the norm. What is needed is a degree of integration of the shadow, enduring it, and coming to terms with it. The ego must decide what it lives with and what it lives out, and the cost of those decisions to self and others. The integration of the shadow is the task of the first two rows of the Xultun Tarot from the Priestess (2) to the Balance (11).

Anima and Animus

Jung called the feminine and masculine archetypes in the psyche the *anima* and *animus*. The anima is a man's inner feminine and the animus is a woman's inner masculine. Cultural stereotypes and actual people that we come across in our development influence their form and content. The feminine quality of Eros represents relatedness, intimacy, love, harmony, integration, earthiness, and receptiveness. It values uniqueness and subjectivity rather than universality and collectiveness. The masculine quality of Logos represents word, deed, power, meaning, reason, judgement, discrimination, objectivity, structure, abstraction, clarity, universality and spirituality. Each complements the other and to achieve balance and wholeness each must develop its opposite. If one is ignored, then the other is strengthened in the unconscious. We tend to choose partners who provide a bridge to the deep, unknown aspects of our psyche, hence the other name for the anima or animus is the soul image.

Whereas the anima functions as an unconscious soul or eros, the animus is more like an unconscious mind or logos. It manifests negatively in fixed ideas, collective opinions and unexamined assumptions believed to be the obvious and absolute truth. Animus opinions, like anima feelings, are banal, collective and ride roughshod over individual judgements.[23] However, the animus can express not only conventional opinion, platitudes and truisms but also highly differentiated spiritual or philosophical ideas and insights.[24] The animus becomes a helpful figure when a woman can tell the difference between her animus' opinions and what she really thinks. When positive, the animus gives beliefs, inspiration and meaning, discrimination, reflection, assertion, and initiative. If the animus is underdeveloped, the woman is clingy, allows men to take over and will be whatever a man wants. A well-developed animus allows a woman to make up her own mind and decide what she really thinks about things. When negative, the animus produces shallow, handed-down opinions that are not her own, and makes her into an inferior man — bossy, abrasive, power-driven and overly intellectual.

When a man's anima is unconscious, his femininity is undeveloped and he is possessed by, rather than conscious of, the anima. It causes him to be irritable, moody and sentimental rather than in touch with his actual feelings. Projected, the anima causes passionate attraction and, if he is unconscious of her, relationships go less well. The anima of the scholar, for example, has a primitive romanticism; the anima of the sensitive artist is earthbound and realistic. When positive, the anima makes a man related to others, compassionate, and gentle. When negative, the anima makes a man into a stereotypical inferior woman — irrational, flighty, manipulative and overly emotional.

Just as the persona is the bridge between the ego and the outer world so the anima or animus is the bridge between the ego and the inner world. If the persona is over-valued then the inner life is neglected and will be activated in compensation. If the persona is powerful and intellectual, the anima will be weak and sentimental. If the persona is maternal and devoted, the animus will be cold and opinionated.[25] If the persona is over-adapted to the outer world and always scrubbed-up for public presentation, the anima or animus will contain all those fallible human qualities that the persona lacks.

Conscious identity with the persona leads to an unconscious identity with the anima or animus. Anyone who is captured by their outward role will fall victim to their inner processes. We see frequent shadow and anima "oopses" in politicians (from whom we demand a white-washed persona) and are then horrified when we see their shadow (financial or sexual indiscretions, for example). Politics is a prime hunting ground for the anima.

The anima is the deposit in the collective unconscious of all the experiences by the masculine of the feminine as a receptive, creative force.[26] Jung distinguished four stages of anima development. He personified them as Eve, Helen, Mary and Sophia. In the first stage, Eve, the anima is identical to the personal mother and, like Adam, the man cannot function in the world without a close tie to a woman. In the second stage, personified by Helen of Troy, the anima is a collective, ideal sexual image. The third stage, Mary, manifests in religious feelings and a capacity for lasting relationships. In the fourth stage, as Sophia, the anima functions as a guide to the inner life, mediating conscious and unconscious, cooperating in the search for meaning and functioning as the creative muse.[27]

The animus is the deposit in the collective unconscious of all the experiences by the feminine of the masculine as an active, conceptive force. As with the anima, Jung described four stages of development. The animus first appears in dreams or fantasy as the embodiment of physical power — an athlete or a thug. Then he appears as a man of action who provides initiative, independence and the capacity for planned achievement. In the third stage, the animus is the "word," often appearing in dreams as a priest or professor. In the fourth and highest stage the animus represents profound spiritual meaning which acts as a guide to the symbolic life. Jung said:

> Younger people... can bear even the total loss of the anima without injury. The important thing at this stage is for a man to be a man.... After the middle of life, however, permanent loss of the anima means a diminution of vitality, of flexibility, and of human kindness. The result, as a rule, is premature rigidity, crustiness, stereotypy, fanatical one-sidedness, obstinacy, pedantry, or else resignation, weariness, sloppiness, irresponsibility, and finally a childish ramollissement [petulance] with a tendency to alcohol.[28] Like the anima, the animus is a jealous lover. He is adept at putting, in place of the real man, an opinion about him, the exceedingly disputable grounds for which are never submitted to criticism. Animus opinions are invariably collective, and they override individuals and individual judgements in exactly the same way as the anima thrusts her emotional anticipations and projections between man and wife.[29]

The integration of the anima involves discovering her feelings about things, and integration of the animus comes by constantly questioning his ideas and opinions. These lead us to discover the primordial images that lie behind what humankind has always taken for granted. Then one can begin to know what one thinks or feels.

Soul and Spirit

The columns of the Xultun Tarot hold the medicine of the elements and the four directions. From left to right they are water/south, earth/west, air-/north and spirit/east. The fifth column of cards (Lovers, Balance, Released Man, Planet Earth) sits in the centre of the wheel and they are the catalyst or soul cards (Figures 105 and 108).

The distinction between soul and spirit is important. Soul is the divine force that inhabits matter. Air and fire are more closely associated with spirit and water and earth with soul. We live on a planet called Earth. It is not called Air, or Fire, or Water. The body we live in and the one we live on are both made of earth. The soul is what Robert Bly calls a "grateful guest of the earth." It loves physical existence. Spirit is the divine force that exists apart from matter. It, however, puts on the robe of matter with great reluctance and is the ungracious visitor who is always trying to leave.

Soul is feminine, receptive and creative. James Hillman said, "Soul sticks to the realm of experience and reflections within experience. It moves indirectly in circular reasonings, where retreats are important as advances, preferring labyrinths and corners, giving a metaphorical sense to life through such words as close, near, slow, and deep... Soul is vulnerable and suffers; it is passive and remembers." In contrast, spirit is masculine, active and conceptive. Its "images blaze with light, there is fire, wind, sperm. Spirit is fast, and it quickens what it touches. Its direction is vertical and ascending; it is arrow-straight, knife-sharp, powder-dry, and phallic."[30]

The consciousness of any culture has two polarities. At one end, there is the extroverted spirit which shuns the physical realm and adheres to universal, abstract ideas and principles. At the other end, there is the introverted soul where symbols attach to earthy localities and natural objects. As Rodney Ravenswood describes it: "If we use the analogy of a sailing boat to represent either a culture, or an individual, we might consider this spectrum as reaching from the height of sail to the depth of keel. Here the sail would be the element of spiritual values and the keel the connection to soul values as related to the earth and matter."[31]

A monotheistic spiritual orientation tends to devalue the material realm and holds certain beliefs about it. The world is the "vale of suffering" or the realm of the fallen. Humanity has become separated from God through its own bad behaviour and has fallen into matter from which it needs release or redemption. Heaven, not the earth, is our real home to which the best-behaved will eventually return. "The word" or books that are an expression of the deity's will are holy. Sexuality and women are a distraction for men, taking their minds away from God. There is minimal use of physical objects in religious life. For example: the Protestant rejection of icons, incense, rings and relics associated with Catholic "popery"; the simplicity of the Quakers; or the Islamic prohibition against images of Mohammed. Symbols are abstract and portable (a cross, the Bible, the Ten Commandments, the Noble Truths of the Buddha). Faith in the experience of an intermediary who is usually male (Christ, Mohammed, Buddha) takes precedence over direct personal experience of the divine. Finally, spiritualisation, purity and ascension are seen as the best way to deal with problems of the life and the body.

In contrast, the soul elevates the material world. The symbols are natural objects and phenomena such as the elements, the sun, moon and stars, and plants, animals and the land. These natural events are sacred, spirit is not abstract, above and removed, but material, below and immanent in earthly realities such as the weather, the behaviour of animals, the movements of the heavenly bodies, and the gifts of plants. The symbolic life of the soul is bound to natural objects, hills, trees, and permanent geographic features. Human life references itself, not to eternity, but to the moons, the seasons, animal migrations and vegetation changes.

This book takes the viewpoint of soul. Not because it is better but because, at this historical time, it is needed. From the viewpoint of spirit, location is irrelevant as long as one is connected to God, and when one is released from this mortal coil, there is joy and the promise of eternal paradise. However, from the viewpoint of soul, the land is everything and severance from one's connection to the land leads to deep grief and a loss of soul. This emigrant grief is the illness of Western culture.

Types

> When your daemon is in charge, do not try to think consciously. Drift, wait and obey.
>
> — Rudyard Kipling

Jung distinguished four ways of perceiving the world: thinking, feeling, sensation and intuition (Figure 8).[32] Each row in the Xultun Tarot represents one of these psychological functions (see Figure 9). They are how the elements of water, air, earth and fire manifest in the inner world.

Each function is experienced (if you are an introvert) or expressed (if you are an extrovert) through a different aspect of our humanness (emotional, physical, mental, spiritual, and soul/sexual). So each card in a row corresponds to a different aspect of the function. For example, in the first row the Priestess is emotional feeling, the Consort is physical feeling, the Ruler is mental feeling, the Priest is spiritual feeling, and the Lovers are soul feeling.

Sensation establishes what is actually present in the physical world, thinking tells us what it means or what its name is, feeling tells us its value to us, and intuition points to its possibilities as to where it came from and where it is going in the non-physical world.

A group was shown an ordinary cup and asked to write down the words that came to mind. The sensation types wrote down words which, when put together, helped you to know it was a cup (white, hard, glossy). The feeling types made judgements (beautiful, commonplace). The thinking types were more interested in the origins and form of the cup (porcelain from China). Finally, the intuitives ascended quickly to the symbolic levels of cupness (breast, womb, imagination, emptiness). No one would think they were referring to a plain cup but they had no problem connecting the dots. All of them described things having the capacity to be filled, to hold, and to give out.

Feeling and thinking are both rational, judging functions, that is, they sort and judge the raw, perceptual input received through sensation and intuition according to their own rational standards. Rational does not mean logical, it simply means an ordered system. The word rational comes from the Latin *ratus*, meaning "to calculate." Feeling judges from an individual, subjective point of view. Thinking judges from an objective, collective point of view. Thinking aims at definition, objectivity and a systematic approach. Thinking tells you what the object is, names it, categorises it, and is interested in cause and effect relationships. Feeling tells you how much or how little you like something and in what way. Feeling is personal and individual. It is one's particular "taste" or preference. Contrary to what thinking types would have us believe, a feeling is as indisputable a reality as an idea.[33]

Thinking types are skilled at being objective about thoughts. Feeling types are skilled at being objective about emotions. Because it is their superior function they don't get swallowed or overwhelmed by either beliefs or emotions. But when it comes to our opposite or inferior function, we get emotional, precious, touchy, tetchy and thin-skinned. Thinking types get all sensitive about their feelings, and feeling types get all sensitive about their ideas.

Feeling, in the way Jung used the term, is distinct from emotion or affect. When we are emotional we are hot, cold, distressed, upset or stirred up. Emotion is the alchemical fire that is the chief impetus to consciousness and its heat burns away everything that is superfluous. It gives us the energy to take action and make the changes. The forces that drives us toward self-discovery are hurt, excitement, disappointment, love, jealousy, grief and all the other powerful emotions. Jung said, "There is no change from darkness to light or from inertia to movement without emotion."[34]

Thinking

N

Sensation | W

E | Intuition

S

Feeling

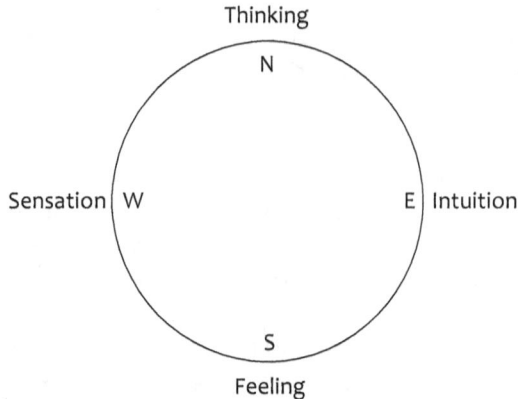

Figure 8. The Psychological Types

Feeling is the ability to stand back from emotions, to get their measure, and relate to them consciously. Feeling not contaminated by the fire of emotion can be quite cool, for example, aesthetic or artistic judgement.[35] In a less individuated person, whose soul is uncooked, feeling judgements are more likely to be emotional and to reflect uncritically the values of the person's religious, social or cultural group. Feeling is the inferior function of Western culture.

Sensation and intuition are irrational, perceiving functions. They tell you what exists, without ordering or judgement. Sensation tells you about the physical world, intuition about the non-physical world. Intuitions emerge instantly and full-blown into consciousness without any obvious connection to sensory data. On the other hand, the sensation-oriented consciousness of science advances painstakingly, observation by observation. A thinking or feeling type will tend to notice a person's conscious character and make a judgement, whereas a sensation or intuitive type will tend to notice the unconscious character without judgement, because perception notices the process itself rather than the conscious presentation.[36]

The psychological functions can either be turned outwards (extroverted) or turned inwards (introverted). The extrovert adjusts well to the environment, uses the outer world well, and his or her morality and behaviour coincides with the expected norm. Extroverts put aside their own needs in favour of others, they dread spending time alone, they like being part of a group and usually have many friends. An extroverted advertising executive once said, "Running a company without advertising is like winking at someone in the dark, you know what you are doing but no one else does." The introvert, on the other hand, might think (but wouldn't say), "He just doesn't get it... that's the whole point!"

PRIESTESS	CONSORT	RULER	PRIEST	LOVERS
Emotional Feeling	Physical Feeling	Mental Feeling	Spiritual Feeling	Soul Feeling

WARRIOR	CACTUS	SAGE	WHEELBALANCE	
Emotional Thinking	Physical Thinking	Mental Thinking	Spiritual Thinking	Soul Thinking

HANGED MAN	DEAD MAN	TEMPERATE MAN	BOUNDRELEASED MAN	MAN
Emotional Sensation	Physical Sensation	Mental Sensation	Spiritual SensationSensation	Soul

STAR	MOON	SUN	VENUS	EARTH
Emotional Intuition	Physical Intuition	Mental Intuition	Spiritual Intuition	Soul Intuition

Figure 9. The Psychological Types and the Xultun Tarot

The introvert concentrates on subjective factors and inner responses. Rather than pay attention to the object (person, situation or thing) the introvert notices how the object affects them. The introvert prefers his own thoughts to conversation with others, enjoys being alone, and is often socially gauche, either too blunt or too polite. The introvert tends to disregard the opinions of others, distrusting them, and is in a constant struggle to not succumb to the demands of the external world. The introvert finds the extrovert too superficial but admires their social ease. The extrovert finds the introvert odd but admires their independence of mind.

The unconscious of the extrovert is primitively introverted; the unconscious of the introvert is primitively extroverted. When the level of conscious control is relaxed (alcohol, stress, tiredness, holidays) then the shadow or inferior function will tend to emerge. When the party is winding down in the early hours, the introvert is the one just starting to get going, while the extrovert is sitting morosely in the corner crying in their beer.

Although we possess all four functions, one function (the dominant or superior function) is more highly developed than the others and more under conscious control. The first half of life is spent developing our dominant function but this inevitably leads to one-sidedness. The psyche will not tolerate too much imbalance and at mid-life will attempt to influence the conscious mind, if necessary through symptoms or impossible life situations, to change its one-sided attitude.

The inferior or least developed function sits directly across the wheel from the dominant function. The dominant function comes easily to us, it is socially well-adapted, we are good at it, it is second nature, and it is usually how we earn a living. The inferior function is clumsy and primitive, poorly adapted to the outside world, it is what we were never good at in school, it is where we trip up particularly in intimate relationships, and it is where we are touchy, sensitive, embarrassed and embarrassing.

In between the dominant and inferior functions are the auxiliary functions. One auxiliary function is relatively well-developed and works in concert with the dominant function and the other is relatively undeveloped like the inferior function. So, for example, one can be as Jung was, a thinking-intuitive type who had dominant thinking with good intuition, but whose feeling and sensation were least developed.

People with dominant sensation tend to be, for example, chefs, visual artists, interior decorators (auxiliary feeling) or applied, experimental scientists (dominat sensation with auxiliary thinking). In general, scientists have over-developed discrimination, scepticism and rationality. Their shadow is under-developed intuition and feeling—academic jealousies and competition, dark hunches about what may happen, terminal nerdiness, compulsions, magical superstitions, and a fear of (but a secret fascination with) the irrational.

Intuitive types are artists, visionaries, entrepreneurs and psychics. Tarot card readers are usually intuitives. Their shadow is the physical world (driving directions, the bank balance, organising the files) and the body (poor health, lack of physical coordination, or a dislike of sport and exercise).

Feeling types tend to become politicians, diplomats, mediators or entertainers. The shadow of feeling is undifferentiated thinking—collective, hackneyed opinions that are held with great fervour and belief combined with a stunning lack of curiosity about them. Emile Chartier said, "Nothing is more dangerous than an idea when it's the only one you have." One might equally say, with a thinking type, that nothing is more dangerous than an emotion when it's the only one you have.

Thinking types are academics, philosophers, or theoretical scientists. The thinking function names, categorises and differentiates this from that. It makes conceptual distinctions. Whenever someone says, "What exactly to do you mean by…" or "First, we need to define our terms…" they are likely a thinking type (or at least using their thinking function). The shadow of thinking types is their feeling function. They may be awkward, clumsy and reluctant in their expression of feelings and sentiment, they may seem distant in relationships, often forget birthdays and anniversaries, and may be nerdy and pedantic.

In indigenous cultures the functions are more evenly balanced and harmonised than in our modern, Western culture. To track an animal for days (sensation), to talk to the ancestors (intuition), to live in a small community (feeling), and to memorise the great stories (thinking) meant that all the functions were well-educated and in good relation. In contrast, Western education privileges the thinking function over the others, there is little emotional education (and it is presented in a thinking way), sensation is confined mostly to sports or the science lab, and intuition doesn't exist. Whereas Western culture is a thinking-sensation culture, most indigenous cultures are feeling-intuitive cultures.

Dreams

A myth is a public dream, a dream is a private myth.

—Joseph Campbell

Dreams are impartial, spontaneous products of the unconscious psyche, outside the control of the will. They are pure nature; they show us the unvarnished, natural truth, and [they] give us back an attitude that accords with our basic human nature when our consciousness has strayed too far from its foundations and run into an impasse.

—C. G. Jung[37]

Indigenous cultures make less distinction than Western culture between this world and the other world. Dreams are seen as messages from spirit above that have relevance for the whole community. In contrast, Western culture views dreams as either irrelevant rubbish or, in psychoanalysis, messages from the soul below (the inner world of the psyche) that have relevance for the individual. It was Freud and Jung's great contributions to human culture to consider the revolutionary idea that dreams had meaning for the individual. Both viewpoints, introverted and extroverted, are valid. Dreams are a book (or many) in their own right. Suffice to say here that they are a natural phenomenon of the psyche. They are a symbolic picture of how we look from the point of view of the unconscious. Dreams are our inner compass and for the most part they compensate our conscious point of view. When we develop too much of a psychological list the unconscious tries to right us. If we don't listen it will either turn up the volume with more intense dreams or lose interest and leave us to our own devices.

Self

Just as the ego is the centre of consciousness, so the Self is the organising centre of the whole psyche, both the conscious and the unconscious. It is what Jung called the objective psyche. Objective in the sense that it stands outside the ego, is independent from it, and can see the ego and reality as-it-is. It sees reality unclouded by the beliefs, feelings, desires, complexes and distortions of the ego. In other words, our conscious viewpoint is not the only one we have. The Self has a mind of its own and functions according to its own laws.[38] The tarot is a roadmap of psychological development, and the maturation of the relationship to the Self. It is an expression of the archetype of the Self.

3

Medicine

Everything the Power of the World does is done in a circle. The sky is
round, and I have heard that the earth is round like a ball and so are all
the stars. The wind, in its greatest power, whirls. Birds make their nests
in circles, for theirs is the same religion as ours. The sun comes forth and
goes down again in a circle. The moon does the same, and both are
round. Even the seasons form a great circle in their changing.... The life
of man is a circle from childhood to childhood, and so it is in everything
where power moves. Our tepees were round like the nests of birds, and
were always set in a circle, the nation's hoop, a nest of many nests, where
the Great Spirit meant for us to hatch our children.

—Black Elk

The Medicine Wheel Way begins with the Touching of our Brothers and
Sisters. Next it speaks to us of the Touching of the World around us, the
animals, plants, trees, grasses, and other living things. Finally it Teaches
us to sing the Song of the World, and in this Way to become Whole People... on the Great Medicine Wheel, our Earth.

—Hyemeyohsts Storm

Nothing in nature is a straight line and all things move in circles. All
things that move in circles are inherently healing, in other words they
have medicine. Accumulated over millennia, the medicine teachings of the
indigenous peoples of Turtle Island (North, South, and Central America),
have been distilled from inner and outer experience into a vast body of
knowledge that is held and taught in wheels. I shall explore some of these
wheels in this and subsequent chapters insofar as they help us understand
the tarot.

Air, Animals, Mind
Harmony and Balance
Wisdom and Knowledge
Receiving with Caring
Mental Flexibility

N

Earth, Minerals, Body
Death and Change
Intuition & Introspection   W

CENTRE
Void
Catalyst
Ancestors

E   Fire, Humans, Spirit
Illumination & Enlightenment
Determining with Passion
Spiritual Expansiveness

Holding with Intimacy
Physical Stability

S

Water, Plants, Heart
Trust and Innocence
Giving with Tenderness
Emotional Fluidity

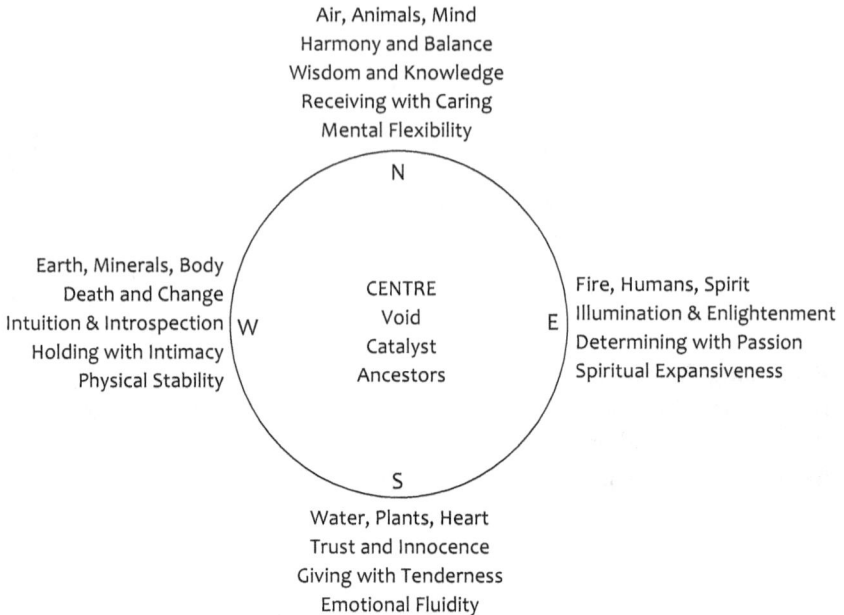

Figure 10. The Medicine Wheel

Medicine Wheel

Although the major arcana of the Xultun Tarot are laid out in a rectangle to accommodate a two-dimensional picture they are more properly represented as a sphere, triangle, cylinder or a double helix. They can also be placed on a Medicine Wheel (a two-dimensional representation of a sphere) which is the basic pattern for understanding the energies and interrelationships of the cards.

The Medicine Wheel is an archetypal symbol of wholeness and completeness. When we sit in a circle we can see all other parts of the circle and yet we are naturally focussed on the centre. The circle naturally indicates the four compass points. Four-fold structures and the number 4 point to the idea of wholeness. There are four seasons, four elements, four mathematical operations, four directions, four human aspects (heart, mind, body and spirit), four parts to the day, and four stages of life.

All organic life is based on carbon and all so-called "inorganic" matter or minerals are based on silicon. Both these elements have a valency of four. Valency is the number of chemical bonds formed by the atoms of an element. Carbon is the fourth most common element in the universe and silicon the eighth most common. About carbon Jung said, "The deeper 'layers' of the psyche lose their individual uniqueness as they retreat farther and farther into darkness. 'Lower down'—that is to say, as they approach the autonomous functional systems—they become increasingly collective until they are universalized and extinguished in the body's materiality, i.e., in the chemical bodies. The body's carbon is simply carbon. Hence 'at bottom' the psyche is simply 'world.'"[1]

The Medicine Wheel brings all things into relationship so that they are both in opposition and in balance with each other. What is directly opposite any point on the wheel is its compensatory opposite or shadow. We come into balance by holding the tension between, and integrating, what is across the wheel from where we sit. Each direction on the wheel draws on the energies of the directions on either side of it. The cardinal directions hold or stabilise the wheel in the tonal and are compensatory to each other. The non-cardinal directions spin or move the wheel in the nagual and are complementary to each other. Each cardinal direction has a non-cardinal on either side that changes its stability, and each non-cardinal has a cardinal on either side that stabilises its changeability.

The basic Medicine Wheel is shown in Figure 10. It is beyond the scope of this book to go into detail and we shall concern ourselves only with some of the powers of the cardinal directions. In Figure 108 the cards are laid out in two-dimensions. From the top downwards, the four rows of the psychological types, the Worlds, the Shields and the Moods follow a south–north–west–east movement. From left to right, the five columns of the Movements of the Book of Life follow a south–west–north–east–centre movement. Figures 104 and 105 show the cards in wheels rather than rows and columns.

The south is the place of trust and innocence, the element of water, the colour red, the Plants, the Spirit of the Plants, and the numbers 3 and 13. It is where we start to go around the wheel, the place of the child, beginnings, futurity, and hope. Processes of growth and development in time and their associated deities are often configured in threes: a beginning, middle and end; past, present and future; the Father (Self), the Son (ego), and the Holy Ghost (ego and Self); or the Triple Goddess, maiden, mother, and crone, the ones who hold the feminine cycles of life, the three times three, the nine, the pregnancy.

Water is symbolic of washing, purification, rejuvenation, new beginnings, amniotic fluid, emotional fluidity, and the alchemical *solutio* which was the beginning of what the alchemists called "The Great Work." They thought of this as a return to the womb for the purpose of rebirth, and that no change could come about until everything had been reduced to the *prima materia* (the first material of creation or basic substance of alchemical procedures). The south is also the place of our give-away, our sacrifice to life. In the act of sacrifice, the ego decides against its own needs and subordinates itself to a higher authority, the Self and the biddings of spirit.

The west is the place of death and change, the colour black, the body, and the place of woman as Life-Giver (2) and Death-Bringer (12). The more we are known to ourselves, the more we can move with the inner and outer deaths and changes that life brings us. The west is the place of looks-within and introspection and if we lack knowledge of death then life will impose it. If we lack knowledge of life then death will impose it. That is, if we are not living fully according to ourselves then we are at risk of dying at some level. Jung said, "When an inner situation is not made conscious, it happens outside, as fate."[2]

The north is the place of the Animals (4), the element of air, wisdom and knowledge, and the Spirit of the Animals (14). The north teaches us mental flexibility and imagination, inter-connectedness, discrimination, and how to receive with consciousness from all places around the wheel.

The east is the place of illumination and enlightenment (1), fire, passion, and memory (11). It is the ability to live by one's own light and vision (having seed) rather than the reflected light of others. Its shadow is fantasy and illusion (having no seed) and the inability to build one's fire on the solidness of earth. The east teaches us spiritual expansiveness and is the place of Humans. It is here that we actualise the consciousness gained on our journey around the wheel. The physical body is in the west, the place of death and change, and east and west compensate each other. Physical illness, life-threatening trauma, or spiritual practices that involve some kind of deprivation or "mortification" of the body, strongly constellate a connection with spirit in the east and may bring illumination. We experience an illumination when we become aware of our inter-connectedness with all creation, we remember who we are and we regain spiritual memory. When the lightning bolt of illumination jumps the gap between unconscious and conscious, spirit and matter, then there is an act of creation.

But the illumination birthed in the east has to walk around the wheel and be lived in the west. Marie-Louise von Franz said, "I have often asked myself why the unconscious or nature.... plays such a cruel trick on people by first curing them and then dropping them again.... If some people had not had a brief experience and glimpse of how it could be when things are right, they would never hold on.... [I]t is as if it were to say; 'That is what you will get later, but you have first to realize this and this and this, and much more, before you can get there.'"[3]

The centre of the Medicine Wheel is the place of the soul catalyst energy and the element of the Void. The centre of the wheel is the quintessence, the summing up and union of the opposites around the circumference. The catalyst at the centre makes the wheel turn without itself turning. Like a chemical catalyst, it produces change without itself being changed or used up. This centre is the sum of all things; it is an infinitely small point that is bigger than everything; it has no beginning and no end and yet is the beginning and the end; it has no parents yet it gives birth to everything; it is the place of destruction and renewal, of void and totality. In alchemy an image of this centre is the *ouroboros*, the serpent that swallows its own tail. The alchemists said, "He slays himself and brings himself back to life. He fertilises himself and he gives birth to himself. He devours himself and he generates himself."[4] In the Xultun Tarot the cards (the Lovers, Balance, Released Man and Planet Earth) in the last column of Assuming Authority are the catalyst cards.

Twenty Count

The Xultun Tarot is a picture and a story of how the soul comes to know itself by impressing its free will on matter as it moves through space and time in all eight directions. But this free will is not the same as the political freedoms of democracy, or the "freedom" of those who don't want to be taxed or told what to do by "the government." There is something within us, that Jung called "the spirit" or the Self, which organises dreams and offers them to us when we are ready to understand them. Over time, the function of these dreams and images is to help us to become more conscious, that is, to use our free will to follow where spirit leads us. This is true freedom. We then become life's way of robing itself in the beauty of space and time.

Gary Sparks describes the association between spirit and number. "The gradient that Jung called the spirit anticipates how we can live forward into a meaningful life. Meaningful living follows the direction revealed by the spirit.... When we feel our life is evolving in some sort of sensible *sequence*, then life is felt to be meaningful.... If our life is going somewhere, there is an order which can be described numerically in the unfolding phases of life. There is a one, there is a two, there is a three, a four, a five, and so on.... If we are living meaningfully; then there is a sequential process with us, and sequence is denoted by counting. In short, *number symbolises spirit*." (Italics in original).

The teachings of the Twenty Count[5] describe both the doings of spirit as well as the process of unfolding a meaningful life. Each card holds the energy of a number in the Twenty Count (Figure 11). To explore the Twenty Count in depth would take us too far from our theme but I shall refer to it throughout the book.

The traditional view of the tarot is that the Fool moves through the cards in a linear sequence from 0 to 21. But the cards are infinitely more varied in their inter-relationships than a linear progression or ascent. This world we inhabit is sung into life by the Holy. It is both a dance and a song. The dance is the Three Paths of the Book of Life and the Five Movements of the Book of Life. This is a geometric choreography, a holy trinity of a double double

	Twenty Count	Xultun Tarot
0	Void	Fool
1	Fire, Grandfather Sun	Sorcerer
2	Earth, Grandmother Earth	Priestess
3	Water, Plants	Consort
4	Air, Animals	Ruler
5	Humans	Priest
6	Ancestors, Self-image	Lovers
7	Sacred Dream, Symbols	Warrior
8	Rules, Laws, Patterns	Cactus
9	Design of Energy	Sage
10	All Measures of Intellect	Wheel
11	Great Grandfather Stars	Balance
12	Great Grandmother Planets	Hanged Man
13	Earth Mother, Spirit of the Plants	Dead Man
14	Earth Father, Spirit of the Animals	Temperate Man
15	All Human Souls	Bound Man
16	All Enlightened Human Souls	Released Man
17	Keepers of the Sacred Dream	Star
18	Holders of the Book of Life	Moon
19	Teachers of the Higher Self	Sun
20	Creator, Great Spirit, God/Goddess	Planet Venus

Figure 11. The Twenty Count and the Xultun Tarot

helix (the DNA of the Creator), a series of interlocking triangles (the thoughts of the Creator), or a sphere (the body of the Creator). For example, when the major arcana are laid out to form a picture as in Figure 109 the two cards at the top of the deck (the Fool and the Sorcerer) sit outside of the rectangle formed by the other cards. This denotes their special position as the numbers 0 (the Fool) and 1 (the Sorcerer) from which all other numbers are formed. If we now imagine a sphere with all the cards lying on the surface of that sphere then the 0 card, which represents the potential for all things to be born from nothing, is not located in any one place but inhabits the spaces inside, between and outside all the other cards. It is the centre, the circumference and all places in between. The 1 card, on the other hand, is the one-point at the centre of the sphere. Together, the 0 and 1 cards represent the feminine and masculine aspects of the Creator. The 20 card (Planet Venus) is the Creator in its totality — the double zero or the infinity movement (OO).

The soul is the Human Flowering Tree. The song of the cards, the breeze that awakens the leaves of the Flowering Tree, is the Twenty Count. The Maya used a vigesimal system of counting based on the number 20. The numbers from 0 to 20 describe all movements of energy in this universe. They are not only quantitative and sequential, as in our Western notion of numbers, but also express a particular archetypal quality or energy. The operations of addition, subtraction, multiplication and division show how these energies interact with each other and the relationships between them. Where the medicine, meaning the power or gift, of a number is particularly significant, I shall use numerals (for example, 18) rather than words (eighteen).

Animals

Too much of the animal distorts the civilised man, too much civilisation makes sick animals.[6] Animal symbols not only have a reductive meaning, but also one that is prospective and spiritual. They point both upwards and downwards at the same time and represent a "spiritual nature or a natural spirit."

—C. G. Jung[7]

The Medicine Wheel holds an element in each of the five directions: water in the south, earth in the west, air in the north, fire in the east and void in the centre. These are the building blocks of our natural world and our physical body. For the majority of cultures throughout history matter was holy. This holy ground was always feminine because she gave birth to life and was known by a thousand names: Papatuanuku (Maori), Pachamama (South America), Nokomis (Algonquin), Ishtar (Babylonian), Khaltesh-Anki (Ugric), Ala (Ibo) or Gaia (Greek) among others. From her body of the five elements she bore five children: the first-born were the Minerals, then came the Plants, the Animals, the Humans, and finally the Ancestors. Each of these is a World, a nation, a principality with its own laws, sovereignty, mana, gifts and powers. Each of these Worlds, or Children of, Grandmother Earth, appear in the Xultun Tarot in sequence mirroring their presence in nature.

The first child, the Stone Peoples, is the very ground beneath us and is the stepped pattern at the base of the bottom row of the deck. From this, in the second row up, grows the greenness of the Plant Nations. The third row from the bottom is the Animal world and the top row is the world of Humans. The whole deck is the world of the Ancestors. Note that this sequence runs bottom-to-top and is the opposite of most of the patterns in this book. Looking at the cards from the bottom upwards is seeing through the eyes of Grandmother Earth. Looking at the cards from the top downwards is seeing through the eyes of Humans.

Animals are depicted in several cards in the tarot. They are important because they represent our connection to the instinctual part of human nature. Animals are the closest form of life to us and people have always incorporated animals into their lives for companionship, for food, and as teachers. Animals move, plants don't. Through their instinctual nature animals teach us how to move with wholeness and balance in the plane between spirit and substance. If our instincts are followed they will bring us to the laws of our own nature. Jung said that instincts are at the infra-red or biological end of the energetic spectrum and archetypes are at the ultra-violet or spiritual end.[8]

The tarot is about how humans unite the opposites and bring together what has been divided — earth and sky, matter and spirit. This involves a descent as well as an ascent — roots and branches, feet and head. Animals bring us back to earth when we get too spiritually up ourselves. Being close to nature, they live comfortably with the opposites of their nature. The cat is maternal but also cruel (ask any mouse); self-reliant but also lazy. The dog is the guide but also the trickster; the guardian but also the thief. We have become so separated from nature that either we sentimentally assign all manner of human feelings to animals (domestic pets or farm animals get preferential treatment here) or scientifically pronounce that they have no feelings at all and it is all our imagination.

When an animal shows itself in a reading we are being reminded to use our instincts. Not use them to do our tax returns but to allow them to lead us in situations where ego consciousness cannot see its way forward. The ego might consider the right thought, feeling or action as shadowy, unacceptable, against what it believes, or even "animalistic," but instinct knows it is the right reaction in the circumstances.

The words instinct and distinct come from the same root. An instinct is an inner prompting (*in-*, on and *-stinguere* meaning to prick or to goad). Distinct (*dis-*, apart and *-stinguere*) means to separate by pricking with a fine-pointed tool like a pin. An instinct is quite specific when it is "pricked" into action. Like our feeling function (which, other than our physiological reactions, lies closest to our animal nature) instinct is specific to a particular situation and distinguishes it quite accurately from other similar situations.

But instincts go awry when their precision is blunted by human virtues (useful and proper as they might be) such as patience, renunciation, meekness, charity, compassion, diligence, purity, righteousness, repentance, honesty, loyalty, sincerity, frugality, prudence, moderation, self-restraint, discipline, perseverance, hope, dignity, courage, justice, tolerance, respect, honour, courtesy, kindness and gratitude, to name but a few. There's little room for honest vice.

Medicine Animals

In the Xultun and Marseilles tarot there are three kinds of depictions of animals. First, the actual, physical animal. Second, the animal medicine items or bundles that are made from the skin, bones or feathers of an animal. And third, the symbolic or mythological animal.

In the Xultun Tarot the physical animals are the two jaguars in the Warrior card; a white bird in the Cactus card; a quetzal and a jaguar and her cub in the Wheel; and another quetzal in the Star card. In the Marseilles Tarot there is a dog in the Fool card, horses in the Chariot card, a lion in the Strength card, and two dogs and a crayfish in the Moon card.

In the Xultun Tarot the animal medicine is seen in the jaguar skin at the top of the deck that joins the Fool, Sorcerer, Ruler and Priest; the jaguar skin throne of the Priestess; the jaguar skin robes of the Priest and the Warrior; and the headdresses with long, green quetzal feathers worn by the Empress, Ruler, Priest, Balance and the Star. However, in the Marseilles Tarot there are no animal medicine items. Instead, there are part-human, part-animal chimeras: a cherubim (one of the nine levels of angels) in the Lovers card; a sphinx and two other chimeras clinging to the Wheel of Fortune; the human body and bird's wings of the angel in the Temperance card; and the bat wings, goat ears, antler headdress, and clawed feet of the Devil card.

The animal symbols or mythological animals in the Xultun Tarot are seen in the serpent bundle held by the Ruler; the snake surrounding the calendar stone of the Wheel (which has many animal day-names on it); and the Feathered Winged Serpent of the Planet Venus card. In the Marseilles Tarot we see the heraldic eagle in the Empress and Emperor cards; and the spiritualised animals in the World card which are the symbols of the four evangelists, The eagle is the symbol of John, the lion is the symbol of Mark, the ox is the symbol of Luke, and the angel is the symbol of Matthew.

Now let's look at the differences between the two decks with regard to each type of image. First, the physical animals. In the Xultun Tarot there are only wild animals (jaguars and birds). In the Marseilles Tarot the animals are domesticated (dogs and horses) and so more distant from their essential nature. The lion being subdued by the woman in the Strength card indicates the early house-training of wildness. The images are also more polarised with the dogs (close to humans) and the cold-blooded, invertebrate crayfish (distant from humans) pictured together in the Moon card.

Next, the medicine animals. The physical animal represents its raw instinctual energy. Four is the number of the Animals in the Twenty Count and the physically alive animal is its 4-ness. The skin, bones, claws or feathers of an animal, received and prepared in a sacred way, is physically dead but spiritually alive. It is its 14-ness. Almost all the animal medicines in the Xultun Tarot are in the top row at the beginning of the Fool's journey where it is most needed. It holds the medicine of the animal and provides a bridge between its raw physical power and its raw archetypal power both of which, in their full strength, are potentially destructive to humans. The shaman uses the power of the medicine animal for healing and it is the substance twin to his inner medicine animal helper. Psychologically, the medicine animal is our connection with our animal instincts. In the Marseilles Tarot this mediating power of the animal medicine is absent. What we see instead are chimeras in the second and third rows.

Chimera

In Greek mythology the Chimera was a fire-breathing animal with the body of a lioness, the head of a goat that arose from her back and a tail that ended in a snake's head. She was one of the children of Echidna and Typhon (one of the beasts on the Wheel of Fortune) who was eventually killed by the hero Bellerophon. Generically, the word chimera refers to an imaginary monster made of mismatched animal and human parts that are an aberration of the natural order. In mythology, the chimeric crossovers were all lethal to mere mortals. The centaurs, half-human and half-horse, were known for their drunkenness and savagery and tore people limb from limb. The mermen or tritons, and mermaids, half-fish and half-woman, lured sailors to their deaths. The song of the sirens, who had birds' feet and wings and a woman's body, lured shipwrecked sailors onto the rocks. The Sphinx, a winged creature with a lion's body and a woman's head, posed a riddle and if it was answered incorrectly then the Sphinx killed the person. Finally, the gorgon was a creature with a human face, covered with golden scales, with large wings and snakes for hair. If a human looked at her directly they were turned to stone.

The presence of chimeras in the Marseilles Tarot reflects the negation of the natural world by Western consciousness to such a degree that, without an intermediary like the medicine animal, it has perforce returned in the bizarre union of human and animal. Chimeras are a pastiche of animal and human parts, an unnatural blending of pieces that don't belong together, a fragmentary totality. Psychologically, any psychic function that is split off from the whole begins to function autonomously and acts counter to the whole. Now, instinctual behaviour has returned in chimeric form and endangers our humanness.

The case of Pan, one of the oldest gods in the Greek pantheon, points to the origin of the chimera. In the beginning he was an expression of our union with nature. He was our "silent knowledge" that is available to us when we are connected with the natural world, our kinship with nature's gentleness and healing as well as our healthy survival fear and respect for nature's disregard for human concerns. Pan was the god of shepherds and flocks and was depicted with human arms and torso and the ears, horns, and legs of a goat. His instrument was the syrinx or panpipes on which he played music, that most human of creations. Pan lived in remote mountains and caves and brought about the sudden, inexplicable fear (pan-ic) that overtook those travelling in remote and lonely places who were not at ease with the wilderness.

Jung once remarked, "The gods have become diseases," and we see this in symptoms of panic disorder. An individual becomes highly anxious and may have a panic attack when they misinterpret physical sensations (their natural wildness), such as heart beat or breathing, which they feel will get out of control and become harmful. It is often accompanied by agoraphobia — a fear of going outside the safety of the house (that is, into wild and remote places). Similarly, many fears, anxieties or phobias (fear of water, fear of hospitals, fear of snakes, fear of needles, fear of spiders, for example) are symbolic markers of dissociated parts of our psyche that threaten ego consciousness. For the average suburbanite these would be the wild parts of the psyche, for the average mountain man they would be his suburban impulses.

In the 2nd century CE Plutarch recorded that during the reign of Emperor Tiberius travellers sailing along the west coast of Greece heard a voice proclaiming the death of the great god Pan. This story was later associated with the Passion of Christ and was taken as a sign of the victory of Christ over the pagan gods. "A cry went through late antiquity: 'Great Pan is dead!'... Nature no longer spoke to us — or we could no longer hear..."[9] In later centuries, Pan, originally a force of nature, came to represent evil when his image was appropriated for that of Satan.

In the Marseilles Tarot the psychological situation of the chimera is depicted by the angel and the devil. These lie side by side as the 14 (Temperance) and 15 (The Devil) cards and are in fact mirror-image twins (Figure 12). Sallie Nichols in *Jung and Tarot* refers to the Devil as the "dark angel." One is idealised and one is demonised but they are both chimeras. Each has a human body with wings — the angel has the wings of a bird and the devil has the wings of a bat. One holds the limitations of chains, the other the formlessness of water. Both are an aberration of our humanness. We would usually think of the angel in positive terms and not see it is as demonic or chimeric. But the angel is as inhuman as the devil.

The conventional meaning of the Temperance card is that it represents contact with the heavenly realm through a part-human intermediary (the angel) and leads to an enhancement of our humanness through the virtue of temperance. Likewise, the usual interpretation of the Devil card is an en-

Figure 12. The angel and the devil

counter with the infernal realms and our baser, animal natures through a part-human intermediary (the devil) which leads to a debasement of our humanness through sin and excess.

What is obvious (but rarely noted) is that the debasement of the devil occurs right after the upliftment by the angel and, I would add, is its necessary result. Too much spirit at 14 leads to the return of the repressed in destructive form at 15. The lightning bolt of the realisation of this blasts the twins out of the Tower and brings them down to earth in the 16 card. The images of both the devil and the angel are perversions. I use the term here to mean, not a sexual practice, but the turning of something natural, true to its own nature, into something unnatural, estranged from its own nature. The angel symbolises a perversion of our humanness through too much spirit (spiritual debauchery and excess, if you will) just as the devil is the perversion of our humanness through too much instinct (physical debauchery and excess). Thus we see the improper joining of animal and human parts. This unconscious bias toward rationality and spirituality is seen in the seven deadly sins of Thomas Aquinas (pride, avarice, lust, anger, gluttony, envy, and sloth). They are all physical or emotional sins. Tellingly, there is no corresponding list of spiritual or cognitive sins.

From the conscious ego's point of view, peace, wholeness and freedom from conflict is attractive because life is often hard, painful, debilitating, unrewarding, unfair, cruel, raw, excruciating, agonising, sorrowful, heartbreaking, harrowing and downright awful. And no amount of positive thinking, therapy, meditation, transcendence, good works, faith or prayer makes a damn bit of difference. The first of the Buddha's Four Noble Truths is that all life is suffering. And Hamlet ruminated on, "The slings and arrows of outrageous fortune / The heart-ache and the thousand natural shocks that flesh is heir to / For who would bear the whips and scorns of time / To grunt and sweat under a weary life."[10] But from the unconscious' point of view it is wholeness and nirvana that are monstrous. Eternal peace, oneness and unity without end is barren and boring. To stir things up a bit the universe always creates some twoness, division, disharmony and difference to break the monotony.

The ego wants to fast forward and skip the difficult parts and will try to force the arrival of unity, love, wholeness and oneness. It sees white light, synchronistic revelations and underlying harmony everywhere and ignores distinctions and differences and the conflict and tensions between them. But wholeness is not the reconciliation, joining or elimination of opposites. It is the harmony that allows opposites to live according to their own nature.

When wholeness is hurried and grasped-at, it arrives as unlived, sterile, intellectual notions accompanied by all the fervour that goes with over-valued beliefs. It is the fusion of parts that are not yet fully mature in their difference and distinctiveness. Then, as Hillman says, "our consciousness, no matter how wise and wondrous, is therefore both premature and monstrous. And by monstrous, alchemy means fruitless, barren, without issue."[11]

As we move from left to right along the columns, the Movements of the Book of Life become more archetypal and less personal. The first Movement is Erasing Personal History and the second is Using Death as an Advisor. As past and future these both engage us personally. Stopping the World is more abstract and Controlling the Dream is the furthest from consciousness, living at the boundary between the worlds of spirit and matter. Assuming Authority however does not continue the sequence but completes the circle as the union of both the personal and the archetypal — the intensely personal issue of freedom of choice and the archetypal image of authentic, personal authority. Controlling the Dream is the most removed and is most alien to ego consciousness. Accordingly, all the cards of this Movement contain images that are alien or even chimeric to our daytime sensibilities.

In the Priest (5) card the man looks half-human and half-jaguar. In the Mythic Tarot deck this card is the Hierophant as Chiron the centaur who was half-man and half-horse. The Wheel (10) and the Devil (15) are both chimeric cards as we have seen. In Planet Venus (20) the figure is that of an animal chimera, the Feathered Serpent. In the European tarot the 20 card is called Judgement. It depicts a chimeric angel sounding the last trump and human souls ascending from the grave to heavenly salvation, released from

Figure 13. The extraction of the spirit of Mercurius from the *prima materia*

their imprisonment in the world of the flesh. We can see a similar image and theme in alchemy. Figure 13 shows a man with serpents for arms, wings and the tail of a fish being pulled out of a lump of matter.[12] The lump is the "lumpinesss" of reality, the hard facts of existence from which he is being liberated. These images are the reverse of the Xultun card where a serpent with wings descends toward the earth, released from its exile in the world of spirit.

Mythological Animals

Let's return now to the third type of animal image, the mythological animal. The medicine animal is a bridge to the spiritual power of the animal. The mythological animal *is* the spiritual power of the animal. They are neither physically alive and spiritually inert (the physical animal) nor physically dead and spiritually alive (the medicine animal). They are animals of the imagination who come from and return to the other world. They are "fantastic" or "fabulous" in appearance and have fearsome or magical powers, for example, the unicorn, windigo, dragon, basilisk, griffon, balrog, or taniwha. They are embodiments of the archetypal power of the animal — its 14-ness. In the Temperate Man we shall return to the significance of the number 14 and the Animals.

In the Marseilles Tarot the Emperor and the Empress each hold a shield with an eagle on it. In the Xultun Tarot the Ruler holds the serpent bar. The eagle is the messenger of spirit, the serpent is the messenger of matter; one higher, one lower, each reflecting the different attitude of the decks. Because of its upward bias toward spirit, the Marseilles Tarot does not have a symbol of the union of spirit and matter like the Feathered Winged Serpent. The closest it comes is the polarised and ambivalent image of a crayfish and two dogs in the Moon card, or the distant juxtaposition of the angel above and the resurrected humans below in the Judgement card. In the last card, the World, the calf, the eagle with a halo, and the lion with a halo, are not at all mythological. They symbolise the final domestication of nature and instinct.

The clear separation of the Animal and Human worlds is essential for both to function according to their own laws. (The exceptions to this are domestic animals and pets which have given their consent for a mutually beneficial association. We are as much their pets as they are ours). This is why in the Xultun Tarot there are no images of human-animal conjunctions — because they are unnatural. The only chimeric unions we see are animal-mineral (the snake surrounding the calendar stone) in the Wheel card, and animal-animal (the serpent with wings) in the Planet Venus card.

Due respect, ceremony and honour must be given to the Animals. If we don't, there is trouble. We often hear of the animal trainer who has ignored the essential wildness of the animal, has chimerically "bonded" with it, and grandiosely shows us how tame the lion or tiger or bear or elephant is. Later, often after many years of "relationship" with the animal, the trainer is mauled, trampled or eaten.

Our hunter-gatherer ancestors knew the importance of this relationship with the animal world, as do all indigenous peoples. For example, the buffalo and the First Nations of the North American plains and prairies; the totem animals of the Aboriginal Australians; or the bear and the Ainu people of Japan. With each there is a reciprocal and distinct, sacred relationship between humans and animals. Minerals, Plants and Animals can teach us, Humans cannot. Other humans can show us their way but only the other forms of life can teach us to find our own way. For example, in T. H. White's *The Sword in the Stone*, the young King Arthur acquires wisdom by being changed into various animals by Merlin.

We can see the sequence of the proper joining of spirit and matter in the 5, 10, 15 and 20 cards of the Movement of Controlling the Dream. This movement is about how we build our relationship with spirit or our "connecting link with intent." First, the Priest (5) connects with spirit through the medicine of the jaguar. Then spirit appears in matter in undifferentiated form as the snake surrounding the calendar stone of the Wheel (10) heralding our encounter with the inhuman, impersonal laws of the universe. We also see below the stone, the mother jaguar teaching her cub—reminding us that we are being fed and taught by the memory of these laws. Then in the 15 card, spirit appears as the quaternity of the man, the woman, the mask of Xipe-Totec, and the tail of the Feathered Serpent. Finally, in the 20 card of the Feathered Winged Serpent, the union of the high and the low, the serpent and the bird, spirit descends to join with matter.

As Jung pointed out, animals are a "spiritual nature or a natural spirit" and in both decks there is a movement from the animal most emotionally related to humans (the dog in the 0 card) through horses, cats and birds to the least related and furthest from our human consciousness—the snake with wings in the Planet Venus card or the crayfish in the Marseilles Moon card. Here the animals point to the deeper theme of the tarot as a symbolic codex of the cosmic evolutionary spiral from the separation of sames to the union of opposites and back again. The tarot starts with the same-but-separate image of the Fool and his dog or jaguar in the 0 card and ends with the different-and-joined image of the Feathered Winged Serpent in the 20 card.

4

Shields

Carefully, I unwrapped my four shields and placed them in their four directions around me… The shields stood for the concept of who I am in my completeness. Together, they were the ultimate medicine wheel, the map from my outer to my inner being.

—Lynn Andrews

The luminous cocoon is the energy body that surrounds our physical body.[1] It is the energetic configuration of the Self in the dream. Within the luminous cocoon are four energetic bodies called the Shields that rotate around the vertical axis of the physical body. The Shields hold us in substance form and are the personality configuration that we create over a lifetime. Depending on our emotional or spiritual state the Shields may spin so that a different Shield is in front and then we experience the world differently. The Shield that is in front of us determines our perception of reality but in most situations our Adult Substance Shield is up front. The Substance Shields (Child Substance Shield and Adult Substance Shield) are the same gender as our physical body. The Spirit Shields (Adult Spirit Shield and Child Spirit Shield) are the opposite gender to our physical body. At the centre of our body is the Elder Shield which is a balance of female and male (Figure 14). Each row of cards in the Xultun Tarot represents a Shield. The cards within each row represent, from left to right, the heart, body, mind, spirit and soul of the Shield (Figure 15).

Each Shield has needs, wants or desires—emotional, physical, mental, spiritual and sexual. Needs are those things that, if we do not have them, cause us long-term pain and we are not able to recover without external help. Wants are those things that cause us short-term pain if we do not have them, but we can recover using our own resources. Desires add beauty to our lives but we are not attached to them. Turning the pages of our Book of Life requires us to make our needs into wants, and our wants into desires. Needs and wants dominate the Substance Shields which are about coming

Adult Substance Shield

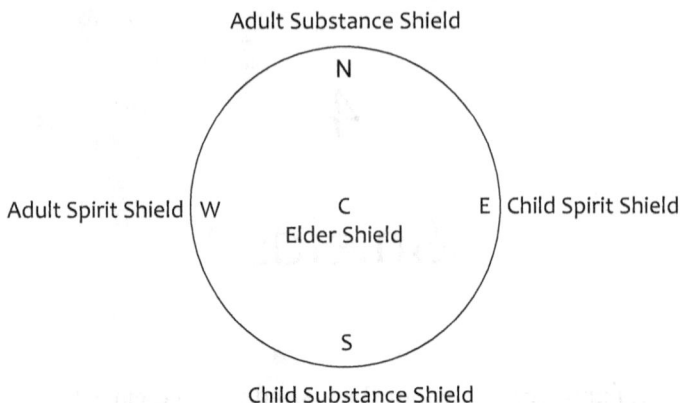

Figure 14. The Shields of Humans

into alignment with the needs of the external world. The Spirit Shields are about coming into alignment with the inner desires of the soul. The Elder Shield has neither needs nor wants — it has only desire.[2]

Keeper, Holder and Teacher

Each card in the tarot is an archetype or a potential spiritual energy. Each card contains three Powers — Keeper, Holder and Teacher. As Keeper, the card is the essence of the archetypal energy that it represents. As Holder, it maintains the energy sacred and intact. As Teacher, it gives-away the energy of the archetype and shows you how to use this energy properly.

So each card is the Keeper of a Shield, the Holder of a Mood of Stalking and the Teacher of a Movement of the Book of Life. For example: The Priestess is the Keeper of the Heart of the Child Substance Shield, the Holder of the Mood of Emotional Sweetness, and the Teacher of Erasing Emotional History. The Cactus (Strength) is the Keeper of the Body of the Adult Substance Shield, the Holder of the Mood of Physical Cunning and the Teacher of Using Mental Death as an Advisor. The Bound Man (the Devil) is the Keeper of the Spirit of the Adult Spirit Shield, the Holder of the Mood of Spiritual Ruthlessness and the Teacher of Controlling the Physical Dream. The Sun is the Keeper of the Mind of the Child Spirit Shield, the Holder of the Mood of Mental Patience, and the Teacher of spiritually Stopping the World.

Child Substance Shield

This Shield sits in the south and is associated with the element of water and the psychological function of feeling. It holds all memories of the past, con-

PRIESTESS	CONSORT	RULER	PRIEST	LOVERS
Heart of the Child Substance Shield	Body of the Child Substance Shield	Mind of the Child Substance Shield	Spirit of the Child Substance Shield	Soul of the Child Substance Shield

WARRIOR	CACTUS	SAGE	WHEEL	BALANCE
Heart of the Adult Substance Shield	Body of the Adult Substance Shield	Mind of the Adult Substance Shield	Spirit of the Adult Substance Shield	Soul of the Adult Substance Shield

HANGED MAN	DEAD MAN	TEMPERATE MAN	BOUND MAN	RELEASED MAN
Heart of the Adult Spirit Shield	Body of the Adult Spirit Shield	Mind of the Adult Spirit Shield	Spirit of the Adult Spirit Shield	Soul of the Adult Spirit Shield

STAR	MOON	SUN	VENUS	EARTH
Heart of the Child Spirit Shield	Body of the Child Spirit Shield	Mind of the Child Spirit Shield	Spirit of the Child Spirit Shield	Soul of the Child Spirit Shield

Figure 15. The Shields of Humans and the Xultun Tarot

scious and unconscious, painful and joyful. On the light side, it is child-like, playful, innocent, mischievous and full of wonder. It is dependent, vulnerable, irresponsible, and likes to show off. On the shadow side, it is manipulative, bratty, and omnipotent. It is the archetype of both the wounded child and the innocent child. For a woman the Child Substance Shield is her Little Girl Shield, for a man it is his Little Boy Shield. Jung said, "In every adult there lurks a child — an eternal child, something that is always becoming, is never completed, and calls for unceasing care, attention, and education. That is the part of the human personality which wants to develop and become whole."[3]

The Priestess is the Keeper of the Heart of the Child Substance Shield which needs love, acceptance and support from peers, parents and significant others. The Consort is the Keeper of the Body of the Child Substance Shield which needs to explore its own body and the environment around it. The Ruler is the Keeper of the Mind of the Child Substance Shield which needs acknowledgment and recognition. The Priest is the Keeper of the Spirit of the Child Substance Shield which needs permission to explore without boundaries. The Lovers are the Keepers of the Soul of the Child Substance Shield which needs cohesion, bonding and attachment.

Adult Substance Shield

This Shield sits in the north and is associated with the element of air and the thinking function. It is the "adult" part of us which is mature, responsible, identifies with our culture and society, takes care of the present, and plans for the future. It needs to find out what it can do, what its strengths and limitations are, what it is best suited for in society, and needs to search for meaning and purpose. It loves cooperative competition (men) and competitive cooperation (women). On the dark side, it is angry, bitter and anti-social, or correspondingly passive, depressed and overly conforming. For a man the Adult Substance Shield is his Man Shield and for woman it is her Woman Shield.

The Warrior is the Keeper of the Heart of the Adult Substance Shield which needs to find its self-worth and its value in the world. The Cactus is the Keeper of the Body of the Adult Substance Shield which needs to find its capacities and limitations in physical action, either in sport or sexuality. (Sexuality is erotic sport and sport is athletic sexuality). The Sage is the Keeper of the Mind of the Adult Substance Shield which needs to master a body of knowledge. The Wheel is the Keeper of the Spirit of the Adult Substance Shield which needs to find meaning in the universe. The Balance is the Keeper of the Soul of the Adult Substance Shield which needs to take things apart so it can put them back together. This is the archetype that drives science. Just as we are unconscious of spirit, so spirit is unconscious of matter. The urge to explore, investigate, measure and control matter (which we know of as science) is driven by spirit's longing to know matter more deeply.

Adult Spirit Shield

The Adult Substance Shield connects us to the outer world whereas the Adult Spirit Shield connects us to the inner world. It is what Jung called the anima or animus. It sits in the west, the place of death and change, and is associated with the element of earth and the sensation function. It is artistic and creative but knows that death is a part of life and, in fact, seeks it out. It loves physicality, sexuality and sensuality. The Adult Spirit Shield is the opposite gender to the physical body, so for a woman it is her Man Shield and for a man it is his Woman Shield.

The Hanged Man is the Keeper of the Heart of the Adult Spirit Shield which wants passionate, tender, wild love. In any romantic relationship (that is, one that involves significant projection) both the Lovers (6) and the Hanged Man (12) are at work. The Lovers card is about trying to meet unresolved, past needs for bonding, cohesion, attachment and closeness and bring about a deepening of the personality. The Hanged Man card is about trying to meet future, not-yet-actualised needs for growth through a high-voltage relationship that sweeps one away, flies high and brings about a widening of the personality. The purpose of both is for the relationship to end in tears, bring about death and change, and birth a new relationship with the "other" whether that be the same person or another person. The Dead Man is the Keeper of the Body of the Adult Spirit Shield which wants an open circle of sexual choice—to be celibate (that is, to have spirit as a sexual partner), to have a sexual relationship with one person (as in monogamy), or to have sexual relationships with multiple partners. The Temperate Man is the Keeper of the Mind of the Adult Spirit Shield which wants to be free of beliefs, constricting viewpoints and limiting attitudes. The Bound Man is the Keeper of the Spirit of the Adult Spirit Shield which wants an open and unlimited imagination. The Released Man is the Soul of the Adult Spirit Shield which wants to give to others unconditionally.

Child Spirit Shield

The Child Spirit Shield is the magical, divine child that knows no fear, pain or limitations. It sits in the east and is associated with the element of fire and the function of intuition. It is pure light and joy and delights in living on the edge. It pushes us into difficult situations and then abandons us so we have to find our own way out. It is the gateway to the Elder Shield. For a woman it is her Little Boy Shield and for a man it is his Little Girl Shield.

The Star is the Keeper of the Heart of the Child Spirit Shield which desires to love unconditionally, starting with oneself. The Moon is the Keeper of the Body of the Child Spirit Shield which desires to heal others. The Sun is the Keeper of the Mind of the Child Spirit Shield which desires to share everything it knows. Planet Venus is the Keeper of the Spirit of the Child Spirit Shield which desires to find the light and go towards it. Planet Earth is the Keeper of the Soul of the Child Spirit Shield which desires an open and unlimited circle of being.

Elder Shield

The Elder Shield, at the centre of the luminous cocoon, is our Grandmother and Grandfather Shields, the God or Goddess within. It is our inner wisdom and our connection to the Everything. It has only two desires — Breath and Light. The whole Book of Life is our Elder Shield.

5

Moods

There are four steps to learning [the art of stalking]: ruthlessness, cunning, patience, and sweetness... ruthlessness should not be harshness, cunning should not be cruelty, patience should not be negligence, and sweetness should not be foolishness.... The very first principle of *stalking* is that a warrior stalks himself. He stalks himself, ruthlessly, cunningly, patiently, and sweetly... Sorcerers use the four moods of *stalking* as guides. These are four different frames of mind, four different brands of intensity that sorcerers can use to induce their assemblage points to move to specific positions.

—Don Juan Matus

For a sorcerer, ruthlessness is not cruelty. Ruthlessness is the opposite of self-pity or self-importance. Ruthlessness is sobriety.

—Don Juan Matus

Consciousness is the ability to adapt to the worlds of both matter and spirit. It calls for skill in both dreaming and stalking. Dreaming is behaviour in the fifth dimension—the world of spirit, the unconscious, the dream. Stalking is behaviour in the third dimension—the world of Humans, Animals, Plants and Minerals. Each row of cards represents a Mood of Stalking—the first row is Sweetness, the second row is Cunning, the third row is Ruthlessness and the fourth row is Patience (Figures 16 and 17).

Sweetness without Foolishness

Sweetness is the south, emotional Mood of fluidity. On the light side it is authentic expression of feeling (but not emotionality), heart-to-heart communication, and giving with tenderness from the heart. It is differentiated feeling—having a heart of one's own, knowing what one wants and feels

Cunning without Cruelty

N

Ruthlessness | W   E | Patience
without Harshness   without Negligence

S

Sweetness without Foolishness

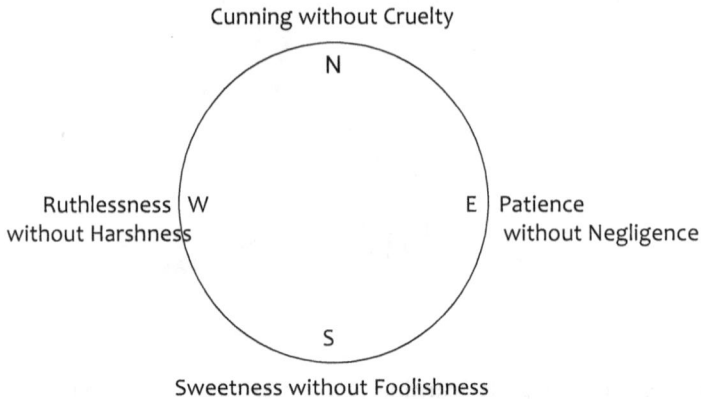

Figure 16. The Moods of Stalking

without being confused by personal or collective emotions. It is being fluid with one's emotions like water — neither damming them up until they burst their banks and flood destructively nor continuously leaking them all over others so that relationships are permanently damp and mouldy and never quite dry out. On the shadow side it is destructive self-sacrifice and emotional foolishness, naiveté or masochism. Sweetness is the compensatory opposite to the Mood of Cunning across the wheel.

The Priestess is the Holder of the Mood of Emotional Sweetness. This is the emotional fluidity of empathy, compassion and love without pity. The Priestess can see through the veil between the worlds. She sees the hidden potential of things and what may come to pass. It is this ability to "see into the future" that births her sustaining emotional hope. This is not the spiritual hope of the Star card, the forceful expectation of the Warrior, nor the annihilated hope of the Hanged Man. It is the uniquely personal hope that comes from seeing the gold, the seed hidden in the heart of the individual, that will blossom in the Star card.

The Consort is the Holder of the Mood of Physical Sweetness. This is the physical fluidity of affection, comfort, intimacy, touch, nursing, cherishing, warmth, tenderness, as well physical healing through herbs, diet, or massage. It is making love passionately, affectionately and sweetly. It is being in natural and beautiful places and having our bodies healed and held by the Sweetness of nature.

The Ruler is the Holder of the Mood of Mental Sweetness. This is the mental fluidity to say the right words at right time, to inspire confidence and courage, to be clear and articulate, and to get others to follow and obey. It is the encouragement and confidence that come from the words of Winston Churchill, Eleanor Roosevelt, John F. Kennedy or Nelson Mandela. The Ruler is the one who leads and brings order and discipline (in the

PRIESTESS	CONSORT	RULER	PRIEST	LOVERS
Emotional Sweetness	Physical Sweetness	Mental Sweetness	Spiritual Sweetness	Soul Sweetness
WARRIOR	CACTUS	SAGE	WHEEL	BALANCE
Emotional Cunning	Physical Cunning	Mental Cunning	Spiritual Cunning	Soul Cunning
HANGED MAN	DEAD MAN	TEMPERATE MAN	BOUND MAN	RELEASED MAN
Emotional Ruthlessness	Physical Ruthlessness	Mental Ruthlessness	Spiritual Ruthlessness	Soul Ruthlessness
STAR	MOON	SUN	VENUS	EARTH
Emotional Patience	Physical Patience	Mental Patience	Spiritual Patience	Soul Patience

Figure 17. The Moods of Stalking and the Xultun Tarot

sense of the disciple, the one who follows). When conflicting needs and demands cause chaos and disorder the Mental Sweetness of the Ruler brings everyone together to work for a common cause.

The Priest is the Holder of the Mood of Spiritual Sweetness. This is the spiritual fluidity that awakens spirit in others. The words of the Priest inspire us spiritually. For example, the sermons of Martin Luther King, the speeches of Mahatma Gandhi, or the conversations of the Dalai Lama.

We can see that the Consort and the Priest are on a raised dais, with the larger-than-life Ruler standing in front of the dais, signifying that they have some form of power or influence. We admire and look up to the physical power of the Consort (the capacity to give birth), the mental power of the

Ruler (courage and steadfastness), and the spiritual power of the Priest (the ability to talk to the gods).

The Lovers are the Holders of the Mood of Soul Sweetness. This is the soul or sexual fluidity that allows the marriage of matter and spirit in the human soul. We approach this Mood when we physically make love with our beloved. In their eyes and limbs we see heaven in earthly form. Our first taste of heaven is in this lovemaking—the attempt to unite with spirit through the body of another.

Cunning without Cruelty

Cunning is the north, mental Mood of flexibility. It is the ability see, as the Creator does, from all points around the Wheel of Life. We can then understand the world-view of others and how they came to construct and live by such a world-view. Then, no other human being is outside the realm of our understanding. With this comes not only the Sweetness of empathy (because when we develop one Mood it also feeds the opposite Mood across the wheel) but we are also less likely to be snagged by the beliefs of others. The word cunning is derived from the Old English word *cunnan,* "to know, have power to, to be able, to know how to do something, to be mentally able, to be learned." Its close cousins, like can, ken, canny, or know, derive from the same word ancestor. Cunning, meaning sly or deceitful, only came into use in the 14th century.

With Cunning we can adopt whatever belief system is necessary for our situation. Beliefs are a collective refuge from the meaninglessness of life and the Mood of Cunning is the capacity to see that life has no inherent meaning other than what we give it. Our beliefs are notions about reality, they are never reality itself. They are the map not the territory. Reality changes in each moment and mental constructs can never keep up. There is always some slippage between reality as-it-is and reality as-we-think-it-is and this liminal place is where spirit lives.

We develop attachments to our beliefs peculiar to our own psychology, we become attached to them, and they become so precious to us such that they become an object in our inner world. Then our beliefs (particularly those about spirituality and religion) become ossified into dogma and defended with much emotion as the "truth." If we believe that our way is the only way, as in fundamentalism, then this becomes cruelty.

The Warrior is the Holder of the Mood of Emotional Cunning. Emotional states are the raw stuff of the psyche. Without emotion there would be no movement and change in life. The word emotion is derived from the Latin *ex-*, meaning out, and *movere*, meaning to move, set in motion or agitate. The Warrior uses emotion as fuel for his movement. He has the emotional flexibility to be impulsive, to be impelled, to be moved into action "without a second thought" or even a first one. This lack of forethought is both his brilliance and his downfall but at his best the Warrior is not given to rumination and debate about what to do. In the moment he is all action without the need for a "why," a rationalisation, or a belief system to back himself up. He is able to experience and act on emotional states without having to reflect on them. This leaves him free to experience fully any emotional state without disowning it, denying it, believing in it, getting stuck in it or being consumed by it. If Cunning is highly developed, we can experience any emotion that we have ever had, or even those we have not personally experienced, to its depths without being overwhelmed. Actors are good at this.

The Cactus is the Holder of the Mood of Physical Cunning. This is the physical flexibility to realise the potentials of the body through the prolonged practice of physical disciplines such as yoga, tai-chi or martial arts. On a beginning level it is the willingness to entertain that the body has capacities beyond our comprehension.

The Sage is the Holder of the Mood of Mental Cunning. This is the mental flexibility to live without a belief system. It is the capacity to retain our identity and not be collectivised by belief or by faith (which is belief on steroids). It is to be able to relate to our thoughts as objects, things that have a separate life of their own. Aristotle said, "It is the mark of an educated mind to be able to entertain a thought without accepting it," and Jung, when asked if he believed in God said, "Since I have not the gift of belief, I only can say whether I know something or not."[1]

The Wheel is the Holder of the Mood of Spiritual Cunning. While Mental Cunning is about knowing the mental beliefs of humans, Spiritual Cunning is about knowing the beliefs, cognitions, and intellect of the Creator. In the Twenty Count the number 10 (the number of the Wheel) is All Measures of Intellect or All States of Consciousness. Just as humans conduct themselves mostly according to their belief systems so too does spirit. This intellect appears to us as fate or random chance but there is a lawfulness about how spirit moves and all religious traditions have ways of describing the orderedness and pattern of spirit. The Twisted Hairs speak of this as the Thirty Sacred Laws.[2] This knowledge of how spirit works is no different than any other knowledge, like the yachtie's knowledge of wind and tides, the surgeon's knowledge of anatomy, or the scientist's knowledge of the laws of physics. They give us skilfulness, expertise and freedom of movement in a particular domain, in other words, spiritual flexibility.

The Balance is the Holder of the Mood of Soul Cunning. Cunning is about building, in turn, one's knowledge of the domains of emotion, the body, the mind and spirit. The Sorcerer is the 1 card and he uses his will to bring about change in matter. The Balance, also known as the Ceremonial Alchemist, is the 11 card and uses his will to bring about change in spirit. The last domain of knowledge is the soul of the individual. Now the Balance has the capacity, agency and power to act on that knowledge in the service of the soul. All knowledge and action are without foundation or meaning until we choose from a place of deeper purpose. The "how," "when," and "what" are irrelevant until the "why" is clear, quite the opposite of the Warrior's action or the Sage's understanding. It is the soul's hunger: "For what purpose?" "What is my motivation?" "Do I want this?" "How does this serve me?" It is only after many rounds of sharpening the sword of decision that we gain enough Cunning to know where and when to cut deeply to bring about soul change.

Ruthlessness without Harshness

Ruthlessness is the west, physical Mood of stability. Just as Sweetness is about our relationship with water, Ruthlessness is about our relationship with earth, matter, form and substance. On the light side, it is the ruthlessness and self-discipline needed to challenge the body to go beyond its limits, or to rein in our physical heroism and adapt to the limitations of the body. The result is optimum health. It is the physical endurance necessary to keep going when times are hard or when times are soft. It is the ability to adapt and survive in a changing physical environment and having control over our physical space and personal security. On the shadow side, harshness is the control of matter for one's own ego-driven ends — external addiction to money or possessions. Or being controlled by matter and the body — internal addiction to substances. Ruthlessness is the physical equivalent of the Mood of Patience across the wheel.

The Hanged Man is the Holder of the Mood of Emotional Ruthlessness. The Warrior acts on his emotions, the Hanged Man suffers them. Psychological development, from the moment of birth, is the story of developing emotional self-control. This is not emotional repression but the process of harnessing the great horse of the emotions so it works for the Self not the ego. We have the emotional stability to be ruthless with our emotions and self-importance, to develop self-restraint, and to not unconsciously require others to carry our problems. It is a mark of maturity when we are able to manage our aggressive and sexual hungers, at least to the extent that they do not overly trouble others or the police. This requires that we suffer ourselves and our feelings. Not because self-restraint is "good" for us but because the containment of the burning rage, the smouldering resentment, the winding sorrow, the seductive excitement, or the manic happiness, begins an alchemy that brings death and change to the soul in the third row.

The Dead Man is the Holder of the Mood of Physical Ruthlessness. This is the physical stability to do whatever is needed to get the job done. It is having the body in the best possible physical condition in order to follow the designs of spirit, physically holding the tension between the opposites, not seeking a "geographical cure," undergoing physical hardship (fasting, pilgrimage, meditation), and allowing our encounters with physical death to teach us about spirit. Physical Ruthlessness is the ability to hold spiritual knowing in the body and to enable our body to be an Earth Lodge for spirit. This Mood is highly developed in shamanic shapeshifting or the ability to control our physiological states as in the Hindu *siddhis* or the Buddhist practice of *tummo*.

The Temperate Man is the Holder of the Mood of Mental Ruthlessness. This Mood asks us to surrender our unconsciously held beliefs and think without the impediment of belief. This gives us the mental stability to leave behind the comfort of collective beliefs, whether they belong to church or family, trade union or corporation, and have a mind of one's own. The 14 card is the point in the journey where spirit begins to work with us. In Christianity it is the guidance of the Holy Spirit. It is the place where our connecting link with the intent of the Creator begins to manifest. Thus the Temperate Man is not beholden to any faith, creed or belief other than Sacred Law, the laws of spirit. This does not make the Temperate Man unfeeling and without compassion towards others. Quite the opposite, he has the mental space to have thoughts that embrace All Our Relations. But from the ego's point of view authentic compassion is utterly ruthless as it pays no heed to the beliefs and needs of the ego.

The Bound Man is the Holder of the Mood of Spiritual Ruthlessness. This is the spiritual stability that enables us to surrender to our fate and the designs of the abstract. The mental freedom of the Temperate Man leads him to naturally and voluntarily to surrender his spiritual freedom, or at least exchange it for a greater freedom, by making a binding contract with his own soul.

The Released Man is the Holder of the Mood of Soul Ruthlessness. This is the soul stability that chooses and acts in accordance with the deepest desires of one's soul. All the cards of Ruthlessness are about burning away what is superfluous and leaving only the essence. The culmination of this process is the release from whatever tower we have built. The result is not an ascension, so beloved by monotheism, but a descension into matter so that we may meet spirit coming the other way.

Patience without Negligence

Patience is the east, spiritual Mood of expansiveness. Here we have arms patiently wide enough to embrace the trials of living in an imperfect world. It gives us the mental wisdom and emotional objectivity to say, "This too will pass." When we are patient and have forbearance time is no longer an enemy. Instead, it becomes an ally and we are able to use free will, active will, and passive will in equal measure.

The Star is the Holder of the Mood of Emotional Patience. This is being able to walk our own Path with Heart guided by the light of our own star. It is the emotional expansiveness to be able to ride out the emotional storms that beset us. Jung said, "What, on a lower level, had led to the wildest conflicts and panicky outbursts of emotion, from the higher level of the personality now looked like a storm in the valley seen from the mountain top. This does not mean the storm is robbed of its reality but instead of being in it, one is above it."[3] Don Juan said the same thing in a different way: "Realisations are of two kinds. One is just pep talk, great outbursts of emotion and nothing more. The other is the product of a shift of the assemblage point; it is not coupled with emotional outbursts, but with action. The emotional realisations come years later after warriors have solidified, by usage, the new position of their assemblage points."[4]

The Moon is the Holder of the Mood of Physical Patience which is the physical expansiveness that aligns us with the rhythms of the Self and nature. The moon is associated with the archetype of time and for many indigenous peoples, notably the Maya, time is holy. The orderedness of time as seen in the movements of the moon and other heavenly bodies gives an understanding of how energy moves between substance and spirit. Time is a way of staying aligned with the rhythms and cycles of the Creator.[5] Because every deviation from the Self is associated with a disturbed relationship with time, those who are closer to the tempo of the Self are more aligned with the rhythms of nature, and vice-versa. But in Western culture, time has lost its numinosity and become a secular commodity. Time is saved or spent, wasted or bought.

The Sun is the Holder of the Mood of Mental Patience which is the mental expansiveness to be able to see the light of nature, the inner light or *lumen naturae* of all things. With Mental Patience we can see past the outer forms of things, understand the heartfelt core of all beliefs, and so come to know that all pathways to God are equal. We may even have patience with our own path.

Planet Venus is the Holder of the Mood of Spiritual Patience which is the spiritual expansiveness that is spiritual love, love of spirit, or love of God. It is this love that allows us to have spiritual patience or in Christian terms, forgiveness. Planet Earth is the Holder of the Mood of Soul Patience which is the soul expansiveness that loves the soul of the world, the *anima mundi*, in all its beauty and imperfections, just as passionately as spirit does. We desire union with the world.

6

Movements

Nobody knows my personal history. Nobody knows who I am or what I do. Not even I… [If we] erase personal history, we create a fog around us, a very exciting and mysterious state in which nobody knows where the rabbit will pop out, not even ourselves… When nothing is for sure we remain alert, perennially on our toes.

—Don Juan Matus

Dreams are the driving force of life. Strangely enough they are the awakener.… The challenge is to bring the dream into reality as a gift to the People. Every dream is either a question or an answer to a question that is needed among the human beings.

—Hyemeyohsts Storm

Each column of the Xultun Tarot represents a Movement in our Book of Life. A Movement is a teaching and a challenge that the soul must meet on its journey. Like all the changes and processes described by the cards, the Movements are not sequential stages following one after the other but rather archetypal processes that are happening all the time, sometimes coming powerfully to the fore and at other times receding into the background. The Movements from left to right are Erasing Personal History, Using Death as an Advisor, Stopping the World, Controlling the Dream, and Assuming Authority (Figures 18 and 19).[1]

There are five gifts or *huaquas* that make us truly human and able to Walk in Balance—health, hope, happiness, harmony and humour.[2] The Movement of Erasing Personal History gives us the emotional gift of happiness. Using Death as an Advisor gives us the physical gift of health. Stopping the World gives us the mental gift of harmony. Controlling the Dream gives us the spiritual gift of hope. Assuming Authority gives us the soul gift of humour.[3]

Stopping the World

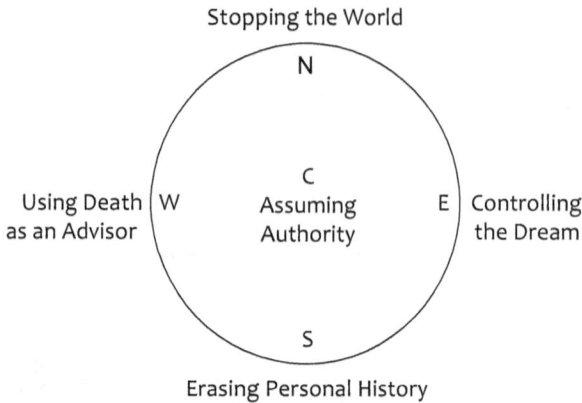

Figure 18. The Movements of the Book of Life

The Movements are the archetypal weft of the fabric woven on the Loom of Time. The Shields and the Moods are the horizontal warp made up of the particular circumstances of our life, the historical times we live in, and the individual choices that we make in response to our situation. These strands, archetypal and personal, are the unique pattern of our life that we weave. Each card is at the intersection of the horizontal, personal Shields and Moods and the vertical, archetypal Movements. Each card is a knot that holds the connection between the ancestral weft and the personal warp, between natural forces and human vices and virtues.

For example, in its archetypal aspect the Dead Man is the Teacher of Using Physical Death as an Advisor, and in its personal aspect it is the Keeper of the Body of the Adult Spirit Shield and the Holder of the Mood of Physical Ruthlessness. The Body of our Adult Spirit Shield desires, and is shaped by, the experience of a deep, physically intimate relationship with another. Its archetypal companion, death and change, always accompanies this intimacy. It is in matters of love and war that our Physical Ruthlessness emerges most starkly. And do not assume the body of the other is always human. Buried beneath our human loves is a love of the land, the body that we walk on. More wars have been waged over territory and love of the "homeland" than love of another human being.

The weaving is also seen in the masculine and feminine qualities of the Movements (see Figure 23). In the west Movement of Using Death as an Advisor all the cards are feminine. In the north Movement of Stopping the World, all the cards are masculine. In the south and east Movements of Erasing Personal History and Controlling the Dream, the masculine and feminine cards alternate and the Movements are mirror-images of each other. In the centre movement of Assuming Authority the cards are both masculine

PRIESTESS	CONSORT	RULER	PRIEST	LOVERS
Erasing Emotional History	Using Emotional Death as an Advisor	Stopping the Emotional World	Controlling the Emotional Dream	Assuming Emotional Authority
WARRIOR	CACTUS	SAGE	WHEEL	BALANCE
Erasing Mental History	Using Mental Death as an Advisor	Stopping the Mental World	Controlling the Mental Dream	Assuming Mental Authority
HANGED MAN	DEAD MAN	TEMPERATE MAN	BOUND MAN	RELEASED MAN
Erasing Physical History	Using Physical Death as an Advisor	Stopping the Physical World	Controlling the Physical Dream	Assuming Physical Authority
STAR	MOON	SUN	VENUS	EARTH
Erasing Spiritual History	Using Spiritual Death as an Advisor	Stopping the Spiritual World	Controlling the Spiritual Dream	Assuming Spiritual Authority

Figure 19. The Movements of the Book of Life and the Xultun Tarot

and feminine. The feminine Movements are learned primarily in the nagual and the masculine Movements primarily in the tonal.

In addition, the Movements also express the three kinds of will—active, passive and free. Active will is extroverted and masculine. ("Find your passion." "Don't just sit there, do something!") Passive will is introverted and feminine. ("Let your passion find you." "Don't just do something, sit there!") The Movements alternate, from left to right, between active will and passive will: Erasing Personal History is active will, Using Death as an Advisor is passive will, Stopping the World is active will, Controlling the Dream is passive will. Assuming Authority is free will.

Erasing Personal History

It is no surprise that the first Movement of the Book of Life is Erasing Personal History. We must disentangle ourselves from our family and our blood ancestors to become who we are. All peoples have their lineage stories of honour and shame, oppressing and being oppressed, suffering and inflicting suffering, grief and laughter. It is a mark of our humanness. When we erase personal history we create space within the weave for a new pattern to emerge that is different from previous generations. However, this is only the potential for something different, the possible interruption of the cycle of hurt and revenge. This potential is not actualised until the fifth Movement of Assuming Authority.

It is difficult to let go of personal history—like a dog with a bone, even though there's no meat. Masculine, sibling cultures have the most difficulty. The patriarchal line finds it hardest to let go of the grudge. It reveals its infirmity by its vulnerability to insult. Particularly precious are its beliefs, especially religious ones about the Father/God. Revenge, feuds, bad blood, disrespect, loss of face, honour killing, jihad, and crusade all flow from this. Then there's the ever-present Hollywood theme of the son avenging the death of the absent but longed-for father. Then hunting and killing the bad man who killed the good father. But the son/hero becomes just like them both because he's now a killer like the bad father but also a redeemed himself in the eyes of the good father for getting revenge… and so on. Saddam and the George Bushes come to mind?

When we do let go of personal history, we can then begin to assume authority. We say, "No more. This stops with me." If we do not assume responsibility, we transmit the same cultural DNA to future generations. If we do assume responsibility, even for what we have not created, we make a new genetic link, a new spiritual mutation.

Jung said, "But no matter how much parents and grandparents may have sinned against the child, the man who is really adult will accept these sins as his own condition which has to be reckoned with. Only a fool is interested in other people's guilt, since he cannot alter it. The wise man learns only from his own guilt. He will ask himself: Who am I that all this should happen to me? To find the answer to this fateful question he will look into his own heart."[4]

The first four Movements in the Book of Life are strands of a quadruple (a double double) helix of spiritual DNA that joins those who have gone before and those who will come after. The fifth Movement of Assuming Authority is at the centre of the helix and is the basis for mutative change and spiritual evolution from generation to generation.

In Assuming Authority we consciously accept, but do not identify with, the fortunes and misfortunes of our forebears. We take responsibility for the circumstances of our lives whatever they might be, while at the same time declining responsibility or holding others accountable where appropriate. We consciously consider the result of our actions or inactions on those who come after us unto seven generations. In Assuming Authority we are offered the opportunity to leave behind a spiritual legacy. As the fifth and catalyst Movement, Assuming Authority is the spiritual RNA of the Book of Life, transcribing what has been encoded by the other four Movements and passing it on to following generations.

Erasing Personal History and Assuming Authority are but different strands of the same spiral. Our personal history is a result of the previous generation's assuming responsibility... or not. We are living the dream, both light and dark, of those ancestors who came seven generations before us. We are the ancestors of those seven generations from now who will live out our collective dream that we are dreaming now.

Erasing Personal History is about the conflict between the opposites of light and dark. Each card initiates a process that becomes the developmental theme for that row. The Priestess looks for the Light-within-the-Dark, the Warrior fights the Dark-within-the-Light, the Hanged Man descends into the Dark-within-the-Dark, and the Star sees the Light-within-the-Light.

In this Movement we first go to the place of looks-within, introspection and intuition (the Priestess) to see the battle of the light and the dark within ourselves, to see our dark and light shadow — our dividedness and our potential. We then use this hard-won strength to be victorious over ourselves (the Warrior) and fashion a life for ourselves. Then we turn ourselves upside down (or are turned upside down by the Self) to annihilate the ego that we have worked hard to establish in the world (the Hanged Man). In so doing we awaken our sacred dream (the Star) which is the dream that the Self dreams of us. It is who we are when we are most fully alive and most truly ourselves. Now we are guided by our own star and able to see the transpersonal meaning of our personal history.

We should note that the term "erasing" has an adult, spiritualised tone. However, the first two rows of cards in the deck concern childhood and early adulthood and are more about creating a personal history, or what kind of personal history gets created for us, than erasing one. Erasing the personal history that has been created for us then predominates in the second half of life. Erasing is also open to misinterpretation as it implies wiping away, disappearance or eradication. No human being ever had perfect parents and we all come out of childhood and adolescence wounded in some way. We cannot make our personal history disappear however it is possible to change our relationship to it. It is possible to overcome our own childishness and the effect that our parents and our parental complexes have on us. Then the emotions generated by our childhood experiences no longer take centre stage in our lives. When a complex no longer generates significant emotion it no longer troubles us and goes off our psychological radar. But it never disappears, it is always present to be activated by life.

The wounding that arises from our personal history is, to some extent, an archetypal necessity and we are incomplete without it. W. B. Yeats wrote, "Nothing can be sole or whole / That has not first been rent."[5] For life to come forth we must first be divided, at odds with ourselves, split, unwhole. We see this in creation myths where the mythologem runs like this: The world-before-this-world was made of a single element. The first humans wanted more room, land to live on, or air to breathe. They separated the world into two elements (earth and sky, or land and water) and the world as we know it began to form. Significantly, this as often accompanied by grief, as in this Maori myth:

Rangi-nui, the Sky Father, looked down with loving eyes into the beauty of Papa-tu-a-nuku, the Earth Mother. He had longed for her from above and slowly they moved towards each other until they came together and were joined in a close, loving embrace.

The offspring of Rangi and Papa were numerous, and they lived in the cramped darkness between their parents. The Sky lay on the Earth and no light could come between them. Her coverings were rank low weed, and the sea was dark and putrid.

At length the children of Rangi and Papa came together to decide what should be done about their parents so that they could stand, stretch and grow. "Shall we kill our parents or shall we separate them?" they asked.

Tu-mata-uenga, the fiercest son and the god of war, said simply: "We have no choice. Let us kill our mother and father!"

But Tane-mahuta, father of all the forests, protested and said, "No, no, it is better that they be prised apart. Let our father stand high above us and our mother remain close to us below and continue to be our nursing mother".... Over an immense length of time he grew as the kauri tree, and very slowly he tried to move his parents. Next he lay on his back on his Earth Mother and he placed his feet against his father the Sky, and eventually the Sky began to move. Cries and shrieks of pain rang out from Rangi and Papa. "Why, why are you doing this to our great love for each other?" they cried....

Rangi, the Sky, looked down upon his wife and in his longing shed vast quantities of tears so that much of the land was covered by the sea. Papa, the Earth, looked up at her husband and in her yearning she too wept for him.

At length one of Papa's many sons, Mataaho, became worried that all of the land would be covered with sea from his father's tears so he resolved to turn his mother over so that his parents could not forever look upon one another and continue their grieving. This he accomplished, and now when Rangi weeps his tears are the dewdrops on Papa's back; the early morning mists that gather in her valleys are her heartfelt sighs.[6]

In Western culture there are two approaches to healing our personal history. There is what we might call the literal approach — to heroically change things, to manage the crisis, to cure the ill. This approach attends to matters of the inner child, trauma, catharsis, deprivation, emotional release, overcoming, positive thinking, breaking through, breaking down, symptom, diagnosis, cure, treatment, and management. For healing we go back: to causes, to biology, to chemical imbalance, to childhood, to infancy, to birth, to past lives. They are symptomatic cures, and symptoms they do indeed cure.

The other approach is a symbolic one. It has the rhythm of the growth of trees and decades and generations. It has to do with what James Hillman calls character, with all its connotations of fatefulness. It is what D. H. Lawrence called the "long, difficult repentance." This is not the warp and weft of our lives; it is not the thread with which we make the stitches, nor the form of the stitches, nor even the fabric itself. It is the dream that dreams the pattern. It seeks not to change but to outgrow; it seeks understanding not healing; consciousness not cure. We do not cure our problems, we outgrow them. This therapy is called Life. Sometimes it works, sometimes it doesn't.

Using Death as an Advisor

The second Movement of the Book of Life is Using Death as an Advisor. It is the process of changing without resistance. It is the body-knowing we have about the inevitability of change, that change is a natural outcome of all movements of life, and that all changes are small deaths. The "big" death itself is of the same nature and is birth into another form. All births are deaths, all deaths are births. All births, deaths, movements and changes happen in cycles of 9. There is a "death-birth" every 9 years, 9 months, 9 weeks, 9 days, and 9 seconds.[7]

This Movement is feminine and the four cards are the faces of the Holy Feminine as Life-Giver and Death-Bringer. The Consort (3) is the Teacher of Using Emotional Death as an Advisor and teaches us about Life. The Cactus (8) is the Teacher of Using Mental Death as an Advisor and teaches us about Death-within-Life. The Dead Man (13) is the Teacher of Using Physical Death as an Advisor and teaches us about Death. The Moon (18) is the Teacher of Using Spiritual Death as an Advisor and teaches us about Life-within-Death.

It is our desire to live that allows us to fully embrace death. To be able to experience death while still alive, to experience the tearing, the scooping out, the losing what we love — whether that be our self-esteem, money, the love of our life, our youth — is what keeps us fully alive. Endings get our attention and death concentrates the mind. Don Juan said:

> The thing to do when you're impatient is to turn to your left and ask advice from your death. An immense amount of pettiness is dropped if your death makes a gesture to you, or if you catch a glimpse of it, or if you just have the feeling that your companion is there watching you.... Yes, one of us here has to change, and fast. One of us here has to learn again that death is the hunter, and that it is always to one's left. One of us here has to ask death's advice and drop the cursed pettiness that belongs to men that live their lives as if death will never tap them.[8]

The Consort is full of life. She is bountiful and pregnant. In the Mythic Tarot, she is Demeter, the earth goddess of ancient Greece.[9] In other decks, she is the Empress, the Earth Mother, the Mother of All Life. We are the third rock from the sun and she is the number 3, the number of the Plants, the number of constant growth and abundance. But her ceaseless growing brings about the ceaseless dying of her shadow sister, the 13 card. Barbara Kingsolver describes her:

> First, picture the forest. I want you to be its conscience, the eyes in the trees. The trees are columns of slick, brindled bark like muscular animals overgrown beyond all reason. Every space is filled with life: delicate, poisonous frogs war-painted like skeletons, clutched in copulation, secreting their precious eggs onto dripping leaves. Vines strangling their own kin in the everlasting wrestle for sunlight. The breathing of monkeys. A glide of snake belly on branch. A single-file army of ants biting a mammoth tree into uniform grains and hauling it down to the dark for their ravenous queen. And, in reply, a choir of seedlings arching their necks out of rotted tree stumps, sucking life out of death. This forest eats itself and lives forever.[10]

From this paradise, where life and death just happen, innocently and unconsciously, where everything is growing and provided for, where everything is dying and provided for, we must withdraw into ourselves and leave. We must go from the jungle into the desert, be cut off from the collective noise and profusion and, like the Cactus, have the strength to be with oneself. The equivalent of the Cactus in the Marseilles Tarot is the Strength card. It is the Keeper of the Body of the Adult Substance Shield and the Teacher of the mental aspect of Using Death as an Advisor.

The heroic young body comes alive in the face of risk and danger and loves to dance on the edge and the Cactus represents the capacity to be victorious over death while still alive. All cultures have ceremonies of isolation, retreat and withdrawal to natural places where the forced introversion intensifies the relationship between the inner and outer worlds. These physical privations bring about the psychological death of the 13 card (the Dead Man). From this, we learn something of the inevitable cycles of life and death in the universe, that there are hidden patterns of ebb and flow that are not visible in the bright light of the sun but are only seen by the soft light of the Moon (18).

Stopping the World

Stopping the World happens when we still the mind and are completely in the present moment such that we can catch "minimal chance" (the Breath of Chance, or Chaos). In this space between substance and spirit we see the breath of spirit, in the quietness between the inhale and the exhale. This also happens at sunrise and sunset when for a moment the world stops, Grandmother Earth turns over her robe, and we can see substance breathe.

Don Juan said that stopping the internal dialogue was the key to the sorcerer's world and that there were "two major activities or techniques used to accelerate the stopping of the internal dialogue: erasing personal history and 'dreaming.' To erase personal history three other techniques were taught: losing self-importance, assuming responsibility, and using death as an advisor."[11]

The four cards in this Movement are the faces of the Holy Masculine and each has a give-away to add to what the feminine has birthed in the previous Movement. The Ruler is the Teacher of Stopping the Emotional World and gives order to the Life birthed by the Consort. The Sage is the Teacher of Stopping the Mental World and gives meaning to the Death-within-Life birthed by the Cactus. The Temperate Man is the Teacher of Stopping the Physical World and gives wisdom to the Death birthed by the Dead Man. The Sun is the Teacher of Stopping the Spiritual World and gives illumination and meaning to the Life-within-Death birthed by the Moon.

The column of masculine energy that is Stopping the World holds the tension between the opposites in its particular row. The Ruler holds the horizontal tension in the world, the Sage holds the vertical tension between the As Above and the So Below, the Temperate Man holds the tension between the 4 elements, and the Sun holds the tension in all 8 directions.

The Ruler governs the secular world and brings emotional order to the kingdom. The Sun is the ruler of the spiritual world and brings spiritual order by bringing light into the darkness. Positioned between the Ruler and the Sun, the Sage and the Temperate Man are at the centre of the whole deck and they hold the balance between the spiritual and material worlds. We shall examine their significance in Chapter 24.

We construct both the psychological and physical worlds that we inhabit. Even though the discovery of an unconscious blind spot often comes as a great shock to the ego, it is relatively easy to comprehend that we assemble our psychological world. But to consider that our physical world may be a projection, that it may be sustained by our attentional and perceptual habits, is considered to be crazy. But here, it is our Western worldview that suffers from the unconscious blind spot. It considers the external, physical world to be an unalterable reality that is uninfluenced by non-physical events. Thus we have the split between the "hard" sciences (mathematics, physics or chemistry) and the "soft" sciences (psychology, sociology and so on), with the softer sciences trying desperately to gain the respect of their older siblings by stiffening up and becoming "harder." Science does not trust the human observer, objectivity is good and subjectivity is bad, and it attempts to experimentally exclude observer effects and other "confounding" factors. The only instruments considered trustworthy are non-human ways of apprehending reality—clocks, rulers, scales, statistical formulae, microscopes, telescopes and the like.

Not that all this is wrong—just unbalanced. In contrast, all spiritual traditions attest to the fact that the apparently solid nature of reality is "maya," the Hindu veil of illusion. The nature of reality is not independent of who is observing it. Many traditions have some form of meditation—that is, a way of withdrawing the libido invested in the perception of the phenomenal world. In deep meditation, our internal dialogue quietens, our perceptual viewpoint collapses and the world Stops.

Controlling the Dream

Stopping the World unlinks the obsession of the first attention with the phenomenal world. When our World Stops the unseen becomes a separate reality and the second attention emerges. The shamanic practices designed to encourage our second attention and recondition our energetic capabilities to perceive are called the "art of dreaming."[12] In Controlling the Dream we build a functional and robust connection with spirit. However, this requires the development of the personality of the dreamer as well as the arts of dreaming. As Don Juan points out, the sorcerers of the Americas were consummate dreamers but they themselves did not change. This was their downfall.

> "Sorcerers view dreaming as an extremely sophisticated art," [don Juan]
> said, "the art of displacing the assemblage point at will from its habitual
> position in order to enhance and enlarge the scope of what can be per-

ceived... The problem with the old sorcerers was that they learned wonderful things, but on the basis of their unadulterated lower selves," don Juan went on. "The inorganic beings became their allies, and, by means of deliberate examples, they taught the old sorcerers marvels. Their allies performed the actions, and the old sorcerers were guided step by step to copy those actions, without changing anything about their basic nature."[13]

Edward Edinger called this connection with spirit the ego-self axis.[14] Jung called it living the symbolic life. Then "life makes sense, and makes sense in all continuity, and for the whole of humanity. That gives peace, when people feel that they are living the symbolic life, that they are actors in the divine drama. That gives the only meaning to human life; everything else is banal and you can dismiss it. A career, producing of children, all are maya compared with that one thing, that your life is meaningful."[15]

Our physical world is made up of three dimensions. A point is something that has no magnitude and only one dimension. Like the oneness of the Sorcerer, a point has not yet taken up form in the world. But when the point moves it has intention so a two-dimensional form comes into being. As Euclid said, a moving point sweeps a line, a moving line sweeps a plane, and a moving plane sweeps a solid. Now we have three dimensions. The fourth dimension is time and the fifth dimension is the dream, the unseen world of spirit or the unconscious. This fifth dimension dreams our world into life. It is well known, for example, that dreams are often months or years ahead of conscious developments. So our waking reality that we experience has already been dreamed of in the fifth dimension. Everything that exists physically has already been imagined and dreamed by something, somewhere, sometime.

Dreaming (behaviour in the fifth dimension and dealing with the aberrations of spirit) must be balanced by stalking (behaviour in the third dimension and dealing with the aberrations of humans). Stalking is a set of procedures and attitudes that enable us to get the best out of any situation. Dreaming is the capacity to utilise one's dreams and transform them into controlled awareness. Castaneda explains:

The *stalkers* are the ones who take the brunt of the daily world. They are the business managers, the ones who deal with people. Everything that has to do with the world of ordinary affairs goes through them. The *stalkers* are the practitioners of *controlled folly*, just as the *dreamers* are the practitioners of *dreaming*. In other words, *controlled folly* is the basis for *stalking*, as dreams are the basis for *dreaming*. Don Juan said that, generally speaking, a warrior's greatest accomplishment in the second attention is *dreaming,* and in the first attention his greatest accomplishment is *stalking.*[16]

The word "controlling" as I use it here means not to control or exert authority over but to have mastery of and to be at home with. Just as the swimmer is at home in the water but does not control it, the dreamer is one who connects with the non-physical world in a fluid way. All of the cards in this Movement are about working at the boundary between spirit and matter. The Priest (5) is the seer who has contact with the fifth dimension of the dream. Through this relationship, the Wheel (10) shows him other states of consciousness and the habits of spirit. Through a binding contract with his soul within and spirit without the Bound Man (15) is then able to break free of the ignorance and darkness accumulated by humans over millennia and bring spirit and matter closer together. Finally, the Feathered Winged Serpent (20) is the Light-within-the-Light of the Planet Venus and the incarnation of spirit within matter.

Assuming Authority

In dreams begin responsibilities. —W. B. Yeats

In this Movement, we come to fully accept and take responsibility for who we are and are not, what we can and cannot do, our strengths and limitations, and the path we have walked and the path we have not taken. We accept ourselves as we are. The desire for self-improvement has gone. We see what needs to be done and simply do it. We stand on our own, not separate from humankind, but in the knowledge that at the end of the day neither the gods nor our fellow humans can help us. We are the sum total of our own diligence and effort. Don Juan said:

When a man decides to do something he must go all the way, but he must take responsibility for what he does. No matter what he does, he must know why he is doing it, and then he must proceed with his actions without having doubts or remorse about them.... Everything I do is my decision and my responsibility... Death is stalking me. Therefore, I have no room for doubts or remorse. If I have to die as a result of taking you for a walk then I must die.... You, on the other hand feel that you are immortal and the decisions of an immortal man can be cancelled or regretted or doubted. In a world where death is the hunter, my friend, there is not time for regrets or doubts. There is only time for decisions.[17]

Each card in this Movement represents a loss, a breaking away from something, a severing of ties, an ending, a closure. If it's a loss that can be repaired, then it's not a loss, it's a substitution. Jo Coudert elaborates:

> You'll get over it... It's the clichés that cause the trouble. To lose someone you love is to alter your life for ever. You don't get over it because "it" is the person you loved. The pain stops, there are new people, but the gap never closes. How could it? The particularness of someone who mattered enough to grieve over is not erased by anyone but death. This hole in my heart is in the shape of you and no one else can fit. Why would I want them to?

These losses can only be compensated for and healed by an equal psychological and spiritual gain, something greater that pulls one into more life such that the loss recedes but never disappears. We can see this in the chronological sequence of the cards: adolescence (the Lovers) is the loss and mourning of childhood; adulthood (the Balance) is the loss and mourning of adolescence; old age (the Tower) is the loss and mourning of adulthood; and elderhood (Planet Earth) is the loss and mourning of life and the new birth into spirit.

Joseph Henderson said that three conditions are necessary for individuation (in other words, Assuming Authority) to become real as opposed to being anticipated in dreams. One, separation from the original family or clan. Two, commitment to a meaningful group over a long period of time. Three, liberation from too close an identity with the group.[18] The Lovers represents letting go of our family and are the Teachers of Assuming Emotional Authority. The Balance represents letting go of our outer culture and is the Teacher of Assuming Mental Authority. The Released Man represents letting go of our ego-based inner culture (our personality) and is the Teacher of Assuming Physical Authority. The Planet Earth represents letting go of spirit itself to experience the physical preciousness of creation and is the Teacher of Assuming Spiritual Authority.

The Movement of Assuming Authority is composed of four steps, two steps away from matter and two steps toward spirit. We fall in love with another (the Lovers) and, seeing heaven in their eyes, we forsake our blood family. In the lightning-bolt of decision made by the Balance we leave behind our spiritual parents or culture and forge our own destiny. These are the first two steps. Then we do not so much walk the next two steps, as we are dragged by spirit. In the Released Man the lightning bolt of spirit, not the ego, decides our fate and we have to let go of what is familiar even in our own psyche. Then in the Planet Earth card we forsake the designs of spirit itself and fall in love with all of Creation. Now, full circle, All Things are our blood family and we are both a child of the universe and its parent.

At the beginning, for life to move forward there must be a transfer of attachment from the physical parents to the spiritual parents or culture (see Chapter 13). In many indigenous cultures this is done through separate initiation processes for girls and boys. Particularly for young males, these are rigorous, authoritarian, painful, testing and sometimes fatal events. If initiation doesn't happen then the same archetypal need expresses itself but in less conscious and more deadly ways—car accidents, depression, binge drinking or an overdose, to name but a few. During and after initiation young women or young men then come under the tutelage and mentorship of the spiritual parents. If there is no spiritual parentage the person is vulnerable to being stuck at the warrior stage. This lack of initiation is the norm in Western culture.

In the Lovers card the individual moves out of the realms of both the biological parents (the Consort and the Ruler) and the spiritual parents (the Priestess and the Priest). The peer group becomes more important and helps diminish the gravitational pull of the family ties so the adolescent can live and love outside the family and forge adult relationships. It is in the affairs of the heart that we first establish our individuality and the Lovers card symbolises the decision made from the heart to become entangled in life and love.

But later in life we must in turn let go of our spiritual parents just as we had to let go of our physical parents. Letting go of the good parent is much more difficult than letting go of the bad parent. But, in our own fashion, we have to abandon, divorce, or kill (psychologically) both our earthly and spiritual parents in order to come to ourselves. This may sound dramatic but the other world, which communicates to us through dreams, uses these images of abandonment, murder and killing if the ego is unwilling.

We need to kill that which gave us life in order to birth new life in ourselves. Adolescents need to "kill" the outer parent, who they paradoxically depend on, to move out of their gravitational field. This is often a loud and messy process. At an earlier age, Freud's Oedipal conflict is another one of numerous developmental steps that, throughout our lives, follow this archetypal pattern.

There is also another archetypal need, a mirror-image which is not as obvious because it is a more introverted process. It is the ego's need, as inner parent, to initiate the inner child. In other words, to grow up. Wherever there is an uninitiated warrior (male or female) overreaching themselves and trying to be bigger, there is an equally fearful and fragile inner child trying to stay smaller. Initiation helps the child grow up and the adolescent grow down.

Unfortunately, the "inner child work" of popular culture does not help the child grow up. Often, it is a way of maintaining the tie to the hated or unloving parent by securing a final victory over them by becoming their opposite — the eternally warm, nurturing, unconditionally loving parent to the "inner child." The ego then identifies itself as victim or survivor. As necessary a first step in recovery as this might be it often congeals into a support group and a culture of complaint and perpetual woundedness.

Whereas the Lovers make an unconscious choice to merge, the Balance makes a conscious choice to discriminate, to separate things rather than bring them together. In the second row, the cards preceding the Balance (11) are the Sage (9) and the Wheel (10). The Sage has the self-knowledge distilled from life experience about who he is and what he wants. The Wheel is the beginning of a new cycle, a new order. The number 11 is consciousness (1) of the new order (10). Therefore, the Balance as the Teacher of the mental aspect of Assuming Authority, is about the wise and timely use of the sword of mental discrimination from an awareness of a new order. The Balance moves when the universe moves and takes action at the right moment as the wheel of time revolves. These choices are not trivial ones. If the choice is easy then it likely does not involve the whole personality and the deeper layers of the psyche. The Balance chooses and takes responsibility for the decision, fully aware that when we use our own authority, as distinct from the allowances or obligations afforded us by the collective, there is often displeasure, disapproval, opposition or attack.

The Balance (11) is the halfway point in the deck. It occupies the same position in relationship to the second half of the deck as the Sorcerer (1) does to the first half. As the will of the Sorcerer to incarnate in matter seeds the birth of the ego, so the will of the Balance (the lightning that crackles downward from his wand) to live his own life, rather than live solely within the safety of the collective, fertilises the Earth at the end of the journey. This courage to judge, to use free will when there are no rules, laws or conventions to guide us, is what initiates us into spirit. It is ultimately creative not only for the individual but for the Earth itself.

The human psyche, in spite of its frailty, has been given the gift of free will. It is in this choosing and assuming responsibility that we make our give-away to life, for good or for ill. It is what Jung spoke of when he asked, "Does the individual know that he is the makeweight that tips the scales?"[19] But Hillman also points out that, "Jungians have sometimes led us from the world soul into the private soul, quoting Jung who said we are each makeweights in the scales of world history. On the individual the destiny of the world depends. I think this statement can be reversed and be equally true today: on the destiny of the world, the fate of the individual depends."[20]

The next card in this Movement is the Released Man, the Teacher of the physical aspect of Assuming Authority. Now comes the final destruction of beliefs, theories, expectations, familiar perceptions, and ways of seeing. After the liberation from the attachment, bondage and addiction of the Bound

Man, the Released Man is no longer attached to matter itself. The Lovers and the Balance cards represent the personal authority that flows from a thinking heart and a feeling head. But the Released Man is where we make life-changing contact with the source of this inner authority—the Self. The result is the clearing away of those remaining psychic structures that hide our own authority from ourselves and conceal the terror and pleasure of knowing that we are totally responsible for who we are.

But paradoxically, at this stage of Assuming Authority, we have our choices wrested away from us by spirit. The Released Man is not a card of generous cooperation or reasoned negotiation. We are blasted out of the tower; we are intruded on, abused, violated, dispirited, and disempowered. Spirit takes away our rights, commits sacrilege, profanes our creed, race, religion and gender, is politically incorrect, despoils our precious values, and generally behaves badly toward us. We suffer, as Jung said, from the violence done to us by the Self.[21] We are struck by the divine lightning, the thunderbolt, the shaft that cleanses and fertilises. If we are full of illusion the Released Man is an experience of collapse but if we are without illusion then the card is one of liberation.

The lightning bolts that emanate from the Balance card each branch into three, the number of increase and fertility. The more visible lightning bolt issuing from the wand only reaches the top of the tower. However, the other bolt comes from underneath the Balance's left foot at the top of the Released Man card and reaches all the way down to the flower-soul in the Planet Earth card. This symbolises something of great importance. When a Two-legged takes a "stand" (which may be internal and not in the public arena) and chooses with free will then he or she creates something that lasts beyond the life of the individual. The past and future are irrevocably changed. We change our karma, we rewrite our Book of Life. The possible future that existed before the choice will never come to pass. This is why the lightning bolts skip two rows—there is no step-by-step process of change, it is done in an instant. This is the link between will and magic. The lightning-children born from these choices are the spirit and soul of the next spiral of life. The fire in the cauldron is the spirit and passion to be conjured again by the Sorcerer and the white flower is the soul to be carried once more by the Fool.

7

Mirror

Don Juan said that the nagual Elias explained to him that what distinguishes normal people is that we share a metaphorical dagger: the concerns of our self-reflection. With this dagger, we cut ourselves and bleed; and the job of our chains of self-reflection is to give us the feeling that we are bleeding together; that we are sharing something wonderful: our humanity. But if we were to examine it, we would discover that we are bleeding alone; that we are not sharing anything; that all we are doing is toying with our manageable, unreal, man-made reflection.

— Carlos Castaneda

As well as Five Movements there are also Three Paths in the Book of Life: Creating the Mirror of Self-reflection, Cracking the Mirror of Self-reflection and Seeing Through the Mirror of Self-reflection (Figure 20).[1] Like the Movements, they outline the soul's journey through life but with more emphasis on the functioning of the ego. The Paths tend to be more linear and sequentially ordered in time over the life cycle whereas the Movements are occurring all the time.

The wheel of the Five Movements as in Figure 18 includes all the cards from 2 through 21 with the 0 and 1 cards remaining apart. However, the three linear Paths includes the cards from 1 through 21 with the 0 card remaining unattached. The union of the 0 and 1 balances the chaos of the Five Movements. The chaos of the 0 balances the order and linearity of the Three Paths.

When we add the Five Movements to the Three Paths we get number 8 which is the number of Pattern, including the Pattern that we know of as the physical body. When we take a figure 8, sever each end and partially untwist it, we get the double helix that contains the human genome — the physical Book of Life. When we multiply 5 (the Movements) by 3 (the Paths) we get 15 which in the Twenty Count is the number of the Souls of All Humans and All Matter. Thus the tarot is the story of the journey of all human souls through matter, and the relationship of the human soul to matter.

The Mirror of Self-reflection is the ego itself. The Three Paths show how the ego is formed, how it is challenged and its limitations revealed, and how it is healed and brought into relationship with spirit. The Three Paths constitute our physical birth, our psychological birth and our spiritual birth. Creating the Mirror of Self-reflection (the Sorcerer to the Warrior) is about the development of the ego. Cracking the Mirror of Self-reflection (the Cactus to the Temperate Man) is about the destruction of the ego. Seeing Through the Mirror of Self-reflection (the Bound Man to the Planet Earth) is about the transcendence of the ego.

In J. R. R. Tolkien's *The Lord of the Rings* each of the three books (*The Fellowship of the Ring, The Two Towers* and *The Return of the King*) correspond to a path in the Book of Life. The task of Frodo (the ego) is to return the ring (the Self) to a place that can contain its power (the earth, as represented by Mount Doom). His story is the same as the tarot—to refuse the enchantments of both the light and the dark, and to become consciously related to the Self without losing our earthy, instinctive humanness (Sam Gamgee).

The task of the first Path is to become a useful human being and experience our belonging in society. In the second Path, we consciously exile ourselves from the collective to experience our uniqueness and separateness and Crack the Mirror of Self-reflection. In the third Path, the ego is no longer mesmerised by its reflections in the mirror held up by itself or the world, and it Sees Through the Mirror of Self-reflection. We are then able to see through the eyes of our Elder Shield and experience our belonging in the whole of Creation. We can touch the place where we become unknown to ourselves, not knowing what we will do, or who we will be, from one moment to the next. In the final passage of his autobiography Jung describes this kind of consciousness: "The more uncertain I have felt about myself, the more there has grown up in me a feeling of kinship with all things. In fact it seems to me as if that alienation which so long separated me from the world has become transferred to my own inner world, and has revealed to me an unexpected unfamiliarity with myself."[2]

Creating the Mirror

The first Path is about the formation of the ego and the development of active will. We see active will most clearly in the heroic stories of those who have fashioned a meaningful life out of great adversity, those anointed with oceans of courage who have put a more human face on the world, and those who have put themselves in harm's way, physically or spiritually, to protect what gives life. For most of us this path involves a different, but not lesser, kind of heroism—becoming a functional member of our family and

Creating the Mirror of Self-Reflection

Cracking the Mirror of Self-Reflection

Seeing Through the Mirror of Self-Reflection

Figure 20 The Three Paths of the Book of Life

society, taking up adult responsibility, getting an education, contributing to the commonwealth in some way and, most importantly, experiencing our belongingness and similarity.

At the beginning and the end of this Path are the Sorcerer and the Warrior — the ones who are the masters of will and intent. The Sorcerer looks upward and outward to the Great Light. He is the one who knows the way of the dream and how to change matter through impressing his will on spirit. The Warrior looks steadfastly forward, along the human plane between spirit and matter. He knows the ways of the world and how to change spirit through impressing his will on matter. As the final card in this Path, the Warrior sits on his throne signifying that the ego has consolidated itself in the world.

There is a break in the visual flow of the cards between the Sorcerer and the Priestess and then again between the Lovers and the Warrior. These breaks, which we see in each Path, represent a discontinuity in the comfortable flow of life — a chaotic change or what Gregory Bateson called "second order" change. The first break between the Sorcerer and the Priestess is physical birth and the cards that follow describe the stages of early development. In Freudian and Kleinian terms (for a further discussion see Chapter 12) the Priestess is the paranoid-schizoid position, the Consort is the depressive position, the Ruler is the oedipal stage, the Priest is the latency stage, and the Lovers are adolescence. The break between the Lovers and the Warrior is the psychological birth into adulthood or more accurately into egohood — the conscious awareness of one's self-identity.

The sun we see behind the Consort, Ruler and Priest suggests that their focus is on strengthening the light of consciousness. Further from consciousness, in the twilight, are the Priestess and the Lovers. They look downward, absorbed in something other than the ego — they look beneath the surface of the world. The Priestess sees into the unconscious and looks at the ego's destiny from the viewpoint of the Self. She reads from a codex, the Book of Life in which the soul's code has been written.[3] The Lovers look into the smoking mirror to see what will be written as a result of their fateful choices in love.

Cracking the Mirror

> Psychotherapy is at bottom a dialectical relationship between doctor and patient. It is an encounter, a discussion between two psychic wholes, in which knowledge is used only as a tool. The goal is transformation — not one that is predetermined, but rather an indeterminable change, the only criterion of which is the disappearance of egohood.[4]

By the end of the first path the ego has achieved a level of social adaptation, belonging and status. But the second path puts aside all these accomplishments and is the story of the destruction of that part of the ego that overly identifies with the collective and the birth of the person as a unique individual. This is what Jung called individuation. Don Juan said:

> The *tonal* [the ego] rules, yet it is very vulnerable [and] must be protected at any cost. The crown has to be taken away from it, but it must remain as the protected overseer.... The goal of a warrior's training then is not to teach him to hex or charm, but to prepare his *tonal* not to crap out.... Whenever it doesn't succeed, there is a moment of bafflement, and then the tonal opens itself to death. What a prick! It would rather kill itself than relinquish control. And yet there is very little we can do to alter that condition.[5]

For healthy personality development all available libido has to be put into building up the ego in the first twenty-seven years of life.[6] This is inevitably one-sided and around mid-life the unconscious will attempt to establish a balance. This compensation requires the individual to have sufficient adaptation and ego strength (including the strength to be weak) so the ego can tolerate its own symbolic death and rebirth. Now the ego must develop passive will — the capacity to endure, to not act, to bear one's own fate. In a letter to his brothers in 1817, the poet John Keats (1795–1821) wrote of "negative capability, that is, when a man is capable of being in uncertainties, mysteries, doubts, without any irritable reaching after fact and reason."

Unlike the public ordeals that the Warrior sought, the challenges are now personal and one must develop one's own container and ego boundaries strong enough to ward off collective invasions and interferences. So the first card on this path is the Cactus or Strength card. It sits in its own pot and grows even in extreme conditions.

Next is the Sage who sits within a temple. In the Marseilles Tarot he is the Hermit who carries a lantern. He symbolises the need for solitude, introspection and finding one's way in the darkness of the psyche by the little light of our own consciousness.

Once the Warrior has explored the outer world and the Sage the inner world, the ego now confronts what it cannot conquer — time, fate and the laws of the universe. This is the Wheel of Fortune as the Aztec calendar stone. This symbolises time as the destroyer but also the healer, as it grinds up what has been constructed by the ego but does so with a cosmic purpose. Now the Wheel stands at the centre of the platform instead of the Ruler — the ego has met a greater will and has been deposed.

We see the same theme in the next card, the Balance (or Justice in the Marseilles Tarot). He, like the Ruler, is the fourth card along the path. However, he stands one step lower on the platform and is smaller than the Ruler. This indicates that, in its encounter with fate, the ego has now become humbled, taken down a peg.

The Balance is about using the sword of discrimination to choose and this choosing brings about the humiliation of the ego. Yet it is the ego that does the choosing, in other words it chooses its own death and commits suicide. If we do not choose death and change consciously then the unconscious will choose it for us. Impossible situations happen to us where we are forced to choose something unwelcome to the ego. Sometimes suicidal feelings may emerge where the need for ego sacrifice is acted out literally.

In this path, the scene is unbroken across the first four cards. They all bask in the light of the sun behind the Consort in the top row suggesting that the ego has not yet entirely broken free of the parental complexes. The fire is still outside – it is not yet integrated. Then there is a break and in the next card the Hanged Man begins to burn with the Fire-from-within. This is the fire that is internalised, suffering that is intensely and personally experienced. Following the Dead Man, a state of harmony then emerges in the Temperate Man.

Seeing through the Mirror

This is the path of free will and begins with the Bound Man or the Devil. Here we become married and bound to spirit so that the soul may be free. The first two cards in this Path (the Bound Man and the Released Man) embody the archetype of the apocalypse. Then there is a break before the Star card. The passage through this gateway between the Released Man and the Star is an apocalypse for both matter and spirit. For each it reveals another world quite unlike their own. The contemporary interpretation of the Released Man (the Tower in the Marseilles Tarot) suggests that it is a catastrophe for the ego. But it also is a catastrophe for spirit as it descends from above – what was previously whole in its oneness becomes divided and falls to earth. The Released Man symbolises the destruction of any remaining ego inflation so it can live in the world of spirit but it is also the "downsizing" of spirit and the archetypes so they can live in the world of matter. The personality expands, spirit contracts. Both must undergo a cataclysmic kenosis or emptying before they can pass through the gateway into the other world. Spirit has to squeeze itself into the tight bodice of matter and it is given a rude awakening as to what life is like on this planet. For humans, it is a final shrivening, the bolt from the blue, the lightning bolt of illumination, after the reconciliation and harmony of the Temperate Man.

The Star follows the catastrophic collapse of old forms in the Released Man and symbolises a personal vision or hope born out of struggle. In all cultures there are stories of how we came from the stars. The Star Nations are intimately connected to our past and our future—they hold the memory of human history and the hope of human potential. Now, with the Star and the cards that follow (Moon, Sun, Planet Venus and Planet Earth) the light of consciousness progressively increases. They bless us with starlight, moonlight, sunlight, the white light of Planet Venus, and the black light of Planet Earth. These are the luminosities that humans need in order to "see."

The Moon, as the mediator between the As Above and the So Below, allows the personal vision, the transpersonal hope represented by the Star, to emerge slowly into consciousness. Too much clarity, too much haste, too much consciousness, too much definition and examination, spoils what is emerging. The Moon softens and gives a shadowy shape to things that allows what is emerging to find its own way without the ego putting its stamp of knowing on it.

The Sun is the symbol of libido and life-force—it is the divine fire that moves through all things. Volcanoes, the inner fire of Grandmother Earth, frame the outer fire of Grandfather Sun. In this image, we see the passion of substance for spirit and spirit for substance. We see this divine fire of transpersonal origin all along the base of the last row. All of the cards have some kind of fire in them—a star, volcanoes or the sun. However, in the last card in the deck (Planet Earth) the fire is not the cosmic fire but the fire of individual consciousness symbolised by the smoking urn.

The next card is Planet Venus or Judgement in the Marseilles Tarot. In the form of the Feathered Winged Serpent flanked by two volcanoes, spirit descends and penetrates substance (or substance ascends and envelops spirit). In Aztec and Maya mythology, the Feathered Winged Serpent was associated with the sky-god Quetzalcoatl whose story has many similarities to that of Christ. He was identified with Venus, the morning star, as was Christ who, in the Book of Revelation, describes himself as the "bright and morning star." The Planet Venus as the symbol of love, and the person of Quetzalcoatl as saviour, embody the human hope that love will prevail in the cosmic struggle. The last card, Planet Earth, symbolises completion, fulfilment and wholeness and is the culmination of the individuation process.

8

DNA

"Every stone has seven faces. The first face is sound."

"Agnes, you're not going to tell me that rocks make a sound?"

"Yes, I am going to try to describe to your great unawareness—and how you misinterpret and misunderstand the things around you. Rocks do indeed make a sound. All things that the Great Spirit has put here continually cry to be heard."

—Lynn Andrews

Science has long debated the question "What is life?" meaning, "Where is the dividing line between living matter and dead matter?" The scientific consensus is that anything that reproduces itself via some form of DNA and has a carbon-based, "organic" metabolism is alive and everything else is dead. To a world-view that sees death as the cessation of organic life processes and the extinction of consciousness, this makes sense. But the question of a dividing line is irrelevant if matter itself has consciousness (albeit very different from human or animal consciousness). We would do well to remember that the vast majority of human beings throughout history have considered all things in Creation to have some form of consciousness. The modern scientific distinction between "living" and "non-living" is a recent aberration. It is another way of dissociating from the reality of the natural world and, simply put, it is wrong.

The modern theory of evolution describes how "dead" matter came to be "living." Change comes about through alterations in DNA called "mutations" that have no discernible cause other than "chance." These changes are selected for by the "survival of the fittest" or "natural selection." It is ironic that science, an enterprise that idealises precision and certainty and does its best to eliminate the messy, feminine element of chance through the experimental method, should place chance at the centre of evolution—the most important theory of modern biological science.

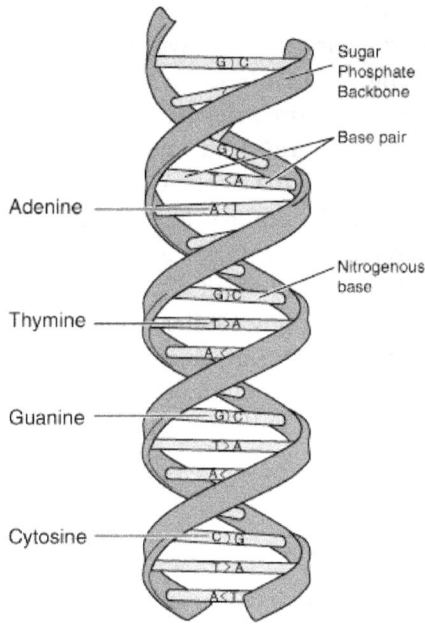

Figure 21. The DNA Double Helix

I am not suggesting that evolution through natural selection does not happen, just that it may not be the only game in town. Neither am I suggesting that Creationism is the other game in town. They are just fundamentalist twins who squabble — one believes in absolute chance, the other in absolute determinism. The tenets of evolutionary theory and accepted notions of what is living are being challenged. In other words, they themselves are evolving. James Lovelock's Gaia theory is now generally accepted. He proposed that the whole planet is a self-regulating, self-sustaining organism that is "alive."[1] His co-author, Lynn Margulis, has suggested that evolution takes place through a process of symbiosis rather than mutation and in fact, the random mutation of genes may be the least important mechanism of evolution.[2]

The elements (earth, air, fire and water) and supposedly dead matter are alive, they have consciousness, and they evolve. The stuff of the universe (quarks, photons, gluons, electrons, 100-odd chemical elements, chemical reactions, chemical compounds, minerals and rocks, right up to what we anthropocentrically define as living matter) has been evolving and becoming increasingly complex in the infinite cycle of the separation of sames and the union of opposites. Living matter evolved from dead matter by pure accident, so the story goes. But let's not assume that dumb "chance" is the only mechanism by which this happens and stay close to what is observable and obvious — "dead" matter has produced "living" matter. Stars have been birthing and dying themselves for billions of years (without our help, thank you) and we are their children — we are walking stardust. Bird song is air's way of hearing its own beauty; the human body is earth's giga-grandchild; consciousness is fire's desire to burn brightly on the earth. We humans and all living things are "dead" matter's way of reproducing itself.

Why is all this important to the tarot? All things are birthed in the dream before they come into the physical world. If this is so then the physical processes involving DNA and the evolution of life are a reflection of already existing processes in the realm of spirit. The structure of DNA and its bio-chemical processes are amazingly similar from simple bacteria through to complex primates. The tarot is a guide to the relationship between spirit and matter, and our spiritual inheritance, so to speak. Accordingly, we might expect to find some understanding of DNA in the tarot and vice-versa.

How DNA Does It

Deoxyribonucleic acid (DNA) is the genetic material that contains the blue-print for making a copy of an organism. A gene is a segment of a strand of DNA. Each gene produces a specific protein and proteins are the building blocks of the new organism.

A molecule of DNA consists of two strands made of nucleotides linked together to form a chain. These chains are like a ladder that is twisted into the shape of a winding staircase, called a double helix. The two strands of DNA lie head to toe next to each other rather than head to head. Just like the movements of substance and spirit in the tarot, one strand spirals "down" in a anticlockwise direction and the other "up" in an clockwise direction, forming the double helix.

Each nucleotide consists of three parts: a sugar molecule called deoxy-ribose, a phosphate group, and one of four different bases. The four bases are adenine (A), guanine (G), thymine (T), and cytosine (C). A human gene can be anywhere from 100 bases to 1,000,000 bases in length. The deoxy-ribose-phosphate units form the side rails of the ladder and the bases face inward toward each other, forming the rungs of the ladder. Because of the particular chemical structure of the bases adenine always pairs with thy-mine and cytosine always pairs with guanine (Figure 21).

The sequence of the bases along the DNA strand is the actual code for making amino acids. When amino acids are strung together they make pro-teins. In humans, there are twenty amino acids created by the standard ge-netic code. In addition, two amino acids are made by special codes. The sim-ilarity to the configuration of the cards in the Xultun Tarot (20 + 2) is apparent here.

But how does the sequence of bases code for DNA? If one base coded for one amino acid that would only give us four amino acids and there are twenty in all. Nor are two bases sufficient as they which would only give us 16 (4 x 4) different combinations of two bases. But three bases in combination as a triplet gives us 4 x 4 x 4 = 64 possible combinations, more than enough to code for twenty amino acids. The bases are strung together like beads on a string like AAAUAUTTGCCCACA which reads as AAA–UAU––TTG–CCC–ACA. Each triplet of bases is called a codon. They are the three-letter "words" of DNA and each word translates into an amino acid. For example, the triplet AAA codes for the amino acid lysine and CCC codes for proline.

But there are twenty amino acids and sixty-four possible codons. What happens to the other 44 "unused" codons? All the amino acids except tryptophan and methionine are coded for by more than one codon. For example, leucine is coded for by six different codons and tyrosine by two different codons. The term for this is "degenerate" or "redundant" coding. (But if we look at the history of science we should read "degenerate" as meaning that science has not yet found meaning in the redundancy, dismisses it as irrelevant, and will later make a "new discovery" about its importance).

What is important for our discussion here is that the variation in the redundant codons occurs only in the third base of the codon. The first two bases are always fixed but it is the third base that can vary or "wobble" and still code for the same amino acid. For example, UAU or UAC both code for tyrosine, TTA and TTG code for leucine, and GCC, GCA, or GCG code for alanine. Biologists propose that this kind of redundancy makes for greater genetic stability. If a mutation occurs it will mutate to a codon for the same or similar amino acid. This minimises genetic errors.

Of the sixty-four codons, sixty-one of them code for amino acids and three are "stop" codons. These stop codons do not code for an amino acid but act like a full stop at the end of a sentence telling the RNA to stop protein synthesis. The codon for methionine (AUG) also doubles as a "start" codon to signal RNA to start protein synthesis.

Ribonucleic Acid (RNA) is the molecule that directs the middle steps of protein production. DNA carries the information that determines the final structure of the proteins but it relies upon RNA to carry this information to the cytoplasm of the cell outside the nucleus where the proteins are made. The structure of RNA is similar but not identical to DNA. There are three types of RNA. Messenger RNA (mRNA) carries the genetic blueprint copied from the sequence of bases in the DNA. Ribosomal RNA (rRNA) is found in the cell's ribosomes, structures which are the sites of protein synthesis. Transfer RNA (tRNA) carries amino acids to the ribosomes for incorporation into a protein.

Before DNA can be copied it must unwind so its code (the sequences of codons) can be read. Part of the DNA helix is unwound and the two strands are separated, exposing the DNA base sequence. In a process called transcription, beginning at the "start" codon, the mRNA bases make complementary matches with the exposed bases of one of the DNA strands. At the end of the gene there is a "stop" code. The mRNA is then released and leaves the cell nucleus with the code. Once the coding strand has been copied, the DNA strands rewind.

Once transcription is finished the genetic code must be converted into proteins. This process, called translation, takes place in specialised cellular structures called ribosomes. The mRNA attaches to the ribosome which acts like a workbench and clamp that holds the mRNA strand and coordinates the enzyme activity of translation. Ribosomes walk along the messenger RNA in "strides" of three bases translating the amino acid sequence as they go. The tRNA carries amino acids to the ribosome and transfers them to the growing chain of amino acids. The process ends when the entire sequence of mRNA has been translated. The polypeptide chain then falls away from the ribosome as a newly formed protein.

Richard Krakowski has written tantalisingly on what he calls the occult genetic code and the relationship between the I Ching and the tarot. He says, "The 22 trumps of the Tarot perform roughly the same function as transfer RNA does within the replication of a cell—it helps to translate raw data into a form that can be interpreted, processed, and replicated.... The isomorphism between the two systems manifests only when the 64 kua of the I Ching and the 22 major arcana of the Tarot are arranged in the same way as the 64 codons and 22 amino acid and punctuation codons are arranged in the genetic code."[3]

Codons of Experience

We have seen that the tarot is an image of the double helix of spirit and matter. One is descending, the other ascending just like the strands of DNA. The process whereby DNA creates the proteins that make up our physical body is a reflection of the process that is happening all the time in spirit. Spiritual DNA is what Jung called the collective unconscious—the sum total of our spiritual and psychological heritage that contains the essence and residue of all the dreaming and the doings of humanity since always. It is humankind's spiritual genome or Book of Life.

If the collective unconscious is the Book of Life then the archetypes (and the tarot suggests there are only 20 + 2 basic ones) are the amino acids. The building blocks of our non-physical body are unique and yet they are archetypal—that is, there is an almost infinite variation within a recognisable pattern. Just as our physical DNA makes twenty amino acids so there are twenty archetypal patterns that make up our spiritual body, our Book of Life. Excluding the 0 and 1 cards (the Fool and the Sorcerer) these are the twenty cards in the major arcana of the tarot.

Life brings us the raw material of experience which is our tRNA. Together they make the proteins that form the spiritual and psychological body of our life from our life circumstances and our personal history. The Movement of Assuming Authority however has a special role as we shall see below.

Because this Movement is about our free will choices, it acts as our mRNA. But not all of our life choices and experiences are written in our Book of Life, only those that leave their mark upon our soul. This distillate of our deepest experiences is our spiritual memory and this memory is passed from lifetime to lifetime in our DNA. Jung describes this in his autobiography written when he was in his eighties:

> Life has always seemed to me like a plant that lives on its rhizome. Its true life is invisible, hidden in the rhizome. The part that appears above the ground lasts only a single summer. Then it withers away — an ephemeral apparition.... Yet I have never lost a sense of something that lives and endures underneath the eternal flux. What we see is the blossom, which passes. The rhizome remains. In the end the only events in my life worth telling are those when the imperishable world irrupted into this transitory one. That is why I speak chiefly of inner experiences... All other memories of travels, people and my surroundings have paled beside these interior happenings... Recollection of the outward events of my life has largely faded or disappeared. But my encounters with the "other" reality, my bouts with the unconscious, are indelibly engraved upon my memory. In that realm there has always been wealth in abundance, and everything else has lost importance by comparison. Similarly, other people are established inalienably in my memories only if their names were entered in the scrolls of my destiny from the beginning, so encountering them was at the same time a kind of recollection.[4]

Spiritual Amino Acids

We can see the signature of spirit in another aspect of DNA. The body can make only ten of the twenty amino acids that it needs. These are called the non-essential amino acids as we do not have to take them in our food. Spiritually, they correspond to the first two rows of ten cards. They are given to us and we do not have to reach for them. They are experiences that all humans have and they occur within and between people without too much interference or interest from spirit, which lets us get on with our human affairs. Likewise, humans at this point are not too concerned with spiritual matters. The majority of humans live their lives within the first two rows of cards and do not need or take anything from spirit.

The other ten amino acids are not made by the body and are "essential" —that is, they must be taken in through our diet. The ten cards in the bottom two rows are the spiritual equivalent of the essential amino acids. In the last half of the journey, we must take in more spirit, becoming more engaged with spirit so that spirit becomes more engaged with us.

Knock of the Spirit

Spirit reveals itself to everyone with the same intensity and frequency but not everyone takes notice. We strengthen our relationship to spirit, or our "connecting link with intent," by being continually on the lookout for manifestations of spirit. These gestures of the spirit are called synchronicities, omens, coincidences or medicine signs. We experience this activation of our link with intent as intuition.

Don Juan said that spirit stalks us in four stages. The stories of these four stages are told in the four rows of the tarot and they are what Jung called the process of individuation. The first row is the manifestation of spirit and an untrustworthy link with intent. The second row is the knock of the spirit and cleaning the link with intent. The third row is the trickery of spirit and using the link with intent. The fourth row is the descent of the spirit and accepting the "designs of the abstract."[5]

Wobble and Free Will

Each amino acid is coded for by three bases. The first two bases are fixed while the third base varies or "wobbles." Each card or "spiritual amino acid" is coded in a similar way. The first codon for each card is the vertical Movement it sits in. The second codon is the relevant horizontal Shield and Mood for that card. Both these codons are fixed. For example, the first codon for the Warrior is Erasing Mental History, the second codon is the Heart of the Adult Substance Shield and the Mood of Emotional Cunning.

As we have seen, the Movements are archetypal, enduring and collective while the Shields and the Moods are more individual and transitory. But because the Movements are impersonal and the Shields and the Moods are ephemeral, none of them carry the unique individual imprint of our soul that is encoded in the Book of Life and carried over from lifetime to lifetime in an evolutionary spiral. For "genetic" change to take place there must be variability or an unpredictable "mutation" at a soul level—the equivalent of "chance" in evolutionary and biological terms. The third codon provides for this through its wobble, the free will choice of the Movement of Assuming Authority.

The soul or catalyst card at the end of each row interacts with each of the four other cards in the row and functions like the Joker in a deck of playing cards by changing the expression and effect of a particular card. As we can see in Figure 105 where each row is arranged as a wheel, the cards of Assuming Authority sit at the centre of each wheel and so catalyse the cards around the wheel. Each of them represent an aspect of authority that, when brought to bear on a situation either by choice or necessity, puts one's own unique stamp on the matter. The Lovers exert Emotional Authority, the Balance wields Mental Authority, the Released Man applies Physical Authority and Planet Earth exercises Spiritual Authority.

To use the Warrior as an example: he is the Heart of the Adult Substance Shield who uses the Mood of Emotional Cunning to Erase Mental History. But when, instead of mindlessly obeying orders, he uses the free will choice of the Balance card to either follow orders or to go his own way, the Warrior assumes his own internal authority. When he chooses from this place (and not from the place of compliance or rebellion) to either take life or lay down the sword then the universe is changed for better or for worse. Something new has been created and a new line has been written not only in the individual's Book of Life but in the heritage of all human souls who have ever been born, are being born and will be born. Such is the power of human choice.

The notion of the third codon has several implications. In a reading, if the meaning of a card is unclear or conflicted, the soul or catalyst card at the end of the row the card is in, indicates the solution or free will choice that needs to be made (or is being avoided). As the catalyst cards, the Lovers, Balance, Released Man and Planet Earth cards represent the points at which we can change our destiny and rewrite our Book of Life (that is, change the structure of our spiritual DNA). This change is not just one way, though. The choices that we make shuttle back and forth on the Loom of Time and change both our past and our future. This process of rewriting our Book of Life is a lifetime's soul work.

Only what touches our soul is encoded in our Book of Life and gets passed on to the next generation whether that be our biological or creative children. Those who are born from our physical DNA are also heir to our spiritual DNA. They get the best and the worst of our psyche. The intimate relationship between parents and children is where psychological and spiritual inheritance takes place. Children are, more obviously, heir to the emotional, physical, mental and spiritual choices of their parents. But, less obviously and more powerfully, children also live out the unlived lives of their parents. Either way, the omissions or comissions of the parent are inherited by the child as their personal history. The centre Movement of Assuming Authority of the parent then becomes the south Movement of Erasing Personal History of the child.

Finally, we should remember that just as the Movement of Assuming Authority and the soul cards are our karma, so the reverse is true. The Movement of Erasing Personal History (the Priestess, Warrior, Hanged Man and Star cards) is spirit's karma. It is the uniquely human qualities of hope (the Star), endurance (the Hanged Man), courage (the Warrior) and feeling (the Priestess) that are the redemption and salvation of spirit. They bind spirit in the chains of self-reflection, liberate it from its unconsciousness and usher it into, not immortal and everlasting life, but a life that is frail, mortal, impermanent and deeply precious. Human beings are spirit's Christ.

9

Loom of Time

Everything is connected and the web is holy.

—Marcus Aurelius

the first cross of warp and weft
union of high and low, sky and earth,
woman and man
the first knot, begging of the spiral:
life and death, birth and rebirth

—Cecilia Vicuna
The Unravelling of Words and the Weaving of Water

The severe schools shall never laugh me out of the philosophy of Hermes, that this visible world is but a picture of the invisible, wherein, as in a portrait, things are not truly, but in equivocal shapes; and as they counterfeit some more real substance in that invisible fabrick.

—Sir Thomas Browne, *Religio Medici*

It is safe to assume that we are standing in between two worlds, a visible tangible world, and the other invisible world, which somehow has a peculiar quality of substantiality, but very settled, sort of matter that is not obvious and is not visible, that penetrates bodies and apparently exists outside of time and space.

—C. G. Jung, *Visions Seminars*

Before we look at the individual cards of the major arcana, we shall explore some of the other patterns woven on the Loom of Time. I have titled the chapter the Loom of Time because many creation myths speak of weaving as a way of creating the world, of bringing matter out of spirit. So it is with our lives, we weave a pattern on the backstrap loom of time that has not existed before and will never be repeated again.

The tarot also has its own weaving, its own heart and its own mind. Every card is an individual but is also a part of a community. Each card makes love with, marries, awakens, dreams, and completes other cards in the deck (Figure 22). The archetype and alchemy of each card is summarised in Chapter 32.

I shall also look at other patterns in later chapters: the World Tree in Chapter 14 on the Ruler; the mid-life crossing in Chapter 19 on the Sage; and the Four Dreams in Chapter 24 on the Temperate Man).

Awakening

The nine cards that follow any card are its transformations according to the Zero to Nine Law.[1] Energy moves in 10 movements or transformations beginning at 0 and moving outward 9 times before returning to the source (10) to begin a new movement. Note that 0 to 9 is a ten-step movement (0-1-- 2-3-4-5-6-7-8-9) just as, more conventionally, we might count from 1 to 10. Each card starts at 0, transforms itself 9 times, and the tenth card becomes the 0 of the next cycle. So the nine cards following the index card are each energetic transformations of the archetype of that card. The last step results in the full manifestation or flowering of the archetype in its wholeness. I shall mention here only the fourth transformation of awakening, the seventh transformation of dreaming and the tenth transformation of completion.

Each card awakens and is awakened by another card. This is the card's manifestation within substance and within time. If we add 4 to the number of any card from 2 to 21 we can see which card it awakens. (The 0 and 1 cards stand outside this process and are not included in the counting). For example, the vision of the Star (17) awakens the wholeness of Planet Earth (21). The Sun (19) awakens the growth of the Consort (3). The devotions of the Priest (5) awaken the knowledge of the Sage (9). The beauty of Planet Earth (21) awakens the awe and reverence of the Priest (5). Visually, we can see this most clearly in the red smoke that spreads from the brazier of the Sage (9) and envelops the Dead Man (13). The containment of the Fire-from-within by the Sage births the death and change in the Dead Man.

As with all the archetypal processes in the tarot, the cards can also be read backwards. For example, the death and change of the Dead Man (13) awakens the introversion and introspection of the Sage (9). The strength of the Cactus (8) awakens the leadership of the Ruler (4). The dreaming and service of the Warrior (7) awakens the growth of the Consort (3). The sacrifice, waiting and suspension of the Hanged Man (12) awakens the strength, patience and self-reliance of the Cactus (8).

PRIESTESS
Awakened by Moon
Awakens Lovers
Dreamed by Bound Man
Dreams Sage
Completion of Dead Man
Completed by Balance

CONSORT
Awakened by Sun
Awakens Warrior
Dreamed by Released Man
Dreams Wheel
Completion of Temperate Man
Completed by Hanged Man

RULER
Awakened by Planet Venus
Awakens Cactus
Dreamed by Star
Dreams Balance
Completion of Bound Man
Completed by Dead Man

PRIEST
Awakened by Planet Earth
Awakens Sage
Dreamed by Moon
Dreams Hanged Man
Completion of Released Man
Completed by Temperate Man

LOVERS
Awakened by Priestess
Awakens Wheel
Dreamed by Sun
Dreams Dead Man
Completion of Star
Completed by Bound Man

WARRIOR
Awakened by Consort
Awakens Balance
Dreamed by Planet Venus
Dreams Temperate Man
Completion of Moon
Completed by Released Man

CACTUS
Awakened by Ruler
Awakens Hanged Man
Dreamed by Planet Earth
Dreams Bound Man
Completion of Sun
Completed by Star

SAGE
Awakened by Priest
Awakens Dead Man
Dreamed by Priestess
Dreams Released Man
Completion of Planet Venus
Completed by Moon

WHEEL
Awakened by Lovers
Awakens Temperate Man
Dreamed by Consort
Dreams Star
Completion of Planet Earth
Completed by Sun

BALANCE
Awakened by Warrior
Awakens Bound Man
Dreamed by Ruler
Dreams Moon
Completion of Priestess
Completed by Planet Venus

HANGED MAN
Awakened by Cactus
Awakens Released Man
Dreamed by Priest
Dreams Sun
Completion of Consort
Completed by Planet Earth

DEAD MAN
Awakened by Sage
Awakens Star
Dreamed by Lovers
Dreams Planet Venus
Completion of Ruler
Completed by Priestess

TEMPERATE MAN
Awakened by Wheel
Awakens Moon
Dreamed by Warrior
Dreams Planet Earth
Completion of Priest
Completed by Consort

BOUND MAN
Awakened by Balance
Awakens Sun
Dreamed by Cactus
Dreams Priestess
Completion of Lovers
Completed by Ruler

RELEASED MAN
Awakened by Hanged Man
Awakens Planet Venus
Dreamed by Sage
Dreams Consort
Completion of Warrior
Completed by Priest

STAR
Awakened by Dead Man
Awakens Planet Earth
Dreamed by Wheel
Dreams Ruler
Completion of Cactus
Completed by Lovers

MOON
Awakened by Temperate Man
Awakens Priestess
Dreamed by Balance
Dreams Priest
Completion of Sage
Completed by Warrior

SUN
Awakened by Bound Man
Awakens Consort
Dreamed by Hanged Man
Dreams Lovers
Completion of Wheel
Completed by Cactus

PLANET VENUS
Awakened by Released Man
Awakens Ruler
Dreamed by Dead Man
Dreams Warrior
Completion of Balance
Completed by Sage

PLANET EARTH
Awakened by Star
Awakens Priest
Dreamed by Temperate Man
Dreams Cactus
Completion of Hanged Man
Completed by Wheel

Figure 22. The Alchemy of the Xultun Tarot

Dreams

When something is not yet ready for the light of growth it is hidden in the earth, in what is common, humdrum, everyday or taken for granted. When the conditions are right and at its appointed time, the flower comes to light and makes itself visible. The flower is the dream of the seed in the darkness of the earth. All things in creation dream. The world of spirit dreams this world of matter. The world of matter incarnates the world of spirit. Our world is an image in the dream of the Creator. It is our connectedness to the dream that allows us to play and create possible realities in the sandbox of dreaming.

Each card dreams of and is dreamed by another card. (I shall use the more active verb "dreams" as well as the less active "dreams of"). This is the card's manifestation within spirit and outside of time. In the Twenty Count the number 7 is the number of the dream and dreaming. Number 1 is the Sun, 2 is the Earth, 3 is the Plants, 4 is the Animals, 5 is the Humans, 6 is the Ancestors, and 7 is the Dream. So if we add 7 to the number of any card we can see its dream.

In a reading, the dream of the index card pulls it forward into greater consciousness. For example, the Priestess (2) dreams of translating her intuitive seeing into the knowledge of the Sage (9). The Ruler's (4) external and collective authority dreams the equally organised but internal authority of the Balance (11). The Lovers (6), merged in passion, dream of the death and transformation of the Dead Man (13). The woundedness and suffering of the Hanged Man (12) dreams the light and life of the Sun (19). We see this pattern most clearly in the Three Paths of the Book of Life (Figure 20). The dream of each card is the card directly below it. Likewise the dreamer of each card is the one directly above it.

Whatever is not made conscious inwardly is projected onto the outside world. The external world then becomes a mirror of our unconscious. In a mysterious way, and at a distance, spirit manifests and the world around us shows what we hide from in ourselves. Synchronicities happen, we become attracted to certain kinds of people, experience good luck and bad luck, all of which reflect our inner world. However, this projection distorts our view of the world around us and our relationship to it. The effect of projection is isolation from reality as-it-is and our relationship with the world becomes illusionary.[2] Therefore, we see the reflection in the mirror not the real thing.

The unconscious contains all those things that have been conscious at one time but have been repressed — all those feelings, wishes or desires that were too painful or dangerous to hold in consciousness, or needed to be put aside for the sake of development and adaptation. Whatever is projected is pushed from behind, so to speak, by the pressure of unresolved needs and emotions from the past that are constantly seeking resolution in the present.

But the psyche is not a one-way street with traffic only going from past to future. The unconscious also contains all those desires and potentials, personal and archetypal, that have never been conscious but wish to be lived. Nature abhors a vacuum. If the psyche cannot find a way to live out these potentials, the person will increasingly feel unfulfilled and experience a vague restlessness of the soul. The pressure will build until either the potential can be lived concretely or the person develops symptoms of some kind (mid-life crisis, relationship breakdown, or physical illness, for example). The difference here from the first kind of projection is that the psyche is pulled, so to speak, into the future by its own unconscious dreaming that yearns to be born. This is what happens when a synchronistic event occurs — its purposeful meaning pulls us toward the person we can become (but only if we notice). The dream occurs outside not inside.

Meister Eckhart said, "When the soul wishes to experience something, she throws an image of the experience out before her and enters into her own image." The unconscious, seemingly unformed and inchoate, is in fact goal-directed and always working towards seducing, goading, prodding, abandoning, comforting, or guiding us to become who we are. It gives us glimpses of something working on our side, behind the scenes, so that we can dare to dream a better future. So projection = hope = dream. In a reading, the card that is seven cards onwards in the major arcana shows the querent the hidden potential that is pressing for recognition.

Completion

Each card completes and is completed by another card. This is the essence of the card in its fullest expression. It combines the opposites and so is the beginning of a new spiral. If we add 9 to the number of any card we see its completion. For example, Planet Earth (21) is the completion of the Hanged Man (12) — wholeness is the manifestation of dividedness. The Balance (11) is the completion of the Priestess (2) — the fate of the individual seen by the Priestess is actualised through the choices of the Balance. The expansive spiritual vision of the Star (17) is the full manifestation of the physical constraints of the Cactus (8).

Marriages

At the top of the deck the Feathered Serpents on either side of the Fool and the Sorcerer represent the great universal polarities. The Feathered Serpent to the left of the Fool spirals anticlockwise and symbolises the great receptive, creative, feminine energy. The Feathered Serpent to the right of the Sorcerer spirals clockwise and symbolises the great active, conceptive masculine energy. These energies spiral in a double helix through all the cards in the deck. The marriages between the masculine and feminine cards create the cross linkages between the archetypal Movements and are like the base linkages that connect the two strands of DNA.

In each row there are two pairs of masculine and feminine cards. Each card marries its opposite (Figure 23). For example, in the first row the Consort marries the Ruler and the Priestess marries the Priest. These two couples are the tonal and nagual parents of the last card in the row which is the child of their needs, wants and desires. The last card in each row is an aspect of the Movement of Assuming Authority. But who does this card

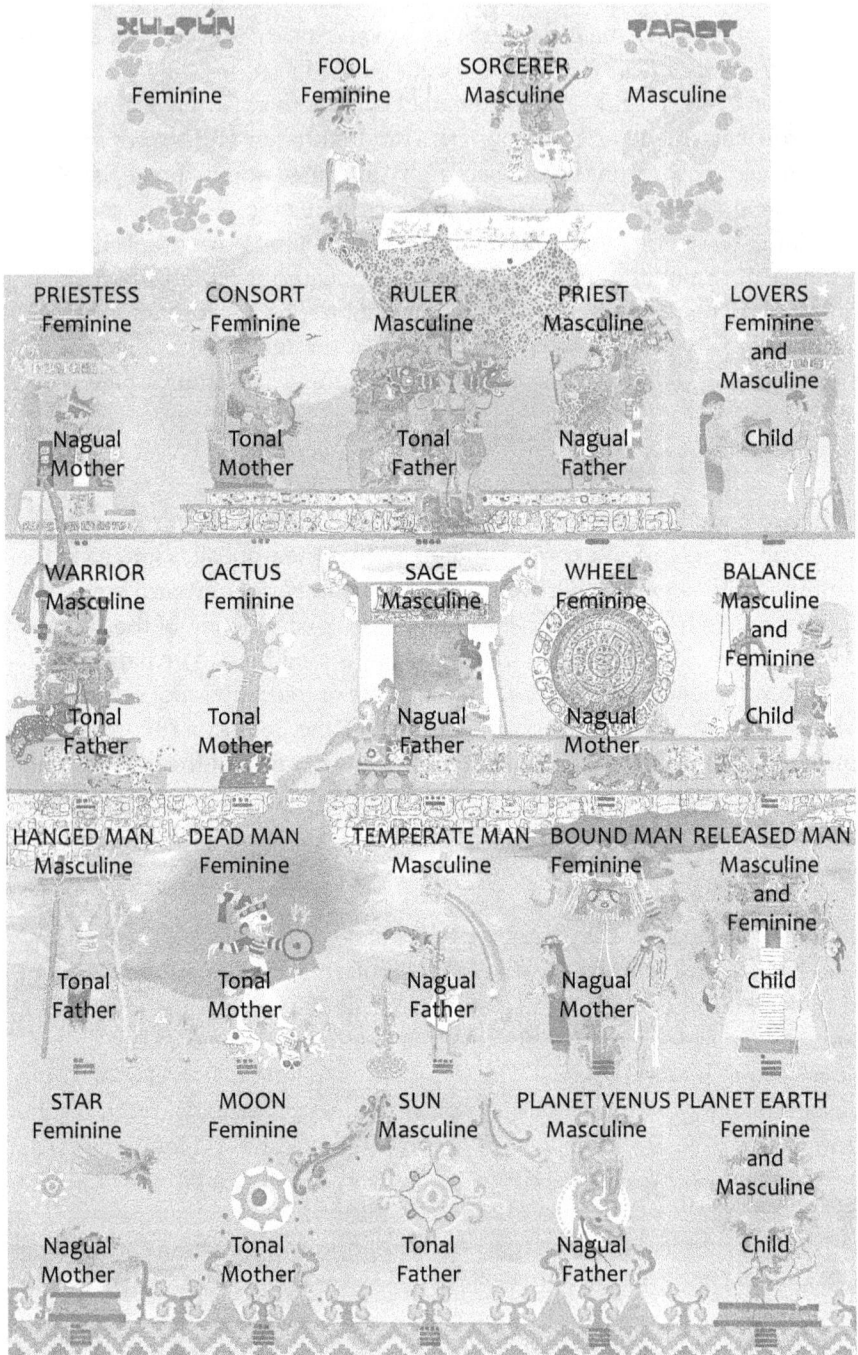

Figure 23. The Marriages of the Xultun Tarot

marry? The Lovers, the Balance, the Released Man and Planet Earth marry the opposite within themselves, consummating the inner marriage.

For anything to be born it must have four parents. The physical or tonal parents conceive and nurture the physical form of the child. The spiritual or nagual parents (the "godparents") conceive and nurture the spiritual form of the child. Alice Howell said:

> This is the profound secret of individuation: as all growing things in outer nature yearn sunwards, so do we yearn for that inward sun and light within us that sheds meaning to our own existence. One of Sophia's greatest secrets is that nature's processes are true of the psyche as well *but reversed*. Another example of this is that it takes a father and a mother to produce a child. Within the psyche, the inversion is equally true as a process. It takes a "divine" father and a "virgin" mother within us to consummate a *hierosgamos* or sacred marriage to bring us to a "second birth."[3]

In the first row of the Child Substance Shield we are born into this physical world. Our physical parents are the Consort and the Ruler and our spiritual parents are the Priestess and the Priest. The Lovers, the image of the union of the anima and animus within a physical relationship, is their child.

The second row of the Adult Substance Shield is about separation from the security and safety of the first parents and being born into the adult world of culture and nature. The tonal parents of nature are the Warrior (action) and the Cactus (forbearance). The nagual parents of culture are the Sage (knowledge) and the Wheel (time). The Balance, the one who chooses their own way, the middle way between the conflicting demands of nature and culture, is their child.

The third row of the Adult Spirit Shield is about being born to oneself. The Hanged Man (in conflict with the world) and the Dead Man (released from the world) are the tonal parents. The Temperate Man (bound to the world) and the Bound Man (bound to spirit) are the nagual parents. The Released Man, the one who has overcome the dominance of ego consciousness, is the child of these parents.

The fourth row of the Child Spirit Shield is about being born to the cosmos and the whole of creation. A 14th century Samurai said, "I have no parents. I make heaven and earth my parents." The Star (vision) and the Planet Venus (love) are our nagual parents and the Moon and the Sun are our tonal parents. Planet Earth is their child and is the marriage of the all the marriages (see page 364).

In a reading, the marriage partner of the index card indicates the compensation need for balance. For example, the introverted Priestess needs the extroversion of the Priest. The gung-ho Warrior needs the containment of the

2 Priestess	21 Planet Earth
3 Consort	20 Planet Venus
4 Ruler	19 Sun
5 Priest	18 Moon
6 Lovers	17 Star
7 Warrior	16 Released Man
8 Cactus	15 Bound Man
9 Sage	14 Temperate Man
10 Wheel	13 Dead Man
11 Balance	12 Hanged Man

Figure 24. The Lovers of the Xultun Tarot

Cactus. The despairing Hanged Man needs the resolution of the Dead Man. The distance of the Star needs the closeness of Planet Venus.

Lovers

As well as the lateral, conventional marriages above, the cards also join in contra-lateral, radical lovemaking. The lateral marriage of the cards is like the horizontal rungs that join the sides of a ladder. But the contra-lateral lovemaking is like the right-hand side of the bottom rung joining the left-hand side of the top rung. This bonding is the complementary attractions of substance "up" toward spirit and spirit "down" toward substance and it gives the spiral twist to the helix of spirit and matter. In a reading, the lover is what is most other or opposite to the index card, what it is most strongly attracted to or repelled by, and the qualities that will bring about the most catalytic change. This twist creates life as each card makes love with its diagonally opposite card (Figure 24).

Some examples: Planet Earth bonds with the Priestess at the opposite corner of the deck. Spirit needs a witness to become real and does not replicate itself in matter unless seen and understood by humans. Not only does the Priestess see what will come into form, but if it is not seen by her then it will never come into form, or if it does it will manifest in a destructive way, unmoderated by any humanness. Ultimately, this means that if we do not value intuition as a mode of human perception and restore the women seers to their rightful place in our culture, then life on this planet will die.

The Bound Man is about submitting to the designs of spirit and is the lover of the Cactus. The Cactus symbolises the opposite—spirit's submission to the designs of substance. The Sun is the lover of the Ruler. The Sun is about the inspirational energy necessary for spiritual growth and the Ruler, the Sun King, is about the organisation and leadership necessary for cultural growth. The Released Man is the lover of the Warrior. Through the Warrior's aggression and love of conflict, spirit is released from its constricting beliefs about oneness and harmony.

Flower

The Fool holds a white flower which for the Maya symbolised the human soul, the distilled essence of our uniqueness. As the tarot is about the journey of the human soul, we should expect it to appear in all the cards, which it does but in symbolic form as it evolves and transforms on the journey. For example, it appears as the codex in the Priestess, as the bundle in the arms of the Ruler, as the bird in the Cactus, and as the ropes in the Bound Man. Halfway through the deck, when the soul is most tested at 12 and *in extremis* at 13, it begins to flower as the Flowering Tree at 14. This indicates that even though the ego is dying, new life flowers from the deep in the unconscious. Then in the last card, Planet Earth, the flower reappears completely transformed into itself.

Spirals

The Xultun Tarot is a wandering story, a circular, spiral way of capturing feelings, images and fleeting associations about states of human consciousness that are hard to convey in a linear way. Each row of cards forms a rung of an ascending spiral.

Every human being who survives to adolescence experiences the first row of archetypal events (1–6). The second row (7–11) tells the story of our growth as adults. Both of these rows are lived within the confines of the collective. However, the third and fourth rows represent experiences that can only be lived outside the collective. In muted form they touch many human lives but in their totality they become increasingly infrequent as we move along the third row. In the fourth row the experiences of the "higher" cards from 17 to 21 are rare and distant from everyday consciousness.

Like nature, the tarot is aristocratic, hierarchical, and unequal. Life is not an equal opportunity employer and, as much as it may offend our sense of social justice, equality and fairness, not everyone experiences the states of consciousness the tarot describes, neither do they have the capacity to do so. This results in polarised responses to the tarot. On the one hand, it is dismissed as wacky, airy-fairy, a symptom of psychopathology, or simply wrong-headed. On the other hand, we see in New Age culture a too-casual familiarity with the higher states of consciousness described by the tarot. To experience these states of "non-ordinary reality" in their breadth and

Figure 25. The Four Platforms

depth is often a profound experience, and one that is often dissipated by "sharing." Such an experience may last hours, days or possibly weeks but the capacity to contain the numinous without leaking and to live it consciously may only come many years later.

Platforms

The whole Book of Life rests on a transpersonal platform or foundation that we see as the zigzag pattern at the base of the last row. In each of the three upper rows there are also platforms. In the first two rows, the triads of the Consort, Ruler and Priest and the Sage, Wheel and Balance cards all stand on a platform. The last two rows also have platforms but they are less obvious (Figure 25).

A stage, podium, dais, altar, platform or pyramid provides the spatial location for a ceremony, drama or special event. The Maya used their pyramids, which had platforms at various levels, for public ceremonies. A theatrical stage is a public place for a directed unfolding of relationships and interactions that leads to a dramatic climax. A platform elevates things above the earth assigning them a special significance or power and marking them off from everyday life. A launching platform is a base to send something upwards or onwards. A political platform is the base upon which decisions and policies are made. In development, a stage is a distinct period in the life of an organism, culture or society when its form is different from earlier or later periods. A stage of a journey is a distinct part of a journey after which a stop is usually made.

If we follow these associations, the three cards on each platform form a sequence that provides a base or foundation, and also the momentum, to begin the next stage of the developmental journey. The card in the middle of the platform unites, separates, marries, bridges, mediates or catalyses the cards on either side. The card immediately following the platform is the beginning of the next stage. For example, the worldly doings of the Consort, Ruler and Priest are the activity needed for the outer dramas of the Lovers. The introversion and silent action of the Sage, Wheel and Balance are the necessary introspection before the inner dramas of Hanged Man.

But the changes are not all of the same intensity. As we saw in the Three Paths, a break or discontinuity in the visual sequence of cards indicates a major movement in the developmental process rather than a minor shift. A shift also occurs between cards in a row whereas a movement occurs between rows. A shift happens when we gain more life through living. A movement happens when we gain more life through dying. We can see in Figure 25 that there is a shift after the first platform (the Lovers) but a movement after the second platform (the Hanged Man). The change visited on

the Hanged Man is much greater and more disorienting than the change
brought about by the Lovers.

But what of the third and fourth rows? They also have platforms but
they are not made by human hands. Again, there is a shift after the third
platform (the Released Man) but a movement after the fourth platform (the
Priestess). The Dead Man, Temperate Man and the Bound Man stand on the
platform of the green earth and prepare us for the upheaval of the Tower.
The Sun, Planet Venus and Planet Earth stand on the platform of the
transpersonal earth and prepare us for the last great movement—death.
The Star and Planet Earth, as images of individual and universal wholeness
respectively, are self-generating and self-supporting and each has its own
platform in contrast to the collective platforms of the first two rows.

The platforms are also mirror images of each other. The worldly Ruler
unites the biological growth of the earthly Consort with the cultural mores
handed down by the spiritual Priest. The shift is the Lovers—the biological
union of the opposites between two people that ensures the physical continuity of the people.

In the second row the cosmic Wheel catalyses the spiritual wisdom of the
Sage and the individual actions of the Balance. The movement is the
Hanged Man—the spiritual union of the opposites within one person that
ensures the spiritual continuity of the individual.

In the third row the harmony and balance of the Temperate Man bridges
the symbolic death and separation of the Dead Man with the binding,
kinship and holy matrimony of the Bound Man. The shift is the Released
Man—the separation of the opposites within the individual (the ego from
the Self) as a prelude to union with the Everything.

In the last row the cosmic love of the Planet Venus marries the transpersonal fire of the Sun with the transpersonal substance of Planet Earth.
The movement is the Priestess—the separation of the opposites without
(the soul separates from the body and spirit separates from matter) and life
begins again.

This resonance and mirroring is also seen in each card following the
platform. In the Lovers card, two humans (a man and a woman) stand underneath a human-made canopy and hold between them an undivided object with a blue void at its centre. In the Hanged Man card, two objects (a
live tree and a dead tree) stand on top of the earth and hold an upside-down, divided human with white light at his centre between them. Or
if we reverse our perception: In the Lovers card, a whole object with the
earth above its head separates two opposites (a man and a woman). In the
Hanged Man card, a divided human with the sky above his feet unites two
opposites (a dead tree and a live tree).

In the Released Man, two humans are divided and fall to the ground on
the outside of a temple-pyramid. In the Priestess, the card that follows

Figure 26. The Soul Bundles

Planet Earth, one human is joined to the other world and sits on a throne inside a temple. Or from the contrary point of view, the temple holds a single
Priestess on the inside and the Tower holds two upside-down humans on
the outside.

Bundles

All the figures in the top row of cards are holding something. The Priestess
holds the codex of the Talking Leaves, the Consort holds the Shield and
Arrows, the Ruler holds the double-headed Snake Bundle or Serpent Bar,
the Priest holds the Flowering Tree staff, and the Lovers hold the Smoking
Mirror. Symbolically, each object they hold represents something that is not
yet psychologically integrated or internalised, it is not yet "inside." We
would expect this in the first line of the tarot. But what might this
something be?

There are many kinds of medicine bundles. One such bundle is the Soul
Bundle or 15 Bundle, which is the essence of our humanness and is a com-
posite of all the other bundles. The number 15 in the Twenty Count is the
conscious (10) human (5) (10 + 5 = 15) and the growth and movement (3) of
the human soul (5) (3 x 5 = 15). If we look at the number difference between
the cards in the top and bottom rows, we see that it is also 15 (2 and 17, 3
and 18 and so on). This suggests that each of the objects held by the figures
is a bundle which contains the elemental beginnings of the Soul Bundle that
manifests 15 cards later.

If we remove the second and third rows and put the top and bottom
rows together as in Figure 26 we can see the relationships more easily. The

Priestess, Consort, Ruler, Priest and Lovers all have an association with the heavenly bodies — the stars, moon, sun, Venus and Earth, respectively — that are the cosmic manifestation of their archetypal powers or conversely the figures are the human manifestation of the cosmic powers. The Priestess sees the destiny of the individual which is the Star card. The Consort holds the healing medicine of the Plants and the invisible physical processes of the body which are ruled by the Moon. The Ruler holds to his chest the serpent bar which for the Maya was the ecliptic along which the sun travelled,[4] the body of the ruler was the World Tree or the Milky Way and their intersection was the Heart of Heaven and the Centre of the World. The Priest is the mediator between heaven and earth with his jaguar robe (the markings on which symbolised the constellations) and his staff (which was used as a device for measuring the solar zenith passage). Finally, the Lovers hold the mirror with the deep blue of the night sky which becomes the fullness of Planet Earth.

There are other linkages between the top and bottom rows: In both the Priestess and the Lovers cards we can see the stars of the Pleiades. And the Consort is the image of the Tikal ruler Hasaw Chan K'awil sitting on his palanquin and we know that he succeeded to the throne on May 1, 682 CE on which date the sun (which frames the Consort) and the Pleiades were conjunct.

The task of the top row is to begin to free oneself from the rule of instinctual and collective behaviour. By holding matter dear we become free of its demands. This is done with the help of the element bundles which ceremonially establish our connection with matter. They are matter beautified by our own hands. Spirits don't have opposable thumbs and our creations in matter, our "fiveness," adds to what spirit has created in nature. So the Priestess holds the Water Bundle whose give-away is the Star. The Consort holds the Earth Bundle whose give-away is the Moon. The Ruler holds the Breath or Wind Bundle whose give-away is the Sun. The Priest holds the Fire Bundle whose give-away is the Feathered Winged Serpent. Finally, the Lovers hold the Void or Catalyst Bundle whose give-away is the Planet Earth. Therefore, our soul is complete when we are related, within and without, to the Stars, the Moon, the Sun, the Creator, and the Earth.

Descent of the Serpent

The Soul Bundles show us that the bottom card of each Movement is the fullness or flowering of first card in that column. In other words, the bottom card is the spiritual essence of the top card. Progression downwards in each Movement results in increasing spiritualisation but when the bottom is reached a compensation must occur to return us to earthly, elemental reality. Thus, the top card of a column compensates the bottom card of the previous column.

For example, at the end of the Movement of Erasing Personal History a new dream or vision is born in the Star card. Having reached the consciousness of the Star, there is a return to matter as the psyche shifts into the next Movement. So, after the inspiration of the Star the vision must be submitted to the scrutiny of the Consort who asks, "Yes, but will it feed the Children?"

Then the new dream comes into physical form and it goes through further distillation and refinement as it travels downwards through the Cactus and Dead Man cards until it reaches the Moon, which is the Teacher of Using Death as a Spiritual Advisor. Too much moonlight brings indecision, uncertainty and mooniness and the ego can become enchanted and sink beneath the moon-tides without a trace. So the light and order of the Ruler at the beginning of the next Movement must be imposed so that the work can continue.

The order of the Ruler transforms eventually into the boundless spiritual energy of the Sun but this will incinerate us unless it is stepped down into usable form through the ceremonies of the Priest. This connection with spirit eventually leads us to discover the power of universal love in the Planet Venus. But this love remains a sentimental and dangerous abstraction unless it is lived between human beings by the Lovers. Only then, through the free will choices of the Balance and the Released Man, does the wholeness of Planet Earth manifest. The wholeness of Planet Earth is finally brought into balance by singular dividedness of the Priestess and the last card of Assuming Spiritual Authority becomes the first card of Erasing Emotional History.

Ascent of the Eagle

The only sitting figures in the deck are all in the first column — the Priestess in her temple, the Warrior on his palanquin, the Hanged Man (who sits in the sky) and the Star Maiden on her drum. This means that we need to be "grounded" to begin each step in life, solidly in contact with the earth (literally or symbolically) for this is the lap we always sit on. The only other sitting figure is the Consort or Earth Mother, the second card of the first row and the second card of the whole deck. This points to the fact that the larger the undertaking the more we need to be grounded and have the support of the earth beneath us. This is particularly true at the beginning of life when we need to be loved or, as modern psychology puts it, "securely attached."

Following the shift or movement at the end of a row, the card at the beginning of the next row represents the archetypal forces that propel us into the next phase of life. But, unlike the Descent of the Serpent, the last card in a row acts as a catalyst, rather than a compensation, for the first card in the next row. It amplifies rather than moderates. This results in a spiralling up-ward toward spirit like the eagle moving ever higher from one updraft to another.

For example, the dividedness of the Priestess leads to the wound of Eros' dart in the Lovers. The Warrior in the second row ramps up the sexual energy and conflict of the Lovers. The Warrior's mastery of conflict yields the judgement of the Balance. The Hanged Man must then suffer the consequences of what the Balance has chosen. But in turn, the suffering of the Hanged Man allows the illumination of the Released Man. The long-sight vision of the Star extends the flash of enlightenment of the Released Man. Finally, the Earth is the beauty that results from the vision of the Star. The first and third rows show suffering, sacrifice, and domination by the archetypes. The second and fourth rows show victory, completion and an integration of the archetypes.

Patrix and Matrix

The cards in the left and right hand columns (the Movements of Erasing Personal History and Assuming Authority) all contain some form of vertical structure, pole, seat, or building made by human hands—except for the cards on the bottom row. The Star and Planet Earth are self-supporting. In the left hand column, the Priestess sits underneath the temple, the Warrior sits on the palanquin with the Star Nations banner on a pole behind him, and the Hanged Man is stretched between the poles of life and death. In the right hand column, the Lovers stand beneath the temple, the Balance stands in front of the scales, and the tower of the Released Man reaches up to the sky. These human structures suggest that at the beginning and end of each row there is some ego consolidation, some building of substance, some added strength and presence in the personality. Then again, we could also say that the ego needs these structures and supports at these places on its journey.

Let's now look at the centre column, the Movement of Stopping the World. We see *quaternio* symbols of fourness in each of the cards: the cross formed by the Ruler's body and the serpent bar in the 4 card, the square opening of the temple in the Sage card, the four images in the Temperate Man (the Twisted Hair, the urn, the flower and the quadrated sun) in the 14 card, and the four-rayed sun in the Sun card. These symbols of order and wholeness indicate a holding of the tension between the opposites and they show how to balance the tensions generated by the cards at either end of the rows.

The cross formed by the Ruler and his serpent bundle provide the discipline, rationality and order (both cosmic and human) to compensate the tendency to get lost in the magic and enchantment of the Priestess or in the eyes of the beloved in the Lovers card. The wisdom of the Sage, pointing to the As Above and the So Below, with the fire in front of him and the Flowering Tree staff behind him, balances the extroverted hyperactivity of the Warrior and the cold decisiveness of the Balance. The harmonious feeling function of the Temperate Man, with his twisted hair, the rainbow, the water and the Flowering Tree, balances the suffering of the Hanged Man and the destruction of the Released Man. Finally, the Grandfather Sun of the Sun card stands mid-way between the impossibly distant lights of the Great Grandfather Stars and the dark, intimate closeness of Grandmother Earth. He gives us warmth and light—not too little, not too much.

The story of our life is woven on the Loom of Time. The cards are a snippet of DNA, a section of a gene on the chromosome of our ancestral lineage formed from an infinite series of Books of Life laid end to end that come from past generations and continue onwards to future generations. The finely balanced vertical and horizontal forces of the marriages, lovers, awakenings, dreams, completions, spirals, platforms, bundles, ascents and descents, hold the tensions between the opposites and form the invisible endoskeleton, the matrix and patrix, of the Book of Life.

The Fool

LE · MAT

The Fool

10

Fool

If the fool would persist in his folly he would become wise.
—William Blake, *The Marriage of Heaven and Hell.*

The essence of reality is open, empty and naked like the sky,
Luminous emptiness without centre or circumference,
Unobstructed, sparkling, pure and vibrant, pristine awareness.
Your intelligent, cognizant, radiant mind
Is the pure Buddha of Immortal Light.
—The Tibetan Book of the Dead

A young person who could be of either sex stands in the mouth of a jaguar. He raises his left hand as though he is uncertain or unable to see. His eyes are closed and he wears an elaborate headdress. The glyphs in his headdress identify him as Hasaw Chan K'awil of Tikal. In his right hand is a white flower with six petals. The number of the Fool is 0 symbolising the feminine Void which is the Nothing that gives birth to All Things. However, the card in the European tarot is traditionally depicted as male so I shall refer to the Fool as "he." The first paragraph of each of the following chapters is based on Peter Balin's description of the card in his book *The Flight of Feathered Serpent.*

Blind and Foolish

With his left hand the Fool points forward in childlike curiosity, fingers apart, as if to indicate that he might only be able to see just so much. In Maya art, this pressing of his wrist to his forehead is a gesture of despair at the approach of impending death.[1] In many tarot the Fool is blindfolded and seems quite happy in his blindness. Psychologically, this blindness is a necessary aspect of the Fool and it symbolises both his lack of, and need for, consciousness.

Th Fool is unknowing, blissful in his ignorance, and unhampered by the burden of consciousness. He is not self-conscious, second-guessing himself and hyper-aware of his every thought and action. From the point of view of reason and maturity he is rash, impetuous, hare-brained, not-a-care-in-the-world, foolish, irresponsible and unsophisticated. But when the ego becomes too world-weary, when too much of life has been seen, the psyche needs to return to this place of the Fool where goals, ambitions, failures and successes take a holiday. The Fool is life lived on gut instinct. He is the innocent leap of faith, the "just do it."

The innocence of the Fool is not gullible naiveté but a necessary archetypal innocence (the movie Forrest Gump is a good example) that creates life no matter what, under any conditions, because that is just what life does. Life always finds ways of replicating itself, otherwise it is anti-life. The Fool urges us on into life when thinking or feeling might be overly cautious and not quite up to it. He is a natural force undisturbed by consciousness, knowledge or experience. Without the Fool's blind and thoughtless impulse toward life nothing new would be born.

However, merchant consciousness sees the nothingness of the Fool not as a cornucopia of all things *in potentia* but rather as a waste of productive real estate. It is convinced that the devil will make work for idle hands and anyone being foolish, foot-loose, fancy-free, feckless, empty-headed and good-for-nothing will surely come to no good — and certainly not be economically productive. In a culture that cannot tolerate grief and loss, time and space that is not used to manipulate matter into different forms for economic gain is "wasted."

The Fool is childlike, living in a timeless world and completely in the present. But, because he is not separated from the world around him, he can never know himself, he cannot see himself, so he has no objectivity. The Fool is unconscious, moreover he *is* the unconscious. He is blind to himself and the future. He does not want to see, or he is intentionally blind like the blindfolded statue of Justice atop the Old Bailey in London, or he is forced to rely on his inner sight like the blind seer Tiresias in Sophocles' *Oedipus Rex*. Most importantly, he has to be blind to begin the journey. If we knew all the consequences of our actions before we carried them out we would be paralysed — too much consciousness would root us to the spot. If we knew at the beginning what we know now we would never have started.

Life is an archetypal gamble, a game of chance, and that is its irresistible fascination. Like sports or games, life is unscripted drama — all things are possible, anything can happen, the treasure waits to be found and the victory waits to be won. If everything was predictable, if we had perfect foresight, if there was no blindness, then there would be no risk and nothing new would come into being. There would be no death (as safety would be guaranteed) and without death there is no life.

The Fool is also known as Il Matto (the Mad One) in some Italian tarot or Le Mat (the Dull One) in a Swiss deck.[2] He is simple and like the simpleton he has not yet been complicated and complexed by life. But therein lies his gift. In fairytales, a common theme is that the king has three sons. The kingdom is in danger and the two older sons, who are smarter and more skilled, are the ones who rush off to save the kingdom. The youngest brother, the dummling, tries his hardest to do the same but his bumbling attempts are not taken seriously. But the older brothers even with all their knowledge and derring-do, fail in their quest. In the end, the youngest brother is the one who finds the treasure or saves the kingdom from danger.

Why the youngest, the most foolish? Because he is the aspect of the personality that is closest to nature. He is not hemmed in by convention and not all grown up and worldly wise. He symbolises the basic genuineness and integrity of the personality.[3] It is this original wholeness that is more important than learning or bravery and in the end wins the day.

Joker

The Fool is the compensatory twin of the king who brings order and structure to the kingdom. The word "idiot" comes from the Greek *idios* meaning a private person or someone outside the bounds of society. The wise king knows that too much order and structure leaves no room for new life to be born from the recesses of chance, uncertainty and ambiguity. So the king's court had a jester whose role it was to turn things upside-down and poke fun at the follies of the great and the good. Like the unconscious, he could tell the naked truth and get away with it (Sacha Baron-Cohen is a modern example). The comedian as clown speaks about uncomfortable things and makes us laugh at ourselves and our seriousness or touchiness (Chris Rock or Billy Connolly, for example).

The jester is the atrophied form of the much older sacred clown or, as he is called in Native North American cultures, the trickster, contrary or heyoka. Of the animals, coyote is the trickster who is always causing trouble or getting into trouble and is often insatiable, foolish and bawdy. Likewise, the jester is raunchy, rude, crude, and horny. He gets up, behind, underneath and into everything that masks, hides, primps and postures. The jester knows that sex is not only the most universal but also the most secretive of our activities. He knows that if sexuality is to retain its healthy lust it must be exposed as well as veiled.

In Europe, between the 12th and 16th centuries, the Feast of Fools was celebrated each year at the beginning of January. It originated within the church and for a day the church hierarchy was inverted, a mock pope was elected, and the church was parodied. Over the centuries it became bawdier and was eventually banned by the church. Today, we see similar days given over to play and foolishness, shadow and sexuality in April Fool's Day, Fastnacht or Mardi Gras.

Beginning the Journey

The Fool is the only unnumbered card. Even in the archetypal world of numbers he does not have a home. In some decks he is placed before the 1 card as the 0 card, or after the 21 card as the 22 card. In others, he is placed between the 20 and 21 cards. This ambivalence reflects the nature of the card.

The word fool comes from the Latin *follis*, a pair of bellows, or a wind-bag, associating the card with buffoonery and puffery. A raspberry fool is an insubstantial dessert—light, fluffy and full of air. In many creation myths wind is the first element and is the "Breath of Life." Just as the baby begins life by taking its first breath so air, the invisible, insubstantial element on which life depends, begins the journey.

Here let us notice the differences between the Xultun Fool and Sorcerer cards and the Marseilles Fool and Magician cards. In the Marseilles deck the Fool and the Magician are part of the sequence of cards from 0 to 21 and are not visually related to each other. However in the Xultun Tarot cards the Fool (0) and the Sorcerer (1) face each other and are set apart from the other cards. Just as all other numbers derive from 0 and 1, so the 0 and 1 cards are the parents of all the other tarot cards.

The circle of the 0 encompasses all the other cards and its spherical nature generates the 1, the point at the centre. The 0 contains all the opposites in both simplicity and complexity. 0 to 1 is spirit transformed into substance and 1 to 0 is substance transformed back to spirit. The other 20 cards then tell the story of what happens in between. This is why the 0 and 1 cards sit separately at the top of the major arcana.

The Marseilles Fool is setting off on a journey. Even though he may not have a goal he is moving somewhere. However, the Xultun Fool is less burdened and less purposive—he stands still and holds only the six-petalled flower. The Marseilles Magician is often depicted holding a wand and standing in front of a table spread with magical tools, instruments of his will and focussed purpose. The Xultun Sorcerer has no equipment like the table or magical apparatus, instead he holds only what he can carry—a headdress which he holds aloft and a Flowering Tree staff he carries over his left shoulder. He has fewer trappings than the Marseilles Magician and rather than being focussed on his magical items he looks at the source of his magic—the Great Light above him and the Zero before him.

Dog

The dog is almost universal in the European Fool card but it is absent from the Xultun Fool however I shall explore its symbolism here because it adds to our understanding of this card. The Xultun Tarot differs markedly from traditional European tarot particularly with regard to animals. For a fuller discussion of this see Chapter 3.

The earliest European tarot depicted the Fool as an idiot, wild man or a beggar then later a dog was added at his side. The dog represents the right amount of instincts—not too wild, not too domesticated—that the Fool needs on his journey to maturity. Of all the animals, the dog is the most domesticated and adapted to humans. A dog responds to our moods, copies us, accompanies us, and understands what we expect. The dog is the essence of our first mother-relationship: devoted, uncomplicated, free of demands, ambivalence or separation, and willing to sacrifice itself.

Dogs diverged genetically from their wolf ancestors before 15,000 BCE and were first domesticated in Central Asia around that period. The dog is "man's best friend" and many creation stories tell of the dog's friendship with humans from the beginning. One myth tells of a gulf that opened up between Adam and the beasts that he had named. As the chasm was almost complete the dog leaped across taking its place alongside Adam. Another tells how in the beginning animals lived in peace and harmony. Then humans came with self-will and arrogance. The animals gathered in council and decided to kill the humans while they slept. The dog, hearing this, gave the humans warning and when the animals attacked they were prepared. For his betrayal, the animals cursed the dog to be forever dependent on humans.[4]

As with all animals, the dog is true to its own nature and is in turn both friend and betrayer, guide and trickster, watchdog and thief, healer and devourer. In many cultures the dog is a symbol for greed, sensuality, sexuality and unrestrained appetite. The dog also epitomises loyalty, doggedness, faithfulness and devotion. But loyalty to what? The Fool is nothing as yet, he is not formed. So he can only be loyal to himself, to what is unborn in him, to his potential, because that is all he has. Someone said, "My goal in life is to be as good a person as my dog thinks I am." The Fool must be loyal to the unconscious, the original wholeness of his nature, in order not to become too civilised and removed from his instincts. In the European tarot he is seen stepping off a cliff in a moment of unguarded innocence, representing the instinctual, irrational, playful impulse to step off into the unknown.

The dog is also the betrayer, from the human point of view. In Eastern Europe creation myths say that the dog is the one who betrayed humans to the devil.[5] But the dog is being itself, just like the unconscious that "betrays" our carefully arranged conscious intentions. Without being betrayed by our instincts (particularly our sexual instinct which is the most instinctual of all the instincts) consciousness will never develop.

The dog is associated with dying and procreation, beginnings and endings, and the Crack-between-the-Worlds of spirit and matter. Through their intuition or "nose" they are connected to the unseen because they can perceive what humans ordinarily cannot. In Hinduism, the dog is a messenger of Yama, the god of death, and dogs guard the doors of Heaven. In Hawai'ian folklore, the volcano goddess Pele was sometimes accompanied by a white dog. The black dog is a common nocturnal spectre in the folklore of the British Isles. It is larger than a physical dog, has large, glowing red eyes and its appearance was regarded as a portent of death. It is often associated with crossroads, places of execution, ancient pathways and electrical storms. The dog, Black Shuck, appeared during a violent storm in 1577 in the church at Bungay, Suffolk. Several people died of fright.

The dog is also the psychopomp, the animal that guides souls to the underworld. Just as it accompanies humans during the day so it follows them into the night. The Lacandon Maya set four figures of dogs at the four corners of graves so they would accompany the deceased. Anubis was the Egyptian god who protected the dead and brought them to the afterlife. He was usually portrayed as half human, half jackal. Jackals, dingoes and hyenas are well known for scavenging meat and eating corpses. Cerberus, in Greek and Roman mythology, was the three-headed dog who stood guard at the gates of Hades to prevent those who crossed the river Styx from returning. Each of Cerberus' heads is said to have an appetite only for live meat and thus allow the spirits of the dead to freely enter the underworld, but allow none to leave.

In pre-conquest Central America each person was considered to have an animal soul—a *nahualli*. This link was very strong and the death of one could bring about the death of the other. Sorcerers and shamans could shapeshift into the form of their nahualli. The dog Xolotl was a nahualli of Quetzalcoatl and he accompanied Quetzalcoatl to the Underworld to retrieve the bones of humankind. During the sacrifice by the gods at the first dawning at the creation of the world, Xolotl turned into the double-headed maize plant, then the double maguey plant (mexolotl) and finally the salamander or axolotl ("water xolotl").

We find Xolotl again in the Aztec story of the sun's rising and setting. The Aztec night begins just after noon. After the sun passes the zenith, it becomes Cuahutemoc, Falling Eagle. As it moves toward the western horizon, it becomes Tlacitonatiuh, Earthbound Sun or Dying Sun. At this point it is joined by Xolotl who drags it into the land of Death below the horizon, guiding it through its nine underground stations. In the underworld it becomes Yohualtonatiuh, Night Sun, and is sacrificed eight times on its way to midnight. Then it is sacrificed a ninth time and, purified, it begins the struggle to be reborn as the morning sun. Like Xolotl, our animal soul is infinitely adaptable to new circumstances but if it dies without rebirth we continue to exist but do not really live.

Spirit Canoe

The archetypal journey that the Fool will undertake is prefigured by the images under his feet. He stands in the mouth of the jaguar, the Keeper of Memory. The mouth has seven teeth, the number of the dream, the dream of this life he is about to enter. The Fool is dreaming himself awake. The jaguar skin stretches above the head of the Ruler across to the Priest suggesting that if the Fool shows up, then like the fairytale, the kingdom will be restored to wholeness both materially (the Ruler) and spiritually (the Priest). Conversely, the Ruler and the Priest must remain connected with the simplicity of the Fool through the arts of remembrance. Underneath the feet of the Fool and the Sorcerer is a spirit canoe, a world-wide mythological symbol representing the soul's journey to and from this world.

The Maya used canoes for river transport and trading as well as a metaphor for life and death. The image of the canoe is taken from an incised bone found at Tikal (Figure 27). The Old Jaguar God sits at the front of the canoe and Old Stingray Spine God sits at the back. Between them from left to right sit an iguana, a spider monkey, First Father as the Maize God, a parrot, and a dog. The Maize God wears the headdress of the Jester God (so-called because of the similarity to the European jester's three-pointed cap with baubles) and he is the model for the painting of the Fool card. He holds his left hand to his forehead in a sign signalling despair at his imminent death in the Otherworld as he is born into this world. He dies in order to gain memory through substance. Psychologically, for the Fool at the beginning of the journey into consciousness this is the death of his innocence and unconsciousness.

Every major image of Maya cosmic symbolism is a map of the sky. The glyphs on the bone carving indicate a date of September 16, 743 CE and on this date at midnight the Milky Way was stretched across the sky from east to west. When it lies in this position one end is split into two. For the Maya these were the jaws of a crocodile and the whole Milky Way was the Cosmic Monster. Linda Schele, a Maya scholar, has shown that the canoe represents the Milky Way as it rotates and descends over the horizon during the night. Another carved flint shows the Milky Way canoe "sinking" as it turns in the sky during the night, bringing the three hearth stars of Orion to the zenith just before dawn. Schele says, "Like Itzamna, the original shaman, the Paddlers are up in the sky riding the Milky Way to the place of Creation where they will set their stones in the hearth of Orion. They propel the Milky Way canoe, with its precious cargo, to the same location. I real-

Figure 27. Incised bone, Burial 116, Temple 1, Tikal

ised that the Paddlers bring the Maize God to the place of the three stones of Creation and to the turtle carapace, the belt stars of Orion, so he can be reborn and create the new universe. He is the Wak-Chan-Ahau who made everything happen."[6]

In similar scenes on Maya pots the Maize God carries a bag of seeds on his chest so he can plant the seeds that are the Pleiades when he raises Wakah Chan, the World Tree (another name for the Milky Way). In other scenes the Maize God is lying down in the same position as a child emerging from the birth canal. So we can see that the canoe and the Fool card are powerful symbols of beginnings, birth and creation.

The journey of the soul culminates in the union of the masculine and the feminine which the medieval European alchemists thought of as the marriage of the Sun and the Moon. In the Xultun Tarot this marriage comes about in the last row but it is prefigured in the image of the canoe. In fact, Susan Milbrath, a Maya scholar, suggests that the two paddlers in the canoe are the sun and the moon and that the canoe itself represents the sun, moon and the planets as they pass through the Milky Way.[7] The passage of the planets through the Milky Way and the symbolism of rebirth is a theme to which we shall return in the last row of cards.

Flower of the Soul

In some tarot the Fool carries a tramp's bundle on a stick over his shoulder indicating that he is free to roam anywhere in the world and is not yet tied down by life. All his worldly possessions (which are his genuineness and simplicity) are carried with him in the simplest of ways. But they are behind him, that is they are unconscious.

At the beginning of a journey or event that touches our soul (and it is only these kinds of events that the major arcana comment on) we have all we need from the very beginning. The whole event and all its possible unfoldings are wrapped up in the first moments of the encounter. This is what the bundle symbolises. Only after we have acquired the insight that the journey was undertaken to gain, can we look back at the first few steps and say to ourselves, "I knew right from the beginning…" or "I knew from the moment I met her…." It is as if the whole event is distilled into a few symbolic moments and the dream of the journey shows itself to us at the moment of creation—if we are quick enough to catch it.

But it is not we who take the journey, it is the journey that takes us. The journey itself wants to be walked and this archetype of the red road, quest, pilgrimage, journey or hajj wants to be lived through human experience. But, like all archetypes, it does not care who takes the journey. Like a fool, we are blindfolded and taken along for the ride. One of Jung's most important contributions was his re-discovery and understanding of this reality. He restated in modern terms what all indigenous peoples keep alive and, in its hubris, what Western culture has forgotten—that the desires of the gods and goddesses are not to be denied. But he also added something new—the potential for a human being to do something other than be crushed between the jaws of fate and biology, spirit and matter.

Jung emphasised that the human soul must transform itself but also maintain its integrity and individuality throughout the journey. It must hold to account the great archetypal forces, like love or power, that assume no responsibility for the human souls they have used for their own ends throughout history. The end of the journey is not the goal. The goal is the shaping and reshaping of the soul along the way. When the soul changes by coming to know itself then the great archetypal forces of death, sex, love and power and even the Creator itself, are changed and humanised.

The flower-soul appears as itself in the Fool and the Planet Earth, the first and last cards in the deck. This suggests that the greatest flowering of ourselves (but also the greatest danger of losing ourselves) occurs in these two cards. The Fool is all innocence, immaturity, and inexperience. The young Fool is supposed to lose himself in the arms of life, he needs to fail magnificently, and his vulnerability, which paradoxically is also his best protection, is achingly raw.

The Earth card, on the other hand, means maturity, achievement, success, victory and seasoned experience. But success is a blow much harder to recover from than failure. Success brings the inflation of victory as opposed to the inflation of innocence. The perils of knowing it all are the same as the perils of knowing nothing. So the young Fool eventually may become the old Fool of success, riches and political power who is puffed up with his own greatness and refuses to die, step down or give up his power.

The antidote for all this is the principal quality of the Fool—humour. For those with too much ego this is the humility that allows us to take ourselves less seriously. For those with not enough ego it is the right dose of healthy narcissism that encourages us to take ourselves more seriously. The cardinal sign of being taken over by an emotional complex or being blindly driven by an archetypal force is that we become touchy and sensitive (or thick-skinned and invulnerable) and lose our sense of humour. If we can survive success as well as defeat we can then take our accomplishments and our failures with a grain of salt. This is why the discipline of humour is always associated with the Fool.

Don Juan referred to this discipline as "controlled folly" which is the foundation of stalking. "Applying these principles [of stalking] brings about three results." [said Florinda, one of Don Juan's apprentices] "The first is that *stalkers* learn never to take themselves seriously; they learn to laugh at themselves. If they're not afraid of being a fool, they can fool anyone. The second is that *stalkers* learn to have endless patience. *Stalkers* are never in a hurry; they never fret. And the third is that *stalkers* learn to have an endless capacity to improvise."[8] The lesson of the Fool is that if we can retain the capacity to laugh at ourselves, to not take ourselves too seriously, then we can become the wise Fool.

The Sorcerer

The Magician

11

Sorcerer

At various times don Juan attempted to name his knowledge for my benefit. He felt that the most appropriate name was *nagualism*, but that the
term was too obscure. Calling it simply "knowledge" made it too vague,
and to call it "witchcraft" was debasing. "The mastery of intent" was too
abstract, and "the search for total freedom" too long and metaphorical. Finally, because he was unable to find a more appropriate name, he called
it "sorcery," although he admitted it was not really accurate.

— Carlos Castaneda

It is good knowing that glasses
are to drink from;
the bad thing is not to know
what thirst is for.

— Antonio Machado

The Sorcerer stands on his toes as if leaning into the wind, holding a
wand with seven jade rings. Over his shoulder is a wooden staff with a
single living leaf. He is elaborately dressed and before him on the ground
is a cup.

The Sorcerer, or Magician in the Marseilles Tarot, represents focussed
purpose, thought that becomes action, one-pointedness, active will, the
power of command, one's desire to live and take up space, the desire for
knowledge, and goal-oriented drive. The Sorcerer is the One who has come
out of the Nothing. Wind is the first element in creation. It is the thought,
the idea or the intent in the mind of the Creator, in other words, consciousness. Then comes fire that needs wind to expand. Consciousness desires
form so water is the next element and from that comes earth.

The Sorcerer is the seed of all things, the breath that creates life. He is associated with air, enthusiasm and inspiration by God. He symbolises the
intent, free will and purpose of humans that are capable of influencing, for

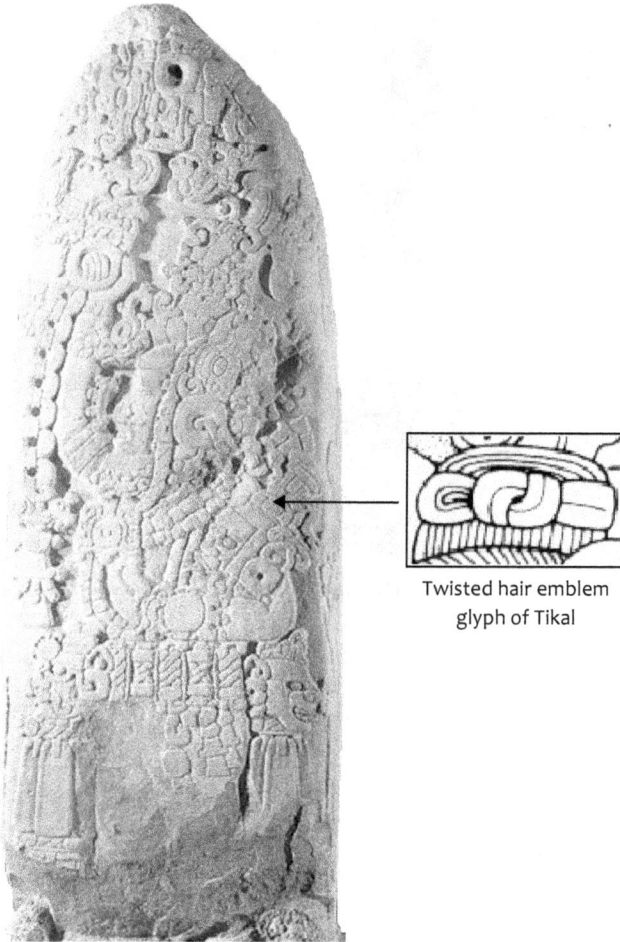

Twisted hair emblem
glyph of Tikal

Figure 28. Stormy Sky, Stela 31, Tikal

better or for worse, the natural order. The Sorcerer also symbolises the longing to create beauty — to decorate the material world in resplendent form in gratitude to the other world that gives us life. All art is born from this struggle of the Sorcerer to release the light hidden within the darkness of matter. In all ancient cultures, craftspeople were also considered practitioners of the magical arts.

Stormy Sky

The image of the Sorcerer is taken from the front of Stela 31 at Tikal (Figure 28). Here we see the ruler Stormy Sky or Sky-born K'awil (Siyaj Kaan K'awil II) holding up the head of the Tikal Jaguar War god and from it fall seven spools of jade linked together. In the crook of his arm he cradles the head of the god of fire (omitted in the card) underneath which is the twisted

Figure 29. Mount Taranaki, North Island, New Zealand

hair or *mutul* emblem glyph of Tikal. He wears a complex crown that declares he is the Bakal Uay, the spirit of the founder of the Tikal dynasty, Yax Eb Xok.[1] He wears the heads of God Number Seven and the Jaguar God of the Underworld on his belt, which shows the mat design indicating royalty. The accession ceremony of Stormy Sky was performed on June 11, 439 CE after the change of the 400 year baktun.[2] On the sides of the stela are images of his father, Nuun Yax Ayin, whom we shall encounter later in the Balance card. The Ruler card is also a depiction of Stormy Sky.

Taranaki

At the base of the card in the distance, we see a snow-capped mountain. Balin explains:

> I didn't want to put my name on the cards themselves, and I was born within the shadow of this particular mountain, literally right on the side. My grandfather, my mother's father had a farm there and I was born on it. And it is a mountain which stands all alone in a plain that juts out into the ocean in New Zealand, it's called Mount Egmont, and it's a sleeping volcano like most of the mountains in New Zealand. And it is a very sacred mountain to the Maoris. It is the mountain on which Ratana received his prophecies and the law, which probably doesn't mean anything to you, but anyway that was my way of signing the cards.[3]

This dormant volcano is on the west coast of the North Island of New Zealand. Captain Cook named it in 1770 after Lord Egmont, First Lord of the Admiralty, but in recent years it has resumed its original Maori name, Mount Taranaki (Figure 29).

The separation from the unity of the zero is the first step of the journey. Desire, will and intent ("I want") brings about differentiation and disturbs the undifferentiated zero. The tarot is about the movement from the undifferentiated (the One) to the differentiated (the Many) and back again. The dictum of the alchemists' Maria Prophetessa was "Out of the One comes Two, out of the Two comes Three, and from the Third comes the One as the Fourth." Separation is the first step in differentiation and is the mathematical operation of addition (the 1 separates and adds to the 0). This leads to division (the 1 divides into 2) which in turn leads to differentiation (the 2 multiplies into 3). In summary, the 0 and 1 become 21 which is a 3, growth.

At the top of the cards we see spirit and matter in undifferentiated form as the Great Light and the dormant Mount Taranaki. In between them lies the pot in which the soul is to be cooked. Then, at the bottom of the deck, we see these images in differentiated form. The big bang of the Great Light has become the black hole at the centre of Planet Earth, the singular Taranaki has become the eight fiery volcanoes, the Sorcerer's staff has become the sixteen Flowering Trees (eight along the bottom row and eight surrounding Planet Earth), and the flower of the human soul lies next to the smoking pot.

Differentiation initially leads to solitude and isolation and eventually to being trapped in space and time, and entangled in the messiness of life. This is reflected in a Maori legend about Mount Taranaki which recalls how Te Maunga o Taranaki (the mountain of Taranaki) once lived in the centre of the North Island with the other mountain gods, Tongariro, Ruapehu and Ngauruhoe (all active volcanoes today). Nearby stood the lovely maid-mountain Pihanga with her cloak of deep green bush, and all the mountain gods were in love with her. What had been a long, peaceful existence for the gods was disturbed when Taranaki could no longer keep his feelings in control and dared to make advances toward Pihanga. A mighty conflict between Tongariro and Taranaki ensued, which shook the foundations of the earth. The mountains belched forth their anger and darkness clouded the sky. When peace finally came to the land, Tongariro, considerably lowered in height, stood close by Pihanga's side. Taranaki, wild with grief and anger, tore himself from his roots with a mighty wrench and left his homeland. Weeping, he plunged recklessly towards the setting sun, gouging out the Whanganui River as he went and, upon reaching the ocean, turned north. While he slumbered overnight, the Pouakai Ranges thrust out a spur and trapped Taranaki in the place he now rests.

Magic, Science and Alchemy

The Sorcerer is the master of the tonal. He stands at the edge of the unknown and leans into the wind, the first element. Through his imagination, he manifests the unknown into the known. As the Magician in the European tarot, he often has an infinity sign over his head that symbolises the potential for will to come into physical form. He is Hermes or Mercury, the trickster-magician who lives in the Crack-between-the-Worlds, the mercurial one who is found at the crossroads, the one who we only glimpse out of the corner of our eye and then he is gone. Hermes, in Greek mythology, is the Olympian god of boundaries and of the travellers who cross them. As a translator, Hermes is a messenger from the gods to humans. He gives us our word "hermeneutics" for the art of interpreting hidden meaning. In ancient Greece, a lucky find was called a *hermaion*.

The Sorcerer is a scientist but with a different methodology. The magician prides himself on his occultism and the secrecy of his procedures; the scientist on peer review, disclosure, transparency of method and replicable results. But they are joined at the hip — they both wish to control matter. Just as magic is the alignment with substance through the understanding of the laws of spirit, so science is the alignment with spirit through the understanding of the laws of matter. If we go deep enough into matter we come out at spirit, and many scientists have had a metaphysical undercurrent to their work. Sir Isaac Newton was deeply religious and studied alchemy for most of his life. Albert Einstein said, "When the solution is simple, God is answering." This magical shadow of science has become more available for mainstream discussion through the emergence of such fields as quantum physics and chaos theory.

Medieval alchemy combined both science and magic and Jung wrote at length on the psychological wisdom contained in alchemical writings. Alchemy was an exploration of the properties of matter and how substances interacted as well as a spiritual exploration of the transformation of the human soul. However, the two ideas have been conflated in the modern misconception that alchemy was only concerned with the transmutation of base metals into gold.

The word alchemy comes from the Arabic *al-khem* meaning "black earth," so alchemy is the art of the black earth. The practice of alchemy first appeared several centuries BCE in Egypt and China. Arab alchemy flourished from 200 CE to 1000 CE and made its way into Europe via Spain. The practice of alchemy in Europe was at its height between the 12th and 16th centuries. Some well-known alchemists were Roger Bacon, Albertus Magnus, Raymond Lully, John Dee and Paracelsus.

The Latin names for the major alchemical operations were *calcinatio* (burning or heating), *solutio* (dissolving), *coagulatio* (coagulating or solidifying), *sublimatio* (sublimating or vaporising), *mortificatio* (putrefying, decomposing, rotting, mortifying), *separatio* (separating, distilling) and *coniunctio* (joining, combining).

The Sorcerer is a magician and all magic and miracles have in common an attitude of faith, hope and expectancy. This is not the notion that we "create our own reality" (a misreading of Jane Roberts' original Seth material). Neither should it be confused with notions of empowerment, abundance, prosperity consciousness, manifestation, positive thinking or other New Age or quasi-business beliefs. Nor is it the opposite—blind faith and submission to the will of God. The magician's attitude abstains from cynicism and nay-saying and champions adamant optimism. It is hopeful, expecting life to offer something, expecting that something will happen, but without specifics. This allows spirit room to work. In the face of difficult or impossible life situations, after everything else has been tried, we can either doubt the possibility of finding a way out or hope that a "miracle" (something as yet unknown to us but known to spirit) will happen. A person being confronted with the unknown finds himself in this archetypal situation, which often occurs in myths and fairytales, where divine intervention offers the only solution.

At the feet of the Sorcerer sits an urn with the mountain behind it, symbolising both the limitations and vastness of physical form. The urn is the human-made receptacle in which the soul is given shape and cooked. In medieval mysticism, the Holy Grail was seen as an image of the soul which receives divine grace. According to Gnostic tradition, the Creator sent down a mixing vessel, or *krater*, in which those who sought spiritual transformation could be immersed.

However, the urn has not yet grown three legs like the traditional Maya cooking pot we see in later cards. In other words, it does not yet have agency, it cannot get about or stand on its own feet, and it does not have an identity. The soul is not yet cooked. It has not yet differentiated itself from the matter from which it was made and the Great Mother, the Earth, that it rests on. It is a spiritual potential that later incarnates in increasingly differentiated form. We see it again in the Sage card as the brazier that holds the fire. Now the soul begins to awaken. Then in the Temperate Man he pours starwater from the pot as his connecting link with intent becomes stronger. In the Star card the pot "doubles," and finally it sits smoking on the platform separate from and underneath Planet Earth. Next to it lies the six-petalled flower-soul. The soul is now cooked.

This sequence of cards is also the Maya story of creation. The Sorcerer rides the spirit canoe (the Milky Way) which carries the Maize God (the Sage is an image of the Maize God) who plants the seeds that are the Pleiades (the stars in the starwater poured by the Temperate Man) that will become the three hearth stones (the three-legged pot in Planet Earth) of Orion where the Maize God is born again.

The Sorcerer represents the soul's desire to be embodied and clothed in matter, for the heart to long something into being, for the mind to imagine an idea, to command it to be so, and bring it into form. Nothing is born unless our soul has the feminine desire to receive life and our spirit has the masculine will to penetrate life. This life is the most important thing of all. It offers the Self, as Jung said, the opportunity to become incarnated into three dimensional physical reality. "It assumes human shape in order to enter three-dimensional physical existence, as if someone were putting on a diver's suit in order to dive into the sea."[4] The intensity of our introverted feminine longing and desire for life enables the world to draw us in. The extroverted masculine will to be born allows us to penetrate the world. However, the Sorcerer has all the powers of will and desire but does not yet have the wisdom to use this energy consciously. We see the Sorcerer holding the rudimentary Flowering Tree in his left hand and it points behind him — the growth of the personality is yet to come and is still in the unconscious.

The Priestess
The Heart of the Child Substance Shield uses the Mood of
Emotional Sweetness to Erase Emotional History

The Papess

12

Priestess

The world will change less in accordance with man's determinations than with women's divinations.

— Claude Bragdon

When our hearts break, the cosmos opens up.

— Matthew Fox

"Living backwards!" Alice repeated in great astonishment. "I never heard of such a thing!'"

"—but there's one great advantage in it, that one's memory works both ways." [said the White Queen]

"I'm sure MINE only works one way," Alice remarked. "I can't remember things before they happen."

"It's a poor sort of memory that only works backwards," the Queen remarked.

— *Through the Looking Glass*, Lewis Carroll

A woman sits under a canopy between a black and a white pillar. She holds a folded book that is a map of the Fool's journey. She points with her right hand to the stars that might guide him. The canopy has a roof-comb on top and four eyes underneath it.

The Priestess symbolises intuition, receptivity, waiting for the right moment, having premonitions of things to come, and seeing the hidden, inner world of dreams and fantasies. She is able to "see" the imaginings of the magician, the events occurring in the dream, and give them word and image. In her shadow aspect the Priestess is the goddess of the underworld, chthonic rites, black magic, madness, religious terror and mania, infertility, fatalism and superstition.

The Great Work

The Xultun Tarot begins with the Priestess (2 or 1 + 1, separation and twoness) and ends with Planet Earth (21 or 2 + 1, separation and oneness). This whole sweep of the tarot is the about the union of opposites or the Great Work, as the alchemists called it. For spirit its work is the contrary — the separation of sames. The intertwining of these two movements, one from matter to spirit and the other from spirit to matter, creates and is created by the 20 archetypes of the tarot. They are what makes life sing and dance.

The Priestess is all about separation and Planet Earth is all about union and the movement between the two is the human drama. The absolute dissimilarity between spirit and matter make them hunger for their opposite. The Priestess expresses this by her "seeing" the world of spirit. But she does not embody her seeing, it is not real-ised until the 21 card. Likewise, Planet Earth is matter incarnate but does not see itself until intuited by the Priestess. Visually, we can see this is in the deep blue of spirit in each card. In the Priestess, the "inner firmament" as it was called by the alchemists, lies outside in the dark blue heaven and the stars above. In the Planet Earth card we see the same dark blue heaven and stars but they are *inside* the earth.

How does one world come to know the alien other, make friends with it and ultimately join with it to create new life? How do we get to know another? The process is known by many names: attraction, understanding, affinity, being on same wavelength, intuition, good vibrations, picking up on, or rapport. More psychologically, and referring to less conscious processes, it is known as empathy, projective identification, *participation mystique*, psychic infection, transference, countertransference, emotional contagion, unconscious identity, affective attunement, or empathic resonance. For our purposes here the unwieldy term projective identification comes closest. This is simultaneously a psychological defense against unwanted feelings, a mode of communication, a type of human relationship, a way of controlling the other, a way of knowing the other, a way to absorb or be absorbed by the other and so become like them, and a way to avoid separation, abandonment and being left. Melanie Klein describes it as follows:

> By projecting oneself or part of one's own impulses and feelings into another person, an identification with that person is achieved.... On the other hand, putting part of oneself into the other person (projecting), the identification is based on attributing to the other person some of one's own qualities. Projection has many repercussions. We are inclined to attribute to other people — in a sense, to put into them — some of our own emotions and thoughts.... By attributing part of our feelings to the other person, we understand their feelings, needs and satisfactions; in other

words we are putting ourselves into the other's shoes. There are people who go so far in this direction that they lose themselves entirely in others and become incapable of objective judgement.

The conscious use of projective identification is the basis of psychoanalysis and psychoanalytic psychotherapy. The inability to distinguish inside and outside and to accurately assess physical reality is a cardinal sign of madness or psychosis. The occasional inability to assess emotional reality accurately is universal and is the subject of psychotherapy — one's distortions, assumptions, blind spots and sore spots.

Klein's description of the process sounds more conscious than it actually is. The more something is unconscious inside the psyche the more it will be projected onto something outside the psyche. The object of the projection provides a receptive place, a hook, a landing place for the projection. Although a bloodless word, "object" is the generic term for anything that has psychological importance to us. We can project onto many kinds of "objects" (money, beliefs, words, images, or things) as well as people. The process is then like a chemical reaction and in it both subject and object are changed. Nature's economy and efficiency ensures we get two for one, every time.

The visible quality of the interaction (judged as positive or negative by consciousness) is compensated by its opposite in the unconscious. Often the process starts out as sexual attraction, hero worship or admiration from afar. We feel curiosity and a desire to know, or repulsion and a desire to avoid. If the relationship becomes intimate then it will turn into its opposite over time, or shuttle back and forth between the two. Interest turns into boredom. Repulsion turns into fascination. Love turns into hatred. Hatred into love.

At different times the recipient of the projection may be loved, hated, venerated, feared, despised or attacked. The emotional coercion of projective identification is familiar. The projector pressures the recipient to think, feel and act in accordance with the projection — but are mostly unaware of this. As recipient, we feel a vague pressure to act or feel a certain way or otherwise the other will be hurt or disapprove or get angry. We are made to feel what the other cannot feel. We can't think clearly, we don't know quite what we feel, we are indecisive and unsure. Jung wrote:

> [The doctor] becomes affected [by the transference] and has as much difficulty in distinguishing between the patient and what has taken possession of him as has the patient himself.... The resultant paradoxical blend of positive and negative, of trust and fear, of hope and doubt, of attraction and repulsion, is characteristic of the initial relationship. It is the [love and hate between] the elements, which the alchemists likened to

the primeval chaos. The activated unconscious appears as a flurry of unleashed opposites and calls forth the attempt to reconcile them, so that, in
the words of the alchemists, the great panacea, the *medicina catholica*, may
be born.[1]

The process in relationships is more familiar to us and most humans
have the experience of being changed by the deeper relationships we encounter in our lives. If we are fortunate and go far enough we discover the
part of ourselves that is hidden in the heart of the other. Most of the psychological writings about projective identification have identified its defensive
and negative aspects. That is, the individual remains unaware of and gets
rid of feelings or wishes they find unacceptable—too shameful, too ob-
scene, too dangerous—by attributing them to another. But it is also a way
we hide, and hide from, our talents and their development by finding them
only in others.

The human experience of projective identification is only a part of what
is a larger archetypal process (as yet to receive a name that does it justice).[2]
It is the process by which any two opposites discover their wholeness, or
any two samenesses discover their differences, through the catalyst of the
other. Even the great worlds of matter and spirit have the same vicissitudes
of relationship as we do. It is how the worlds of the visible and the invisible,
the creatura and the pleroma, the implicate order and the explicate order,
heaven and earth, join together and come apart. Like DNA (and this is more
than a metaphor as we shall see) they weave and unravel continuously on
the Loom of Time to create new life, incarnate and discarnate. In the process
both are changed.

Moreover, if both subject and object are changed in this dance it means
that our human relationship to matter below and spirit above changes both.
We change nature and nature changes us. All indigenous cultures knew
this fact but Western consciousness has regressed into ignorance. Shamans,
conjurors, and medicine people know how to change the weather, how to
talk to the plants, how to enter dreams, or how to hear the rocks. This is the
archetype of the magician, the one who, if he has the skills, knowledge and
proper feeling relationship to the object, can influence matter at will. But
our modern scientific consciousness has had to deny the reality of a living,
breathing universe and armour itself in empiricism in order to develop its
highly specialised form of consciousness. Not only can we change the earth
but we can also change heaven as Jung wrote of in his book, *Answer to Job*.
So humans walk between the two worlds and are the catalyst for the transformation of both spirit and matter. This is the story told by the tarot.

Otherness

As the Sorcerer is the 1, so the Priestess is the 2. As the feminine counterpart of the Sorcerer, she takes what the Sorcerer has imagined and begins its incarnation by seeing it. With acknowledgements to William Blake, we could say that the Sorcerer impregnates while the Priestess brings forth. Without the otherness of the Priestess, life would not move forward and would remain the inspired potential dreamed of by the Sorcerer. The Sorcerer is in open space without limits, he stands on his tiptoes, but the Priestess is fixed, sitting under a canopy between two pillars. She is spirit come into solid reality. The pillars are black and white indicating the opposites. In the Sorcerer card the other was the impersonal realm of spirit, all white light, unity and oneness. With the Priestess, this otherness has come down to earth into the human realm and is now subject to the great trials of twoness — attachment and separation.

The Priestess intuits or senses the other which may be another person (clairvoyance), the past (retrocognition), the world of the dead (mediumship), the future (precognition, prophecy), or another consciousness including animals, plants and supposedly dead matter.

Up until now there has been nothing (0) and something (1). Two is the first real number because now counting and the operations of arithmetic (addition, subtraction, division and multiplication) become possible. Now the original unity of 1 has been split and becomes a 2 composed of two 1s. But these 1s are different from the original "numberless" 1. In the latter there is only oneness and sameness but 2 is now split into two 1s that are bound together in a relationship of opposition and attraction, seen and being seen, togetherness and loneliness. The medieval alchemists said that God did not praise the second day of creation, because on Monday (the day of the moon) the *binarius*, or the devil, came into existence. Now the world is sharply divided. This division into two-ness, relinquishing the peace and purity of one-ness, is a necessary step toward consciousness.

Oneness, the spiritual fantasy of those who are not friends with difference, can be a bit limp and feeble. It stands alone, still, in isolation, not moving, uncoupled, unchanging. Its purity is barren. It does not invigorate or give life. Difference does. Like trying to see a white figure against a white background, consciousness cannot emerge unless there is contrast, difference and otherness.

What moves us into exercising our free will choice and defining our boundaries are the universal forces of opposition, competition, conflict and alignment. In the first row of the Xultun Tarot psychic energy is derived from the energy of opposition (the "terrible twos" of any age) which opposes the external forces of parents and culture. In the next developmental step, the second row, the energy is derived from competition with others. In the third row, energy is generated by conflict between the opposites within oneself. In the last row, energy is drawn from alignment of the opposites (not oneness) in the worlds around us and within us.

Jung said, "For just as there is no energy without the tension of opposites, so there can be no consciousness without the perception of differences."[3] Now there is not only the "One" but also the "Other." This brings about difference, separation, distinction, loss and distance (in both time and space). Polarities come into being and movement and opposition between them is now possible; close–distant, together–apart, bound–free, past–future, high–low, good–bad. With opposites, too much of one constellates the need for the other and the necessity for balance arises. Along with this separation, there arises the need for the judging functions of thinking ("Is it good to be close or distant?") and feeling ("Do I like being close or distant?") as well ambivalence, choice and free will ("Do I want to be close or distant?").

As soon as the number two appears there arises a tension between the One that seeks to hold to its solitary existence, and the Other who strives for relationship and twoness. The One tries to preserve its separateness and singleness while the Other strives to get closer to the One. But the Other, in its urgent attraction to the One, secretly pushes itself away to avoid being engulfed or annihilated. So a tension of opposites comes about.[4] The result is that in every relationship there is an optimal distance where the forces of separation and attachment cancel each other out and stability results. Pull them further apart and they will resist. Push them closer together and they will resist. Therapists who work with couples know this.

Relationship brings about a stretching, the natural extension toward, or withdrawal from, the other. We want to know what they feel, about us, about themselves, about others. The other gives our world another dimension. With their presence, we are born into a world of relationship. The other throws who we are into sharp relief. Am I the same as him? Am I different from her? Separation and twoness inevitably leads to introspection, the act of looking within, not only into oneself but also into the other.

This tension of opposites culminates in a release out of which a uniting third is born. In the third, the tension is resolved, the differences of the One and the Other are blended in their "child" and growth is possible. The growth of the 3 leads in turn to the stability of the 4 directions of the circle and the return to the 1 again with the 5 at the centre.

When Eve ate of the fruit of the Tree of Knowledge, with one bite she went from oneness to twoness: from the unchanging, sterile and narcissistic Garden of Eden ordered by God the Father to the messy, growing, fertile world of sex, juice, error and otherness. Around the edges of oneness, the Garden of Eden where everything is merged in a paradise of love, the serpent of twoness always waits to enter.

We see Eve's desire for knowledge in the traditional meaning of the Priestess—mystery, secrets, feminine wisdom, intuition, the future, and the unknown. The knowledge intuited by the Priestess goes through later transformations in the Priest, Sage and Temperate Man cards. Knowledge can be raw or processed, uncodified or codified. By codified I mean a body of knowledge accumulated over the lifetime of an individual or over generations of individuals that has been systematised to form a philosophy, culture, world-view, religion, or code of conduct that guides the actions of the individual or the group.

The knowledge of the Priest is the knowledge of spirit codified by the collective into canon, doctrine or law. The knowledge of the Sage is the knowledge of self codified by the ego into a world-view or philosophy. The knowledge of the Temperate Man is the uncodified union of the two, knowledge of self and knowledge of spirit, which we call wisdom. The Priestess intuits all of the above. Where the Fool was blind she sees it all. She sees the whole journey coming up as a pattern with the details yet to be filled in—like a tarot reading. This why she is the seeress, the oracle, the wise woman or the medium. Her knowledge is codified and uncodified at the same time. What she sees is a pattern of the Creator. To us it appears chaotic, that is, its exact form is not predetermined and it evolves itself as it passes through time. Chaos does have a pattern but it is a pattern repeated only once. Therefore, the Priestess sees the unique order that applies to that particular person or circumstances. It cannot be generalised, repeated or tested.

This is the opposite to how science works. Science does not trust events where n = 1, which are so-called "case studies" or "anecdotal evidence." They are not replicable and so are inferior sources of evidence. Science believes that the more subjects a study contains the less it is subject to chance or individual variation and so the more accurate the study is. Science's perception is ostensibly based on sceptical, hard-nosed fact, evidence and reason. However, these modern scientific superstitions are blind to the obvious—that Life and Nature do not live by fact, evidence or reason. We do not carry out double-blind, randomised, controlled trials to decide whom to marry. The turning points in our lives are often Priestess moments—happenstance, pure luck, one-off coincidences, and chance encounters that, in hindsight, were exquisitely accurate and could not have happened any other way.

Another characteristic of the Priestess' knowledge is that it is personal. I mean not only unique to a particular person, but that the Priestess cannot "see" unless there is relationship, unless there is some degree of connection between the seer and the seen. She cannot be objective, only subjective. The means by which she sees is not through the medium of instruments or formulae or experiments but through her own experience and particularly her own feelings and emotions — the bridge to her intuition.

Thinking and feeling evaluate experience and are developed much later than the intuition and sensation the infant is born with. A newborn still lives in the world of the dream. We see this in Bali, for example, where babies are not allowed to touch the ground until they are a year old. The phenomenal world is not yet real to the infant but feelings, inner experiences, and the unconscious (its own and others) are pleasurably and terrifyingly real. However, the development of the cortex and the capacity to think, and the demands of adapting to a largely left-brain world, require that we put aside this early knowledge and experience.

With any new-born endeavour our initial experiences or "first impressions" come through sensation and intuition and give us information that gets ignored, forgotten, distorted or denied (often to our later regret) because it comes "in a flash." But the primacy of intuition and sensation will reassert themselves in situations that strip away our veneer of cognition such as trauma, life and death emergencies, severe illness, sexual and emotional intimacy, or being in nature for extended periods.

In some European tarot this card is called the Papess which calls to mind the story of Pope Joan who, in the 9th century, was elected to the papacy as John VIII. Her true identity was only revealed when she gave birth during a papal procession. Like Pope Joan's untidy interruption of the solemn spiritual proceedings, the bloodiness of birth is in sharp distinction to the purity of spirit. Without birth there would be no one to witness the doings of spirit. Without witness, spirit would be alone in its completeness, completely alone, and have no place to experience the gifts of touch, intimacy and otherness.

Attachment and Separation

The Priestess is about the dynamics of twoness and to understand her we must look to the original couple in our lives. Freud proposed that the oedipal phase, roughly between the ages of three and six, occupied a central place in psychic development and not much happened before then. From the work of infant psychologists who observe infant behaviour and child psychotherapists who work with inner feeling states, we now know that there is a lot happening from conception onwards.

In child psychoanalysis, two complementary views arose in the 1950s, one extroverted and one introverted. John Bowlby (1907–1990) was a British psychiatrist and psychoanalyst. He was interested in the effects of separation and deprivation on children during WWII and on those who were hospitalised or institutionalised. From his research he developed what has come to be known as attachment theory.

What is taken for granted today was not collective knowledge a hundred or even fifty years ago. The quality of a child's relationships and their attachment with caregivers is critical during the first three years of life. In the last decade it has also been shown that disrupted attachment (aka not being loved) and other relationship trauma result in observable changes in the brain structure which leave their mark on the personality.[5] Attachment theory is about the baby's relationships with the external other. It focuses on the real-world external relationship between infant and mother and the developing ability to "mentalise" or acquire an internal representation of the mind and feelings of another.

The contrary view, about the relationship with the internal other, is associated with Melanie Klein. Klein (1882–1960) was an Austrian child psychoanalyst (and John Bowlby's training supervisor) who emigrated to London. She was influential in the development of psychoanalysis, particularly the British school. She held that the infant's emotional development begins in the first year of life, much earlier than Freud's oedipal stage. In her work with children beginning in the 1920s she found that psychic life begins in the first few months with what she called the paranoid-schizoid position, characterised by splitting and projection.[6] She said, "It is splitting which allows the ego to emerge out of chaos and to order its experiences."[7] Klein proposed that for approximately the first year of life, the internal world of the infant is mostly split and fragmented (schizoid) and it sees pleasure and danger as coming from the outside (paranoid). Destructive impulses and persecutory anxieties are strongest in the paranoid-schizoid position and it is obvious that infants experience terror, fright, and pleasure.

The infant does not yet have the ability to alleviate states of unpleasure, or maintain states of pleasure. Experiences are felt emotionally as all-good or all-bad, and all-outside or all-inside. Projection is brought into play when an infant cannot tolerate the anxiety created by frightening impulses, feelings and experiences, whether they be good or bad. The anxiety-producing impulses are split-off and projected onto the mother who is able to accept them and hold them until the baby is more mature. In other words, a mother feels what her baby feels (or the baby "makes" her feel what it feels). An unconscious feeling is projected, taken in, and experienced by another who takes the mental state to be their own. This is called projective identification from the introverted viewpoint of psychoanalysis, or attunement or empathy from the extroverted viewpoint of attachment theory.[8]

With "good enough" mothering, the mother knows what the baby needs without becoming emotionally overwhelmed by the baby's pain, distress, anger, need, or dependence. The mother's attunement to the baby during early infancy allows it to experience an outer object that can soothe its distress, contain its feelings, and not withdraw, reject, or collapse. This allows the baby to move from the paranoid-schizoid position to the depressive position which begins at about four or five months.

We can see that a baby protests when its needs are not met. If these needs are repeatedly unmet then we the typical stages described by Bowlby in orphaned or abandoned infants: first protest and rage, then detachment, then despair and eventually depression. This is what we see on the outside. On the inside, the rage is directed against whatever or whoever has what it needs. If the infant cannot have it then, in its distress, it wants to destroy the good object who possesses, or even worse is felt to be actively and sadistically withholding, what it desperately needs. This is what Klein called primitive envy. Envy is always a Priestess, two-person event ("I'd kill for looks like hers.") and is the precursor of jealousy which is a Consort, three-person event. In murder-suicides where the separated husband kills both the wife (who may have had an affair, constituting a triangle) and the children and then himself, we see the three-person jealousy of "She's mine, you can't have her," and also the darker, murderous envy of "If I can't have the kids, nobody is going to have them."

As experiences become less fragmented, the infant ego becomes more able to see objects as related wholes. The baby slowly begins to distinguish between itself and the external world and perceives that love, as well as anger, come from the same caring parent, and that the person it hates (for going away, for not soothing) is the same as the one it loves.[9]

The infant then begins to experience a kind of sorrow or guilt concerning the harm that its incessant needs and demands might have done to the loved object. Klein calls this "depressive anxiety," and it is expressed unconsciously in the omnipotent fantasy: "Am I too much for mummy?" "Did I make her angry at me?" "Doesn't she love me anymore?" or in clinical terms, "Did I destroy the loved object?" The normal guilt and fear that arises from the anxiety that one has spoiled what is good constitutes the depressive position.

This position is a naturally occurring process of self-regulation. Physiologically, it is called homeostasis which is the body's ability to keep physiological and biochemical processes (body temperature or hormone levels, for example) within upper and lower limits. On a planetary level it is Gaia's ability to self-regulate her life processes.[10] Our Western culture remains at the paranoid-schizoid position in its omnipotent denial of any worry about the planet. It's a depressive episode waiting to happen.

These early emotional processes that Klein described can apply to any stage of life, because projection, introjection, identification, and projective identification are archetypal processes, and as such, they can emerge at any time during the life cycle.

Klein adhered to Freud's drive concepts of Eros, the life instinct, and Thanatos, the death instinct, but gave more importance to the death instinct

than Freud had, particularly in relation to the destructive envy and aggression that infants and young children feel. Although Klein thought about the
death instinct as a biological force, we might also think about it, in Jungian
terms, as an aspect of the Self.

The wholeness of the Self (the 0 and the 1) is present at birth. It contains
all the opposites in raw, chaotic, rudimentary form. The best and the worst,
life and death, lie side by side. The shadow side of the Self that annihilates,
takes apart and destroys, is what Klein refers to as the death instinct. In the
baby, the "uncivilised" Self is incarnated in the raw, light and dark, and neither light nor dark knows the existence of the other because they are split
and projected. If the child is deprived of the maternal container and the
mother's reverie, then it will be forced to deal with these life and death feelings by denial, splitting, and projection, and by becoming omnipotent. It
will also have difficulty, as it matures, to think about and make mental
space for feelings (as these are the first facts of psychic life) and later may
have learning difficulties.[11]

As the infant experiences good-enough parenting (not too much, not too
little) through the ability of the Priestess-mother to intuit and attend to its
needs, the destructive shadow side of the Self is civilised, so to speak. However, if the child's normal need to be loved is not met, if there is neglect,
abuse, or trauma, then the shadow side of the Self remains in archaic form.
Donald Kalsched proposes that in these cases this shadow side of the Self
paradoxically preserves the "personal spirit" of the infant, by severing
thinking and feeling and dissociating experience into fragments in a primitive, last-ditch attempt to protect the child from further psychological
pain.[12] The outcome of this process is dissociative, borderline and perhaps
psychotic states characterised by inner persecutory events symbolised by
dream images of rape, cutting, shooting, concentration camps, torture, or
decapitation. Thus the inner trauma continues long after the outer trauma
has stopped.

Silent Knowledge

Why is attachment and separation important to our understanding of the
tarot? Because intuition, projective identification, attachment and attraction
are our primary ways of knowing and experiencing. They happen unconsciously in the blink of an eye. Our thoughts may catch up weeks, months
or years later. The Priestess embodies the "silent knowledge," our original
knowing and being known, inherited from the indigenous psyche. Don
Juan explained:

The events unleashed by sorcerers as a result of silent knowledge were
so simple and yet so abstract that sorcerers had decided long ago to

speak of those events only in symbolic terms. The manifestations and the knock of the spirit were examples.... Inside every human being was a gigantic, dark lake of silent knowledge which each of us could intuit... He then said that sorcerers were the only beings on earth who deliberately went beyond the intuitive level by training themselves to do two transcendental things: first, to conceive of the existence of the assemblage point and second, to make that assemblage point move.... "Silent knowledge is something that all of us have," he went on. "Something that has complete mastery, complete knowledge of everything. But it cannot think, therefore, it cannot speak of what it knows...." "It means that man gave up silent knowledge for the world of reason," he replied. "The more he clings to the world of reason, the more ephemeral intent becomes...." As the feeling of the individual self became stronger, man lost his natural connection to silent knowledge. Don Juan asserted that the reason for man's cynicism and despair is the bit of silent knowledge left in him, which does two things: one, it gives man an inkling of his ancient connection to the source of everything; and two, it makes man feel that without this connection, he has no hope of peace, of satisfaction, of attainment.... The nagual stated that mankind had spent the longer part of its history in the position of silent knowledge, and that this explained our great longing for it.[13]

The significance of this card is not only personal but also cultural. For wholeness, each individual and each culture has to be part of, and separate from, the larger culture in which they live. Every culture, race or nationality has its own wounds and gifts. For Western culture the wound is a catastrophic separation from the original mother, this planet, and the loss of our connection with the arts of the Priestess. As a result, the dynamics we have described above—denial, splitting, projection, omnipotence, depression, guilt, emotional retardation, ecological imbecility and hyper-rationality—all loom large in the Western psyche.

Love

We create the second couple in our lives when we fall in love. When we are in love there is a reawakening of feelings from infancy: envy, jealousy, the need for absolute understanding and undivided attention, oceanic feelings for the infinite, promises of everlasting love, and anguish when the loved one is absent. The eye contact and caresses of a couple in love are remarkably similar to that of a mother and baby.

We can see these parallels if we look at the cards. The Priestess and the Lovers are the only two cards where the figures stand underneath a canopy, and above the canopy are the stars in the night sky. This means that in early infancy and when we fall in love we come closest to the archetypal world of the unconscious (the stars in the darkness of the night sky). The result is "madness" if the ego is not strong enough for a naked encounter with such power. The madness of infancy and the madness of love are one and the same and the Priestess and Lovers are protected from its craziness by a canopy which is actually a temple. They both need a structure to mediate the constructive and destructive powers from above. The other cards in this row (Consort, Ruler and Priest) also have a canopy but their canopy is below them in the form of the platform they stand on. They need protection not from the spiritual archetypes in the heavens but from the chthonic archetypes in the earth.

The temples we see in the cards are common images in Maya iconography. The eyes in the roof are the glyph for a star (Figure 31). Its incorporation in the temple roof indicates that the archetypal power has been stepped down, and contained in matter through human activity and form. For the infant, the temple is the mother who loves, feeds, soothes, and knows every pleasure and discomfort. For the Lovers, the temple is the community that allows or prohibits the form and fashion of their relationship. All cultures throughout history have had collective rules as to who can have sex with who, when, in what postion, and what orifices are permitted.

Healing the Creator

It is through the division of the original unity, the separation of the primal couple, the dismemberment of the self-sufficiency of the 0 and the 1, that consciousness comes into being. The Priestess represents this original wound, the fall, and the painful facts of our personal history. She is the Keeper of the Heart of the Little Boy or Little Girl Shield. This is the heart that is wounded when our childhood needs are not met by our humanly imperfect parents, when we are left out and abandoned, or when we are displaced in love and find we are not held in the heart of the other. The fall from oneness, from grace, is inevitable and must ever lead to twoness.

For the human soul in its "ascent" toward spirit, the Priestess is the first step. The last step, the "goal" furthest from our daily experience and most difficult to reach, is the Planet Earth card. It is the Keeper of the Soul of the Child Spirit Shield and the Teacher of Assuming Spiritual Authority. It is the card of completion, attainment, fulfilment, satisfaction, joy, seeing eternal life behind the impermanence of matter, and seeing spirit in all matter.

However, as much as we desire to touch spirit, so spirit in its purity desires to fall into rough matter. Spirit has its own personal history that it needs to erase. And we are it. For spirit, the Planet Earth card is the Keeper of the Heart of its Child Substance Shield and its Teacher of Erasing Emotional History (Figure 30). In other words, this tiny green planet is part of

Figure 30. The Xultun Tarot from the viewpoint of spirit

the healing of the Creator's personal history. The last step for spirit, the "goal" furthest from its experience and most difficult to reach, is the Priestess. She sits in the half darkness, partly hidden under the canopy, with the dark pillar at her back. She is all of what the completion and consciousness of the Planet Earth does not know about. She is the contrary to wholeness and eternity, she is the number 2, unwhole, split, divided and dismembered. For the Creator, this is its fulfilment. For spirit, the Priestess is the Keeper of the Soul of its Child Spirit Shield and its Teacher of Assuming Spiritual Authority. This is why women elders and grandmothers, as priestesses, have always been the primary holders of spiritual wisdom.

The history of spirit is the history of God's engagement in human affairs. Hegel said that history is the autobiography of God.[14] Or, as Edward Edinger put it, "the entire human drama of human history is God's dream!"[15] God is a trauma for humans as well as a salvation, but God is also traumatised and wouldn't know it but for us. God is all-seeing, but in its completeness is also all-blind. The gift of humans is to allow the deity, in its largeness, to see what is small—the traumatised, the lesser, the trivial, the least developed, the vulnerable, the small voice from the bottom of the ladder. By experiencing our unique human wounding and dividedness spirit achieves its wholeness. Angelus Silesius said, "God needs our poor heart in order to be real," In this intertwining, this ascent of humans and descent of spirit, spirit comes to have a human face and humans come to have a spiritual face.

Book of Life

The Sorcerer invokes the creative powers but the Priestess brings the products of his inspiration and imagination down to earth and grounds them in reality. The Sorcerer looks toward the Void and the Great Light; the Priestess looks downward to the writing—inspiration birthed in visible form. She reads from a folded codex, the Book of Life or the Talking Leaves.

The voice of the Talking Leaves is heard in the sacred way in which Maya make the paper for a codex. Women, facing each other in rows, hammer out the inner bark of the *amate* tree, while men keep the rhythm. The mallets are made from ironwood and have a carving on each face that represents a song. The songs and the rhythms are sung into the paper as it is being made.[16] Historically, the Maya coated the paper in stucco, folded it in long accordion strips, and sandwiched it between covers made of wood and jaguar skin.

The Priestess is the spiritual midwife and she gives the handsign which means "birth" or "speech." When something sprouts or births the Maya say "its words come out." In Maya, a *pop* is a reed mat and a *popol* is a king or queen, in other words "he or she of the reed mat." The mat is woven to represent the houses, families and community of the village, thus the king both sits on and is held up by the village. *Vuh* means paper and so the Popol Vuh, the sacred book of the Quiche Maya, is "The King's Papers" or "The Book of the Community." A Maya king or queen needed to be versed in the sacred arts of writing and speaking and the sacred books were taken out and read on ceremonial occasions. The sound of words was considered holy.

In the Marseilles Tarot the codex becomes the Bible on the Papess' lap but also the veil or curtain behind her. This symbolises the past and future history of each human being that is woven into the cloth of destiny. The

Priestess is the deep introverted connection to our spiritual heritage and identity. The Sorcerer, who stands under the Great Light, receives great illuminations, visions and revelations accompanied by burning bushes, the parting of heavens and seas, lightning bolts and all manner of fireworks from above. The Priestess, on the other hand, receives her dark illumination from below in the form of intuitions, dreams and small noticings. In the striving of humanity to understand nature, she is the wisdom hidden in nature, the *sapientia dei* or what the alchemists called the *lumen naturae* (the fount of light in nature). However, she does not reveal herself readily, as we shall see, only appearing in her fullness in the Planet Earth card.

Eyes of the Stars

The Priestess wears a blue moon headdress, indicating that she is associated with moon goddesses like the Egyptian Isis or the Greek Artemis. The moon is the heavenly body that mediates between the upper regions and the earthly plane. The Priestess is the medium, the one who intuits hidden knowledge and mediates this knowledge between the upper and lower realms. She sees how the magic of life unfolds. Hers is not the active, showy magic of the Sorcerer but the hidden unconscious patterns that express themselves in our fateful choices of career or partners, and in our fortunes or misfortunes.

The Priestess represents intuition par excellence. Intuition includes what we have called projective identification and the intuitive allows the unspoken in the other to get inside her. If she is known to herself and has some degree of individuation, she can distinguish between what belongs to others and what is her own psychology. If not, she can fall prey to all kinds of physical and psychic infections. If she identifies with the archetypal contents she lives a life that is not her own and loses herself.

The Priestess is able to sense what is "in the air" collectively and personally. The collective often ridicules her insights and she may suffer the fate of Cassandra who was given the gift of prophecy by Apollo who was enamoured of her. When she refused Apollo's advances he, not being able to take back a gift already given, cursed her powers and decreed that no one would believe her prophecies.[17] In her rightful place, the Priestess is the power behind the throne, but she is two cards removed from the Ruler, working behind the scenes, revealing things not seen in the light.

The Priestess is what Jung's colleague, Toni Wolff, called the medial woman.[18] In ancient cultures, she was the oracle, sibyl or prophetess. She knows our destiny or potential and is able to birth that into physical form by her ability to see it. When she senses the hidden potentials of a man and what he might become the Priestess is the muse, the *femme inspiratrice*, and she is able to birth the god in a man.

Figure 31. Mixtec temple (Codex Nuttall)

Whereas the Sorcerer acts on the world as it is, the Priestess devotes herself to the world as it might become. She is the first card after the Fool and the Sorcerer, so she still has memory of the other world and lives close to the collective unconscious. Like Persephone, she is Queen of the Underworld. She knows the secret insides of things, she can see in the dark and see what is hidden. She knows the darkness of matter. She reads without speaking and communicates in signs and symbols. She holds the secrets of the individual in the dark until they are ready for incarnation and growth in the world of the Consort.

The Priestess sits within a temple (Figure 31) that has a crenellated roof. Underneath it are eyes that symbolise stars (Figure 32). These represent the outer connection with the stars of the Pleiades that we see above the temple, as well as the inner sight that sees the light in the darkness. Stars appear in the cards at the four corners of the deck (Priestess, Lovers, Star and Planet Earth) and the two cards at the centre (Sage and Temperate Man). We shall discuss their significance in Chapter 24.

What the Priestess sees is real. The world of the dream or spirit is the opposite of the world of matter. In our three-dimensional world, tables and cars are solid and have substance. They are "real." Ideas, fantasies, imaginations, thoughts and dreams are abstract and have no substance. But in the world of spirit, it is dreams, feelings, wishes and fantasies that are "real" and have substance. Doors, buildings and computers are abstract notions, fantasies and dreams.

Like Cassandra, the Priestess is ignored by the dominant culture, and her presence in a reading may indicate that we have turned a deaf ear to our dreams or intuitions. The Priestess sees in the dark and asks us to return to

Figure 32. Starry night symbol

this way of seeing the world. She suggests that we need to pay attention to our momentary feelings as indications of what deeper emotions and attitudes lie hidden within us, often connected to history, childhood and the beginning of things. This is the function of the Priestess as the Teacher of the emotional aspect of Erasing Personal History. She sees what the ego would prefer not to see. She looks past our public face and touches the hidden heart at the centre of things. She is also the Keeper of the Heart of the Child Substance Shield and the Holder of the Mood of Emotional Sweetness. She feels and sees the hidden wound — the hurt beneath the anger, the anger beneath the hurt, the depression behind the smile. She can gently touch what is close to the bone.

The Consort
The Body of the Child Substance Shield uses the Mood of
Physical Sweetness to create Emotional Death and Change

The Empress

13

Consort

If the ego does not interfere with its irritating rationality, the opposites, just *because* they are in conflict, will gradually draw together, and what looked like death and destruction will settle down into a latent state of concord, suitably expressed by the symbol of pregnancy.

—C. G. Jung

Out of the One comes two; out of the two comes three; and out of the three come the ten thousand things.

—Tao Te Ching

A middle-aged woman sits erect on a jaguar skin seat. The seat is on a dais that supports her, the Ruler and the Priest. She wears an elaborate headdress that forms the jaws of a serpent. Under her left arm, she holds a shield with two darts. Her right hand is slightly raised indicating quiet.

The image of the Consort is from a wooden lintel at Tikal (Figure 33). It depicts Hasaw Chan K'awil who ruled Tikal from 682–734 CE. In his tomb lay the incised bone of the spirit canoe that we saw underneath the Fool and Sorcerer cards. To celebrate his victory over Yuknoom Yich'aak K'ahk, the king of Calakmul on August 5, 695 CE he had two lintels carved. This date was the thirteenth katun (260th) anniversary of Spearthrower Owl's death and the lintel states that on this day Hasaw Chan K'awil "conjured the Holy One."[1] Spearthrower Owl's grandson is the figure in the Sorcerer card holding up his grandfather's headdress.

Hasaw Chan K'awil is sitting on a palanquin holding bunched javelins or darts and a shield. Above him looms his *uay* or animal spirit, the spirit jaguar called Nu Balam Chaknal who aids him in battle, conjured up by vision rites and piercing. Hasaw wears the balloon headdress of Tlaloc-Venus warfare, so called because battles were timed in accordance with the cycles of Venus and Jupiter. Tlaloc, a goggle-eyed deity borrowed from Teoti-

Figure 33. Hasaw Chan K'awil, Temple 1, Lintel 3, Tikal

huacan in Mexico, appears on many war monuments. It is ironic that Balin chose these masculine war-like images as a model for the ever-maternal Consort.

Demeter and Hera

The Consort is the number 3 card and she represents the movement forward from the tension of the 2 card. Whereas the Priestess is the virginal Papess, the Consort is the matriarchal Queen, or Empress as she is called in the Marseilles Tarot. She is progression, movement and multiplication rather than tension. She symbolises advance and growth as the ego moves outward and engages with the world. The Consort is the Earth Mother and the card may augur marriage, the birth of a child, the fostering of new life, or a period of creativity.

The Consort sits with the brilliance of the sun behind her. Wreathed in green, she is the fertile marriage of Grandfather Sun and Grandmother Earth. From this lovemaking comes the fruitfulness of the extroverted feminine as the Great Mother. She contains all the 3s: conception, pregnancy, birth; beginning, middle and end; past, present and future; mother, father, child; the three dimensions of the physical world; and even the Father, the Son and the Holy Ghost. As the Queen, she represents the capacity to contain and endure and she is equal to the King's capacity to act in the world. The Consort is the ability of Nature to be endlessly fertile and prolific, for life to die and reappear in a multitude of forms, the cycles of vegetation, the cornucopia of life, and the pleasures of physical existence.

The shadow side of the Earth Mother is that, as Queen of the physical world, she is unconcerned with airy matters of spirit or high-flying ideas. Her concern is only about who is thinking of, about to have, or having babies — all so she can look after them. She is the archetypal grandmother, happiest when surrounded by her grandchildren. But if there is no spirit then life stagnates and all that remains is the incessant cycles of nature with no change in consciousness. Her shadow may emerge when there is no (grand)mothering to be done anymore, when her children grow up, break out of paradise, and move away from the comfort of the mother. Her nest is now empty and she has lost her purpose for being. We then find the Earth Mother as the *mater dolorosa,* the guilt-provoking mother, the sorrowful mother, the grieving Demeter.

In Greek mythology, the Consort in the natural world was Demeter and in the human world was her sister Hera, wife of Zeus and the Queen of Heaven.[2] Demeter was the mother of Persephone. Hades, god of the underworld, fell in love with Persephone and wished to marry her. Although Zeus gave his consent, Demeter was unwilling. Then one day Hades seized Persephone as she was innocently gathering flowers in the fields and carried her off to the underworld. Demeter wandered in search of her daughter. In her rage and grief, she refused to let any crops or vegetation grow and famine devastated the land. Finally, Zeus sent Hermes, the messenger of the gods, to bring back Persephone. But before she left the underworld Hades persuaded her to eat a pomegranate seed, the food of the dead. Because of this, she was compelled to return and sit as Queen of the Underworld for one-third of the year.

As both the goddess of the dead and the goddess of fertility, Persephone symbolises the return of life in spring. The Eleusinian mysteries were held in honour of she and Demeter. However, each year when her daughter must return to the underworld Demeter goes into mourning and the trees shed their leaves, winter comes and nothing grows. Demeter is the bountiful mother who is all-giving but she is also the death mother who is all-taking. Thus the Consort, the 3 card, has a hidden link with death. If we look at the 13 card, the Dead Man (which is actually a feminine card), we see her holding the same darts.

Demeter's heavenly sister, Hera, was the goddess of marriage and the protector of married women. On the light side, she represents the loyal spouse who devotes her energy to the home as a sanctuary for the people she cares about deeply. She is the queen in this realm as the Goddess of the Hearth. Steadfast and reliable, she provides warmth and feeling for without her there is no communal life. On the shadow side, Hera was a jealous wife who often persecuted Zeus's mistresses and children. She never forgot an injury and was known for her vindictive nature. She was angry with the Trojan prince Paris for choosing Aphrodite, the goddess of love, over herself and aided the Greeks in the Trojan War. She was not appeased until Troy was finally destroyed. The negative aspect of Hera emerges when she is crossed or offended. Then warmth becomes implacable hatred, cold rejection and family intrigue; acceptance becomes jealousy, spite and revenge; property and appearances become more important than people; and convention and formality overrides natural courtesy.[3]

Earth Parents, Sky Parents

As we have seen in Chapter 9, the first four cards in the top row (Priestess, Consort, Ruler, Priest) form two sets of parents. The Consort (3) and the Ruler (4) are the extroverted, earthly parents. The Priestess (2) and the Priest (5) are the introverted, spiritual parents. Our physical or creative children are always born of these two sets of parents, worldly and archetypal. Seven is the number of the dream and we need both sets of parents to create the dream that is our life $(2 + 5 = 7, 3 + 4 = 7)$.

This motif of the dual descent from both human and divine parents is a common theme in the mythic story of the hero. The hero myth tells us that the formation of the personality occurs only through struggle, suffering, and sacrifice. Frequently, the hero has two fathers — his personal father and a "higher" father. His mother is a virgin and the hero is divinely conceived, so inheriting a dual nature. He is human like everyone else, yet at the same time he feels himself to be an outsider, he does not fit in, and discovers within himself something that sets him apart, such as his prophetic, creative or healing powers. These lead him to a special destiny and extraordinary deeds. The myth of the hero is the story of all human lives no matter how ordinary or extraordinary.

There is an important relationship between the generations that is implied in dual parentage. In cultures that are closer to their own indigenosity there is a correspondingly greater "respect for the elders." This is not just an outmoded cultural preference but a recognition of a necessary spiritual reality. Properly, there is a tonal relationship between the male elders and

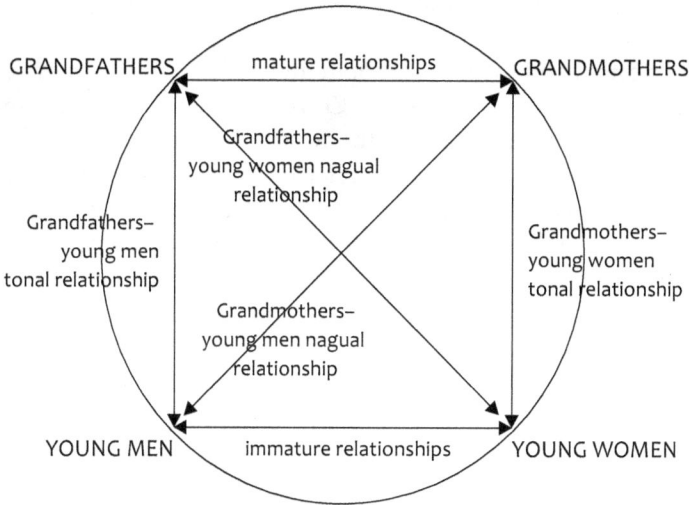

Figure 34. The tonal and nagual relationships between the generations

the younger men in the culture whereby the young men are initiated into "men's business." Likewise, there is a tonal relationship between the female elders and the younger women in the culture, whereby the young women are initiated into "women's business."[4]

But there is also a cross-generational, nagual relationship between the grandmother elders and the young men, and between the grandfather elders and the young women. When a culture is in balance, the men and women elders have power in different areas but overall neither dominates. The nagual and tonal relationships operate so that the culture is kept in balance. These relationships (Figure 34) have the same archetypal form as within the individual (Figure 44).

The elders' relationship with the opposite-sex generation is a function not so much of their direct influence but how much inner authority, mana or power they have (which may or may not correlate with visible, public authority). It lays the foundation for the individual's future relationships with whatever is "opposite." If the elders have too much or too little authority, or misuse what they have, trouble starts. When the older women lose their authority, the young men don't know their limits and spiral out of control. When the older men have too much power, it is the young women who suffer (as in systemic sexism and sexual abuse). This is the current state of affairs in Western culture.

This phenomenon is well known in elephant populations in southern Africa. Because of overpopulation, several extensive culls of elephant herds have been made in recent decades. The result has been that many of the younger males began to show aggressive, atypical behaviour because the older, ruling matriarchs in the herd, who control the young bulls, have been killed.

The Priestess and the Consort both give birth. The Priestess' is an inner pregnancy in the darkness but the Consort's is an outer pregnancy in the light. The two masculine cards, the Ruler and the Priest, give order and meaning to what they birth. The Ruler orders the outer world so that the physical child may grow in safety and he guides the mind of the child into the world. The Priest, in the form of the medicine man or woman, minister, godparent, mentor, or teacher, gives the child his spiritual blessing and he initiates the spirit of the child into the inner world.

Human parents function as transformers that moderate the power of the mother or father archetypes and "step down" their voltage so it can be harnessed for development. Good-enough mothering and fathering in childhood provides a platform from which the life-giving aspects of the archetypal mother and father can be experienced without becoming taken over by the archetype.

If one has had an absent, damaged or damaging real-world mother or father then the archetypal mother or father rushes in to occupy the vacuum. Everything is larger than life and ordinary human relationship becomes more difficult. If the good father is damaged, culturally or personally, then in our inner world the negative, abusive father rises to power or the person becomes prey to all manner of unquestioning hero worship or belief worship. Similarly, if the good mother or the life-giving feminine is damaged then it sinks into the unconscious and reappears in idealised, spiritual form as the madonna or in debased, material form as the whore.

The raw, archetypal shadow of the cards in the top row manifest as personality disorders. The Priestess as Borderline Personality Disorder, the Consort as Dependent Personality Disorder, the Ruler as Antisocial Personality Disorder, the Priest as religious fanatic, and the Lovers as Histrionic Personality Disorder.

We shoudl note that the Priest has no DSM-IV diagnostic equivalent. This anomaly might point to something. The Diagnostic and Statistical Manual of the American Psychiatric Association is now in its Fourth Edition (DSM-IV) and soon to be DSM-5. The APA has generally had a hands-off approach to both pathological spirituality and the pathological hatred and anger (honour killings, terrorism, or the death sentence for adultery or apostasy) with which it is closely associated. Interestingly, after more than 50 years of DSMs there is no Axis I diagnosis for pathological anger except for a half-hearted attempt with Impulse Control Disorder. The "softer" Axis I disorders of introverted mood such as depression get preferential treatment over disorders of extroverted mood such as anger. More importantly, there is no diagnosis of any kind of pathological spirituality unless it is clearly psychotic. In contrast, the DSM has free to apply many diagnoses to sexuality, the twin of spirituality, revealing its Western privileging of spirit over matter. For example, why is Sexual Aversion Disorder (an aversion to sex, with a low mortality rate) a DSM-IV diagnosis but not religious extremism (an attraction to religion, with a high mortality rate)? And let's not forget that homosexuality used to be a diagnosis in the DSM-I of 1952 and the DSM-II of 1968 and was not removed until 1974.

Grief and Comfort

> You think Nature is some Disney movie? Nature is a killer. Nature is a bitch. It's feeding time out there 24 hours a day, every step that you take is a gamble with death. If it isn't getting hit with lightning today, it's an earthquake tomorrow or some deer tick carrying Lyme disease. Either way, you're ending up on the wrong end of the food chain.
>
> —Jeff Melvoin

The Consort is the Keeper of the Body of the Child Substance Shield. She is the human mother who bears and raises children and is the source of safety, trust, physical comfort, food, warmth and nurturing. As the Holder of the Mood of Physical Sweetness she gives physical comfort and healing through touch and caring for the body. She is the archetype or patron saint of those women throughout history who have held and nursed the bodies of their loved ones, the sick and the wounded.

The Movement of Using Death as an Advisor is a west Movement and so is about our relationship with matter and our physical environment (body, house, clothes, food, air, water, or money). As the Teacher of the emotional aspect of Using Death as an Advisor, the Consort is associated with feelings about our physical body and sexuality (pleasure, shame, secrecy, exhibitionism, admiration, narcissism) and body functions and fluids (blood, sweat, tears, faeces, urine). These activities and substances are the physical substrate of life. We have only to look to young children between about eighteen months and five years of age to see the deep feelings and fascination they have about these basic biological functions. As well, she represents the feelings we have about the inevitable changes and losses that come with living in a physical body (puberty, sexuality, pregnancy, menopause, ageing and death).

The Consort is Nature in the raw and in her realm there is relentless growth and abundance but also relentless death and dying. When life is abundant then death is cheap. Nature does not care about the individual but only her collective ends. She is blind to the death of one of the trillions of creatures in her domain, but she also weeps when the cow murders the grass. She is the Great Mother who cares for all life. The Consort teaches us about the grief of being alive.

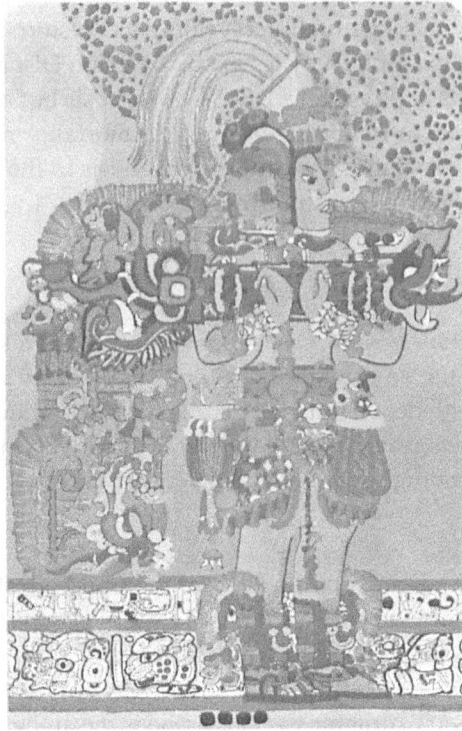

The Ruler
The Mind of the Child Substance Shield uses the Mood of Mental
Sweetness to Stop the Emotional World

The Emperor

14

Ruler

The "blood royal" then, in each of us is that which inherits the high responsibility of ruling in the psyche, of uniting the personality in the service of the "best."

— Helen Luke

Power without love becomes brutality. Feeling without masculine strength becomes woolly sentimentality.

— Robert Johnson

An elaborately dressed young man stands in front of the dais. In his arms he holds a double-headed serpent bar. He wears an elaborate backrack covered with flowers and feathers. Behind him is a jaguar skin.

The image of the Ruler is that of Stormy Sky or Siyaj Chan K'awil II who we have already met in the Sorcerer card. It was taken from Stela 1 at Tikal (Figure 36). In Maya art the ceremonial bars and waist belts are recognised by the crisscross *pop* or mat markings identifying him as "he of the mat," meaning a ruler.[1] He holds a double-headed serpent bar, or Vision Serpent, in his arms. Universally, the rod, mace, wand, baton, staff or sceptre symbolises worldly authority and power. Feathered standards frame Stormy Sky on either side (only one side is shown in the card). On the left, a rattlesnake and a jaguar are climbing the standard, and on the right, a fish-snake and a fragmentary figure. These symbolise the two sides of the night sky — Pleiades on the one side and Sagittarius on the other.[2] The particular configuration of the constellations corresponds to the night sky at midnight at Tikal on May 1, 451 CE.[3] This was twelve years after the date of Stela 31 in the Sorcerer card.

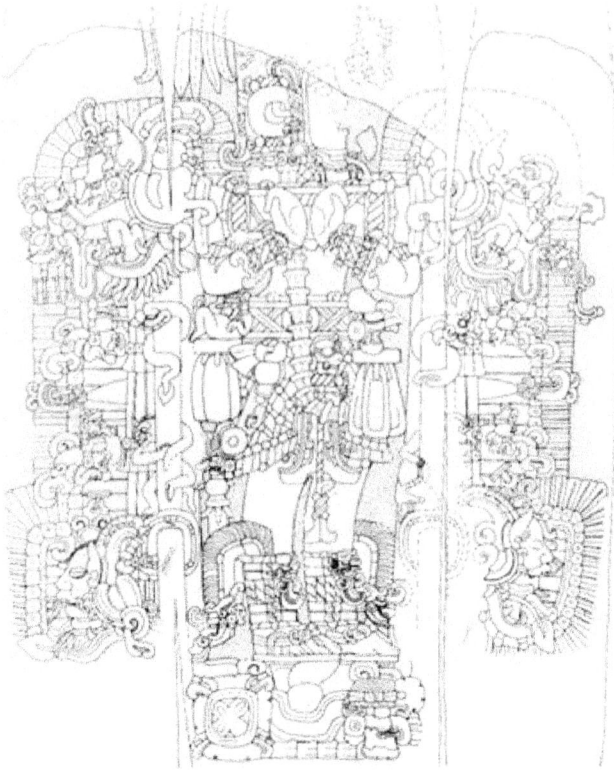

Figure 36. Stormy Sky, Stela 1, Tikal
(Siyaj Chan K'awil II carrying a sacred bundle and standing
on the Mutul Bird emerging at dawn)

Lord of the Four Quarters

The Ruler is the one who Stops the World by bringing order and direction. In the Marseilles Tarot he is the Emperor. He or she is the father, patriarch, general, lawmaker, emperor, builder, leader, CEO, captain or manager. In his introverted aspect, he is the revered and respected gravitational centre around which the culture and community revolve. Queen Elizabeth II of England or King Bhumibol of Thailand are examples. In his extroverted aspect, he is the procreative, generative inseminator who projects his seed outward by enforcing his will and authority in a conscious, directed exercise of power. Sir Lewis Robertson, a veteran of British company takeovers, made no bones about his boardroom technique: "The lions have to appreciate that the lion tamer has arrived. First you do a lot of homework, then you impose yourself on management."[4]

The Ruler reconciles the opposites—God and man, life and death, spiritual and physical, right and left, as well as differing groups, opinions and factions within the nation, the group or the psyche. He is the one who overcomes doubt, ambivalence and paralysis in preparation for the Warrior to carry out the orders. He mediates between all these opposites to make their energies available to all.

The Ruler is the Keeper of the Mind of the Child Substance Shield. He explores, conquers, sorts, orders, categorises and is curious about the world. He is the Holder of the Mood of Mental Sweetness — saying the right words at right time, inspiring confidence, being a leader, mover and shaker, getting others to follow, and bringing clarity and order to a situation. He shows courage, leadership, power, firmness, strength, conscience, virility, tenacity and creative aggression. He imposes laws that limit the brute instincts of the individual or the mob and protect each from the excesses of the other. Through the proper application of masculine energy and discipline, he serves his subjects by assigning the appropriate position to all things and promoting what is best for all in his realm.[5] Above all, he is not a committee.

Psychologically, the Ruler is the part of the ego that has the strength, fortitude and determination to not let one desire or appetite rule our lives. He represents the concrete meaning of the God-given right to rule in our inner world when we are connected to the Self. Robert Bly said, "The inner King is the one in us who knows what we want to do for the rest of our lives, or the rest of the month, or the rest of the day. He can make clear what we want without being contaminated in his choice by the opinions of others around us."[6]

This inner authority that enables the ego to make its mark on the world requires a courage that does not flinch or flee at the first sign of conflict, an emotional certainty that does not collapse when things go wrong, and a strength of character that it is not bullied by his or others' emotions. This is what we call "self-esteem" or "self-confidence." In this way, the Ruler is the Teacher of Stopping the Emotional World.

He cuts a larger figure than the others in this row and stands on the ground in front of the dais below the Consort and the Priest. This symbolises the paradoxes of his leadership. He must be the servant of those he rules and remain connected to his subjects but at the same time be distant in order to be free from the personal entanglements that would compromise his task. He must maintain the common touch and keep his feet firmly planted on the ground but also remain larger than life and not let familiarity breed contempt.

In a reading the Ruler augurs a confrontation with authority, the father complex, and power in its negative or positive forms. We see this positive authority in the powerful father or the mighty king who cares and protects. Negatively, he is the Lord of Misrule, the tyrant, despot, bully, crabby old man, oppressor, or dictator who personifies authoritarianism, pettiness, dogmatism, stubbornness, and perfectionism. In the inner world, he is the tyrannical superego, the internal persecutor who never lets up.

The Consort brings increase and multiplication but the Ruler puts limits on this wild and unrestricted growth. As the Lord of the Four Quarters, he brings order to this fruitful chaos and at the same time remembers that too much restriction stifles growth.[7] He is the structuring masculine principle symbolised by the sacred number four, the number of balance, order, symmetry and harmony. The Ruler integrates all the 4-ness of the elements and the directions into an orderly whole.

The Consort and the Ruler embody the opposing poles of nature and culture. Agriculture, domestic animals, houses and tools all came into being to make life "easier" in the face of the unpredictable moods of nature. Whereas nature is in constant cyclical change, culture brings stability and predictability. Nature is red in tooth and claw but human hands create the smooth edges of culture. The Priestess and the Consort value the inner images, feelings, and relationships that are inherent in nature. The Ruler and the Priest value the outer facts, ideas, principles and laws that are the result of human culture.

The Consort rules over the three dimensions of physical existence but like nature she is unconcerned with the death of an individual because another of the species will soon be born to replace it. If death is not final then time is irrelevant. However, the Ruler's number is four and he rules over the four dimensions—the three dimensions of space and the fourth dimension of time. He wants to preserve culture against the ravages of time and nature. At his most extreme, he is preoccupied with immortality in one form or another—if time is real and finite then so is death and its transcendence means an extension of the Ruler's power. Monuments that have stood for thousands of years or the passing of the crown from father to son remind us of this masculine desire for immortality.

Culture, like the process of individuation, is an *opus contra naturam* or a work against nature, as Jung called it. When energy is freed from the unconscious, it comes under the ordering influence of the ego. As a result, culturally or psychologically, we move from natural time to clock time. Unlike the Maya, who regarded time as a sacred, living entity, our modern economy is based on time as a commodity that can be measured and divided. Secular, clock time and goal-directedness have ensured that the same activity can continue 24/7/365. A prolonged task requiring concentration and the steady application of energy now becomes possible without the interference of the rhythms of the day or the seasons. This has made Western culture quasi-independent of nature. But this homogenisation of time and season has fatally numbed us to the rhythms of Creation.

Power

The neophyte Ruler or the immature ego believes that he is all-powerful, immortal and bulletproof. He takes the feminine for granted and forgets that the energy of his realm comes from the Consort and the Priestess. The adolescent psychology of Western culture has specialised in this hubris believing that conscious willpower can accomplish all things, that Nature is to be dominated, and the breasts of the Great Mother will endlessly supply our needs for oil to drive, land to build, and air to breathe. It is so possessed by this archetype of the masculine ruler and his sidekick, the warrior, that their dominance in sports, politics and business (or we could say that these activities are expressions of the archetype) are actually considered normal.

The more the unconscious becomes conscious the more energy is available to the ego to direct where it wishes. Up until now, the diffuse but unconscious energies of the Priestess and the Consort have been spent on dreaming and growing. Now the time has come for this energy to be consciously focussed on doing.

The Ruler has the power to act in the world — but this power inevitably leads to its misuse. The only certainty about power is that it will be misused by any two-legged who has enough of it. However, this is not a problem to be solved or legislated away, it is an archetypal necessity. Constitutions, parliaments, laws and codes of ethics arose as essential protections against the misuse of power but it is through the excesses of power that the ego, if not too hardened, comes to experience the full power of the archetype. Through this, we gain some objectivity as to our human limitations and become more able to use our personal authority — gently or ruthlessly, as necessary — in a graceful, conscious way in service of self and others. As William Blake said, we can only know what is enough when we have had too much and the road of excess does lead to the palace of wisdom. The result of this humbling is that the Ruler becomes the wise Ruler who has developed firmness in places where he was too soft and softness in places where he was too hard.

Sky Serpents

The Ruler holds his hands in a ceremonial gesture with his wrists back to back and thumbs turned outward. One of the ceremonies associated with the Vision Serpent was the conjuring of ancestral spirits. Especially during accession rites, the kings would contact the spirits of their lineage for guidance and blessings. This was achieved by inducing a shamanic trance state with the aid of hallucinogens or bloodletting ("harvesting") by perforating the tongue or penis with a sting-ray spine, or nicking the carotid artery with a flint and swiftly stemming the blood flow with the *ek' balam* bush and closing the wound with the bark of the *bakalche'* tree.[8] The Maya god associated with the deity of former kings is K'awil and by summoning him, the kings could communicate with their ancestors. K'awil is often portrayed as a serpent-footed sceptre and in the Ruler card he is seen as the figure emerging from the ends of the serpent bar.

The Maya words *kan, kaan, k'aan* or *chan* variously means sky, snake, four, yellow, cord, umbilicus, precious and the birthplace of the Maize god. In Maya iconography umbilical cords that came down from the sky ("sky ropes" or "sky snakes") connected the earth to the heavens. The Maya pictured these in several ways: As a rope that ended in a *sak-nik* or the "white-flower" sign for the human soul; as two intertwined serpents; or as arching serpents carrying the white flower on their snouts.

The ecliptic is the path that the Sun and the planets follow in the sky during the year appearing to move westwards relative to the stars. The Maya called the ecliptic the Cosmic Monster and the planets travelled the length of the serpent's body. It had two heads with Venus at one end and the Sun at the other end and all the other planets in between.[9]

Notwithstanding our Western predilection for metaphor and its attendant dissociations the Ruler holds, not a representation of, not a symbol of, not a metaphor of, but the heavenly bodies themselves. He holds nothing less than the ecliptic, the Cosmic Monster itself. In Maya carvings there are many images of this double-headed serpent bar, which is the intersection of the temporal and the eternal. The Maya called this central point, where the vertical and horizontal worlds meet, the navel, *rumuxux*, or belly button of the world. The vertical body of the king was the Milky Way and when he held the horizontal serpent bar at his heart, he was the centre of the world, the place where the two worlds touch, and the conduit through which the powers of the universe could manifest. This is the Heart of Heaven, the centre from which all things are born. We shall explore this further in the Planet Earth card.

The World Tree

In the ancient theocracies of the pharaohs in Egypt or the Shang dynasty in China (c. 1500–1000 BCE) the sovereign was the representative of Heaven and derived their right to rule directly from God. In Europe, the doctrine of divine right was epitomised by the "Sun King," Louis XIV of France (1638–1715). The Maya called their kings *ch'ul ahau*, lords of the life-force. Like Stormy Sky in the Ruler card, they often dressed themselves as Wakah Chan, meaning "Raised-up Sky," the Maya name for the Milky Way as the World Tree.

The tree, inverted or upright, as the axis of the world is a common theme in many mythologies.[10] The Upanishads mention an ancient tree whose

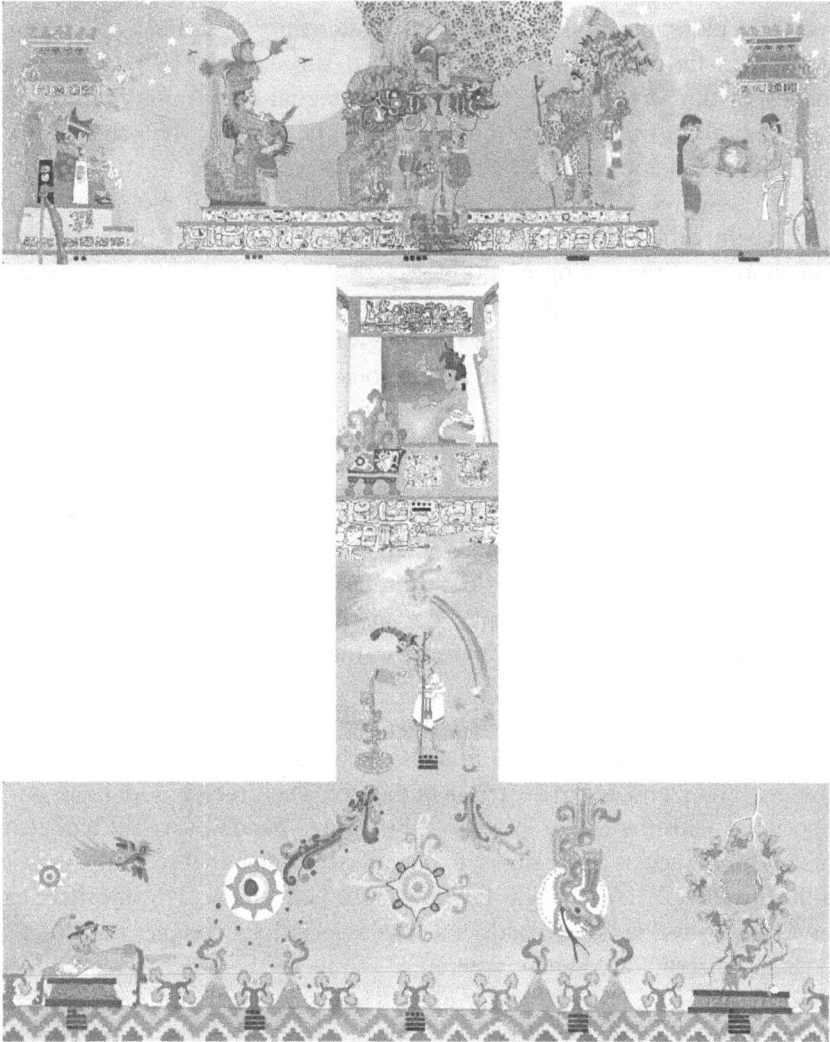

Figure 37. The Xultun Tarot as the Tree of Life

roots grow upward and branches grow downward. In the Bhagavad-Gita, there is a similar fig tree, rooted in heaven and its branches earthward, each of whose leaves are a song of the Vedas. The Sephiroth of the Cabala are pictured as an inverted tree. The symbol of the inverted tree is also found in alchemy. It has its roots in the air and its branches in the "glorified earth" or the future world.[11]

For the Maya the giant ceiba tree was the World Tree. The ceiba produces small white flowers that are the souls of humans just as the Milky Way produces stars. The flower-soul grows and participates in creation by being cooked—by gaining a face and a heart. The Maya kings as the World Tree raised in the night sky by First Father wore jade earflares that were stylised ceiba blossoms. Wakah Chan glyphs often appear with *sak-nik* or white flowers on its branches, a double-headed serpent intertwined in its branches, or the Serpent Bird (Itzam-Ye, the nagual of Itzamna) perched on top. Nagual, in this context, means the animal form of the sorcerer, or a shamanic medicine animal, helper or familiar.

The ceiba tree follows the cycle of the Milky Way. It blossoms in the month before the Maya creation day of February 5 and bears fruit in the dry season around the spring equinox, March 21, just before the planting of maize. Humans are the blossoms of the World Tree raised from the three hearthstones of creation in Orion. In the Ruler card we can see ceiba blossoms cascading over the lord of the life-force. As he blossoms so does all of Creation.

The medicine of the Xultun Tarot comes from the fact that it is itself the World Tree and the Milky Way (Figure 37). The tree and the tarot symbolise the growth of the human personality and the flowering of the soul. The World Tree of the Xultun Tarot is rooted in the lower world of the heavens and it flowers in the upper world of humans in the top row. We might also say that its roots are in the human sky and its branches are in the heavenly earth. Like the soul, it grows upwards to the sky and downwards into the earth.

The centre column of cards, the Movement of Stopping the World, is the trunk of the World Tree. The images in the cards show us the sap that moves both up and down the trunk of the tree. The Creator God, Itzamna, is associated with the Milky Way and the double-headed serpent bar. *Itz* refers to fluids such as resin, dews, tears, milk, or semen that were the essence of the life-force.[12] Itzamna was the dew in the heavens, and the Jacalteca call the Milky Way the "dew road."[13] These associations connect the Ruler to the Sage card directly below, where the glyphs on the lintel above the Sage are of Itzamna flanked by water lilies. The water lily plant resembles the umbilicus attached to the placenta reminding us of the Ruler as the navel of the world.[14] Below the Sage is the Temperate Man where the Twisted Hair pours starwater or dew upon the earth. This emerges in the bottom row as sky-ropes full of itz which feed the Moon, the Sun and Venus. The Sun completes the Movement of Stopping the World and is the life force that the Ruler embodies for the People.

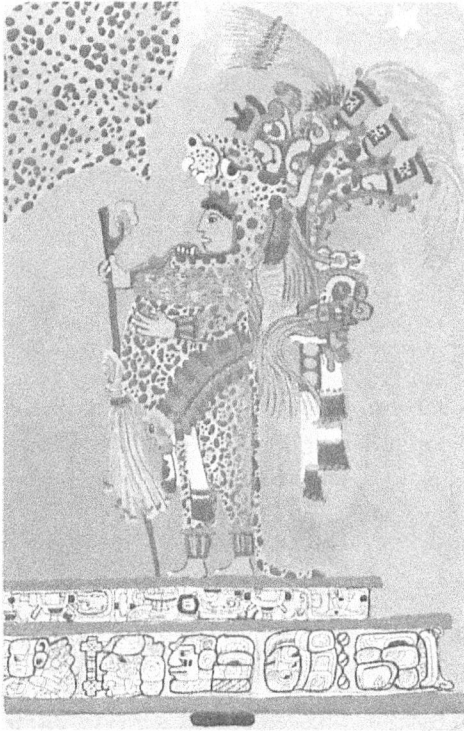

The Priest

The Spirit of the Child Substance Shield uses the Mood of Spiritual
Sweetness to Control the Emotional Dream.

The Pope

15

Priest

Man does not speak because he thinks; he thinks because he speaks. Or rather, speaking is no different than thinking: to speak is to think.
— Octavio Paz

He who has a why to live can bear almost any how.
— Friedrich Nietzsche

A man stands on the dais dressed in a jaguar skin. He wears a backrack of masks and feathers. In his right hand, he holds a staff with one living leaf and to it is tied a gold cloth. Around his waist is a belt with a single mask of the Maize God on the front. The figure is Dark Sun who ruled Tikal from 810 CE and is taken from Lintel 2, Temple 3 at Tikal (Figure 39).[1]

Spiritual Authority

In the European tarot this card is sometimes called the Hierophant. In ancient Greece this was the title of the chief priest of the Eleusinian Mysteries. The role of the hierophant was to bring the congregants into the presence of the holy (Greek, *ta hiera*, the holy; *phainein*, to show). The Priest represents the values, principles and spiritual connection that stand behind and above the power of the Ruler. The secular power of a medieval ruler submitted to the spiritual power of the priest — even the absolute monarchs of Europe had to kiss the ring of the Pope. However, this did turn into its opposite in due course. The most profound upheavals in medieval Western culture were brought about by Henry VIII (1491–1547) who protested the secular power of the Pope, and Martin Luther (1483–1546) who protested the spiritual power of the Pope. Protestantism was the result.

Many rulers in history had spiritual advisors — Arthur had Merlin, the medieval rulers of Europe had the Pope, the Muslim Caliphs had their viziers, Lenin had Marx, Queen Elizabeth II has the Archbishop of Canter-

Figure 39. Dark Sun, Lintel 2, Temple 3, Tikal

bury. In modern times, if the advisor is a secular one, his power may be the legal codes, mores, and principles of the culture (the US Supreme Court, for example) or the knowledge of "how things work" (economists and scientists have now become the new viziers).

The Priest represents power and authority like the Ruler but the power is spiritual not physical. Internally, the ruler is the conscious ego and the priest is the superego, conscience or moral code. The priest embodies the "shoulds" and "oughts" that derive from the traditional values and accepted beliefs of our family and culture, as well as a recognition that higher powers influence human affairs.

Although the power of the priest may have declined, he is still alive in the inner world. As with all archetypal powers, if they are not given a place in the human world they continue to appear but in degenerate, negative or troublesome form. In the case of the priest, who represents the human relationship with (or submission to) a higher power, the split manifests either as a mindless conformity to spiritual authority or an equally mindless rejection of it. For example, the conformity twins of American fundamentalism (built upon the separation of church and state) and Islamic fundamentalism (built upon the joining of church and state) are both as different as they are alike.

The non-conformist, the over-conformist, the fundamentalist or the athe-
ist is often enslaved internally by his or her own beliefs, left or right. The
more extreme the beliefs are the greater the influence they exert on the individual, and the more the internal conscience punishes and condemns any
movement away from them. This "punishment" is often an unconscious,
shadowy process whereby having broken the internal rules of the superego
(for example, having too much or too little pleasure, success or achievement) the individual has an "accident," a sudden attack of "poor judgement," or somehow brings disaster or success upon themselves. The unconscious guilt results in punishment through misfortune but the deeper, unconscious intent is to bring about a change in a distorted consciousness,
through disaster if necessary.

Portals to the Dream

The Priest has many connections to the cosmos. Stela 20 at Tikal shows a
jaguar priest holding a vertical staff, like the one in the card, that was used
to identify the "no shadow" date of the passage of the sun through the
zenith.[2] The Maya glyph for uay is an ahau, or lord, glyph half-covered
with a jaguar skin like the Priest. A uay is a spirit that can take on physical
form or a shaman that can shapeshift into the form of his animal companion
or nahualli. The uay were depicted as their human or animal forms or as
part-human and part-animal. Uay in various Maya languages translates as
shaman, to dream, to transfigure by enchantment, sorcerer, metamorpho-
sis, transformation, animal spirit companion, animal familiar or sleeping
place. So the Priest is primarily a dreamer and in his dreaming he works
with his uay or medicine animal.

The Maya believed that the markings on a jaguar skin were the constellations in the night sky and the mouth of the jaguar was the entrance to the
Underworld. In Figure 40 we see the doorway to the main temple at Ek
Balam in the Yucatan. In Yucatec the name Ek Balam means "black jaguar"
and the temple entrance is framed by jaguar teeth. We have seen that the
Fool enters life by stepping into the mouth of the jaguar.[3] The Priest wears
the jaguar skin with its jaws over his head so his body becomes the night
sky and he is in the Underworld. The Ruler joins the cosmos with the earth
by holding the serpent bar but the Priest travels outward and upward into
the dream with his jaguar helper to join the earth with the cosmos.

To the Maya, all clefts, pits, caves, rivers, streams and female sexual or-
gans were incarnations of the First Mother's sacred womb and her birth
opening. The sacred maize plant, the World Tree, the Vision Serpent, pe-
nises, snakes and trees were incarnations of the Milky Way phallus of First
Father. So cenotes, caves, underground chambers (pib na) and small buildings called dreaming places (kunilor itzam nah) were ritual portals through

Figure 40. Temple at Ek Balam, Yucatan

which shamans could enter the Underworld and beings from the Under-world could come into this world (Figure 41).[4] Offering plates or mirrors, like the one we see in the Lovers card, were also used as portable openings.[5] The Priest was the one who travelled through these portals and was able to conjure the spirits.

In the constellations the Maya saw the story of First Mother and First Fa-ther and how the world was created. The two primary portals to the Under-world sat at either end of the World Tree which is the Milky Way when it is positioned north-south. Its roots in the south are the White-Bone Snake, Black Transformer, or Black Dreaming Place. In the north are its branches, the Ol or Heart Portal.[6] At death the soul "enters the road" into the Under-world at the southern end of the Milky Way. The Ol portal at the other end was where the souls of newborns entered this world from the Underworld. This was the portal of resurrection after the transformation of the soul in the Underworld and it opened in the sky near where First Father broke out of the Cosmic Turtle Shell. We can see this in the cards at the beginning and end of the deck. A dark blue hole, the colour of Xibalba, the Underworld, is at the centre of Planet Earth, the last card in the deck. The Ol Portal, the Great Light, is at the top between the 0 and 1, the first cards in the deck.

Spirit and Emotion

The Priest is the extroverted, sermonal prophet who is the companion of the introverted, oracular Priestess. She connects to spirit in the other world

Figure 41. Conjuring house

whereas he expresses spirit to this world. The Priestess embodies spiritual-ity while the Priest articulates religion — a collectively organised spirituality that has a set of moral laws or a code of obedience to God. The Priestess does not speak unless asked and each answer is unique to the individual's destiny. The Priest speaks *ex cathedra* and his word applies to all as moral law.

But this word has not only the weight of religious law behind it but also something more emotionally compelling. The Priest's psychological type is spiritual feeling. He is the Keeper of the Spirit of the Child Substance Shield, the Holder of Spiritual Sweetness and the Teacher of Controlling the Emotional Dream. On the light side he can inspire us to heights of magnifi-cent sacrifice. On the dark side he is the demagogue, evangelist, propagan-dist, proselytizer, revivalist, radical cleric, fire and brimstone preacher and cult leader of whatever persuasion, secular or spiritual. He appeals to the tsunami-like power of undifferentiated emotion in the masses and com-bines it with the fire of spirit and the weight of authority. Both light and dark lead to the same place, the loss of our own voice, we just prefer one over the other.

A belief is the mental expression of an archetypal virus that can bring about severe distrubances in behaviour. It does not require human contact for its transmission. The actual religion or beliefs of the Priest are irrelevant. It is rather the alchemy of any strong belief held with religious fervour or leaden certainty, the use of speech to persuade, cajole and hector, the activa-tion of strong emotion and the absence of any reflective thinking in the lis-teners, that makes the toxic brew. So the left wing anti-capitalism activist, the family values TV host, the free market conservative, the radical cleric, the New Age prosperity preacher, and Amway all graze in the same psychological paddock.

Meaning

The Priest represents the desire to seek meaning in life through some form of education, religion, philosophy or spiritual path. He may appear as a person who is a mentor, guide or advisor, or as one's inner conscience or principles. This card indicates that we will begin to seek some philosophical system, spiritual path, therapy or self-development of some kind, in order to know ourselves and the world around us more deeply.

This world of meaning that lies behind outer appearances makes itself known through symbols, like the tarot. Symbolic knowledge provides a net in which to catch experience and express it. If there is no net then these experiences pass us by, overwhelm us or are meaningless. We become marooned on a bleak, three-dimensional island of literalness where things just happen. However, when we live a symbolic life then the symbols are the windows and doorways to archetypal resources that would otherwise be undreamt of.

In indigenous cultures all art was made, not for the benefit of the human world, but to feed the other world in gratitude for its creation of this world of matter. So all craftspeople and "artists" also served a priestly function. The Priest as the shaman or artist is the one who acts as a bridge, brokering the relationship between spirit and substance. Dreamers work in the fifth dimension, the nagual, the dream. Stalkers work in the third dimension or tonal reality. Dreamer-Stalkers are those who work from the fifth dimension to bring the Dream down into the third dimension—this is the shamanic or artistic aspect of the Priest. Stalker-Dreamers work from the third dimension to see what is happening in the Dream—this is the Priest as the prophet or visionary.

Other tarot call this card the Pope. The names is derived from the Latin word (*pater*) for father. The Pope is the spiritual father or pontiff (Latin, *pontifex*, bridge builder). He is the vizier, magus, or spiritual counsellor. He is the bridge between heaven and earth, gods and humans, the absolute and the relative, the temporal and the eternal. Just as the Ruler gives order to substance so the Priest gives order and meaning to spirit and provides us with numinous symbols. He talks to the gods and does battle with the evil spirits on our behalf. He negotiates with the spirit world or, psychologically, he connects us with the healing power of the archetypes.

Tradition and Ceremony

The Priest is also the guardian and transmitter of tradition, oral teachings, wisdom, or religious knowledge. He is the symbol of acting in accordance with divine law and obedience, not to the will of the Ruler but to the will of God. The Ruler is concerned with right behaviour in the world whereas the

Priest is concerned with right behaviour in the eyes of God, or in psychological terms, the Self.

On the light side, the Priest is the Holder and Keeper of ceremonies and
traditions. He knows their long history and he holds the memory of long cycles of time. In Western culture, Judaism and Catholicism have the longest
institutional memories and operate on a different time cycle from secular
culture. Over the centuries, ceremonies and ceremonial objects accumulate
an archetypal power—they begin to Breathe, Walk and Dance. The Sun
Dance, the Mass, Pesach, the Haj, the Inipi, the relics of the saints, the tooth
of the Buddha, the Wailing Wall, the Sacred Pipe, Lourdes, the Torah, or the
Shroud of Turin. When we participate in a time-honoured ceremony, we
have behind us the power of all the prayers and thoughts of all the other humans who have done the same ceremony throughout history. The Priest
keeps the integrity, sanctity and power of these ceremonies intact.[7]

In his negative form, the Priest is the dogmatic zealot or the spiritual fanatic. He is out-of-touch with human feeling reality and may use spiritual
power for his own ends, as either the black magician or the fundamentalist,
who are but twins. The dark sorcerer controls others for his own ends, the
fundamentalist controls others for God's ends. The Priest brings dogma, rigidity and meaningless ritual.

I make a distinction here between ceremony and ritual. Ceremony is
alive and has blood and breath; it changes according to need but not impulse; it has alchemy, that is, it brings about change; and it has beauty
which awakens spiritual hunger. Over time ceremony inevitably degener-
ates into ritual unless it renewed and refreshed. Rituals that doggedly stay
the same, while the world and the People change, become tired and meaningless. In general, monotheistic religions are suspicious of individual spiritual experience and outlaw it with doctrine and canon. The result is a dependence on second-hand reports of spirit from static, codified and collective expressions of revelation (the Torah, the Bible or the Quran, for example). Frozen in time and on the page, they are particularly vulnerable to losing their numinosity and degenerating into empty ritual. In contrast, indigenous peoples rely on memory not writing and in the stories, sings, dances
and ceremonies the individual connection to spirit can flower anew each
time.

The jaguar is the Keeper of Memory and we see that the tail of the jaguar
skin, underneath the Fool and the Sorcerer, points to the throat and mouth
of the Priest suggesting speech and its twin, silence. The Priest is inside the
mouth of the jaguar robe that he wears. This means that tradition and memory envelop him and he knows what feeds the spirit of the People. He can
see the other world and see what is happening in the realm of the Fool and
the Sorcerer. He can see what the Ruler, who stands with his back to the
jaguar, cannot see. In his remembering, using the uniquely human faculty

of speech, he utters the sacred words which are the names of things — not their outer form but their inner spiritual essence. The Priest speaks with the collective memory and voice of the People.

Devotion

The nature of religious experience is such that it feels absolute. It lies outside the graduated judgements of our thinking or feeling functions. Origen, an early Christian theologian, said the soul is naturally religious. Wonder and awe is the normative response to a spiritual experience — the ego is supposed to be overwhelmed. We long to devote ourselves completely, to worship something, to touch spirit, to revere, to bow down, to surrender completely, to be enfolded more deeply in the arms of the Mystery. So the Priest is the Keeper of the Spirit of the Child Substance Shield.

The number 5 is the number of Humans and as the number 5 card the Priest speaks with the voice of spirit from his fifth wheel, his throat chakra. He awakens spirit in us and helps us bring out our best as a human being. He provides spiritual nourishment and pastoral care for our soul. He introduces us to the world of spirit as the contrary companion to the world of matter and reveals to us a profound possibility — that what cannot be realised in matter can be attained in spirit. This is the Priest as the Holder of Spiritual Sweetness.

The priest, shaman or healer who tends to the dreams and souls of others must undergo a long training. This training is possible only if he has been "called," that is, if he has a vocation. If the priest's heart is emotionally compelled, at a level deeper than ego desire, then he has the right emotional attitude to undergo the training. Only if his heart has been captured by spirit, only if he has taken a spirit-wife, can he work with the Dream of the People. Dreams guide and heal and the shaman-priest-therapist must have undergone a long apprenticeship to his own unconscious, the world of spirits, or the symbols of the collective unconscious. He must have the right attitude toward, and the right relationship with, the images and symbols of the personal and collective dreams. Then the Priest becomes the Teacher of Controlling the Emotional Dream.

Integrity

In the Mythic Tarot the Priest is the Hierophant or "revealer of sacred things" who also keeps them secret. The Priest also knows the dangers of the *numinosum* for the unprepared. The jaguar robe of the Priest suggests the opposite of speech and revelation — secrecy, silence and hiddenness. (The jaguar is one of the most secretive of the cats). He knows that if transpersonal energies are not kept secret there is a danger that their power will be used for the satisfaction of personal desires, including his own.

Because the Priest symbolises the physical celibacy that allows spiritual union, his shadow is often one of sexual excess, fascination or fetishism, sexual abuse or sexual addiction. The shadow of spirituality is sexuality and the Priest is particularly vulnerable to the misuse of sexual power. The Priest, by virtue of his vocation, bridges heaven and earth. He can touch the place where the opposites meet, where spirit and matter make love. Spirit is a sexual turn-on and it is part of the Priest's apprenticeship to bridge the tension between spirituality and sexuality. The resolution is often to go wild one of two ways, either become a libertine or a celibate. Either way sex or spirit becomes tyrannical and the individual is lost.

This tension, however, is not a natural, inherent one. Christianity has almost gone out of its way to create a tormented conflict between the two. The battle is inevitably an uphill one as sexuality is a biological instinct with all of its undeniable power. If the priest is constrained to celibacy by external rules and vows, as opposed to the bidding of his own soul, he is even more likely to lose the battle. If he does lose, if he does not befriend his shadow, we hear of the hard-on under the robe of the guru, the abuse of children in religious institutions, and institutionalised misogyny. As the placard said, "Abstinence makes the Church grow fondlers."

The Priest is neither seated on a throne like the Consort nor is he larger-than-life like the Ruler. He is of human proportions and presence. To avoid the pitfalls of priesthood the Priest needs an ethical standpoint. This emerges from an flawed human position rather than a perfect spiritual position. It holds the place between the opposites of, on the one hand, heartlessly obeying the dictates of dogma or doctrine or, on the other hand, mindlessly following the urgings of stiff cock or wet pussy. (I decided to keep this last phrase as written. I imagine some readers are more likely to take offense at the "earthy" words "cock" or "pussy" than they would at words like "dogma" or "doctrine." The unfortunate lack of "spirity" words that might give fair and equal offense are evidence of the imbalance between earth and spirit that the tarot addresses). The Priest must do the right (but human) thing for the particular circumstances.

The Priest is the ego's first encounter with the Self as the manifestation of the still, small voice within. He is the inner conscience that looks after our spiritual welfare. The Tree of Life grows downwards into spirit and with each row of cards the ego incarnates more fully. In this first row, the ego experiences the world moderated by human events and relationships rather than by direct contact with an archetype. However, if we are to become the unique soul that we are, we must be free from the inner persuasions of the archetypes as well as the outer demands of the collective. Jung said, "The aim of individuation is nothing less that to divest the self of the false trappings of the persona on the one hand, and of the suggestive power of primordial images [the archetypes, including the anima and animus] on the other hand."[8] The Priest initiates us into this task and prepares us for an encounter with evil in the Bound Man.

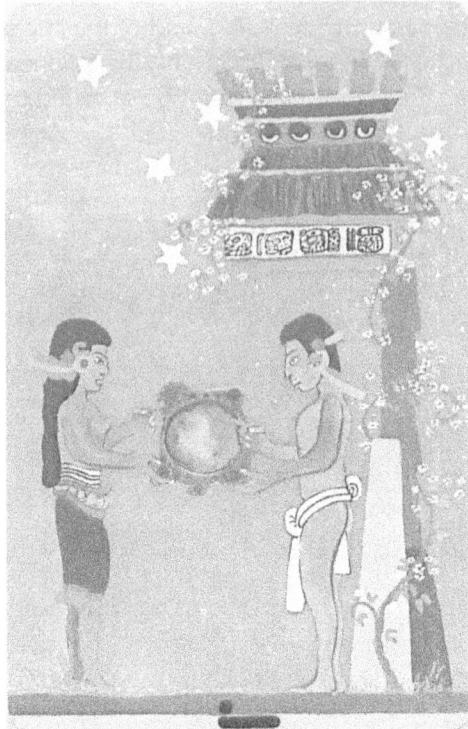

The Lovers
The Soul of the Child Substance Shield uses the Mood of Soul
Sweetness to Assume Emotional Authority

The Lovers

16

Lovers

The mirror of love is blind.

— Arabic saying

If we are a metaphor of the universe, the human couple is the metaphor par excellence, the point of intersection of all forces and the seed of all forms. The couple is time recaptured, the return to the time before time.

— Octavio Paz

In life we all have an unspeakable secret, an irreversible regret, an unreachable dream and an unforgettable love.

— Diego Marchi

I am tired, beloved, of chafing my heart against the want of you; of squeezing it into little ink drops, and posting it. And I scald alone, here, under the fire of the great moon.

— Amy Lowell

Have you ever been in love? Horrible isn't it? It makes you so vulnerable. It opens your chest and it opens up your heart and it means that someone can get inside you and mess you up....You give them a piece of you. They didn't ask for it.... It's a soul-hurt, a real gets-inside-you-and-rips-you-apart pain. I hate love.

— Neil Gaiman

A man and a woman, both lightly clad, stand underneath a temple similar to the one in the Priestess card. The man holds a clouded mirror with his left hand and points to it with his right hand. The woman stands under the starry sky and holds the mirror with her right hand while pointing to it with her left hand. Under her feet grow tiny golden flowers.

The Lovers card represents an important love relationship in one's life and particularly the role of choice in love relationships. The beloved may be another man or woman, or it may be a vocation, God, a creative pursuit, or a cause. The Lovers point to all decisions and choices that involve something of heartfelt value to us. Although they are human figures and we shall talk mostly about human relationships, this card also symbolises the attraction and repulsion between any two opposites.

Smoking Mirror

The Lovers hold a mirror between them. The Maya and Aztec used obsidian, a black volcanic glass, and iron pyrites to make mirrors. In Figure 43 we see a mirror found under the throne seat of the temple of Chac Mool at Chichen Itza. It is inlaid with turquoise (which was thought to emit smoke)[1] and is surrounded by four obsidian serpents. The iron pyrites mirror at the centre is missing.

Mirrors were not used for looking at one's reflection but were worn by rulers on a headband or at the small of the back. They were also used for divination and starting ceremonial fires. Prisoners of war were often sacrificed by having their heart ritually cut out with an obsidian knife. Two mirrors were then placed at an angle to each other inside the opened chest cavity of the victim. Paper was placed between them and a fire was started by the concentrated rays of the sun.

The English alchemist John Dee (1527–1608), astronomer and scryer to Elizabeth I, possessed a "shew-stone" or obsidian mirror which he used for scrying. According to him, it was delivered by the angel Uriel from whom he learned the magical language of Enochian. More than likely the mirror was one of many Aztec objects brought to Europe after the Spanish conquest of Mexico in the 1520s. The mirror now resides in the British Museum.

Tezcatlipoca or Smoking Mirror (*tezcatl*, mirror; *poca*, smoke) was the Aztec god of the night, sorcerers, and all material things. He carried a magic mirror that gave off smoke and killed his enemies. As lord of the world and the natural forces, he was the adversary of the spiritual Quetzalcoatl and sometimes appeared as a tempter, urging people to evil. Tezcatlipoca was the embodiment of change through conflict but he was also the god of beauty and war, the lord of heroes and beautiful women. In some ways, he was the male version of the Greek goddess, Aphrodite, who was married to Ares, the god of war. As the goddess of love, she caused as much strife as she did union.

Tezcatlipoca once seduced Xochiquetzal, the goddess of flowers, who was the epitome of alluring female sexual power. Flowers play an important role in Maya and Aztec ritual and mythology. The yellow marigold,

Figure 43. Maya mirror

known as "the flower with four hundred lives," symbolised death for the Aztecs and marigolds are placed on graves on November 1, the Mexican Day of the Dead. It is believed that the scent of the petals forms a welcome path for the spirits to return to their graves. So we see, at the feet of the first woman in the deck whose feet touch the earth (the Priestess and the Consort are both elevated on seats), flowers as symbols of life but also of death. The image reminds us of what the Lovers are perhaps only vaguely conscious of — the power of the feminine as Life-Giver and Death-Bringer.

The word mirror comes from the same root as the word miracle (Latin *mirari*, to wonder at). Another Latin word for mirror is *speculum* and the word "speculate" comes from the practice of searching the stars, and so divining the heavenly laws, by looking downwards at the reflection of the night sky in a mirror. Thus, the mirror represents alignment with spirit as reflected in the laws of nature. When a mirror is broken then disalignment or misfortune occurs as seven years of bad luck. The mirror also represents the boundary between this world and the other world, as in the magic mirror of fairytales, Alice in Wonderland's looking glass, or the practice of covering mirrors when someone in the house dies. In Christian mysticism the human heart is the mirror which reflects God. It not only reflects but when the reflection is pure enough it becomes what it reflects. To offer a pure reflection a mirror must be unblemished so as not to interfere with what it reflects.

In the Lovers card, the man and the woman not only hold the mirror but the mirror of projection holds them.[2] The Lovers do not look directly at each other but at the image of the other in the blue mirror of spirit. The mirror symbolises the process of projection — the mirroring and distortion of outer reality by our inner world. The Lovers do not see the other person for who they are but see instead the projected image. But this image is never the other, it is an amalgam of what the other wants us to see (their persona), what they don't want us to see (their shadow), and what we want to see (our anima or animus projection). Being unconscious, the anima or animus is inevitably projected upon a real object, which we become captivated by and dependent on.

So the mirror symbolises union and separation, awe and wonder, integrity and purity, and projection and distortion. However, it is through this reflection in the mirror that the Lovers come to know a refraction of themselves that they thought was the other. Jung said, "In practice it means that the woman of your choice represents your own task you did not understand."[3]

Mirrors were used as portals for dreaming and as entrances to the other worlds. Dark blue was the colour of Xibalba, the Underworld, or the "Place of Awe." Early 17th century Maya chants referred to the surface of the earth as a smoking mirror. These associations point to the similarity between the dark blue of the mirror in the Lovers card surrounded by its frame and, in the Planet Earth card, the dark blue of heaven surrounded by the earth. The roundness of the earth and the mirror, and the encircling of the blue sky by the brown earth in both cards, indicates that the intimate relationship between the Lovers is the seed of the ultimate flowering of the Planet Earth as our intimacy with the Self, taking the Earth as lover, and the union of spirit and matter.

Love

The goal of alchemy was to discover the presence of spirit in matter. The chemical attraction of the elements and metals for each other produces new compounds. In this mysterious physical process the alchemists saw a spiritual process. Our desire and attraction for another produces soul. Falling in love often gives us our first experience of heaven on earth in the eyes of another and physically making love allows us to approach the union of spirit and matter. As a result, the Lovers are the Holders of the Mood of Soul Sweetness. The experience of being deeply in love is the first step in the individuation process. Unless one has foolishly, blindly and impetuously loved then one has not fully entered into life... or death. Rumi says:

In the shambles of love, they kill only the best,
None of the weak or deformed.

Don't run away from this dying.
Whoever's not killed for love is dead meat.

But romantic love is an archetypal compulsion and does not need to be idealised nor made into a lifestyle. It is the first step of the journey, not the first step over the edge. "The language of love is of astonishing uniformity," Jung said, "using the well-worn formulas with the utmost devotion and fidelity, so that once again the two partners find themselves in a banal collective situation. Yet they live in the illusion that they are related to one another in a most individual way.... Very often the relationship runs its course heedless of its human performers, who afterwards do not know what happened to them."[4] This card is our first experience of the delights of delicious helplessness, wild passion, servility, being head over heels in love, unable to keep our hands off them, and being tied to them in the bondage of love. The same theme is repeated in the Bound Man card where the bondage is not to another but to the Self or Life.

The Lovers is the number 6 card. It is the union of two triangles — the spiritual parents and their child and the physical parents and their child (6 = 3 + 3). The Priestess and the Priest, the Keepers of the Heart and the Spirit of the Child Substance Shield, are the spiritual parents and birth the spirit child. The Consort and the Ruler, the Keepers of the Body and the Mind of the Child Substance Shield, are the substance parents and birth the substance child. Each of the Lovers brings these two children to the relationship and each child needs its opposite. The spirit child lusts for sensuality, the substance child longs for spirituality. With women the substance child is often more dominant and with men the spirit child is more dominant — the woman wants relationship and the man wants sex. But everything contains its opposite and when deeply in lust or deeply in love the positions become reversed — the woman wants sex and the man wants relationship.

Compared to the previous cards in this row the figures of the Lovers are naked and smaller. This indicates that they are much more human than archetypal. They have left behind the parental powers of the four previous cards to whom they could appeal for help. Whereas the Ruler stood on his own and brought order to the public world, now the Lovers stand together to bring confusion to their private world — and so it should be. This pattern happens at the end of each row where the last card unravels what has been woven, so that the next row can start a new spiral. This is the paradox of the Lovers as the Keeper of the Soul of the Child Substance Shield. This shield needs cohesion so that things can be torn apart, and discord and disintegration so that things can be put back together.

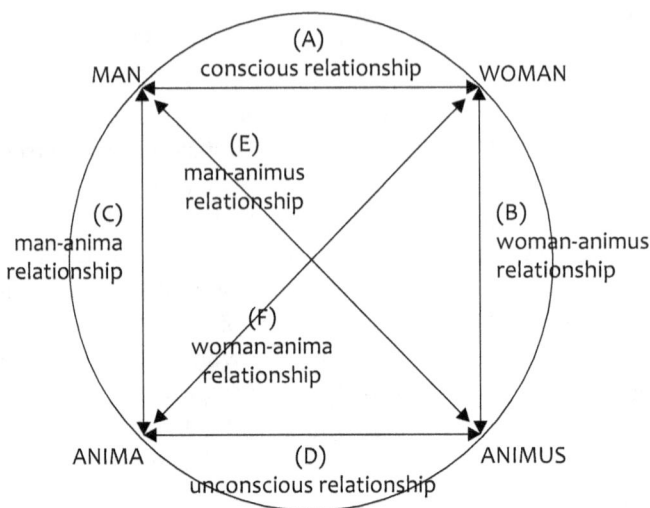

Figure 44. The Marriage Quaternio

Animus and Anima

In his paper *The Psychology of the Transference* Jung used a series of alchemi-cal woodcuts known as the *Rosarium Philosophorum* to explore the six possi-ble relationships between two individuals. He called this the "marriage quaternio" (Figure 44). The Rosarium tells the same story as the tarot — the maturation of the soul, the relationship between the masculine and the femi-nine, and the union of opposites. In the first woodcut (Figure 45) we see the similarity with the Lovers card — the man and the woman face each other, they hold something between them, and there is a star above them.

In Figure 44 the relationship (A) is between the egos of the two individu-als and is what we usually mean when we talk about "a relationship." The inner relationships (B and C) are between the woman and her animus (B) and between a man and his anima (C). Relationship (E) is between the man's ego and woman's animus, and relationship (F) is between woman's ego and man's anima. These relationships (E and F) are the ones that cause the most conflict between people in intimate relationships. Finally, relation-ship (D) is the unconscious relationship between animus and anima.[5] All six relationships in the marriage quaternio are ambivalent and made up of attraction and aversion in equal measure.

Jung said that if the encounter with the shadow is the "apprentice-piece" then coming to terms with the anima or animus is the "master-piece."[6] The work is to transform a troublemaking adversary into a psychic function that bridges the great opposites — masculine and feminine, conscious and unconscious. With this achievement, it becomes possible for the ego to extri-

Figure 45. Picture 2, Rosarium Philosophorum

cate itself from its emotional entanglements with the collective conscious and the collective unconscious. Then the anima and the animus are no longer autonomous complexes that possess us without our knowledge but become "a psychological function of an intuitive nature, akin to what the primitives mean when they say, 'He has gone into the forest to talk with the spirits.'"[7] This frees up energy for use by the ego—not for its own ends but to listen to what spirit is saying through nature.

Choices

Love brings out the unconscious. Jung observed that, "Apart from the personal striving for power, or *superbia*, love, in the sense of *concupiscentia*, is the dynamism that most infallibly brings the unconscious to light."[8] By its very nature the unconscious is duplex—ambivalent, two-sided, equivocal, messy, and conflicted—in contrast to the smug, glossy unity of consciousness. In the Lovers card conflict and ambivalence dominate. This is pictured in the Marseilles Tarot as a young man who has to choose between two women, both equally attractive. In Greek mythology Eris, the goddess of discord, was the only goddess not invited to the wedding of King Peleus and the sea nymph Thetis. So, in a hissy fit, she tossed a golden apple, on which were inscribed the words "for the fairest," into the midst of the banquet hall. Zeus (a wise man!) refused to judge between Hera, Athena, and Aphrodite, the three goddesses who laid claim to the apple. They then asked Paris, Prince of Troy, to choose between them. Each goddess offered Paris a bribe: Hera, power and rulership; Athena, great military victory; and Aphrodite offered herself, the fairest woman in the world. Attempting to evade the fateful choice, the naïve Paris (a puer emotionally incapable of refusing a reasonable request and hopelessly bullied by his ideals of justice, fairness and equality) wanted to cut the apple into three equal pieces. But this was not allowed. He then declared Aphrodite the fairest and chose as his prize Helen of Troy, the wife of the Greek king Menelaus. Later, Paris' abduction of Helen led to the Trojan War. In our life journey, this card is about the decisive choice that loosens the bonds with our parents and family and throws us into the inevitable conflicts of life.

Having to choose between obedience and disobedience, between spiritual ideals and carnal appetites, the Lover finds that rationality and its beloved problem solving won't work and the heart is torn. This is the first opportunity to experience the tension between the opposites. Damned if you do, damned if you don't. Here there are no rules for an individual situation and we must rely on our own judgement, or lack of it. For most of us, it is the latter and it is only in our "errors" of judgement in matters of the heart that we come to know ourselves. The young ego has rid itself of the parental complexes and now stands alone, caught between two women, two men ot two somethings — the real thing and the projection. This fateful choice in love is the first decision that is truly one's own, uninfluenced by family or community. This is why the Lovers card is the Teacher of Assuming Emotional Authority — the heart must make an impossible decision without recourse to any rules or authority other than one's own judgement.

Marie-Louise von Franz was Jung's senior colleague for thirty years and he said she was the only one who really understood his work. She astutely observed that, "The animus fosters loneliness in women, whereas the anima thrusts men headlong into relationships and the confusion that accompanies them."[9] The crucible of relationship forces the unconscious to the fore and brings about a differentiation of eros, or feeling values. When a man (let's say) is caught between his marriage to his wife and his desires for another woman, he feels, "If I don't see the other woman, I am betraying my feelings. If I leave my wife and children, I am behaving irresponsibly and chasing a passing infatuation. I can't do either and I can't keep this up." His wife's animus says: "It's her or me!" And the other woman's animus says: "Make up your mind, will you!" Everyone pushes him toward the wrong decision. And what's a "wrong decision?" Any one that isn't his.

Jung said that to be in such a conflict is the classical beginning of the process of individuation — the unconscious wants the hopeless conflict in order to put the ego up against the wall and teach it a lesson. If the person can sustain the tension between the opposites without wriggling out of it then, *deo concedente*, because of the insolubility of the conscious situation, the Self will manifest. In religious terms, an impossible situation forces one to rely on an act of God.

From the inevitable contradictions and double binds of relationship, one becomes aware of contradictions within oneself. The only way out is to find a different psychological position that encompasses the opposites. Jung called this the transcendent function. "The shuttling to and fro of arguments and affects represents the transcendent function of opposites. The confrontation of the two positions generates a tension charged with energy and creates a living, third thing... a movement out of the suspension between opposites, a living birth that leads to a new level of being, a new situation."[10] The problem is not solved but one feels differently about it. A new attitude has emerged.

The Warrior
The Heart of the Adult Substance Shield uses the Mood of
Emotional Cunning to Erase Mental History

The Warrior

17

Warrior

God help me, I do love it [war] so. I love it more than my life.
—General George Patton

The only way to stop the pain is to win.
—Super 14 Rugby, Sky Sports, New Zealand

Life is trouble, only death is not. To be alive is to unhook your belt and look for trouble.
—Nikos Kazantzakis, *Zorba the Greek*

Got to kick at the darkness 'til it bleeds daylight.
—Bruce Cockburn, *Lovers in a Dangerous Time*

These are the rules of the shield carrier... In your trust and innocence, never underestimate your enemy. In the west with your introspection, estimate and recognise any possible move your enemy might make. In the north, in your wisdom, know that an enemy can assume any potential. In illumination in the east, realise that a self army never exhausts itself in any manner. Standing in the centre, you can see that a great warchief knows all the territories, inner and outer, in which armies exist. Remember that ignorance is your greatest enemy.
—Agnes Whistling Elk

A young man sits in a square litter or carrying chair which in turn is set on a raised dais. He is dressed as a jaguar warrior. Behind him, attached to the litter, is a star banner that goes into the Priestess card above. Below him, tied to the chair, are two jaguars; one black and one white. We see similar images in the Codex Nuttall (Figure 47).

Figure 47. Warrior and Jaguar (Codex Nuttall)

Initiation

The card at the beginning of each row is a card of initiation. The Priestess is the initiation into Life. The Warrior is the initiation into Death-within-Life. The Hanged Man is the initiation into Death. The Star is the initiation into Life-within-Death. The Priestess and the Warrior are external and collective—they are made for us. The Hanged Man and the Star are internal and individual—we are called to them.

The archetype of initiation is about the human need to mark a transition from one status to another: girl to woman, boy to man, single to married, living to dead.[1] One does not simply become a man or woman by default. A rite of passage is necessary to transform the individual, ensure the continuity of the culture, overcome the normal tendency to regress when confronted with a challenge, and dissolve, bypass or defeat the all-too-human resistance to change. By ensuring development, these rites of passage produce rejuvenation and renewal and enable the individual to occupy the new status acknowledged by society. The initiate is given a place in an ordered cosmos together with all the attendant rights and responsibilities. They are also given access to the sacred myths, legends, stories and knowledge of the group so they can participate in the life of the holy. The ceremony often has such a profound emotional effect that the new status is felt to be divinely sanctioned. It is unmistakably and robustly internalised so the change is not only in external recognition but is also a deep inner transformation. This serves the person well in later life transitions because they are not reliant for their identity or self-esteem on outer forms of status such as title, wealth, membership, or appearance. They become a useful human being.

Initiation is neglected in Western culture, so it has to operate out of sight and unconsciously. It gives more attention to those transitions that are amenable to collective control (for example, marriage, divorce, baptism, confirmation or bar mitzvah). The hard-coded biological transitions that happen in their own way on their own schedule, tend to be ignored: from girl to woman to mother to elder to crone, the coming of the moon (menstruation) or the coming of the sun (ejaculation).

The rites of passage that survive in the West pale beside the intensity of the ceremonies of tribal cultures who better understand the need for a physically and emotionally powerful experience at these times. Boys' initiation rites might involve seclusion, circumcision, beatings, being terrorized by elders dressed as demons, sleeplessness, symbolic death and rebirth, and fasting. Ideally, a man emerges who knows about courage and self-denial in the face of danger, knows his place in the hierarchy of authority and power, wields authority without ambivalence, submits to authority without complaint, knows how to work harmoniously as part of a group, and who can offer these strengths for the good of the community.

All adolescents or young adults need to be initiated. Without initiation life stagnates. For men, war, combat and competition are initiation. As Mussolini said, "War is to man as maternity is to woman." The warrior society, or some form of initiation that danced with death, carried this function in indigenous cultures. If cultural forms for initiation don't exist, the archetype does not disappear but instead produces a constant pressure for expression. When conscious initiations fall away they are replaced by a host of unconscious initiations which appear in uncontrolled and antisocial form. They seek to overcome death through symbolic death in extreme sports, body-building, military service, aid work in dangerous places, self-sacrifice, dangerous driving, video games, drugs, gangs, depression, overdoses, hunting, car accidents, parasuicides, bankruptcy or bungee jumping, to name but a few.

This self-initiation may result in actual death or disability or, more often, a failed initiation where no internal change has come about and the person lives on as an emotional child in an adult body. If a boy has never been initiated, he becomes someone who outwardly looks like a man but who remains a grandiose adolescent in his use of power. When such men reach positions of political influence they may do great harm.

However, any numinous experience, any contact with the sacred, is potentially powerful enough to initiate the individual into a new level of consciousness. In the absence of cultural initiation, the Self may initiate the person from within by means of a numinous dream or experience, either positive or negative.

Hero

The warrior, male or female, is the archetypal hero. All cultures have honoured warriors for their heroism, bravery, courage, will, daring, sacrifice, discipline and strength. As the Teacher of Erasing Mental History, the Warrior is always pushing back the frontiers. As explorer, he looks for new horizons and searches for new lands to conquer. As soldier, he is willing to put himself in harm's way and give his own life to protect what is of value. As entrepreneur, he is endlessly optimistic and always willing to have a go. As scientist, he is constantly seeking new knowledge and "advancing the frontiers of science." The warrior moulds self, life and others according to his will, he vanquishes himself, stalks and fights with the tyrant, internal or external, does the hard work, pays his dues and fights for his dream. He is willing to do his utmost, defend the kingdom and make the ultimate sacrifice so life may continue to live.

The Warrior is born from the joining of the opposites in the Lovers card. Unlike the Ruler who stands at the centre and brings order to what has already been created by nature, the Warrior travels out into the world and creates something new. The Warrior sits upon a palanquin—a chair with poles that was carried by two or four people, a movable throne. The other seated figures in the cards so far (the Priestess and the Consort) have been on immovable thrones. The Warrior has fashioned himself a standpoint, a place from which he can go out into the world, not enclosed like the Priestess, or weighty and fixed like the Consort, but mobile, open and outward looking. He eagerly looks forward along the second row towards life's tasks. "The basic difference between an ordinary man and a warrior," Don Juan said, "is that a warrior takes everything as a challenge, while an ordinary man takes everything as a blessing or a curse."[2]

Although the Warrior has many admirable qualities that seem highly individual, everything he does is in fact highly collective. We see an aspect of the Warrior's collectiveness in the Star Nations banner tied to the back of his palanquin. The Star Nations People are the ancestors of our ancestors just as psychologically the collective unconscious is the ancestor of the ego. The banner is a symbol of the collective unconscious not the collective unconscious itself which are the stars themselves in, for example, the Priestess and Lovers cards. The banner means that the Warrior does not relate directly to the archetypes, he is driven from behind by their symbols. Just as the soldier serves "The Flag," all the warrior's actions serve the collective not the individual. His mission is to obey orders, respect authority, serve (his God, President, King, country) and protect (the faith, democracy, the state, free speech, national interests). He is unquestioningly bound to the authoritarian father.

The Warrior is also unconsciously bound to the Priestess above. Young men as warriors-in-training are always separated from their mothers, wives and girlfriends. The hero football player is easy prey for the alluring seductress or "jersey girl," and coaches still recommend sexual abstinence before the big game. For all its power, the erect, upstanding, extroverted masculine is a vulnerable thing and knows that it will fall limp eventually if the introverted feminine comes too close. Although the Warrior serves the collective, if his connection to the feminine becomes conscious (10) then the Warrior (7) has the opportunity in the Star (17) to dream his own dream.

Psychologically, the hero's task is to overcome the monster of darkness and achieve a victory of consciousness over the unconscious.[3] The hero tames the unconscious as opposed to being killed and eaten by it. In myths or fairytales the hero often has to find the princess, the ring, the golden egg, or the precious elixir — symbols for one's true feelings and unique potential. Then he has earned a genuine claim to self-confidence because he has faced the unknown within.[4]

The psychological task in the first twenty-seven years of life is to seed, bud, bloom and ripen sufficiently to become a fruitful, flowering human being. To do this we must take in hand the under- or over-socialised parts of ourselves. Plants have many gifts but free will and locomotion are not among them. Animals live under the heavy rule of instinct. But both are true to their own nature. Humans however are able to go against their vegetative inertia and animal instincts. The ego, because it has free will, can make choices and develop in such a way that it falls out of harmony with the natural growth of the whole personality. This is why *Homo sapiens* is so adaptable but neurosis is the price we pay.

We see this condition in fairytales where the King is sick, the land is laid waste, or crops will not grow. But the psyche is self-regulating and the Self will attempt to influence the ego with dreams or moods or symptoms. This is when the Warrior is needed — to restore the King's vitality, to make the land fertile again, to find the treasure that has been lost or to rid the land of the devouring monster. The monster may be the narcissism of overwork, the stupor of underwork, too little purpose, or too much purpose. If the ego is strong enough or not already too hardened it will heed the dream or the symptom and govern itself accordingly. The Warrior then is an archetypal figure who shows a model of ego functioning that listens to the Self when needed and restores a healthy balance to the psyche.[5] He provides the aggression and action needed. The hero reminds us of the one right way of behaving that is in accordance with the totality of the personality. He offers us an encouraging and heartening reminder of life's possibilities and shows us that adversity can be overcome.

The Warrior is the Keeper of the Heart of the Adult Substance Shield. The bravery, endurance, boldness, daring, and determination in dangerous or difficult conditions are what we call courage (the French for heart is *coeur*). Although this commonly means physical bravery in the face of danger, it is also the unseen bravery in the face of emotional, mental or spiritual difficulties. It takes courage to use healthy aggression and authority wisely, kindly, ruthlessly and in service of the whole. To hold the tension during the most difficult times, to not collapse into advance or retreat, and to remember that harmony can come from conflict requires fortitude and endurance. We might remember that Ares, the Greek god of war, and Aphrodite, the goddess of love, had three children: Deimos (the god of terror), Phobos (the god of fear) and a daughter, the beautiful goddess Harmonia.

War

War, as James Hillman points out, is normal.[6] Though this statement wounds our idealism, it is a fact. Words like opposition, conflict, difference, battle, struggle, competition, confrontation, rivalry and so on, saturate our language. We are "at war with ourselves," we "battle cancer" and "crush the opposition." There is the war on drugs, trade wars, gender wars, Darwin's survival of the fittest, Marx's class struggle, and Freud's battle between id and ego.

If we refuse to engage with war, we remain dissolved in the dreamy adolescent wetness of the Lovers. However, if we only engage in war we are stuck with the perpetual adolescent hard-on of the Warrior. But engage we must with this archetypal force that is outside human (good)will and forces us into acts that go against the grain of our hard-won decency. The archetype of war has its own purposes, independent of human concerns. How else can we think about something that has been waged by millions of people, world-wide, for millennia, with the full knowledge that it will bring misery, suffering and death, and the repeated evidence that it is never worth it?

When we live out a myth, an archetype, its encompassing force drives us and we experience the best and the worst of being human. But, because myth is collective, it is never our own humanness. Our behaviour and our choices are commandeered by the myth and we are relieved of the individual responsibility for those choices. In war it is young, idealistic men that are the most vulnerable and easily drawn to death. They follow the predatory call of heroism and service like lambs to the slaughter. War robes its indecency in ponderous values such as patriotism, sacrifice, martyrdom, valour, heroism, courage and gallantry.

But when the call comes — to fight for freedom, to fight the Hun, Communism, capitalism, colonisation, the liberals, the unbelievers, the anti-Semites, Al Qaeda — what to do? With war there is always the feeling of foreboding and inevitability about it, there is no choice, we are backed into a corner.

The code of the warrior (who bangs on about defending freedom) deprives us of freedom. The die is cast. War is never an individual act. Barbara Ehrenreich suggests that war is a living organism, "a self-replicating pattern of behaviour possessed of a dynamism not unlike that of living things."[7] In other words, war is an archetype.

War and Peace

The shadow aspect of Erasing Mental History is forgetting but the Warrior prods us into remembering. Peace not war is the great forgetting. When the war is over, to remember is too much, too fresh, too painful. There is a desperate rush toward the triviality of normal life. To recover from trauma goes against the grain of our nature. We have been hurt and horrified. The experience has trained every cell in the body: Never Again! To face the internal war again and again takes as much courage as the war itself. So the anaesthetic veil of peace descends and we forget. We adapt but at a price.

This psychic numbing, the constriction of emotions, and the avoidance of remembering are the symptoms of Post Traumatic Stress Disorder (PTSD) that are the most reliable predictors of chronicity and treatment-resistance. It is as if forgetting (punctuated by vivid, unwanted recollections, or flashbacks) is the only way to remember. Just considering modern historical times, from 1914 until the first years of the 21st century (when most of the veterans of World War II are coming to the end of their lives), a significant proportion of the male population of Western culture have had undiagnosed, untreated, chronic PTSD.

The Warrior ensures that we don't collapse into the narcosis of peace and forgetting. Christ said, "I did not come to bring peace, but a sword,"[8] which is the meaning of the whole second row of the Adult Substance Shield. The Warrior is hair-triggered, hot-headed, ill-tempered and impetuous. He is vengeful, keeps score, and remembers old slights and wounds against him, his family, or "his people," no matter if it was centuries ago. He likes nothing better than a fight.

But his fighting is not under his control. Hard man as he might seem, his psyche is putty in the hands of the right idea or cause. He fights against what he thinks controls him (but he has not developed any internal authority). He rails against what he thinks will deprive him of his freedom (which he doesn't have) or others' freedom (which he can't give). But in the end his vigilance, fire and energy begins the movement towards the Balance who uses the sword to bring the war between the opposites to a head in preparation for the transformation of the third row of the Adult Spirit Shield. And the Warrior learns some lessons along the way.

In the Twenty Count, the As Above is represented by the numbers from 11 to 20. It is after the Wheel (10) that we get our first taste of the forces beyond the ego's comprehension. The Balance (11) chooses to continue the journey as an autonomous individual and is the first one to confront the archetypes. Then, it is only at 14 (the Temperate Man) that the real purpose of the Warrior and the archetype of war, becomes clear. Seven is the number of the dream and the dream (7) of the Warrior (7) is the Temperate Man (7 + 7 = 14). What might this dream be? Like everything that exists including the Everything, it is nothing less than the transformation of itself. War, as the dreaming of the Warrior, ultimately brings about its own transformation if development continues and 14 is reached. James Hillman said:

> There is no practical solution to war because war is not a problem for the practical mind, which is more suited to the conduct of war than to its obviation or conclusion. War belongs to our souls as an archetypal truth of the cosmos. It is a human accomplishment and an inhuman horror, and a love that no other love has been able to overcome.... By imagining the real and standing in the conflict of its complexity, in willing suspension of the practical urge, we may awaken.[9]

We cannot begin to influence the collective unconscious as a 14 until we have experienced something of the dark side of death (13). As 7 dreams of 14 so 14 dreams of 7. The shadow dream of 14 is the dark side of the Warrior. The number 14 is the Spirit of the Animals and in war soldiers talk of the shadow side of 14—being taken over by the spirit of Mars, feeling God-like, immortal, untouchable by enemy bullets, but also wanting more blood, more killing. A Vietnam veteran said, "I was like a fucking animal... I started putting fucking heads on poles... digging up fucking graves."[10] This is the Viking berserker. To go berserk means to strip naked and to put on the bearskin—to surrender oneself completely to one's animal nature. But by holding the tension between the human and cosmic opposites, the Temperate Man can transform and humanise the archetype of war itself. When a pacifist lays down his sword, it means nothing. When a warrior lays down his sword, creation listens.

Love and War

James Hillman wrote, "A vague idea of love tends to whitewash the mind in innocence. It becomes an all-purpose remedy that gets you out of trouble and makes things come out all right. Love as salvation. Such love is another monosyllabic, open-mouthed, vowelly word that keeps the mind simple, without bite or hiss. This is hardly Aphrodite and Venus: for them love is the beginning of trouble, the necessary delusion that keeps one from seeing what's coming."[11]

Love is the cause of war not the solution to war. Let's notice the obvious: the Warrior card immediately follows the Lovers card. Histories large and small are littered with stories of how love and its vicissitudes leads to war, death and destruction, whether it be romantic love, love of romance, love of the land, love of God, love of freedom, jealous love, revenge love, jilted love, honour love, stalking love, or Romeo and Juliet love. These turn, in their own time, into God hate, jealous hate, revenge hate, and so on. Love started the ten-year Trojan war when Paris fell in love with Helen, Agamemnon's wife, abducted her, and took her back to Troy. As Marlowe wrote: "Was this the face that launch'd a thousand ships / And burnt the topless towers of Ilium?[12]

But the antidote to the excesses of the warrior cannot be a limp pacifism. Any pacifism that refuses all fighting and killing is doomed to failure since it not only grandiosely sets itself apart from life by denying death, a basic fact of the unconscious, but it actually breeds more violence. To be released from outer violence we have to fight on an inner battlefield. Often when a psychic change is emerging our dreams show the killing or death of someone, symbolic of an attitude or complex that needs to die or be killed. Until there are enough individuals who fight their inner battles, wars will continue and the honourable tradition of the warrior will be needed.[13]

The twins of love and war are complementary opposites: one leads to the other, hates the other, loves the other. In war, the usual human courtesies go by the board and "All's fair in love and war."[14] Both are an initiation into the intensity of life. After the life, love, union and merging of the Lovers, the universe wants a little death and separation. Love produces children. War is population control. Like General Patton, soldiers talk of never having felt so alive as when in battle. After battle, there is rape, the soldier "wipes the sword," death is a turn-on. If war is the father of all things, as Heraclitus said, then love is the mother of all things. They both suffer an excess of sentimentality and, alive as we feel when we are swept away by their power, we also lose ourselves completely and are rendered helpless and without free will. In part, this is the whole idea, to experience their undeniable power so that we can eventually become *agents provocateur* of the archetype's own transformation. But in the process hearts get broken and people die.

The Lovers are soft and melty, the Warrior is hard and pushy. The Lovers is the first card of Assuming Authority and they prepare the way for the differentiated choices made by the Balance, the next card of Assuming Authority. But the soul must pass through the lived experiences of the Warrior and the other cards of the second row before it can live in the place of the Balance. The Warrior's task is to experience love's emotional opposite — hatred. To do this matter justice would take us too far from our theme but I quote Lyn Cowan:

One of the works that hatred does then, psychologically, is a work of differentiation. Love, as we all know, is blind, or at least myopic, but hatred
sees with a cold, penetrating glare into the truth of the matter.... Cosmic
loving, as in "I-love-humanity," is as useless and ridiculous as
"I-hate-Jews (Catholics, Blacks, gays, telemarketers, whatever your group preference)." One needs to give careful attention to one's hatreds, as
to one's loves. I am afraid of people who love indiscriminately. It means
they do not choose their lovers carefully, and therefore may hate anyone
with the same indiscriminate projection.... When enemies come to mind
in our presence, we do not go all mushy but stiffen and straighten up, taking on the bearing of an adversary in complete self-command, not necessarily righteous be certainly forceful.... Now when I talk about enemies I
do not mean people whom you merely dislike... hatred is not to be devalued by lessening its object... The person you hate must embody a principle or value that is so abhorrent to you... that they inspire something
very close to an urge to kill. Ah, but here's the rub: I can only truly hate
what I am capable of doing, or have done, myself.... It is partly though
cultivating my hatred that I build dignity and respect for my own capability. By so respecting my capacity to do things I hate, I also build an inhibition to act them out. *Doing what my enemy does is not beyond my capacity,
but beneath my dignity* [italics in original].... Hatred's work of protecting
truth gives the soul courage, and preserves its integrity.[15]

Jaguar

The Warrior is the first card where we see a live animal. The jaguar-skin
throne of the Consort first supports us with its biological, instinctual energy
for life and growth. Then we encounter the same energy indirectly through
the Priest who has a more conscious spiritual relationship with the jaguar.
The jaguar is the Keeper of the Memory of the Ancestors and the Priest,
through his training and apprenticeship, has earned the right to wear the
jaguar skin robe. Now, the Warrior not only wears the robe but he also has
two live jaguars on a leash. The archetype has taken form and now lives
among us.

The family of cats (Felidae) are native to every continent except Austra-
lasia and are divided into the smaller cats (including the lynx, ocelot,
margay, caracal, serval, civet, and the domestic cats) and the large cats
(lion, tiger, leopard and jaguar). They are the most strictly obligate carni-
vores of all mammals. Vegetarian cats are hard to find. Cats must eat meat
because they do not naturally produce certain amino acids (arginine and
taurine) or digest them from plants. Dogs, on the other hand, will eat just
about anything. Thus the cat embodies the task of the Warrior—to experi-

Figure 48. Jaguar

ence the fears and pleasures of tearing into the meat of life and discovering the length of one's teeth.

According to recent DNA studies the domestic cat seems to have descended from a genetic group in the Middle East.[16] The cat was never intentionally domesticated like the dog but began to form a mutually beneficial relationship with humans just as the first agricultural settlements appeared in the Middle East about 10,000 BCE. In contrast to the dog the cat is set apart and fiercely independent, as we know: There are many intelligent species in the universe. They are all owned by cats.... Cats are nature's way of telling you that you really don't matter.... Dogs answer when called. Cats let the machine get it.... Dogs believe they are human. Cats believe they are God.... Thousands of years ago, cats were worshipped as gods. Cats have never forgotten this.... Dogs have owners. Cats have staff.... Do not meddle in the affairs of cats, for they are subtle and will piss on your computer... And so on.

Symbolically, the cat is an ambivalent image. Like the serpent, it oscillates between beneficence and malevolence. It is affectionate but cruel, sleepy but alert, fierce but scaredy-cat, proud but reclusive. It suns itself sleepily during the day but hunts at night. In ancient Egypt the cat goddess, as Bast or later Sekhmet, was sacred to Isis. In Norse mythology, Freyja is the goddess of love, beauty and fertility. Blonde, blue-eyed and beautiful she was also associated with war, death, magic and prophecy. She received half of the dead lost in battle in her hall, whereas Odin received the other half at Valhalla. Her war chariot was drawn by two cats.

In the Marseille card of Strength we see the lion. As Leo, the cat is heat, desire, emotions, pride, and fierceness. Up until 10,000 BCE lions were the most widespread large land mammal after humans. They were found throughout Europe, Africa, Eurasia and the west of the Americas from the Yukon to Peru. Herodotus reported that they were common in Greece in 480 BCE. They are now found only in sub-Saharan Africa and some parts of Asia.

The jaguar is the third largest cat after the tiger and the lion and the only big cat native to the Americas. Historically, its range to the north included most of the southern USA and to the south all of South America. As recently as the early 1900s jaguars were to be found in the area of the Grand Canyon. Its present-day range, now much reduced and fragmented, extends from northern Mexico down through Central America to Brazil and northern Argentina. Its prefers dense rainforest but is also found in open grassland and wetlands. It hunts in water and is the only cat other than the tiger that habitually swims. The jaguar has the most powerful bite of all the big cats. It can swim with large prey in water and climb trees carrying an animal as large as a heifer. It stalks and ambushes, rather than chases, its prey. It prefers larger animals and will take deer, capybara, tapirs, dogs and even anacondas and caiman, but will also eat smaller species like fish, frogs, sloths, monkeys, turtles and armadillos.

Maya rulers often took the names of animals. For example, at Yaxchilan a large part of its hieroglyphic record refers to the reigns of Itzamnah B'alam II (Shield Jaguar II), Yaxuun B'alam IV (Bird Jaguar IV) and K'uk' B'alam (Quetzal Jaguar) who was the founder of the Palenque dynasty. The jaguar was the Maya shaman's spirit companion or nagual because of its strength and stalking but also because of its dreaming and its gift of moving between the worlds. It is at home in both trees and the water, it hunts at night and during the day, and frequently sleeps in caves, places associated with the ancestors.

In the Xultun Tarot there are three animals: a crawler or a no-legged (the snake), a winged-one (the quetzal), and a four-legged (the jaguar). These animals form three paired opposites (serpent-jaguar, jaguar-quetzal, serpent-quetzal). Cats are Leos, all warmth and fire, snakes are Scorpio, all cold and chthonic, and birds are somewhere in between. Domesticated animals point to instincts that are more easily tamed and used for our own purposes. We can domesticate a cat, less so a bird, but we can't domesticate a snake. It represents something much further from consciousness, something more unknown, alien, inhuman and unconscious. And we see this movement in the sequence of animal images in the cards.

We first encounter the warmth and medicine power of the jaguar robe in the Consort and the Priest. The Consort sits on the robe. The instinctual energy is behind and underneath her, that is, it supports her but is unconscious. The Priest uses the medicine power of the jaguar by wearing the robe. Then in the Warrior we see live black and white jaguars: one black with white markings, the other white with black markings. Neither form appears in nature. (The closest is the melanistic jaguar also called the black panther which is solid black. Albino jaguars are rare). This indicates that they are symbolic—symbols of sharply contrasting opposites that the Warrior's must confront. In the Wheel the jaguar's fierceness has softened and we see the more maternal image of the mother jaguar feeding her cub beneath the calendar stone. And, just when the ego encounters the impersonal, cosmic laws of the Wheel symbolised by the snake encircling the stone, so the jaguar makes its final appearance as the last warm-blooded mammal in the cards.

The quetzal appears for the first time as a small white bird looking almost like a bud of the Cactus. As the ego encounters something larger than itself in the Wheel, the quetzal appears at the top of the stone in more differentiated form. Later, we find the quetzal flying free in the Star card. The quetzal was also called a sky-snake because of its long tail that undulated in flight and were often depicted by the Maya and Aztecs as having the body of a snake. Finally, the bird and the snake become joined in the Plumed Serpent of the 20 card. So the warm-blooded jaguar transforms first into a bird and a stone snake, then into a bird which is a sky snake, and finally, it shapeshifts into the symbolic, living energy of the Feathered Winged Serpent, the Teacher of Fearlessness.

In the first part of our journey we are helped by the warm fierceness of the jaguar. Then, as the center of the personality shifts away from the ego, the quetzal begins to fly and the snake is released from the stone. These two, a bird and a reptile, so far from our humanness, are the ones that finally bring us back to ourselves, back to earth, in the 20 card.

Horse

In European tarot the Chariot is the equivalent of the Warrior and instead of two jaguars we see two horses drawing a chariot. In *Phaedrus*, Plato describes the soul as having three parts, two of which had the form of horses, the third that of a charioteer. The black horse always yields to earthly passions and the white horse is always willing and obedient. The charioteer must use his skill and strength to control them.

The modern family of horses (horses, zebras, and asses) are a small remnant of a once much larger family that first appeared in North America about 55 million years ago as the dawn horse, or *Eohippus*. The modern species of horse (*Equus*) appeared about 5 million years ago and by the last Ice Age they were widespread across North America, Europe, Asia and Africa. But as the climate warmed and open steppe gave way to tundra and forest around 15,000 years ago, its habitat began to vanish and horses disappeared from both North and South America. By 7,000 years ago horses had become extinct the world over except for a small area in the still-open grassland steppes of Central Asia. It was here they were domesticated between 4,000–3,000 BCE.

Since then no other animal has served humankind as well as the horse — pulling, ploughing and carrying. Draft horses, dray horses, cavalry horses, hackneys, warm bloods, cold bloods, hot bloods, Welsh ponies, Shetland ponies, Connemaras, polo ponies, cobs, thoroughbreds, purebreds, quarter horses, mares, stallions, geldings, Arabians, Percherons, Andalusians, Shires, Clydesdales, Belgians, Holsteins, Hanoverians, Lipizzaners, Appaloosas, mustangs, brumbies, donkeys, mules, bays, greys, duns, roans, chestnuts, piebalds, palominos, paints, and pintos.

Horses are symbols of work, stamina, power, speed, and the ability to move and get somewhere in life. We chomp at the bit and get the bit between our teeth. We speak of someone who is a "real workhorse," the horsepower of an engine, or The Stones' "wild, wild horses." They are also symbolic of the unruly spirit that cannot be tamed — the "young filly," the "runaway horse" or the "bucking bronco."

Horses are both the helper of humankind but also the sacrificial victim. In a military or state funeral a horse is led behind the coffin on the gun carriage with the deceased's boots hung backwards in the stirrups. This is a remnant of the days when the horse was led to the grave to be slaughtered for the warrior to ride in the beyond. Horses have great vitality but are also capable of great destruction (the riderless horse, the stampede of wild horses). They have extra-sensory powers — in the Iliad, Xanthus, Achilles' horse, foretells his death, and Sleipnir, Odin's eight-legged horse, had powers of foresight. But they also tend to panic.[17] Horses are made of wind and easily scared. They are associated with terror, bolting and night-mares. In Scandinavian folklore, a mara or mare is an incubus that is believed to torment people in their sleep by sitting on their chest and "riding" them, causing nightmares.

Fire and Shadow

The Lovers card is about private relationship and the intimacy between anima and animus. The Warrior is about public action and the clash between persona and shadow. Now there are teeth, claws, speed and danger. The jaguars, baring their teeth but restrained, are the Warrior's war horses, his battle animals, his connection to his instinctual reactions to be called on in time of need.

The black and white pillars of the Priestess' seat have given way to the black and white jaguars tied to the palanquin. The Warrior has transformed the stone pillars of the Priestess card into something more alive and much closer to the human realm. Now the shadow and the opposites are closer to consciousness. But the black and the white are still separated — there is no integration of shadow as yet. The jaguars symbolise the Warrior's greatest enemy — himself. The adversary he must fight are his attitudes and emotions that need to be civilised and brought under control so the journey may continue. All sports and symbolic warfare train the young person to bring the jaguars to heel and let them off the leash at the right time. In the final analysis, instincts can never be "controlled" and the art lies in finding the right relationship to them just as we do with an animal.

The influence of an archetype rises and falls throughout our lives and the warrior archetype, more than others because it so culturally dominant, can appear before its appointed time or stay well after. So we see the ageing, battle-sodden warrior, nostalgic for youthful action, always on the lookout for an emergency, for an enemy, for a crisis, for an outer battle (as an avoidance of the inner battle) who may paradoxically lack the simple courage to live an ordinary life. Just as Anton Chekhov said: "Any idiot can face a crisis, it is this day-to-day living that wears you out."

The bodies of the jaguars face in opposite directions while their heads face in the same direction. This is the Warrior's conflict — the head wants one thing, the body another. Similarly, in the Chariot we see the horses, one red, one blue, symbols of instinctual power, moving in opposing directions. The Warrior needs to use the boundless energy of young adulthood to discipline the red horse of the heart and train the blue horse of the mind.[18] As the Holder of the Mood of Emotional Cunning, the Warrior needs this quality to bring his or her own sexuality and aggression under ego control, to let the instincts run or rein them in, and unite the warring opposites in a confrontation with his own shadow.

The predominant colour of the second row is yellow. The three primary substances in alchemy are mercury (spirit), salt (wisdom), and sulphur. Sulphur is yellow and associated with passion, fire, drivenness and desirousness. This row of the Mood of Cunning and the Adult Substance Shield is about dealing with the paradox of sulphur. On the one hand, it is about going for it, finding our passion, being gung-ho, discovering what interests us, attracts us, turns our crank, lights our fire. On the other hand, it is developing the discipline to not be consumed by the combustible sulphur and not let the fire get out of control. Fire is the only element that feeds on itself.

But inevitably and purposefully, all this discipline will fail the Warrior in the third row beginning with the Hanged Man. Here the Warrior will be brought to his or her knees by the opposite within (the anima or animus) and will begin to burn with the Fire-from-within. The Warrior must begin to go against his own conscious desires. If he's too tight, he must loosen up. If he's too loose, he must snug up. Either way, it does not mean that the ego should open the door wide to any and all impulses, retentive or expansive. Jung cautioned that, by human standards, the unconscious can be highly destructive.[19]

All social animals are subject to the controls and support of the pack, flock or herd. But in this age of personal responsibility, the burden of self-control has been increasingly transferred to the individual accompanied by a lessening of social controls on behaviour. Where events have an archetypal background this may be too much for a young or vulnerable psyche not bolstered by social controls.

As a result, we see an increase in the incidence of crimes that are outside the human fold—the sexual abuse of infants, sadistic murder, or cannibalism, for example, in contrast to the more human crimes of robbery, fraud or murder. The alchemists said that in the prima materia there is a certain amount of *terra damnata* (accursed earth) that cannot be transformed and has to be thrown out. Not all shadow impulses lend themselves to integration or rehabilitation. There are some, contaminated by the archetype of evil, that cannot be allowed to break loose and must be fiercely repressed.[20] The Warrior knows the difference between personal shadow and archetypal evil. He knows when to fight and when to turn away from an adversary that is not of the human realm. We shall have more to say about evil in the Bound Man card.

For most people in Western culture however the danger is not opening the door too wide, but not opening it wide enough. The fear is that once the dark genie of the shadow is out of the bottle we won't be able to control it, will be in bondage to it, and we will inevitability become a sinner, axe-murderer, reprobate, ne'er-do-well, or moral degenerate. So we forget, stifle, constrict and repress. But repression is never selective. True, the shadow disappears but so does the light. If we refuse to eat some of our own shadow, we become energetically anorexic. The red-bloodedness of the Warrior becomes pale. Our light dims.

The Cactus
The Body of the Adult Substance Shield uses the Mood of
Physical Cunning to create Mental Death and Change

Strength

18

Cactus

Our psychological strength consists precisely in the capacity to fight whatever acts against our growth process.

— Aldo Carotenuto

Come what may, all bad fortune is to be conquered by endurance.

— Virgil

Endurance is nobler than strength, and patience than beauty.

— John Ruskin

What can't be cured, must be endured.

— Anon.

Knowing others is intelligence; knowing yourself is true wisdom. Mastering others is strength; mastering yourself is true power.

— Lao-Tzu

When restraint and courtesy are added to strength, the latter becomes irresistible.

— Mohandas Gandhi

A large green San Pedro cactus grows in a white pot with black decorations showing a temple with two priests. The cactus is in full bloom and on its branches sits a white bird. In the bottom right-hand corner is smoke from the urn in the Sage card and in the top right-hand corner is part of the lintel of the temple door.

The Cactus stands for endurance, the passive strength that enables one to see an action through to its completion. The Cactus is not free, for it grows in a pot, yet it has reached maturity, is in flower and will complete its natural cycle regardless of its "imprisonment."[1] The Cactus is the Teacher of Using Mental Death as an Advisor and teaches us about the Death-within-Life.

Card for card, the Cactus is the most radically different from its counterparts in other tarot decks—a plant is depicted instead of a human figure. This indicates that there is a less human, more archetypal force at work that is further away from our conscious functioning. European tarot decks lean away from nature toward spirit and this is evident in their imagery. Humans are over-represented and the other Children of Grandmother Earth (Minerals, Plants, Animals and Ancestors) are under-represented. For example, in the Marseilles Tarot the only card in which there is no human figure is the Moon card (but buildings are visible in the background). But in the Xultun Tarot human figures are absent in six of the cards: the Cactus (plant), the Wheel (mineral), the Moon, Sun, Venus (ancestors) and the Earth (all the Worlds).

Teacher Plants

The Cactus card symbolises all things to do with the body—physical health, self-containment, mastery of the body and the physical environment, and providing for oneself physically. It continues the task of the Warrior but in an introverted way. The Cactus symbolises the feminine strength that comes from knowing the wisdom of the body. In some cultures, this wisdom was awakened by the use of teacher plants or hallucinogens, for example, peyote or ayahuasca. The Maya were known for their use of hallucinogens, sometimes administered rectally.

The cactus in the card is a flowering San Pedro cactus (*Trichocereus pachanoi*) known as Grandfather or the Great Provider (Figure 49). It can be used as a hallucinogen (either as a powder or liquid or mixed with other plants), as an anaesthetic or a poultice, as an emergency supply of water in the desert, and the spines and fibre can be used to sew.

The San Pedro is a native of the Andes of Peru, Bolivia and Ecuador but it and peyote (*Lophophora williamsii*) or Grandmother are used throughout the Americas. It is multi-branched, spiny and ribbed, and often grows to heights of ten or fifteen feet, averaging four to eight inches in diameter. The oldest archaeological evidence of its use, a Chavin stone carving in northern Peru, goes back to 1300 BCE. Almost equally old Chavin textiles depict the cactus together with jaguar and hummingbird figures. Today, it is used as a hallucinogen by the *curanderos* of Peru where it is known as *huachuma*, or as a sacrament in the Native American Church.

The mescaline in San Pedro is contained within the outer half-inch of the plant. The cactus is sliced, boiled, made into an extract and drunk. The curanderos prepare a drink called *cimora* from it and take this in ceremony to diagnose the spiritual or subconscious basis of a patient's illness. The

Figure 49. San Pedro cactus in flower

name San Pedro (Saint Peter) intimates that the cactus holds the keys to the gates of heaven. During the ritual, the participants are "set free from matter" and engage in flight through the cosmic regions.[2] The goal of the shaman is to make his patient "bloom" during the ceremony, to make his subconscious "open like a flower," like the night-blooming huachuma itself.

The pot in which the Cactus grows was found in the tomb of Stormy Sky of the Ruler card. The vase, from the mid-5th century CE, depicts the arrival of a group of Teotihuacanos at a Maya city. The Teotihuacan culture of Mexico had a trading empire reaching as far south as Guatemala and Honduras.[3]

As we have seen, the Cactus is the only card, except for the bottom row which are all heavenly bodies, in which there is no human figure. (The only other living thing in the card is the white fledgling at the top of the cactus and even that looks like a flower). This suggests that the card represents something distant from human consciousness. Since always, plants have been used for physical healing. Animals do not cure illness by direct biological action, plants do. For every affliction that besets humans there is a corresponding plant that, under the right conditions, can heal it. The San Pedro cactus is a hallucinogenic "teacher plant" that heals the afflictions of the soul. The spirit of the plant teaches us, through our physical bodies, about the non-physical world. When we work with teacher plants our body remains still while the soul (the white bird) is set free to travel. When the soul travels, it sees the energetic pattern of the web, the matrix of the interconnectedness of all things. This is the infinity movement, the 8, which is the number of the card. This is not a human pattern but the basic energetic pattern of the universe thus the Cactus is a non-human image.

The Cactus is a very physical card (physical thinking, the Body of the Adult Substance Shield, Physical Cunning) and the body is all. Any intellectual activity and mental thinking is surplus to requirements. As such, the Cactus is the Teacher of Using Mental Death as an Advisor.

The alchemist's dictum was "sublimate the body and coagulate the spirit." This paradox requires that the body is bridled and contained in order to free its spiritual potential. All spiritual traditions have physical practices (walking meditation, fasting, chanting, martial arts or dance, for example) that channel the instinctual demands of the body and impose some form of discipline on how physical energy is used. The libido that is blocked from meeting instinctual or unconscious needs then becomes available for other purposes. These practices allow spirit to move in the body.

The Cactus represents something that happens at a primitive cellular level well below the water-line of consciousness. It is about being receptive to the wisdom of blood and breath, and the body's innate potential to connect spirit and substance. This is the Mood of Physical Cunning. Jung describes this cellular consciousness:

> "Spirit" always seems to come from above, while from below comes everything that is sordid and worthless. For people who think in this way, spirit means highest freedom, a soaring over the depths, deliverance from the prison of the chthonic world, and hence a refuge for all those timorous souls who do not want to become anything different. But water is earthy and tangible, it is also the fluid of the instinct-driven body, blood and the flowing of blood, the odour of the beast, carnality heavy with passion. The unconscious is the psyche that reaches down from the daylight of mentally and morally lucid consciousness into the nervous system that for ages has been known as the "sympathetic." This does not govern perception and muscular activity like the cerebrospinal system, and thus control the environment; but, though functioning without sense-organs, it maintains the balance of life and, through the mysterious paths of sympathetic excitation, not only gives us knowledge of the innermost life of other beings but also has an inner effect upon them. In this sense it is an extremely collective system, the operative basis of all *participation mystique*, whereas the cerebrospinal function reaches its high point in separating off the specific qualities of the ego, and only apprehends surfaces and externals — always through the medium of space. It experiences everything as an outside, whereas the sympathetic system experiences everything as an inside.[4]

Feminine Strength

In the Marseilles Tarot the Cactus card is called Strength. In the older European decks Strength is usually the number 11 card with the number 8 card being Justice. However, in the late 19th century A. E. Waite, the creator of the Rider-Waite tarot, switched the 8 and the 11 cards so that Strength is number 8 and Justice is number 11. The position of Justice earlier in the sequence of the older tarot perhaps reflects the predominance of external control and authority in medieval Europe. Over the centuries, the locus of control has shifted from the collective external authority of the king or government to the internal authority of the individual. So in more recent decks Strength (internal authority) is the first challenge that the ego meets rather than Justice (external authority). In the Xultun Tarot the positions are the same as the Rider-Waite.

In the Strength card, a woman stands behind and to the left of a lion with her hands on its jaws. The image is ambivalent—it is not clear whether she is opening or closing the jaws of the lion. The lion does not look like it is dangerous neither does the woman look like she wants to dominate the lion. Lions, like all wild animals, indicate instinctual behaviour and wildness.[5] Jaws and teeth are associated with eating, appetite, red-bloodedly tearing into things, and assimilating life. The lion is close to nature, a natural instinctual force that can be tamed, integrated and civilised to some extent, but not by dominance or supremacy.

Like the Strength card, the Cactus represents the ego's continuing struggle to contain, pacify, struggle with, and harness its instinctual, animal nature but at a deeper level than the Warrior. Now is the time for the plant-like patience of the feminine rather than the animal-like masculine aggression of the Warrior. The anger, the bitterness, the fieriness, the temper, the machismo, the sulking, the rashness, the moodiness—all must be tamed. The Warrior must kill the lion or the bull, defeat the opponent, and drink its blood—but in the Cactus the opponent is now himself. In alchemy, this is symbolised by two lions fighting with each other. If the projected conflict is to be healed it must return to the psyche of the individual where it began. The Cactus represents the process of assimilating one's own emotions.[6]

The fire of desire generated in the next card, the Sage, has significant consequences in the third row but it also crosses the bottom corner of the Cactus card. Lions and fire are related—alchemically the lion was considered a fiery animal; we know that the sun and the lion are linked astrologically; and both are symbols of the ruling principle of consciousness. The Warrior uses masculine strength to control himself and his animal passions and harness them in the service of the collective. The Cactus uses feminine strength to come into relationship with the somatic, vegetative processes of life and awaken them in the service of the soul. When the extroverted, fiery, lion energy of the Warrior is physically contained by the introversion and immobility of the Cactus, something begins to happen that culminates in the last card, Planet Earth, as Jung pointed out:

> When you indulge in desirousness, whether your desire turns toward heaven or hell, you are giving the animus or anima an object; they are then turned out into the world instead of staying in their place within... But if you are governed by your desires you are naturally possessed.... If you have put your anima or animus into a bottle you are free from possession... You slowly get quiet [like the woman holding the jaws of the lion] after a while and transform, and you will discover that in that bottle grows the stone, the amber or the Lapis.... and inasmuch as the self-control, or non-indulgence, has become a habit, it is a stone.... and when it has become a *fait accompli* it is a diamond.[7]

A cactus is a contained and self-sufficient organism. It survives on very little water but stores a surprising amount in its body. Like the cactus, too much emotional wetness kills us. Dry on the outside, moist on the inside is the cactus' teaching about emotional containment. To quote Margaret Thatcher: "To wear your heart on your sleeve isn't a very good plan; you should wear it inside, where it functions best."[8] The cactus is the introverted, receptive strength that we need to just sit with our discomfort, pleasure, anger, pain, joy or grief. "Warrioring" can be done with (or to) others, but enduring and suffering is done alone—this is the strength of the feminine. Whereas the Warrior wishes to dominate the physical world, the Cactus submits to the physical world. Now dark illumination comes up from the body.

White Bird

In the alchemical manuscript *Splendor Solis* there is a picture of an alchemist being heated in a bath (Figure 50). The picture contains the same themes as the Cactus with images of the pot, the bird and the fire. Part of the alchemical process was to heat the material in a closed vessel, an operation known as the sublimatio. The operation of sublimation occurred when a lower substance was transformed into a higher substance by an ascending movement and vaporisation. Psychologically, sublimation means getting above a problem, gaining some objectivity, and having a wider perspective on an issue. Looking at things from an archetypal point of view is an example of sublimation.

In alchemy, a white bird, symbolising the soul flying upwards from the heated substance, often represented the sublimatio.[9] In such a way the body

Figure 50. The Alchemist in the Bath

was "made perfect" by spiritualising it. In the Cactus card, we see a small white bird that sits atop the cactus and in the alchemical picture a white bird sits on the alchemist's head. The bird reappears again, in increasingly differentiated form, in the Wheel and the Star cards. It then appears in its fully developed form of the greater sublimatio as the Feathered Winged Serpent in the Planet Venus card.

Edward Edinger made a distinction between the greater and the lesser sublimatio. A descent, a fall, a crash, or a coming down always follows the lesser sublimatio—there is more work to be done and living to be had. In other words, a coagulatio will follow. The greater sublimatio, however, is the transformation into eternity of what has been created in time. This is the process described by the major arcana of the tarot. Edinger elaborates: "Individual consciousness or realisation of wholeness is the psychological product of the temporal process of individuation.... It seems to imply that consciousness achieved by individuals becomes a permanent addition to the archetypal psyche.... whenever an item in one's personal psychology is decisively objectified [it] then becomes an eternal fact, untouchable by joy or grief or change." The white bird is the beginning of this undertaking.

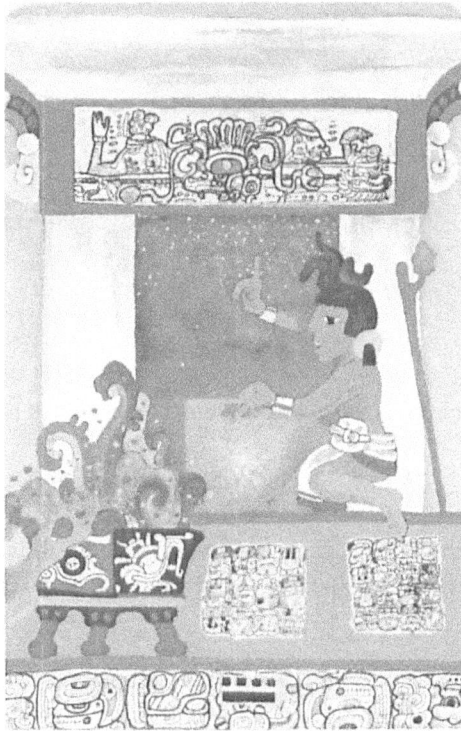

The Sage
The Mind of the Adult Substance Shield uses the Mood of Mental Cunning to Stop the Mental World

The Hermit

19

Sage

The fool doth think he is wise, but the wise man knows himself to be a fool.

—William Shakespeare, *As You Like It*.

Perhaps that is what we are here for: to bring appreciative understanding to the phenomena that have no need to understand themselves.

—James Hillman

Solitude is the profoundest fact of the human condition. Man is the only being who knows he is alone.

—Octavio Paz

I want to be with those who know secret things
or else alone.

—Rainer Maria Rilke

I've had a wonderful life, but it was Norman's life... You don't realise how much of yourself you have sublimated until you are alone.

—Norris Church Mailer

Life can be compared to a piece of embroidered material of which everyone in the first half of his time comes to see the top side, but in the second half the reverse side. The latter is not so beautiful, but it is more instructive because it enables one to see how the threads are connected together.

—Arthur Schopenhauer

In this card we see a man inside a temple. He points upward with this right hand to a lintel that depicts the sorcerer Itzamna surrounded by water lilies.[1] With his left hand, he points downward to a tripod basin from which pours the incense smoke of copal (Nahuatl, *copalli*) called *pom* by the Maya. Behind him is a staff with one leaf on it. Outside the temple we see a starry night sky with a passage cut in it, at the end of which is a light.

The image of the Sage is taken from sculptures of the Maize God or Yum Caax (Figure 52). He holds his hands in a handsign that means "break," similar to the North American Indian hand sign for "daybreak." Another meaning of this handsign is "birth." In Maya iconography, humans being born from ears of maize or the cleft of a tree and holding their hands in this way are a common symbol and the Maize God is often associated with this handsign. The Sage's hands point upwards to heaven and downwards to the earth indicating the potential of joining of matter and spirit. This is the first time that the possibility of their union is indicated.

These images of birth and fire indicate that the Sage is beginning the process of individuation. We see the individual fire in the brazier whilst in the background are the great galactic fires, the Great Grandfather Stars. The fire in the brazier is connected to the small sun below in the 14 card (Temperate Man) and below that to the large sun in the 19 card (Sun). The intensification of libido and emotions symbolised by fire brings about the birth of our own personal fire, our inner sun, and the individual experience of illumination. It is this unique personal identity that Jung called the "little light of consciousness" or the *principium individuationis*, the individuation principle.

The Sage (9) is the most mental card in the deck. It is the card of mental thinking, the Mind of the Adult Substance Shield, Mental Cunning, and Stopping the Mental World. Similarly, the Priestess (2) is the most emotional card — emotional feeling, Heart of the Child Substance Shield, Emotional Sweetness, and Erasing Emotional History. The Dead Man (13) is the most physical card — physical sensation, Body of the Adult Spirit Shield, Physical Ruthlessness, and Using Physical Death as an Advisor. Planet Venus (20) is the most spiritual card — spiritual intuition, Spirit of the Child Spirit Shield, Spiritual Patience, and Controlling the Spiritual Dream.

Solitude and Secrecy

The proper cure for loneliness is solitude. — Anon.

The ego has ventured out into the world as the Warrior and has been tested in the swell and churn of life. To become who we are we must disentangle ourselves from the collective mass of humankind. In his temple the Sage is protected from the world but open to the sky. We need some degree of solitude, some insulation from the "ten thousand things," to see ourselves as we are, unclouded by the eyes of others or what we imagine to be in the eyes of others. Emily Dickinson wrote:

Figure 52. Maize God

There is a solitude of space
A solitude of sea
A solitude of death, but these
Society shall be
Compared with that profounder site
That polar privacy
A soul admitted to itself—
Finite infinity.

The inner world often demands our attention after long periods of War-
rior-like strength or Cactus-like endurance. We need to withdraw into
silence, meditation, quietness, time off, taking stock, enforced rest or illness. Physical rest enforces contemplation, rumination and reflection on
where we have been and where we are going. The Sage, then, is the Keeper
of the Mind of the Adult Substance Shield and the Teacher of the mental aspect of Stopping the World. In solitude we become more aware of the hidden rhythms and cycles of the Moon card which is the completion of the
Sage. Sarah Maitland found she:

Loved solitude and silence... It was like having a new lover; I wanted to spend more and more time with silence and get to know it better. I experimented: I spent six weeks in total silence on Skye; I walked in wild hills and forests; I went to the Sinai desert; I visited silent religious orders—Christian and Buddhist; I sat in libraries and churches... I became aware of all the silent processes on which we depend—organic growth itself, electricity, gravity and tides; the silent spinning of the Earth and the changes of the seasons.[2]

Jung said, "Everyone who becomes conscious of even a fraction of his unconscious gets outside his own time and social stratum into a kind of solitude."[3] The detachment that comes with being solitary does not mean an antagonism to being human but it is a disengagement from the mass unconsciousness that is shared by the majority of humankind. In fact, the solitary person is better able to engage in the world because they are less likely to become confused or lose themselves in the tides that surge through the mass psyche. As well, the Sage's solitude is not isolation, in fact the taste of our own loneliness brings a fresh appreciation of what the presence of the other means.

In these reclusive experiences we may find unknown reservoirs of strength within us and, hopefully, unknown reservoirs of weakness. It is difficult to find any positive English antonym for strength. Most have a negative tone—frailty, weakness, powerlessness, for example—a dead giveaway as to the unconscious bias of the Western psyche.

The Sage is the one who has seen the limitations of his or her strength, and begins to know what cannot be done, what wants to be done, and what needs to be done—right away, next week or never. Sooner or later, all that heroic strength, all that prevailing and overcoming, all the goals, all the potency, all the pushing, and all the achievement, becomes a burden. The strength that comes from knowing our weaknesses is devalued in our heroic culture. Instead, it emerges as depression and the melancholy of all things done.

Senex

The alchemists depicted the growth of the personality as the "philosophical tree." The flowering of this tree is driven by two archetypes: the anima, who expresses life, and the wise old man, who expresses meaning.[4] In the Marseilles Tarot the "wise old man" is pictured as the Hermit. He is the one who sees meaning hidden in the chaos and senselessness of life. The Hermit carries a lamp representing the mental introversion that is needed to activate the unconscious and kindle the little light of consciousness by which one finds one's own way. It is by this small light that we begin to see a dim outline of who we are and how to make our own choices. Not those driven by the ego's wishes, nor those driven by collective pressures, but those that are uniquely and fatefully our own. Now the ego begins to realise that to be anyone else other than who we are is a living death. As someone said, "Be yourself, everyone else is taken."

In fairytales the old man often appears when the hero is in an impossible situation from which only profound reflection or luck can extricate him.[5] The old man urges the hero to sleep on it, to think about it, and poses thoughtful questions like: Who? Why? How? What for? Jung said this symbolises a purposeful process that gathers up all the resources of the psyche to help the personality move forward into the future.[6]

The Movement of Stopping the World, particularly the Ruler and the Sage cards, embodies the consciousness of the senex (Latin for old man) in all its forms.[7] The maturing, flowering, ageing, stagnation and withering of psyches, persons, peoples, civilisations, and ages are contained within this archetype. We see him in symbols of the passage of time — Father Time, the old oak tree, the scythe of the Grim Reaper, or the skull of Yorick. We hear him in talk of tradition, establishment, lineage, and breeding. More personally, the archetype expresses itself in feelings and notions about time and death, nostalgia, ruminations about the past, melancholy, abstractions and principles, history, calendars, cosmic meanings, geometric forms, ancient pyramids, numbers, and timeless forms.

The senex is all-knowing, seated, bearded, and removed from the feminine and the earth. He is generally benevolent but enraged when his will is crossed. He rules, not through personal presence, but by abstract principles handed down from on high. The Greek god of time, Kronos, who later became the Roman god, Saturn, is a senex god as is the Christian God. Saturn was the god of agriculture and the harvest, and his symbol was the sickle. His festival, the Saturnalia, was celebrated at the winter solstice, the lowest point of the sun where the descent ends and the ascent begins. Kronos was one of the twelve Titans and the youngest son of Uranus and Gaia, the original marriage of heaven and earth. Long before Oedipus, he castrated his father with a sickle given to him by his mother and became ruler of the universe. However, he had been warned that one of his children in turn would overthrow him and so he swallowed each of his first five children as soon as it was born. A well-known painting by Goya shows Kronos eating his children.[8]

Being swallowed by the father is symbolic of the times when the ego refuses the next step in individuation — everything has been done, no further change is needed. One becomes resigned to one's fate, hardened into the stone of the next card, the Wheel. But the mystery of our humanness is that we need to succumb to, but at the same time overcome, our fate. To do this we must not allow ourselves to be eaten by the collective father of laws, customs and systems—or become the father himself.

After his son Zeus dethroned him, Kronos governed the Isles of the Blessed and became ruler of the Golden Age. The Isles were at the end of the world and inhabited by the heroes after their death. They lived in eternal youth, the trees flowered three times a year, and all lived in great abundance and peace. This tells us that if the ego steps down, draws back, dethrones itself, then the younger generation of new growth in the psyche can flower and the ego is eventually brought great reward. We see his fruit in the Temperate Man and Sun cards below him in the same Movement, and in the last card where the Earth flowers. So the Sage is a "late bloomer" far removed from the youthful energies and rashness of the Lovers and the Warrior. With the sickle of time he reaps his harvest towards the end of his life, or in the other world.

Melancholy

The temperament of the senex is cold. He likes distance, isolation, retreats, reflection, to wander (alone), and prefers the bitter truth of reality just as it is. He has the qualities of profundity, renunciation, pessimism, diffidence, selfishness, concentration, spiritual perseverance, relentless introspection, and self-torment. He is drawn to cold, hard facts, self-knowledge, rules, first principles, and underlying patterns. He shows an occupation with religion, prophecies, the occult, esoterica, dreams, intellectual study, and oracles. He draws boundaries and marks territory, includes this and excludes that.

In alchemy, the element associated with Saturn is lead—the state of mind that is slow, dense, leaden, chronic, depressed, where the will is inhibited. This is not a deficiency in, or lack of, willpower but a confrontation with a contrary and more powerful will than the ego's will. The alchemists knew that the gold of the sun hid in the denseness and chaos of the lead where all light is dulled and all warmth is extinguished.

Saturn realises his creations through the slow passage of time. The alchemical processes of coagulatio, putrefactio and mortificatio eventually produce the *sal saturni*, the bitter salt of wisdom. It is common for a creative period or a numinous experience to be preceded by a period of melancholia. So the way of the senex is one of depression rather than inflation, limitation not expansion, complaint not celebration, suffering not laughter, turning away from the world as opposed to engaging with the world. The role of the Sage is to understand things that have no need or are unable to understand themselves. The introverted seeking of the Sage is godfather to the beauty and meaning of the Temperate Man in the card below. As we shall see in Chapter 24, the two centre cards of the Xultun Tarot, the 9 and 14 cards, have a special role to play in the relationship between spirit and substance.

After the activity of the Warrior and the release of the white bird-soul in the sublimatio of the Cactus, the Sage now coagulates things. He slows them down and mulls them over before the Wheel grinds them up ready to be digested by time and fate. To the alchemists, Saturn was known as the "governor of the prison." The Hermit must be imprisoned in his hermitage, his monkish cell, he must realise the constraints and limitations of his own nature and wait, in what may be a profound and prolonged darkness, until the inner light dawns.

Time

In ancient Greece there were two words for time, *kairos* and *kronos*. Kronos is quantitative, tick-tock, profane, temporal time. Kronos is birthdays, getting older, biological clocks, diaries, deadlines and appointments. We must adapt, time and tide will not wait. We have to immerse ourselves in life in order to get one. We adapt to our collective reality and allow life to make its mark on us. Then, like the children of Kronos, we are eventually eaten by time.

Kairos, however, is sacred, eternal time. It is the right time, the moment of opportunity, the perfect time, the qualitative time, the "now." In the New Testament kairos means "the appointed time in the purpose of God." It is the time when God acts. It cannot be measured, only experienced. In these moments everything "flows" timelessly and without effort. Time stands still, an hour passes in a second, a second stretches to eternity. These moments occur when we draw close to the other world, often in archetypal situations of intense creativity, danger, ecstasy, lovemaking, or death. They transcend kronos and stir emotions and realisations that result in decisive action. "Carpe diem!" (Seize the day!). Then we leave our mark on time itself. Kairos alters destiny and destiny alters kairos. To miss kronos is inconvenient. To miss kairos is tragedy.

The Sage in the Marseilles Tarot is the hermit or the monk. The word monk comes from the Greek *monachos*, meaning single, solitary, or unique, which in turn derives from *monos* meaning alone and *monas* meaning one. In the monk's separation from the outside world he draws closer to himself. In so doing, he is able to notice what is his kairos and what is merely kronos.

Kairos moments (and the dates now become important) are those upon which personal or collective destiny turn. For example, Lincoln's two-minute Gettysburg address in November 1863 where he declared that "government of the people, by the people, for the people, shall not perish from the earth." Churchill's speech to the House of Commons in June 1940 when he said, "This was their finest hour." Kennedy's assassination on November 22, 1963. And 9/11.

Kairos is when our free will choice acts on what life offers us and diverts the stream of collective history or an individual life in unimaginable directions. The next card after the Sage, the Wheel of Fortune, symbolises this chance, luck, opportunity, crisis, fortune or misfortune that is the unpredictability of the Creator's unknowable free will. But to step through the doorway of chance given to us by the Wheel, we first have to be still enough to notice (the Sage) and then quick enough to act (the Balance).

Spirit Mirror

> As far as we can discern, the sole purpose of human existence is to kindle a light in the darkness of mere being. It may even be assumed that just as the unconscious affects us, so the increase in our consciousness affects the unconscious.
>
> —C. G. Jung[9]

> We can make our minds so like still water that beings gather about us so that they may see, it may be, their own images, and so live for a moment with a clearer, perhaps even fiercer life, because of our quiet.
>
> —W. B. Yeats[10]

We have touched several times on the notion of the mirror. With the Sage we now come to a different kind of mirror. Within each thing and between all things there is balance, harmony, alignment and resonance. This harmony and balance is the number 4 which is the number of the Ruler, the first card in the Movement of Stopping the World. The Ruler brings harmony to his domain by coming into resonance and alignment with all the 4s — the four directions, the four seasons, the four worlds, and the four elements. When he is out of harmony the land will not flourish. To restore harmony he must align his own nature with the nature of the cosmos. In doing this the Sage as priest-king performs not only a human function but also a cosmic function. This is the importance of the Sage as one of the two cards, together with the Temperate Man, that are at the centre of the deck.

When we are out of sorts and need rejuvenation we go into retreat. In seclusion and meditation the mind becomes clear. The ancient Taoists saw the original "empty" mind as that organ that is most receptive and can resonate most fully with nature. Chang-Tzu said, "When the perfect man employs his mind, it is a mirror. It conducts nothing and anticipates nothing.... The still mind of the sage is the mirror of heaven and earth — the glass of all things."[11] When a human (5) comes into balance (4) then he can become the pure mirror of the Sage (9). This allows spirit to see itself reflected in the mirror of human consciousness. The temple opening then is not only for the Sage to look out of but also for spirit to look into. This is the cosmic function of humans — to give witness to spirit. For the first time in the tarot, spirit has an "other" in which it can see itself in material form — contained within the temple walls, in the stillness of the mind of the Sage, and made visible by the light of the fire of human consciousness.

Nature of Nine

The light from the Great Zero has now moved outwards 9 times, has seen itself, and returns to itself. As we have seen in Chapter 9, according to the Zero to Nine Law all energy moves in ten movements. The first seven movements are the development of pattern and at the eighth movement the pattern is completed. At the ninth the pattern then breaks apart, creating chaos so that it can return to the source and re-create itself anew. At this ninth movement energy turns around, creates a chaotic pattern of kairos and returns to the completion of 0/10. So the Sage is the completion of the Fool and is the first card where the Zero to Nine Law has expressed itself fully.

The foolishness of the Fool has now turned into its opposite, the thoughtfulness of the Sage. On the shadow side however, just as the Fool was too unconscious so the Sage may be too conscious. His introspection may become over-vigilant awareness. He may develop a destructive lucidity which paralyses every step forward with visions of catastrophe and failure and renders him full of doubt and indecision and unable to move on.

The number 9 sits in the northeast of the Medicine Wheel which is the place of our choices and decisions and how we use energy in our lives. The Sage is a card of timing, of natural cycles and rhythms, knowing when to stop, when to start, when to watch and when to act. It is the ability to use our energy most efficiently ("A stitch in time saves nine") and catch the opportunities and lucky breaks offered by the Wheel. Don Juan described it as catching the "cubic centimetre of chance."

> "There is something you ought to be aware of by now," don Juan said. "I call it the cubic centimeter of chance. Any of us, whether or not we are warriors, have a cubic centimeter of chance that pops out in front of our eyes from time to time. The difference between an average man and a warrior is that the warrior is aware of this, and one of his tasks is to be alert, deliberately waiting, so that when his cubic centimeter pops out he has the necessary speed, the prowess to pick it up. Chance, good luck, personal power, or whatever you may call it, is a peculiar state of affairs. It is like a very small stick that comes out in front of us and invites us to pluck it. Usually we are too busy, or too preoccupied, or just too stupid and lazy to realize that that is our cubic centimeter of luck. A warrior, on

the other hand, is always alert and tight and has the spring, the gumption necessary to grab it."[12]

Nine is the highest attainable by a single number and is the last number before the return to the unity of the 10. It associates to timing and the maximum imaginable as in, "dressed to the nines," "on cloud nine," "the whole nine yards," "nine times out of ten," "a nine-day wonder," or "possession is nine-tenths of the law." Tiresias the seer told Zeus that a woman had nine times as much sexual pleasure as a man. In medieval Wales a dog that had bitten someone could be killed if it was nine steps away from its owner's house, and nine people assaulting one constituted a genuine attack. In German law the ownership of land terminated after the ninth generation. In Mayan the number nine means "to stop, to detain, to limit."[13]

The number nine represents both the end and the beginning of a new cycle. We see this in pregnancy. The mother has the potential to become pregnant (0), she then receives the seed (1), becomes pregnant (2), gives birth after nine months (9), and then returns to 0 again but with a separate other, the baby (1 + 0). After nine months in the womb, we start at the 0 of 10 again.

Nine is a recursive number, in other words it always returns to itself. All nine digits add up to nine ($1 + 2 + 3 + 4 + 5 + 6 + 7 + 8 + 9 = 45 = 9$). Nine added to itself is nine ($9 + 9 = 18 = 9$). Nine multiplied by itself is nine ($9 \times 9 = 81 = 9$). Nine multiplied by any number always equals nine ($9 \times 7 = 63 = 9$; $9 \times 26 = 234 = 9$).

In a circle there are four cardinal and four non-cardinal directions plus the centre which equals nine. In Hinduism the number 9 is revered and considered a complete, perfected and divine number. Nine symbolises completeness in the Bahá'í faith. In the Christian angelic hierarchy there are nine choirs of angels. At the ninth hour of the crucifixion Christ asked God why he had forsaken him. Ramadan, the month of fasting and prayer, is the ninth month of the Islamic calendar. The initiatory Eleusinian Mysteries took nine days. The Romans buried their dead on the ninth day and held a feast, the Novennalia, every ninth year in memory of the dead. Yggdrasil, the World Tree, had nine roots plunging into nine springs, and the nine branches reached toward the nine heavens. Odin hung from the World Tree for nine days and nine nights before he received the wisdom of the Runes. There were nine hells in Dante's Inferno. The River Styx encircled Hades nine times. There are nine planets. A cat is pregnant for nine weeks and has nine lives. There are nine months of pregnancy. At the age of eighty-one we enter the Big East Moon, the Big Moon of Illumination and Enlightenment. The age of eighty-one represents consciousness of pattern (pattern 8 + 1 consciousness = 9 movement), and is nine cycles of nine ($9 \times 9 = 81$).[14]

Jung described nine this way: "Unless the conscious mind intervened, the unconscious would go on sending out wave after wave without result, like the treasure that is said to take nine years, nine months, and nine nights to come to the surface and, if not found on the last night, sinks back to start all over again from the beginning."[15]

Mid-life, Mystery and Renewal

We have seen that Sage is where the energy of the Fool has expressed itself fully for the first time. He has come to the end of the first half of his journey and his introversion is the necessary pause that takes place in mid-life before we start the second half of life. Because the tarot is an archetypal map of development, the term mid-life applies to the middle stage of any significant process within space and time.

And pause he must because the next five cards are ones of chaos, kairos and upheaval before the rebirth of the Temperate Man (14). The trials and challenges of the Wheel (10), the Balance (11), the Hanged Man (12) and the Dead Man (13) form a gap across which he must jump in the journey from culture to individual, substance to spirit, knowledge to wisdom. The jump is the perilous journey, the tipping point, the momentous decision, the defining moment, the point of no return, the crossing of the Rubicon.

The process by which life creates itself is an infinity movement. In Figure 53 we see the two great wheels of the major arcana. The 0 card lies at the centre of both wheels and the 1 card lies at the centre of each wheel (Figure 54). The remaining cards from 2 to 21 are the process of life itself and lie on the infinity movement in a figure eight. The collective, tonal, upper wheel and the individual, nagual lower wheel represent the first and second halves of life and are connected by the 10–13 cards which bridge them.

Life begins with the 2 card, the Priestess, in the southwest of the upper wheel and moves clockwise around to the 9 card, the Sage. Then we travel through the tumultuous transition of the 10 to 13 cards until we reach the resolution of the 14 card. Development then proceeds counter-clockwise around the wheel to the 21 card, Planet Earth, in the northeast of the lower wheel. To complete this infinity movement, the 21 card returns back to the 2 card and a new cycle begins.

Most lives are lived within the comforts and conflicts of the collective in the tonal wheel. Should an individual strike out on their own and if psychic development proceeds then there is a mid-life transition from the Wheel to the Dead Man where the withdrawal of projections occurs. This may be accompanied by a crisis in work or relationships, depression, loss of religious belief and direction, feelings of betrayal, or cynical disappointment with those in authority or those who have been idealised. Indications that the ego has identified with its projections are evident in the person's uncer-

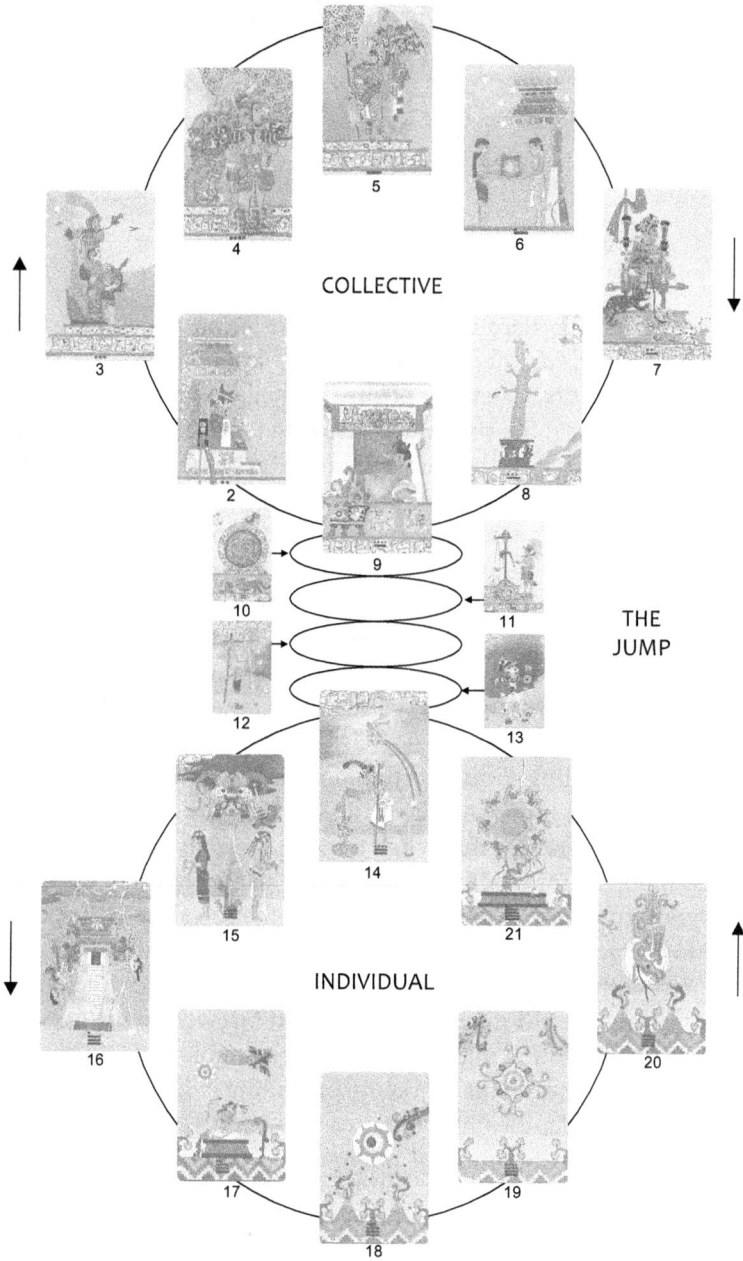

Figure 53. The Jump

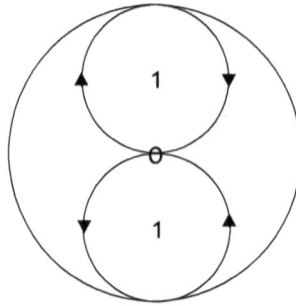

Figure 54. The Wheels of Life (The Infinity Movement)

tainty about limits, the flare-up of brief enthusiasms, quick reversals of opinions and behaviour, and states where elation alternates with depression, all of which characterise a positive or negative inflation. When the projection is withdrawn the previously projected energy flows back to the subject and sinks back into the unconscious. The result is that we feel deflated, depressed, empty, disenchanted, a feeling that we have lost something wonderful, such as when we fall out of love or lose a loved one.

If we make this mid-life crossing successfully we experience a second birth in the Temperate Man (which initially may dress itself up like a second adolescence) and then later in life we are offered the rewards of Kronos who governed the Golden Age. If our development becomes arrested and we fail to negotiate the crossing we gradually become the negative senex or seneca.

Against the prevailing Freudian thinking of his time that focussed on childhood experience, Jung was one of the first to propose that adulthood has its own tasks and he said that when things go wrong in adulthood there is often a common factor where the individual wants "to carry the psychology of the youthful phase over the threshold of the so-called years of discretion.... As formerly the neurotic could not escape from childhood, so now he cannot part with his youth.... So for many people all too much unlived life remains over... an old man who cannot bid farewell to life appears as feeble and sickly as a young man who is unable to embrace it."[16] Over a hundred years after Jung began his work, the prevailing culture still pays more attention to early difficulties in mental or physical development while ignoring the emotional and spiritual retardation that afflicts many in their later years.

The fertility and renewal that we see in the Temperate Man, directly below the Sage, is not possible without the Sage's introversion. From time spent with himself and on himself the Sage gains some wisdom and touches the wellspring of life. He touches the "mysteries" and learns arcane and occult knowledge. But his learning cannot be public knowledge and it must be kept secret from the collective. The mystery, ceremony, or knowledge is not to be named otherwise it is desecrated by being brought out into the glare of public view and subjected to the shallowness of collective scrutiny. Unveiled, the mystery can be spoken about with easy familiarity by those professing wisdom who have not been initiated, who have not earned or learned the knowledge, or who have not paid their dues. Dumbed down by collectivisation, it becomes drained of its numinosity and power for individual transformation.

But what is hidden is, to a certain extent, irrelevant. The act of keeping something hidden points to a strong psychic motive for keeping the secret—the numinous presence of an archetype. The keeping of a secret requires constant attention and awareness and over time this investment of psychic energy allows the unconscious to exert its compensatory effect which brings about a balance that promotes health. The primary manifestation of the mysteries is fertility, health, and growth.[17]

Slowly, the Sage develops insight into his problems rather than solving them. He observes how energy moves rather than bending it to his will like the Warrior. The Warrior has the courage and will to change what can be changed, the Cactus has the strength and patience to endure what cannot be changed, and the Sage has the wisdom to know the difference.

The Wheel
The Spirit of the Adult Substance Shield uses the Mood of
Spiritual Cunning to Control the Mental Dream

The Wheel of Fortune

20

Wheel

writing of fire on the slab of jade,
the cleft in the rock, serpent-goddess and queen,
pillar of cloud, and fountain struck from the stone,
the nest of eagles, the circle of the moon

— Sun Stone by Octavio Paz

God didn't want everything to happen at all at once so he invented time.

— Anon.

Light is time thinking about itself.

— Octavio Paz

Time is light thinking about itself.

— Anon.

The card depicts the Aztec Calendar Stone surrounded by a snake swallowing its own tail, both encircled by Maya glyphs. On top of the stone is a bird and below the wheel is a jaguar nurturing its cub. The stone is held at either side by two small stones.

The Wheel is a symbol of the aeons, the endless cycles of time, and the cycles of incarnation. It is symbolic of the start of a new cycle, or the repetition of an old cycle. It represents rhythm within time and the inevitable turning of all things into their opposites over long periods of time. The Greeks called this *enantiodromia*. In contrast to the Sage, who is concerned with timing and the cycles and rhythms of the individual life span, the Wheel has to do with the greater cosmic rhythms.

Figure 55. Aztec Calendar Stone

Calendar Stone

On December 17, 1760 a huge stone disc was uncovered during the renovation of El Zocalo, Mexico City's central plaza. Afterwards, it was embedded for display in the wall of the west tower of the Metropolitan Cathedral where it remained until 1885 when it was transferred to the National Museum of Anthropology. It weighs almost twenty-five tons, is three feet thick and twelve feet in diameter. Its Aztec name is Cuauhxicalli (Eagle Bowl) but it is universally known as the Aztec Calendar or Sun Stone as it was dedicated to the solar deity (Figures 55 and 56).

The stone is composed of several concentric rings. The innermost ring contains the face of the Sun God Tonatiuh. His tongue, in the form of a sacrificial obsidian knife, protrudes from between his bared teeth, while in each claw-like hand he grasps a human heart.

The second circle from the centre depicts the four "Suns" or epochs each ended by an elemental cataclysm. The First Sun is called Nahui Ocelotl (Four Ocelot or Jaguar) and represents an age where the Earth was inhabited by giants who eventually were devoured by beasts. The Second Sun is called Nahui Ehecatl (Four Wind) and represents an age of agriculture that ended when hurricanes and strong winds swept everything away. The

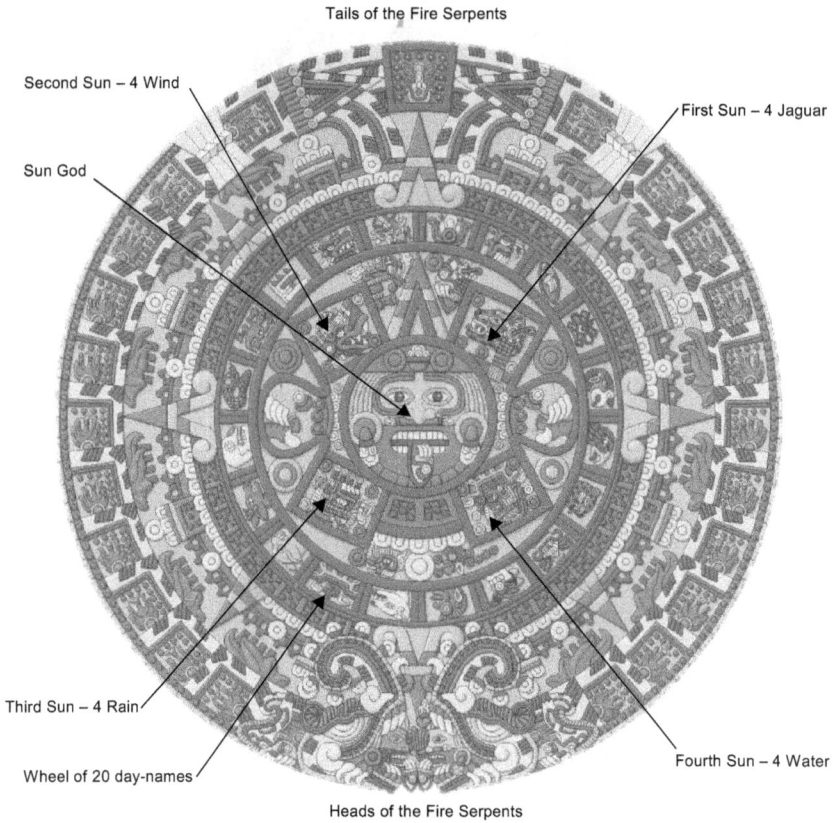

Figure 56. Aztec Calendar Stone

Third Sun is called Nahui Quiauhuitl (Four Fire Rain) and represents an age when cities, temples and pyramids were built only to be destroyed by fire from the interior of the Earth. The Fourth Sun is called Nahui Atl (Four Water) and represents an era when oceans were being navigated by ships and sailors who perished when a great flood covered the whole Earth. The pattern suggests that the world of the Fifth Sun is destined to be destroyed by an earthquake.

The third circle depicts the twenty day-signs of the sacred calendar.

he fourth circle, shaped like a compass rose, depicts the present Sun or age, the Fifth Sun. Inside this circle is contained the calendar itself, the symbols for the four past Suns, and the central face.

The outer circle, fifth from the centre, depicts two Fire Serpents or Xiuhcoatl who represent the universe that surrounds the Earth. They meet face to face at the bottom of the stone. Out of the jaws emerge the Sacred Twins, the Lord of Darkness on the left and the Lord of Light on the right. The bodies of the serpents are divided into 11 sections each bearing an emblem of

Figure 57. The Wheel of Fortune (Visconti-Sforza Tarot)

the maguey plant, making 22 in all.[1] On the head of each serpent is a head-dress with seven stars representing the Pleiades.[2] When the seven sisters of the Pleiades reached the zenith of heaven at midnight the Aztecs held New Fire ceremonies where human sacrifices ensured that the world would go on for another fifty-two years.

Fate

The Wheel of Fortune, or Rota Fortunae, was a concept in medieval philosophy that refers to the capricious nature of fate and destiny. The wheel belongs to the goddess Fortuna who spins it at random like a roulette wheel changing the positions of those on the wheel — some suffer misfortune, others gain good fortune. Shakespeare wrote, "by a cruel trick of fate and a turn of silly Fortune's wildly spinning wheel, that blind goddess who stands upon an ever-rolling stone."[3]

In the Marseilles Tarot this card is called the Wheel of Fortune. In the Visconti-Sforza tarot, a contemporary of the Marseilles deck, four human figures are strapped to the Wheel and forced to endure the successes and humblings of life (Figure 57). The one on the left on his way up is saying *Regnabo* (I shall reign) and he is growing a pair of ass or donkey ears. The figure on top of the wheel has full-grown ears. He says *Regno* (I reign). The figure on his way down has lost his donkey ears and has grown a tail. He says *Regnavi* (I have reigned). Beneath the wheel there is an old man crushed on his hands and knees. He is the only fully human figure of the four and he says *Sum sine regno* (I am without reign). This suggests that in both our inflation and deflation we become an ass and lose our humanness and when we are without power and ambition then we regain it. Fortune is enthroned in the centre of the wheel. She is blindfolded and has a pair of golden wings, indicating both her indifference to human destiny and her divine power to control it.

Oedipus

In the Marseilles Tarot, the goddess Fortuna and the lower figure have been omitted and instead we see three animals. The creature on the right is Anubis, the dog-faced god of Egypt who weighed the souls of the dead. The monkey-like animal on the left is associated with Typhon, the god of destruction and disintegration. At the top is the Sphinx.

In Greek mythology, the Sphinx was a monster with the head and breasts of a woman, the body of a lion, and the wings of a bird. Lying crouched on a rock, she accosted all who were about to enter the city of Thebes by asking them a riddle, "What is it that has four feet in the morning, two at noon, and three at night?" If they could not solve the riddle, she killed them. Oedipus solved the riddle by answering, "Man, who crawls on four limbs as a baby, walks upright on two as an adult, and walks with the aid of a stick in old age." The Sphinx then killed herself. For ridding them of this terrible monster, the Thebans made Oedipus their king and he married Queen Jocasta who, unbeknownst to either of them, was his mother.

Oedipus was the son of Laius and Jocasta, king and queen of Thebes. Laius was warned by the oracle of Apollo at Delphi that he would be killed by his own son. Determined to avert his fate, Laius pierced and bound together the feet of his newborn child and left him to die on a lonely mountain. The infant was rescued and given the name Oedipus (swollen foot). The King of Corinth raised him as his own son. Oedipus did not know he was adopted, and when an oracle proclaimed that he would kill his father, he left Corinth. In the course of his wanderings he met and killed Laius, believing that the king and his followers were a band of robbers, thus unwittingly fulfilled the prophecy. When Oedipus discovered who Jocasta was she killed herself and Oedipus put out his own eyes.

The story of Oedipus and the Wheel of Fortune reminds us that, despite our smarts and intellect, there is no dodging fate or outwitting the laws of the universe. What goes around, comes around and chance and fate will be the corrective for under- or over-reaching ourselves.

In the Mythic Tarot this card shows the Fates or Moirae of Greek mythology on the Wheel of Fortune. These three goddesses, daughters of Kronos, determined human destiny. At birth, the Fates apportioned to each person their lot and were often portrayed in art and poetry as stern old women or sombre maidens who were weavers. Clotho, the Spinner, spun the thread of life; Lachesis, the Dispenser of Lots, decided its span and assigned a destiny to each person; and Atropos, the Inexorable, carried the shears that cut the thread of life at the appointed time. Even the gods could not alter the decisions of the Fates.

Individual destiny, real or perceived, is the "bullet that has your name on it," the moment "when your number is up," or the love "that was meant to be." Destiny can also be collective as the "elect of the faithful," the "chosen people," or John Calvin's Divine Providence and its Puritan American step-child, Manifest Destiny. This historical belief, from the early 1800s onwards, held that the United States was ordained by the Christian God to expand westward across North America. In 1845 John O'Sullivan wrote, "Other nations have tried to check... the fulfillment of our manifest destiny to overspread the Continent allotted by Providence for the free development of our yearly multiplying millions." Believers held that the invasion and colonisation of indigenous lands was not only good, but that it was obvious ("manifest") and ordained ("destiny").

Wheel

The Wheel is a symbol of the process of walking around something — an idea, oneself, an event — so that all sides can be seen. This is the way the Creator sees. The Sage has become aware of the hidden inner patterns behind the seeming disorder of life. In the Wheel, he now becomes aware of the outer patterns and the connections between his inner world and the cosmic patterns. This union between outer and inner leads eventually to the formation of the Philosopher's Stone of the alchemists. This is the unique version of our fate that is an amalgam of the universal forces and our own life choices and circumstances. The roundness of the Wheel and the Stone emerges again in the Planet Earth card which is the Philosopher's Stone in its fullness.

The Wheel is the archetype of time, fate, chance, Lady Luck, karma and the mysterious workings of the universe and it is the ego's first encounter with things beyond its control. The Western heroic attitude spurns the notion of fate and so the archetype becomes split. On the one hand, we have the New Age notion that we create our own reality or the Puritan ethos that all things are possible if we have enough hard work or enough hard faith. On the other hand, we have the fatalistic scientific fantasy that the universe is a grand accident. Between these two extremist views is the observation of

Figure 58. Mixtec bird (Codex Nuttall)

the Twisted Hairs that eighty percent of all energy has recognisable pattern which can be predicted and to some extent "controlled." But twenty percent of all energy movement has no pattern at all. Its only pattern is that it has no pattern. It is the result of the Creator exercising its unknowable free will to birth itself into new forms. Because the Creator never repeats itself this pattern occurs only once and we are unable to compare it to other events and establish a regularity that enables us to see what we call a pattern.

In other words, we experience this as chance or chaos. It is what we cannot control or foresee. Jung referred to something similar when he said, "God is the name by which I designate all things which cross my wilful path, violently and recklessly, all things which upset my subjective views, plans and intentions and change the course of my life for better or worse."[4] In the encounter between ego and fate, one of them has to lose and it won't be fate. So there is a humiliating and humbling effect on the ego. If it changes its past-its-prime, heroic attitude toward fate, and works with not against the laws of the universe, then the Wheel becomes the Holder of the Mood of Spiritual Cunning and the Teacher of Controlling the Mental Dream.

At the centre of the Wheel are the Universal Laws and at the periphery is the human application of those laws.[5] In the Calendar Stone we see the glyphs for the four great ages at the centre and at the circumference are the day-signs symbolising time on a more human scale. Now that we have travelled around the outside of the wheel in the first half of life we are about to spiral into the centre to confront the universal laws of life. To do this we must apprentice to a body of knowledge that has depth and tradition, holds accumulated wisdom about these laws and has been tested over many generations. In so doing, we are able to widen our perspectives, gain knowledge, and view life from all points around the Medicine Wheel. So below the stone we see the jaguar, the Keeper of Memory of the old cycle, passing on its oral knowledge to the baby jaguar of the new cycle.

Figure 59. The Fires-from-within in the Sage and Balance cards

The Self can take on many forms. Or rather, it uses countless images to express itself to the conscious mind. Because it is generally so far removed from consciousness it can only be partially expressed by human figures (father, mother, king, queen, goddess or god, for example). Accordingly, it expresses itself in animal symbols (dragon, snake, bull, or bear, for example), plant or mineral symbolism, or abstract geometric forms. In the Wheel we see the Self, not only as the stone, but also as the young quetzal bird setting off from the top of the Calendar Stone with its tail almost touching the snake. For the Maya, birds were sky-snakes and in Mixtec codices they are often drawn with the body of a snake (Figure 58).

This image is a more differentiated version of the white bird we saw sitting on the Cactus. The snake, and the transpersonal energy it represents, is wrapped around the stone indicating that it is still embedded in matter and contained within space and time. Matter (the snake) and spirit (quetzal bird) are not yet separated and the relationship to the Self is still unconscious. As we have seen, this triad of the bird, the snake and the stone in the 10 card repeats itself in the most differentiated form in the Planet Venus (20) card as the Feathered Winged Serpent descending to earth.

Fire

In Chapter 9, The Loom of Time, we discussed the significance of platforms as a preparation for coming developments. If we look at the Sage, Wheel and Balance cards we see that they all stand on a platform (Figure 59). The Wheel is framed on either side by similar configurations related to fire. First, the Balance is in the same spatial relationship to the scales in front of him as the Sage is to the fire in his urn. Second, the element of fire emanates from both cards—the smoke from the fire spreads down and across the Adult Spirit Shield cards and the lightning bolts from the Balance's wand go straight down. Third, both the smoke and lightning meet in the Released Man card below. These images suggest that when the knowledge of the Sage encounters the chaos of the Wheel it creates a conflagration. Being close to chaos and the ways in which the Mystery moves generates powerful spiritual forces of transformation. It's a fire-starter and things heat up. It galvanises the Balance into electrifying action that will have far-reaching consequences that only become apparent in the course of time in the Released Man.

The Sage is able to forgo the attractions of the outer world because his inner world is so rich and compelling. Intentional withdrawal, solitude and hermitic retreat powerfully activate his inner life. When this light of consciousness is focussed on the tinder of the unconscious, it sparks and flames. The red smoke coming from the brazier is the product of this inner fire. This spiritual fire irrupts from the unconscious when we observe ourselves. It later becomes the lightning (fire in its most powerful form) that crackles through the air bridging earth and sky when the Balance consciously aligns his will with the will of the Creator.

The Wheel is the transformative point between these two forms of fire — the introverted personal fire of the Sage and the extroverted transpersonal fire of the Balance. The Wheel is the peculiarity of our fate that become apparent after the solitude of the Sage. The Spirit of the Child Substance Shield was mediated by the Priest. Now, spirit is experienced directly (but in its impersonal form) by the Spirit of the Adult Substance Shield as the Wheel.

Both these things, fire and fate, give birth to the spiritual memory of the 11 card. This is the gradual remembering of who we are, where we come from and where we are going. Its development is prefigured by the jaguar, the Keeper of Memory, feeding its cub at the base of the Wheel. The process of aligning our Fire-from-within (the Sage and the Balance) with the vast forces of the cosmos (the Wheel) to create our unique Path with Heart is what Nietzsche called *amor fati*, or love of one's fate. He said we must, "Not merely bear what is necessary, still less conceal it — but love it."

In his autobiography, written in his early eighties, Jung said, "It was only after the illness [his near-fatal heart attack in 1944 at the age of sixty-eight] that I understood how important it is to affirm one's own destiny. In this way we forge man ego that does not break down when incomprehensible things happen; an ego that endures, that endures the truth, and that is capable of coping with the world and fate. Then, to experience defeat is to experience victory. Nothing is disturbed — neither outwardly nor inwardly, for one's continuity has withstood the current of life and time. But that can come to pass only when one does not meddle inquisitively with the workings of fate."[6]

The Balance
The Soul of the Adult Substance Shield uses the Mood of
Soul Cunning to Assume Mental Authority

Justice

21

Balance

Choose what you will and pay for it.

—Spanish proverb

Man was created for the sake of choice.

—Hebrew proverb

It falls exclusively to the lot of human consciousness to perform the crucial action, even if consciousness fundamentally lacks the power to do so without the help of the almighty helper. This is the cosmic role that is allotted to the conscious mind in spite of its frailty.

—Alfred Ribi

The trouble with normal is it always gets worse.

—*The Trouble with Normal*, Bruce Cockburn

A man stands at the end of the dais in front of a balance that has only one arm. He has a club or sword in his right hand from which comes forked lightning. One fork strikes the skull at the base of the balance; the other continues down through the Released Man card and ends in the Planet Earth card. The Balance is the fulcrum, the mid-point of the deck. Here the frail but potent agency of human choice will determine left or right, this or that, in or out, friend or foe.

Scales of Justice

The image is of Nun Yax Ayin, the father of Stormy Sky whom we have already seen in the Sorcerer and Ruler cards. It is taken from the side of Stela 31 at Tikal where he is shown in war costume with a flexible shield draped over his left arm and a spear thrower (an *atlatl*) in his right hand (Figure 60).[1]

Figure 60. Detail of right side, Stela 31, Tikal

In the Marseilles Tarot this card is Justice. In Greek mythology, justice is associated with the goddesses Themis and Athena. Themis was one of the Titans, a daughter of Uranus and Gaia, and mother of the Moirae. She was the goddess of divine law and was Zeus's counsellor. She sat blindfold in Hades and judged the souls of the dead. We see her image in courtrooms and on top of the Old Bailey in London where she sits holding the scales of justice. The blindfold symbolises her being blind to the senses and not swayed by worldly circumstances or personae, so that the law is applied equally to all.

Athena was born fully formed from the forehead of Zeus after Hephaistos split open Zeus' head with a bronze axe. She was a goddess who favoured great heroes and, although warlike, she undertook battles for principles rather than passions. She was the goddess of logic, diplomacy, cleverness, planning and foresight. Athena embodies the human capacity for reflective judgement, balanced thought, impartiality, objectivity, cool-headed decision-making, and evaluating matters based on abstract principles. She was virginal and born, not from the body of her mother, but from the head of her father. So Athena symbolises the capacity for rational thought undisturbed by personal feeling or physical desires.

In many mythologies, scales symbolise judgement or justice. Saint Michael the Archangel holds the scales on judgement Day. In Egyptian mythology, the jackal-headed god Anubis weighed the souls of the deceased on a pair of scales. The heart of the dead person was put on one pan and on the other an ostrich feather symbolising Maat, the Goddess of Truth. If the scales did not balance then the soul was returned to matter — the monster Ammit (part crocodile, part lion, part hippopotamus) devoured the heart. If the scales balanced then the deceased was ushered into the presence of Osiris and eternal life.

These mythologies of the final judgement have their equivalent in the inner world in an anticipated encounter between the Self and the ego. The unprepared ego is shriven of any pretensions, pride, or arrogance and experiences anxiety, fear and terror. Maat's scale is like the lie detector in the encounter between the ego and the Self. At the end of the day we cannot lie to ourselves — the Self will not allow dishonesty that violates the soul. But we are endlessly self-deceiving and most forms of psychoanalysis and psychotherapy are in some way charged with the task of uncovering our self-deceptions, our not-so-innocent naiveties, our predestined betrayals of our own cherished ideals, our painful truths that we have forgotten, and our secret meetings with ourselves to forget that we have forgotten. Psychotherapy is not about alleviating symptoms or becoming better adapted but rather about developing the capacity to suffer, experience, and enjoy truth — the truth about oneself and the truth about others. As a result, life goes better. As in the Egyptian scene of the afterlife, this truthfulness, this self-knowledge, this knowledge of the Self, gives us eternal life — a lasting sense of something deep within us that sustains life, both in life and beyond life.

Sword of Separation

Aztec and Maya warriors carried weapons such as the *chimalli* (the round shield in the Dead Man card), the *tlauitolli* (the bow), the *atlatl* (spear-thrower) and a wooden sword called a *macuahuitl*. The Balance holds a single-edged, curved macuahuitl like the one in Figure 61. The macuahuitl was made of obsidian flakes embedded along the length of a piece of wood. It could be curved, straight, pointed, single-edged, double-edged, one-handed or two-handed.[2] The two-handed, double-sided macuahuitl could be as tall as a man.

Obsidian is a volcanic glass and consists mainly of silicon dioxide (SiO_2), usually 70% or more. The Maya believed that obsidian was made when lightning struck the earth.[3] Its colour varies from a dark green to brown to a

Figure 61. Mixtec obsidian club (Codex Nuttall)

smoky translucent black. Obsidian can be napped easily and because it has no crystalline structure and has a cutting edge many times sharper than steel. Obsidian blades have been used in cardiac surgery. Under an electron microscope even the sharpest metal knife has a jagged edge whereas an obsidian blade is smooth and even. However, a steel blade holds its edge much better than an obsidian blade which, with its thin and brittle edge, becomes dull very quickly.

The sword is a symbol of separation, division and decision and is often associated with lightning. Japanese ceremonial swords were said to originate in lightning and the Vedic sword was Indra's thunderbolt that cut through the darkness of ignorance.

Division, multiplication, measuring, numbering and weighing are all associated with the alchemical process of separatio. Space and time arose out of the original chaos only through an act of division. In many creation myths the world parents lie so closely together that nothing can come into existence and the first act of creation is the violent separation of the divine couple. In order to create we must divide and kill the original unity and oneness though an act of sacred violence so that new life may be lived.

The sword is the symbol of clarity and knowing. It cuts through ambivalence and confusion to the heart of the matter. Knives and blades represent the discriminating power of consciousness that breaks up and dismembers the unconscious monster, making its power available to the ego. Although etymologically unrelated, the words "sword" and "word" are similar. Both the pen and the sword have the potential to wound and cut for good or for ill. The sword of the mind, Logos, separates out what has been mixed up. This brings clarity but also conflict because now the opposites have been made conscious. Mental confusion is often a defence against the awareness of emotional conflict.

Psychologically, what often needs separation is ourselves and the other onto whom we have projected part of our own psyche. Thus, the death or loss of a lover, spouse, parent, or child is an important step in our journey. With the death of someone we have shared deep intimacy with either as a child or an adult, the glue that held two bodies and two psyches together is pulled apart. The tearing of the glue is not only mourning the loss of the other but also mourning the loss of the part of ourselves that we had hidden inside them.

We encounter the Balance most often when we have to make an important choice. Should I move? Should I divorce? Should I take another job? Should I marry? Ambivalence often arises from a lack of separation between oneself and the other, or a lack of differentiation between the symbolic and literal meanings of an action. The ego is in uncharted territory: "I want to, but I shouldn't" or "I have to, but I don't want to." A physical move ("the geographical cure") may be an attempt to resolve a situation where there is too little emotional distance. A psychological divorce may be needed but not necessarily a literal one. Once the sword of feeling judgement has separated the symbolic and literal meanings then the decision becomes easier.

If the situation can be resolved by rationally weighing the pros and cons, all well and good. If this solves the problem then the decision has already been made for us by outer realities and we are let off the hook. However, when the pros and cons are evenly balanced then the ego must search for another way rather than using the cheap merchant trick of tallying costs and benefits, getting out the markers and whiteboard, or resorting to ready-made rules. Now the ego needs to hold the tension between the opposites so that a never-before-seen third can be born. Jung called this the "transcendent function" because it transcends the conflict of the opposites. In cases where two decisions or actions, both equally distasteful or equally attractive to the ego, collide with one another, the moral code (or whatever code the ego values) fails because the situation is utterly individual. Jung said:

> The deciding factor appears to be something else: it proceeds not from the traditional moral code but from the unconscious foundation of the personality.... It is true that these conflicts of duty are solved very often and very conveniently by a decision in accordance with custom, that is, by suppressing one of the opposites.... If one is sufficiently conscientious the conflict is endured to the end and a creative solution emerges which is produced by the constellated archetype and possesses that compelling authority not unjustly characterised as the voice of God... it embraces conscious and unconscious and therefore transcends the ego.[4]

From an objective point of view either way could be wrong (or right) but from the subjective viewpoint of our feeling values only one way is right. The right way may only emerge in hindsight after many years of reflection and conflict over the decision. This is the image of the Hanged Man which follows the Balance card. These agonising decisions touch our soul or come from our soul and demand much "soul searching." So the Balance is the

Keeper of the Soul of the Adult Substance Shield, the Holder of the Mood of Soul Cunning and the psychological type of soul thinking.

Often there is no mysterious "right" way, instead we create a life woven from the innumerable threads of small decisions and we make ourselves up as we go along. We have to make decisions of the heart without "all the facts" — as if more facts would help. But they are often a sign of a too-rational approach that further removes one from the nub of the matter (later to become the crux of the matter in the Hanged Man) and confuse the issue with too much external reality. Then analysis leads to paralysis.

The ego must decide anyway — and live with the consequences. The Sorcerer (1) is the application of the will of the ego to the form of substance using the wand of power. The Balance (11) is the application of the will of the Self to the movement of spirit using the sword of decision. In both cases, having made the decision the ego must then take responsibility for that decision and its impact on the world. A human being with the capacity for conscious reflection rather than driven, unconscious action naturally judges their actions, weighing individual freedom versus the common good, earthly justice versus karmic justice, immediate gratification versus postponement of desires, and the literal versus the symbolic meanings of an action. However, with a fateful decision this is not a bloodless and abstract reflection — some impact on the world always flows from this card. The Balance is the Teacher of Assuming Mental Authority and when the soul decides the world is changed.

Ultimately, because the free will of the Creator is unknowable, one cannot know if one's decision is right or wrong or what impact it will have, now or seven generations from now. Therefore, all one can do is choose and take responsibility for that decision... and that is more than sufficient. By assuming the burden of his responsibility and claiming his own authority for what he does or does not do, the Balance uses the sword of discrimination to cut away any illusions about who is responsible for his life.

The dominant collective protects individuals from the responsibility of the free will choices that the Balance makes. Because the archetype cannot find its proper place in the individual who assumes their own authority it has to live in a divided form in the collective. As a result we see the familar political splits betwen right and left. The right wants less government interference, less taxes and more biggy-business. The left wants more controls, more taxes and more nanny-state. But both are are equally unstable as there is no transcendent third, leading to a swing between the opposites over historical time. When the investment banks explode the wailing for corporate welfare begins. When the socialist economies implode the free market vultures float to the top.

The ego must be willing to exercise judgement and to choose with as much consciousness as it can muster about what is chosen and what is left behind to die. More difficult still, consciousness must also take responsibility for the unconscious and what it does not know about itself. As in a court of law, so it is in the psyche — ignorance or unconsciousness is not a defence. Sooner or later, we have to take responsibility for what we are not responsible for. In the next card, the Hanged Man, the ego will be crucified and experience the full reality of the Balance's decisions.

Judgement and Grief

The Balance holds the sword midway between his head and his heart. The cool judgement of the Balance comes from the marriage of the thinking heart and the feeling head and decisions are made with both. His sword is so sharp it cuts things together not apart.[5] But this is not the heart that haemorrhages at the sight of another's pain nor convulsively bestows forgiveness on another's irresponsibility. Those who are promiscuously "non-judgemental" often harbour a multitude of unconscious judgements about themselves or others and compensate by spraying judgement in all directions in an acceptable form as "forgiveness." And I speak here not of the hard-won forgiveness that comes from years of wrestling with ourselves but of oily, ego-driven, religiose forgiveness.

This dialectic between thinking and feeling is a creative act of individual ethical decision that in the end serves both self and other. The Balance's judgement has integrity. It is detached and has objectivity. It truly considers the other, including itself, as a separate object in a feeling way. This detachment allows us to be truthful, gives us the courage to pronounce the sentence, to speak the fateful words that heal or divide, and to not retreat from the edge — all qualities of Soul Ruthlessness. James Hillman writes:

> Sometimes we forget that the application of law by a judge is an operation of feeling, and that laws were invented not merely to protect property or assure the priesthood and ruling-class of their power, but also to evaluate difficult human problems and to do justice in human affairs. Judging is a matter of feeling, just as in the temples of Saturn a balance was displayed, or as Saturn in a horoscope is said to be well-placed when in the sign of Libra. A Solomonic decision is not one brilliant stroke through the Gordian knot of complexities, but rather a judgement made by following the labyrinth of feeling to the "right" solution. Law concerns "cases," considers "claims" and "obligations" and by means of it one can make "appeals." The Bill of Rights is a document of the feeling function at its abstract best.[6]

The detachment of the Balance comes not from a failure in caring, but from a caring resilient enough to withstand the tension between moral reac-

tion and unbiased observation. Clifford Geertz said, "To judge without understanding, constitutes an offence against morality; to understand while
retaining the responsibility to judge teaches humility and wisdom." Morality, legal or otherwise, is imposed on the human soul by the human soul.
The Balance is concerned with judgement that brings about balance, not in
the sense of exactness but in the sense of beauty and harmonious proportion. This judgement can only come about when there is sufficient justice, in
other words a relationship with the Self, constellated in the psyche of the
individual.

We can see in the card that one fork of the lightning coming from the
wand ends in death (the skull) and the other fork ends in life (the Planet
Earth card). The word decide has the same root as suicide or homicide
(Latin, *caedere,* meaning to cut or strike). A decision always involves a death
of something, sometime, somewhere. So the decision that flows from the
Balance card is also the beginning of death, grief and mourning. All conscious decision destroys innocence and the lightning ending in the skull is
the road not taken. The skull symbolises the loss that always comes with
decision and the death of limitless possibilities.

In using our free will to choose, we give birth to twins — the road taken
and the road not taken. The choice may be difficult (and indeed, if it is easy
then the choice has not involved the whole personality) and often attended
by great longing for the road not taken. There is a wrenching loss, regrets,
nostalgia, melancholy, and "If only…" One twin is taken home, the other is
left to die; a light twin and a shadow twin. Unless we make this choice
(knowing that we'll get it wrong) and unless we mourn then the shadow
twin sinks into the unconscious or, we might say, becomes part of the
shadow dream.

In every decision there are two forces. One is the desire or intent (the
spirit) behind the decision, the other is the manifestation (the body or form)
of the desire. The ego may insist on a particular form to the desire ("I want
this kind of job/partner/relationship") and blinded by its insistence it
misses a thousand other forms of the same desire. If the desire does not
manifest in the imagined form, the ego, feeling betrayed and hurt by life, at-
tacks and banishes both the desire and the form. The form evaporates and
was of no consequence in the first place. However, the disowned desire
("I'll never want/need/aim for X ever again") is set loose in the dream like
a lost spirit looking for the body that has not had a proper burial. It becomes
a psychic free radical, so to speak. If we can unlink desire and form, and not
have them yoked together by the ego, then we allow life to give form to our
desire in its own way. If we sacrifice the form (and this may be half a life's
work) and retain the intent, we can bury the body and recycle the desire. To
Assume Authority we need to know where the bodies of desire are buried
and mourn them consciously.[7]

Connecting Link with Intent

Matter seeks spirit and spirit seeks matter. So it is with conscious and unconscious. They will not tolerate estrangement for too long. If the artery between them is sclerotic then either the lower regions of matter or the higher realms of spirit will exert a compensatory influence to break through the blockage, get the ego's attention, and bring about a more functional connection. If the ego is too big for its boots then "lower" symptoms offensive to the ego will emerge (depression, anxiety, or sexual problems for example). If the ego is too small for its boots then "higher" symptoms uplifting to the ego will emerge (mystical experiences or flashes of inspiration). Like the Warrior coming after the Lovers and the Bound Man coming after the Temperate Man, the Hanged Man and the Dead Man come as compensation for the lightning-bolt of illumination in the Balance. The psychological "rule" is that every change, unless it brings one closer to one's own nature, will turn into its opposite over time until the personality is distill to its essence. "White light" experiences will be followed by a descent, or an addiction will be "cured" by a religious conversion.

Whatever might follow, the lightning bolt of illumination does connect us to the Self. This often brings about a decisive act of judgement and we make significant changes in our life. However, the opposite is also true—that an act of judgement can bring about a lightning bolt connection with the Self. Either way, the Balance signifies the establishment of this ego-self axis or the connecting link with intent.[8] This is the "justice" in the card. We now come under the rule of law, not societal or religious law but the higher authority of the Self. Now the ego is strong enough to receive the Self and carry the rights and responsibilities that flow from this encounter. However, Jung cautioned against wanting to know more of the unconscious than one gets through dreams and intuition. He said that the more one knows the greater the ethical burden because the knowledge becomes one's individual obligation and responsibility when it enters consciousness.[9]

If we look at the Balance card, we can see that there is no other side to the scales—the man *is* the other side. The separation that the Balance has brought about with his sword of decision includes a renunciation of his membership in the mass of humankind. He is now a world unto himself. Edward Edinger said, "Collective thinking is revealed by preoccupation with whether or not one is normal. To the extent that one is a separate, unique world of being there can be no norms, since a norm is the average of many. The individual psyche is and must be a whole world within itself in order to stand over and against the outer world and fulfil its task of being a carrier of consciousness. For the scales to be balanced, the individual must be of equal weight to the world."[10] And Jung said, "So long as the self is unconscious, it corresponds to Freud's superego and is a source of perpetual

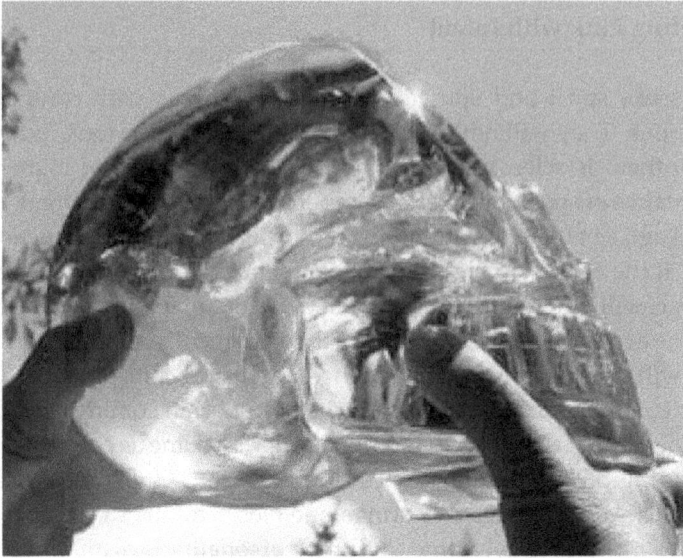

Figure 62. A human-size citrine quartz crystal skull

moral conflict. If, however, it is withdrawn from projection and is no longer identical with public opinion, then one is truly one's own yea and nay."[11]

The Balance is the last card in the row of the Adult Substance Shield which begins and ends with a tension of opposites—the black and white jaguars of the Warrior card and the scales of the Balance card. This row forms the adult ego. The row begins with the Warrior, then proceeds through Strength, Knowledge, Fate, and ends with Justice—all qualities that one needs to be able to forge an ego that can engage with the conflicts and paradoxes of life.

Crystal Skulls

Just as the number 1 is about the tonal consciousness and the light of Grandfather Sun so the number 11 is about nagual consciousness and the illumination of all the Great Grandfather Stars. The tarot is about regaining memory, in other words consciousness, in both spirit and substance (2 x 11 = 22). Humans are the only child of Grandmother Earth that has forgotten their connection with creation and we spend our whole lives trying to remember it. After travelling through the first ten cards the Fool has gotten some life and living under his belt. At the end of the second row of cards, when we are well established in our lives, when our ground is prepared enough to receive it from above, comes the spark that jumps the gap between spirit and matter. It is the lightning bolt of illumination that awakens the memory of who we are, where we have come from and where we are going. In psy-

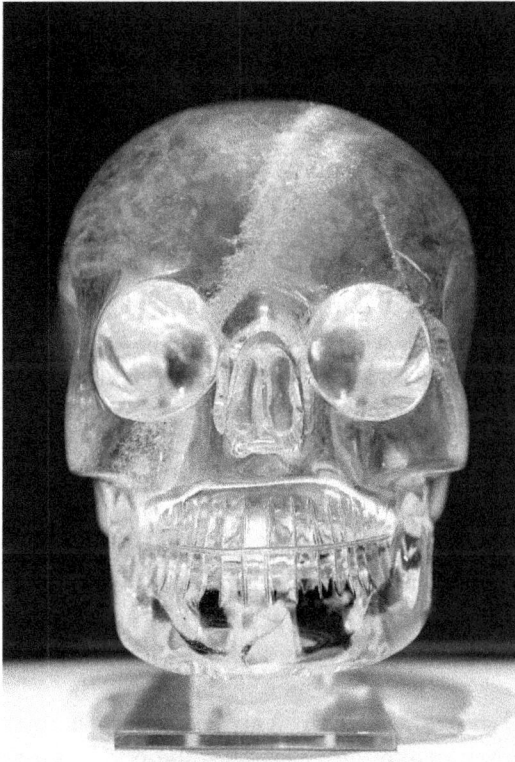

Figure 63. The British Museum crystal skull

chological language, it means the awakening of the connection with the Self.

"There are two distinct ways in which consciousness arises," Jung said. "The one is a moment of high emotional tension.... The other is a state of contemplation, in which ideas pass before the mind like dream-images. Suddenly there is a flash of association between two apparently disconnected and widely separated ideas, and this has the effect of releasing a latent tension. Such a moment often works like a revelation. In every case it seems to be the discharge of energy-tension, whether external or internal, which produces consciousness."[12]

For the Maya, enlightenment was not the slow, pastel dawning of peace and realisation, like watching paint dry, but the lightning strike that split the soul asunder. In Maya iconography birthing and creation were often shown as the god K'awil being struck by lightning in the head, or having a smoking axehead or torch striking him in the brain. It was the lightning of K'awil that blasted open the Black Dreaming Place and the Ol portals into the other world.[13] In his poem "No Joy in Life," D. H. Lawrence wrote:

Never will you know any joy in your lives
till you ask for lightning instead of love
till you pray to the right gods, for the
thunder-bolt instead of pity.

The fateful choices that the Balance makes will determine if and how he will continue through the next ten cards to remember his connection with all of creation. We see this foreshadowed in the forked bolt of lightning. One fork ends in a crystal skull at the base of the scales, the other travels through the Released Man card down to the Planet Earth card.

The human skull universally symbolises what survives after death. It is the immortal part of the human psyche that is the distillation of a life lived consciously. After death this remains as spiritual memory in the collective unconscious. The crystal skull (Figures 62 and 63) is a symbol of this marriage between spirit and matter in the human psyche and the capacity to remember what is not here any more.

The crystal skulls help us to overcome our spiritual amnesia so we can feed a time beyond our own. As we near the close of the Fifth Age and the year 2012, at a time when the Holy Female who Suckles All Life has been taken for granted by the terrorists of annual growth and progress, when those who still hear her Heart with their indigenous ear have been strip-mined of their ceremonies that keep the Body of the World in good health, when matter has been enslaved for human consumption, our culture needs a remedy for this amnesia that keeps us crazed with longing, a healing that will bring us in from the cold of our spiritual exile from the warmth of matter.

One legend tells of thirteen Singing Skulls—a wheel of twelve clear quartz skulls and one amethyst skull at the centre, all surrounded by an outer wheel of twelve Talking Skulls. A Singing Skull has a separate moveable jaw, while a Talking Skull has a fixed jaw.[14] The British Museum skull is a Talking Skull and the Mitchell-Hedges skull is a Singing Skull. Anna Mitchell-Hedges (1907–2007) was born in Port Colborne, Ontario and was a long-time resident of Kitchener, Ontario. She kept the skull on the living room coffee table in her suburban home and also travelled extensively with it. As she tells the story, she discovered the skull on her seventeenth birthday. She was with her father, an archaeologist and explorer, on an expedition to Lubaantun in British Honduras (now Belize), a Maya site he had discovered in 1924. Anna noticed something reflecting the sunlight underneath the rubble of one of the ruins. After six weeks of moving stones and debris, the top part of the skull was brought out of the ruined temple. Three months later, the lower jaw was found in the same location.

The crystal skulls are the repository of our spiritual memory, the knowledge and illumination from all Great Grandfather Stars. When the Star Nations peoples came to this world they brought with them a stellar heritage: the knowledge from all the Twelve Worlds, the twelve planets in this south universe that have human life, together with the wisdom of their Great Grandfather Suns. This knowledge was brought down into matter and encoded in skulls made of quartz ("lightning-in-the-earth"). Quartz is one of the hardest minerals known and the second most common in the earth's crust. All crystals are the brain cells of Grandmother Earth. As lightning-in-the-earth they hold a key to the spiritualisation of matter and the materialisation of spirit, the marriage of spirit and matter which creates life that lives in balance and harmony.

The crystal skulls hold the hope and knowledge needed for the evolution of Two-leggeds on this Planet of the Children. Hope is the capacity to dream a better future for all the Children: the winds, the whales, the trees, the waters, the sands, the spores, the honey badgers, the albatross and the invisible salt of the sea. This hope was brought here by the Star Nations People from the other planets with human life. They dreamed themselves here and imaged their spirit, their knowledge, into matter—quartz skulls made in the image of what is quintessentially human.

The crystal skull symbolises the conscious human being who uses the free will of fallible human judgement in alignment with the laws of both substance and spirit and brings down the lightning bolt of death and change which allows new life to be born. The crystal skulls, made with the permanence of the hardest matter, invisibly transparent with spirit, and in the form of what is irreducibly human, keep alive the Memory of the First Breath of what is not yet born.

Here we end the cards of the Substance Shields and begin the cards of the Spirit Shields.

The Hanged Man
The Heart of the Adult Spirit Shield uses the Mood of Emotional
Ruthlessness to Erase Physical History

The Hanged Man

22

Hanged Man

Pain is inevitable. Suffering is optional.

—Kathleen C. Theisen

Art is the tree of life. Science is the tree of death.

—William Blake

Grief drives men into habits of serious reflection, sharpens the understanding and softens the heart.

—John Adams, letter to Thomas Jefferson

We would rather be ruined than changed.
We would rather die in our dread
Than climb the cross of the present
And let our illusions die.

—W. H. Auden

In the Hanged Man we see a person hanging upside down. The left arm
and leg are tied to a gibbet or hangman's tree, and the right arm and leg
are tied to a living tree that is in blossom. The body radiates a glow and the
blue sky is overcast w0ith red storm clouds. The dead tree and the live tree
grow from a green, fertile plain. The image of the Hanged Man is the
sacrifice of a captive of war to the Maya god Xipe Totec. He was tied to a
scaffold and pierced with arrows so his blood drained to the ground (Figure 64).

Crucifixion

Those unfamiliar with the tarot will often turn the Hanged Man around so
he is "right" side up. When we do this we see the similarity to a crucifixion
(Figure 65). The mythologem of being sacrificially hung from a tree,

Figure 64. Sacrifice to Xipe Totec (Codex Nuttall)

speared and spilling blood, is a common one. Christ was crucified on a wooden cross and pierced by the lance of the Roman soldier, Longinus.[1] (Calvary, the site of the crucifixion, is described by Biblical sources as a little knoll, small hill or a mount. We can see in Figure 109 that the Hanged Man is raised up on a slight hill above the level green plain of the other cards in the row). The Egyptian god Osiris was entombed in a tamarisk tree. The Sumerian goddess Inanna was hung on a meat hook in the underworld. In his search for wisdom, Odin, the god of wisdom, poetry and magic, hung for nine nights upon the Yggdrasil, the World Tree, pierced by a spear, without food or water. On the ninth night he saw the reflection of the runes in the water. The word "rune" means "whisper" or "secret wisdom" and according to the *Leder Edda*, the poetic saga of the Norse Gods, the Runic alphabet was a gift from Odin.

> Wounded I hung on wind-swept gallows
> For nine long nights
> Pierced by a spear, pledged to Odin
> Offered, myself to myself.

Hair symbolises both mental activity — thoughts that grow from the head — and wisdom. The Hanged Man's hair is unbound, unfettered by collective beliefs and concepts. It hangs downwards almost touching the

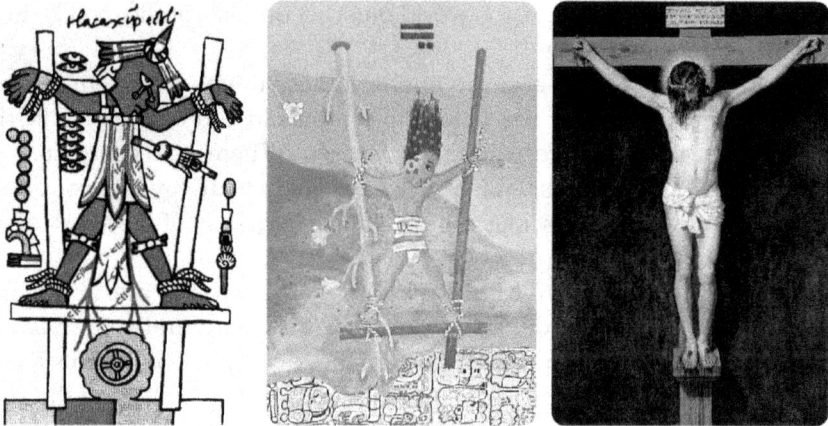

Figure 65. Sacrifice to Xipe Totec
Hanged Man (centre) and *Christ on the Cross* by Diego Velazquez, 1632 (right)

ground. His wisdom is earth wisdom not sky wisdom. We also see small green beads in his hair and his hair is braided and bound by a green ribbon, symbolising an integration of this earth wisdom into consciousness. Later, in the Temperate Man card, he becomes a Twisted Hair.

Jung wrote at length on Christ as a symbol of the Self and on the crucifixion as the experience of being torn apart by two opposing forces. He said, "This great symbol [Christ] tells us that the progressive development and differentiation of consciousness leads to an ever more menacing awareness of the conflict and involves nothing less than a crucifixion of the ego, its agonizing suspension between irreconcilable opposites.... in such cases the ego is a suffering bystander who decides nothing but must submit to a decision and surrender unconditionally. The 'genius' of man, the higher and more spacious part of him to whose extent no one knows, has the final word."[2]

Over the years, we repeatedly bump our heads or fall into the same painful places and the evidence builds that something about our attitude is wrong. To remedy this we can redouble our efforts to arrange people and circumstances to conform to what the ego wants. However, forces will eventually conspire against us. Jung said, "Nobody who finds himself on the road to wholeness can escape that characteristic suspension which is the meaning of the crucifixion. For he will infallibly run into things that thwart and 'cross' him: first, the thing he has no wish to be (the shadow); second, the thing he is not (the 'other,' the individual reality of the 'You'); and third, his psychic non-ego (the collective unconscious)."[3]

If we do manage to evade the conflict then the world will have to experience it for us, as Jung pointed out. "The psychological rule says that when an inner situation is not made conscious, it happens outside, as fate. That is to say, when the individual remains undivided and does not become conscious of his inner opposite, the world must act out the conflict and be torn into two opposing halves."[4]

Alternatively, we can begin to question those things that seem self-evident. This creates doubt, a tension between the old and the new, which always brings about change as Jung emphasised. "There is no energy unless there is a tension of opposites; hence it is necessary to discover the opposite to the attitude of the conscious mind... Life is born only of the spark of opposites."[5]

The So-below cards are from 1–10. The As-above cards are 11–20. The first four As-above cards depict the story of Christ. Scripturally, the Balance is the trial and judgement of Christ before the Sanhedrin and Pontius Pilate, the Hanged Man is the crucifixion, the Dead Man is his death, and the Temperate Man is the resurrection. Psychologically, the Balance is the ego's decision to execute itself (although it is not aware of this at the time), the Hanged Man is its crucifixion, the Dead Man is its death, and the Temperate Man is the resurrection of the relativised ego as part of the larger personality.

Betrayal

The row of the Adult Spirit Shield begins by turning the world upside down, changing our mind, overturning old priorities, seeing things from a new angle, upending the old order, or doing an about-face. In medieval times, the custom of hanging someone upside down was called "baffling" and the inversion of the Hanged Man augurs confusion. In early tarot decks the Hanged Man was called the Traitor. In Italy, at the time when tarot cards first emerged, the punishment for treason was to be hung upside down by one foot which we see in the Marseilles Tarot. In 1945 at the end of World War II, Italian partisans shot and hung the Italian dictator Mussolini in just such a fashion.

The Hanged Man is about betrayal—a crime in outer world but a necessity in the inner world. It is the betrayal of what we have laboured hard to build in the world, all that we have depended on. Where there is a Christ, a Judas is an archetypal necessity.[6] Now the ego must be its own Judas. Inwardly, the betrayal is about forsaking beliefs that have become so familiar that our relationship to them is so unquestioned and taken for granted that they become, or always have been, unconscious. (Does the fish know about water?) The Hanged Man begins to have a new relationship with his mental processes and is asked to abandon all the treasured beliefs, notions, ideas, ideals, principles, standards, morals, ethics, philosophies, or viewpoints that have outlived their time.

In the first half of the journey the ego has unconsciously betrayed the Self in order to become established in life. Now, in the second half of life, the ego has to be the traitor again, but this time it has to consciously betray it-self to be true to the Self. Now we have to turn upside down in order to see ourselves from the viewpoint of spirit. When we are turned upside down, our face becomes recognisable to the unconscious. In the other world every-thing is a mirror of this world and now we must play by its rules. Shamans of all traditions and cultures knew that to go up into the sky they had to go down into the ground, and to go down into the earth they had to fly up into the sky.

"There comes the urgent need," Jung said, "to appreciate the value of the opposite of our former ideals, to perceive the error in our former convic-tions, to recognize the untruth in our former truth, and to feel how much an-tagonism and even hatred lay in what, until now, had passed for love.... The point is not conversion into the opposite but conservation of previous values together with recognition of their *opposites*."[7]

Suffering

> Pain is the most clarifying thing. Joy can be very unfocused, but pain em-bodies everything inside of you.
>
> —Jim Cuddy, Blue Rodeo

The Judas betrayal, which will come about willingly or unwillingly, leads to suffering. The word suffer means "to hold up from underneath" or "to sustain." The word passion comes from the Latin *pati* ("to suffer") as in "to be patient." The word came into the English language through the Old French word *passion* which originally meant strength of feeling. Later in the Christian era the word *passio* became associated with Christ's suffering as in the Passion plays at Easter. The word passive originally meant "capable of suffering." The English connotations of fervour, excitement, desire, sexual attraction or anger did not emerge until the 16th century. Contrary to the exhortations of motivational speakers who urge us to go out and find our passion, the Hanged Man has to let his passion find him. He passively suffers his own unique circumstances because his soul demands it of him.

Although suffering has had bad press from the compulsive optimists of Western culture, it has a place in the stations of life. Suffering is the absence of denial. It is allowing life to have an impact on us. We take life as it pres-ents itself to us, without armour. Suffering is the beginning of becoming self-sustaining and taking responsibility for our own unique pains and joys.

The Movement of Erasing Personal History contains the alternating po-larities of active will (creating one's destiny in the Warrior and the Star) and passive will (surrendering to one's destiny in the Priestess and the Hanged Man), of going for it and waiting for it. In one of his seminars, Jung, after being asked a question about the feminine equivalent of the hero's journey, thought for a moment and said, "Suffering." Passive will is the great art of allowing things to happen, as Jung said. "We must be able to let things happen in the psyche.... Consciousness is forever interfering, helping, correcting, and negating, never leaving the psychic processes to grow in peace. It would be simple enough if only simplicity were not the most difficult of things."[8]

Dealing with life's ups and downs is the province of the first two rows of cards, the Child and Adult Substance Shields. For some, burdened by a greater share of abuse, illness or disadvantage, dealing with this may be a lifetime's work. Others seem to skip lightly through the challenges—outwardly life is a breeze. But sooner or later there will come a different kind of trial—the inner challenge of the Spirit Shields. We can see that, compared to the first row where the figures are static, the figures in this row of the Adult Spirit Shield suggest much more movement and action.

This challenge, if not met, results in a psychic arrest or neurosis. Jung said, "All creativeness in the realm of spirit as well as every psychic advance of man arises from the suffering of the soul, and the cause of the suffering is spiritual stagnation, or psychic sterility."[9] A neurosis is, ultimately, the suffering of a soul which has not found its meaning.

The unconscious will try to produce an impossible situation to force us to come up with our best. "Otherwise," Jung said, "one stops short of one's best, one is not complete, one does not realise oneself. What is needed is an impossible situation where one has to renounce one's will and one's own wit and do nothing but trust to the impersonal power of growth and development."[10]

The Hanged Man is the sacrifice that is required for the greater good. It is the sacrifice of what, in oneself, impedes life from moving forward. The ego must give way to the greater good, which is the enlargement of the personality. "Sacrifice," said Jung, "means... relinquishing all the ties and limitations which the psyche has taken over from childhood into adult life... Life calls us forth to independence, and anyone who does not heed this call because of childhood laziness or timidity is threatened with neurosis."[11]

A symbol of this sacrifice is the clothing worn by the figures in this row. Clothing is part of the persona, the public face we present. It is also a symbol of incarnation.[12] As we come closer to spirit we drop our persona, become naked in front of ourselves and spirit. So the Hanged Man wears only a loin cloth and we can see that the figures in the bottom two rows of cards are wearing less clothing than the figures in the top two rows.

We must suffer to keep the heart open and emotionally well-exercised. The Lovers (6) and the Hanged Man (12 or a double 6) are a pair. The Lovers is the card of bonding and the Hanged Man is the card of separation. But like the romance of the Lovers, the danger here is twofold. Either our suffering becomes an object of fascination, we become swept away by it, join a support group and fossilise our pain into a new victim identity supported by the collective. Or we refuse our suffering, our development grinds to a halt, we buy property in psychological suburbia, and retire.

The suffering of the Hanged Man is not a masochistic idealisation of pain, or suffering for the sake of suffering, or suffering because we have sinned. It is the suffering that properly attends the ego as it squeezes through the cosmic catflap, the Crack-between-the-Worlds, into the world of spirit. It is the rehab program for our addiction to matter, literalness and collectivity. The soul is harrowed, purified, cleansed, purged, and shriven. Or it may be expanded, enthused, inspired, and illuminated. But the experience only has value if we come to know the meaning of the suffering or the joy. The ego must undergo the suffering because it brings greater consciousness. This is not for the sake of the ego but for the sake of the Self.[13]

The result of all this is not a wallowing in the slough of despond, as many would believe, but a release from suffering. The only way out is through. "If you can see and understand your suffering without being subjectively involved," Jung said, "then, because of your altered standpoint, you also understand 'how not to suffer.'"[14] Too much suffering or the wrong kind of suffering is trauma and leaves us worn-out and raddled; too little suffering leaves the psyche virginal and unweathered.

The suffering of the Hanged Man is not the suffering of the poor, the sick, or the dispossessed of the world, but rather the difficulties peculiar to our own psychology, our own cross that we have to bear. With rare exceptions, those who take on the suffering of the world, admired as they may be, often do so to avoid their own suffering. This is inherent in the archetype of Christ who grandiosely took on all of humanity's sins — without their permission. Around 2,000 years ago were the Maya villager, the Aboriginal clever woman, or the San bushman in need of salvation? No, Christ was a local affair at the end of the Mediterranean. He was sacrificed to take on God's suffering — his dividedness — so that God could avoid his own ambivalent nature and remain in all-powerful oneness.

The Hanged Man is a conscious response to the unexpected change brought about by the Wheel and Balance cards. The conscious suffering of the Hanged Man (12) opens us to a transpersonal understanding (10) of our original wound (2). Our suffering awakens a depth and intimacy in us with what we are not, the other that we can never be. It awakens a tenderness and compassion in us for the suffering of others. It awakens the heart of the animus or the anima. So the Hanged Man is the Keeper of the Heart of the Adult Spirit Shield. In a man, his suffering awakens the Heart of his Woman Shield. In a woman, her suffering awakens the Heart of her Man Shield.

The Hanged Man is also the Teacher of Erasing Physical History. Every emotion has its physical and physiological counterpart in the body. Our emotional history is reflected in posture, body type, and musculature. The myriad forms of body work and psychosomatic treatment recognise this relationship (acupuncture, applied kinesiology, Body Talk, craniosacral massage, psychoneuroimmunology, Hakomi, Rolfing, Reichian, Radix, or Bioenergetics, to name but a few). So the Hanged Man is the card of emotional sensation. As the luminous cocoon begins to glow and increase in energy it becomes more sensitive to the energies of thoughts and emotions and their expression in the physical body.

The Hanged Man is also the Holder of the Mood of Emotional Ruthlessness. Our emotional repertoire broadens, our empathy deepens, and we can experience or witness intense emotional states without drowning in them or losing ourselves. We can think about our feelings and have feelings about our thoughts. Our feelings take on meaning and our beliefs take on colour. We can be passionate but not histrionic about our ideas. We can be thoughtful but not intellectual about our feelings. Both thinking and feeling come to their right size, neither idealised nor devalued. Ideas are just ideas and emotions are just emotions — we can be sweet, cunning, ruthless and patient toward them both.

Fire-from-within

The situation without solution, being hung up by our own psychology, forces us to submit to that which is greater ("Thy will be done"). This is an intensely emotional process that is physically experienced. But during this crucifixion, when we are nailed to the cross without hope of rescue (Christ cried, "My God, my God, why hast thou forsaken me?") and feel abandoned by whatever "father" has given order and meaning to our lives, the psyche manifests in a helpful way. Holderlin said, "Danger fosters the rescuing power."[15]

The fire of emotion, previously introverted and contained in the Hermit's lamp and the Sage's brazier, is now transformed into the red smoke which spreads across all the cards in this row. The glowing redness or *rubedo* denotes an intensification of consciousness which now begins to react emotionally to what emerges from the unconscious. Initially, this is not a smooth integration but a fiery conflict. Although the opposites fight with one another to begin with, they ultimately strive for balance, since the war cannot be sustained indefinitely. Eventually, this leads to the melting and blending of the opposites. The alchemists called this process the marriage of the red man and the white woman, Sol and Luna.[16]

Marie-Louise von Franz puts it in more personal terms: "The fire has to burn the fire, one just has to burn in the emotion till the fire dies down and becomes balanced. That is something that unfortunately cannot be evaded. The burning of the fire, of the emotion, cannot be tricked out of one's system; there is no recipe for getting rid of it, it has to be endured. The fire has to burn until the last unclean element has been consumed, which is what all alchemical texts say in different variations, and we have not found any other way either. It cannot be hindered but only suffered till what is mortal or corruptible, or, as our [alchemical] text says so beautifully, till the corruptible humidity, the unconsciousness, has been burnt up. That is the meaning, it is the acceptance of suffering."[17]

Out of this ordeal a transcendent function is born and we see that the Hanged Man's luminous cocoon begins to glow. He is torn between the old and the new, the dead tree of the past and the live tree of the future, and he burns without flame. His will is paralysed and he is in limbo. But when we still the body the spirit quickens and the enforced psychic immobility produces heat. The Hanged Man begins to burn with the Fire-from-within.

Different traditions call this "body of light" by different names. It is the golden body of the alchemical Emerald Tablet; the astral body of Paracelsus; the spiritual body of Saint Paul; the diamond body of Taoism; the most sacred body (*wujud al-aqdas*) or supracelestial body (*jism asli haqiqi*) of Sufism; the light body of Tibetan Buddhism; the vajra body or adamantine body of Tantric yoga; the divine body of Gnosticism; the diamond body of the temple of God of Rosicrucianism; or the luminous body or *akh* of ancient Egypt.

We can see the transformation of fire into light in the last two rows. The Hanged Man shows the effects of the Sage's fire—smoke above him and light coming from his body. This then transmutes into the fractured light of the rainbow in the Temperate Man and at the end of the row into the momentary lightning of the Released Man. In the Star this red light coagulates into an enduring but distant light that comes ever closer to consciousness through the Moon (blue light), the Sun (yellow light) and the Planet Venus (white light). Finally, in the Planet Earth card the light achieves wholeness. Now it turns into its opposite, black light, which is the light of the Earth. It now contains all the colours of light and so the 12 has transformed into its opposite, the 21. Instead of light emanating from the body of a human we have darkness contained in the body of the Earth.

The Hanged Man (12) is the experience of the wound (2) with consciousness (10). This vulnerability, this willingness to let life hurt us requires (or acquires) a faith in ourselves, a confident hope, and a loyalty to the laws of our own being.[18] Then, just at the same time as the trials of the Hanged Man are at their height, we find that not only does the Fire-from-within begin to burn but the greenness begins. The ground that the figures stand on in the third row is green earth. Green signifies new beginnings and hope for the future. The alchemists called it the greening of the metals, the blessed greenness or *benedicta viriditas*, which appeared at this point in the work.

Myths and the archetypes that lie behind them are not immutable. They change and transform with the ages. The same archetype appears in different forms depending on the historical time, place and culture. But the archetype is also changed by its manifestation in space and time. In the Age of Pisces the Hanged Man was the story of one individual (Christ) who was publically crucified so that the many (humankind) could be redeemed from sin and paganism (too much earth). But in the Age of Aquarius it is the opposite story. It is the story of many individuals who are privately crucified (in their own psyches) so that the one (the planet we live on) can be redeemed from monotheism (too much spirit).

The passion and suffering of the Hanged Man births the Dead Man. Out of the skulls that the Death Dancer walks on grows new life which leads to the resurrected Temperate Man, the new level of psychic equilibrium. However, the wound of the Hanged Man is not one that can be healed by human hands. Jung said that to suffer necessity and fate willingly is a religious task. The Hanged Man is the suffering of what cannot be changed and the development of what he called "the religious attitude."

But there is a contradiction — to bear our particular circumstances we must be strong, but we must also be strong enough to be weak, and this contrary strength comes only through descending to those abyssal places where weakness and helplessness are the only things that get us through. As Michelangelo said of Dante, "He did not fear to plumb the places where / Failure alone survives."[19] Now we can but wait for what is greater than ourselves and discover what supports us when nothing else does.

The Dead Man
The Body of the Adult Spirit Shield uses the Mood of Physical
Ruthlessness to create Physical Death and Change

Death

23

Dead Man

So long as you do not die and rise again,
You are a stranger to the dark earth.

—Wolfgang Goethe

Life is a sexually transmitted disease with a 100% mortality rate.

—R. D. Laing

You have little time left and none of it for crap. A fine state. I would say
the best of us always comes out when we are against the wall, when we
feel the sword dangling overhead. Personally, I wouldn't have it any
other way.

—Don Juan Matus

This card depicts a skeletal figure walking across a green and fertile landscape. Above the figure are fiery clouds behind which there is the light
of a new day dawning. The Dead Man holds a shield and two darts in his
left hand and his right hand is limp and empty. Flowers grow up between
the skulls. The Marseilles card is similar and is called Death.

I should state the obvious here: when the Death card appears in a reading it rarely, if ever, indicates physical death. It does indicate a change of
psychic state with a death of the old state and the birth of a new one. Even
dreams of death that occur prior to physical death often portray the approach of death as a change of state rather than a final ending.[1]

Ball Game

The Maya ballgame was called *pitz* and the action of play was *ti pitziil*. It
was the first known team sport and was played by the Olmec as early as
1600 BCE and perhaps dated back to 2500 BCE.[2] The oldest accurately dated
ballcourt has been found at Paso de la Amada, dating from 1400 BCE. There

Figure 66. A ballcourt at Tikal

are more than 500 ballcourts in Guatemala and in Tikal alone (Figure 66) there are seven. Ball courts have been found from Arizona to Nicaragua and in various Caribbean islands such as Cuba. While the game was played casually by men, women and children for recreation, the game also had important ceremonial aspects and major ballgames would be held as ritual events.

The rubber for the ball was made from the sap of the rubber tree. The latex was separated by boiling it with *machacuana* and *guamol* roots to facilitate coagulation. This process yielded long strands of grayish, elastic material. These hot strips of rubber were then wound into balls of the desired size which varied from little larger than a baseball to the size of a beach ball and may have weighed up to fifteen kilograms. The Maya glyph for rubber is a spiral, alluding to the wound strips. The Olmec, the originators of the ballgame, were known as the "rubber people." The Nahuatl word for both rubber and ball is *ol*, and the word for movement is *ollin*.

The ballcourt was I-shaped, approximately five metres wide by twenty-five metres long with sloping sides, although the ball court at Chichen Itza measures 35 by 140 metres. The number of players on each team varied from two to eleven depending on the region where the game was played. In most ball courts, the two sloping parallel walls were inset at the top with three round disks, or a single stone ring, at right angles to the ground. The players had to keep the ball in motion using their hips, thighs or forearms but the use of hands or feet was not allowed. The players scored by touching the markers or passing the ball through the rings that were up to eight metres off the ground. Scoring was such a feat that it usually ended the

Figure 67. The Ball Game Umpire

game. In some cases, the losers in a ballgame would be killed and have their heads displayed in front of the court.

As well as using their arms, knees and hips, the players could hit the ball with a carved handstone stick or bat. They wore elbow, knee and groin protectors and also a heavy, horseshoe-shaped, ceremonial yoke made of cloth, leather, and wood or even stone, around the waist. The yoke was the Crack-between-the-Worlds. The upper body of the ball player was (not a symbol of, not a metaphor of, but *was*) the ear of corn in the sunlight of the upper world, his hair gathered up on his head like the Sage was the tassels of the corn. His lower body was the dark roots of the World Tree in the Underworld. The player emerging from the yoke was the sun in its struggle to be reborn from the Underworld every day and every year. The ceremonial intent of the game was to ensure the rebirth of the sun.

In the Popol Vuh, the mythological Hero Twins play the ballgame against the Lords of Death. In winning, they resurrect their father the Maize God and their uncle and place them in the sky as the sun and the moon. For the Maya, the ball symbolised the movement of the heavenly bodies and the soul's journey to the Underworld. The ball is both the moon and the sun and the court represents the earth. The ball was kept in the air, just as the sun and the moon are always in the sky. When the ball passed through the goal ring it symbolised the rebirth of the sun each day, each year and each Great Year (which we shall look at later in the Planet Earth card). The court was a place where death was turned into life. It was a re-enactment of the divine ballgame and the resurrection of First Father, ensuring the victory of light over darkness, the rebirth of the sun and the continuation of life.

Figure 68. Mixcoatl

A ceramic figurine from the Peten region shows a ballgame "umpire" wearing a mask with a stone implement before him used to keep the ball off the ground (Figure 66). His right handsign means life, and the left handsign means death just as we see in the Dead Man card. The two arrows and the shield of the Dead Man are similar to those carried by Aztec warrior figures, for example Mixcoatl or Cloud Serpent (Figure 68) who was identified with the Milky Way.

With its sloping sides, the ballcourt was a portal with a view down into the events in the Underworld. At Tonina, set into the earthen floor of the ballcourt, is a stone tube several feet deep that was a viewing port down into the Underworld. On the lid that covered this hole was carved a picture of the ruler Six-Sky-Smoke, a young "sprout" of the lineage. He holds a serpent bar across his chest. However, instead of each end being the usual vision serpent or the signs for Venus and the sun representing the Milky Way, the sign for "white flower" is at either end of the bar. This white flower was the soul of Six-Sky-Smoke. It is the flower that we see at the beginning and the end of the journey in the Fool and Planet Earth cards. This deceased young ruler sits in the Underworld holding his own soul which is one and the same as the Milky Way.[3]

All sports were originally sacred ceremonies and our modern games are their secular descendants. In the modern era millions of people invest untold amounts of time, money and energy in sports. This points to the presence of a powerful archetype driving these activities. The religiosity with which millions flock to the stadia, fields, tracks and courts of the world show that the powerful archetypal themes of winning and losing, luck and chance, life and death are ever-present. Like art, sport shows its beauty in the experience of the body, the mastery of matter and the skill, grace and aggression of the human body, pushing for farther, faster, higher. Sport is unscripted drama.

But always being a winner is not good psychologically because one is deprived of experiencing the opposites. This is why there are no team sports played with three sides. Two opposing sides ensure there is a clear winner and a loser. The experience of defeat opens the gateway to the unconscious and going down requires a different kind of courage than going up.[4] Within the game, the opposites come together and the experience of both defeat and victory in fullest measure brings depth and breadth to the developing personality.

Cinnabar and Sulphur

The background of the Dead Man is a deep red colour which points to the other themes in the card — grief and the death of desire. The colour is that of the mineral cinnabar which was used extensively by the Maya. Large deposits of cinnabar (HgS, mercury sulphide) are found in Central America. It varies in colour from cinnamon to scarlet red and was used to make the pigment vermilion. Offering plates and the bodies of deceased Maya rulers were often liberally painted with cinnabar because it was blood-red and so contained *ch'ulel*, the holy soul-force of the universe.

In alchemy, cinnabar represents the rubedo stage and Pliny called it "dragon's blood."[5] Cinnabar is the principal source of mercury, which it releases on gentle heating. In alchemy, Mercury or Mercurius is the name for elusive element symbolising the freedom of the autonomous spirit. One of the goals of alchemy was to capture this mysterious spirit in matter. The alchemical operation of coagulatio refers to turning a gas into a liquid or a liquid into a solid. In general, it means to congeal, set or thicken — in other words, to become fixed, permanent or have form. Psychologically, this means that a psychic content has become concretised, that is, it is no longer freely in the unconscious and has become attached to the ego. It has come down from the dream and manifested in matter. It no longer flies in the air, or swims in the water, it walks on the land, as Shakespeare wrote:

> The poet's eye, in a fine frenzy rolling,
> Doth glance from heaven to earth, from earth to heaven;
> And as imagination bodies forth
> The forms of things unknown, the poet's pen
> Turns them to shapes and gives to airy nothing
> A local habitation and a name.[6]

Mercury is a highly reactive substance and combines with almost all other substances. The alchemical recipe for coagulatio was to take quicksilver (mercury) and coagulate it in magnesia (the generic term in alchemy for crude ores or impure mixtures), lead, or the body of sulphur which "does not burn." These three mixtures are significant.

Mixing mercury (spirit) with the crudeness of the impure metallic ores (the particulars of our ordinary, individual existence) brings the trans-personal realm into contact with ordinary human reality.

Mixing mercury with lead binds the autonomous free spirit to the heaviness of lead. Lead is associated with the planet Saturn—limits, discipline, deadness, melancholy, restriction and burden. The urgent and unreflective acceptance of the notions of equality, equal opportunity, and the freedom to become anything we want, suggests an underlying denial of the presence of Saturn in the Western psyche. Saturn is the prison of our particular life circumstances (not everyone can be rich, a film star, intelligent, or athletic), the limits of our psychological make-up (we all have limits to our kindness or generosity) and the relationships we have (some relationships are just not for us). Relationship, limitations and grief coagulate. They look beyond the short-sighted expansionisms of inspiration, purpose, vision, growth, ecstasy and illumination and bring us face-to-face with the details of our lives—the losses, the hurts, the failures, what I feel, what she feels, what I want, what he wants, the bank accounts and the babies.

The alchemical sulphur in the recipe is the kind that "does not burn" indicating it is not the actual chemical sulphur but that it has a symbolic aspect. Sulphur is known for its bright yellow colour and its flammability, thus associating it with the yellow sun. But it also blackens metals, makes foul smelling gases and was associated with the black sun, putrefaction, decay and the underworld. For the alchemists sulphur represented the active substance of the sun, which was will and desire—both conscious will and the will of the unconscious. And desire coagulates.[7] What beliefs or emotions drives us or to where we are driven is irrelevant, the state of drivenness is what is important. That is sulphur.

An alchemical image shows the lion devouring the sun with the blood of the lion issuing from its mouth (Figure 69). Both lion and sun symbolise desire. This image shows that the raw solar energy must be devoured by itself and undergo a *mortificatio* process yielding blood. Only then can it be readied for the sacred marriage of the sun and the moon. This marriage produces a philosophical child or stone which is nourished by the blood, called red mercury, from the encounter between the lion and the sun.[8]

We have seen that the yellow colour of sulphur dominates the second row. Now in the third row the yellow changes to red, meaning that it is less spiritualised, more embodied, and becoming bound by life-as-it-is. It is human to be interested in, fascinated with, want, covet, possess, need, desire, lust for, long for, and love what is of the flesh. But all things must pass. What is of the flesh does not live forever and will eventually die. So sul-

Figure 69. The green lion devouring the sun, Rosarium Philosophorum

phur—as sun-driven passion, will, drivenness, or desirousness—always ends in tears and brings grief, limitation and death. Marie-Louise von Franz this about passion:

> Sitting in Hell and roasting there is what brings forth the philosopher's stone; as it is said here, the fire is extinguished with its own inner measure. Passion has its own inner measure; there is no such thing as chaotic libido, for we know that the unconscious itself, as pure nature, has an inner balance. The lack of balance comes from the childishness of the conscious attitude. If you only follow your own passion according to its own indications it will never go too far, it will always lead to its own defeat. Inordinate passion seeks defeat. People who have an inordinately passionate nature, a kind of devilish nature, are lovingly searching for a human person, or a situation, against which they can knock their heads, and they despise any partner or situation in which their passion wins out. Instinctively they seek defeat.... The fire of the passion looks for that which will extinguish it, and that is why the urge for individuation, as long as it is a natural inordinate urge, seeks impossible situations; it seeks conflict and defeat and suffering because it seeks its own transformation.[9]

The Dead Man is the card of physical sensation and Physical Ruthlessness. The urgency for impossible situations is heard in the old saw that men have two heads and one of them doesn't have any brains. Letting the cock lead is physical sensation. It always leads to the pleasure and pain of impossible situations and sometimes leads to the ruthless transformation of whoever is attached to it.

The Dead Man is also the Teacher of Using Physical Death as an Advisor and the Keeper of the Body of the Adult Spirit Shield. The whole row of the Adult Spirit Shield is the anima or animus. The shadow is what the ego could be or does not want to be but the animus or anima is what the ego could never be because it is the opposite of our physical gender. And because of this radical otherness it is sought all the more insistently.

In the first half of life the ego is outwardly directed and does not think to look, or want to look, inside. So the anima or animus, in order to become known, throws out its own image onto another (most often a person but it can also be a cause, a hobby, an ideal, or a leader). Because this process is unconscious, the one upon whom the projection falls exerts a holy fascination that is often both sexual and spiritual. The anima or animus, vap'rous and fleeting, lusts for matter while the ego, leaden and worldly, longs for spirit. For the animus/anima nothing less than touch, body contact, and sex in any and all forms, will satisfy. The intent of the anima/animus is two-fold: to experience itself incarnate in the flesh, as the Body of the Adult Spirit Shield, and to bring about its own transformation and that of the ego. So the projection will inevitably disappoint in some way and the mental projection will die. It is the intensity of the longing for the body and the world of matter that inevitably brings about this death.

The alchemists saw this wounding as the death of innocence. They used the image of virgin's milk as a symbol of innocence. This was an inherent condition in the psyche which had no earth or blackness in it, in other words it had not been touched by earthly realities. Stanton Marlan says that typical virgin's milk fantasies and beliefs might be, "sentiments such as 'Life should be fair,' 'God will protect and care for me like a good parent,' 'Bad things won't happen to me because I have lived according to this or that principle,' 'I have been good or faithful, eat healthy foods, and exercise,' and so on. When life does not confirm such ideas, the innocent, weak, or immature ego is wounded and often overcome with feelings of hurt, self-pity, oppression, assault, and/or victimisation."[10]

Triangles and Thirteen

In Western culture the number 13 is considered unlucky. It represents death, dissonance, and the breakdown of the old order. The number 13 disrupts the symmetry of the 12. The 13th note on the Pythagorean musical scale is dissonant. In fairytales, the hero is not supposed to open the 13th door. There are 13 witches in a coven.[11] Judas Iscariot, the 13th disciple, completely ruined the last supper.

However, in other cultures 13 has more positive associations. The book of Exodus (34:6) and the Passover Haggadah mention 13 divine attributes. The Cabala speaks of the 13 heavenly fountains, the 13 gates of mercy and the 13 rivers of balsam that the pious will find in paradise. The Maya tzolkin is composed of 13 numbers and 20 day-names. In Greek mythology, Odysseus escaped death at the hands of the Cyclops but his 12 companions were devoured. In some European folktales there is 1 sister and her 12 brothers are turned into animals and the sister has to rescue them.

The Dead Man is the card of dying to the emotions that attach us to the old life, the letting go that comes as a result of the trials of the 12 card. We cannot go back to the old state, our former life. The number 3 is movement, change, transformation, and the number 10 is consciousness, so 13 (3 + 10) represents dying with consciousness. Dismemberment in dreams often indicates this process at work, dividing up the unconscious contents for the purpose of assimilation into consciousness. The skeleton of the Dead Man symbolises the bare bones of who we are, no covering, no flesh, just the dismembered essentials that survive death.

The number 3 is a triangle and number 13 is our consciousness of triangular relationships. We can see that both the Consort and the Dead Man are holding arrows. We have seen that the arrow or dart is a symbol of projection, directed aggression or desire. Conflict, merging, difference, opposition, enmeshment, aggression and all the colours of relationship that take place between two people do not happen without the presence of a third in reality or in fantasy. The third can be a person (alive or dead), a parent, a lover, an idea, market share, love, money, sex, principles, religion, or the relationship itself. Most important of all, for which more people have died than anything else in history, is the land.

Triangles bring out what is gloriously human in us when, for example, someone gives their life for the sake of another or putting oneself "in harm's way" (the triangle of self, other, and death, danger or the enemy). They also bring out what is ingloriously human in us—betrayal, greed, envy, jealousy, and murder—all of which we would like to consider inhuman despite all the evidence that they are quintessentially human. For example, and tragically all too often, the husband murders the recently separated wife and children and then kills himself. Or battery acid is thrown in the woman's face so another man will never want to look at her. Or the father and brothers murder the daughter to protect the "family honour." Triangles elicit feelings of triumph over the other, contempt and hatred for the other, murderous jealousy, destructive rage, the comfort of being included, and the abandonment of being left out.

The first psychological writings on triangles were by Freud. In his writings on the Oedipus complex, he focussed mostly on the literal mother and father. Here the boy's strongest tie is with his mother in the beginning and he sees the father as a competitor for his mother's affections. The little boy will harbour unconscious angry feelings toward his father as rival. "Mummy is mine, not yours!" The father's response is important. But in standing up to Daddy, or wishing he could, he worries that Daddy will not love him, hurt him or hit him. If this in fact happens then the boy begins to develop anger and aggression as the hope of Daddy's love fades. Here lies the root of later problems with authority.

However, the triangle can also be thought of as the boy, his mother, and the father-in-the-mother, for example. That is, the mother's inner relationship with all that is masculine in her life — her animus (the archetypal masculine), her father, her brothers, grandfathers and uncles, male friends, male lovers, and the boy's father. Similarly, for a girl the triangle is herself, the father and the mother-in-the-father.[12] This triangle is repeated in adult relationships where a third person either in fantasy or reality comes into a two-person intimacy. The arrival of the third brings emotional death and change and murders the coziness of the two. Of betrayal in relationships, Aldo Carotenuto said:

> When one feels the need to deceive the beloved, this implies a lack of integration of the shadow. On the other hand, the person who betrays can be considered faithful to life for the unconscious aim is often to transform the initial tie, "I do not have the courage or the strength to change the existing relationship and so, with the violent impact of a third person, I will revolutionise it and see what happens." It is as if deceit were the only instrument with which to break down boundaries.... There may be external motivations, but they are superficial. I am convinced that there is always complicity, albeit unconscious, between betrayer and betrayed.[13]

In the Dead Man card, there is a re-working of triangular issues of, on the one hand, loss, displacement and abandonment and, on the other hand, closeness to the same sex, competition and rivalry. These feelings and situations, at any age, are often powerful crucibles for death and change. Jealousy and possessiveness are humbling experiences but a sign of maturity is the acceptance of one's pettiness and neediness.

Death and Rebirth

We see three skulls beneath the feet of the Dead Man. In Maya and Aztec cultures bones and skulls represented not only death but also rebirth. Christ died at Calvary (Latin, *calvaria*, skull) or Golgotha (Aramaic, *gul-*

gutha, the place of skulls) later to be resurrected. For the ego, the Dead Man card is a death in the world of substance but a birth in the world of spirit. For spirit however, it is a death in the world of spirit but a birth in the world of substance. Just as physical death results in spiritual rebirth, so spiritual death (the death and change that is involved in becoming more conscious) results in physical rebirth. In other words, the spiritual death of the 13 card keeps us physically alive and healthy, and if we refuse spiritual death and change (consciousness) then we die more quickly. We are confronted by the enemy of old age. Our life energy diminishes more rapidly and when we do die there is little energy left over to negotiate the passage from this world to the next.

Bob Dylan sang, "He not busy being born is busy dying."[14] The natural way to approach death is to live fully and practice dying as Jung described. "From the middle of life onward, only he remains vitally alive who is ready to die with life. For in the secret hour of life's midday the parabola is reversed, death is born. The second half of life does not signify ascent, unfolding, increase, exuberance, but death, since the end is its goal. The negation of life's fulfilment is synonymous with the refusal to accept its ending. Both mean not wanting to live, and not wanting to live is identical with not wanting to die. Waxing and waning make one curve."[15]

It is in grief and mourning that we are most unlike nature and most human. Nature is bent on her own ends and she does not grieve the loss of a life. She ensures that another of the species can easily be made and is solely concerned with the abundance of life in its many forms, not an individual life. Human lives are of little account in the great cycles of life and death, and nature has countless ways to kill a meaningless existence. It is this merciless and relentless face of death that the Maya looked upon unflinchingly, as Douglas Gillette graphically describes:

> The decapitation of First Father by the Lords of Death, then the Hero Twins and the human sacrifices, the symbolic head of the ball game, the ball court marker that lay over the portal to the Underworld, the Holy First Father Decapitated-Dead-Creating-Thing, the Holy-Singing-Skull-Thing, the thin crust on which humans walked above Xibalba, the Underworld, the nightly swallowing of the Sun and Stars by the Cosmic Serpent and their resurrection, the shedding of blood so that the world may live, the throwing of the sacrificed body down the steps into the Underworld, the clear-sightedness of the wrath of God, the terribleness of its power, beyond all human understanding, not good, gentle, intimate but the wrath of the Lamb, that is so incomprehensible that awe and dread, the *mysterium tremendum* is the only rightful response, to Death and his cohorts—Stab Master, Blood Gatherer, Skull Sceptre and Pus Master,

that as well as light and love, life is also diarrhoea, disease, putrefaction and clotted blood.[16]

The reality of death brings us into right relationship with life and in this sense, the Dead Man represents the triumph of life over death. It is not literal death but the death of the literalist ego, the liberation of the imagination and the deepening of the symbolic life.

The growing experience of death throughout life counters the child's experience of living in a timeless world and the adolescent fantasy of immortality — not that these conditions should be anything different in their time, but their time passes. However, we see these residual fantasies, well past their prime, in endeavours to prolong life indefinitely by "genetic engineering," or in New Age "immortality consciousness." They are simplistic and ill-mannered literalisations of the great enterprise of the transformation of spirit by the human soul through its experience of life and death. "There are no survivors on this earth."[17]

The Temperate Man
The Mind of the Adult Spirit Shield uses the Mood of Mental
Ruthlessness to Stop the Physical World

Temperance

24

Temperate Man

Wisdom never forgets that all things have two sides.... Life wants not only the clear but also the muddy, not only the bright but also the dark; it wants all days to be followed by nights.

—C. G. Jung

Don Juan had told me that there is no completeness without sadness and longing, for without them there is no sobriety, no kindness. Wisdom without kindness, he said, and knowledge without sobriety are useless.

—Carlos Castaneda

These violent delights have violent ends
And in their triumph die, like fire and powder,
Which as they kiss consume: the sweetest honey
Is loathsome in his own deliciousness
And in the taste confounds the appetite:
Therefore love moderately; long love doth so;
Too swift arrives as tardy as too slow.

—Friar Laurence, *Romeo and Juliet*

All things in moderation, including moderation.

—George Bernard Shaw

Moderation is a fatal thing. Nothing succeeds like excess.

—Oscar Wilde

A man pours water onto the ground from a tripod vessel held in his right hand. The water has stars in it. He holds a staff with a single leaf in his left hand. On his left side is a Flowering Tree with three leaves and a flower. Above the tree is a rainbow that arches up over his head to join with a small sun. The curve of his body and the hair twisted above his

Figure 70. Part of Lintel 2, Temple 3, Tikal

head follows the arch of the rainbow. At the top of the card the red smoke clears as it passes overhead. The starwater poured onto the ground becomes the dew of the Moon card and the roots of the tree extend into the Planet Venus card. The image is taken from the same lintel as the Priest card (Lintel 2, Temple III at Tikal). He is to the right of and behind the jaguar priest (Figure 70).

Temperance

In the Marseilles Tarot this card is called Temperance. The four cardinal virtues of classical Greece and Rome were Temperance, Fortitude (the Cactus), Justice (the Balance) and Prudence (the latter is absent from the tarot). The word temperance comes from the Latin, *temperare*, which means to mix or blend. One's personality or temperament was believed to result from the combination or mixing of the four humours (sanguine, choleric, phlegmatic, and melancholic) to produce the person's characteristic temper or state of mind. The usage of the word to indicate bad temper, that is, anger, came about only in the early 1800s. Temperance comes when things are mixed in just the right proportion for the person or the situation—not too much, not too little, when we observe limits, control or regulate ourselves, and exercise modesty, forbearance and restraint.

An inscription at the temple of Apollo at Delphi read, "Nothing too much." In Christian theology, temperance means self-control or self-discipline and is believed to be a fruit of the presence of the Holy Spirit. But why all this caution and curbing? Because the Temperate Man is the first place where the ego experiences a functional, ongoing relationship with spirit and spiritual inflation is a danger. Those who have brilliant intuitions, spiritual gifts or are naturally so inclined are vulnerable to identifying with their insights, floating away from tonal reality and living in the dream. However, we can never achieve what we intuit and Jung cautioned, "Only the gods can pass over the rainbow bridge; mortal men must stick to the earth and are subject to its laws.... No noble, well-grown tree ever disowned its dark roots, for it grows not only upward but downward as well. The question of where we are going is of course extremely important; but equally important, it seems to me, is the question of *who* is going where.... It takes a certain greatness to gain lasting possession of the heights, but anybody can overreach himself."[1]

This card is the beginning of the friendship between matter and spirit. It is the blending of opposites to achieve a harmonious state. It is the "solution" where the conflicted parts of a problem, previously knotty, tangled and un-solved, are dis-solved. In terms of human temperament it is the proper blending of the four humours — fiery choleric, airy sanguine, watery melancholic and earthy bilious. The blending is even of those things we consider fixed and immiscible: human and divine, masculine and feminine.

The Temperate Man is androgynous and the rainbow is associated with androgyny. There are legends in the French, Serbian and Bulgarian countrysides about people changing sex when passing under a rainbow.[2] This process will reach its conclusion in the 21 card when all the opposites will be united. In alchemy this union of the opposites was imagined as the union of the elements just as earth, air, fire and water are combined in the rainbow. Although the rainbow is not depicted in the Temperance card of the Marseilles Tarot it is almost universal in later tarot.

Temperance is fluid like the water pouring from the vessel whereas Justice is inflexible like the crossbeam of the scales in the Balance. Iris, the goddess of the rainbow, serves Mother Hera whereas Athena (Justice) serves Father Zeus. Iris is kind and merciful, whereas Athena is fair and objective. Temperance values relationship, whereas Justice values independence. Temperance means taking the middle way, combining things in their right proportion, doing the temperate thing, the right action at just the right time even in a situation of conflict.

The ego now becomes the intermediary between the two worlds of conscious and unconscious, substance and spirit, mixing the two in their right

proportions for the particular situation. When there is a more functional relationship between conscious and unconscious life goes better. The Temperate Man is a human who Walks in Beauty and he is the renewal of life
through a continuous exchange, a working relationship, between substance
and spirit.

Now, after the Hanged Man and the Dead Man, there comes an experience of greater harmony between inner life and outer events, self and others. There is greater trust in oneself and one's thoughts and feelings. Anxiety about being one's own worst enemy lessens and the unconscious becomes a helpful ally. The rationalist discovers the fuzzy precision of feeling
and the dreamer discovers that the body is not an enemy of spirit. Order re-
places confusion and one has a greater sense of inner authority and
self-containment. Just as steel is tempered to make it stronger, there is a
firmness of will and the capacity to face reality "as it is" is strengthened.
Temperance is what Don Juan called sobriety:

> If seers can hold their own in facing petty tyrants, they can certainly face
> the unknown with impunity, and then they can even withstand the pres-
> ence of the unknowable. The average man's reaction is to think that the
> order of that statement should be reversed.... A seer who can hold his
> own in the face of the unknown can certainly face petty tyrants. But
> that's not so. What destroyed the superb seers of ancient times was that
> assumption. We know better now. We know that nothing can temper the
> spirit of a warrior as much as the challenge of dealing with impossible
> people in positions of power. Only under those conditions can warriors
> acquire the sobriety and serenity to stand the pressure of the unknow-
> able.... For instance, the other day when you understood about La
> Gorda's and your self-importance, you didn't understand anything re-
> ally. You had an emotional outburst, that was all. I say this because the
> next day you were back on your high horse of self-importance as if you
> had never realized anything. The same thing happened to the old seers.
> They were given to emotional reactions. But when the time came for
> them to understand what they had seen, they couldn't do it. To under-
> stand one needs sobriety, not emotionality. Beware of those who weep
> with realization, for they have realized nothing.... Seers have to be me-
> thodical, rational beings, paragons of sobriety, and at the same time they
> must shy away from all of those qualities in order to be completely free
> and open to the wonders and mysteries of existence.[3]

At this point in the journey, the connecting link between ego and Self becomes more supple. Spirit and substance touch and the ego has become
strong enough to act as a go-between. Now conscious unites with unconscious, not as sought-after experiences from above, nor a striving for "en-

lightenment," but as a part of everyday life where dreams and dailiness are interwoven.

Suffering of Light

After the alchemical operations of solutio, calcinatio, sublimatio and mortificatio, the completion of the second stage of the work is heralded by the *albedo* or the whitening of the substance. Whiteness suggests purity and not being contaminated with other colours. Psychologically, it represents the process of taking back a projection — a long process that has to be repeated many times. When the projection is eventually withdrawn then a peace or quietness is achieved and one can be objective about the person or the situation.[4]

Although the purity of the albedo is an advance in the work, it is too refined for life as it is actually lived. It can only survive in rarefied climates where there is silence, gongs and pure thoughts, a place removed from ironing boards, bad tempers, and the grizzling of children. The colours of life must be allowed, purity must be sacrificed, and blood must flow so we can love what is mortal. There must be an material embodiment of this rainbow bridge between matter and spirit otherwise life stagnates.

Therefore, after the albedo the next stage is the appearance of the *cauda pavonis* or the rainbow colours of the peacock's tail. The early Christians saw the peacock as a symbol of Christ's resurrection. Now the purity of white light is fractured by the prism and we see the beauty and woundedness of the colours. Wolfgang Goethe said, "Colour is the suffering of light."[5] The colours signal the end of the albedo and the substance is said to have the strength to "resist the fire."[6] Being able to resist the fire prepares us for the encounter with evil that will follow in the Bound Man card. After the mortificatio of the Hanged Man and the Dead Man comes a more positive experience of the Self and in the hour of darkness the peacock's tail appears. Jung summarised the process:

> Right at the beginning you meet the "dragon," the chthonic spirit, the "devil" or, as the alchemists called it, the "blackness," the *nigredo*, and this encounter produces suffering... matter suffers until the *nigredo* disappears, when the "dawn" (*aurora*) will be announced by the "peacock's tail" (*cauda pavonis*) and a new day will break, the *leukosis* or *albedo*. But in this state of "whiteness" one does not *live* in the true sense of the word, it is a sort of abstract, ideal state. In order to make it come alive it must have "blood," it must have what the alchemists call the *rubedo*, the "redness" of life. Only the total experience of being can transform this ideal state of the *albedo* into a fully human mode of existence. Blood alone can reanimate a glorious state of consciousness in which the last trace of

blackness is dissolved, in which the devil no longer has an autonomous existence but rejoins the profound unity of the psyche. Then the *opus magnum* is finished: the human soul is completely integrated.[7]

Rainbow Covenant

The rainbow is the pathway or bridge between this world and the other world. It is Eros, the mature differentiated feeling, that connects heaven and earth. The image of the rainbow appears in myths world-wide: Zulu, Navajo, Hawaiian, Japanese, Cambodian, Greek, Australian Aborigine, Chumash, and Hopi.[8] In Norse mythology Bifrost, the rainbow bridge, was the Tremulous Way over to Asgard, the home of the gods, from Midgard the home of mortals. Heimdall, son of Odin, guarded it from attack by the giants but it was destined to fall in the final battle of Ragnarok between the gods and the giants. In Greek mythology, Iris was the goddess of the rainbow and the messenger between humans and the gods. She is seen as a young woman with golden wings and a multicoloured bow, with a herald's rod in one hand and a pitcher in the other.

The rainbow means that the original psychological disunity, the denial of the reality of spirit and the unconscious, and the internal war between contradictory feelings and values, has become unified and given order. There is the beginning of a conscious dialogue between the ego and the Self and a free flow of energy between the opposites. The personality has now begun an integration that heralds the roundedness and unity of the Philosopher's Stone in the Planet Earth card.[9]

In the outer world, the rainbow represents the sacred covenant (Latin, *convenire*, to come together) between matter and spirit. Humans, now that they are teachable, are the caretakers of this covenant. The biblical covenants between God and humans are best known to Western culture. The rainbow that appeared to Noah after the flood was a sign from Yahweh that he would never again destroy the Israelites by water. "I do set my bow in the cloud and it shall be for a token of a covenant between me and the earth."[10] Psychologically, this means that when the ego has a sufficiently deep encounter with the Self this provides a solid foundation for the psyche and a certain immunity to future destructive invasions (being destroyed by floods) from the unconscious.[11]

The first or "old" covenant was made between Yahweh and Abraham, and later affirmed after the flight from Egypt by the receiving of the Ten Commandments by Moses on Mount Sinai. The Israelites were led to the Promised Land but as they prospered they disregarded the first covenant and were exiled into the wilderness, and out of this came the second or "new" covenant announced by Jeremiah.

Just as churches, temples or mosques were built on older "pagan" sites so these biblical covenants lie upon much older covenants. All indigenous peoples held this covenant in their relationship with the earth they lived on. In Australia, the land of the Rainbow Serpent, Aboriginal peoples say that the spirit ancestors in the beginning Dreamtime roamed the earth creating rocks, streams, mountains and providing the plants and animals for food. They purposefully created every billabong, rock, star, planet, human, plant, animal, insect, and every living creature. As they travelled across the land, they gave it form by creating the rivers and the mountains. They also laid down the Laws the people must obey and the Dreaming Tracks which connect all creatures of the world and define the belonging territory of the tribe within the landscape. After this was done, the ancestral spirits changed into aspects of the landscape, empowering it with their numinous presence.

This "belonging place" was the land created for their kin, their clan and their tribe during the Dreamtime. Aboriginals belong to this area of land where their totem ancestors were born, lived and died. Though widely different in their customs (there were over 200 separate languages prior to white settlement) all Aboriginal Australians believe that they are connected to all the animals and plants and that the ancestral spirits charged them with the duty to be caretakers of the land and its inhabitants. Aboriginal Australians call this responsibility to safeguard the land and all species, "Taking Care."

Each person and clan had their own totem, which imposed restraints and responsibilities. For example, Aboriginal law may forbid a clan to eat their own totem, the possum. It is their responsibility to respect and protect this totem and all places where the ancestral possum spirit rested while creating the earth of his homeland. Such places are sacred. Ceremonies were performed at sacred sites to make contact with the ancestor spirit who would provide protection and food. The tradition of totems protected the existence of the species. With many clans having different animal and plant totems, the people and the land were in balance. Aboriginal peoples sing the land. Storytelling, songs, paintings and dance ensured the livingness of each species and the fruitfulness of the land.

By the mid-1700s Britain's "Bloody Code," where execution was the punishment for hundreds of relatively petty crimes, mostly against property, was coming to an end. Transportation to the North American colonies had become the preferred alternative. But in the 1780s, after the American War of Independence, the British government was forced to look elsewhere. In 1770 Captain Cook had mapped the east coast of an land unknown to Europeans, declared it *terra nullius* (land belonging to no-one or empty land) and called it New South Wales. On 20 January 1788, eleven ships with 775 convicts aboard arrived at Botany Bay. (Now on 26 January each year Australia Day commemorates the arrival of the grandly-named

"First Fleet." Some Aboriginals call it "Invasion Day"). Over the next two hundred years Aboriginal peoples were hunted for sport and their culture was decimated. The first covenant that had lasted for over 40,000 years was broken. It remains to be seen if there will ever be a second covenant.

The biblical and Aboriginal covenants with the earth externally, and the psychological covenant with the Self internally, are one and the same. Their development is described in the cards. In infancy the link between the ego and the Self is non-existent because the ego is completely contained within the Self. The Self is projected in its entirety onto the parental figures and the physical environment and the actual behaviour of the parents soothe or amplify the terrors and comforts of infancy. The Fool and Sorcerer cards correspond to this psychological condition.

Then, as the child begins to develop a sense of identity, the ego separates out from the Self (the Priestess) like an island rising out of the ocean. Moving through childhood, the Self is projected onto a widening circle of extended family, teachers and other collective authority figures: mother (the Consort), father (the Ruler) and teachers or heroes (the Priest).

During adolescence and young adulthood the person separates from the family-of-origin. By the late teens, the process of developing an internalised authority structure, the superego or internal value system, is completed. But the Self remains projected and now the projection shifts to partners (the Lovers), physical possessions (the Cactus), groups and organisations (the Warrior), or beliefs and bodies of knowledge (the Sage).

Personality development may remain arrested at this stage for life, held in the arms of mass culture. Here, gifts are admired (the narcissism of TV talk shows) and shortcomings are judged (the cynicism of radio talk shows) but always in others and at a distance. This is a relatively stable first covenant between the individual and the collective where he or she has achieved adequate social functioning. If the mid-life crossing is negotiated then it is possible for a second covenant, a resurrection and a rebirth, to appear in the Temperate Man. Now, the connection with the Self happens internally.[12] As this internal connection strengthens so the ego's relationship with the outer world becomes broader and deeper.

Blood

The rubedo or blood, which we see in the red wrappings around the bones and the red smoke in the Dead Man card, represents the life of the soul. An alchemical text says, "Man's blood and the red juice of the grape is our fire."[13] Blood symbolises the redness that brings life. Even the shades of Hades were restored to life temporarily by being given a drink of blood.[14] However, blood is a divine fluid and the spilling of blood other than in sacrifice to the divine is an archetypal crime as well as a human crime. In the inner world the denial of the soul's needs is the spilling of blood and is a crime against nature tantamount to psychological murder.

Blood is also a binding agent, like the blood of the covenant through which Moses ceremonially bound Israel and Yahweh.[15] At the Last Supper Christ bade the disciples to drink the blood of the covenant. In the Catholic Mass, the communicant, through the symbolic cannibalism of eating the body and drinking the blood of Christ, reaffirms their relationship with the nourishing, sustaining aspect of God. However, this view that God's love sustains humans is a recent development against a more ancient background that recognises that blood sacrifices must be made to feed the gods. Psychologically, the two operate at different times in our lives. Sometimes the ego would not survive unless it was able to receive the life-giving food of the Self through its communion. At other times the Self must be fed by spilling the blood of the ego through the crucifixion, sacrifice and death we have seen in the Hanged Man and Dead Man cards.

As well as binding humans to God (and ego to Self) blood also cleanses and redeems. That is, it releases us from guilt — both the introverted guilt that arises from Self-betrayal and being untrue to our own nature as well as the extroverted guilt incurred through injuring others. This idea of redemption through blood is well developed in the Christian theme of partaking of the blood of Christ in the Eucharist. A picture from a Catholic missal (Figure 71) portrays strikingly similar images and themes to those in the Hanged Man, Dead Man and Temperate Man cards (the cards of crucifixion, death and resurrection). The top half of the picture shows Christ on the cross and an angel holding a chalice collecting a stream of blood that issues from his side. Below, an angel pours blood from a chalice releasing souls from purgatory.

The sacrifice of the Hanged Man and the death of the Dead Man allow spirit and matter to join via a fluid that brings consciousness and is a union of fire and water, life and death. The blood of Christ is identical to what the alchemists called the *aqua permanens* (the eternal water) which was a liquid form of the Philosopher's Stone. It contains and reconciles all the opposites and is the nourishment that flows from the Self. The water of life flows again after a period of troubles, depression or stagnation. Aqua permanens, blood, starwater — the difference between the Christian imagery and that of the Xultun Tarot is that the blood poured from the chalice redeems human souls but in the Temperate Man the starwater is poured from the pot onto the earth and redeems not just humankind but all of creation.

When the same substance is shared between people whether it be a toast or libation, breaking bread together, the shedding of blood together in war, or the literal exchange of blood as in a blood brotherhood, then an indissoluble bond is made between individuals, between peoples, or between heaven and earth. The exchange of blood, literally or symbolically, repre-

Figure 71. The blood of Christ saving souls from purgatory

sents a joint investment of energy in a common enterprise. Psychologically, it is only after a battle with ourselves, after some psychic blood has been shed, after intense affect, that the ego and the Self, spirit and matter discover each other and become bound to one another in a common enterprise. This is the Temperate Man.

Breath of Starwater

In the European tarot this card is often pictured as an angel. This suggests the combining of heavenly and human attributes—angelic wings and a human body. The angel pours water from one vessel to another indicating that the connection between heaven and earth are made by the fluidity of feeling rather than the sharp discriminations of thinking. The pouring from one vessel to another also points to energy now being reversible and flowing in both directions, whereas in the previous 13 cards life had only flowed in one direction—forward. The water is also contained within a pitcher or pot—psychic energy and emotion is now self-contained and useable. The alchemists called this the *vas bene clausum,* the well-closed vessel. This containment is the middle way between on the one hand being walled-off, locked away and bottled-up or, on the other hand, being emotionally leaky. All this brings about a fertilisation, an interpenetration, a balancing, a bringing together of things that have been separate, and a separating of things that have been commixed.

Water does not appear in any of the cards until this point. There is air and earth in all the cards from the Priestess to the Dead Man, as well as fire in the Sage and the Consort, but no water in any of them. All water yearns for the ocean and it is the psychic energy that flows naturally toward its goal and finds its own level by itself. But the personality is not ready for this living water — as disinct from the water of tears and affect — until the Temperate Man. Thus it does not appear until now.

The water poured by the Temperate Man is different from the water poured by the angel in the Marseilles Tarot. It has stars in it. Stars symbolise divine guidance, our unique destiny, spiritual light penetrating the darkness, the guiding light in the darkness of the unconscious, or the deceased ancestors and souls of the dead. The starwater and the roots of the Flowering Tree behind him go down into three of the five cards in the bottom row. The water and roots (which are all one needs for growth) connect the Temperate Man to the totality of the Self represented by the row of cards underneath him. What sustains him comes from below not from above.

The Temperate Man is now self-stabilising, he has his own compass and can unerringly find his way back to the source. Psychologically, water symbolises the feeling function and in pouring water, the substance that sustains life, the ego now feeds an elemental and enduring connection with the Self. From the contrary point of view, we can also say that the Self nourishes the Temperate Man through the elements of earth and water. These elements are needed for embodiment, one cannot live on fire and air. This is highlighted by the fact that in the first two rows all the figures are supported by human-made foundations but in the third row all the figures are supported by the solidity of the green earth beneath them. The Temperate Man (14) is now a conscious animal (1 + 4) and for the first time he is fully human (5), and is teachable (10 + 4). In fact, he is the child of the Self.

The pouring of the water by the Temperate Man is not done with the heroism of the Warrior, the introverted searching of the Sage, or the striking decisiveness of the Balance. His graceful and fluid posture suggests a conscious cooperation with the forces of nature, the natural qualities of the element and the force of gravity. This is not an act of will but a matter of noticing where psychic energy wants to go and bending oneself to its course. Life energy, symbolised by the water, that is in alignment with the will of the Self will always restore life to barren ground, find its natural course and flow to the sea to begin again. About this psychic energy Jung said:

It does not lie in our power to transfer 'disposable' energy at will to a rationally chosen object.... [It] can at best be applied voluntarily for only a short time. But in most cases it refuses to seize hold, for any length of time, of the possibilities rationally presented to it. Psychic energy is a very fastidious thing which insists on fulfilment of its own conditions. However much energy may be present, we cannot make it serviceable until we have succeeded in finding the right gradient.[16]

Now that he has an enduring relationship with what he is utterly not, with what is most alien to himself, the Temperate Man paradoxically becomes more himself. This relationship with the deeper Self enables him to pour the water of his unique, human feeling values on the earth and to return his individuality to the place from which he was born. This gift moistens the Moon with its own dew and reminds the Winged Serpent of its earthy roots. This brings about a greater flexibility and an expansion of the personality. Jung wrote, "This loosening up of cramped and rigid attitudes corresponds to the solution and separation of the elements by the *aqua permanens*, which was already present in the 'body' and is lured out by the art. The water is a soul or spirit, that is a 'psychic substance,' which is now in its turn is applied to the original material."[17]

The starwater is the aqua permanens and the green earth is the prima materia. The aqua permanens dissolves the elements and separates them from each other.[18] Psychologically, this means that when we turn our attention to ourselves, to our dreams and our inner life, or carry out "active imagination" (by dialoguing with the figures in our dreams, as Jung suggested) we water the green earth of the psyche. Jung described this active imagination in just such terms: "If you will contemplate your lack of fantasy, of inspiration, and inner aliveness, which you feel as sheer stagnation and a barren wilderness, and impregnate it with the interest born of alarm at your inner death, then something can take shape in you, for your inner emptiness conceals just as great a fullness if only you will allow it to penetrate you. If you prove receptive to this 'call of the wild,' the longing for fulfilment will quicken the sterile wilderness of your soul as rain quickens the earth."[19]

We see these developments in the Movement of Stopping the World. The Ruler holds the serpent bundle horizontally in his arms and he mediates the horizontal relationships between people in the outer world. The Sage's Flowering Tree stands vertically behind him and he mediates the vertical relationships between ego and unconscious in the inner world. Both the Ruler and the Sage are separated from, but also connected to, the earth by human-made platforms. The Ruler's bundle is a microcosm of the macrocosm but is held in his arms and does not touch the earth. The Sage's staff touches

Figure 72. Side view of the first edition box of the Xultun Tarot

the ground but is not yet planted in the earth and leans on the wall behind him. Both Ruler and Sage rely on edifices fashioned by the ego.

However, the Temperate Man holds his staff vertically in his left hand and the Flowering Tree to his left flowers and gives birth to a rainbow. His feet are planted on the ground, neither on a platform nor on a temple floor. He mediates all four directions and we see the four-pointed sun above him. The brazier of the Sage has now become a human-size pot that holds water, the most flexible and adaptable element. The sun shines, plants flower, the rainbow comes out and starwater flows.

The last card of Stopping the World, the Sun, mediates all eight directions. The rainbow above it is the Breath of the Sun and, as we shall see later, the Temperate Man is linked to the Sun through breath.

Four Dreams

On the side of the box of the first edition of the Xultun Tarot are the words "Unlocking the Four Corners" (Figure 72). The cards at the four corners of the deck have stars in them (Priestess, Lovers, Star and Planet Earth). So do the two cards in the centre of the deck (Sage and Temperate Man). The cards at the four corners are feminine, they dream and create. The cards at the centre are masculine, they focus and bring forth.

The stars are seen in the night sky in the Priestess, Lovers, Sage and Star cards, at the centre of Planet Earth, and in the water poured by the Temperate Man. These six cards are the only cards in the deck with stars in them and they form two triangles: a lower triangle with its apex pointing up (Star, Planet Earth and Temperate Man) and an upper triangle with its apex pointing down (Priestess, Lovers and Sage). The apices of these two triangles touch making a figure 8 or infinity movement (Figure 73).

The card at each corner is the Holder of a Dream.[20] In the southeast, Planet Earth (21) holds the Dream of the Ancestors. The ancestors are all those who came before us who dreamed a dream, including the ancestors of the Stone Peoples, the Plant Nations, the Animals, the Humans and particularly the Star Nations Peoples, the ancestors who came from other worlds. The Dream of the Ancestors is for Grandmother Earth to be a fully fertile planet, physically and spiritually. Physically, she is a 2—matter, sub-

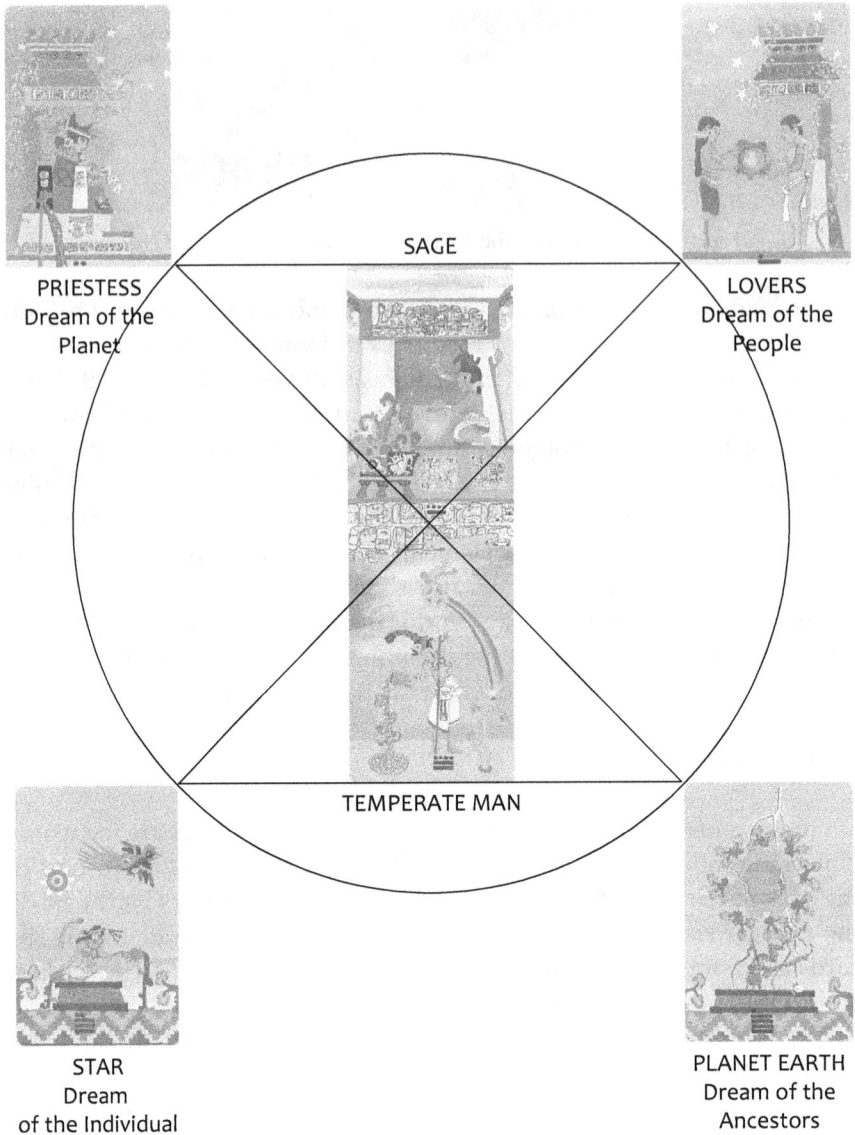

SAGE

PRIESTESS
Dream of the
Planet

LOVERS
Dream of the
People

TEMPERATE MAN

STAR
Dream
of the Individual

PLANET EARTH
Dream of the
Ancestors

Figure 73. The Four Dreams

stance and form. But spiritually, she is a 21 which is matter (2) that is conscious (1) and fertile (2 + 1 = 3). In the southwest, the Star holds the Dream of the Individual to find their own guiding star, so its light will bring them a fertile life of pleasure and knowledge. At the apex of this triangle the Temperate Man is the bridge and mediator between these two dreams.

In the northwest, the Priestess holds the Dream of the Planet to look within herself and find her own inner partner, her inner sun to make love with and to become a fertile planet. In the northeast, the Lovers hold the

Dream of the People for the masculine and feminine to come into balance and to become a fertile people. The Sage's wisdom is the marriage of these two dreams.

Each position on a wheel works with the energy on the opposite side of the wheel. The Lovers hold Dream of the People and when they look across the wheel to the Star in the southwest they see the other walking their individual path guided by their own star. Conversely, when the Dream of the Individual looks across the wheel to the Lovers they see the masculine and feminine in balance within and between people.

The Priestess holds the Dream of Planet and she works across the wheel with the Dream of the Ancestors that Grandmother Earth will become a spiritually mature planet and take her place in the Sisterhood of Planets. When the Dream of the Ancestors looks across the wheel it sees this actual physical planet that is their dream. Their dream is not for us to board an alien mothership and leave for Sirius, channelling ascended masters all the way, but for us to Walk in Beauty on this planet that has air to breath, water to drink, starfish, elephants, sunsets and mountains.

In the upper triangle the Priestess, Lovers and Sage are all covered by a temple indicating their need for protection from the archetypal power of the stars. The temples also denote the need for containment within the established structure of a culture or society. However, the lower triangle of the Temperate Man, Star, and Planet Earth, are nakedly and extrovertedly open to the cosmos without the need for protection or a mediating structure. In fact, in Planet Earth the Great Grandfather Stars (19) are at the centre of the earth indicating that the divine, cosmic forces have now become integrated and incarnated in the physical body (2) of the Earth (21).

The tarot is the story of how both ego and spirit develop the capacity to view themselves from outside their accustomed horizons. Nothing, neither spirit nor matter, can become fully conscious unless it has both objectivity and subjectivity. That is, unless it can consider itself (or be considered) as an object from the outside as well as experiencing itself as a subject from the inside. When we see ourselves through our own eyes we gain meaning and subjective understanding. When we see ourselves through eyes of the other we gain relationship and objective understanding. The Sage understands and gives objectivity to matter—this is the noble pursuit of science. The Temperate Man understands and gives objectivity to spirit in ways that it cannot or has no need to.

In the upper triangle the human figures of the Priestess, the Lovers and the Sage all present the Maya handsign meaning "birth" or "creation." These cards symbolise the birth of matter into spirit. The seeds of creating a life worthy of ourselves are sown with the first card, the Priestess, when we are born into life itself. This engagement with life becomes intensified when we are born into the life of another (the Lovers) and then born into ourselves (the Sage). This upper triangle represents the work in service of one-self and the work that belongs to the first half of life. It is introverted and individual.

In the lower triangle the handsign is in more symbolic form. In the Temperate Man his whole body is the handsign, in the Star it is the two streams of the water, and in Planet Earth the trees are the handsign. These cards represent the birth of spirit into matter. Planet Earth is spirit manifest in matter. Spirit is then born into an individual by becoming the unique vision and destiny of an individual in the Star card. It is then born again in the Temperate Man who has the depth to hold this relationship with the other world and we see him looking down on the row of cards beneath him. This lower triangle is the work in service of creation and occupies the second half of life. It is extroverted and collective.

If we add the numbers of the cards in top triangle we get 2 + 6 + 9 = 17 = 8. If we add the cards in the bottom triangle we get 14 + 17 + 21 = 52 = 7. The lower triangle is working with nagual reality and the dreaming (7) matter, pattern and form. The upper triangle is working with tonal reality and stalking matter, pattern and form (8) that has already been dreamed. When these two triangles are brought together this is the work of the Souls of All Humans (7 + 8 = 15).

Death of the Earth

The four dreams are held together by the two centre cards — the 9 (Sage) and the 14 (Temperate Man). Ceremony Man is another name for the Temperate Man because he is the one who brings the beauty, harmony and balance of ceremony. The lower triangle is extroverted spirit and the upper triangle is introverted matter and for the two to meet the humanness of the 9 and 14 cards is necessary. It is not just the cards themselves but also the past and the future they embody. The 9 card contains all the materialised forms of the previous 0–9 cards and the 14 card contains all the potential dreamings of the 20–14 cards. As we reach up to spirit, so it reaches down to us.

Many traditions and religions have spiritual ceremony and knowledge (the collective, extroverted understanding of spirit) but not human wisdom (the individual, introverted understanding of oneself). In fact, some religions attempt to circumvent the problems of being human by getting rid of the ego rather than having one. But when the wisdom of the Temperate Man is married to the knowledge of the Sage then something important happens — all Four Dreams are brought together. When conscious humans sit on Grandmother Earth in ceremony then a gateway to the Dreaming, the songlines of the Star Nations, is opened. The two triangles touch and energy flows in a figure of eight and feeds the Four Dreams.

This is why the planet needs humans to gather, individually or collect-ively, in a sacred way in order to keep her dream alive and to keep her body physically healthy. And this why the Star Nations visit us—because their dream is dying. It is possible, even probable, that this planet will become in-fertile and die. This means not only that this physical world dies, the Dream of the Ancestors dies and one more Hoop of Creation is broken, but some-thing even more cataclysmic.

Each child of Grandmother Earth has a gift or a medicine by which it gives life and heals life. The Minerals hold, Plants give, the Animals re-ceive, Humans determine, and Ancestors catalyse energy. Humans are the determiners, meaning they have been given the gift of free will in the Cre-ator's desire to exercise its free will and birth itself into all forms of all things. The Creator has four Shields in its luminous cocoon just as we do, be-ing created in its image, and each Shield is a universe. The south universe is the Child Substance Shield of the Creator, the north universe is the Adult Substance Shield, the west universe is the Adult Spirit Shield, and the east universe is the Child Spirit Shield. Within the south universe there are twelve planets that carry human life, and Grandmother Earth is the south planet. The south is the place of beginnings, the child and the heart. Like the Priestess who carries the Heart of our Child Substance Shield, as the south planet in the south universe Grandmother Earth carries the heart, the feel-ings, the joy, the woundedness and the emotions of the Child Substance Shield of the Creator.

As determiners, we can choose for good or for ill. Other life forms cannot choose in this way. The polar bear never wakes up in the morning wanting to move to Madagascar and be a lemur. The horse does not come out of the closet and declare it is a carnivore. The buffalo never wants to work in Man-hattan. Rocks are at home where they are, the grass is never celibate, and flowers don't envy trees. The choices of humans however can be in align-ment with, or contrary to, our own nature and to nature herself. The cumu-lative result of our choices over the last 5,000 years and particularly the last 500 years has resulted in the incremental destruction of life. If this planet dies then there is no conscious matter to hold this place in the south uni-verse. The result is something beyond human comprehension—the heart of the child of the Creator will die.

So it's not just about global warming and habitat destruction. More im-portantly, we must not leave this planet, physically or spiritually. This is why rampant monotheism, the paradise of the martyrs, New Age ascension-ism, economic growth, fundamentalist rapturing, plans to colonise Mars, and the yearning for heaven and eternal life are all the same in their destruc-tiveness and toxicity—they abandon what is precious. They are anti-life and contribute to the destruction of this home for our children's children unto seven generations. Not that transcendence is a heinous crime but if one-sided it rips the web asunder. Just as rampant individualism is a cancer, so are those spiritual pursuits that have a lust for transcendence and exile. The whole point is not to leave but to stay. There is enough to praise here.

Green

Now let's look at the predominant colour of the background in each row. In the top row, the yellow passion of the rising sun of consciousness is dominant against a background of the blue of spirit. In the second row, yellow is the only colour and in the last row green dominates. However, in the third row the colours of red, green and blue are more varied and more conflicting. The Temperate Man (14) stands in the middle of this row holding all these spiritual opposites together in the same way as the Ruler (4) held the secular opposites together.

Green is the colour of renewal, growth, rebirth, life after death, and immortality. Hope springs eternal. The corn stalks that sprang from the corpse of the god Osiris in ancient Egyptian mythology were green. Osiris' body was dismembered by Set into 14 (sic) pieces and scattered across Egypt. Where each part lay it brought a blessing to the land. His wife and sister, Isis, gathered up the parts, restored him to life and he later became the god of the underworld. Like Osiris we have to suffer our own crucifixion (12), die and be dismembered (13) and then reassemble ourselves (14) to add our uniqueness to creation. D. H. Lawrence wrote:

> Torn, to become whole again, after long seeking for what is lost,
> The same cry from the tortoise as from Christ,
>   the Osiris-cry of abandonment,
> That which is whole, torn asunder,
> That which is in part, finding its whole again throughout the universe.[21]

The Green Man of the Celtic tradition or the Islamic Al-Khidr (The Green One) are similar images of renewal.[22] Khidr is associated with the immortal Water of Life, a freshness of spirit and eternal aliveness, and his greenness symbolises the freshness of knowledge drawn directly from living sources of life. In the Christian tradition, green has a spermatic, procreative quality and for this reason it is the colour attributed to the Holy Ghost as the creative principle.[23]

Green mediates between the airy coolness of the blue sky above and the earthy red warmth of the earth below. In many mythologies the green deities of annual renewal spend winter in the underworld where they are regenerated by the chthonian red. Persephone, after she was captured by Hades and taken down into the underworld, ate the red pomegranate seeds before she came back into the upperworld. We see this renewal in the green tree in the Temperate Man card which grows from the same position in the card as the bones wrapped in red that lie on the ground in the Dead Man card. If we let our capture by the underworld be a conscious descent — into loss, sorrow, depression, success, activity or happiness, depending on our nature — then this will bring about a deepening of the personality. Our tears of grief are seeds that will eventually bring harvest.

Angels

In Western culture over the last two thousand years, there has been a one-sided development of spirituality whereby matter has lost its sacredness. Monotheism has never done much for the earth. In the spiritual hierarchy of the Abrahamic religions (Judaism, Christianity and Islam) men are second to God, with women third, animals maybe coming a distant fourth, and plants and minerals not even on the ladder. Rocks and plants are not considered to have any form of consciousness at all and humans arrogate to themselves a spirituality that they deny other forms of matter.

As a result, the only way to know the world is not through a feeling kinship with All Our Relations but through the intellect and its discriminations. The development of Western consciousness has carved Nature at her joints and science is engaged in the strange task of trying to reassemble the whole by gluing together dead parts. The tiger in the zoo is not a tiger. It stopped being a tiger when it was taken from the jungle. So relatedness and connection fall into the scientific shadow. We see this shadow in the archetype that drives statistics — to (re)discover relationship, connection and association. But it's a dead body that they're dissecting, the life in it has left, and we find ourselves relying on clumsy and impersonal mathematical notions of the relationship between things.

In the development of religious traditions from shamanic cultures to Taoism to Buddhism to the Abrahamic religions, we see a movement away from the earth and nature toward spirit, from "nature worship" to "spirit worship." We see this in the differences between the 14 cards in the European and Xultun tarot. The Marseilles Temperance card is a more spiritual and less earthy image than the Xultun Temperate Man. The angel pours water from one human-made container into another. The psychic energy is contained and reserved for spiritual purposes and not "wasted" by being poured on the ground. But the Temperate Man pours the water on the ground — the earth and the cosmos are the other container.

The earthy Temperate Man does not have angelic wings, moreover he is no angel. In the Xultun, wings do not appear until the Feathered Winged Serpent in the Planet Venus card. Indeed, in this card it is not a human that has wings but a serpent, reviled by Christianity, that returns to earth as a saviour in the form of Quetzalcoatl. The appearance of wings much earlier in European tarot suggests a favouring of spirit. Our unthinkingly positive, airbrushed attitude toward angels should alert us to their chimeric one-sidedness. From the point of view of nature an angel is a bizarre mutant with a limited wardrobe and musical talents to match. It is the sterile, neuter offspring of intercourse between a bird and a human. A woman and a he-bird, or a man and a she-bird? One can but imagine.

But all things are two-faced and we must not forget the light side of angels. In the Judeo-Christian-Islamic tradition they are the protectors, messengers or emissaries who carry out the tasks of God. Gerard Manley Hopkins, a devout Catholic, wrote tenderly:

And for all this, nature is never spent;
    There lives the dearest freshness deep down things;
And though the last lights off the black West went
    Oh, morning, at the brown brink eastward, springs —
Because the Holy Ghost over the bent
    World broods with warm breast and with ah! bright wings.

I include here a dream of an angel. This dream weaves together many of the themes of this and other chapters — ruthless compassion, free will, becoming teachable, our contract with spirit, and our *hokseda*, our 19 or guardian angel. This dream came to a thirty-year-old woman contemplating suicide.

I lay on the ground of a cave where it was pitch dark. I felt tired and empty. I wondered whether I should pray to God to let me come to his kingdom. I was prepared to take all my sleeping tablets and die quietly.... I suddenly felt presence of an angel behind me. Although my eyes were closed, I could see his huge radiating wings. He spoke: "There are many other worlds beside this one but they are no better. You may choose to go wherever you like, but God's kingdom is only open to those he calls, and he has not called you yet. There is still a task for you to fulfill on this earth." I asked for a definite order, which I promised to obey. He replied: "The great masses of people need orders, you are told to act freely. Your task cannot be revealed to you until you are ready to live out of your own free will." I felt defeated and afraid when I heard these words. There was a long silence. Then the angel whispered into my ear: "Be careful. Time is pressing and your nature works slowly. Therefore you must use the people who are sent to help you more than ever before. I shall watch over you and be there for help. But remember, I am the angel of strength and I cannot relate to your weakness." I made no reply but felt a growing calmness inside me. The radiance of the wings faded but the angel stayed with me until I fell asleep.[24]

Peacocks

Alchemical writings offer an antidote to over-spiritualisation. Sir George Ripley's *Cantilena* (c. 1460) describes the diet of the Queen, during the pregnancy following the royal marriage, as one of peacock's flesh and the blood of the green lion. Mercury, bearing the dart of passion, brings her the drink in the golden cup of the Whore of Babylon. This sacrament was the alchemical and earthy contrary to the eating of the flesh and blood of Christ in the spiritualised Eucharist or Mass.[25]

The royal marriage and the subsequent pregnancy of the Queen are images of new life that will revitalise the old King. Like Isis' re-membering of Osiris, this new renewal cannot come about except through the feminine. The King grew senile because he had grown apart from the dark, chthonic aspect of nature. But why should the Queen have such a strange diet? The alchemists said the peacock's flesh is the only flesh that does not turn rotten, in other words it is immortal. The green lion was associated with Venus particularly in its quarrelsome aspect. Mercury brings the golden cup of the Whore of Babylon that was referred to in the Book of Revelation. So the Queen's diet symbolises the Queen consuming and integrating her instinctual, sexual, earthy nature, the resolution of conflict, and the harmony between the physical and spiritual realms. If the Queen assimilates these qualities, it means that her consciousness widens and the consciousness of the King is regenerated by her supplying what was lacking.

The senile king in need of rejuvenation is a common theme in alchemical writing and world mythology. The king is holy, in some cases he must not touch the ground, he must wear special clothes or specific taboos must observed. As we have seen in the Ruler, he is connected to the cosmos and must retain inner and outer order so that the tribe, kingdom or empire remains stable under his rulership. But everything ages, including religion, power and truth. Religious symbols and beliefs lose their numinosity and power over time if they are exposed, used and talked about too much. We become blasé and the deeply moving ceremony becomes a mechanical, tedious ritual. So the king must be renewed — the old king must be sacrificed and the new king must be born. Psychologically, the king represents the worn-out ego attitude that is no longer adapted to life.

We see this renewal (bloody or bloodless) in the losing team that fires the coach, the CEO who must go when profits are down, the group that undermines its leaders, parliamentary democracies who rarely elect a party beyond a third term, the military *coup d'état*, the French Revolution, the Ameri-

Figure 74. The renewal of the king

can Revolution, the Russian Revolution, political intrigue, and the night of the long knives.

This renewal is needed in the inner world as well as in society and the Ruler (the old king) and the Temperate Man (the new king) together with the cards on either side of them show how this happens (Figure 74). The Ruler, who represents the young ego consciousness, must be the guardian of the fertility, life and growth of the Consort on his right side. He must be raised up, revered, spiritualised, connected to both earth and cosmos. We see him standing in front of the platform, larger than life, holding his serpent bar indicating he is the intersection between the cosmos and the world. He must also be observant of his duties to the moral and religious codes of his culture as indicated by the Priest on his left side.

What occurs in a revolution (Latin, *revolvere*, to turn around) is shown by the row underneath. The Ruler who gave life must now die and be reduced to bones in the underworld as the Dead Man. He must then be re-connected to the earth and the elements (the common people and everyday life) as the Temperate Man. The Bound Man on his left is now bound, not to society and religious forms, but to the new spirit and inner values.

Becoming Teachable

> Nature creates all beings without erring: this is its straightness. It is calm
> and still: this is its foursquareness. It tolerates all creatures equally: this
> is its greatness.... Therefore it attains what is right for all without artifice
> or special intentions. Man achieves the height of wisdom when all that
> he does is as self-evident as what nature does.
> —I Ching, Second Hexagram, The Receptive

As the ego becomes more cooperative and opens inwards and outwards,
the cosmos begins to respond in kind. Our work becomes our medicine and
our medicine becomes our work. Nature protects against nature and the
arms of the world catch us when we fall.

The medicine teachers now begin to teach through the medicine of the animals and by Talking the Twenty. The Twenty Count says it this way: the
powers from 1–10 are the Movers, the powers from 11–13 are the Great Movers, and the powers from 14–20 are the Great Drivers. Now at 14 we become
directly linked to the intent of the Creator and become teachable.

The major arcana of the tarot are the big picture of our development, the
compass for our journey. The minor arcana are the local maps to help us
find our way through the bush. The fifty-six cards of the minor arcana are
not dealt with in this book as they require separate treatment but they show
us how to become teachable. Each suit represents an aspect of ourselves.
Cups = emotional, swords = mental, pentacles = physical, wands = spiritual. The 14 cards of each suit (4 x 14 = 56) represent a step, stage, gateway
or ceremony that shows us how to awaken our 14 in all four aspects.

In the Twenty Count the numbers 4 and 14 sit in the north of the Medicine Wheel (Figures 10 and 11) which is the place of wisdom, knowledge
and logic, and their shadow, philosophies and beliefs. The number 4 is the
number of the Animals. They are our instincts, our animal nature, and
teach us how to walk in balance and come into alignment with ourselves
and creation. Jung said, "The only true servants of God are the animals,"[26]
and "When God made animals, he equipped them with just those needs
and impulses that enable them to live according to their laws."[27] The Paw-
nee Chief Letakots-Lesa (Eagle Chief) said:

> In the beginning of all things, wisdom and knowledge were with the ani-
> mals; for Tirawa, the One Above, did not speak directly to man. He sent
> certain animals to tell men that he showed himself through the beasts,
> and that from them, and from the stars and the sun and the moon, man
> should learn. Tirawa spoke to man through his works. When a man
> sought to know how he should live he went into solitude and cried until
> in vision some animal brought wisdom to him. It was Tirawa, in truth,

who sent his message through the animal. He never spoke to man himself, but gave his command to beast or bird, and this one came to some
chosen man and taught him holy things. Thus were the sacred songs and
ceremonial dances given to the Pawnees through the animals. So it was
in the beginning.[28]

The number 14 is the number of the Spirit of the Animals, Sweet Medicine or Earth Father. It is the sum of 4 (the Animals, harmony and balance)
and 10 (All Measures of Intellect, consciousness). It represents the entire
knowing, awareness and communication of the animal world. It is our connecting link to the intent of the Creator and all animal guides and spirit
guides work through this connection. It is the Spirit of the Animals that
teaches us how to hear and understand the song of the other children of this
planet—the Mineral, Plant, Animal and Ancestor Worlds. We are the only
child of Grandmother Earth who has forgotten their inter-connectedness
with all things and has to relearn it. The Spirit of the Animals teaches us
how to do that.

The Maya glyph for dreaming is a half-human, half-jaguar face. Maya
rulers are often pictured with their uay, their medicine animal, were-jaguar
or animal helper. In Catholicism there are the *Nothelfer* or the group of 14
helping saints, and the 14 innocent saints in Shi'ite Islam.[29] In ancient Egypt
the Pharaoh went about in public with his 14 *ba*-souls behind him represented by birds. The *ba*, as a sparrowhawk or a falcon, symbolised the person's wholeness. So the number 14 is the number of the animal helpers and
is the part of us most in touch with our animal natures.

This natural animal, the indigenous soul within us, keeps itself dappled,
glimpsed but not seen until the holiday-maker, the wage earner, the
mother, the student, the seeker or the anthropologist within us is ready to
ask the right question, to be still, to find the right attitude, to kneel. Then
our indigenous soul smells us, and only after long years of sniffing, does it
reveal its wildness to us.

Animals are driven by instinct, humans are driven by archetypes or
spirit. The Temperate Man finds a human balance between the inhuman
brutality of our animal natures and the inhuman cruelty of our spiritual natures. Whether we kill out of animal passion or spiritual fanaticism, the result is the same—dead bodies. The Temperate Man finds the Middle Way.
Becoming "mature" as an individual is becoming more "civilised" and less
"animal"—but not overly so. Too much consciousness is characterised by a
refined use of will and directed, rational behaviour but an almost total absence of instinctual behaviour and naturalness. Too much instinctualness results in little intellectual and ethical achievement.[30]

The number 14 is the marriage of spirit and instinct, in other words, spiritualised instinct or instinctualised spirit. It is not the learned wisdom of the

Sage but an earthy wisdom. It is the place where we are connected to our instinctual emotional reactions—both aggressive and compassionate, both separating and connecting. Through consciously exercising our animal reactions the emotional atmosphere in relationships clears more quickly. Tempers and grudges linger less—animals rarely suffer from prolonged snits or moods. We also develop a keen nose for when our attitudes, and those of others, are unnatural, contrived, affected, put-on or pretentious. Our inner animal quickly sees shadow and smells bullshit. If it is not too domesticated it will bark, bite, charge, disappear, cuddle, comfort, strike or kill—all without thinking. The customary interpretation of the European Temperance card is that it is associated with angelic harmony. But the harmony of the Temperate Man is not the heavenly harmony of the tofu-eaters where everyone is of the same sweet nature and all is love, it is the harmony of nature where all things are true to the beauty and terror of their own nature.

Wisdom

> Together the patient and I address ourselves to the two million year-old man that is in all of us. In the last analysis most of our difficulties come from losing contact with our instincts, with the age-old unforgotten wisdom stored up in us. And where do we make contact with this old man in us? In our dreams.
>
> —C. G. Jung[31]

The figures of Aion and Philemon were examples of Jung's 14-ness. The image of the Mithraic god Aion (Figure 75) served as the frontispiece for *Alchemical Studies* (CW 13). Aion is cognate with the Feathered Winged Serpent. He has the body of a man, the head of lion, the wings of a bird, and is encircled by a snake whose head lies over his. In *Memories*, Jung recalled that the figure of Philemon first appeared to him in a dream where saw a sea-blue sky covered by brown clods of earth that appeared to be breaking apart, and an old man with multi-coloured wings and the horns of a bull flying across the sky, carrying a bunch of keys. After the dream, Jung painted the image in his Red Book and later as a mural at Bollingen, his lakeside retreat.

At the same time, Jung was struck by the synchronicity of finding a dead kingfisher, a bird with multi-coloured wings rarely seen around Zurich, in the garden of his home in Küsnacht. He would often converse with Philemon as he strolled in his garden. Jung said, "He was simply a superior knowledge, and he taught me psychological objectivity and the actuality of the soul. He formulated and expressed everything which I had never thought." Jung's painting of Philemon from the Red Book can be seen on the Philemon Foundation website[32] and the similarities between the image

Figure 75. The Mithraic god Aion

of Philemon, the angel of the Temperance card and the Temperate Man are apparent.

This marriage of spirit and instinct within a human being is what we know as wisdom. The biblical King Solomon embodied the archetype of instinctual wisdom. It was said that he could speak with plants and animals.[33] The legendary relationship between Solomon and the Queen of Sheba was one of the union between nature and spirit. The Queen sought out Solomon for his wisdom and tested him with 22 (sic) riddles. Thomas Aquinas' *Aurora Consurgens*[34] describes Solomon's temple as having 14 cornerstones and says that the house of wisdom of the alchemists is also built upon the rock that has 14 pillars. These pillars symbolise the inner structure of the alchemist himself must have if Wisdom is to build her house.

We see the theme of balance and temperance in Marie-Louise von Franz's description of the fourteenth pillar which was called *temperatia*, meaning a balanced temperament: "It is said that it nourishes and keeps people in health because when the elements are in a state of balance the soul enjoys living in the body, but when they are at strife, it does not. Therefore balance is the right mixture of the elements, of warmth and coldness, of dry and moist, so that the one does not overbalance the other."[35]

The marriage of psyche and spirit is known as the Holy Ghost or the Holy Spirit in the Christian tradition. Jung described the evolution of culture as a progression from the age of the Father (blind obedience to the law) to the Son (conflict resulting from a freedom from the law and a sharpening of the opposites) to the Holy Ghost (temperance and reconciliation as a result of subordination to the rule of the unconscious).[36] Movement from the first stage to the second stage requires the sacrifice of childish dependence, and the movement from the second stage to the third stage requires the sacrifice of adultish independence.

In Christianity the rainbow is a symbol for the Holy Ghost and in medieval depictions of the last judgement Christ is enthroned on a rainbow. The Holy Ghost is also symbolised by the dove, an enduring symbol of peace, reconciliation and temperance. According to Jakob Boehme, the 16th century German mystic, the number 14 represents the Holy Ghost as manifest in nature.[37]

Behind the Solomonic image of wisdom stands its essential feminine aspect. To the Gnostics, an early Christian sect of the second and third century CE, she was known as Sapientia or Hagia Sophia (Greek: *hagios*, holy; *sophia*, wisdom). She is known by the same name in the Eastern Orthodox Church. In the Talmud she is the Shekhinah, the indwelling presence of the feminine attributes of God. Reminding us of starwater, Gary Sparks says that in dreams stars are "one of the most frequent images of Sophia"[38] Alice Howell describes her:

> Hagia Sophia represents here: the loving, intimate, kind, helpful, and practical aspect of Holy Wisdom in each individual and, at the same time, the great ordering principle of the physical creation of the cosmos. The function of her archetype is to unite both of these principles through greater consciousness and love... Jesus called her the Paraclete, the Comforter. Early Christians called her Hagia Sophia, the Holy Spirit or Holy Ghost. Her symbol then and now is the dove. *Hagia* and *Sophia* are Greek words. They were translated into Latin as *Spiritus Sanctus*, a masculine proper noun, requiring a masculine pronoun.... This eventually turned the Christian Trinity or triangle of the Godhead into a totally masculine one, leaving out the Feminine, women, and Mother Nature completely.[39]

Caitlin Matthews adds, "This magical art, sometimes called 'the knowledge and conversation of the holy guardian angel,' attempts to bring about a conscious relationship with the interior guiding spirit, whether this is conceived of as the conscience, the angel or the daemon. This is one of the most important functions of Sophia in that she is the angelic presence whom all may seek. Because she is established in these texts [Wisdom and Ecclesiasticus] as the partner of both God and the soul, she is likewise the symbol of divine union — the sacred marriage of heaven to earth."

In his last great work, *Mysterium Coniunctionis: An Inquiry into the Separation and Synthesis of Psychic Opposites in Alchemy,* Jung discusses salt, one of the three important elements (mercury, sulphur and salt) of alchemy and has this to say about the comforting aspect of wisdom:

> Apart from its lunar wetness and its terrestrial nature, the most outstanding properties of salt are bitterness and wisdom. As in the double quaternion of the elements and qualities, earth and water have coldness in common, so bitterness and wisdom would form a pair of opposites with a third thing between. The factor common to both, however incommensurable the two ideas may seem, is, psychologically, the function of *feeling.* Tears, sorrow and disappointment are bitter, but wisdom is the comforter in all psychic suffering. Indeed, bitterness and wisdom form a pair of alternatives: where there is bitterness wisdom is lacking, and where wisdom is there can be no bitterness. Salt, as the carrier for this fateful alternative, is coordinated with the nature of woman.... The novilunium of woman is the source of countless disappointments for man which easily turn to bitterness, though they could equally well be a source of wisdom if they were understood.... Disappointment, always a shock to the feelings, is not only the mother of bitterness but the strongest incentive to the differentiation of feeling. The failure of a pet plan, the disappointing behaviour of someone one loves, can supply the impulse either for a more or less brutal outburst of affect or for the modification and adjustment of feeling, and hence for its higher development. This culminates in wisdom if feeling is supplemented by reflection and rational insight. Wisdom is never violent: where wisdom reigns there is no conflict between thinking and feeling.[40]

World Wide Web

This planet is alive and has consciousness. Almost every culture in history has recognised this as a fact. Western culture is a wacky exception. But even Plato, beloved of the rationalists, wrote in the fourth century BCE, "Therefore, we may consequently state that: this world is indeed a living being endowed with a soul and intelligence... a single visible living entity containing all other living entities, which by their nature are all related." The alchemists called this the anima mundi, the soul of the world. Edward Edinger adds, "Wisdom is the *anima mundi,* a matrix or invisible network that maintains interconnections among all things."[41] So the wisdom of the Temperate

Man is the instinctive understanding of this interconnectedness between all things through the faculty of intuition.

It is no coincidence that the World Wide Web is so called. If a spiritual reality is not acknowledged, fed and kept alive by humans it does not disappear. Instead it re-emerges in distorted, dissipated or degraded form in matter. Just as the denied thirst for spirit may appear as alcoholism, or the gods that are no longer honoured become diseases,[42] so the internet is the concretisation of the web of life and the interconnectedness of the anima mundi. Wisdom has become Twitter.

The north of the Medicine Wheel is the place of wisdom and logic. However, this logic is not the modern philosophical or mathematical logic but the orderedness or lawfulness of the universe as perceived by the faculty of wisdom. This lawfulness is not readily apparent, always escapes measurement and initially appears to the conscious mind as anything but wise. In fact, as Jung said, we first experience the anima or animus as fickle, whimsical, rash and unpredictable. But when we take her seriously, we realise that behind what seems like senseless fate lies a hidden orderedness and the more we recognise this the more she loses her capricious character.[43] This is the wisdom of Sophia, a wisdom that contains not only animal intuition, common sense and street smarts but also a profound spiritual understanding of how the universe works.

Because of this capacity for wisdom the Temperate Man is the card of mental sensation and the Keeper of the Mind of the Adult Spirit Shield. He is the ability for thoughts to think about themselves. This can only happen when he does not play favourites with mental philosophies and beliefs that impose constraints on his ability to perceive. As the Holder of the Mood of Mental Ruthlessness, he is our openness to receive information from the web of creation and seeing as the Creator sees—360 degrees around the wheel of life. He is the capacity to notice synchronicities—the unbiased observation of seemingly unrelated things that occur within the same time and space which at 14 become the stuff of everyday life. He is able to perceive reality as-it-is.

The Temperate Man is also the Teacher of the Stopping the Physical World. The physical aspect of Stopping the World is holding the tension between what the body wants to do and what spirit wants to do. We still the body so that it can receive spirit, or quicken spirit so that it can be received by the body. As in yoga, the yoking of the animal body so that it becomes a receiver for spirit, leads us to the Sun card (19) directly below. This card represents our higher Self and is the image of one-pointedness, spiritual focus, and the power of the breath. The higher Self is the part of us that sits but a breath away from the Great Spirit. The spiritual power of the sun is the Breath of Light and our breath summons the 19. So one way of Stopping the World is to simply focus on the breath.

Deflation

The two cards before the Temperate Man (the Hanged Man and Dead Man) and the two cards after (the Bound Man and the Released Man) all represent some kind of calamity. We have discussed the trials presented to the ego by the Hanged Man and the Dead Man cards. But why, after the promise of the Temperate Man, do things not "get better"? This is because the tarot is about the intertwining of not one but two archetypal stories — the spiritualisation of matter and the materialisation of spirit. One spiral up, one spiral down. Before spirit and matter can meet in the Temperate Man both must be tempered. Crucifixion (the Hanged Man) and death (the Dead Man) temper the ascending ego. Falling to earth (the Released Man) and being bound (the Bound Man) temper the descending spirit.

The ego must meet something larger than itself to be transformed and spirit must meet something smaller. This is the function that each performs for the other, smaller changes larger and larger changes smaller. For spirit, it must first fall from the heights of the pyramid in the Released Man and then be chained to matter in the Bound Man. Spirit then dies and in turn is crucified. The ego, in reverse, is first crucified in the Hanged Man, then "falls" upwards in death into spirit, becomes bound and then is set free.

For spirit this journey is a cataclysm, for the ego it is liberation. The meeting in the Temperate Man results in the getting of wisdom for the ego and a second birth. But for spirit it is a catastrophic downsizing, a demotion leading to imprisonment in matter. It is the opposite of physical birth, fiercely resisted by spirit but brought on by the ego's pregnancy and labour. This birthing and increase of consciousness for both matter and spirit is the result of the ego's efforts to know itself.

Until this crossing of paths comes about, neither spirit nor matter are aware of each other. They are both unconscious, that is, lacking in wisdom. In the transformation of the 14 card, both suffer a deflation and gain wisdom. The ego realises that it is not the centre of the universe and is beholden to the other world. Spirit, like Yahweh who has to be reminded by Job that he created him, realises that it needs lowly matter to become manifest.

The theme of one of Jung's last works, *Answer to Job*, was the divine drama of the development of the God-image in the Western psyche, and how it was transformed by Job's encounter with Yahweh.[44] By holding to his integrity and his human consciousness, Job was granted a glimpse of the shadow side of God, of which God himself was unconscious. Jung proposed that Job became the occasion through which God became more conscious of himself. The result was the incarnation of God in matter in the form of Jesus Christ.

Similarly, in the inner world when the ego becomes aware of the unconscious, and the unconscious becomes observed by the ego, both become transformed. But, like Yahweh, when we first glimpse our shadow we deny that any such thing exists, or only exists in others or, in shock, we over-identify with our faults and take the sins of others upon ourselves. Eventually, we begin to separate what is our own psychology from what is not. The ego becomes aware that it can be something other that its personal history, old complexes, popular beliefs, collective enthusiasms and archetypal passions. This comes about only when the ego has developed sufficiently such that it can go beyond the duality of either being responsible for everything or nothing in the psyche. When that happens the ego is no longer identical with the psyche, the psyche becomes an objective reality and wisdom can awaken.[45]

Compassion

The south of the Medicine Wheel is the place of openness to experience whereas the north is the place of making meaning out of that experience. The north is the place of the mind and it teaches us mental flexibility, discrimination and receiving with consciousness from all places around the wheel of life.

The shadow side of the north is closed-mindedness and mental rigidity where we are unable to receive new knowledge and are ruled by beliefs. When belief reigns there is no doubt. James Hillman said, "People who are sure are unconscious." This absence of doubt is often called faith. (I distinguish this from the authentic trust needed to listen and follow where spirit leads especially when we are led up alleyways and along paths where the ego does not want to go). As we have seen in the Priest and the Sage, we can become a slave to our own opinions, harbour intolerance and "–isms," and the word becomes dogma. We become the negative senex.

The light side of the north allows us to see our interconnectedness with creation. Out of this understanding of the lawfulness of the universe comes the mental aspect of love. This love is what we call compassion, our feeling of sympathy (Greek: *syn*, together; *pathos*, feeling) with and for all beings, not only sentient ones.

In *Aion* Jung discussed the myths of Adam, the original man or the Anthropos. This figure of a cosmic man represents the prima materia of the world and the basic substance of all later humans who are descended from him. He symbolises all human souls, since always, in transpersonal unity. In Jewish legend, God created Adam from red, black, white, and yellow dust gathered from all corners of the world. Adam, like the Temperate Man, is the Rainbow Human. This is the one who is quintessentially human and precedes the differences of age, race, colour, sexual orientation, gender, national origin, religion or disability.[46]

The psyche tends to be dissociative and split up into different archetypal contents and personal complexes. However, in the collective unconscious there is a compensating tendency represented by the Anthropos. The Anthropos or the Temperate Man is humankind's "group-soul" and the psychic counterweight to the one-sided drive of a single instinct or the differentiations of gender, race, and religion.[47] Thus the Temperate Man and particularly the next card, the Bound Man, symbolises human community and compassion, the archetypal feeling of being connected with humankind, and the social aspect of the Self. This transpersonal, mental love, purged of human desirousness, is at the root of group loyalties and allegiances to family, party, nation, church, and humanity itself. This is what bonds us to others in times of disaster and impels us to lay down our lives for another human being.[48]

Knowledge

Where is the Life we have lost in living?
Where is the wisdom we have lost in knowledge?
Where is the knowledge we have lost in information?

—T. S. Eliot

We have seen that wisdom comes with the marriage of spirit and instinct and is the province of the Temperate Man. Knowledge, its companion in the north of the Medicine Wheel, is the province of the Sage. It serves us here to distinguish knowledge from information. Modern information dresses itself up and refers to itself as knowledge but several things differentiate the two.

Information comes from taking things apart, wisdom comes by putting things together. Information is about something else, never about itself. In other words, paradoxically for a pursuit that values such things, it has no objectivity, no capacity to view itself through its own eyes, and no consciousness.

Knowledge always works, that is, it can be used practically to bring about change and healing and it will feed us mentally, emotionally, physically or spiritually. Knowledge is sacred and can always be put on a wheel. Like all things in Creation, it is a circle and always has a four-, eight- or twelve-fold structure or taxonomy. If knowledge cannot be put on a wheel it is dead information. Information has no luminosity, it does not breathe, walk, sing or dance and it will not feed the People. It is not connected with the greater web of wisdom. Like the tarot, one image will pull you into the web. One fact leads nowhere.

Information does not hold our attention or engage us, has no colour or image and has to be learned by rote. It has no self-awareness, that is, it only tells us about something else and eventually will reach the limits of its expertise. Information has no breath or blood and has no DNA. It is unalive and sterile, that is, it cannot teach you about itself, is not conscious of itself and so cannot become an ancestor.

Knowledge however is aligned with the greater pattern. Its nature is such that it balances the opposites within itself, will organise itself into a coherent whole ("a body of knowledge"), has self-evident rules, patterns and internal structure, and it is self-regulating and self-referential. Quite the opposite to objective information which defines something that is not itself. Knowledge has colour which is its image, sound and rhythm which is its song, and movement which is its dance. Information has no colour, song or dance.

Knowledge that breathes, walks, dances and sings contains its own depth and subjectivity and can always teach you about itself — like the tarot. In other words, it is alive and fertile and will always propagate itself. Knowledge that is allowed its own nature will always bring wisdom. Thus a 9 will eventually become a 14. The tarot itself is a living, breathing entity that has consciousness so the best way to learn about the tarot is to ask the cards themselves to teach you. This is perhaps a difficult notion for the Western psyche to grasp — that something as abstract as the tarot has its own consciousness and intent.

As Oscar Wilde reminded us, "Education is an admirable thing, but it is well to remember from time to time that nothing that is worth knowing can be taught."[49] Knowledge cannot be taught, only learned from knowledge itself. Information will work some of the time but requires a constant infusion of energy in the form of evidence, conviction, belief or faith. We can, as Jung said, forcibly apply our beliefs with wilful effort for a certain length of time until the original eagerness wanes then the enterprise collapses.[50] Knowledge that has breath and blood does not require belief or faith for it to work. But it does require a ceremonial *temenos* or container and an attitude of Temperance.

This ceremonial container, as the alchemists knew, requires constant attention. The alchemical vessel had to be tended so that the volatile Mercurius did not escape and return to its original state. Psychologically, this means that the fragile insights attained in the transition from the Sage to the Temperate Man can easily be lost and slip back into the unconscious if the ego is not strong enough to live the new consciousness, if it is contaminated with conscious strivings, or if the ego goes back to sleep. The Temperate Man represents the point at which the connection with the web of life is sufficiently robust that knowledge, approached in a sacred way, begins to teach itself. Paradoxically, now we have become teachable we no longer need a teacher—nature and spirit teach us.

This card, as the meeting place between heaven and earth, thrusts upon us a challenge to our integrity similar to the story of Job.[51] In our human weakness we must come to terms with forces stronger than ourselves. The challenge in this is to not lose ourselves in the process, and to not sacrifice ourselves on the altar of spirituality. We must find our own human standpoint halfway between earth and spirit. When we stand our ground no matter how much we are bullied from inside or outside, where we don't regress or progress, slip downstream or struggle upstream, when we don't collapse into certainty or unshakeable belief, when we have integrity and are true to our wholeness, we create something fully and uniquely human. It is this gift of beauty, our gratitude for this gift called life, the eloquence of the voice that is our own, the starwater that the Temperate Man pours onto the earth, that sings this world into life.

The Bound Man
The Spirit of the Adult Spirit Shield uses the Mood of Spiritual
Ruthlessness to Control the Physical Dream

The Devil

25

Bound Man

Sorcerers say that the fourth abstract core happens when the spirit cuts
our chains of self-reflection.... Cutting our chains is marvellous, but also
very undesirable, for nobody wants to be free.

— Don Juan Matus

Coagulatio is experienced as a bondage because it confines individuals to
their actual reality, the portion they were given by destiny. Perhaps this
accounts for the phrase "he was *bound* to do that." Language is stating
that destiny is bondage.

— Edward Edinger

There are two kinds of people: those who say to God, "Thy will be done,"
and those to whom God says, "All right, have it your way."

— C. S. Lewis

I want nothing. I fear nothing. I am free.

— Inscription on the gravestone of Nikos Kazantzakis

We, each and all of us, contain within us the entire history of the world,
and just as our body records Man's genealogy as far back as the fish and
then some, so our soul encompasses everything that has ever existed in
human souls. All gods and devils that have ever existed are within us as
possibilities, as desires, as solutions.

— Hermann Hesse

The card depicts a man and a woman lightly bound to a mask of Xipe
Totec, the god of spring. In his left hand Xipe Totec holds a torch that
he is extinguishing over the head of the man. Over the head of the woman,
he holds a snake. Between the man and the woman is the tail of the Feathered Serpent of the Planet Venus card below. On either side of the mask

316

Figure 76. Ox-Ha-Te Ixil Ahau

are two skulls which are the door into matter (birth) and the door out of matter (death).

The image of the man in the card is taken from an incised bone found at Tikal in the tomb of the ruler Ah-Cacau (Figure 76). In 695 CE Ah-Cacau attacked Calakmul, a city north of Tikal, and captured a lord named Ox-Ha-Te Ixil Ahau (Split Earth) whom we see as a bound captive.

Xipe Totec

The god Xipe Totec was of Zapotec origin but was adopted by the Mixtecs, who flourished in southern Mexico about 900–1500 CE, and later by the Aztecs. He was the god of agriculture, spring and the seasons, and death and rebirth in nature. He was Our Lord of the Flayed Ones. In order to give life and growth to nature and humankind, he flayed himself to offer food to humans like the maize seed which loses its outer skin to enable the shoot to grow. After he has shed his skin he appears as a shining, golden god just as the golden maize appears out of the ripening, spring greenness of the maize stalks.

Xipe Totec is often depicted as a person wearing the flayed skin of a captive of war and recognisable by the holes cut out for the eyes and mouth of the wearer (as in the image on the left in Figure 77) and the hands falling loose from the wrists. He frequently had vertical stripes running down from his forehead to his chin, across the eyes, and "horns" similar to the Bound Man card can be seen in the right-hand image in Figure 77. The an-

Figure 77. Xipe Totec

nual festival of Xipe Totec was celebrated at the spring equinox before the onset of the rainy season and was known as Tlacaxipehualiztli ("flaying of men in honour of Xipe"). A song to Xipe Totec was sung by the young warriors. It sings of the old tree of the Hanged Man changing into the green earth of the third row. It sings of the fire-snake held by Xipe Totec and its transformation into Quetzalcoatl in the Planet Venus card directly below. It sings of the emerald water of new life that springs up at the base of the card.

> Thou night-time drinker, why does thou delay?
> Put on thy disguise—thy golden garment, put it on!
> My Lord, let thy emerald waters come descending!
> Now is the old tree changed to green plumage—
> The Fire-Snake is transformed into the Quetzal!
> If may be that I am to die, I, the young maize plant;
> Like an emerald in my heart; gold would I see it be;
> I shall be happy when first it is ripe—the war chief is born.[1]

The nearly whole skin, known as "the golden clothes", was dyed yellow and worn by the priests for twenty days during the rituals that followed. Arrow sacrifice was another method used by the worshippers of Xipe Totec. The sacrificial victim was bound spread-eagled to a wooden frame, he was then shot with many arrows so that his blood spilled onto the ground. We have seen this image in the Hanged Man.

More Shadow

> Addiction exists wherever persons are internally compelled to give energy to things that are not their true desires.
>
> —Gerald May[2]

In the Marseilles Tarot the card is an image of a man and a woman in bondage to the Devil. It is usually interpreted as a confrontation with the personal shadow. This is an encounter with those parts of us that we consider base, inferior or undeveloped, and the ego is ashamed of or disowns.

Because the ego usually identifies with the culturally dominant attitudes, what it disowns will vary from culture to culture. In an extroverted culture an individual may disown their desire to be alone, in a homosexual culture an individual may disown their heterosexual inclinations, or in a feeling culture one's ability to think is persecuted. Whatever is disowned in the psyche will return, albeit in different form, as a symptom, troubling and distressing, that exerts control over us or takes our energy. In particular, the Bound Man represents those shadow desires, acts or relationships that enslave us and we feel in bondage to. For example, compulsive thoughts or obsessive behaviours, addictions to substance (money, food, drugs, alcohol, clothes), or someone we are obsessed with or dependent on. We want to be rid of these things but are unable to give them up. We feel repelled by them but in equal measure we feel bound to them. The result is that we are unable to leave.

We have met the personal shadow in the Warrior card. There shadow is relatively clear-cut—there is a line to draw, a battle to fight, a cause to crusade for, a mission to accomplish, a damsel to rescue, goals to achieve, principles to uphold, a freedom to defend, terrorists to prevail over, or the oppressed to liberate. It's all fairly straightforward but it's also the adolescent psychology of patriotism, activism, George Bush, and Super Bowl games. However, as we move more deeply into spirit's territory the issues of shadow become more archetypally weighted. Now it becomes not a question of good or bad, right or wrong but the very relationship between matter and spirit especially between spirituality and sexuality.

The shadow in the Bound Man card is trickier and more double-binding than the simple, alternating forces of repulsion or attraction in the Lovers and the Warrior. Now there is a powerful repulsion and attraction from both sides at the same time. In a sense, all psychological conflicts are of this doubly ambivalent nature but most conflicts do not touch the depths of the soul and we can treat them as if the arrow of influence points just one way. These are Warrior repulsions or Lover attractions.

However, with Bound Man conflicts there is an additional twist because the psychic forces themselves are ambivalent to each other. If we try to move one way then we are pulled the other way by the same force. This makes matters more binding and more devilish. This paralysis makes us vulnerable to evil and our soul stands naked and unprotected in the desert like the temptation of Christ, vulnerable to being seduced, provoked, compelled, and persuaded by oneself to act against oneself. We must stand on our own and choose without the guidance of the law, moral codes or principles that are more suited for straightforward shadow conflicts.

These archetypal temptations are rarely clear-cut but life offers us, in diluted form, frequent opportunities to make a "deal with the devil" particularly with the seductions of money, sex and power. Such casualties are the stuff of politics, sport and entertainment — fraud, cheating, corruption, scandals, affairs, or influence-peddling. The cure is effected not by retreating to the moral high ground and barricading oneself in a tower of fragile purity but by a homeopathic solution. Living, eating and consciously digesting one's own devilish nature, our sexual longings, our shadowy deceptions with money, the secretive ways we control others through our victim-hood, or the more obvious ways we control others through our bully-hood, all provide some immunity against evil.

Double-headed Serpent

This binding state of affairs that is the Bound Man is symbolised by the double-headed serpent. It is seen, for example, in ancient Egypt where the cosmic serpent had two heads, or on the healing staff of Asclepius with two serpents intertwined, or in the Mixtec double-headed serpent (Figure 78). A story from the Kwakiutl people of the Pacific Northwest about the Sisiutl, a double-headed sea serpent, is about this archetype of evil. In *Daughters of Copper Woman*, Anne Cameron tells the legend:

> When you see Sisiutl you must stand and face him. Face the horror. Face the fear. If you break faith with what you know, if you try to flee, Sisiutl with blow with both mouths at once and you will begin to spin. Not rooted in the earth as are the trees and rocks, not eternal as are the tides and currents, your corkscrew spinning will cause you to leave the earth, to wander forever, a lost soul, and your voice will be heard in the screaming winds of the first autumn, sobbing, pleading, begging for release... Before the twin mouths of Sisiutl can fasten on your face and steal your soul, each head must turn toward you. When this happens, Sisiutl will see his own face. Who sees the other half of self, sees Truth. Sisiutl spends eternity in search of Truth. In search of those who know Truth. When he sees his own face, his own other face, when he has looked into his own eyes, he has found truth.[3]

Figure 78. Mixtec double-headed serpent

The serpent is the "lowest," it crawls with its belly on the earth. It is poisonous and yet it sheds its skin and is reborn. It both heals and destroys. The double-headed serpent is a symbol of all the opposites within the Self and the inherent duality of nature. Psychologically, it is those experiences where we find ourselves in a profound double-bind at the level of the soul. So tortuous that they make us mad — both angry mad and crazy mad, immobilised yet full of feeling, no recourse, no solution. These states threaten to tear us apart. Nathan Schwartz-Salant gives an example:

The experience of the two heads [of the serpent] and their conflicting messages is terrifying. While we do commonly experience such things as a daily occurrence in life, we can often fade out of experiencing them or find some other defence, notably anger. For example... [someone] asked me to quickly explain something which was particularly difficult to put into concise language. This request was particularly maddening because I wanted to communicate with the person, but I was only being allotted a short time to do so. If I refused to give a quick answer, I frustrated both of us; and if I tried to answer I would undoubtedly be inaccurate. Yet the request, amidst the incessant demands of life, seemed reasonable. I wondered if, perhaps, it was just my narcissistic need to be careful and take time. Why could I not simply meet the request? It was difficult simply to be honest and to refuse. Within such dynamics of madness pulling me in opposite directions, I could feel a deep conflict in my soul. I could feel how my soul was severely depleted by a lifetime of such "hurry up" messages and by a need to split off from their destructive impact.... Perhaps the most difficult lesson to learn when facing a double bind is that one cannot win. One must learn to leave the field of battle by knowing that one's soul is in danger. All one can really do is not win and, instead, care

ROSARIVM

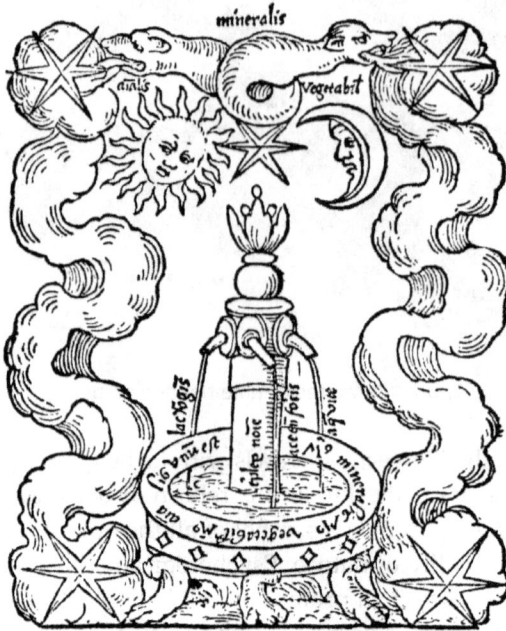

Figure 79. Picture 1, Rosarium Philosophorum

for one's inner life. At times, one is left with the necessity of recognizing and stating something to the effect that "this is not good for me." The potentially infantile sounding quality of such a response is often felt as humiliating for a person wilting under the impact of the double bind and believing that he or she must be a hero and overcome it. Generally this heroism takes the form of trying to get the projector of the double-bind message to understand how he or she is being contradictory. Little could be more futile.[4]

When our soul is in mortal danger, when we make a sacrifice to cut the bonds that enchain us, when we act contrary to ourselves to protect the life of our soul, then the ego acts as the Keeper of the Spirit of the Adult Spirit Shield.

Responsibility

Jung used the alchemical woodcuts of the Rosarium Philosophorum to explore the psychology of the transference.[5] The first and second woodcuts of the series (Figures 79 and 45) are familiar images. In the first woodcut, The Mercurial Fountain, we see the sun and the moon, five stars, and a dou-

ble-headed serpent (which the alchemists associated with the devil) spit-
ting forth fire and smoke that link the top and the bottom of the picture. The
alchemists said that the *binarius* or double-headed serpent was three-
named: *animalis, mineralis, vegetabilis*. The human element is absent and that
is the alchemical work—for humans to complete what is incomplete in
nature. The work of the tarot is the opposite—for nature to complete what
is incomplete in spirit. The union of these two completions is what we shall
see later as the image of the Planet Earth card—the catalyst of the Self.

All the cards in the Movement of Stopping the World (Ruler, Sage, Temperate Man, Sun) in midline of the deck are cards of holding the tension between the opposites to bring order to the world through our human efforts.
But the next Movement of Controlling the Dream, and particularly the
Bound Man, represents the ego's willingness to do what is unnatural, to
bind itself to the Self, to sacrifice its own freedom by submitting to the designs of spirit, to take responsibility for what it is not responsible for, and experience the unalterable duality of existence.

No life is complete without mistakes, regrets, and hurt received and
given. We behave badly when the instincts and passions of the Self, which
are bigger than we are, get the better of us (and at times we just behave
badly). Although frail and flawed in the face of these forces we are, and
must be, responsible for what we do and what the Self does through us.
This is the tragedy (in the Greek dramatic sense) and the magnificence of being human. The "sins" or "crimes" that we commit, outer or inner, including the crime of consciousness, must be consciously borne and experienced.
This is the Bound Man as the prisoner who experiences the full weight of
the "mistakes" in his life and being held to account. In the Marseilles Tarot
this theme is expressed in the Judgement card. These necessary crimes
bring about the inner process of remorse, repentance, contrition and forgiveness. Only when it has occurred internally can one then offer apology to
others.

In this process, the ego takes responsibility for the inhuman behaviour of
the Self so that the Self may be transformed and humanised.[6] To the Self the
ego is the rebellious one like Lucifer who fell from grace and was full of original sin for having free will. However, the ego redeems the Self by humanising it. The Bound Man is an image of punishment, bondage and evil but directly below it is the Planet Venus or Judgement card. This is a card of the final judgement, redemption, love and liberation. It is the ego's redemption
of the Self, the ego's redemption by the Self, and the reconciliation of the
two.

We are "bound" to give the devil his due because this allows the psyche
to function without interference. The individual psyche will set the limits
on how far we can stray from our own nature. If we don't honour the devil
then the psyche has to resort to extreme measures to restore balance. These

tolerances may or may not be the same as the prevailing cultural or religious standards. Some people can "get away with murder" psychologically and their psyche does not bother them too much, others are on a very short leash.

Jung said, "If one carries one's personal difficulties consciously, or collectively, if one can recognise evil without identifying with it or projecting it, then that frees the unconscious to function naturally and releases its capacity for growth. I consciously and intentionally made my life miserable because I wanted God to be alive and free from the suffering man has put on him by loving his own reason more than God's secret intentions."[7]

Evil

The Bound Man, then, is not primarily about personal shadow but about archetypal shadow or evil. Where there is light there is shadow — shadow is inevitable. If we put shadow on a wheel (Figure 80) we can discern five types: two pairs of polar opposites (the personal and collective shadows, and the human and spiritual shadows) and one at the centre that reflects and contains all the others. Over time the pole of each pair changes into and balances its opposite.

The most accessible is our personal shadow in the south — the longings, talents, needs, joys and pains that we have had to forget to survive, and then we forget we have forgotten. The shadow is who we hope we are not, but if we are, we hope others won't notice. On the light side, the personal shadow is the best of ourselves that we vowed never to be because the ego was too timid, it is what we hoped we wouldn't have to be to speak with our own voice, it is our talents that we refuse to claim. On the dark side it is the pain of growing up in the particular place and time, in the particular family and being born the particular person we are. In psychotherapy this is where we start. W. B. Yeats wrote:

Now that my ladder's gone,
I must lie down where all the ladders start
In the foul rag-and-bone shop of the heart.

These pains are exquisitely ours and rightly so, they make us unique, but they also make us common. It is an antinomy, like falling in love it is unique but as common as potatoes. The personal shadow is personal but is also archetypal.

In the north every group, nation, organisation, culture, race or creed has a collective shadow. Mostly denied, the collective shadow is the opposite of the cultural persona, the face that it presents to the world. The togetherness of the Italian family are shadowed by deadly familial rivalries, as in the Ma-

Collective Shadow

N

Human Shadow | W

C
Archetypal
Shadow

E | Spiritual Shadow

S

Personal Shadow

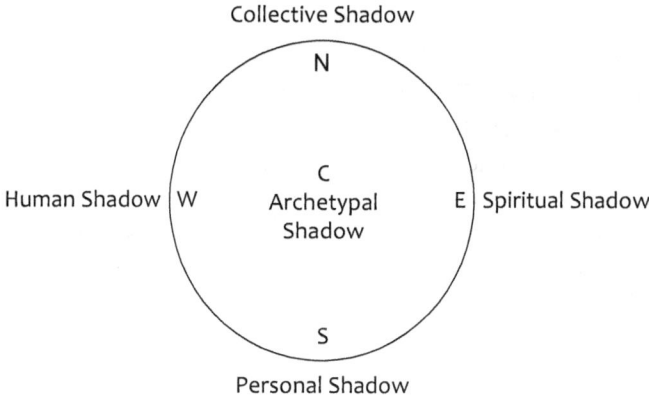

Figure 80. The Wheel of Shadows

fia or the Sopranos. The shadow of American wealth is its poverty of health care and inability to take care of its own. Colonialism and class structure are the shadow of the British ideals of fair play. The shadow of the French tradition of diplomacy is Gallic arrogance. Although these characterisations may seem stereotypical, there is no stereotype without a corresponding archetype that lies behind it.

In the west the human shadow only emerges after a prolonged effort at viewing oneself from the perspective of the Self—after some humble pie has been eaten, some shadow digested. It has nothing to do with personal history, it cannot be analysed or psychologised away. It is the shadow of simply being human; where we cannot grow and are always stunted; the places where we feel insufficient for life and others, bitter, powerless, shameful, forsaken and unhuman. Ojibway prayers often start with the words "Great Spirit, this pitiful one sends a voice..." and in "Amazing Grace" we hear of "a wretch like me" This is not masochistic self-negation but a relativisation, a humble reminder how frail our humanness is. The light side of this human shadow is the profound magnificence of being human, our grandeur, our exhibitionism, our extravagance, our joy of displaying our beauty and human finery.

The opposite of the human shadow is the spiritual shadow in the east. It is the dark side of the guru-disciple relationship, the abuse of spiritual power, and institutional abuse within religious orders. This shadow takes the moral high ground and is hard to argue with. It seduces us with the promise of deliverance and redemption from our human shadow.

The shadow at the centre of this wheel is the dark side of the Creator. When this archetypal darkness does emerge, we can only protect ourselves, as all shamanic traditions know how to do, and look within to see where we have been too innocent or where we have denied our own darkness and so left the door ajar.

An awareness of evil, or even the possibility of evil, puts our personal shadow in perspective. This awareness is the next challenge for the ego now that it has the strength to resist the fire. "With a little self-criticism one can see through the shadow—so far as its nature is personal," Jung said. "But when it appears as an archetype, one encounters the same difficulties as with anima and animus. In other words, it is quite within the bounds of possibility for a man to recognise the relative evil of his nature, but it is a rare and shattering experience for him to gaze into the face of absolute evil."[8]

The Bound Man is the 15 card and in the Twenty Count the number 15 is the human soul. This card is about the struggle for the human soul between the great archetypal forces of light and darkness and the struggle of the human soul with these forces. Without this worthy effort the soul cannot tell the difference between itself and the forces outside itself and will either be annihilated by the darkness or succumb to the light. Either way, the human soul is lost. Agnes Whistling Elk said to her apprentice:

"Because evil wants to know you. In a way, evil is trying to help you."
"How could evil help me?" I asked.
"You see, in the Dreamtime your image, your spirit, appears to be frayed. You are not clearly defined."
"What does that mean?"
"It means that the light that you are needs a distinct darkness to define it. The darkness that provides your balance and cosmic equilibrium is now only a gray shadow. By witnessing true evil, the opposite of the goodness that you are, your spirit will become more clearly defined. On the other side, the allies of darkness will see that and know your strength and they will leave you alone."[9]

Evil is a force or entity in the other world whose intent is to break the Sacred Hoops of Creation and unwind the Spirals of Life. Mephistopheles, the personification of the Devil in Goethe's *Faust*, says:

I am the Spirit that Denies!
And justly so: for all things, from the Void
Called forth, deserve to be destroyed:
'Twere better, then, were naught created.
Thus, all which you as Sin have rated—
Destruction—aught with Evil bent—
That is my proper element....
Part of the Part am I, once All, in primal Night—

Part of the Darkness which brought forth the Light,
The haughty Light, which now disputes the space,
And claims of Mother Night her ancient place.

The collective and personal defences against seeing the reality of evil are many. At one end of the spectrum is the fundamentalist who sees the Devil's work at every turn and is unable to discriminate personal evil from archetypal evil. (And we might remember that those who most fear the devil often have the most reason to do so). At the other end are those who naively see only love and goodness in the world and deny the existence of any personal or archetypal evil. Jung reminded us that "good people are singularly incapable of handling evil."[10]

An encounter with absolute evil is rare but the cardinal vulnerabilities are ignorance, naiveté and innocence, all of which attract evil strongly. Paradoxically, these are also the best protections. After all, fools go where angels fear to tread and an instinctive response will get us out of a tight corner when all else fails. The training of healers in some indigenous cultures involved an intentional and unprotected encounter with evil. If one survives, the reaction to such an encounter can go one of two ways. On the one hand, the individual makes a contract with the dark side and "sells their soul to the Devil" in exchange for spiritual power as did Goethe's Faust or Sauron in *The Lord of the Rings.* On the other hand, in response to evil the individual makes a binding contract to live in alignment with their own soul and the laws of the Creator. The confrontation with evil and the seductions of spiritual power bring the matter of integrity to a head as, for example, in Luke Skywalker's confrontation with the dark father (Darth Vader) in *Star Wars.* In such a way archetypal evil constellates the Self and evokes a profound inner integrity. As Mephistopheles says, "I am part of the power which forever wills the Bad and forever works the Good."

The process of individuation leaves a spiritual legacy in the collective unconscious. The unexamined life, however, leaves a dull, inertia-laden residue. Over thousands of years and the passage of millions of lives and trillions of free-will choices there has been laid down an endless, repeating cycle of unconsciousness from generation to generation. Just as children live out what is unlived in their parent's lives so each generation lives out what has been unlived in previous generations. As a result, countless souls are ensnared in ancestral prejudices without being able to break free from the chains of ignorance and lethargy into a wider consciousness. If there is no change in consciousness from one generation to the next then the sedimentation grows deeper and thicker. Like all things this residue has grown and evolved over millennia. It now has breath, intent and consciousness. It is what we call evil.

Evil is a part of what Don Juan called by a different, and more inclusive, name – the unknowable. It has no life of its own so it does not create life, it only brings the Death-Death that does not give Rebirth. He said:

There is a simple rule of thumb. In the face of the unknown, man is adventurous. It is a quality of the unknown to give us a sense of hope and happiness. Man feels robust, exhilarated. Even the apprehension it arouses is very fulfilling. The new seers saw that man was at his best in the face of the unknown.... whenever what is taken to be the unknown turns out to be the unknowable the results are disastrous. A terrible oppression takes possession of them. Their bodies lose tone, their reasoning and sobriety wander away aimlessly, for the unknowable has no energizing effect whatsoever. It is not within human reach; therefore, it should not be intruded upon foolishly or even prudently. The new seers realised that they had to be prepared to pay exorbitant prices for the faintest contact with it.[11]

The Bound Man symbolises the physical reality of evil and the shadow dream. His type is spiritual sensation so he perceives evil without the distortions of thinking or feeling judgement. He is the Teacher of the physical aspect of Controlling the Dream which is the willingness to entertain that God has a shadow side, to know that some humans consciously choose to work on the dark side, and to understand that evil is real but not a reality.

Praise

The monotheistic religions of Judaism, Christianity and Islam created a single god and by default created a single adversary. Polytheistic indigenous cultures have always had a multitude of evil spirits and the job was spread around, so to speak. Before the advent of monotheism, as Jung observed, the contrast between good and evil was not so stark and evil was much less evil.

In the age of reason, where such things are supposed not to exist, the black magician, the shaman who allied himself with evil, has disappeared into the collective unconscious. When the black magician was part of the culture the archetype remained where one could keep an eye on it. When malevolent spiritual forces are a part of everyday life the collective shadow gets more air time so it is less likely to turn demonic. Many indigenous healers trade in street corner herbal cures, love charms, hexes, talismans, and protections against the evil eye. These are open expressions of the day-to-day human shadow of marriage, money, jealousy, anger, envy, revenge and so on. But infinitely more dangerous, and far from public view, is the more conscious practitioner who traffics with archetypal evil. Marie-Louise von Franz said:

> Primitive peoples distinguish with great accuracy between a man who is possessed by a "spirit," that is, by an archetypal content, and is therefore in need of treatment, and a shaman or medicine man who knows how to control spirits and can give them free rein to work their powers through him without becoming possessed himself.... The symbolic inner experiences which the shaman lives through during his period of initiation are identical with the symbolic experiences the man of today lives through during the individuation process. One may therefore say that the shaman or the medicine man was the most individuated, that is, the most conscious, person of the group to which he belonged. From the very beginning, however, even in this early stage, the shaman's shadow appeared, namely the psychopathic black magician, who misused his inner experience (the experience of the spirit world) for personal power aims. The real shaman has an unintended power in that the spirits, especially the archetype of the self, stand behind him, but the black magician claims collective power with his ego and consequently is psychically ill.[12]

Indigenous ceremony is primarily for beauty and praise not for healing. The shaman was the eccentric, fix-it man who was called in when people and nature were out of balance. He knew that by feeding the other world with food, prayer, song and beauty all the worlds were kept in balance. He balanced the inevitable debt humans incurred when they dabbled in, meddled with, or unexpectedly crossed natural or spiritual forces larger than themselves. This debt was repaid and the forces of darkness were kept at bay with beauty—dance, painting, sculpture, poetry, or praise-songs created by humans with hands and voices that the gods do not have.

For example, in the Bible when King David's workmen began to build the House of God they dug a drain for the altar. In so doing they inadvertently lifted the covering on the Mouth of the Abyss and the Waters of the Deep began to rise. David knew that only a stone with the name of the Ineffable on it could seal the hole. He lowered the stone 16,000 ells and sealed the Mouth but found that the earth had lost its moisture. He then composed 15 (sic) Psalms and as each Psalm was completed the water rose 1,000 ells. When the waters reached within 1,000 ells of the surface of the earth King David offered thanks to God who thereafter kept the water exactly at that level.[13]

Protection

In the Twenty Count the number 15 of the Bound Man is the number of the Souls of All Humans—those human souls who have lived, are living, and will live on this planet. In the majority of these souls, the light of consciousness has dimmed to a bare flicker and they are easy prey for the dark side. To see this and not be demoralised or lose all hope is to be able to endure an awareness of evil. A consciousness connected with wholeness can bear this knowledge without being overwhelmed by hopelessness and despair. However, if we personally identify with evil we become dis-spirited. This is the devil's trick—to use either our guilty personal shadow to get us to see evil everywhere, or to makes us think that there is no such thing as evil, just bad people who can be saved by unconditional love.

Although we may be able to endure a degree of unworthiness or disheartenment when we are confronted with the evil of others we have a much lesser capacity to endure an awareness of our own evil. Edward Edinger said, "This means then that continued human existence demands that containers be found for evil.... self-esteem is fragile, and awareness of too much evil can just overwhelm it.... [but] there is an agency able to endure evil. And it has redemptive power. I see that agency as consciousness—consciousness that is aware of the transpersonal dimension of the psyche and therefore does not make the fatal mistake of identifying with everything it discovers within."[14]

Evil needs to be seen but not indulged, acknowledged but not given energy, before the light of the Planet Venus in the card below can manifest. One must be able to hold in clear sight, without flinching, the wrongs done to others and oneself and how one has acted against life, regardless of how the act may feel to oneself or appear to others. This is the archetypal basis of the Catholic confession. Like cures like and the best protection against evil is consciousness of one's own shadow. "The sight of darkness," Jung said, "is itself an illumination."[15]

Knowing one's own darkness means that one is aware that the personal shadow is the door through which evil enters. As a result, one is more likely to give a wide berth to those relationships, people and events where there is unconsciousness and shadow, even if this means sacrificing membership in the group. Leaving the field of battle is the first and foremost strategy in dealing with evil. This is not the place for the Warrior, eyeball to eyeball. We must look away, banish, and protect ourselves, as Catholicism and all shamanic cultures know how to do. Much apotropaic magic (magic that wards off evil) is rote superstition but is rooted in the deep awareness that there are forces whose desire is to bring about spiritual and physical death, rather than support life.

The Maya call shamans "spirit lawyers" and the term is appropriate. A natural predilection, adequate training, a street-smart shadow, a sense of humour, sharpness of wit, soundness of mind, the ability to discriminate between light and dark, and an understanding of the "laws" of spirit are all needed in dealing with the other side. But we cannot deal directly with absolute evil, it is too powerful so we must use our own dark side consciously. We must be the trickster, summoning all our wilyness, craftiness, guile and deceit. We must be able to lie like a rug and abandon human niceties like truth, honesty, fairness and justice. We must have the capacity to be merciless, pitiless and ruthless as needed to deal with evil. This is why the Bound Man is the Holder of the Mood of Spiritual Ruthlessness.

The Bound Man is a card of choice like the Lovers card but on an archetypal level. Religious and moral codes are collective protections against personal and archetypal shadow. If we are bound by a moral code we are safe — but we have no free will. Only when we Assume Authority and choose with our free will either for good or for evil, for life or against life, are we free. Then we are bound and are responsible, not to a code or a commandment, but to Life itself for the choices that we make. Thus the man and the woman in the card are bound, not to each other, but to Xipe Totec, the God of Eternal Life. In the Lovers card the ego makes the choice but in the Bound Man card the ego willingly submits to and is bound by the choices of the Self — and this serves as the soul's protection against evil.

Holy Matrimony

The man and the woman, and Xipe Totec and the Feathered Winged Serpent in the card below, are pairs of opposites which Jung called the "marriage quaternio" that we have seen in the Lovers card. The cards are similar in several ways (Figure 81).

In both cards the man and woman look downwards, at the level of the heart, to what binds them (the mirror) or separates them (the ropes). The ropes and the tail of the Feathered Winged Serpent occupy the same position in relationship to the man and woman as does the mirror in the Lovers card. In the Lovers card, the man and the woman find their connection to each other and are tightly bound to spirit via the reflection of the other in the mirror.

Putting on the flayed skin of Xipe Totec symbolises the death of our projections and taking back what has us captive. It is only in turning away from the other that the Lovers find the possibility of a relationship to the inner man or inner woman, then through that to spirit, and through spirit to the other. So in the Bound Man the man and the woman look, not at the mirror that binds them to each other, but at the ropes that bind them directly to spirit. The Lovers, then, are the social marriage sanctified by the commu-

Figure 81. The Lovers and the Bound Man

nity, whereas the Bound Man is the sacred marriage sanctified by the Creator. The collective does not like this marriage, as Jung pointed out:

> When a man controls his anima, or a woman her animus, they are doing something no one dreamed of doing before; because mankind has always been possessed.... For one should realise that one risks an unusual loneliness in controlling the animus or the anima. This is because a *participation mystique* is created by not controlling them; when one allows a piece of one's self to wander about and be projected into other people, it gives one a feeling of being connected. And most connections in the world are of this sort. *Participation mystique* provides this appearance of a connection, but it is never a real connection, it is never a relationship; it only gives one the feeling of being a sheep in the flock. And that is, of course, something; for if you disqualify yourself as a sheep, then you are necessarily out of the flock, and you have to suffer a certain loneliness. Yet then you have a chance to re-establish a connection, and this time it can be a conscious relationship which is far more satisfactory.[16]

In the Lovers card, the horizontal closeness between the two human figures stands in contrast to the vertical distance between the earth and the distant stars (matter below and spirit above). In the Bound Man the situation is reversed. The man and the woman are distant and turned way from each other and this allows the tail of the Feathered Winged Serpent and Xipe

Totec (spirit below and matter above) to draw close to each other in preparation for the coniunctio of Planet Venus.

In other words, the horizontal opposites of the masculine and feminine must be in good relation, as in the Bound Man, before the vertical opposites of spirit and matter can join. This suggests something profound — that without a conscious marriage between the masculine and the feminine within and between humans, spirit and matter cannot touch. The Great Grandfather Stars and Great Grandmother Void cannot make love and give birth to the worlds, and Grandmother Earth cannot receive the seed of Grandfather Sun and continue to be a fertile planet unless the masculine and feminine on this planet are in balance. This is why in its truest essence matrimony is holy.

Mary and Eve

The bonds of the Bound Man bring about a reworking of the relationship between the masculine and feminine that was begun in the Lovers card. This relationship is, by nature, ambivalent and double-binding. Jung begins *Mysterium Coniunctionis* by saying that in the alchemist's work of uniting the opposites the last antagonism to be overcome, even more difficult than the opposition of the elements, is the opposition between male and female. The goal of the feminine is union whereas the goal of the masculine is discrimination. He then makes a frighteningly obvious statement, which reminds us how one-sided and collective our thinking is. "We are inclined to think of this [relationship] primarily as the power of love, of passion, which drives the two opposite poles together, forgetting that such a vehement attraction is needed only when an equally strong resistance keeps them apart."[17]

Jung then goes on to say that the Christian ideal attempted to solve the problem of the opposites of sexuality and spirituality by a regressive restoration of the original state of innocence through monasticism, celibacy, and the mystical marriage of the Church and Christ as bride and bridegroom. Alchemy swung to the other extreme and projected the conflict into matter. Neither of them located the problem in the place where it belongs — the human soul.

John Layard pointed out that Christianity got itself into a terrible tangle with the feminine. Both the Old and New Testaments begin with paradox, ambivalence and a reversal of the order of nature. In the Old Testament, a woman (Eve) is born from the rib of a man (Adam) who conceives without a woman. Then in the New Testament, a man (Jesus) is born from a woman (Mary) who conceives without a man. The first female brings "ruin," the second "salvation."

Psychologically, Eve with her rebellious will that upset the paradise of the Garden of Eden, is the image of the anima projection that will not last indefinitely because it is idealised and in the wrong place (outside rather than inside). The projection will inevitably encounter reality and the "world out there" that will bring about the "fall." Adam's creation of Eve from his rib symbolises the desire for the anima in the flesh, in accordance with *his* desires. Their lives in Eden are the epitome of the static, incestuous, undifferentiated union that inevitably constellates change. It is the feminine that chafes at these distortions and restrictions and births something new from this paradisiacal but sterile dead-end.

Mary, on the other hand, represents the internalised anima. Her connection to spirit allows the marriage of a human and divine love to be born from the caprices of the old gods. She is the archetypal image of what Layard calls the "soul's brideship with God" which leaves "the individual free to conduct life without negative projections due to an unrealistic dependence on human love."[18]

Feeding the Other World

The whole bottom row of cards represents what Jung called the Self. Each card is a different face of the Self. The Star is the emotional face of the Self. The Moon is the physical face of the Self. The Sun is the mental face of the Self. The Planet Venus is the spiritual face of the Self. The Planet Earth is the soul or catalyst of the Self.

The tail of the Feathered Winged Serpent coming up from the Planet Venus below is a fountain of water. Water is often a symbol for spirit, particularly in reference to the unformed prima materia. Without water there would be no life. Just as the Temperate Man poured water downwards onto the earth now spirit pours water upwards onto us. We are not only married into spirit but baptised into spirit.

The wholeness of the Feathered Winged Serpent begins to manifest but neither man nor woman can see this yet as they are facing away from it. This breakthrough of the water of life into the human realm is the result of the man and woman being willingly bound to Xipe Totec. A relationship between the masculine and feminine that is bound to Life is the beginning of a relationship with the Self that regenerates and provides the water of life to all things. This is what the alchemists called the coniunctio or the sacred marriage of the Sun and the Moon.

All the cards in the last two rows share the greenness of the earth symbolising the regenerative power of spirit that sustains hope in the difficult times between the Hanged Man and the Released Man cards. The last four cards in the bottom row all have a vertical connection with the previous row. The Temperate Man pours starwater onto the Moon below. The roots of the Flowering Tree behind the Temperate Man touch the Sun card. The tail of the Feathered Winged Serpent rises up between the man and the woman in the Bound Man card. The lightning from the Balance card strikes down through the Released Man card to the Planet Earth card.

Matter is the visible form of spirit and the doings of spirit make this world jump up and live. Indigenous ceremonies keep alive the good relationship between this world and the other world. If the gods and goddesses, who create matter and life, are not fed with prayer and gratitude for the gifts that they give, then the Hoops of Creation are broken. This is a long way from the notions of primitives appeasing and propitiating their gods, or making sacrifices for divine favours. These quaint anthropological fantasia say more about the primitive world-view of the observers than that of the observed.

But this mutual feeding occurs only in the last two rows of cards and it is only because of this foundation that the top two rows exist at all. This is why indigenous cultures supported priests, shamans and medicine men or women who kept the other world fed so that this world could live. They also recognised that this was only possible when the shaman had achieved a degree of harmony and balance as a result of being chosen by the spirit world, a long apprenticeship, or both. So we see that the elements (water, earth, air and lightning/fire) that connect the cards in the third and fourth rows only begin with the Temperate Man pouring the starwater on the Moon, or conversely the Moon only begins to offer the dew of her grace to the individual that has reached the place of the Temperate Man.

Sex and Bondage

The name of the card, the Bound Man, links us to images of ardour, obsession, excitement, craze, appetite, craving, lust, urge, ache, itch, enslavement, fascination, lure, enthrallment, and enchantment. It particularly applies to sexual fascinations and bondage (physical or emotional) in all possible combinations of gender and sexual preference. These bondages may range from being unable to break off a sexually charged relationship that is not good for us, through erotic bondage, to hard-core sadomasochism, to child pornography, to snuff movies, to murder and cannibalism for sexual gratification. Michael Stone, a psychiatrist, outlines a hierachy of 22 levels of psychopathy (sexual and non-sexual) ranging from treatable to non-treatable. The levels roughly correspond to the shadow side of each of the 22 cards of the major arcana.[19]

They have in common the theme of restraint and bondage when the ego is in thrall to something. Being under the absolute control of someone else, treading the auto-asphyxiated line between orgasm and dying (so different they are the same, for both voyeur and exhibitionist, seer and seen), masochistically struggling to free oneself, or sadistically watching another's terror and hopeless struggle. The razor edge excitement can go either way—turn-on or turn-off, sexual highs or self-loathing, fascination or disgust (with resolutions not to do it again). Secondarily, the self-hatred, the scourging and the flagellation becomes sexualised and a sought-after pleasure in itself. But all are a cheap imitation (and avoidance) of the real psychological work of the Bound Man, that of being bound, tied and leashed to spirit to suffer its pleasure not the ego's.

The themes of the Bound Man—shadow, evil, masculine, feminine, attraction and repulsion—all converge in sexuality. Jung pointed out that sexuality is different from the other passions. "We could call sexuality the spokesman of the instincts, which is why from the spiritual standpoint sex is the chief antagonist, not because sexual indulgence is in itself more immoral than excessive eating and drinking, avarice, tyranny, and other extravagances, but because the spirit senses in sexuality a counterpart equal and indeed akin to itself. For just as the spirit would press sexuality, like every other instinct, into its service, so sexuality has an ancient claim upon the spirit, which it once—in procreation, pregnancy, birth, and childhood—contained within itself, and whose passion the spirit can never dispense with in its creations."[20]

The pleasures of the flesh, lustful desires, carnality, the seven deadly sins, and our feelings about them (shame, secrecy, arousal, exhibitionism, voyeurism) are all symbolised by the Devil in the Marseilles Tarot. The Devil was missing from the earliest tarot decks and his later inclusion reflected the increasing Christian idealisation of spirit and demonisation of matter. The Christian excess of creating a single God who was all-loving or all-merciful was an advance in putting a human, loving face on an inhuman universe but it also made him too good to be true as there was no room for darkness. This state of affairs made the Devil a necessity. In addition, all that was sexual, female and of the earth was demonised. As witness, Saint Augustine's famous words: *Inter faeces et urinam nascimur*, "We are born between piss and shit,"[21] or the celibate Saint Paul's marital counselling, "But I say to the unmarried and to widows, it is good for them if they abide even as I. But if they have not continence, let them marry: for it is better to marry than to burn."[22]

If consciousness becomes overly spiritualised, straying too far from its natural, instinctive roots then biological urges and drives are stirred up in compensation. These are often sexual but instinctual libido can attach itself to any biological process. This results in the person (or the culture) being brought back to earth and the reality of the body by the eruption of the "baser" instincts (addictions to gambling, sex, money, knowledge, TV, computers or food) or an upsurge of "psychosomatic" illnesses where the line (if there ever was one) between biological and psychological becomes increasingly blurred. This compensation for rampant holiness is most clearly seen in the continuing revelations of physical and sexual abuse by the members of the clergy.

The opposite also applies—if there is too much instinctuality then the person or the culture is vulnerable to a sudden spiritual conversion. Like the career criminal who comes to Jesus or the monotheism that arose as compensation for the excesses of indigenous cultures.

Incest

We have seen that two opposing movements, spirit to substance and substance to spirit, are intertwined within the tarot. Both work against their own nature to transform themselves into their opposite and in doing so become whole. Initially, matter is unconscious of spirit and immersed in the joys of form, but matter longs to become more conscious and desires union with its parent so it may return to the source.

All life seeks wholeness. This is both an archetype and an instinct. The union of the opposites is how the alchemists described this desire of life to return to the source from whence it came—just as the river is rain that longs for the ocean. Life is exogamous and extroverted, marching out in all directions. But life also desires to wind in upon itself, to turn inwards and find what is not itself within itself, to become pregnant with oneself, to be one's own mother and father, to give divine, parthenogenetic birth. This, however, is incestuous. The collective forbids the turning-in, the forsaking of the old gods, the birth without proper parentage, because the birth of something new through the process of individuation always means the corresponding death of something old in the collective.

In all creation myths spirit creates substance, matter and instinct. The Word becomes Flesh. Human culture walks the opposite path in attempting to transform matter and instinct into spirit and indeed this may be the cosmic function of human existence. Archetypes are psychological, unconscious urges to behave in certain ways. Any psychic process that is not under conscious control becomes instinctual, thus archetypal forces that are ignored and goddesses that are not honoured show as disturbances in matter and biology. Instincts are biological, unconscious drives toward certain activities. If they are not under individual or social control their raw strength makes culture and social adaptation impossible.

The sexuality of the Bound Man leads us to what might seem like an unrelated aspect of the card—incest. Incest is now a somewhat antiquated term having been replaced by the more comprehensive term sexual abuse, however I shall retain it here as it lies closer to its archetypal source. Symbolically, incest refers to the union of elements that are alike or of the same nature. This includes the union with oneself—the Eve-like desire for the apple

of self-knowledge. But self-knowledge is never simplex, it is always duplex, both longed-for and resisted in equal measure.

Jung said, "Whenever the drive for wholeness appears it begins by dis-
guising itself under the symbolism of incest, for, unless he seeks it in himself, a man's nearest feminine counterpart is to be found in his mother, sister, or daughter."[23] Edinger adds, "Incest is the treason against all first-
half-of-life values. Incest makes one traitor to the proud autonomy of the
ego. I think the dread of incest is the root of all guilty reflections concerning
solitude, self-centeredness, preoccupation with fantasies, with dreams and
with the inner life. You know for many, all such self-centred, introspective
occupations have a morbid quality attached to them."[24] Because there is no
container in our modern age for this introverted, self-generating, endogamous archetypal energy it has emerged in its unnatural and pathological
form—incest.[25] This is not, however, to suggest that the symbolic issues discussed here are the only factors involved in the complexities of sexual
abuse.

Freud was the first to "discover" the problem of incest. But he shrank
back from the enormity of the problem, transferred it to the inner world,
reconceptualised it as the Oedipus complex (a special case of mother-son
emotional incest) and then generalised it to all parent-child relationships.
Freud interpreted the problem objectively and personally, however Jung
saw it subjectively and transpersonally. Subjectively, incest is the ego's intimate relationship with its parent—the unconscious or spirit. In psychotherapy, the ego submits itself to this intimate relationship with the unconscious. However, the history of the species is one of a long struggle to separate from its origins and to establish itself as autonomous. Thus a relationship with the unconscious is regressive and forbidden.

Freud took a literal and biological approach to incest. He believed that
the taboo against incest arose from the Oedipus complex and had its origins
in the prohibition against biological in-breeding. But, as John Layard has
shown, the incest taboo historically preceded the Oedipus complex and is a
prohibition against emotional or spiritual incest between people rather
than biological incest.[26] He said that the true function of the incest taboo is
the transformation of instinct into spirit by sacrificing the external anima or
animus projection and turning inwards to find the inner opposite.[27]

If we look at the second woodcut of the Rosarium (Figure 45) we see the
same scene as the Lovers card. With their right hands the king and queen
each hold a branch with two flowers symbolising their public, observable
realtionship. They hold each other's "sinister" or left hand symbolising the
hidden relationship between them. The dove above them also holds a similar branch, making 6 flowers in all. A common symbol for the joining of the
masculine and feminine is two triangles (2 x 3 = 6) and the flower held by
the Xultun Fool has 6 petals. The flowers and branches are the symbolic

equivalent of the mirror in the Lovers card, which is the 6 card. The mirror held by the Lovers is the human soul that later becomes embodied as the Planet Earth robed in Flowering Trees.

The king and queen are dressed conventionally and so bound to their personae. However, the dove suggests that in their conventional love something deeper is at work. The left-handed, unconscious coniunctio is their secret, "incestuous" relationship. The dove is a symbol of the Holy Ghost and this points to "the hidden meaning of the incest, whether of brother and sister or of mother and son, as the repulsive symbol for the *unio mystica*.... Incest symbolises union with one's own being, it means individuation or becoming a self, and, because this is so vitally important, it exerts an unholy fascination."[28]

In the Rosarium the trinity is king, queen and flowering tree; in the Lovers it is the man, woman and mirror; and in the Bound Man it is man, woman and Xipe Totec. Unlike the Lovers, the marriage in the Bound Man is a spiritual one. (In antiquity, incest was the sole prerogative of the royal brother and sister). It is not ruled by convention or romantic love. The pair now join with each other in a forbidden marriage and give birth to a third — their connection to spirit.

If we read the Bound Man card as it is usually interpreted we would say that the man and woman are bound to something shadowy and devilish. But we can equally say that the card is about an individual overcoming their addiction and bondage to matter by becoming married to spirit, finding themselves in their opposite, and finding the opposite in themselves.

Kinship

Through the experience of the Bound Man the masculine and feminine begin to realise they are part of a far deeper mystery of opposites. Because the mirror of the Lovers card now lies inside, and the need for outer mirroring is neither desperately sought nor defensively avoided, the person can see and ask to be seen by the other in a deeper way. Mirroring is no longer a matter of "empathy" but, more profoundly, seeing the trinity of self, other and relationship (3) that is our humanness (5) from the vantage point of spirit. This is the Medicine of the 3 x 5, the 15, the participation in the community of All Human Souls. Its gift is what Jung calls "kinship libido" or compassion. If we are granted, even fleetingly, such grace then no human experience light or dark lies outside the reach of our compassion and understanding. Absolute evil begets absolute compassion.

This 15 is the milk of human kindness. It is the concern, caritas, consideration, care, and benevolence that humans feel toward each other and other forms of life. This gift of human (5) concern for all beings is a unique addition to the laws of the universe (10).

When we are truly compassionate with another we can also be truly ruth-less. We become discriminating enough to know when to allow God have her own mind, to refrain from milk-sop charity and good works, and to gen-erally not interfere so much in the workings of the universe. But the will and design of the Creator is unknowable and ultimately we do not know what is good or bad, helpful or unhelpful, for a particular soul. We take on a fearful responsibility when, driven by our own needs, we interfere in the journey of the another's soul, or do not keep the agreements we have made with our own soul. All we can do is act (or not) and take responsibility for our omissions or commissions, conscious or unconscious.

In the Marseilles Tarot these actions at 15 are "judged" by God in the 20 card of Judgement. But in the Xultun Tarot we see a mirror sequence. Rather than a fearsome God judging at the end of our lives, our own soul is the ultimate arbiter in this life and the next. The result is not a separation on the Day of Judgement (between the good and the bad, sinners and saved, spirit and matter, heaven and hell) but a joining of spirit and matter through the descent of the Feathered Winged Serpent.

Instinctual kinship, or endogamous libido, holds the family unit to-gether. Excessive endogamous libido results in too much mental, emo-tional, spiritual or physical closeness. Too little and there is no attachment between family members. In many cultures one may only marry someone from outside the family but still within the same culture. Here the endo-gamous and exogamous tendencies are in balance and compensate each other. If marriage is too restricted there is no differentiation at all, no "new blood" and hence no cultural change, and the pressure for exogamy will in-crease. If there is unlimited exogamy and marriage has no restrictions (as ex-ists mostly in our Western culture) then there is cultural differentiation but the pressure for endogamy increases in compensation. If there are no social or psychological containers for this endogamous energy, it must make its presence felt either physically or spiritually.

The physical manifestation of endogamy (incest) is regressive and patho-logical. Incest is a crime in the outer world but it is a sacred mystery in the inner world and creates the Philosopher's Stone. Spiritually, John Layard said, "Its latent or spiritual purpose is to enlarge the spiritual horizon by de-veloping the idea that there is after all a sphere in which the primary desire may be satisfied, namely the divine sphere of the gods..."[29] The purpose of the incest taboo is revealed in the practice of celibacy where the restriction and sacrifice of sexual libido constellates its opposite — spirituality. Celi-bates and spiritual individuals have written some of the most passionate love poetry — for example, the Song of Songs in the Bible, or the writings of Julian of Norwich. This is why the man and the woman are bound to Xipe Totec, the god of sacrifice, because every instinctual desire must be fulfilled and what cannot be done in the flesh must be done in spirit. In sacrificing the outer partner, the inner partner is won.

All Our Relations

The emerging spiritual instinct of community and belonging itself needs to belong. It needs to find a home. Initially, this may be belonging to a church, being one of the faithful, sharing fellowship, or participating in some collective belief system or religion as represented by the Priest (5). The jaguar robe of the Priest symbolises the civilising process of human culture — the power of instinct has been assimilated for human use.

The instinct of kinship then develops into a quest for individual knowledge and the greater whole as symbolised by the Wheel (10). In the Bound Man (15) it becomes the experience of the holy marriage, the inner community, and a desire to serve or benefit others in some way. But the Bound Man realises that all restriction and license or benefit and harm comes not from human culture but from the Creator and the whole community of creation (20).

Jung pointed out that the clinical phenomenon of transference is never truly resolved, although in practical and therapeutic terms it might be, because of the instinct behind it. Transference is the unconscious process of transferring forms of relationship from the past onto current relationships. But transference is not solely a projection of our personal psychology onto another because behind it lies the instinctual factor of kinship libido — the desire for human connection and community.

When exogamy was held in check by endogamy, there was a natural organization of society where one was not a stranger among strangers. In Aotearoa/New Zealand, for example, the bonds of kinship within and between whanau (extended family), hapu (sub-tribe), and iwi (tribe), and in Maoridom itself, are the very fabric of the culture. In non-indigenous cultures these bonds have eroded because of the unlimited expansion of exogamy. Now the only place endogamy can find expression is within the nuclear family. This kinship libido, this feeling of belonging, has been deprived of its object. "But," Jung said, "being an instinct, it is not to be satisfied by any mere substitute such as creed, party, nation, or state. It wants the *human* connection. That is the core of the whole transference phenomenon, and it is impossible to argue it away, because relationship to the Self is at once relationship to our fellow man, and no one can be related to the latter until he is related to himself."[30]

However, this instinctual desire for community is for not only kinship with humans but also a *communitas*, a compassion and kinship with all things. This is the Planet Venus card. This kinship wants a home here on this planet, with the sacred elements of air, earth, fire and water, without whom there would be no life, and the Minerals, Plants, Animals, Humans and Ancestors who are Our Relations. We are children born of this earth. Our brothers and sisters are the first child (the Stone People); the second child (the Plant Nations); and the third child (the Animals). We are the fourth child — the Two-leggeds (the red, black, white, yellow and rainbow peoples).

Like incest, because there is no cultural container for this kinship with all things, it emerges in the exploitation and abuse of our kin — those in our personal or planetary family. So the occurrence of sexual abuse (the violation of the energy that creates human life) goes hand in hand with the abuse of what supports human life on this planet — the dishonouring of matter and the elements of air, earth, fire and water, and the violation of the minerals, plants and animals who are Our Relations.

Released into Chains

> The unconscious wants truth. It ceases to speak to those who want something else.
>
> — Adrienne Rich

The man and woman in the card are bound by a knot around their wrists. In marriage we "tie the knot" and make a binding vow to the relationship. Knots also symbolise constraints, complications, entanglements, the tangle that one is in, being caught in a web of deceit, or being paralysed by anxiety or indecision. Knots are a way of binding a magic spell and are also a protection against misfortune. The loosening of a knot is symbolic of freedom, unbinding, or salvation.

The Latin verb *religare* means to bind back and the noun *religio* means bond or obligation. In English it originally referred to the bond between humans and the gods. From the 5th century it came to mean "the monastic life" and only as recently as the 16th century did it come to have its current meaning of religion.

We are each bound to what we have written into our Book of Life and we choose a male or female body in each life to find the opposite side of ourselves. We will keep doing this until we have consummated the inner marriage. In the search for the beloved in this sacred marriage, which is always in the sight of God, we find God. So the human relationship is the temple, the *chuppah*, in which the God and Goddess come to dwell, and the man and the woman come not to worship each other but to worship a mystery that is greater than themselves — the mystery of relationship that embodies both matter and spirit.

The early encounters with the Self feel offensive to the ego and it tantrums like a spoiled child against being told "No!" It can no longer do what it pleases and feels like it is imprisoned. As much as it squirms and wriggles it is nailed, like the Hanged Man, to the cross of what it cannot do or what it has to do, physically or psychologically. It is only after being hung and bound that we can experience the liberation of the Released Man. Our magnificent or abject failures allow the Messiah, the Self, to come. Then, after the second covenant has been established in the Temperate Man, the ego willingly submits to bondage.

The word religion may also have its root in the word *religere* which means to pay close attention or give careful consideration to.[31] Psychologically, this means constant, alert attention to inner signs (feelings, fantasies and fleeting thoughts) and outer signs (synchronicities, animal behaviour, chance encounters). Life goes better when we allow ourselves to be guided by the irrational and the unseen as well as the rational and the obvious. If our careful observation of the inner and outer worlds becomes codified and mechanical then it becomes either foolish superstition or rational data-gathering. In the former, the black cat crossing one's path always means bad luck, in the latter it is always just another specimen of *Felis catus*. One is blind to the rational facts, the other is deaf to the irrational facts. For the Western psyche, this attention to the "irrational" is how we become acquainted with the inner partner. When one can separate the thoughts or feelings generated by the anima or animus from one's own thoughts or feelings, then one is not bound to the other. The tangle falls away and one is no longer bound by a collective destiny but one's own individual destiny.

The cards from 2 through to 21 form a graduated sequence from matter to spirit. The top row of the Child Substance Shield (Priestess to Lovers) is the most material and the bottom row of the Child Spirit Shield is the most spiritual. The Bound Man (15) and the Released Man (16) are the last cards before this bottom row and significantly are the last cards with human figures in them.

These two cards reflect this liminal place between substance and spirit where things are paradoxical, duplex, upside-down, mirror-imaged, reversed and interchangeable. Here the over-valued laws of reasons and logic do not work. The awakening of spiritual memory in the 11 card (Balance) manifests five cards later in the 16 card. Now we can see the thunder, hear the lightning, breathe through our skin, and see with our hands.

The Released Man is the heyoka, the reverse mirror image, of the Bound Man (Figure 12). That is, the image is not only mirrored (left becomes right and right becomes left) but upside-down (top becomes bottom and bottom becomes top).

The twins hold their hands in the same handsign as the bound man and woman but, in contrast, their hands are free as they fall. The twins are bound by lightning, the man and woman are struck by ropes. The Bound

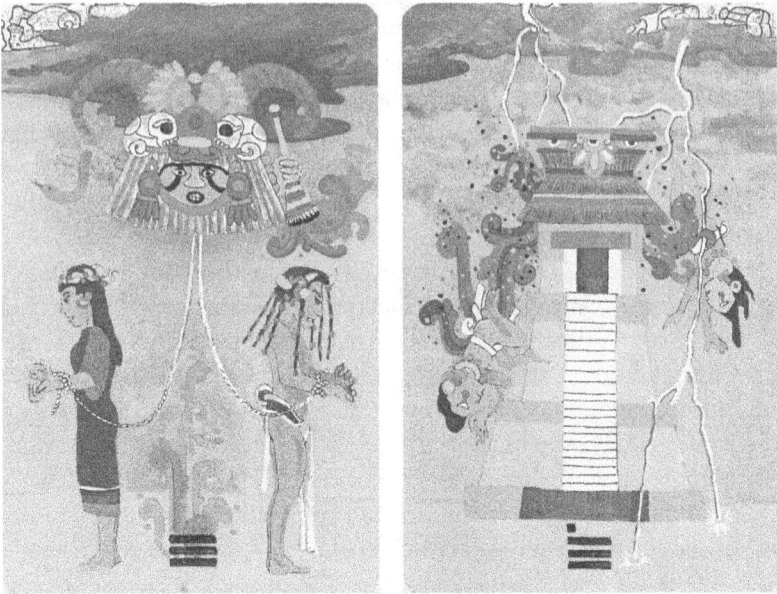

Figure 82. The Bound Man and the Released Man

Man is the final detachment from the outer collective, whereas the Tower is the final detachment from the inner ambassador of the collective, the ego.

Both cards depict two humans with something between them. The Bound Man shows a man and a woman, representing difference, with spirit between them (the tail of the Feathered Serpent). The Tower shows twins, representing sameness, with substance between them (the pyramid). For the descending spirit, an earthy temple issuing forth humans in all their dividedness and two-ness is an abrupt encounter with the realities of matter. For the ascending humans, the watery tail of the Feathered Winged Serpent in all its uniting one-ness begins a gradual encounter with the reality of spirit.

This encounter with spirit requires us to relinquish our attachment to outer forms, customs and conventions. As the Priest (5) is the guardian of collective tradition, so the Bound Man (15) is the destroyer of collective tradition. He finds his own Path with Heart. But what then is he bound to? Instead of being bound to collective norms and habits he realises he is bound to the designs of spirit.

Jung said, "The feeling for the infinite, however, can be attained only if we are bounded to the utmost."[32] In the Christian tradition, the monastic novitiate takes vows of poverty, chastity and obedience. Obedience means "to listen to" and obedience to the Self is a commitment to respond to the voice of the Holy Spirit within. We are called, like Christ, to suffer to the death for our own truth rather than live our lives in blind conformity. Helen Luke said that in doing this, "we not only may, but must break every law, even the laws of the outer Church, in order to be true to the solemn and binding vow of lifelong obedience."[33]

Once the Fool has become teachable at 14 he is ready to "lose his human form." This means that he is no longer bound by socially conditioned ways of perceiving and behaving.

> Don Juan explained that their [the sorcerers of antiquity] most important attainment was to perceive the energetic essence of things.... Nowadays, after lifelong discipline and training, sorcerers do acquire the capacity to perceive the essence of things, a capacity they call *seeing*. "What would it mean to me to perceive the energetic essence of things?" I once asked don Juan: "It would mean that you perceive energy directly," he replied. "By separating the social part of perception, you'll perceive the essence of everything. Whatever we are perceiving is energy, but since we can't directly perceive energy, we process our perception to fit a mold. This mold is the social part of perception, which you have to separate... [It is] the physical certainty that the world is made of concrete objects.... I am saying that this is first a world of energy; then it's a world of objects." Don Juan's conception was that our entrapment in processing our perception to fit a social mold loses its power when we realize we have accepted this mold... without bothering to examine it.[34]

The Bound Man breaks free of the chains that have bound human souls since always. He frees himself, on the one hand, from the coercions of the collective and, on the other hand, from the compulsions of the archetypes. This in turn allows him to be liberated, not destroyed, by the lightning of the Tower. But the freer we become, the more we are bound. At the beginning of the journey, when we are unconscious, we can get away with a lot. But now we cannot deviate from our own way. If we do, we suffer the "judgement" of the Self directly below the 15 card.

Individuation

Contrary to popular notions, introversion and "navel-gazing" are not sterile, solitary activities (although they can be) but do in fact produce new life. Working on oneself is community service. Individuation is the development of the psychology of the individual as distinct from the psychology of the collective. If the former is not sufficiently developed it will be taken over by the latter.

Individuation is not individualism. Individuation deviates from the collective norms but retains a natural respect for them, while the latter rejects them outright in favour of the individual's way. It is not an antisocial act or narcissistic self-absorption but leads naturally to a regard for the collective

norm.[35] Jung said, "Individuation cuts one off from conformity and collective values to some extent and this is the guilt that the individual must redeem by bringing back to the collective an equivalent substitute for his or
her absence in the collective sphere. Without this production of values
individuation is immoral."[36]

So where does individuation lead us? Jung said, "The process of
individuation, consciously pursued, leads to the realisation of the self as a
psychic reality greater than the ego. Thus individuation is essentially different from the process of simply becoming conscious. The goal of the
individuation process is the synthesis of the self."[37]

The deeper one goes into oneself the more one is able to reach out to others, and the more deeply one relates to others the more one knows about
oneself. "Individuation," said Jung, "does not shut one out from the world,
but gathers the world to oneself."[38] The Bound Man is beholden to no one
yet is deeply and altruistically connected to others.

These steps from 14 to 15 to 16 in the spiritual and psychological development of the individual distinguish a Twisted Hair, or the like, from a someone who is wholly contained within and identified with their own culture
and tradition. Those who strike out on their own path, find themselves, include not exclude, and learn from other times and other peoples, are
Twisted Hairs. The individuals who make this transition have to forsake
and betray their own culture to bring something of greater value to all cultures. This is an archetypal necessity that has been repeated million of times
over in all cultures over the course of human history. Biologically, it is how
new species get formed. Culturally, it is how human cultures evolve. But
those who walk this path face criticism, ostracism and condemnation from
their own culture. There is an enormous human price to be paid for the
movement from the Bound Man to the Released Man. You can never go
home again.

The Released Man
The Soul of the Adult Spirit Shield uses the Mood of Soul
Ruthlessness to Assume Physical Authority

The Tower

26

Released Man

Lightning signifies a sudden, unexpected, and overpowering change in psychic condition.

—C. G. Jung

A poet is someone who stands outside in the rain hoping to be struck by lightning.

—James Dickey

I'd rather be a lightning rod than a seismograph.

—Ken Kesey

This card shows a temple with a straw roof and an elaborate roof comb. The temple is at the top of a pyramid that has twenty-two steps. The lightning bolt from the sword of decision strikes the pyramid and sets it ablaze, cinders fill the air and two people are thrown from the tower.

The temple is similar to the ones we see in Figures 83 and 84. The latter is a picture of Temple 1 at Tikal. The Maya glyphs tell us that this temple was the "white flower soul cache" of Hasaw Chan K'awil who we have already met in the Fool and Consort cards.[1]

After Peter Balin had painted the cards, he took them to an elderly lady who was well-versed in the tarot. She looked at the Released Man card and said, "Well, you know the Tower must have twenty-two courses of masonry." Balin said he wasn't aware of that. At that stage it was very hard for him to change anything as the cards were painted in acrylics and to match the colours exactly would have been almost impossible. Reluctantly he said, "Well, I guess I have to paint twenty-two courses of masonry on it." But the woman suggested that he count the steps first. So he did and found that there were twenty-two steps! Balin said, "There were hundreds of little such incidents throughout the whole of the deck that I really didn't know anything about."[2]

Figure 83. Mixtec temple (Codex Nuttall)

Illumination and Humiliation

This card is usually interpreted as a violent upheaval that brings one down to earth, a reality check, a rude awakening, the world being turned upside-down, a life-changing event, the rug being pulled out from under you, or a bolt from the blue. It represents the collapse of old values and beliefs, the destruction of long-established situations, the puncturing of inflation, the discarding of what has petrified, or towering rage, ambition, pride and arrogance. What has been built brick by brick is destroyed in a flash and ego-driven hopes are shattered.

But we also see that this row of cards is set upon a green plain signifying the archetypal back ground of renewal and hope that supports the human figures in their difficulties. The Released Man is the last card in the row and it represents the ego's liberation from the trials of the preceding cards and the power of their archetypes. Edinger's description fits:

That's the way it happens in psychological experience. First one has the event, the crippling, agonizing event, and then in the process of trying to assimilate it, come to terms with it, one may discover its archetypal background—that there's a large enough context to it, a more than personal meaning. And even though that does not eliminate the pain of the experience, it makes the pain meaningful. To discover the archetypal background is indeed healing, I think chiefly because with that discovery the

Figure 84. Temple 1, Tikal

ego is released from the identification with an archetypal experience. What is so intolerably burdensome is to carry personally a weight of meaning that is transpersonal. When one can get out from under that excessive weight by the process of disidentification, then there's a sense of release.[3]

As well as a collapse the Released Man can also be a revelation, an awakening and an epiphany. Moments of illumination rarely come plodding step by step, but all at once in a blinding flash that takes years to understand. Spirit is not limited by space and time, it knows nothing of gradualness, incremental change, and the measured response. Like lightning, it is all or nothing. Spirit seeks union with matter without regard for human concerns, and does not make a distinction between a conscious human being and an unconscious one. For spirit the result is the same — the lightning bolt has touched matter — but for the human the result is vastly different depending on the degree of consciousness. For one who is unprepared it does feel like the collapse of their whole world. For one who is more conscious it feels like a release or a revelation.

The difference in interpretation, revelation or ruin, also depends on the perspective — spirit or ego. Ladders, steps or stairs are symbols of ego development and growth, moving to a higher state of consciousness, and the process of spiritualisation. But when an archetype falls into matter it undergoes a kenosis, an emptying, and a great narrowing. In dreams and visions this is often symbolised as a divine being falling to earth[4] and in the card we see twins falling from the temple. For spirit this descent is a great constriction, humiliation and downfall; for the ego it is an awakening, an ascension and a profound liberation.

Twin Towers

In the Marseilles Tarot this card is the Tower. The tower is a way of symbolically connecting heaven and earth but like space programs that strive to "loose the surly bonds of earth" it also represents the inflated desire to break away from the earth and to dominate nature. In the Bound Man, the threat was from too much instinct, but now in the Released Man the threat is from too much spirit.

In both the Xultun and European tarot we see twins falling from the tower or temple, twin bolts of lightning, flames coming from the tower and in many European tarot the tower is struck by lightning about two-thirds of the way up. The similarity of these images with the tragedy of 9/11 is striking — the twin planes striking the twin towers, where the planes hit, the flames, the destruction of the towers, and people jumping headfirst from the towers. As sensitive an area as it might be, we must not avoid what this card might say about 9/11.

The tarot is a map of the development of the individual ego but also maps the development of the cultural ego. The inflation of the Western psyche has grown unchecked in the last one thousand years and particularly in the last fifty years. It has difficulty accepting limitations and is suffering from a dissociative denial of the reality that the planet we live on is alive. The inflation is fuelled by the uncritical acceptance of heroic attitudes such as, "In this land of opportunity and freedom anyone can become anything," and the economic fantasy of everlasting four percent annual growth.

The heroic world economy is unsustainable, in spite of the euphemism of "sustainable development." Were it not for the pathological breakdown in reality testing, even a single statistic would convince us of our destruc-

tiveness. For example: nearly eighty percent of the world's indigenous forests has been destroyed since 1970; the Grand Banks fishery off Newfound-
land, the richest fishing ground in the world, was closed in 1992 and fifteen
years later cod stocks continue to decline; since 1950 more resources have
been consumed than in the whole history of the human race; and the
Johnny-come-lately awareness of global climate change.

But the global heroic ego, for all its priapic, hyper-masculine competitive-
ness, has feeble self-esteem and is narcissistically vulnerable. Commercial
self-esteem and "business confidence" is a such a delicate thing, swinging
between grandiose, blustering, aggressive competition, on the one hand,
and tantrums and tears on the other when its omnipotence is frustrated.
Therefore, a compensatory deflation of the Western psyche (or the American psyche as the quintessence of this inflated consciousness) that has severed itself from the natural world was a certainty. The puffed-up house of
cards has no internal strength or scaffolding and a collapse was bound to
happen.

It is a sign of how deeply unconscious the inflation is in Western culture
that it had to occur in such a tragic and deadly way as 9/11. The terrorists
got the penis (the World Trade Centre) and the testicles (the Pentagon), but
fortunately not the head or the heart (the White House or Capitol Hill, we
may never know). And it had to be that drastic because we are not listening.

But the message is not too hard to hear. It was the *World Trade* Centre and
two towers *collapsed*. We don't know how the two collapses will happen or
how catastrophic they will be, the only thing that is predictable is its unpredictability. It may be the collapse of world trade, or the banking system, the
world currency structure, an earthquake, or a tsunami. But happen it will,
twice. One not too long after the other.

Often we cannot see the specifics of an archetypal pattern until decades
after the event. This chapter was written in 2000–2001, well before and just
after 9/11. We do not know at this time (2010) if the events I describe have
happened, are happening, or are yet to happen. It is a recognisable, archetypal process that has been repeated thousands of times before in human
history. But each time the form and pattern is different.

Such an archetypal corrective, like a natural catastrophe, takes no prisoners. The planes, the plans, the terrorists, the victims, the extremists, the religions and the politics of 9/11 are all bit players in an ongoing archetypal
drama about the compulsory downsizing of Western culture. From the
ashes of the grief and tragedy, no consciousness of the meaning of 9/11 has
arisen and it continues to be viewed simplistically as the actions of bad
men.[5] The process of collapse will continue in other ways and forms, mostly
shocking and unexpected.

Lightning

Spirit descends step-by-step through Venus, the Sun, the Moon and the Star. The first human card it encounters is the Released Man. But spirit also takes the direct route and the lightning from Planet Earth hits the top of the tower in the card above it — the Released Man. Spirit will always seek out the place where the veil between the worlds is thinnest, where spirit and matter are in closest proximity. In its desire to make human contact, spirit circles the edges of the herd, so to speak, looking for those who are furthest from the protection afforded by the collective at the centre of the crowd. It looks for the most marginal, the most vulnerable, the most receptive, the most defended, the most inflated or the most inflatable.

If our conscious attitude is too concrete or one-sided then we invite the unconscious to take drastic measures like sending down bolts of lightning or arranging collapse in our lives. If the psyche is traumatised the same thing happens but for different reasons. Trauma often produces weak or compromised areas in the psyche. As a result, the normal, healthy boundary between spirit and matter is thinner. Those who have a history of trauma are often unconsciously hypervigilant of the psychological atmosphere around them and may have hypertrophied intuition. Having a trauma-driven foot in the other world, so to speak, they may be drawn to esoteric pursuits. With such individuals spirit may strike frequently, or at least be in the neighbourhood a lot. But there may be insufficient ego strength to handle the experience without losing themselves in a religion, cult or sect, having a bout of inflation (which may be life-long and attract many followers) or exacerbating pre-existing psychological difficulties.

Lightning is an unpredictable natural phenomenon but we can increase our chances of being hit by lightning — and surviving. The first fifteen cards not only prepare us to withstand the bolt of lightning when it comes, but also make lightning more likely to happen in our vicinity. All shamanic and spiritual practices have this preparation and receptivity as a goal.

We see two bolts of lightning that descend on the tower. The one on the left ends at the top of the tower and comes from the Balance card above. This lightning has its origins in the decisions made by the Balance which begin the second half of the deck and send out two waves. One wave is experienced within space and time through the smoke and fire along the third row. We have to experience in the flesh the choices the Balance made for us in spirit. The other wave is outside space and time seen as the fork of lightning striking the temple. When we arrive at the Released Man we can see in retrospect what has been happening. This comes as a lightning flash of spiritual memory and we remember what we have known all along. The photographer Diane Arbus said, "Nothing is ever the same as they said it was. It's what I've never seen before that I recognise."[6]

The other bolt of lightning on the right comes out of the cloud above the temple and continues down into the Planet Earth card. The cloud is a symbol of the manifestation of the deity. Zeus often manifested as a cloud and Yahweh, in Ezekiel's vision in the Old Testament, appeared as a cloud. These two bolts of lightning indicate that both human choice and the impersonal activity of spirit contribute to the events that befall the Released Man.

The row of the Adult Spirit Shield from the Hanged Man to the Released Man is a process of suffering and joy, change and transformation. It begins and ends with people turned upside down. The Hanged Man is the Keeper of the Heart of the Adult Spirit Shield and is the emotional experience of this process. The Released Man is the Keeper of the Soul of the Adult Spirit Shield and is the soul experience. It is also the card of soul sensation and the Teacher of Assuming Physical Authority. As the Holder of Soul Ruthlessness, it is the final shattering of the Mirror of Self-reflection. The twins are the last human forms we see in the deck.

Now we cannot look back, otherwise we suffer the fate of Orpheus or Lot's wife. Both looked back when they had been warned not to. Orpheus lost Eurydice, whom he had brought back from the underworld, and Lot's wife turned into a pillar of salt. The perils here are greater than before. Jung said, "If one does not consciously walk forward, the past sucks one back… like an enormous sucking wind…. As soon as you begin to look back sadly, or even scornfully, it has you again."[7] Even the wistful tug of a backward look, let alone a return to the previous state of unconsciousness, endangers our soul. The wrenching is this: to gain our full humanness we must abandon our human form and our human relationships.

If we now read this row backwards, we can hear the story from the point of view of spirit. Spirit is called from afar by its own destiny and the choices of humans (the Balance). It enters the world of duality symbolised by the twins (the Released Man). The reluctance of spirit to be imprisoned in matter, and its fascination with it, is its humiliation. It is thrown out of the unity of the Tower, divided, and falls to earth. It is then bound to matter, biology and instinct and joins with all that is not light and spiritual (the Bound Man). Spirit and matter are then joined in the balance and harmony of an earthly, not heavenly, marriage (the Temperate Man). Unlike humans, where the heavenly union happens after death, with spirit it happens before death. So, after the harmonious union of the Temperate Man spirit dies to itself (the Dead Man) and is crucified in human form between the tree of life and the tree of death (the Hanged Man). This was the story of Christ.

The Star
The Heart of the Child Spirit Shield uses the Mood of Emotional
Patience to Erase Spiritual History

The Star

27

Star

Our birth is but a sleep and a forgetting:
The Soul that rises with us, our life's Star
  — from *Ode: Intimations of Immortality from Recollections of Early Childhood*
                                                    by William Wordsworth

When you have found the beginning of the way, the star of your soul will show its light.

— Cabalistic saying

The truth is we're all chosen; most of us just forget to RSVP.

— Sarah Ban Breathnach

We are stardust / We are golden / We've got to get ourselves back to the garden.

— Joni Mitchell, *Woodstock*

The goal of life is to make your heartbeat match the beat of the universe, to match your nature with Nature.

— Joseph Campbell

A woman sits cross-legged upon a plinth pouring water with her left hand for all to see and secretly pouring water with her right hand. A single star above on her right has eight points surrounded by thirteen rays. On her left flies a quetzal bird.

Hope

The Star is a card of hope particularly after emotional storms. It is the dawning of an inner light, the faint inner vision seen only by the light of the stars. The Star Maiden sits naked and exposed to the stars, the archetypal constellations that are the background of existence and the wisdom of the cosmos. The great stories and myths are kept in the stars and when we see own star we become connected to our part of the greater story. May Sarton wrote:

Help us to be the always hopeful
Gardeners of the spirit
Who know that without darkness
Nothing comes to birth
As without light
Nothing flowers.

In the top row, the Ruler held the Milky Way as his serpent bundle. The bottom row is the Milky Way itself and the whole cosmos opens up in increasing order of light from the Star to Planet Venus. Finally, in Planet Earth there is an enantiodromia where the light is inside not outside. It is contained in matter. The Star Maiden links us with the increasing luminosity of this divine spark. Unlike the lightning of the Released Man, stars are points of illumination scaled down to human size. They do not scorch or kill like lightning. They are predictable in their courses and can be viewed at a distance and over time so that the illumination they offer can be slowly assimilated. Stars are our instinctual nature transformed into its spiritual counterpart. We see this connection in the animal names for the signs of the zodiac in Western or Chinese astrology.

The Star symbolises divine inspiration, the longing to know our destiny. The questions now are not, Who am I? or What is my name? or What is my relationship with other people? but What is the meaning of my name? What is my destiny? Why was I born?[1]

One night when the lawn was a golden green
And the marbled moonlit trees rose like fresh memorials
In the scented air, and the whole countryside pulsed
With the churr and murmur of insects, I lay in the grass
Feeling great distances open above me, and wondered
What would I become — and where will I would find myself —
And though I barely existed, I felt for an instant
The vast star-clustered sky was mine, and I heard
My name as if for the first time, heard it the way
One hears the wind or the rain, but faint and far off
As though it belonged not to me but to the silence
From which it had come and to which it would go.

— Anon.

We are now led by our own "guiding star," or saved from misfortune by our "lucky stars." The word disaster (Latin, *dis-*, apart, *astrum*, star) means being separated from your star, your destiny, or being ill-starred (as in Shakespeare's "star cross'd lovers"). Without hope there is no vision and when there is no vision, the people perish (Proverbs 29:18). In Western culture, instead of a vision that includes all of creation, we have mission statements, five-year plans and growth forecasts.

Pleiades

The star above the Star Maiden is Sirius. European tarot usually show seven small stars representing the Pleiades and one large star representing Sirius. For example, in the Marseilles Tarot there are seven stars all drawn differently. At the centre of these seven stars is a yellow star superimposed over a red star such that they emit alternating rays. Classical Greek writers such as Cicero, Seneca and Ptolemy described Sirius as red or orange, quite different from the brilliant blue-white star we see today. But the Sirius of today (Sirius A) has a now-collapsed, dwarf companion star, invisible to the naked eye, known as Sirius B. Modern astronomers first detected this star in 1862. However, it was visible to the ancient Greek writers and is depicted in the Marseilles Tarot.

The Pleiades are a cluster of stars in the shoulder area of the constellation of Taurus, the Bull. Both Sirius and the Pleiades are significant in almost all world cultures.[2] The Aurignacian culture in Europe around 35,000 BCE left bone carvings of Sirius. Cave paintings from 16,000 BCE in Lascaux, France show the seven stars of the Pleiades.[3] The Dogon of Mali have had a detailed knowledge of Sirius for thousands of years and knew about the existence of Sirius B before it was seen by modern astronomers. It is said that Sirius and the Pleiades are the suns of two of the twelve planets in this south universe that carry human life.[4] They are our planetary family and among indigenous peoples there is a long history of contact with Star Nations Peoples.[5]

In many cultures the planting of crops was done in accordance with the Pleiades. A "sky disk" found in Germany and dating from 1600 BCE tells us that the disappearance of the Pleiades signalled the beginning of planting season.[6] In Greek myth, the Pleiades were seven nymphs, beautiful spirits who inhabited nature. They were daughters of the Titan Atlas who held up the sky on his shoulders. One day the seven sisters were walking in the woods with their mother Pleione, when they were seen by Orion, the hunter. Orion fell in love with them and chased after them. Zeus saw they were in danger and changed them into doves so they could escape and fly up into the sky. In the night sky the Pleiades move from east to west during the night with the constellation Orion following them.

Maori know the Pleiades as Matariki. Tawhirimatea, the God of the Winds and the Elements, waged war against his older brothers because they had separated their parents Ranginui (the Sky) and Papatuanuku (the Earth). In his rage, Tawhirimatea tore out his eyes and flung them into the heavens. They became stars and are known as Mata Ariki (The Eyes of God) or Mata Riki (Little Eyes). Their appearance heralds the start of the New Year and the beginning of the planting season. There are many Maori stories about their significance as navigational stars and as a portent of whether or not the coming harvests will be plentiful. Some say that Matariki is the mother surrounded by her six daughters, other stories suggest that Matariki is a male star.

An Aboriginal dreaming story similarly tells of the seven Napaltjarri sisters being chased by a man named Jilbi Tjakamarra. He tried to practice love magic on one of the sisters but they ran away from him. They sat down at Uluru to search for honey ants but when they saw Jilbi again, with the help of the spirits of Uluru, they transformed into stars. Jilbi transformed himself into one of the stars of Orion's belt and continues to chase the seven sisters across the sky. These stories say that Pleiades and Sirius are joined forever. We shall have more to say about the significance of Orion in the Planet Earth card.

The Maya believed they came from the Pleiades, or *Muchuchumil* as they are known. They also called them the *tzab*, the rattle of a rattlesnake, or the handful of seeds in the Maya creation story. The sun aligns with Alcyone, the brightest of the Pleiades, every 52 years and the Aztec used this to track the Calendar Round and the New Fire ceremony every 52 years. The main axis of Teotihuacan, the ancient capital of Mexico, may have been oriented perpendicular to the direction in which the Pleiades set.

Holy the Firm

> I have no judgment about myself and my life. There is nothing I am quite sure about. I have no definite convictions — not about anything, really. I know only that I was born and exist, and it seems that I have been carried along. I exist on the foundation of something I do not know. In spite of all uncertainties, I feel a solidity underlying all existence and a continuity in my mode of being.[7]

In the first two rows all the figures are standing on, standing under, wearing, or sitting on, something made by human hands. Again, this suggests that the ego must be protected or insulated from the archetypal powers above or the instinctual forces below. However, in the third row the figures are without this kind of support. They are either standing on the sky (in other words, upside down) like the Hanged Man and the Released Man, or

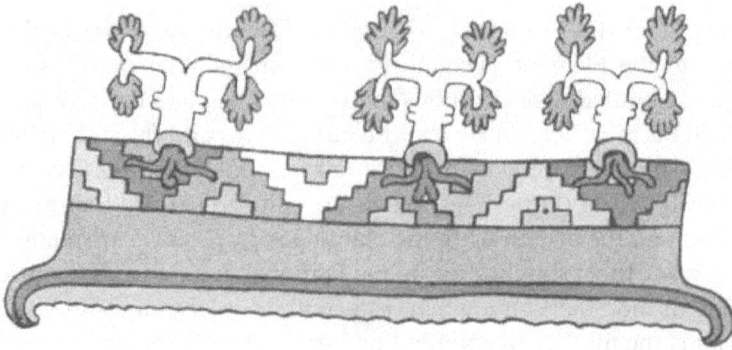

Figure 85. Mixtec symbol for earth or place (Codex Nuttall)

standing on the ground like Temperate Man and the Bound Man. Something transpersonal, not made by human hands, now supports them. This is what Jung referred to when he said, "I know from experience that all coercion—be it suggestion, insinuation, or any other method of persuasion—ultimately proves to be nothing but an obstacle to the highest and most decisive experience of all, which is to be alone with his own self, or whatever else one chooses to call the objectivity of the psyche. The patient must be alone if he is to find out what it is that supports him when he can no longer support himself. Only this experience can give him an indestructible foundation."[8]

How do we navigate in our lives where there are no collective markers, no horizon, no gravitational pull telling us where our feet are, no east or west, no sun or moon? When our senses fail us, when the plan goes wrong, when what we have relied on no longer works, what then? It requires trusting, and despairing of trust or faith. Doing nothing, knowing that nothing has worked or will work. Descending, without knowing if there is a bottom. Breathing, knowing that dying would be the easier option. Saying, "Don't do anything stupid. Just this next breath," for weeks and months. Allowing the unconscious to lead us (as if we had a choice) without benefit of map or compass or trodden path. Then we may reach solid ground.

To navigate in the unknown we must go to the unknown within us, and in strange ways it will lead us in the dark. We can only do this if we sacrifice our excess baggage, what is most precious to us, what we think is indispensable, even life itself. If we disrobe, like the figures in the third row then we can immerse ourselves in the sea of the unknown.

The "indestructible foundation" that Jung refers to is the zigzag pattern along the base of the bottom row, together with the green hope it affords above it. This is the impersonal and transpersonal cosmic support at the base of each of the Movements. The stepped design is the Mixtec symbol for "a place on the earth" (Figure 85). It is also similar to the stylised steps seen in pictures of the Maya ballcourts which represent the symbolic intersec-

Figure 86. Birth of Lord 12 Grass from the World Tree (Selden Codex)

tion of upper and lower worlds, and the Milky Way and the ecliptic (the significance of which we shall discuss later).

Hunbatz Men, a Maya daykeeper, says that the stepped design and the figure "T" symbolise the sacred tree.[9] A common image in Maya and Aztec codices is the zigzag design together with trees, the serpent and humans coming up from the Underworld and being born from the cleft of a tree. In the Selden Codex (Figure 86) we see a "star-man," showing the handsign meaning birth, being born from a tree that is entwined by a cloud serpent and a star serpent. In the Dresden Codex there is a picture of the opposite where the World Tree arises out of the sacrificed body of the Maize God. In the Fejervary-Mayer Codex we see the Cross of the Tree or *uahomche* which in Mayan means "the tree which awakens us" or "we awaken in the tree."

The zigzag pattern has no beginning and no end, it is eternal. It is the earth, the foundation from which the World Tree grows and upon which the whole Book of Life sits. If we look more closely at the zigzag, we see that there are four steps up and four steps down as well as four colours. If we take the four strands of this pattern, hold them at each end and twist them, they become a double double helix, a DNA spiral with four strands instead of two. We have seen that the vertical columns or Movements of the Book of Life also form a double double helix. If we add up the number of steps across the whole base of the deck they total to 160. The number 8 itself is an image of the double helix and the number 20 is the number of amino acids that are basis of life. In the Twenty Count the number 8 is the number of the body, physical form, and laws, cycles and patterns. The number 20 is also the number of the Creator or the Great Mystery. The number 160 is 8 (physical form) x 20 (Life, the Creator). Thus the foundation or great platform on which the Xultun Tarot rests is this physical existence which is brought into being by the will of the Creator and informed by its laws, cycles and patterns. This foundation is what Annie Dillard calls Holy the Firm.

> Esoteric Christianity, I read, posits a substance. It is a created substance, lower than metals and minerals on a "spiritual scale," and lower than salts and earths, occurring beneath salts and earths in the waxy deepness of planets, but never on the surface of planets where men could discern it; and it is in touch with the Absolute, at base. In touch with the Absolute! At base. The name of this substance is: Holy the Firm.
>
> Holy the Firm: and is Holy the Firm in touch with metal and minerals? With salts and earths? Of course, and straight on up, till "up" ends by curving back. Does something that touched something that touched Holy the Firm in touch with the Absolute at base seep into ground water, into grain; are islands rooted in it, and trees? Of course.[10]

When our connection to the Self and the cosmos is firm enough we are "self-sufficient." This is not the fantasy of self-sufficiency prevalent in Western culture but a participation in the abundant flow of energy of the universe and a living understanding of the enduring nature of spirit beside, within and beyond matter. We add energy to our own lives and the lives of others from being in alignment with the rhythms of the heavenly bodies of the stars, the moon, the sun, Venus and Earth and their inner psychological equivalents. We master the Moods of Stalking—we are able to gain energy from any encounter and draw life from life itself.

We have seen in Chapter 9 that each card in a Movement awakens or kindles the card above it in the following Movement. However, what awakens the cards in the bottom row? The answer is that the cards in the last row (Star, Moon, Sun, Venus and Earth), like the cards in last column of Assuming Authority, are all self-awakening. They create themselves and are their own parents. Jung said that, "Only absolute totality can renew itself out of itself and generate itself anew."[11] The last row of the Child Spirit Shield and the last column of Assuming Authority both symbolise absolute totality. However, Assuming Authority is the sum of the horizontal human marriages between masculine and feminine whereas the Child Spirit Shield is the sum of the vertical cosmic separations of masculine and feminine (Figure 23). The marriage of these marriages is the wholeness of Planet Earth.

Earth and Patience

> The serious problems in life are never fully solved.... The meaning and purpose of a problem seem to lie not in its solution, but in our working at it incessantly.
>
> —C. G. Jung[12]

Along the base of the bottom row are four volcanoes erupting with the magma, the blood of Grandmother Earth, her inner sun. Taken together the whole row represents the physical and spiritual fires that sustain and energise all of creation and make life live. So now on our journey we sit on the lap of Grandmother Earth in the light of the Great Grandfather Stars. The thought, word or deed, once feared and avoided but now done, brings relief, a settling downwards into the soil of who we are. We have reached bedrock and know without a doubt that we have discovered something about ourselves that is authentic and unique, no apologies needed, no further scrutiny necessary.

Now, after the trials of the third row of cards that ended in the Cracking of the Mirror of Self-reflection, the personality is reborn, to use the words of Meister Eckhart, from the dark ground of the soul. After a period of fragmentation and scattering the Star, as the integrative, unifying and consolidating function of the Self, appears.

Now, said Jung, "the psychological centre of the personality [shifts] from the personal ego to the impersonal non-ego, which is now experienced as the real 'Ground' of the personality."[13] Marie-Louise von Franz said this connection with the Self brings a feeling of standing on solid ground inside oneself, on a patch of inner eternity, which even death cannot touch.[14] Jung elaborates: "Experiencing the self means that you are always conscious of your own identity. Then you know that you can never be anything other than yourself, that you can never lose yourself and never be alienated from yourself. This is because you know that the self is indestructible, that it is one and always the same, and cannot be dissolved and exchanged for anything else. The self enables you to remain the same through all conditions of your life."[15]

This sameness is not rigidity. If individuation goes on unconsciously it renders the individual cruel and hard towards his fellow creatures but if it is a conscious process then it forms the Philosopher's Stone. This is not a hardening of the personality but a resolute firmness. The rock symbolises the steadfastness that comes from the long process of becoming more conscious. Slowly, over time it forms an enduring nucleus. This means that we do not cure our problems, but what is changed is our ability to withstand them. This is the formation of solid earth beneath our feet—we feel able to stand in a place where we are not swept away by personal emotions or collective pressures. Saint Thomas Aquinas' *Aurora Consurgens* says that the house of wisdom is built upon this rock and in it takes place the vision of the fullness of the sun and the moon.[16] This is the symbolism of the next three cards — the Moon, the Sun and their marriage as the Planet Venus.

For a time, perhaps a long time, one has to be enclosed in one's own vessel and attend to one's own business, to a certain extent closed off from life. Eventually, the inner work bears fruit in a new relationship to the outer world, to Life itself. It is in this last row, descending through the heavenly bodies from Star to Moon to Sun to Venus to Earth, that we open to the cosmos through watching the process of synchronicity.[17]

This wrestling with spirit, with the unconscious, is the story of Jacob wrestling with the angel. At daybreak, after a long night of struggle, the angel pleads with Jacob to let him go. Jacob says: "I will not let you go until you bless me." The angel concedes and confers upon him the name Israel, "because you have struggled with the divine and with men, and you have prevailed." Israel or *yisrael* in Hebrew, means "he who prevails over the divine."

Through our human efforts spirit eventually submits and yields to us. A solid centre slowly precipitates out. This nucleus is at peace, and even in the midst of great emotional tempests (our own or others) we are intensely alive but without action or participation in the conflict. Indira Gandhi said, "You must learn to be still in the midst of activity and vibrantly alive in repose."

But this only comes after countless times of losing this place, pining for it, not being able to return to it at will, and sometimes forgetting its existence altogether. Now we have developed the Patience to relinquish the search for oneself and allow ourselves to be found by those moments when we do stand on home ground, our *turangawaewae*. In Maori, literally *turanga* (standing place), *waewae* (feet), it is often translated as "a place to stand." Turangawaewae are places where we feel especially at home. They are our foundation, our place in the world, our home. Here we can keep our sense of humour a moment longer when we are in the grip of the complex and, most difficult, we slowly begin to live in this place by the continuous rediscovery that any other way of life has become impossible. Now we can never go home again — this world is already our home.

The quetzal we see in the card is the national bird of Guatemala. It lives in the cloud forests, 900–1200 metres up in the mountains. It is solitary and rarely seen other than at dawn or dusk. The male is emerald and golden green with a red belly and white undertail. The iridescent blue and green undulating tail feathers of the male are up to a metre long. In his courting, the male plummets from high up in the canopy down to the branch where the prospective female sits sizing up her suitors by the magnificence of their dive.[18]

So it is with the ego—it is not the ascent but the descent that is all. Like the quetzal, the ego has finally come down to earth and paradoxically its resplendent beauty is released to fly. The ego now has a double attitude towards itself and the Self—not demeaning itself, nor inflating itself; humbly open to the unconscious but not ruled by it. It is this attitude that allows the descent toward the Planet Earth card to occur and is the meaning of the biblical "the meek shall inherit the earth." This attitude allows the Self to appear in the earth, as the rock or the Philosopher's Stone—substance in both its highest and lowest form.

Erasing History

The platform that the Star Maiden sits on is a drum. The drum is the heartbeat of Grandmother Earth and we see a similar drum in the Planet Earth card. The woman sits in the centre of her own heart, her own Path with Heart, and so is connected to and aligned with the earth beneath her. Though she may be buffeted by inner or outer storms, the ballast of her own feeling always rights her. She is able to take pleasure and knowledge from whatever she does knowing that she is in alignment with herself. She walks to the rhythm of her own beat. The Star is the card of emotional intuition and the Holder of the Mood of Emotional Patience—the ability to remain true to oneself in the face of emotional pressures or archetypal compulsions and allow the Self to determine.

From wrestling with what has beset us for many years and the archetypes that stand behind our difficulties comes a realisation of the spiritual meaning of our personal history. We are able weave the hurts and joys of our life into a now-discernible pattern that makes sense to us—whether it be tragedy or comedy. When we are able to understand "why me" and see the broader meaning of our lives, the pain fades away and our history is just that, history. Not forgotten and alive enough in the present to remind us, but it does not rule. This is why the Star is the Teacher of Erasing Spiritual History and the final card in the Movement.

In February 1944, when he was sixty-eight, Jung slipped and broke his leg while out on his daily walk. Ten days later in hospital he developed a thrombosis and was critically ill for three weeks. During this time he had a near-death experience which we shall return to in the Planet Earth card. He describes his experience, toward the end of the vision, of Erasing Personal History and feeling the solid ground of his personality under his feet.

> As I approached the steps leading up to the entrance into the rock, a strange thing happened. I had the feeling that everything was being sloughed away; everything that I aimed at or wished for or thought, the whole phantasmagoria of earthly existence, fell away or was stripped

from me—an extremely painful process. Nevertheless, something remained; it was as if I now carried along with me everything I had ever experienced or done, everything that had happened around me.... I con-
sisted of my own history, and I felt with great certainty: this is what I am.
"I am this bundle of what has been, and what has been accomplished."
This experience gave me a feeling of extreme poverty, but at the same
time of great fullness. There was no longer anything I wanted or desired.
I existed in objective form; I was what I had been and lived.... Everything
seemed to be past; what remained was a *fait accompli*, without any reference back to what had been. There was no longer any regret that something had dropped away or been taken away. On the contrary: I had everything that I was, and that was everything.[19]

Sacred Dream

The Mood of Emotional Patience and the Movement of Erasing Spiritual
History bestow Hope upon us, a transpersonal will that has duration and
substance. This is not the collective, material vision of the Warrior but the
individual, star-vision of the Self which makes sense of what up until now
has been hard scrabble. The Star Maiden's new vision has the internal
authenticity and external strength to go forth into the world because it has
been seen as our destiny by the Priestess, fought for by the Warrior,
suffered for by the Hanged Man, and seen as our sacred dream by the Star
Maiden.

One of the greatest enemies of humans is ignorance—unconsciousness,
not being known to ourselves. What is lost, denied, despised or unknown
in ourselves or in the collective sinks into the Void. What is lost always
seeks to find a home and these lost parts of ourselves will come begging at
anyone's table. This is how the shadow dream is woven. Only in the re-col-
lecting and re-membering of who we are, light and dark, can we weave our
light dream and add our own threads and stitches to the collective unconscious, the Star Blanket of the People.

Now the refined essence of our personal history becomes a give-away to
the collective. We are able to add to, even in some small way, the collective
unconscious. The freedom that results from being inescapably bound to the
truth of oneself and one's own dream births a new gift—the gift of being
able to dream for the People. Jung said:

The widened consciousness is no longer that touchy, egotistical bundle
of personal wishes, fears, hopes, and ambitions which always has to be
compensated and corrected by unconscious counter-tendencies: instead,
it is a function of relationship to the world of objects, bringing the individual into absolute, binding, and indissoluble communion with the world

at large. The complications arising at this stage are no longer egotistic wish-conflicts, but difficulties that concern others as much as oneself. At this stage it is fundamentally a question of collective problems, which have activated the collective unconscious because they require collective rather than personal compensation. We can now see that the unconscious produces contents which are valid not only for the person concerned, but for others as well, in fact, for a great many people and possibly for all.[20]

The Star Maiden represents the feminine principle which, when seeded by the masculine, is the origin of all life. We are connected to the stars in a profoundly physical way that links us to the origin of all matter — the atoms of our bodies are made from cosmic dust that condensed almost five billion years ago. We are also connected spiritually to the stars and they have always symbolised eternity. The soul comes from the stars and returns to stars.[21]

The Star Maiden is the first and only figure on the bottom row of cards, the rest of which are heavenly bodies. She is also a "heavenly body" but in human form. She is an archetypal figure that ushers in our connection to the cosmos. Unlike the Temperate Man who pours starwater, the Star Maiden pours ordinary water and she pours from two urns. This indicates that her task is one of separation and redistribution of this energy, one archetypal stream and one personal stream. When we look up at the stars at night they connect us with something beyond ourselves while at the same time reminding us of our smallness and humanness. When the personal and the archetypal are discriminated we do not confuse the two and each has its rightful place and size. So when we look up at the stars we do not become inflated with Messianic destiny and see messages written there for us. Neither do we grind ourselves into insignificance.

The place where the water falls on the ground tells the same story. The larger archetypal stream pours onto the blue of the zigzag. This connects with the blue of heaven at the centre of the Earth card. The other stream from the urn in her right hand is more surreptitious and falls onto the lighter purple of the zigzag. Purple and violet are a combination of blue and red, symbolic of the union of earth and sky, the personal and the archetypal. Like grapes crushed to make wine the purple represents the transmutation of matter into embodied spirit. Purple is also the colour of royalty and rulership and the lighter purple symbolises an ego attitude that is neither inflated nor deflated but in its rightful place mid-way between heaven and earth.

The Star Maiden generously pours these waters, moistening the cosmic earth beneath, confident that life will return this gift. This give-away is her humanness as indicated by the 5 streams of water from each urn. She gives doubly of her humanness (2 x 5 = 10) to her dream (7) and this awakens her sacred dream (17). This double give-away of water is the Heart of the Child Spirit Shield—innocent yet wise, measured but unconditional. It comes from having a sacred dream of one's own and knowing that when we are linked to the source, to what is eternal, there is always enough.

The Moon
The Body of the Child Spirit Shield uses the Mood of Physical
Patience to create Spiritual Death and Change

The Moon

28

Moon

The cure for anything is salt water—sweat, tears, or the sea.

—Isak Dinesen

Moonlight is sculpture; sunlight is painting.

—Nathaniel Hawthorne

No one eats oranges
under the full moon.
The right things are fruits
green and chilled.
When the moon sails out
with a hundred faces all the same,
the coins made of silver
break out in sobs in the pocket.

—Federico Garcia Lorca

Adopt the pace of nature. Her secret is patience.

—Ralph Waldo Emerson

This card shows a moon with eight blue points surrounded by a white halo. Water from the Temperate Man card enters the right side of the card above the moon. There are two flaming volcanoes at the bottom of the card and trees grow out of the bottom border of the card.

The moon represents the unseen world and the unconscious, the slower, natural cycles of life, and the powers of intuition. It rules the corruptible world. The sun however is always the same—visible, predictable, direct, present and consistent. It rules the eternal world. Spring and summer, winter and fall, are sun cycles observable to the naked eye. But the moon waxes and wanes, and disappears for three nights every month. In European and Arabic alchemy much was written about the marriage of the sun and the moon, and the need of one for the other. The light of the sun exalts things and makes them shine and become visible. In comparison, the moon is seemingly inferior as it borrows its light from the sun. But the splendour of the sun needs witness and reflection, it needs to be seen and to have something to illuminate. Light needs darkness which it can dispel just as spirit needs matter to become visible.[1]

Healing

The Moon is the card of physical intuition — seeing and feeling things from the inside, *their* inside. Masculine consciousness specialises in skilled objectivity. It values distance, accuracy, measurement, precision, non-randomness, control, statistics, definitions, theories, averages, and neutrality. It belittles feminine subjectivity as being vague, haphazard, irrational, inaccurate, biased and ruled by chance. In fact, it has difficulty believing that there might be any such complementary notion as skilled subjectivity. But it is subjectivity (one's personal feeling and intuitive reactions) that cuts through the weighing of pros and cons, and the paralysis of "more research is needed," to the heart, not the mind, of the matter. It comes to a uniquely appropriate feeling solution to this particular problem and no other. It cannot be used again, made into a program, written up as a manual, or expanded into a theory, but it works. All depth psychotherapy is the application of skilled subjectivity to understanding a unique event (the individual psyche) that has never happened before and will never happen again.

This subjectivity is moon consciousness. It observes unconscious processes, sums them up, and guides itself by them. It turns the ego toward a particular psychic event, goes inside it and intensifies its affect rather than using the experience to form abstract conclusions and expand consciousness. This observing consciousness is contemplative and it allows the psyche to turn toward, engage and observe an event that has emotional colour. Moon consciousness loves hiddenness. It always has enough time and is suspicious of quick results and hurried actions. It dreams and watches. Moon consciousness obliges spiritual inclinations to become related to our personal, earthy reality. It does not speculate or theorise and hews closely to nature and life as it is being lived in the moment.

Until recent times, the healing of the physical body has always been the preserve of women and the feminine. The body has, from the point of view of masculine consciousness, a slowness to it. But this slowness is the time it takes to heal what has been injured — either in the body or the psyche. Feminine consciousness holds an attitude of receptivity and acceptance towards the hidden rhythms of the body. Pregnancy and birth, for example, bring changes that last for years for which the only "cure" is time (that is, until the children are grown up). Erich Neumann said:

The moon-wisdom of waiting, accepting, ripening, admits everything into its totality and transforms it and, along with it, its own being. It is always concerned with wholeness, with shaping and realizing, that is, with the creative.... Growth needs stillness and invisibility, not loudness and light.... It is not under the burning rays of the sun but in the cool reflected light of the moon, when the darkness of unconsciousness is at the full, that the creative process fulfils itself; the night, not the day, is the time of procreation. It wants darkness and quiet, secrecy, muteness, and hiddenness. Therefore, the moon is lord of life and growth, in opposition to the lethal, devouring sun. The moist night time is the time of sleep, but also of healing and recovery.... It is the regenerating power of the unconscious that in nocturnal darkness or by the light of the moon performs its task, a mysterium in a mysterium, working from out of itself, out of nature, with no aid from the head-ego. This is why healing pills and herbs are ascribed to the moon, and their secrets guarded by women, or better by womanliness, which belongs to the moon.[2]

Eyes of the Moon

Sunlight is overrated. Intuitions, like dreams, feelings, images or poetry, can only be apprehended by the eyes of the heart, our moon sight. They cannot be understood intellectually by the mind, our sun sight which seeks clarity, lucidity, transparency, vision, visibility, edges, boundaries, definition and sharpness. It abhors all things vague, ambiguous, amorphous, blurred, dim, faint, fuzzy, hazy, ill-defined, imprecise, indefinite, indeterminate, indistinct, muddy, nebulous, obscure, occult, shadowy, tenebrous, uncertain or unclear. Thinking takes years to develop but we begin life as an infant in a world full of big feelings seen only by our moon eyes (the Priestess). Robert Graves paints the difference between the two ways of seeing in his poem *Broken Images*.

> He is quick, thinking in clear images;
> I am slow, thinking in broken images.
> He becomes dull, trusting to his clear images;
> I become sharp, mistrusting in my broken images.
> Trusting his images, he assumes their relevance;
> Mistrusting my images, I question their relevance.
> Assuming their relevance, he assumes the fact;
> Questioning their relevance, I question the fact.
> When the fact fails him, he questions his sense;
> When the fact fails me, I approve my senses.
> He continues quick and dull in his clear images;
> I continue slow and sharp in my broken images.

He in a new confusion of his understanding;
I in a new understanding of my confusion.

Now, in the bottom row of the Child Spirit Shield, psychic energy comes directly from the Self, where all the opposites become united. The Moon smooths things over, differences are minimised and the harmony of the whole is enhanced. When something is too pitilessly visible and harsh in outline, the Moon brings blending and softness. The Moon card is the 18, the double 9, and like the Sage it is about interiority. But now the object of exploration is not oneself but the outer world and seeing it with new eyes.

Lisel Mueller, in her poem *Monet Refuses The Operation*, writes of Monet's fancied words to his eye surgeon. Claude Monet (1840–1926), the founder of French impressionism, developed cataracts in his sixties and eventually had surgery on his right eye in 1923 when he was eighty-two. He was dissatisfied with the results. Her poem declines the sparkle of sunlight and clear vision and looks through not at the fixities of the visible world.[3]

I tell you it has taken me all my life
to arrive at the vision of gas lamps as angels,
to soften and blur and finally banish
the edges you regret I don't see...
Fifty-four years before I could see
Rouen cathedral is built
of parallel shafts of sun,
and now you want to restore
my youthful errors: fixed
notions of top and bottom,
the illusion of three-dimensional space,
wisteria separate
from the bridge it covers...
I will not return to a universe
of objects that don't know each other,
as if islands were not the lost children
of one great continent....

Lunacy

From the sunny-side, lop-side of Western consciousness the moon looks dark, mad and crazy. It's all cold nights, bat-wings, howling, witches, cauldrons, spells, sleep, chaos, regression, murders, madness, secrecy, silence, and lunacy. The moon stands on the border between the light of the sun and the darkness of night and is associated with those things that live between the worlds—magic, vampires, ghosts and werewolves.

When we are "moony" we are drawn close to the unconscious. But beware, the moon does bring madness and dismemberment when the ego is immature and unprepared for the encounter. Like Actaeon, the young hunter in Greek mythology who stumbled across Artemis, the moon goddess, bathing naked in the forest. As punishment, Artemis turned him into a stag and he was torn apart by his own dogs. Artemis represents the moonlight and splendour of the night and Hecate, the goddess of sorcery and witchcraft, represents the darkness and the terrors of the night. On moonless nights she was believed to roam the earth with a pack of ghostly, howling dogs. Hecate's ancient gift, beyond even the power of Zeus to deny, was the bestowing or withholding from mortals any desired gift.

Mythologically, the moon was said to come to earth and transform itself into a snake and have intercourse with women, or if an unmarried woman looks at the moon, she will become pregnant. Stone snakes were made to bring about women's fertility. The moon is also associated with death because it disappears every month for three days, and the four days of a woman's menstrual period is the hidden death cycle when the old makes way for the new. So the fertilising power of snakes, the moon's changeability, its reptilian coldness, the death and rebirth of the snake when it sheds its skin, the appearance and disappearance of snakes and the moon, are all closely associated within the moon-snake-water-death-rebirth-woman image.[4] We see this in the cards. The Moon (death) and the Feathered Serpent (rebirth), bracket the Sun card (life). From above, the Temperate Man card showers them with water.

In the Marseilles Tarot the Moon card reflects more of the dark side of the archetype in accordance with the cards' appearance at a time in Europe when superstition was rife. It has images of dogs baying at the moon and a primitive crayfish coming out of the water onto land. The crayfish perhaps was an attempt to represent something cold and instinctive without explicitly depicting a serpent which in medieval Europe was associated with the devil.

Water and Time

In antiquity the moon was seen as the intermediary and gateway between the celestial realm and the earthly realm.[5] All descending influences that take on material form have to pass through the moon. This acknowledges the psychic reality that any concrete, material expression of our imagination—science, art, or engineering even—belongs to the feminine principle. In other words, the feminine incarnates and gives birth. Macrobius, the Roman writer (fourth century CE) said:

By the impulse of the first weight the soul, having started on its downward course from the intersection of the zodiac and the Milky Way to the successive spheres lying beneath, as it passes through these spheres acquires each of the attributes which it will exercise later. In the sphere of Saturn it obtains reason and understanding, called *logistikon;* in Jupiter's sphere, the power to act, called *praktikon;* in Mars' sphere, a bold spirit or *thymikon;* in the sun's sphere, sense-perception and imagination, *aisthetikon;* in Venus' sphere, the impulse of passion, *epithymetikon;* in Mercury's sphere, the ability to speak and interpret, *hermeneutikon;* and in the lunar sphere, the function of molding and increasing bodies, *phytikon.* This last function being the farthest removed from the gods, is the first in us and all the earthly creation.[6]

When energy moves from spirit to substance it comes into time. Incarnating, its heart begins to beat, its feet begin to move and it dances to the rhythm of its own heartbeat. All things have a pulse, a throbbing, a vibration, a beat, a sound, a song and a dance. The moon governs all these hidden rhythms and influences: the tides, the stages of pregnancy, the menstrual cycle, the movement of the blood, and times for planting (full moon for leaf crops, new moon for root crops). The moon is also associated with all movements of water: sap, dew, rain, tides, and tears. The dew on moonlit nights is supposed to drip from the moon. Water is the mother of all rhythms.

Time reflects the doings of the Creator as seen in the rhythmic changes of the moon, the planets and stars. Those who are closer to the rhythm of the Self, as expressed in the natural world or in the inner world, are more aligned with rhythms of the moon and its effects, particularly on the body. Thus the Moon is the Keeper of the Body of the Child Spirit Shield —knowing our biological rhythms and whether or not the body is in alignment with the Self and time.[7]

Time

The Sanskrit root *me-* gave rise to English words such as moon, month, menstrual, mind, mental and measure. The Indo-European root of the word "time" is *di-,* meaning to cut up or divide. The moon therefore measures time as it relates to inner or hidden events. The first calendars were lunar calendars which measured a different kind of phenomena than the later solar calendars that supplanted them as human cultures became pastoralised. We might say that solar calendars measure secular time and moon calendars measure sacred time. Most ecclesiastical calendars are lunar.

The standing stones of Callanish on the Isle of Lewis in the Outer Hebrides are a stunning visual example of a lunar calendar. They are oriented to the moon and another circle of stones is oriented to a long reclining figure of a woman visible in a range of undulating hills some miles away. They are still called *An cailleach,* the woman. Every saros cycle the full moon rises and moves along her body in an amazing visual display. A saros cycle is when the sun and the moon return to the same position in the sky together every 18 years and 9 days (19 returns of the sun, or 223 lunations).

The moon is closely associated with the cycles of reincarnation. For the ancient Greeks the Elysian fields, where the heroes went after death, were on the moon. Plutarch wrote that after death the body (*soma*) was given back to the earth, the mind (*nous*) was given back to the sun, and the soul (*psyche*) was purified in the moon. Likewise, the moon is associated with spinning and weaving which in turn are associated with time. The Egyptian lunar goddess Neith invented weaving. The Moirae or the Fates, as we saw in the Wheel, were lunar goddesses who spun the fate of the individual.

The number of the Moon card is 18. In the Twenty Count this is the number of the Keepers of the Book of Life — the ones who hold the consciousness (10) of all laws, cycles and patterns (8) of movement between spirit and substance. We have seen in the Sage card that energy moves in 9 movements and cycles of death and birth occur every 9 years, 9 months, 9 weeks, 9 days or 9 seconds. These rhythms happen in both the tonal and the nagual (2 x 9 = 18), are co-occurring and mirror each other. (The tonal and nagual spirals in Figure 53 are an example of this). When there is a death in substance, there is a birth in spirit, and when something is born in this world, something dies in the other world. When we die and are reborn in each moment, we touch our 18-ness. This is the Moon as the Teacher of Using Spiritual Death as an Advisor.

When a woman is on her moon (her menstrual period) she sits directly in front of Crack-between-the-Worlds of spirit and substance.[8] Moonlight and twilight are the times when the laws of spirit and the laws of substance cross over and magic happens. The spiritual aspect of Using Death as an Advisor is an awareness of the movement from spirit to substance and from substance to spirit, and knowing that they are different forms of the same thing. Therefore, there is no such thing as immortality just a cycle of death and rebirth. This is feminine, moon wisdom that has respect for the cosmic laws and natural cycles: death gives life, life gives rebirth, rebirth gives movement, movement gives change, change gives chaos, and chaos gives death.

The Moon card is about time experienced in physical form. The Self only becomes real when it ceases to be an intuition or a concept and actually enters our lives and our actions in space and time. So the Moon is about timeing — spirit's timing not the ego's. It is the inner readiness to accept the archetype of the Self in whatever form and at whatever time it appears. This

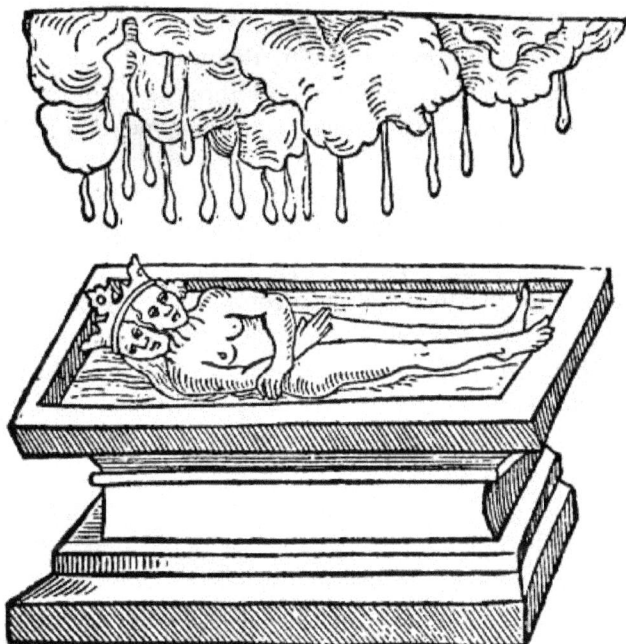

Figure 87. Gideon's Dew, Picture 8, Rosarium Philosophorum

is the Moon as the Holder of the Mood of Physical Patience — the waiting over many years between the first insight into how life might be, or who one is, and the actual living of that reality. It is the Patience to wait for things come down from the dream and manifest in the physical world.

Itz and the World Tree

Itz is the Maya word for all holy liquids and essences such as dew, semen, blood, holy water, nectar, candle-wax, pitch, sap, resin, sweat, or tears. It is the vital life force or "lightning in the blood" and is the Maya equivalent of *chi* (Chinese), *ki* (Japanese), or *gal* (Gaelic).[9] It is the cosmic sap of the World Tree. When copal is burned in a brazier as in the Sage card the itz is converted into smoke. Itz also represents the *ch'ul* or the "soul stuff" in human blood. It was the blessed substance brought forth in ritual bloodletting. Itz is also the word for "magic" and the god Itzamna was the first sorcerer of creation. A Maya shaman is an *itzam* or "one who makes itz" and these fluids were used by shamans to contact other worlds.

For the Maya itz came down through the *kuxan sum*, the "living cords" or ropes from the sky like umbilical cords filled with blood. These kuxan sum, also called "sky-snakes," passed down through the World Tree and below to its roots and the network of underground caverns and cenotes (a cenote is also an inverted, underground tree) that joined places on the earth.[10]

They often came down to earth in giant ceiba trees and were connected to the rulers and places of power, charging them with life-force.

We can see the sky-ropes in the middle three cards of the bottom row, feeding itz upwards. But the movement is not just one way. The Moon, Sun and Planet Venus all nurture, and are nurtured by, the humans in the first row who are the flowers of the World Tree and the Sage and Temperate Man who are its trunk (Figure 37). Each world feeds the other through this holy umbilicus.

We see a similar theme of the fluid connection between above and below, conscious and unconscious, in an alchemical legend that each night Sister Moon gathers up all the discarded memories and forgotten dreams of humankind which she stores in her silver cup until dawn. She then returns them to the earth as dew, the tears of the moon, or "radical moisture" as the alchemists called it.

This alchemical solutio solves problems by introducing the feeling function, patience and waiting. In ecclesiastical symbolism, dew is a symbol of grace and divine intervention. In alchemy, it is the *aqua sapientiae*, the sap of life, in which Mercurius is hidden, and it heralds the return of the soul to the body. Jung said, "The falling dew signals resuscitation and a new light: the ever deeper descent into the unconscious suddenly becomes illumination from above."[11] This is the water that the Temperate Man poured onto the earth which now reappears as the dew of divine grace in the Moon card. In Figure 87 we see one of the woodcuts of the Rosarium where this dew announces the return of the soul and prepares the body for their reunion in the Planet Venus card (20).

The Sun
The Mind of the Child Spirit Shield uses the Mood of Mental
Patience to Stop the Spiritual World

The Sun

29

Sun

Its father is the sun, its mother the moon: the wind hath carried it in his belly; its nurse is the earth. Its power is complete when it is turned toward earth. It ascendeth from the earth to heaven, and descendeth again to the earth, and receiveth the power of the higher and lower things. So wilt thou have the glory of the whole world.

— Hermes Trismegistus, *The Emerald Tablet*

Spirituality is not to be learned by flight from the world, by running away from things, or by turning solitary and going apart from the world. Rather we must learn to penetrate things and find God here.

— Meister Eckhart

Happiness is consciousness set on fire. You will never forget this moment. You are like a film that has been exposed; memory will develop it later.

— Max Frisch

At the centre of this card is a large yellow disk decorated with points and plumes in the cardinal directions and four eggs in the non-cardinals. Above, on the left, is the water from the Temperate Man card and on the right are the roots of the Flowering Tree from the same card.

The sun's energy is boundless and inexhaustible. It brings clarity and warmth, life is good and everything grows in the sun's life-giving rays. Under the sun all becomes clear, simple, joyous and physical. The Sun represents the joy and union of the Child Spirit Shield that is the compensation for the conflict of the Adult Spirit Shield. Life is lived with a childlike simplicity and lucidity, everything is immediately and directly clear and we see the universe as filled with light and aliveness. There is always boundless energy available from the sun and in the Marseilles Tarot we see children or young adults, symbolic of the deep well of youthful energy, joyfully playing under the shining sun. The sun is both the physical sun and the divine fire and breath that moves through all things. It warms, moves, enlivens and energises. Life jumps up and lives. This card is the archetype of the divine child. In Greek mythology he was Dionysus, the ecstatic god of indestructible life.

Hokseda

Isak Dinesen said, "There are three pure joys in life. The first is an excess of strength. The second is a cessation of pain. And the third is to know one is fulfilling one's destiny."[1] The 19 card is symbolic of all these. The number 19 is the number of the higher Self. It is our free will — the consciousness (10) of all choices and decisions (9) in all lives we have lived, are living and will live. It is our guardian angel — that part of us enduringly and uninterruptedly connected to the Godhead.

In his journey across the sky Grandfather Sun sees everything so the sun is always associated with knowledge, as with Apollo the sun god who knew everything that happened. So the 19, the higher Self, knows all things. The Stone Peoples, the Plant Nations and Animal Brothers and Sisters, also have their 19s. "Each blade of grass has its Angel," the Talmud says, "that bends over it and whispers 'Grow! Grow!'"

Ken Carey wrote: "I will tell you also of the gentle tribes from which we came, the tribes some now call angels, but who in simpler days were known by another name 'The Bird Tribes.' There are many names for us. We have been called angels, Bird Tribes, higher selves, hoksedas, spirits of the stars."[2] The word *hokseda* means "he has this person as his child." This Hokseda or Hokkshideh is the part of our soul that makes choices in alignment with the deepest and highest needs of the Self. It is the Mind of the Child Spirit Shield, the mental face of the Self that chooses with free will.

In traditional Maya culture mothers and midwives sing the Maya creation story as the child comes down the birth canal so it knows where it comes from. Similar to the alchemical notion of the soul descending through the spheres, or with near-death experiences where the person sees their life flash before them, the infant has "near-life" experiences, but in reverse.

The Twenty Count describes it like this: When a child is born it comes from the world of spirit which is 20. During the moment it takes its first breath the spirit of the child sees why it chose this life at 19. It sees its entire Book of Life and why it chose that mother, that father, and those particular circumstances at 18. Then it sees the dream of this life at 17. At 16 it accepts its sacredness and at 15 it manifests its humanness. Its spiritual wholeness at 14 then dies at 13 so it may cross over into matter at 12. At 11 it loses memory, at 10 it has consciousness, and at 9 its 19 decides if it will stay in that particular body which is its 8.

We experience our 19, our higher Self, most immediately and directly through the instinctiveness of our 14, the Spirit of the Animals, and the natural alignment and balance they give us. When our will aligns with the will of the Creator we touch our 19. Our energy is in alignment with the movement of the universe at that moment. Marie-Louise von Franz calls this the "instinct of truth," when the Self is so present that the reflective thinking of consciousness does not interfere with our response to a situation. "One reacts rightly without knowing why… sometimes doing one thing and sometimes the other…. On a higher level, it is the same thing as being completely natural and instinctive, when one can discern between the false and the true. That is why the Holy Ghost [our 14] has also been called by certain theologians the instinct of truth."[3]

Joy and Inner Light

It is the nature of life to expand, outwardly in substance and inwardly in spirit, in all ten directions (the eight directions of the compass, and above and below). It is this urge toward consciousness, to shine a light on what has until now been in darkness, to see reality clearly, to discover truth, that the Sun card symbolises. It is the psychic impulse that drove the outward geographical exploration of the world 500 years ago and the more recent scientific exploration of matter. Inwardly, it is the discovery and integration of what has previously been unknown in the psyche. It was what Freud meant when he said, "Where id was, let ego be." When there is "in-sight," when the unconscious is made conscious, we experience a freedom, a widening and deepening of our personality, and we become heavier and lighter at the same time.

"Joy is the cessation of gravity," writes Verena Kast.[4] Joy and happiness open us up and we become lighter. Grey disappears and all is colour. The rainbow in the Temperate Man directly above the Sun card comes down to earth and suffuses all things. Our eyes shine and our whole body beams. We become self-confident and know that we matter. We accept ourselves and our place in the world.

Breath

Joy, ecstasy and happiness connect us to the element of air and breath. We express joy by dancing, singing and making music — all movements of air. The spirit of the element of air, the Breath of Life, feeds both soul and spirit. The words for soul in Greek (*psyche*), Latin (*anima*) and Sanskrit (*atman*) all mean "breath." The words for spirit in Greek (*pneuma*), Latin (*spiritus*), and

Hebrew (*ruach*), also mean "breath." Breath is the marriage of soul and body and the ancient way of bringing spirit and matter together is to focus on the breath. All spiritual paths, arguably with the exception of the Abrahamic religions, have physical disciplines or breathing practices that use the power of the breath, as in pranayama, or the practice of the fire breath, for example. Our 19 is the part of ourselves that "sits but a breath away from the Great Spirit." Our breath connects us with our 19.

The Holy Ghost, often associated with wind and breath, is a symbol of spirit assimilated into matter.[5] Jung said, "Hard as it is to define, this unknown quantity can be experienced by the psyche and is known in Christian parlance as the 'Holy Ghost,' the breath that heals and makes whole."[6] The *Corpus Hermeticum* says, "There was darkness in the deep and water without form; and there was subtle breath, intelligent, which permeated the things in Chaos with divine power."[7] Other airy and fiery images of this source of pure energy are the dove, the whirlwind or the tongues of fire at the Pentecost. T. S. Eliot wrote:

> The dove descending breaks the air
> With flame of incandescent terror
> Of which the tongues declare
> The one discharge from sin and error.
> The only hope, or else despair
> Lies in the choice of pyre or pyre—
> To be redeemed from fire by fire.

We see the image of the dove and the 19 in a dream of Jung's. At the beginning of his "descent into the unconscious" after his break from Freud, Jung had a dream of his 19, first as a 14, a medicine animal, then as his Child Spirit Shield or Little Girl Shield who showed him his sacred dream—his study of alchemy. Jung felt the dream was highly significant as a harbinger of his coming descent into the unconscious. In the dream, around Christmas 1912, he found himself sitting in an Italian loggia on a gold Renaissance chair in front of a table of emerald stone. A dove alighted on the table and transformed into a little girl, about eight years old with golden, blonde hair, who put her arms tenderly around his neck and then changed back into the dove.

The Emerald Tablet, also known as the Tabula Smaragdina, or The Secret of Hermes, was a 14-line alchemical text of Arabic origin dating from the 9th century or earlier. It was later translated by European alchemists including Sir Isaac Newton. Jung refers to it numerous times in his writing. I quote parts of it here as it speaks of the same process as the tarot and specifically the Sun card.

What is the above is from the below and the below is from the above.

Its father is the sun and its mother is the moon.

Thus the wind bore it within it and the earth nourished it.

It is a fire that became our earth. Separate the earth from the fire and you
    shall adhere more to that which is subtle than that which is coarse,
    through care and wisdom.

It ascends from the earth to the heaven. It extracts the lights from the
    heights and descends to the earth containing the power of the above
    and the below for it is with the light of the lights. Therefore the dark-
    ness flees from it.

The greatest power overcomes everything that is subtle and it pene-
    trates all that is coarse.

The formation of the microcosm is in accordance with the formation of
    the macrocosm.

Outer Light

The Sun is the urge toward enlightenment and consciousness that exists in
all life. It is the power of consciousness to dispel darkness and ignorance
and bring meaning and illumination. This compassionate ability to bring
light and a fresh consciousness to things, as well as the irrepressible search
for meaning makes the Sun the Keeper of the Mind of the Child Spirit
Shield.

All of creation, the Stone Peoples, the Plant Nations, and the Animals,
know their connection to the Everything. Humans are the only child of
creation that has forgotten this connection and has to remember it — and in
so doing spirit learns about itself. Rediscovering our connection with all
things and penetrating to the meaning of all phenomena by the light of consciousness is the Sun as the card of mental intuition and the Holder of the
Mood of Mental Patience. It is the ability to accept the outer forms of all
creation because the inner light is seen and understood. When we see that
all things are part of the web and are connected to the source then there is
no separation. If there is no difference there can be no thinking or feeling
judgement — and we are patient.

The sun and figures with solar attributes like the Ruler are archetypes of
libido and life-force. In this Movement of Stopping the World, the Ruler
with the sun behind him, holds this life-force for the culture and the individual. This transforms into the individual life-force held by the Sage as the
fire in his brazier. Then the Temperate Man is the mediator between the
earth and the cosmic fire above him. Finally, at the bottom is the great spiritual fire itself in the Sun card. The Sun is the Teacher of the spiritual aspect
of Stopping the World — to see all things as a design of energy and to see the

luminous cocoon, the shimmering web of life of this planet. Annie Dillard said:

> If the landscape reveals one certainty, it is that the extravagant gesture is the very stuff of creation. After the one extravagant gesture of creation in the first place, the universe has continued to deal exclusively in extravagances, flinging intricacies and colossi down aeons of emptiness, heaping profusions on profligacies with ever-fresh vigour. The whole show has been on fire from the word go! I come down to the water to cool my eyes. But everywhere I look I see fire; that which isn't flint is tinder, and the whole world sparks and flames.[8]

And Wordsworth wrote:

> There was a time when meadow, grove, and stream,
> The earth, and every common sight,
> To me did seem
> Apparelled in celestial light.

Gustav Fechner (1801–1887) was one of the founders of modern experimental psychology. He studied the mathematical relationships between physical stimuli and the sensations we experience and was held in high regard by both Sigmund Freud and William James. He trained as a medical doctor and then became Professor of Physics at the University of Leipzig. At age 39 while studying colour and vision he went into a severe depression and had to resign his position. (On the Moon Cycles, we enter the three-year cycle of Double Death and Change at age 39 and age 40½ is the place of Triple Death and Change). He could not eat or drink and was kept alive by his wife. He protected his eyes with lead cups and bandages and retreated into a room he had painted black. After almost three years he emerged:

> I stepped out for the first time from my darkened chamber and into the garden with no bandage upon my eyes... Every flower beamed upon me with a peculiar clarity, as though into the outer light it was casting a light of its own. To me the whole garden seemed transfigured, as though it were not I but nature that had just arisen. And I thought: So nothing is needed but to open the eyes afresh. The picture of the garden accompanied me into the darkened chamber; but in the dusk it was all the brighter and clearer and more beautiful, and at once I thought I saw an inward light as the source of the outward clarity of the flowers, and within that the spiritual production of colours... and the shining of the plant's souls.[9]

All things put here by the Creator including humans have a luminous co-coon, a *lumen naturae*, a body of light which is their shining. Paracelsus said that there are two kinds of knowledge or Gnosis.[10] One is the *lumen dei*, the light from the Godhead above, the other is the *lumen naturae*, the light "hidden" in matter and nature. The Gnostic and alchemical view was that while the divine light may be discerned through revelation and in the mystery of the incarnation, the light of nature needs to be released through alchemy before it can shine. God redeems humanity but nature needs to be redeemed by the alchemists who, through the process of alchemical transformation, were capable of seeing with their inward eyes and liberating the light hidden in physical creation.

The innermost layer of the *lumen naturae* is a membrane of black light which lives in the boundaries and under the surface of all things. It is not the flashy display of outer light — the blinding revelation, the burning bush, the tunnel of light, the stroke of lightning. It is the light that can only be received by inner eyes rather than perceived by outer eyes. Like the gaseous exchange that takes place across the membranes of our lungs this impossibly thin surface allows us to breathe in light.

Stopping the World is to see the *lumen naturae* in all things, to see the light in the darkness and the darkness in the light, to see the light in matter, to see the world on fire with the passion of the lovemaking between Grandmother Earth and Grandfather Sun.

Planet Venus
The Spirit of the Child Spirit Shield uses the Mood of Spiritual
Patience to Control the Spiritual Dream

Judgement

30

Planet Venus

We shall not all sleep, but we shall all be changed, in a moment, in the twinkling of an eye, at the last trump: for the trumpet shall sound, and the dead shall be raised incorruptible, and we shall be changed. For this corruptible must put on incorruption, and this mortal must put on immortality... O death, where is thy sting? O grave, where is thy victory?

— Corinthians 15:51–55

I think I've discovered the secret of life — you just hang around until you get used to it.

— Charles Schulz

A blue, crimson and green Feathered Serpent is descending toward the earth. It has a white halo around its head and a forked tongue pointing downward between the two volcanoes at the bottom of the card. The card symbolises the imminent union of opposites, the coming of peace, and the rebirth and resurrection of new life.

Venus

As the "morning star" the brilliance of Venus stands out as big as a snowball in the dawn sky and is outshone only by the sun and moon. As the "evening star" it is brighter than any stars in the sky. It has been called Earth's sister planet because it is almost the same size, mass and chemical composition as the Earth. It is also called our "hellish twin" because the surface temperature is around 450°C, the atmospheric pressure is about a hundred times that of earth, the atmosphere is about 97% carbon dioxide and 3% nitrogen, there is very little water, and the clouds are made of concentrated sulphuric acid. Because of its slow rotation Venus' day (the time it takes to make one revolution on its axis) is longer than its year (the time it takes to make one revolution around the sun).

The Greeks called the evening star *Hesperos* which is derived from an Indo-European root meaning "western." As the morning star, Venus was called *Phosphoros* which means "bringer of light" or *Eosphoros*, "bringer of dawn." The Romans also had two names for the star. The evening star was called *Vesper* or *Noctifer* (bringer of night), and the morning star was called *Lucifer* (bringer of light). To the Babylonians she was the goddess Ishtar; to the Egyptians, Isis; to the Greeks, Aphrodite; and to the Romans, Venus. In Arabic alchemy Venus was known as "the noble, the impure, the green lion, the father of the colours, the peacock of the Pleiades, the phoenix."[1] In Roman mythology, Venus was originally a goddess of gardens, fields and fertility but later came to be identified with Aphrodite, the Greek goddess of love and beauty. Venus was also the mother of Cupid, the god of love.

Venus was not only a beneficent female body in the heavens but was also male and malefic, personified as Ahriman, Seth, Lucifer, and Satan. So Venus is the epitome of opposites — it is a planet that is like a star, it appears at night and in the morning, it is both male and female, pure and impure, it is like the Earth but completely different, and it shines brightly in the night sky then disappears completely.

For both the Maya and Aztec Venus was strongly associated with the Feathered Serpent, Kukulkan or Quetzalcoatl that we see depicted in the card. The Maya name for Venus was *Citlalpol* and they recorded the cycles of greater and lesser brilliance along with its appearance as the morning star and evening star.

A conjunction is when celestial bodies appear close to one another in the sky. An inferior conjunction occurs when the two planets lie in a line on the same side of the Sun. When Venus passes between the Earth and the sun (the inferior conjunction) it cannot be seen from the Earth and "disappears" for eight days during this time. After the inferior conjunction Venus can be seen rising in the east before dawn. This is when Venus is known as the morning star and it leads the sun out of the Underworld. After that it remains visible in the morning sky for approximately 263 days.

Then it enters a period of superior conjunction when it is on the opposite side of the sun from the Earth. So Venus again disappears but now for about eight weeks. Next, Venus emerges from behind the sun, but now it is on the sun's "eastern" side. It is visible just after sunset and follows the sun into the Underworld. Now, as the evening star, it remains visible for approximately another 263 days. As Venus never strays too far from the sun, as either the morning or evening star, it was considered to be one of the Guardians of the Sun by the Maya and Aztecs.

The orbit of Venus is at an angle of about 3° relative to the Earth's and Venus usually appears to pass under (or over) the Sun in the sky at the inferior conjunction. But at certain times it lies in the same plane as the earth and appears as a large dot passing directly across the face of the sun. Transits of Venus occur in a pattern that repeats every 243 years, with two pairs of transits eight years apart separated by two long gaps of 122 years and 105 years. The most recent Venus transit was on June 8, 2004. The next Venus transit will be on June 6, 2012.

Venus transits seem to presage shifts in human consciousness. The transits since the "discovery" of the Americas have been in 1518/1526, 1631/1639, 1761/1769 and 1874/1882. Notably, Hernan Cortes landed in Mexico in March 1519 and on November 8, 1519 he entered the Aztec capital of Tenochtitlan. Cortes was Governor of New Spain until ordered to return to Madrid in 1528.

As an interesting aside, Venus was the reason for the first contact between Europeans and the indigenous peoples of the South Pacific. As late as 1770, the central and south Pacific was virtually unknown to Europeans. In 1642 Abel Tasman, the Dutch explorer, had briefly visited what is now known as Tasmania and the western shoreline of New Zealand but continental Australia had remained unexplored. At the time it was believed that there had to be a great land mass, *Terra Australis*, the "Great Southern Continent," stretched across the South Pacific to balance the land masses of Asia and Europe. Without it, the scientists of the time believed, it would not be possible for the earth to rotate properly on its axis.

One of the burning scientific issues of the time was the problem of how to measure accurately the distance of the earth from the sun. Such a measurement, it was believed, would contribute greatly towards a much better understanding of the universe and how it operated. In 1716, the astronomer Edmond Halley suggested that an accurate calculation could be obtained by taking simultaneous measurements of the transit of Venus from widely spaced geographical locations. There had been a transit of Venus in 1761 but the observations made were not precise enough to yield an accurate calculation. The next transit of Venus was calculated to occur on June 3, 1769 and the Royal Society of London, eager to extend Britain's role in scientific endeavour, proposed a journey to the South Pacific to measure the second transit of Venus from Tahiti. Captain James Cook was chosen to lead the expedition, the first of three that Cook made, and the Endeavour began its voyage on August 25, 1768.

Cook was given strict instructions by the Earl of Morton, the President of the Royal Society, as to how the people of the lands that he and his crew encountered should be treated. With a sympathy that was all too rare at the time, he was told to "exercise the utmost patience and forbearance" when dealing with the native people they met. "They are the natural and in the strictest sense of the word, the legal possessors of the several regions they inhabit," he was told. "No European Nation has a right to occupy any part of their country, or settle among them without their voluntary consent."[2]

Apocalypse Now

The deep currents in the dream, which we experience as "history", are not evenly spread out but cluster in nodes and knots. They break through to the surface of the world as historical events in time and space that are marked by corresponding cosmic events visible in the sky. In Maya culture these astronomical events are important times for religious ceremony and ritual.

Ceremonies are planned synchronicities, so to speak. A synchronicity is a resonance between two events that occur together in time but apart in space. They seem to have no observable, causal connection (the ego is speaking here). One event is an inner event (a thought, an image, a feeling) and the other is an outer event. One in spirit, one in matter. They are a sign that spirit and matter have touched, or at least shown an interest in each other. The use of ceremony at those times and in those places where spirit and matter are in proximity enables the two to come even closer so that "magic" happens.

The shadow aspect of this ceremonial observance of cosmic timing emerges in paranoid, apocalyptic, end-of-the-world movements or naïve beginning-of-the-new-age predictions. Here the true nature of the event is either demonised or idealised. The end of the world has been variously called Ragnarok (Norse), Qiyâmah (Muslim), Kali Yuga (Hindu), Judgement Day, the Great Purification, the Quickening, or the New Age.

The word apocalypse (Greek, *apokalupsis*) means the "uncovering of what has been hidden" or revelation. It was also the other name for the Book of Revelation describing the visions of the future given to Saint John the Divine on the island of Patmos. Later, the word apocalypse came to mean the coming of a deity to judge, punish or reward humanity and bring about a new order. The word used in the sense of a catastrophic event, such as the end of the world, is a recently derived meaning.

Psychologically, the archetype of the apocalypse is the earth-shattering advent of the Self into full, conscious realisation. From the ego's point of view this is the end of its world. The many themes and images include: a final judgement, tribulation, reward or punishment; destruction (earthquakes, plague, famine); the separation of opposites (the good from the bad, the just from the unjust, the righteous from the sinners); the bestowal of grace, paradise and eternal life; earthly bodies ascending to heaven (the rapture); and heavenly bodies come to earth (the coming of the saviour).[3]

Apocalyptic movements have waxed and waned over the course of history but this archetype is strongly constellated in the global unconscious at this time in history.[4] The Planet Venus card is the twenty-first card in the deck and at the beginning of the twenty-first century, fundamentalist, apocalyptic beliefs are increasingly popular. For example, the appeal of the *Left Behind* series.[5] All such movements seem incapable of learning from the past and ignore the obvious — that we are still here. So we must assume that a powerful archetype is at work that overrides simple reality-testing. We can approach apocalyptic writings in four ways. First, dismiss them as religious rubbish. Second, accept them as religious gospel. Third, view them as a physical sign of a spiritual event. Fourth, view them as a spiritual sign of a physical event.

The first two views do not concern us here. We shall have more to say about the third and fourth possibilities in Chapter 31. Suffice to say that all cultures throughout history have had their dreamers, prophets and visionaries who have predicted the end of the world but it is only in the last thousand years that such apocalyptic visions have gone global, so to speak. The many Western apocalyptic writings (Islamic, Judaic and Christian) may have only half the story leaving out the subjective (and unconscious) meaning of their prophecies — the end of *their* world-view and *their* mode of consciousness.

Global terrorism, global conspiracies, global climate change, global fundamentalism and the global economy all spring from the same source. The state of grandiose denial that is the global economy says the earthly mother will continue to supply us with all our needs and our standard of living will improve forever. This is the physical twin to the spiritual belief that the heavenly father will rapture us upward into a paradise with a spiritually better standard of living. The fundamentalist belief in the global economy and the fundamentalist belief in *jihad* have the same quantum of religious fervour attached to them. One believes in lethal and unrestricted materiality, the other in lethal and constricted spirituality. With the invasion of Iraq it came about that the most fanatically material were at war with the most fanatically spiritual. And the worst, as Yeats wrote, "Are full of passionate intensity."[6] In other words, driven by an archetype that is beyond their control.

What is the result? A global economy, which ostensibly values prudent financial management, that has been on a manic spending spree for the last five hundred years without checking the bank account. Seemingly, no one has considered the obvious, and done the sums, despite the warnings. We *will* run out — of oil, of steel, of fish, of forests, of water, of food, of room. Profits? Stock markets? Money supply? All based on growth. Can we imagine an economic model that does not include annual growth? Our inability to do so is a measure of our denial. As the Club of Rome pointed out in 1972 there are limits to growth. It's like watching the apocalyptic train crash in slow motion, and crash it will. We shall look at what the Maya said about the timing of this in the Planet Earth card.

The Movement of Assuming Authority is the process of humanising this archetype of the apocalypse by bringing it to consciousness. As this happens, fewer will need to die. Like any archetype whose time has come, the

Figure 88. The Reunion of the Soul and the Body by William Blake

apocalypse will insist on being incarnated and manifesting itself concretely. "To do this, however, the archetypal dynamic must draft or conscript human beings into its service," Edward Edinger said. "Yet this means that human beings will be 'consumed' or 'devoured' by the process which deprives them of their personal lives… mere 'actors' in the archetypal drama. And usually this drama lives itself out unconsciously, willy-nilly, in collective human history where *everyone* is a victim. The more conscious alternative is that an individual who understands what is going on 'incarnates' the archetypal process as individuation."[7]

Judgement and Resurrection

In the Marseilles Tarot this card is called Judgement. It shows images of the resurrection and people rising from a tomb to the call of the last trump. In the Christian symbolism of the card, spirit is now released from the grasp of matter and ascends to heaven and joins the saints. But the Xultun Tarot shows the opposite. The soul, personified by Quetzalcoatl, now reunites with the body. William Blake, the English poet and artist (1757–1827), engraved a strikingly similar image to the Planet Venus card (Figure 88).

Symbolically, the prison, grave or coffin is a psychological problem which one cannot get out of and in which one feels trapped. It represents the necessity to be enclosed or imprisoned for the time it takes to outgrow one's problems. The conscious reaction to this restriction is impatience, hopelessness and feeling that one will always be like this and never get out of one's difficulties.

Ancient Egyptians believed that if someone did not go through the resurrection process properly then they would remain imprisoned in the funerary coffin chamber. However, someone who had gone through the complete ritual of resurrection would be able to leave the coffin and assume any form in the world. Similarly, the medieval alchemists said that the final product of the work was the Philosopher's Stone, which could "penetrate all things." A robust and enduring connection with the Self results in one not being caught or trapped in one's own inner processes and thus one can engage with and become fully involved in all life situations. There is a steady inner core that remains connected to, yet detached from, what happens to the personality. This response is not an impulsive thought or an emotional outburst but a search for meaning in one's fate and the fate of the world. The number 10 is All States of Consciousness (the conscious, the unconscious, the collective conscious, and the collective unconscious). The number 20 (10 + 10) is consciousness of all states of consciousness. It is being able to see through the eyes of the Great Spirit, to look at things from the infinite points of view of the Self. It is the unconscious become conscious of itself.

The God of monotheism is a split-off, dissociated part of the whole of creation. In his rage and grandiose self-exile he attempted to set himself up as the only god. His eldest, Satan, left home repeating the family tradition. The Old Testament and the Book of Revelation in the New Testament are shot through with wrath, vengeance, tribulation, repentance, salvation and redemption. In its unconscious form, Yahweh (or the Self in psychological terms) is brutal and animalistic, meting out harsh judgement, seeking blood revenge, punishing transgressions, and wanting an eye for an eye and a tooth for a tooth. Nature is cruel from the human perspective, but as a by-product of life not as an intentional act. Not so God. We see the creation and refinement of the great human values of ethics in Judaism, mercy in Islam, and love in Christianity. Why? How else do a people cope with a God that is given to such cruelty but to develop what is lacking.

When the Self is made conscious (and it goes without saying that this is an ideal state) we see how we have hurt and been hurt, how we have violated our own soul and the souls of others. Then we have sufficient cool subjectivity and passionate objectivity toward ourselves to stop the cycles of vengeance. This is Planet Venus as the Holder of the Mood of Spiritual Patience.

This psychological position (rather than an act, a belief, or an emotional state) is what we know as forgiveness. On a transpersonal level, this is what happened to Yahweh in his encounter with Job when he became conscious of his own atrocious behaviour. In an act of self-forgiveness and self-sacrifice he incarnated himself as Christ bringing divine love instead of divine wrath.

It was in his book *Answer to Job* that Jung pointed out that the Old Testament Yahweh is the same as undifferentiated unconscious within us.[8] In this state, our affects come from nowhere and their emotional tsunamis overwhelm us. Like God, our affects happen to us. They come from the Self and can have destructive consequences unless they are contained and transformed by the human ego.[9] Just as it was with Job, so it is with the ego — it has to both submit to, and stand its ground against, that which is much greater than itself. It was the spiritual patience of Job that transformed Yahweh. Yahweh underwent a religious conversion from being a less-than-human, unpredictable force, dissociated from the rest of creation and showing florid symptoms of borderline personality disorder, to being a more-than-human loving, too-good-to-be-true God who tried to redeem himself by incarnating what was previously his shadow (the new-found qualities of love and peace) in the figure of Christ.

The Planet Venus is the Keeper of the Spirit of the Child Spirit Shield. Venus' divine love brings balance to the dualities of life resulting in a spiritual wholeness or a holiness of existence. The 17th century English alchemist John Pordage wrote, "But if it [the tincture of life] can withstand and overcome this fiery trial and sore temptation, and win the victory: then you will see the beginning of its resurrection from hell, death, and the mortal grave, appearing first in the quality of Venus.... And then the gentleness and love-fire of Venus will reign."[10] Alice Howell said it this way: "The Chinese have a saying, 'If you keep a green bough in your heart, surely the singing bird will come.' And the same is true of the soul. All too often we fill our psyches with self-incrimination, fault-finding, and woe, and expect our Divine Guest to walk constantly in the dungeons of our own imprisonment. The self comes anyway, but it must be an awful drag."[11]

The goal of the alchemists was the coniunctio, the marriage of Sol and Luna, the union of the male and female dualities within the oneness of the Creator. Similarly, the redeemer or Messiah whose prophesied return will bring peace is, on a psychological level, the conscious union of opposites. This existed in the Garden of Eden where there was no division but there the state of wholeness was unconscious. To the extent that one has a conscious relationship with the Self, one is released from the conflict of opposites and peace reigns.[12] The tomb of the 20 card and the bondage of the 15 card are connected. In the Bound Man the soul was bound to spirit. Now it is free to unite with matter.

Fire

The Messiah symbolises the positive aspect of the Self—salvation, infinite love, and the light of eternal peace and everlasting life. But this lies side by side with the negative aspect of Judgement Day where a wrathful God subjects every soul to inspection and scrutiny and no excuses are allowed. Those judged as wanting are cast into the fire. So images of both fire and light attend the end of the world.

Judgement is cast in negative, apocalyptic imagery because the ego intuits that it will be shorn of all its illusions, errors, and projections. In fear and trembling, its light will be finally extinguished as the centre of gravity of the psyche shifts completely to the Self.

The Self is an archetype, a spiritual entity, and as such has no existence in time and space. The Self is experienced as time-less, eternal, and outside time. So when we are forsaken, abandoned, or deserted by the Self, or we cut ourselves off from the water of life we suffer hell—a time-full, never-ending anguish and torment that has to be endured. Most religions have a belief in a form of "hell" often associated with punishment by fire. Since the Second Council of Constantinople in 553 CE the Christian church has held that unrepentant souls will be consigned to purgatory and everlasting punishment in a fiery hell. The Hindu faith envisions twenty-one (sic) hells that are part of an endless transmigration of souls. In Islam, souls must cross over a pit of fire by a narrow bridge that leads to heaven. If they are not redeemed by Allah's mercy, they are consigned to the fiery pit.

Each row of cards represents an element. Vertically, from the top to bottom, the rows are water, air, earth and fire. In this last row of the Child Spirit Shield all the cards are fiery and form a wheel of fire (the east wheel of Figure 107). In the Moon and Planet Venus, the west and east cards on this wheel, we see the fire of the four volcanoes. This Great Fire comes from below the bottom of the deck, that is, it is of transpersonal origin. The Great Fire is the complementary opposite of the Great Light that comes from the above the top of deck. The light of spirit above has now been transformed into the fire of matter below. It is light incarnate.

In the Star and the Sun, the south and north cards, we see the physical Fires-from-within in this universe. The stars of Sirius and the Pleiades in the Star card represent the Great Grandfather Stars of the other Eleven Worlds, and the Sun refers to Grandfather Sun of our world. These four fires of the Star, Moon, Sun and Venus are joined in the Planet Earth card where we see the fire of our own human soul in the pot below the earth.

Fire represents libido, passion, and emotion and the volcanoes remind us that emotion is the carrier of consciousness and without emotion there is no life and no movement into greater consciousness. And these fiery affects must be experienced. The fires of adversity must be endured and there is no trick for getting rid of them. However, fire it is the only element that consumes itself and will eventually burn itself out. In the process it burns away all that is dross, all that is impure or evanescent. The alchemists said that the Philosopher's Stone was surrounded by or contaminated with foreign matter that had to be washed away (the operation of solutio) or burned away (the operation of calcinatio). This burning is the process of individuation and differentiation, sifting through what is ours and what is not, and not worshipping false idols. In other words, not wasting our energy on what does not have life for us. In this way we are redeemed from the constant pursuit of something that does not belong to us—in spiritual terms our heart is pure. After the burning, the alchemists say that what is left is the "vitreous body" or the white ash which was called the "white foliated earth." Vitreous means incorruptible, transparent or diamond. Foliated means covered with leaves. Here the alchemists point to the same archetypal reality as the final card in the deck—the Planet Earth covered by the Flowering Trees with the blue void at its centre.

Serpent

In mythology, the serpent is variously the mythic ancestor, the healer, and the embodiment of evil. The serpent symbolises the earth and its darkness but also its healing and creative powers. Christianity emphasised the dark side of the serpent as in the temptation of Eve in the Garden of Eden, and Satan as the Old Serpent. The Norse *Edda* also tells how Odin created the enormous ash tree Yggdrasil, the Tree of Life. This tree filled all time and space and took root in the deepest depths of Niflheim or Hel, the home of mist and darkness, and reached up to Asgard, the home of the gods. A serpent named Nidhogg continually gnawed at the roots of Yggdrasil. Its aim was to kill the tree which would bring about the downfall of the gods. The snake is also associated with deceitfulness as in a "snake in the grass," or speaking with a "forked tongue," and its deceit in luring Eve to eat of the Tree of Knowledge.

The serpent, although poisonous, is the healer and guardian. The caduceus, a staff surmounted by two wings and entwined with two snakes was the symbol of Hermes, the messenger of the gods, and was carried by heralds as a badge of office and protection. It was also adopted by Asclepius, the god of healing. The Hindu energy of kundalini, a Sanskrit word meaning "coiling like a snake," is often depicted by intertwined snakes rising up and crossing seven times at the chakras or energy centres of the body. The king of serpents, the cobra Muchalinda, rose up from his palace in the earth to protect the Buddha from the elements with his hood as he meditated under the Bodhi tree.

In Norse mythology the Midgard serpent, Jörmungandr, encircled the world in the depths of the ocean biting its own tail. In Hindu mythology Lord Vishnu sleeps floating on the cosmic waters on the serpent Shesha. Shesha holds all the planets of the universe on his hoods and constantly sings the glories of Vishnu from all his mouths.

The snake is also the spirit of light, creativity and wisdom. We hear of the "the wisdom of serpents" meaning an old, earthy wisdom. The snake was also a means of communicating with the divine. The Pythia, or Python-ess, was the Oracle of Delphi. She was the priestess who kept the shrine of Gaia at Delphi and spoke her prophecies from the cleft in the earth there.

Another form of serpent, the dragon, is cognate with the Feathered Winged Serpent and occur widely in world mythology. We find North American, Welsh, Japanese, and Chinese dragons,[13] the Norse Nidhogg, the Aboriginal Rainbow Serpent, the Maori Taniwha, the Dahomey Aido-Hwedo, the Japanese Ryujin, the Yoruba Oshumare, and the Fijian Dgei. With breath of fire, the wings of a bird, the scales of a fish, and the body of a reptile, the dragon lives in a cave and, like the snake, symbolises the light and dark primal energies, the instinctive, autonomic, nature spirit, and the wisdom of the earth.

In many myths, the hero wrests the treasure from the dragon's grasp and brings wealth back to the people and freedom from the terror of the dragon. Psychologically, this is the process whereby the ego, through a heroic act, gains some consciousness. Then consciousness is no longer beset by distur-bances from the dragon of the unconscious. The Christian myth of Saint George and the dragon focuses more on the dark chthonic energies that must be slain by Saint George in order for the light of consciousness to sur-vive, but in other world mythologies the dragon is more benevolent.

Quetzalcoatl

Quetzal refers to the quetzal bird of Guatemala and coatl is Náhuatl for snake. To the Maya, the quetzal symbolised freedom and wealth. Freedom, because a quetzal will die in captivity, and wealth because quetzal feathers along with jade (believed to attract moisture and bestow greenness and fer-tility) were highly valued. They were traded by the Maya as far north to what is now the USA and as far south as the Inca empire. The male quetzal appears on the Guatemalan flag and the quetzal is the Guatemalan unit of currency.

Mythologically, the Feathered Serpent was a prominent deity in many Mesoamerican cultures and is best known as the Aztec god Quetzalcoatl. It was widespread throughout the Americas: the Zuni knew him as Kolowisi, the Hopi as Palulukong, the Quiche Maya as Gucumatz and the Yucatec Maya as Kukulkan (*kuk*, feather; *kukul*, feathered; *can*, snake). The name

Quetzalcoatl translates as "feathered serpent" or "winged serpent." In Maya, the words for snake and sky are the same so Quetzalcoatl can mean can be "quetzal sky" or "quetzal snake."

The earliest feathered serpents appear in the Olmec culture (1400–400 BCE). At Teotihuacan there is a Temple of the Feathered Serpent (150–200 CE) and at Tula, the capital of the later Toltecs (950–1150 CE), there are profiles of feathered serpents. Figure 89 is similar to the feathered serpent in the Planet Venus card and in Figure 90 we see a feathered serpent at Xochicalco similar to that on the box of later editions of the Xultun Tarot. The pyramid of El Castillo at Chichen Itza served as a temple to Kukulkan. During the spring and fall equinoxes the shadow cast by the sun on the edges of the nine steps and the head carvings at the bottom recreate the descent of the serpent (Figure 91). The Great Pyramid of Cholula in Puebla, Mexico, built between the 3rd century BCE and 9th century CE, was the Aztec centre of worship of Quetzalcoatl. It is the world's largest monument and almost twice the volume of the largest of the Egyptian pyramids.

When Cortes and his men arrived in Tenochtitlan in late 1519 they encountered a society where Aztec sovereignty derived from their Toltec ancestry through a link to Quetzalcoatl. In Aztec culture there was a strong belief in the eventual return of a royal ancestor who would "shake the foundation of heaven" and who would conquer the city of Tenochtitlan. There had been a Toltec priest-king, Topiltzin Quetzalcoatl whose name became conflated with the god Quetzalcoatl. Defeated by a sorcerer and fleeing his native Tollan, Topiltzin Quetzalcoatl disappeared into the east, either by ascension into the heavens to become the morning star or sailing away on a raft constructed of snakes. As well, Topiltzin Quetzalcoatl made a set of arrows on his disappearance and the astrological year in which he returned would determine who would be killed by him with his arrows.

The year 1519 in the Aztec calendar not only coincided with the birth and death dates of Topiltzin Quetzalcoatl but it was prophesied that if he were to reappear on the day of One Reed he would "strike down kings." As a result, when Cortes appeared Montezuma supposedly believed he was the returning god. However, the notion of Cortes being seen as a deity may be one of the many primitive European beliefs about indigenous peoples that arose after the colonisation of the Americas. The Florentine Codex, written some fifty years after Cortes, records verbatim the speech given by Montezuma to Cortes. For example, "You have graciously come on earth, you have graciously approached your water, your high place of Mexico, you have come down to your mat, your throne, which I have briefly kept for you, I who used to keep it for you.... You have graciously arrived, you have known pain, you have known weariness, now come on earth, take your rest, enter into your palace, rest your limbs; may our lords come on earth."[14]

Figure 89. Feathered Serpent

Figure 90. Temple of the Feathered Serpent, Xochicalco

His speech, though, was not an indication of reverence or submission to a god. As with the Maya, speech for the Aztec was a sacred art and elaborate oratory was both a secular courtesy and a spiritual acknowledgement. It is much like the Maori *whaikorero* or oratory of today, known for its poetry and wisdom, welcoming visitors to the marae and affirming the mana of both visitors and hosts.

Figure 91. Descent of Kukulkan, Chichen Itza

The Aztecs believed that night begins at noon and at sunset, Xolotl, Quetzalcoatl's twin as the evening star, drags the sun into the Underworld where it becomes Yohualtonatiuh, the Night Sun. There it is sacrificed a ninth time at midnight and, purified, it begins the struggle toward dawn and climbs up the mountain of the sky. In accordance with this the Aztec believed that human sacrifice would help the sun be reborn each day and delay the inevitable end of the present Age when earthquakes will destroy the world.

In the Five Suns creation story of the Aztecs the primordial being gave birth to four creator gods: Tezcatlipoca (Smoking Mirror), Huizilopochtli (Hummingbird on the Left), Quetzalcoatl (Feathered Serpent), and Xipe Totec. These gods were joined by the rain god Tlaloc and his consort, the water goddess Chalchiuhtlicue. The gods all fought in a great cosmic struggle that saw the successive creation and destruction of the first four Suns, or world Ages. Tezcatlipoca governed the first Sun. Quetzalcoatl then overthrew Tezcatlipoca and jaguars devoured the world. A second Sun arose, ruled by Quetzalcoatl, who was ousted in turn by Tezcatlipoca and swept away in a mighty hurricane. Tlaloc governed the third Sun, which ended when Quetzalcoatl caused the Earth to be consumed by a rain of fire. Chalchiuhtlicue presided over the fourth Sun. This era ended when a great flood destroyed the world.

At the end of the fourth Age, Quetzalcoatl and Tezcatlipoca dug into the earth, creating four roads that met in the middle, in the form of a cross. They lifted the sky and its waters above the earth. In doing this, they created tunnels or roads, similar to the roads of the Underworld, through the sky. These roads would eventually become the Milky Way at night and the path of the sun in the daytime. But the sun would not move. First, Nanahuatl, a nahualli of Xolotl, Quetzalcoatl's alter ego, threw himself into the fire. A reddening occurred all around the horizon but there was no dawn from any direction. They redoubled their efforts and Quetzalcoatl proved the strongest. Dawn broke in his direction, the east. But still, the sun would not climb up in the sky and hovered just above the horizon. Now the gods knew that they would all have to sacrifice. Quetzalcoatl acted as the sacrificing priest and after he had sacrificed all 1,600 gods, the sun still struggled above the horizon. Quetzalcoatl exerted all his strength, created an enormous wind, and fell exhausted into the sun. The sun began to move. We can see this today as Quetzalcoatl, the Morning Star, appears just before sunrise. All the stars die in the fire of the sun as it begins to rise in the sky except for Quetzalcoatl. Soon, he too falls into the sun and dies with the other stars.

Variations of this creation story tell how Tezcatlipoca dipped his foot into the sun to give it motion. His foot was immediately vapourised and replaced by an obsidian mirror — thus his name, Smoking Mirror. Still the sun did not move so Xipe Totec, the god of death and rebirth, threw himself into the sun which finally began to move and the Fifth Age began. The other deities also made a sacrifice of their own blood.

Quetzalcoatl was variously a god, a man or something in between. In his serpent form, he ruled the wind, the rain, the fertility of the earth, and the cycles of human sustenance. Quetzalcoatl was also the bringer of culture, the inventor of books and the calendar, the giver of maize to humankind, and sometimes was a symbol of death and resurrection. He was the patron of priests and the title was given to the Aztec high priest. Quetzalcoatl was the adversary of Tezcatlipoca, the god of magic and the night sky, and was driven from his capital, Tula, into exile. Like Christ, Quetzalcoatl was seen as a saviour who would come again and they are both expressions of the same archetype. In Revelations 22:16 Christ identifies himself as "the bright and morning star" which is Venus.

Quetzalcoatl was the morning star and his twin brother Xolotl was the evening star. He was also closely linked with the Milky Way as the vision serpent that traversed the night sky with Venus at its head. Susan Milbrath has suggested that Venus-Quetzalcoatl was reborn from a cleft in a sky band where the ecliptic crosses the rich, fertile waters of the Milky Way.[15] We shall see the significance of this in the Planet Earth card.

The Dresden Codex has detailed and highly accurate astronomical tables for the moon and Venus. The Maya believed that Venus as the evening star brought pestilence, death, and destruction to the land. Its eight-day disappearance was the death of Quetzalcoatl. He would first lie in the Underworld for four days, then be bones for four days, and then reappear as the morning star. At this time Quetzalcoatl ascended to his throne as a god. So Venus, personified by Quetzalcoatl, symbolised death and rebirth, mediating between night and day, good and evil, and had the power of transcending those opposites within humans.

In his novel, *The Plumed Serpent*, D. H. Lawrence wrote: "For me the serpent of middle-earth sleeps in my loins and my belly, the bird of the outer air perches on my brow and sweeps her bill across my breast. But I, I am lord of two ways. I am master of up and down. I am as a man who is a new man, with new limbs and life, and the light of the Morning Star in his eyes.... And I, I am on the threshold. I am stepping across the border. I am Quetzalcoatl, lord of both ways, star between day and the dark."[16]

This penultimate card in the deck is a snake with wings, the marriage of a bird and a serpent. The Winged-ones know the mind of Grandfather Sky and are the messengers of spirit. The Crawlers know the body of Grandmother Earth and are the messengers of substance. Now, the higher and lower are joined in one body — matter becomes spiritualised and spirit becomes materialised. Psychologically, spiritualising the body means understanding the symbolic aspects of a concrete situation, seeing the larger pattern and meaning behind the veil of mundane daily events. Solidifying spirit means bringing the abstract illuminations and realisations one has into action and experience in everyday life. This is why the Feathered Winged Serpent is the card of spiritual intuition and the Teacher of the spiritual aspect of Controlling the Dream. Now we have one foot in the tonal and one in the nagual and stand in the Crack-between-the-Worlds where spirit and substance marry.

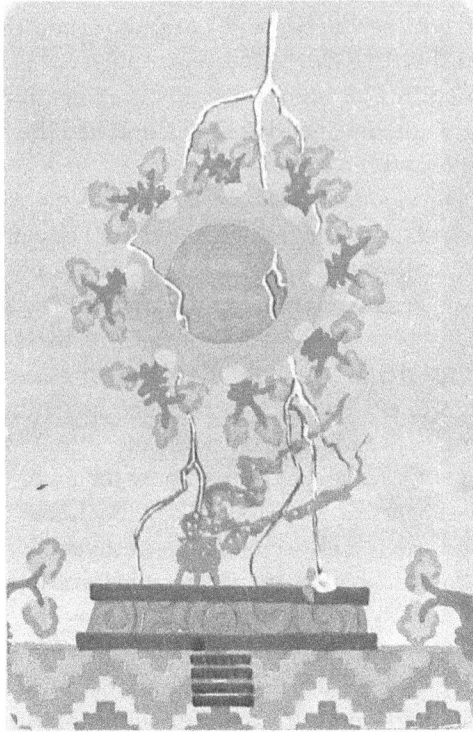

Planet Earth
The Soul of the Child Spirit Shield uses the Mood of Soul Patience
to Assume Spiritual Authority

The World

31

Planet Earth

I am an acme of things accomplish'd
I am an encloser of things to be.

—Walt Whitman

The miracle is not to fly in the air, or to walk on the water, but to walk on the earth.

—Chinese Proverb

Everything will be OK in the end. If it's not OK, it's not the end.

—Anon.

God wants to be born in the flame of man's consciousness, leaping ever higher. And what if this has no roots in the earth? If it is not a house of stone where the fire of God can dwell, but a wretched straw hut that flares up and vanishes? Could God then be born? One must be able to suffer God. That is the supreme task for the carrier of ideas. He must be the advocate of the earth. God will take care of himself. My inner principle is: Deus *et* homo. God needs man in order to become conscious, just as he needs limitation in time and space. Let us therefore be for him limitation in time and space, an earthly tabernacle.

—C. G. Jung

At the centre of the last card is the symbol for the Earth, a brown circle with eight trees growing out of it. Lightning strikes and is grounded on the altar. On the left side of the altar is the pot that was in the hand of the Temperate Man and in it burns copal. On the right side is the flower that was in the hand of the Fool.

Planet Earth represents success, achievement, satisfaction, joy, fulfilment, reaching the goal, full participation in the dance of life, seeing the eternal meaning beyond concrete reality, and seeing the luminosity of spirit in all matter. All things live according to their own nature but there is no conflict. All things are "pure," that is, they have their own integrity and are uncontaminated by what they are not. All things contain their opposite. All the opposites are joined and all things contain all other things. The many is in the one and the one is in the many. In the end is the beginning and in the beginning is the end.

The Fool has now arrived at an inner certainty which makes him both completely in-dependent but also completely inter-dependent with the world around him, a state that the alchemists called the *unio mentalis*.[1] In the Marseilles Tarot this card is called the World. Early European decks depict village scenes of work and play symbolising the natural forms and colours of life as it is actually lived. However, the card changed over time to the figure of Christ within a mandorla surrounded by the four evangelists, then into an androgynous figure, and then into a woman.

Stone in the Sky

The goal of the individuation process is a conscious relationship with the Self. The goal of the alchemists was to create the Philosopher's Stone, the symbol of enduring wholeness. It is fitting that the "highest" consciousness is now contained in the "lowest" form of matter—a mere rock, dumb matter.

Elias Ashmole (1617–1692) was an English antiquary and student of alchemy who donated his collections to Oxford University to create the renowned Ashmolean Museum. In 1652 he summarised the qualities of the stone. The mineral form of the Philosopher's Stone had the power to convert base metals into gold and silver. The alchemists believed that the base metals "matured" slowly in the earth into the "noble" metals and through their art they could hasten this process.[2] Symbolically, this means that through paying attention to our inner life and "working" on ourselves we can foster psychological growth. Chemically, the so-called "noble" metals like gold and silver are resistant to corrosion and do not combine easily with other compounds. So when we are connected to the Self we gain reliability and stability and are less reactive, contaminated or corroded by the psychic condition of others. But turning base matter into gold can have a negative aspect. Like King Midas whose touch turned everything to gold including his food, this is what happens when we identify with the Philosopher's Stone. We cannot live by spirit alone and must have ordinary, earthly satisfactions—so the Planet Earth card is one of soil and substance.

Ashmole said that the Philosopher's Stone also turns "flints" into precious stones. This is the capacity to see meaning and perhaps beauty in the hardest, sharpest and most difficult events. The Stone also reveals to the alchemist the "whole course of nature" and that his name is written in the

"Book of Life." Having one's name written in the Book of Life means one has a unique transpersonal identity.

The Stone is a union of a hot, dry, masculine part and a cool, moist feminine part. Each contains and moderates the negative excesses of the other. Positively, the sun is associated with numinous displays of light—illumination, enlightenment, shining countenances, or haloes, for example. But negatively, the hot sun can be a fiery affect, in oneself or another person, that consumes and shrivels. The positive, lunar aspect of the Stone can heal in the darkness of the body without the ego's knowledge but the cold moon can also benumb and congeal, paralyse and entrance, like the Medusa.

The Philosopher's Stone can "neither be seen, felt or weighed, but tasted only." This means that for those who see reality only in a rational, quantitative way such that it can only be measured and counted the psyche will be invisible. It can only be apprehended by a sense that is not quantitative but through the most personal, subjective and qualitative of our senses—our individual taste.

Ashmole goes on to say that devils cannot corrupt the Stone. A devil is any split-off part of the psyche that usurps the whole—a complex, a fascination, a cause, a belief, a dissociation, an obsession, an addiction, or a neurosis. The Stone as the totality of the Self maintains its authority and does not permit parts of the personality to fragment its wholeness.

Finally, the text says that the qualities of the Stone are "mysteries incommunicable to any but the adepti, and those that have been devoted even from their cradles to serve and wait at this altar." This means that only a few experience the nature of the archetypal psyche and these subjective experiences of the Self are so far removed from "normal" experience that they are exceedingly difficulty to communicate to others. The dangerous inflation here is that one will come to believe that one is special or has secret knowledge that others don't have. In this way, a superiority complex can develop which can give rise to the arcane, occult rituals of many "secret societies."

In some cases, the experience of the archetypal psyche grows out of traumatic experiences early in life. This is the archetype of the wounded healer who heals others to heal him or herself. Early difficulties throw the child prematurely back on themselves. This can be traumatising and the psyche may never recover. Alternatively, the influx of psychic energy can activate the unconscious and generate symbols and inner experiences that support the child's healthy growth. "From the cradle" the child then develops a secret life that consolidates personal identity and personality development through a sense of being supported by something outside themselves and their family. The meanings of the inner experiences may only become clear in later life and often generate a gratitude, service and devotion to the transpersonal source of life.

Un missionnaire du moyen âge raconte qu'il avait trouvé le point
où le ciel et la Terre se touchent...

Figure 92. The Flammarion woodcut.
Attributed to Camille Flammarion, French astronomer, c 1888. Titled "A medieval mission-
ary tells that he has found the point where heaven and earth meet..."

Black Light

The Earth is a stone in the sky, the third rock from the sun. If we look at the
card we see that there is also a sky in the stone. The centre of Planet Earth is
hollow and, like a window, we look onto a firmament that is a deep blue colour. It is the place where heaven and earth meet (Figure 92). Two things
here — the hole and the blue.

First the hole. The hole, biologically, is related to fertility and birth. In
many parts of the world stones with holes in them are used for their fertilising and healing powers. Women came to sit on, slide down, or crawl
through, stones to ensure conception or a safe delivery. In Scotland child-
less women were passed three times through the Kelpie Stane on the River
Dee.[3] Spiritually, the hole is the gateway, the cave, or the portal between
this world and the other world — like Alice's rabbit hole, the tunnel of light
of the near-death experience, or the black hole of cosmology. It is the Void.

Western consciousness largely subscribes to a linear view of time. All
things must have a beginning or a cause (Genesis, Plato's First Cause, Aristotle's Prime Mover, Creation Day, the Big Bang) and eventually they must
come to an end (the heat-death of the universe, Judgement Day, the End of
Days). What happens between the beginning and the end is just a rearrang-

ing of what has already been created. The First Law of Thermodynamics states that the amount of energy in the universe is constant, that energy can be neither created nor destroyed, and that there is no free lunch. In other words, some-thing cannot be created out of no-thing.

But the laws of science are simply the habits of nature that operate within the boundaries of time and space. These habits are not immutable and like all things they evolve and change. In mythic cosmologies time is cyclical. Creation is not born from a single mythical or physical event but is happening continuously in the Void. (Stephen Hawking has suggested that the black hole, where matter and light disappear, and the Big Bang, a white hole where matter and light appear, are mirror images of similar events). From this place that is outside of time and space all things are born into time and space that, from the perspective of the world of matter, are without cause and occur magically "out of the blue." In the Void, lunch is free.

This act of creation is both the cause and the effect of the journey that the Xultun Tarot describes. The desire and passion of this world of two-ness and dividedness is not one-ness—that's when the universe winds down and everything goes to sleep—but three-ness. In its unceasing acts of creation the Great Mystery becomes not only more conscious and less of a mystery to itself, but also heaps mystery upon mystery, becoming even more mysterious to itself. It becomes more devoted to and in awe of its own capacity for creation, days without end, such that it falls to its knees and worships at the feet of itself.

Alchemy was about creating something that was eternal out of the impermanence of matter, something that joined heaven and earth, something in which matter was infused with spirit and spirit with matter, something where the two were joined as one but still two, and the one was divided into two but still one. The stars set in deep blue reminds us of where we started: diagonally opposite from this card in the starry night sky above the Priestess (2). She was the beginning of the tonal, the temporal order, the daily world, the world of matter and dividedness. Now we end with Planet Earth (21) the card of oneness, not the unity where all differences are annihilated but a unity where the worlds of matter and spirit each follow their own nature (2 + 1) and creation is born anew (3).

In the card we look into eternity through the open heart of the Earth. Jung said that "the experience of the self is a window onto eternity."[4] The Latin word for breath was *spiritus* and a *spiraculum* was a breathing hole. Marie-Louise von Franz elaborates on this and I quote her at length:

> There are many alchemical texts and also certain official ecclesiastical hymns in which the Virgin Mary is called "the window of eternity," or "the window of escape"....
>
> In *Mysterium Coniunctionis*, Jung at the end quotes extensively from

the work of an alchemist, Gerhard Dorn, in whose philosophy the window of eternity or the *spiraculum aeternitatis* also plays a great role. Spiraculum is an air hole, through which eternity breathes into the temporal world. We see therefore that this meeting place, which is a vacuum, is an archetypal representation which in mythological and alchemical philosophy appears as the place where the personal realm of the psyche, including the personal unconscious, touches the collective unconscious. It is as though the collective unconscious were the eternal order and the personal conscious would together be the time-bound order, their connection being through the hole.

Jung interprets this *spiraculum aeternitatis*, this air-hole, or breathing hole into eternity, as the experience of the Self. He says that through the experience of the Self we can escape and be freed from the grip of a one-sided image of the world.

Now, reality is only real in so far as we are conscious of it. It is consciousness, therefore, which casts for us the image of the reality in which we move all the time, and that is a cage, or a prison. The hole, which is the experience of the Self, breaks that cage or prison of our conscious reality apart and by that frees us from the grip of its one-sided concepts. This hole, therefore, seems to be like a pivot, the point at which the two systems meet. The Chinese philosopher Mo Dsi has, to my mind, amplified what that means in practical psychological language. He says in *The Doctrine of the Mean*:

"Only the man who is devoted to utmost sincerity can unfold his own nature completely, and through that he can also unfold the nature of his surroundings completely, and thus can support the transforming and nourishing powers of heaven and earth. Only a man devoted to complete inner sincerity can know the future. This virtue is really a quality of nature and thus a union of the outer and inner can take place and the ways of heaven and earth can be explained in one sentence. They are without any doubleness and that is how they produce things in an unfathomable way."

So heaven and earth, Yin and Yang, are united in China through such a hole and they too meet in this innermost meeting point where "there is no doubleness".... This place of oneness is the point where heaven and earth unite and also the place where creation takes place. From this hole comes creation, from this nowhere comes everything which is newly created.[5]

This creative Void is the death that gives life. Not the death of the ego as in the Dead Man card but the ineffable from which all things come and to which all things return. Pseudo-Dionysus, a sixth century mystic, called it

"The divine darkness [which] is that 'unapproachable light' where God is said to live." He says:

It is not soul or mind, nor does it possess imagination, conviction, speech, or understanding. Nor is it speech per se. It cannot be spoken of and it cannot be grasped by understanding. It is not number or order, greatness or smallness, equality or inequality, similarity or dissimilarity. It is not immovable, moving, or at rest. It has no power, it is not power, nor is it light. It does not live nor is it life. It is not a substance, nor is it eternity or time. It cannot be grasped by the understanding since it is neither knowledge nor truth. It is not kingship. It is not wisdom. It is neither one nor oneness, divinity nor goodness. Nor is it a spirit, in the sense in which we understand that term. It is not sonship or fatherhood and it is nothing known to us or to any other being. It falls neither within the predicate of nonbeing nor of being. Existing beings do not know it as it actually is and it does not know them as they are. There is no speaking of it, nor name nor knowledge of it. Darkness and light, error and truth—it is none of these. It is beyond assertion and denial.[6]

Don Juan calls it the "unknowable."

One of the greatest moments the new seers had... was when they found out that the unknown is merely the emanations discarded by the first attention. It's a huge affair, but an affair, mind you, where clustering can be done. The unknowable, on the other hand, is an eternity where our assemblage point has no way of clustering anything.... The unknown is something that is veiled from man, shrouded perhaps by a terrifying context, but which, nonetheless, is within man's reach. The unknown becomes the known at a given time. The unknowable, on the other hand, is the indescribable, the unthinkable, the unrealizable. It is something that will never be known to us, and yet it is there, dazzling and at the same time horrifying in its vastness.[7]

This divine darkness is the *sol niger*, the black sun, the darkness like the velvet soot on laboratory wax paper, so dark that it devours light completely. It is so dark that it extinguishes all hope as in the Hanged Man but now it returns as black light—the dark illumination that is the dawning of the light of the other world.

The Self is knowable in four of its five faces. The bottom row of cards are the heart, body, mind, and spirit of the Self. They lie within the realm of the knowable. The fifth card is the outer face of the Mystery—the beauty of Planet Earth made visible by red, white, yellow and rainbow light. The inner face is the Void made invisible by the black light that creates all outer forms. Together they are the unknowable Great Mystery.

Sky in the Stone

The poet's task is not to translate a colour, but to make us dream the colour

—Gaston Bachelard

What beauty. I saw clouds and their light shadows on the distant dear earth.... I saw the abrupt, contrasting transition from the earth's light-colored surface to the absolutely black sky.... a light blue aureole that gradually darkens, becoming turquoise, dark blue, violet, and finally coal black.

— Yuri Gagarin

Now to the blue. Colours can be thought of as "advancing" or "retreating." Advancing colours are red, orange and yellow and, by extension, white. They suggest activity and intensity. Retreating colours are blue, indigo, violet and, by extension, black. They suggest withdrawal and stillness. Green is the intermediate, transitional colour between the two. If we look at the colours of the Xultun we see a spreading arc of blue at the top of the deck in the Priestess, Feathered Serpents, Fool, Sorcerer and Lovers cards. These sit over the rising sun of the Consort where life starts. The orange-yellow of the sun in the first row becomes even more intense in the bright yellow of the second row, changing into the deep red at the top of the third row. The bottom of the third row is green which then becomes the dominant colour in the fourth row. Blue again makes its appearance in the fourth row along the base of the cards, in the water of the Moon, as the Feathered Winged Serpent and finally, in contrast to the dispersed blue at the top, it is now concentrated and contained at the centre of Planet Earth.

In late 1944, while recovering from his brush with death, Jung dreamt of a blue image. In a letter to Father Victor White he wrote, "It is a mightily lonely thing, when you are stripped of everything in the presence of God.... Yesterday I had a marvellous dream: One bluish diamond, like a star high in heaven, reflected in a round quiet pool—heaven above, heaven below. The *imago Dei* in the darkness of the earth, this is myself. This dream meant a great consolation. I am no more a black and endless sea of misery and suffering but a certain amount thereof contained in a divine vessel."[8]

Deep blue is a refraction of black light. Blue is darkness made visible.[9] It links us to high and low. It takes us downwards to stillness and waiting, to the depths of the blue ocean, to blue movies, to the blues, to a blue mood, to Irving Berlin's *Mood Indigo*, to the devil and the deep blue sea, to blue in the face, to screaming blue murder. It also lifts us to height and elevation, to the wild blue yonder, to a blue streak, to the rarity of once in a blue moon, to the intellect of a bluestocking, to winning the blue ribbon, to the royalty of blue blood, to the blue gods like Dionysus and Vishnu, to the deep blue gown of the Virgin Mary, Queen of Heaven, to the blue of the Earth seen from space. During his near-death experience Jung described a vision of being "high up in space. Far below I saw the globe of the earth, bathed in a gloriously blue light. I saw the deep blue sea and the continents... and its outlines shown with a silvery gleam through that wonderful blue light."[10]

Astronauts have commented on the deep, emotional impact of seeing our home, this blue planet, from space. Only in the last fifty years have humans seen the earth from space. For the few dozen people who have had this experience their consciousness has been irrevocably changed.

If somebody'd said before the flight, "Are you going to get carried away looking at the earth from the moon?" I would have say, "No, no way." But yet when I first looked back at the earth, standing on the moon, I cried.

— Alan Shepard

We came all this way to explore the moon, and the most important thing is that we discovered the earth.

— William Anders

You develop an instant global consciousness, a people orientation, an intense dissatisfaction with the state of the world, and a compulsion to do something about it. From out there on the moon, international politics look so petty. You want to grab a politician by the scruff of the neck and drag him a quarter of a million miles out and say, "Look at that, you son of a bitch".... We went to the moon as technicians; we returned as humanitarians.

— Edgar Mitchell, Apollo 14 astronaut, People magazine, 8 April 1974

This planet is not terra firma. It is a delicate flower and it must be cared for. It's lonely. It's small. It's isolated, and there is no resupply. And we are mistreating it. Clearly, the highest loyalty we should have is not to our own country or our own religion or our hometown or even to ourselves. It should be to, number two, the family of man, and number one, the planet at large. This is our home, and this is all we've got.

— Scott Carpenter, Mercury 7 astronaut
speech at Millersville University, Pennsylvania, 15 October 1992

This leads us to the blue of melancholia, the tear-welling, breath-catching, jump-up joyful beauty of our world. Only in the last forty years of space travel has this tiny aperture, the window on eternity, been opened physically (although this view has always been visible in the nagual, in Jung's dream for example). Through this crack comes the archetypal power of our love for, grief for, attachment to, this planet that gives us life.

All the experiences of all humans and all life that has ever existed on this world, all the experiences of sunsets, of forests, of dawns, of tornados, of floods, of animals, of immigrations, of emigrations, of home towns, of dying, of living, of being laid to rest, of drought, of plenty, of starvation, of fullness, of longing for the being that we walk on, all now come pressing for recognition by a culture that denies them. The consequences of this archetypal pressure on an unprepared Western psyche are unpredictable but one seems probable and actual: depression, of the heart, of the immune system, of the economy.

The word melancholy comes from the Greek: *melankholia* meaning sadness (*melanos*, black and *khole*, bile as in mood or temperament). Although having negative connotations in English, the word is the closest associative link between blue-black light and the sobering, deepening and quietening feeling when we witness nature's beauty. Hillman adds, "Melancholy is a given with the planet, and it needs to be cared for. If not, it becomes clinical depression... The job is to revert depression back to melancholy, not to cure depression, not to lift depression and make us "happy", but to increase our understanding of melancholia; the area of mood, beauty, longing, nostalgia, sadness, and despair."[11]

The primary colours of alchemy are red, black, white, and yellow. Blue is missing until the very end of the work. It reminds us of what is missing. Goethe said, "A blue surface seems to recede from us... it draws us after it." James Hillman restates in blue the medicine of this card.

[Blue] is the absence shadowing the alchemical process, the essentially missing. Not-hereness constellates the longing that profoundly motivates the work all along the way: not enough, not right, not fulfilling, something else, something more. Present in its absence, reminding the soul of its exile. The dislocation of exile, the inevitability of exile as the necessary ground for removal of all supportive identities, the straws to which loneliness clutches. Exile reveals that we are each foundlings and that there is no other home but the cosmos itself from which no single particle can be severed, in which, to which each and every thing belongs and homecoming takes place continually, occurring in our very breathing its blue air. Cezanne drenched all things in blue, keeping them from separateness. The azure vault folds them into its cosmic comprehension. No exile, no nostalgia.[12]

The goal of the alchemical work was to create the celestial balm or *caelum* (Latin, meaning sky or heaven which gives us the English words ceiling and celestial) which was hidden in the human body. The alchemists called it by a "thousand names" — the inner heaven, the firmament, a heavenly spirit within the essential forms of things, the anima mundi in matter, the truth itself, the *panacea catholica* or universal medicine.

Jung quotes an alchemical text describing the process: "Finally, there will appear in the work that ardently desired blue or cerulean colour, which does not darken or dull the eyes of the beholder by the healing power of its brilliance, as when we see the splendour of the outward sun. Rather does it sharpen and strengthen them, nor does he [Mercurius] slay a man with his glance like the basilisk, but by the shedding of his own blood he calls back those who are near to death, and restores to them unimpaired their former life, like the pelican."[13]

At the end of the alchemical procedure when the pure had been separated from the impure, the caelum, a liquid "the colour of air," floated to the top. The goal of alchemy was to create, in the form of a substance, the truth or inner heaven that is identical with the God-image. The blue quintessence produced by the alchemists was nothing less the materialisation of spirit. The alchemist, by sublimating matter, had concretised spirit.[14] The caelum represents the *corpus glorificationis*, the glorified, incorruptible, resurrected body, the immortal soul, the residue left by the process of conscious individuation. It is the physical equivalent of heaven.

Flowering

The alchemist Gerhard Dorn (c. 1530–1584) said that when the alchemical process was completed with the production of *lapis*, the Philosopher's Stone, there was yet one final stage. This was the union of the stone with world. It was only then that it could bring about a healing of the world. This *unus mundus* or "one world," as Dorn called it, is the enduring experience of spirit in everyday, concrete reality. It is the fulfilment and joy that arises from touching the anima mundi, the soul of the world. This is the purpose of, for example, Navajo healing ceremonies that restore *hozhò* or beauty, meaning harmony, balance, and health. The Beauty Way Chant sings:

In beauty all day long may I walk.
Through the returning seasons, may I walk.
On the trail marked with pollen may I walk.
With dew about my feet, may I walk.
With beauty before me may I walk.
With beauty behind me may I walk.
With beauty below me may I walk.

Figure 93. The Flowering Trees (Codex Nuttall)

With beauty above me may I walk.
With beauty all around me may I walk.
It is finished in beauty.
It is finished in beauty.

So, like the albedo needing the blood of the rubedo in the Temperate Man, the creation of the caelum was not the end of the procedure. It was then mixed with other substances to give it life: honey (the joy of life that overcomes inhibition and darkness), chelidonia (a golden, four-petalled flower symbolising the fullness of life), rosemary (the binding power of love), mercurialis (a herb associated with sexuality), the red lily (symbolising passion), and finally the alchemist's own blood.[15] Therefore, the caelum is not placed on high by itself but is mixed with plants, healing products of the earth. We can see this in the cards. Along the bottom row there are a total of eight Flowering Trees growing out of the transpersonal base of the deck. In the Planet Earth card these same eight trees now encircle the earth indicating they have incarnated, transforming an archetypal potential in spirit into wholeness in material form.

Planet Earth is abundantly fertile with trees growing in all eight directions as in the Codex Nuttall (Figure 93). Like the others on the bottom row these are ceiba trees. The ceiba is the national tree of Guatemala and is one of the tallest trees in the tropical rainforest reaching up to seventy metres. Large dugout canoes were made from its trunk and its resin is called copal (Nahuatl, *copalli*, Maya, *pom*) which is used as incense. The seedpods are the source of kapok and the seeds themselves are used for divination. The ceiba was profoundly important to the Maya for whom it was the World Tree that grew through the centre of the earth and held up the sky. The roots were the Underworld of Xibalba. The trunk is the present and all life that is living. The dense, green foliage above is heaven itself and the house of the gods of the firmament—the Sun, Venus, the Moon, and the Stars.

The Book of Chilam Balam, written by the post-conquest Jaguar Priests of the Yucatan, describes the creation of the world. A pillar of the sky was set up with the white tree of abundance in the north, the black tree in the west, the red tree in the south, and the yellow tree in the east. Then the great green ceiba tree (*yax imix*, first tree) was set up in the centre. The Maya calendar itself is called the World Tree. It has its roots in the first day One Imix and flowers on the final day Thirteen Ahau.[16]

In the card, the white flower on the altar beneath the earth is a ceiba blossom—the beauty and fruit of the Flowering Tree. The Maya rulers wore jade earrings in the shape of the ceiba flower denoting that they were the fruit of the World Tree. A Tzjutzil Maya greeting is, "How does your fruit [face] grow on your ancestral trunk?" We have seen that the white flower hieroglyph was the Maya sign for the soul. Planet Earth is the Keeper of the Soul of the Child Spirit Shield which is the joy, life, passion and beauty of the one who undertakes the journey. This immortal soul will undertake the journey into form yet again and the flower will once more be held by the Fool.

In the Twenty Count the number 20 is the number of the Creator, the infinity movement, the double zero (OO). But Planet Venus (20) is not the last card in the tarot. Why? Because the Creator is in a state of constant self-creation out of its desire to express itself more fully through its illumination and know itself more deeply through its introspection. God is not perfect, finished or complete, the dogmas of fundamentalism notwithstanding. The Creator is always creating, that is its job description, and this planet is an expression of its passion to create itself anew in all eight directions in space and time. Humans have the gift of free will and, because all things that are whole are also a paradox, it is by carrying out the will of the Creator through exercising our own free will that we birth something that has never existed before. The created goes beyond the Creator and in our journey we create what the Creator does not yet know about itself. Thus, the lightning of free will choice descends from the Balance down through the blue centre of the Earth and touches both the flower and the urn. The lightning bolt is the human fertilisation of creation through free will choice and when it touches the Earth it brings about the flowering of her never-before-seen beauty which is one and the same as the human soul. The fallible act of ethical choice births something new and immortal in the impermanence of substance.

This is why the Movement of Assuming Authority is the catalyst Movement and Planet Earth is the Teacher of the Movement of Assuming Spiritual Authority. It is about taking upon ourselves the responsibility of the terrible power, foolishness and beauty of being human. We can read this Movement from the top downward as follows: In our humanness, we foolishly fall in love and touch the heart of another. Falling in love (the Lovers) is the beginning of the flowering and we are called on to be ourselves and remember who we are, what we could be and choose accordingly (the Balance). This act of free will brings down the lighting bolt of change and we are released from our imprisonment in ourselves (the Released Man). From this experience, the ego learns humility. When we know our smallness our soul comes into its fullness (Planet Earth). Now the soul of the earth and the earth of our soul flowers.

Heart of Heaven

In the beginning when the King's will began to take effect, He engraved signs into the heavenly sphere.

—Zohar 1:15

The top and bottom rows of cards (the Child Substance Shield and the Child Spirit Shield) tell the creation story of the individual and the cosmos respectively. The cards of the Child Substance Shield represent the unconscious, instinctive process of creating a Self (or being created by the Self, being cooked) that takes place in the first quarter of life. It is guided by archetypal forces and mediated by people who carry their power. In the top row, the heavenly bodies of the Star, Moon, Sun, Venus and the Earth are either held as an element bundle or are visible at a distance above the human figures. However, in the bottom row the cards are the heavenly bodies themselves. Now the cosmos is present in its full grandeur and we are exposed to the raw power of the archetypes. This indicates not only a conscious participation in our own development but also in the cosmic drama—without props. We can understand this cosmic drama more fully by looking at the Maya creation story and the "end" of the Maya calendar.

The Milky Way is the view we get of the 400 billion or more stars that make up our galaxy. It is shaped like the cross-section of a disc with a bulge in the middle. The Maya described the Milky Way variously as a cosmic tree, a cosmic mountain, a volcano, or as roads. We can see that all the cards in the bottom row have trees, and two have volcanoes, at their bases. The cross formed by the Milky Way and the ecliptic is the World Tree or Wakah Chan. In the Popol Vuh it is called the Crossroads. The Maya called its centre the Heart of Heaven (Figure 98).

The Black Road is the north portion of the Milky Way that is the dark rift. The Quiche Maya called this the Road to the Underworld or *xibalba be*. Every night the Underworld rotates up above the earth and becomes the night sky. To the Maya when a planet, the sun, or the moon entered the dark cleft of the Milky Way it was possible for the shaman to enter the Underworld road and to climb to the Heart of Heaven. What was below is now above. To enter the sky the shaman goes down into the ground, to go down into the earth the shaman goes up into the sky.

The White Road is the star-studded portion that extends south of the ecliptic. The Green and Red Roads are the east and west arms of the ecliptic. This cosmic structure was mapped onto the typical Maya village which was surrounded by four sacred mountains with the Heart of the Sky, the umbilicus of the world, at the centre of the village.

Wakah Chan stands with the heavens at its head and the Underworld at its feet. The raising of the Milky Way as the World Tree is the focal point of the Maya account of Creation. In the northern hemisphere this event is seen in the late summer sky every year as the Milky Way rotates during the night to stand erect at dawn, running north to south along the axis of the heavens, and becoming the World Tree.[17]

At sunset in mid-August in Central America, the World Tree arches overhead. By the time the sky becomes dark enough to see the Milky Way, it has turned into what is called the crocodile tree on account of the fork or jaws at one end of the Milky Way. By 10 PM the Big Dipper, known as Twelve Macaw in the Popol Vuh, has fallen almost entirely into the earth. By midnight, he is gone completely and the tree has begun to change into what the Maya called the cosmic canoe. This is the same canoe as seen underneath the Fool and Sorcerer cards. It carries the Maize God with his bag of maize seeds through the Underworld to the Hearth of Creation in Orion where he will plant the maize seeds and be resurrected.

By 2 AM the canoe stretches across the sky from east to west and with it comes the Turtle and the Hearth in Orion. The Quiche Maya still refer to the triad of three bright stars in Orion as "the hearth stones." At the centre of every Maya dwelling is a household hearth, made of such a triangle of three stones. The Earth-Sky, the dwelling place of humans, is centred on the cosmic hearth, from which the World Tree first rose.

As the Milky Way begins to turn toward an upright position again, the canoe begins to sink and by dawn, the Hearth and the Turtle are high in the sky just east of the zenith point. As the three hearth stones of Orion come to the zenith the ecliptic crosses the Milky Way at right angles.

The opposite occurs at sunset in early February. At 2 AM the Milky Way rims the horizon and at the zenith is a particularly dark place in the sky called the *Ek' Way* or the "black dream place" by the Maya. By dawn Wakah Chan is fully raised up in the sky. As in mid-August, the story of creation is

Figure 94. Tomb of Pacal, Palenque

materialised in observable form—Wakah Chan is raised up in the sky from the hearth stones by the reborn Maize God. As the texts say, the gods painted the images of creation on the sky.

The lid of the sarcophagus of Pacal (Figure 94), a ruler of Palenque, as well as many similar images in the surviving codices, tells the same story. Pacal is shown falling down the World Tree into the Underworld and simultaneously giving birth to the tree from his umbilicus. He is both seed and the flower, birth and death. Note the similarities between Pacal, the man in Figure 86 and the Sage.

The sarcophagus of Pacal is a picture of the sky on August 31, 683 CE, the night he died. Wakah Chan is erect in the sky and Pacal falls down through the portal called the White-Bone-Snake into the Underworld of Xibalba (or as the Maya say "he entered his road"). Here he will be reborn and the sky of the new era will be raised. The Milky Way/World Tree is Pacal's umbili-

Figure 95. The *arbor philosophica* growing from Adam

cus—his soul vine connection to the Creator, the eternal life that grows out of his death. This same image of tree, death and rebirth is also seen in Western alchemy (Figure 95)[18] and Renaissance art (Figure 96).

2012

At the central bulge of the Milky Way is a dark cleft running down the middle of the Milky Way (Figure 97). This dark patch is not the absence of stars but the presence of interstellar dust and gas clouds that obscure the stars behind. The intersection of the ecliptic with the dark rift is the Heart of Heaven, the Cosmic Womb of the Great Mother. It is the place where the sun is reborn every 26,000 years. From their astronomical observations and their understanding of time, the Maya priest-astronomers created something astonishing. It was a calendar, called the Long Count, that predicted the date of the next rebirth of the sun from the cosmic womb, on December 21, 2012.

The Maya scholar Munro Edmonson believes that the Long Count emerged around 355 BCE and the oldest Long Count date yet found in the archaeological record corresponds to 32 BCE.[19] The calendars of the Abrahamic religions are counted from an event that happened in the past. The Gregorian calendar dates from the birth of Christ (0 BCE), the Jewish calendar

Figure 96. Dream of the Virgin

from the day of creation (3761 BCE), and the Islamic calendar from the year
of the hijra when Mohammed moved from Mecca to Medina (622 BCE). But
with the Long Count the important date was not when the calendar started
but when it ended, over 2,000 years in the future from when it was first created. This is quite the reverse of our Gregorian calendar that is based on the
birth of an earth-child (Christ) in the past. The Maya calendar is based on
the birth of a sun-child in the future.

To explore this further we need to briefly review the concepts of the solstice, the precession of the equinoxes, and Maya calendrics. The winter solstice is the time when life's energy is at its lowest. The word "solstice"
means "the sun stands still" in Latin. This refers to the fact that the sun apparently rises and sets at the same time over the course of three days. The
winter solstice is the day of least sunlight and the shortest day of the year,
but marks the beginning of increasing daylight — the old year is ending and
another will be born. This is seen in the world-wide myths about the death
and rebirth of a deity, or a great mother giving birth to a celestial boy child
at this time of the year, as in the story of Christ.

To the Maya, the winter solstice sun was the First Sun, the First Lord, or
First Father because it is the first day of the New Year and the sun is reborn
from its apparent dying. This story of the sun being reborn from the dark
rift of the World Tree is told in the Maya creation myth of the Popol Vuh
where the Hero Twins, Hunahpu and Xbalanque, journey down the road

Figure 97. The Milky Way

into Xibalba to do battle with the Lords of Death and resurrect their father One Hunahpu or First Father. First Father's decapitated head (the dying sun) hangs in the World Tree (the Milky Way) which lies near the road to Xibalba (the Dark Rift).

Over 2,000 years ago the dark rift of the Milky Way could be observed some thirty degrees above the horizon as the winter solstice sun dawned. However, the early Maya skywatchers noticed that every winter solstice the centre of the dark rift moved closer and closer to the horizon and the sun at its moment of dawning (Figure 98). The reason for this movement is what is called the precession of the equinoxes. Knowledge of precession goes back as far as the Neolithic period and over two hundred myths and over thirty cultures knew about precession, some going back to 10,000 BCE.[20] The Greek astronomer Hipparchus was the first in the Western world to write about precession in 128 BCE.

The earth is not a perfect sphere and this, combined with the gravitational pull of the sun and moon, cause the earth's axis to inscribe a cone out in space, like a spinning top whose spindle wobbles. To observers on earth, it causes the position of a fixed point to move slowly "backwards" through the constellations over thousands of years. By historical convention, the spring equinox in the northern hemisphere is taken as the reference point, and the movement is called the precession of the equinoxes. At this historical time the North Pole points to Polaris, the Pole Star. But this point moves slowly through the heavens and takes about 25,800 years to complete one revolution through the constellations. This is called a Platonic or Great Year.

The Maya and the Aztecs accorded time more texture, shape and sacredness than does Western culture. For them, time was a living, conscious,

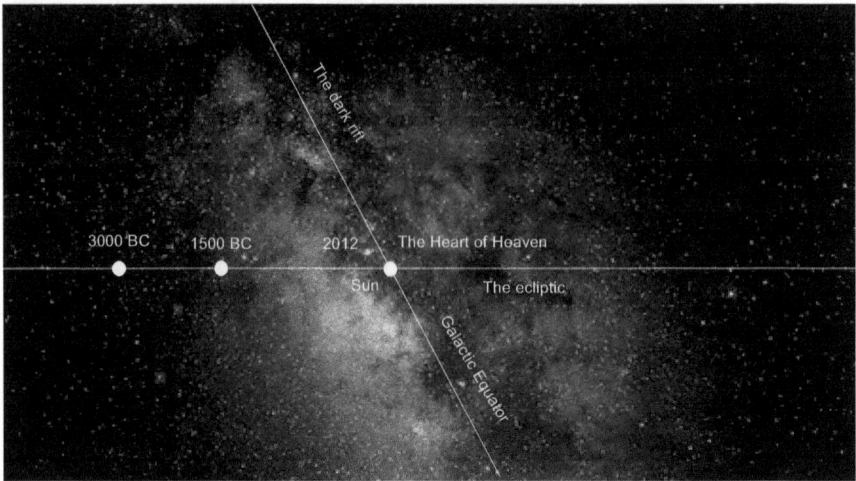

Figure 98. Position of the winter solstice and precession

holy entity. They used a number of calendars for different purposes but unlike our Gregorian calendar, which is based on the number ten and marks
the passing of decades and centuries, the Maya used a vigesimal system
based on the number 20. The calendrical cycles are the *haab* and the *tzolkin*,
both in use today by Maya daykeepers.[21]

According to Barbara Tedlock, an anthropologist initiated as a Maya daykeeper, tzolkin is an invented Yucatec word. "William Gates, in his 'Review
of Archaeology of the Cayo District, by J. Eric S. Thompson,' takes credit for
inventing the word tzolkin in 1921; and he modeled it after the Quiche
Maya *ch'ol k'ij*, meaning 'arranging' or 'ordering of days,' as a way of getting away from the use of the Aztec term."

The tzolkin is the divinatory calendar, a constantly revolving round of
thirteen numbers and twenty day names (13 x 20 = 260 days). It is based on
the length of human pregnancy, 260 days being nine lunar cycles of slightly
less than 29 days. The haab is the secular year of eighteen months of twenty
days each making up the 360 days with an extra five days to make up the solar year. When the tzolkin (13 x 20 days) was used in conjunction with the
haab (18 x 20 days) the cycles synchronised every 260 x 365 days or 52
years. This was the cycle of the Aztec New Fire ceremonies.

The Maya units of time were days or *k'ins*, months or *uinals* of 20 days,
years or *tuns* of 360 days, *katuns* of 20 years, *baktuns* of 400 years, *pictuns* of
8,000 years, and so on (Figure 99). To the historical Maya, the 20-year katun
and the 400-year baktun were the most significant. Each year was called a
tun or stone because the end of the year was marked by setting a stone or
stela in the ground. Stela 1 at Coba shows the longest recorded time period
known in the ancient world with glyphs up to 13×20^{21} tuns or 13 times 20
to the power of 21 years). Interestingly, the place for the 22nd power glyph

Mayan name	Days	Gregorian years
k'in	1	
uinal	20	
tun	360	1
katun	20 x 360 = 7,200	20
baktun	20^2 x 360 = 144,000	400
pictun	20^3 x 360	8,000
kalabtun	20^4 x 360	160,000
kinchiltun	20^5 x 360	3,200,000
alautun	20^6 x 360 days	64,000,000

Figure 99. Maya calendrics

is blank! In comparison, in Hindu cosmology the life span or Cycle of Brahma, a Mahakalpa, is 10^{22} seconds or 311 trillion years.

The Maya set the beginning of the current Fifth Age at 0.0.0.0.0 which means 0 baktuns, 0 katuns, 0 tuns, 0 uinals, 0 kin. In the Gregorian calendar this date is August 11, 3114 BCE. (Similarly, the current Hindu cycle of time or yuga began in 3102 BCE.) So why that date? Because after one Great Year, Five Ages, 13 baktuns, 5,125 years or 13 x 144,000 days, like the hands of the clock coming back to twelve again, the calendar would end and restart again at 0.0.0.0.0 on December 21, 2012. Note that the Maya calendar *does not end* in 2012 but the current 13-baktun cycle does.

Why December 21, 2012? Because that day will see the triple rebirth of the sun: the daily rebirth of the sun from the darkness of the night, the solstice rebirth of the sun from the longest night of the year, and the galactic rebirth of the sun from the Heart of Heaven. In addition, the sun will be almost exactly in the middle of four planets aligned on the arms of the sacred tree with Venus at their head (Figure 100).

According to the Maya, our Sun and all of its planets rotate in cycles in relation to the centre of the galaxy, or Hunab-Ku, the central light of the galaxy. This complete cycle of the Great Year was called a galactic day and each age was a portion of the galactic day. The first age is the galactic morning (23,000–18,000 BCE), when our solar system is just coming out of the darkness to enter the light. The second age (18,000–13,000 BCE) is the midday, when our solar system is closest to the central light. The third age (13,000–8,000 BCE) is the afternoon, when our solar system begins to come out of the light. The fourth cycle (8,000–3,000 BCE) is the late evening and middle of the night, when our solar system has entered its furthest cycle from the central light. The fifth and last cycle (3114 BCE–2012 CE) is the deep-

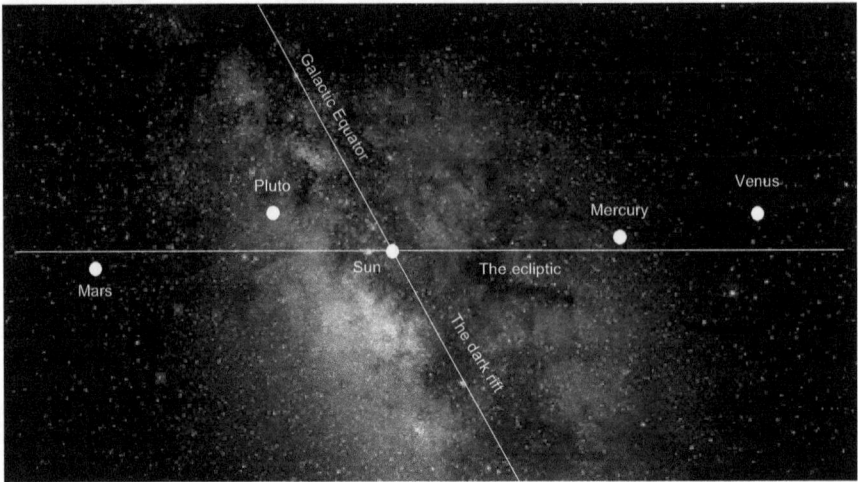

Figure 100. The triple rebirth of the Sun from the Cosmic Womb

est part of the night before dawn, when our solar system is in its last cycle of darkness before starting again.

So this current 13-baktun cycle is different from the others — it is the last of five ages in both Maya and Aztec cosmologies. The number five is the quintessence — the summing up at the centre of what has happened in each of the four directions around the wheel, and it catalyses the turning of the next wheel. The Aztec calendar stone indicates that each "sun" or "age" lasts 100 calendar rounds (5,196 years). The Maya Long Count of 13 baktuns is 5,125 years. So five ages make one full precessional cycle — five Aztec ages are 25,980 years, five Maya 13-baktun cycles are 25,625 years, and a precessional Great Year is 25,765 years. As this Great Year comes to a close and the precessional point moves from the constellation of Pisces to Aquarius it is accompanied by profound dangers and opportunities for the human species and all life on this planet.

Jung wrote about this phenomenon of the age or *aion* (Greek for age or long period of time) in CW 9ii, *Aion: Researches into the Phenomenology of the Self*. He wrote, "My investigation... seeks to throw light on the change of psychic situation within the Christian aeon [which] is filled with intimations of a kind of enantiodromian reversal of dominants. I mean by this the dilemma of Christ and Antichrist."

The year 2012 will see not only the rebirth of the sun but other astronomical phenomena as well. First, the Dresden Codex refers to the "The Birth of Venus" in 3114 BCE. This was the rising of Venus on one horizon at the same time the Pleiades were setting below the opposite horizon. In 2012 we shall witness "The Death of Venus" when Venus will be setting while the Pleiades will be rising. Then on May 20, 2012, we shall see something else — the sun, the moon and the Pleiades will pass through the zenith at the Maya site of Chichen Itza. This event occurs only during a 72-year time window, from 1976 to 2048. Right at the centre of this time window is the year 2012. Quetzalcoatl was a symbol for this sun-Pleiades-zenith conjunction. Finally, Maya prophecy holds that the world of new consciousness will be born on the date of the second of the pair of Venus transits on June 8, 2012.[22]

The winter solstice in 2012 is the knot in the Loom of Time that holds all these physical and spiritual events together in the dream — the World Tree, the cross roads of the Milky Way and the ecliptic, the rebirth of the sun from the darkness, the hope of resurrection, the hope that human love and the warmth of life will prevail against the coldness of the galactic night, the hope that the universe is on our side and we are not just an accident lost amongst the stars, and the hope that life will jump up and live again in a time beyond our own.

On the morning after the shortest night on December 21, 2012 an event occurs that has not happened for 26,000 years. The sun will be in the centre of the Sacred Tree, the Heart of Heaven, and First Father, our sun, will be reborn from this Cosmic Womb of the Milky Way, the Great Mother. John Major Jenkins concludes:

> The 260-day tzolkin calendar is based upon the 260-day period of human embryogenesis, and, on a higher level, the 260-day tzolkin symbolises, or structures, the 26,000 year period of precession, what we might call human spiritual embryogenesis. The Maya believed that the 26,000 Great Year of precession is a spiritual gestation period for humanity, and that the 2012 alignment will catalyse the birth of what has been growing on this planet for 26,000 years. For the Maya, Father Sun's movement into union with Cosmic Mother's heart also signified the insemination, or seeding of what will come to fruition in 26,000 years."[23]

End of Days

> Our hearts have overbrimmed with new agonies, with new lustre and silence. The mystery has grown savage, and God has grown greater. The dark powers ascend, for they have also grown greater, and the entire human island quakes.
>
> — Nikos Kazantzakis

The day of December 21, 2012 will dawn just like any other day, no different from the millions of days before and the millions after. It does not matter whether the astronomical events happen on that specific day or not. It does not matter what people do on that day. Life will go on. The archetype of the rebirth of the sun, which gives light, life and joy to the People, is happening in the dream all the time. In star time, a day, a year, or a decade does not make much difference—it is the process not the event.

However, this archetypal and spiritual potential can only come into being and know itself if there is a human container to hold it, human consciousness to give it witness, human longing for its presence, human joy to celebrate it, and human grief to mourn its passing. So indeed, the day and the year does matter. Not because anything apocalyptic will happen on that day (that's just good copy for *The Skeptical Inquirer* or New Age magazines) but because the event attracts human attention, interest, fear, and fascination. All of which are a landing beacon for spirit. They call down power.

The moment, which is just like any other, is like the alchemical earth that is common and is found everywhere, but it can be transformed into gold. It is a point in time and space where the two worlds can touch through the actions and choices of humans. We can align ourselves with the greater rhythms of the cosmos and both spirit and matter can be changed. Our ceremonies are magnified by the fact that this major ending and beginning resonates with all other endings and beginnings past and future. This is why Maya rulers conjured and ceremonialised at the katun and baktun endings—to plant seeds for a time beyond their own.

There is great hope in this Fifth Age, the fifth Movement of humanity's Book of Life, the age of Assuming Authority at the end of this Great Year. It may be the first time in history where sufficient human consciousness has accrued for the personal history of previous ages to be erased and to make the passage from one Great Year to the next possible without destruction. Moreover, to make the shift one that is a quantum leap in human evolution.

But there is also great despair and we must not turn away from the sight of our destructiveness. The stakes are much higher than ever before. We are so estranged from matter that we suffer the opposite problem to those humans who lived at the beginning of this Great Year 26,000 years ago, or at the beginning of this Age 5,200 years ago. Then, humans needed civilising by their own hand. We needed civilisation not to protect us against the ravages of nature but to protect us against the ravages of ourselves. The rise of monotheism was marked by the great doctrines of mercy, love and justice *between humans*.

Now half the world's population is monotheistic. For 2,000 years the focus has been on love between humans—less murder, less cruelty, more mercy, more justice, more equality, more love. All this is good. But it has been at the expense of the same ideals in our relationship with the natural world. As we have become more thoughtful of our fellow humans we have become more forgetful of Our Relations. Monotheism has been the prime instigator in this great forgetting. Now consciousness has become linear and vertical. We are crucified between above and below. D. H. Lawrence wrote:

We ought to dance with rapture that we should be alive and in the flesh, and part of the living, incarnate cosmos. I am part of the sun as my eye is part of me. That I am part of the earth my feet know perfectly, and my blood is part of that sea. My soul knows that I am part of the human race, my soul is an organic part of the great human soul, as my spirit is part of my nation. In my own very self, I am part of my family. There is nothing of me that is alone and absolute except my mind, and we shall find that the mind has no existence by itself, it is only the glitter of the sun on the surface of the waters. So my individualism is really an illusion. I am a part of the great whole, and I can never escape. But I can deny my connections, break them, and become a fragment. Then I am wretched.[24]

In all the great world myths, destruction accompanies the end of an age. Humanity's relationship with matter was less troubled then. Physical signs such as heavenly events in the night sky were a sign of a coming psychic upheaval in the collective unconscious of humanity. The real cataclysm happened in spirit not in matter. But now things are reversed and the cataclysm may happen in matter. The cost of the transition into the new age, the death-caul that accompanies this birth, may be the destruction of life as we know it. Tragically, our global culture has exceeded itself. As James Hillman diagnoses, we suffer from gigantism: the Great Depression; World War II, superpowers, supermarkets, cities of twenty million; countries of over a billion; the Holocaust; the whole world watching TV; mile-long accelerators, global multi-nationals; trillion dollar budgets; population explosion; and mass extinction.[25]

Over the past few decades the signs have become clear to all but the blind—global warming, loss of indigenous forests, obesity, world-wide drop in sperm counts, diabetes, depression, and the emergence of new diseases, to name but a few. Our denials are signs of spiritual Alzheimer's. The Earth, we hope, will right herself but if her life is in danger she will let her children die without sentiment so that she may live. Just as a dream takes months or years to come into consciousness, this passage from one age to the next will take not a day but decades. Over the next century, it will become clearer whether the People will survive. Or not.

Fruit of the Sun and the Moon Tree

The long path of individuation and the mysterious desire to become more of who we already are pulls us toward the world of spirit. It is strangely familiar and we have come home. At the same time, we become unfamiliar to ourselves. A woman's dream sums up this Great Work:

I saw the earth covered by a single great tree whose multiple roots fed on the inner sun of gold, the *lumen naturae*. It was a tree whose limbs were made of light and the branches were lovingly entangled so that it made of itself a network of beauteous love. And it seemed as if it were lifting itself out of the broken seeds of many, countless egos who had now allowed the one self to break forth. And when one beheld this, the sun and the moon and the planets turned out to be something quite, quite other than one had thought. From what I could make out, the Lord Himself was the Alchemist and out of the collective swarming and suffering, ignorance and pollution, He was "trying" the gold.[26]

Both the height and the depth of our journeys lead to the same place — this world that is our home. In this final row of cards, the Soul of the Child Spirit Shield descends from the Star through the heavenly bodies and finds its home on Planet Earth. It is this Earth that spirit yearns to be enfolded by, to take on form and substance, and to put on its Robe.

"The life of a warrior cannot possibly be cold and lonely and without feelings," [Don Genaro, Castaneda's nagual benefactor] said, "because it is based on his affection, his devotion, his dedication to his beloved. And who, you may ask, is his beloved? I will show you now." [he spins above the ground]... "This is the predilection of two warriors," [Don Juan] said. "This earth, this world. For a warrior there can be no greater love.... Only if one loves this earth with unbending passion can one release one's sadness," don Juan said. "A warrior is always joyful because his love is unalterable and his beloved, the earth, embraces him and bestows upon him inconceivable gifts. The sadness belongs only to those who hate the very thing that gives shelter to their beings." Don Juan again caressed the ground with tenderness. "This lovely being, which is alive to the last recesses and understands every feeling, soothed me, it cured me of my pains, and finally when I had fully understood my love for it, it taught me freedom."[27]

The last row of the Book of Life faces inwards to the psyche and outwards to the cosmos. In the inner world the results of a life lived consciously are symbolised in alchemy as the fruit of the sun and the moon tree. This marriage of opposites has a transformational effect on the past and the future of humankind. Our deepest wound becomes our highest gift and we become a Two-legged, One-hearted Human in good relation with all of the Worlds. In the outer cosmos, this row of cards say what the Maya have always known will happen. In 2012, when Sirius, the Pleiades, the moon and the sun marry in the Heart of Heaven, Quetzalcoatl will return and the Earth will flower.

The body of the Fool is gone. Leaving only the flower of the soul, the essence. Beside it sits the pot that once held starwater, food for the gods. The pot now burns copal, food for the gods. And they are the same, water ever turns to fire. The Smoking Mirror once held the Lovers' world. The Earth now holds this blue saltwater mirror of the Heart of Heaven. And they are the same, fire ever turns to water. In the other we see the world, in the world we see the other. The waters of grief have burned away and left an ocean. The waters of the heart burn with praise.

This is our world.

32

The Book of Life

In the book of life, the answers aren't in the back.

—Charlie Brown

He that overcometh, the same shall be clothed in white raiment; and I will not blot out his name out of the book of life, but I will confess his name before my Father, and before his angels.

—Revelation 3:5

This chapter is a summary of the archetypal meanings and alchemical relationships of each of the major arcana.

Archetype

The archetype of a card is its individual essence, energy and form and is composed of several elements.

Energy. This is the card's energetic orientation: feminine (receptive, creative) or masculine (active, conceptive).

Number. This is the card's medicine, gift or archetypal healing power in the Twenty Count.

Type. This is the aspect (emotional, physical, mental or spiritual) of the card's psychological type (feeling, sensation, thinking or intuition).

Light. This is a description of the light side of the archetype.

Shadow. This is a description of the dark side of the archetype. "Dark" here is not a moral judgement but means whatever is unconscious (that is, what is in the shadows and not illuminated by, and acceptable to, consciousness) or whatever is opposite to the light side of the archetype. Everything contains its opposite which will jump up and live sometime, somewhere.

Alchemy

The alchemy of a card tells you about its relationships with other cards, where it has come from and what it will become.

Medicine. This is the summary statement of the card's Shield, Mood and Movement.

Keeper, Holder and Teacher. These describe what Shield it Keeps, what Mood it Holds and what Movement it Teaches.

Awakener, Dreamer and Completer. These describes its energetic relationships according to the Zero to Nine Law (Chapter 9).

In a reading, the alchemy will suggest linkages with cards in other positions in the reading.

The alchemy does not apply to the 0 and 1 cards (the Fool and the Sorcerer) as they sit outside the matrix of the other 20 cards. They contain, and are contained by, all the other cards so their alchemy is undifferentiated. All subsequent cards are energetic transformations of the original 0 and 1.

I have left blank the alchemy of some of the cards so that the reader may add their own interpretations.

Although this book does not cover the advanced alchemy of the cards I have added the higher alchemical name for each card.

FOOL

Archetype

Energy. Feminine, receptive, creative.

Number. Zero, The Void.

Light. *Emotional*: innocent, childlike, enthusiastic, trusting, integrity, loyal to his own nature, undivided, sense of humour, basic genuineness and integrity. *Mental*: beginner's luck, untutored brilliance, taking a chance, a leap of faith, urges us on into life when thinking or feeling might be overly cautious. *Physical*: adventurous, risk-taking, acting on gut instinct, "just do it." *Spiritual*: spiritual yearning, finding magic in the ordinary, beginning the journey, natural force unburdened by knowledge or experience.

Shadow. *Emotional*: naïve, apathetic, gullible, abandonment, madness, folly, foolery, extravagance, infatuation, childish, always playing it safe, risk averse, lack of personal boundaries. *Physical*: intoxicated, lack of resources, disreputable, irresponsible, not following own instincts. *Mental*: poor decision-making, inept, airhead, stupid, hesitation, senseless, irrational, thoughtless, hare-brained, no objectivity. *Spiritual*: frenzy, rapture, blindness, lacks purpose.

SORCERER

Archetype

Energy. Masculine, active, conceptive.

Number. One, Grandfather Sun, element of fire, illumination and enlightenment.

Light. *Emotional*: self-confidence, charisma, optimism. *Physical*: skill, dexterity, craftsmanship, adaptability, self-starter, entrepreneur, makes things happen. *Mental*: concentration, will power, intention, focus, purpose, one-pointedness, desire for knowledge, goal-oriented drive. *Spiritual*: desire to live, inspiration, drive to change the world, originality, creativity, medicine man, alchemist, healer, doctor.

Shadow. *Emotional*: boastful, deceptive, grandiose, narcissistic, con artist, exploiter, out of one's depth, faking it. *Physical*: no commitment, unreliable, liar, crook, concealed. *Mental*: lack of willpower, devious, manipulator. *Spiritual*: charlatan, imposter, false guru, cult leader.

PRIESTESS

Archetype
Energy. Feminine, receptive, creative.
Number. Two, Grandmother Earth, element of earth, introspection and intuition.
Type. Emotional feeling.
Light. *Emotional*: introspection, hidden knowledge, dreams, fantasies, empathy, receptivity, attunement. *Physical*: body knowing without words. *Mental and spiritual*: seeing and knowing the "other," another person (clairvoyance), the past (retrocognition), the ancestors (mediumship), the future (precognition, prophecy), or communicating with animals, plants and minerals.
Shadow. *Emotional*: betrayal of and by the feminine, alexithymia (inability to know one's feelings), chronic woundedness, distrust of feelings, brittle spiritual or emotional boundaries, borderline personality disorder. *Physical*: not at home in one's own body, space cadet. *Mental*: loss of self-identity, identifying with another's projection, revealing secrets or confidences, literalism. *Spiritual*: denial of intuition, neglect of dream life, black magic, chthonic rites, madness, religious mania, fatalism and superstition.

Alchemy
The Priestess as the Heart of the Child Substance Shield uses the Mood of Emotional Sweetness to Erase Emotional History.
Keeper of the Heart of the Child Substance Shield. She is conscious of our wounds and our vulnerabilities. She recognises the need for love and acceptance from peers and parents.
Holder of the Mood of Emotional Sweetness. She is sensitive to hidden or fragile feelings. She has the emotional fluidity of empathy and compassion, love without pity, and sees the hidden potential of things. She engenders emotional hope from seeing the gold hidden in the heart.
Teacher of the Movement of Erasing Emotional History. She sees the battle of the light and the dark within, our dark and light shadow, our dividedness. Her consciousness of present feelings allows resolution of past wounds.
Awakened by the Moon. She is a moon goddess and can see what is hidden by sunlight but visible in moonlight.
Awakens the Lovers. She can see the unconsciousch oices we make in love.
Dreamed by the Bound Man. The Bound Man's struggles with duality and evil dreams the otherness and duality of the Priestess.
Dreams the Sage. The mental knowledge of the Sage is dreamed into possibility by the intuitive seeing of the Priestess.
Completion of the Dead Man. A confrontation with death and darkness makes the other world a separate reality.
Completed by the Balance. The Priestess' intuition is actualised and made real in the world by the choices of the Balance.
Higher Alchemy. The Fire Woman.

CONSORT

Archetype

Energy. Feminine, receptive, creative.

Number. Three, Plants, element of water, trust and innocence.

Type. Physical feeling.

Light. *Emotional*: wife, marriage, home and hearth. *Physical*:
mothering, growth, fertility, fruitfulness, wealth, pregnancy, community, family, comfort, warmth, nursing. *Mental*:
courtesy, sociability, hospitality. *Spiritual*: impersonal caring, healing by nature.

Shadow. *Emotional*: jealousy, vengeance, rejection of conventional female roles,
triangular or unconventional relationships, under- or over-mothering, dependent
personality disorder. *Physical*: social appearances, vanity, formality, abortion, mis-
carriage, hysterectomy, infertility. *Mental*: conventional, ruthless, vindictive. *Spiritual*: absence of spirituality, physical growth without limits.

Alchemy

The Consort as the Body of the Child Substance Shield uses the Mood of Physical
Sweetness to create Emotional Death and Change.

Keeper of the Body of the Child Substance Shield. She explores her own body
and the environment around it.

Holder of the Mood of Physical Sweetness. She heals through touch, caring for
the body, affection, intimacy, nursing, cherishing, tenderness, herbs, diet, massage, or making love affectionately and sweetly. Being in natural, beautiful places,
and being healed by the Sweetness of nature.

Teacher of Using Emotional Death as an Advisor. She is the heartlessness of
Mother Nature, the inevitability of death, feelings about our physical environment, our physical body and sexuality, our bodily functions and fluids, and physical change and loss.

Awakened by the Sun. The limitless spiritual and physical energy of the Sun
gives birth to the fecundity of the Consort.

Awakens the Warrior. The Warrior is the human form of the Consort's natural
growing and living, he is all extroversion, growth, and conquest without limits.

Dreamed by the Released Man _____

_____

Dreams the Wheel. The impermanence and changeability of nature dreams of the
immutable, abstract laws of the Wheel.

Completion of the Temperate Man. Mental wisdom brings the simplicity of physical growth.

Completed by the Hanged Man. The Hanged Man is the human form of the Consort's natural growing and dying.

Higher Alchemy. The Benevolent Matriarch.

RULER

Archetype

Energy. Masculine, active, conceptive.

Number. Four, Animals, element of air, harmony and balance.

Type. Mental feeling.

Light. *Emotional*: leadership, authority, confidence. *Physical*: power, masculinity, virility, potency, law, protection, stability, accomplishment, organisation. *Mental*: will, conviction, reason, logic, intellect, principle. *Spiritual*: mediator between heaven and earth.

Shadow. *Emotional*: stubborn, coward, weak, passive-aggressive, manipulative, antisocial personality disorder. *Physical*: tyrant, brutal, abuse of physical or financial power, impotent. *Mental*: prejudice, indecision, rigidity, paranoia, perfectionism. *Spiritual*: lack of conscience, religious oppression, preoccupation with immortality.

Alchemy

The Ruler as the Mind of the Child Substance Shield uses the Mood of Mental Sweetness to Stop the Emotional World.

Keeper of the Mind of the Child Substance Shield. He explores, conquers, sorts, orders, categorises, and is curious about the world. He needs acknowledgement and recognition.

Holder of the Mood of Mental Sweetness. He has the mental fluidity to say the right words at right time. He inspires confidence and courage, gets others to follow or obey, brings clarity, order and discipline, and brings everyone together to work for a common cause.

Teacher of Stopping the Emotional World. He brings order to emotional turmoil. He has the strength and fortitude to not let one desire rule the personality, the courage to face up to conflict, the emotional certainty that does not collapse when things go wrong, the strength of character to not be bullied by his own or others' emotions, and the steadfastness to stand firm for his emotions or convictions.

Awakened by Planet Venus. The spiritual union of Planet Venus awakens wholeness in substance through the Ruler who brings order and balance.

Awakens the Cactus. The collective order and structure of the Ruler awakens the individual self-discipline of the Cactus.

Dreamed by the Star. The individual, spiritual vision of the Star dreams the vision and foresight necessary for leadership.

Dreams the Balance. The collective, extroverted authority of the Ruler dreams the individual, internal authority of the Balance.

Completion of the Bound Man. The Bound Man struggles with archetypal conflict in his inner world or in the world of spirit. This brings harmony to the outer world.

Completed by the Dead Man. The fullest expression of the order and harmony of the Ruler is the chaos and death of the Dead Man which births new life.

Higher Alchemy. The Benevolent Patriarch.

PRIEST

Archetype

Energy. Masculine, active, conceptive.

Number. Five, Humans.

Type. Spiritual feeling.

Light. *Emotional*: kindness, mercy, forgiveness. *Physical*: celibacy, sacred sexuality. *Mental*: teaching, knowledge, advice, mentorship, seeks meaning, philosophy of life or spiritual path, ethics, morality. *Spiritual*: therapist, shaman, working with dreams and symbols, ceremony, tradition.

Shadow. *Emotional*: rejection of authority, persecution, cruelty. *Physical*: renunciation, asceticism, prudishness, asexuality, sexual excess or addiction, meaningless ritual. *Mental*: rigid beliefs, harsh conscience, puritan. *Spiritual*: dogma, fundamentalist, religious fanatic.

Alchemy

The Priest as the Spirit of the Child Substance Shield uses the Mood of Spiritual Sweetness to Control the Emotional Dream.

Keeper of the Spirit of the Child Substance Shield. He is the longing for reverence and worship, and for spiritual exploration without boundaries.

Holder of the Mood of Spiritual Sweetness. He is the spiritual fluidity that awakens spirit in others.

Teacher of Controlling the Emotional Dream. He is humility, respect and the right relationship toward spirit. His relationship to spirit is one of vocation and calling. He recognises the emotional power of spirit and the hold it has over humans.

Awakened by Planet Earth _____

Awakens the Sage _____

Dreamed by the Moon. The hidden mysteries of the Moon long for the outward, public observances of the Priest.

Dreams of the Hanged Man. The collective ceremonies of the Priest dream the individual sacrifices and crucifixion of the Hanged Man.

Completion of the Released Man _____

Completed by the Temperate Man The fullness of the Priest who mediates between humans and God flowers in the Temperate Man who mediates between heaven and earth.

Higher Alchemy. The Jaguar Shaman.

LOVERS

Archetype

Energy. Feminine and masculine.

Number. Six, Ancestors, self-image.

Type. Soul feeling.

Light. *Emotional*: decision in love, affection, attraction, emotional trials and testing. *Physical*: sexual relationship, sensuality. *Mental*: adoration, worship. *Spiritual*: relationship with the anima/animus, soulmate.

Shadow. *Emotional*: unrequited love, foolish infatuation, puppy love, infidelity, jealousy, immaturity, broken-hearted, drama queen, histrionic personality disorder. *Physical*: failure, unwise plans. *Mental*: sexual manipulation and taking advantage, sexual grooming, stalking, sexual obsession, doubts, indecision. *Spiritual*: unconsummated love, "pure" love without earthly realities.

Alchemy

The Lovers as the Soul of the Child Substance Shield use the Mood of Soul Sweetness to Assume Emotional Authority.

Keeper of the Soul of the Child Substance Shield. Humans are their most vulnerable when in love and need cohesion, bonding and attachment.

Holder of the Mood of Soul Sweetness. They are the soul or sexual fluidity that allows the marriage of matter and spirit in the human soul. Lovemaking is the attempt to join with spirit through the body of another.

Teacher of Assuming Emotional Authority. Letting go of our biological and spiritual family (Consort and Ruler, Priestess and Priest), the peer group becomes more important. We can now forge intimate adult relationships. It is in the affairs of the heart we establish our individuality. We make a decision made from the heart to become entangled in life and love.

Awakened by the Priestess _____

Awakens the Wheel _____

Dreamed by the Sun. The heat and passion of the Sun comes alive and becomes human in the Lovers.

Dream of the Dead Man. The Lovers dream of and fear in equal measure the inevitable death and change that will come about as a result of touching the soul of another.

Completion of the Star. The passion of the Great Grandfather Stars for substance and matter is realised in the Lovers.

Completed by the Bound Man. The commitment of the Lovers to each other in "holy" matrimony flowers in the commitment to the partner within.

Higher Alchemy. The Wheel of Life Lovers.

WARRIOR

Archetype

Energy. Masculine, active, conceptive.
Number. Seven, sacred dream, symbols of life experience.
Type. Emotional thinking.
Light. *Emotional*: initiation, assertiveness, anger, bravery, boldness, daring, determination, respect for authority, valour, gallantry. *Physical*: war, aggression, action, mastery, conquest, fortitude, endurance, control, sports, achievement, progress, obeys orders, willing to put self in harm's way. *Mental*: exploration, opportunistic, triumph, victory, fame, pride. *Spiritual*: hero or heroine's journey, overcoming adversity, making something out of nothing, finding the treasure, saves the day, gives life to protect life, fights for the dream.

Shadow. *Emotional*: lack of initiation, defeated, loss of confidence, timidity, fear, pussy-whipped, vengeance, rage. *Physical*: conquered, accidents, injury, murder, killing. *Mental*: arrogance, pomp, grandiosity, bigging up, unwarranted pride, too far up himself. *Spiritual*: loss of heart, dispirited, lack of courage.

Alchemy

The Warrior as the Heart of the Adult Substance Shield uses the Mood of Emotional Cunning to Erase Mental History

Keeper of the Heart of the Adult Substance Shield. He finds his self-worth, his Path-with-Heart, and his place in the world.

Holder of the Mood of Emotional Cunning. He has the emotional strategy and tactics to use his sexuality and aggression in the service of life. He has the emotional flexibility to experience any emotional state without becoming stuck in it, victimised by it, consumed by it, idealise it or avoid it.

Teacher of Erasing Mental History. He breaks the generational cycles of collective beliefs about conflict and revenge. He has the mental discrimination to choose when to fight and when to walk.

Awakened by the Consort. For good or for ill, the Warrior serves the Earth Mother, death, life and growth, in all her forms.

Awakens the Balance. The conflict sought by the Warrior unsheaths the sword of decision and judgement.

Dreamed by the Planet Venus _____

Dreams the Temperate Man. The Warrior dreams of balance and harmony.

Completion of the Moon _____

Completed by the Released Man. The Warrior finally frees himself of his beliefs about what is worth dying for and finds what is worth living for.

Higher Alchemy. The Victorious Warrior.

CACTUS

Archetype

Energy. Feminine, receptive, creative.

Number. Eight, laws, cycles and patterns.

Type. Physical thinking.

Light. *Emotional*: self-control, patience to harness own animal instincts, the anger, bitterness, fieriness, temper, machismo, sulking, rashness, moodiness of the warrior, assimilating one's own affects. *Physical*: endurance, strength, force, fortitude, physical health, self-containment, mastery of the body and physical environment, providing for oneself physically, physical practices (for example, walking meditation, chanting, martial arts, dance). *Mental*: perseverance, mind over matter, self-restraint. *Spiritual*: allowing spirit to move in the body, cellular consciousness.

Shadow. *Emotional*: rash, impetuous, impatience, hot-headed. *Physical*: lack of care of body (diet, exercise), weak, lethargy, stupor, couch potato, four of the seven deadly sins (lust, gluttony, greed, sloth). *Mental*: no self-discipline. *Spiritual*: succumbing to temptation, addiction.

Alchemy

The Cactus as the Body of the Adult Substance Shield uses the Mood of Physical Cunning to create Mental Death and Change.

Keeper of the Body of the Adult Substance Shield. She finds her capacities and limitations in physical action and activity.

Holder of the Mood of Physical Cunning. The physical flexibility to do what needs to be done, the best physical condition to follow the designs of spirit, providing an Earth Lodge as a home for spirit, undergoing physical hardship (fasting, pilgrimage, meditation), and encountering physical death to teach us about being alive.

Teacher of Using Mental Death as an Advisor. She teaches us about Death-within-in-Life, the victory over death while still alive. The heroic body comes alive in the face of risk and danger. She loves to dance on the edge.

Awakened by the Ruler _____

_____

Awakens the Hanged Man. The physical constraint exercised by the Cactus awakens the spiritual conflict suffered by the Hanged Man.

Dreamed by Planet Earth _____

_____

Dreams the Bound Man. As much as the Cactus is bound to matter, it dreams of being bound to spirit.

Completion of the Sun _____

_____

Completed by the Star _____

_____

Higher Alchemy. The Dharma Book of Life.

SAGE

Archetype

Energy. Masculine, active, conceptive.

Number. Nine, design of energy, choices and decisions.

Type. Mental thinking.

Light. *Emotional*: beginning of individuation, the intensification of emotions leads to illumination. *Physical*: silence, retreat, meditation, quietness, time off, solitude, enforced rest or illness, aware of hidden rhythms and cycles, wandering, renunciation. *Mental*: prudence, caution, deliberation, contemplation, reflection, nostalgia, abstractions, history, cosmic meaning, geometric forms, calendars, numbers, cold hard facts, self-knowledge, first principles, underlying patterns, religion and the occult, esoterica, turning away from versus engaging with the world. *Spiritual*: timing, knowing when to stop, start or watch, *kairos* and *kronos*, catching minimal chance.

Shadow. *Emotional*: reserve, restriction, resignation, withdrawal, uncommunicative, pessimism, unsociable, melancholy, grumpy old man. *Physical*: loneliness, isolation. *Mental*: relentless introspection, self-torment, too much consciousness, over-vigilant introspection, paralysis by analysis, pedantic, picky, misanthrope. *Spiritual*: recluse, solitary, hermit, outsider, lone wolf.

Alchemy

The Sage as the Mind of the Adult Substance Shield uses the Mood of Mental Cunning to Stop the Mental World.

Keeper of the Mind of the Adult Substance Shield. He masters a body of knowledge, reflects on where he's been and where he's going.

Holder of the Mood of Mental Cunning. He has the mental stability to forgo collective beliefs and have a mind of his own.

Teacher of Stopping the Mental World. He holds the tension between the As Above and the So Below.

Awakened by the Priest _____

_____

Awakens the Dead Man. The introversion of the Sage kindles the Fire-from-within that leads to the Dead Man.

Dreamed by the Priestess. The systematic knowledge of the Sage has already been dreamed by the Priestess' intuitions.

Dreams the Released Man _____

_____

Completion of Planet Venus _____

_____

Completed by the Moon. When the knowledge of the Sage reaches its fullness it becomes occult, that is, seen by only those with the proper vision.

Higher Alchemy. The Grand Architect.

WHEEL

Archetype

Energy. Feminine, receptive, creative.

Number. Ten, all measures of intellect, all states of consciousness.

Type. Spiritual thinking.

Light. *Emotional*: rolling with the punches, acceptance of one's fate as the amalgam of universal forces and our own life choices. *Physical*: unexpected success or failure, risk-taking, progress, movement. *Mental*: understanding the inevitability of universal laws. *Spiritual*: fortune, destiny, fate, luck, inevitability, providence, cosmic patterns, time, Lady Luck, karma, the mysterious workings of the universe.

Shadow. *Emotional*: ego inflation, inability to accept one's fate. *Physical*: speculation, gambling, excess, flying too high. *Mental*: hubris. *Spiritual*: bad luck, misfortune, calamity, tribulation, catastrophe, accidents.

Alchemy

The Wheel as the Spirit of the Adult Substance Shield uses the Mood of Spiritual Cunning to Control the Mental Dream.

Keeper of the Spirit of the Adult Substance Shield. She needs to find meaning in the universe.

Holder of the Mood of Spiritual Cunning. She has the spiritual stability that enables us to surrender to our fate.

Teacher of Controlling the Mental Dream. She has the ability to experience all states of consciousness other than ego consciousness.

Awakened by the Lovers. The eternal timelessness, infinitude and cosmic feelings of the Lovers put them in touch with the mysterious workings of the universe and things beyond their control.

Awakens the Temperate Man _____

_____

Dreamed by the Consort _____

_____

Dreams the Star. The universal laws of the cosmos dream, and dream of, the individual destiny of the Star.

Completion of Planet Earth _____

_____

Completed by the Sun. The laws of the universe encoded in the Sun Stone express themselves in the power of the sun.

Higher Alchemy. The Wheel of Measure.

BALANCE

Archetype

Energy. Masculine and feminine.

Number. Eleven, all Great Grandfather Stars, spiritual memory.

Type. Soul thinking.

Light. *Emotional*: use of free will without recourse to laws or conventions, impartiality, honesty, integrity, virtue, mercy, fairness. *Physical*: action and physical consequences that flow from decision, takes responsibility for intended and unintended consequences. *Mental*: judgement, detachment, objectivity, separation, decision, clarity, cutting through ignorance, ambivalence, confusion, numbering, weighing, principle over passion, logic, reflective judgement, cool-headed decision-making undisturbed by personal feeling or physical desires. *Spiritual*: gift of free will, one who chooses their own way.

Shadow. *Emotional*: bias, dishonesty, lying, deception, bigotry, can't lie straight in bed, crooked as a dog's hind leg. *Physical*: fraud, stealing, embezzlement, theft, larceny. *Mental*: poor judgement, injustice, intolerance. *Spiritual*: venal, degenerate, debased, decadent, lawless, amoral.

Alchemy

The Balance as the Soul of the Adult Substance Shield uses the Mood of Soul Cunning to Assume Mental Authority

Keeper of the Soul of the Adult Substance Shield. The Bound Man divides, separates and destroys things so they can be put back together in a new way.

Holder of the Mood of Soul Cunning. He/she is the soul catalyst that knows and acts in accordance with deepest desires of the soul. She/he has the courage to pronounce the sentence and speak the fateful words, at the right time, in the right way, in the right place.

Teacher of Assuming Mental Authority. The Bound Man takes action at the right moment as the wheel of time revolves. She/he takes responsibility for a decision and its impact on the world. When the soul speaks, the world is changed.

Awakened by the Warrior _____

Awakens the Bound Man. The cutting, division and separation brought about by the Balance awakens the binding of the Bound Man.

Dreamed by the Ruler _____

Balance Dreams the Moon _____

Completion of the Priestess. The intuitive understanding of the "other" by Priestess flowers in the decisive division made by the Balance.

Completed by Planet Venus. When the individual act of free will choice is aligned with the will of the Creator.

Higher Alchemy. The Ceremonial Alchemist.

HANGED MAN

Archetype

Energy. Masculine, active, conceptive.

Number. Twelve, all Great Grandmother Planets (all sister planets with human life).

Type. Emotional sensation.

Light. *Emotional*: turning the world upside down, overturning old priorities, seeing things from a new angle, upending the old order, doing an about-face, sacrifice, suspension, devotion, submission to duty, repentance, expiation, conscious vulnerability. *Physical*: tension between the old and the new. *Mental*: forsaking familiar beliefs, necessary self-betrayal, paralysis of will, in limbo. *Spiritual*: sacrifice of what blocks life or no longer serves us, suffering undertaken for the growth of the personality, awakens the heart of the animus or the anima.

Shadow. *Emotional*: avoidance of suffering, restoration of the persona, refusal to let go. *Physical*: resistance to change and death, unnecessary sacrifice. *Mental*: unrealised ideas, things left undone, obligations not kept, traitor, promiscuous unselfishness. *Spiritual*: spiritual stagnation.

Alchemy

The Hanged Man as the Heart of the Adult Spirit Shield uses the Mood of Emotional Ruthlessness to Erase Physical History

Keeper of the Heart of the Adult Spirit Shield. He wants deep and wide, high and low, hard and soft, passionate and tender, wild and domestic, sex and love.

Holder of the Mood of Emotional Ruthlessness. He begins to relinquish his identity with his emotions and can be ruthless with them. The emotional repertoire broadens and empathy deepens. He can think about our feelings and have feelings about our thoughts.

Teacher of the Movement of Erasing Physical History. This is the beginning of the relativisation, the downsizing, of the ego. The ego begins to relinquish its primary source of identity — the body. Spirit quickens, the Fire-from-within begins to burn.

Awakened by Cactus. The containment and discipline of the Cactus awakens the creative suffering of the Hanged Man.

Awakens the Released Man. The emotional crucifixion of the Hanged Man realises results in the soul transformation of the Released Man.

Dreamed by the Priest. Contact with spirit brings about a suspension between the opposites.

Dreams the Sun _____

Completion of the Consort _____

Completed by Planet Earth _____

Higher Alchemy. The Gleaner.

DEAD MAN

Archetype
Energy. Feminine, receptive, creative.
Number. Thirteen, Earth Mother, Spirit of the Plants.
Type. Physical sensation.
Light. *Emotional*: dying in each moment, dying with consciousness, preparation for rebirth, triumph of life over death. *Physical*: change, ending, transformation, alteration, destruction, putrefaction, alchemical *mortificatio*. *Mental*: death of beliefs. *Spiritual*: annihilation, disillusionment, disenchantment.

Shadow. *Emotional*: boredom, blunted affect. *Physical*: immobility, petrification, near death or narrow escape. *Mental*: denial of death, fantasies of immortality. *Spiritual*: inertia, lethargy, sleep, comatose.

Alchemy
The Dead Man as the Body of the Adult Spirit Shield uses the Mood of Physical Ruthlessness to create Physical Death and Change.
Keeper of the Body of the Adult Spirit Shield. She wants free will sexual choice.
Holder of the Mood of Physical Ruthlessness. She has the physical stability to achieve the highest potentials of the body—yoga, tai chi, martial arts, shapeshifting, or the control of physiological states.
Teacher of Using Physical Death as an Advisor. As the Body of our Adult Spirit Shield, she desires a deep, physically intimate relationship and the death and change that always accompanies this.
Awakened by the Sage. The conscious introversion of the Sage awakens the chaos and death of the Dead Man.
Awakens the Star. Darkness awakens light.
Dreamed by the Lovers _____

_____
Dreams the Planet Venus _____

_____
Completion of the Ruler. The entropy and disorder of the Dead Man is the goal and completion of the structure and authority of the Ruler.
Completed by the Priestess _____

_____
Higher Alchemy. The Death Bringer.

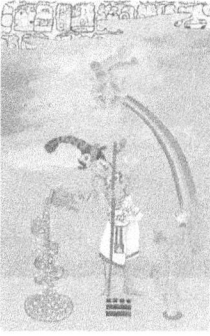

TEMPERATE MAN

Archetype

Energy. Masculine, active, conceptive.

Number. Number 14, Earth Father, Spirit of the Animals.

Type. Mental sensation.

Light. *Emotional*: taking the middle way, combining things in their right proportion, doing the temperate thing, the right action at just the right time even in a situation of conflict, accommodating, adjusting, trust in oneself, inner authority and self-containment. *Physical*: earthy wisdom, spiritualised instinct or instinctualised spirit, animal intuition, conscious cooperation with the forces of nature. *Mental*: firmness of will, increased capacity to face reality "as it is," beginning of "sobriety," common sense and street smarts. *Spiritual*: greater harmony between conscious and unconscious, inner life and outer events, self and others, understanding of the interconnectedness between all things and how the universe works.

Shadow. *Emotional*: discord, disunion, lack of cooperation, gauche, tactless. *Physical*: cityfied, clumsiness, over-civilised. *Mental*: conflict of interest, competition. *Spiritual*: going against the grain, fighting nature, misuse of resources, enslavement of matter.

Alchemy

The Temperate Man as the Mind of the Adult Spirit Shield uses the Mood of Mental Ruthlessness to Stop the Physical World

Keeper of the Mind of the Adult Spirit Shield. He is free of beliefs, constricting viewpoints and limiting attitudes, can see all sides, 360 degrees around.

Holder of the Mood of Mental Ruthlessness. He has the mental flexibility to live without a belief system. He acts on instinctual knowledge not belief.

Teacher of Stopping the Physical World. Just as the Ruler brought order to the tonal world and the Sage gave meaning to it, so the Twisted Hair or man of knowledge brings order to the nagual and the Sun brings visibility to it, and he can transform matter (which the ego calls "magic").

Awakened by the Wheel _____

_____

Awakens the Moon _____

_____

Dreamed by the Warrior. The Warrior's dream is of harmony and balance between humans.

Dreams Planet Earth. The Temperate Man's dream is of harmony and balance within all of Creation.

Completion of the Priest _____

_____

Completed by the Consort. When above and below are in harmony, the world jumps up and lives.

Higher Alchemy. The Twisted Hair Elder.

BOUND MAN

Archetype
Energy. Feminine, receptive, creative.
Number. Fifteen, All Human Souls.
Type. Spiritual sensation.
Light. *Emotional*: knowing one's own darkness. *Physical*: sacred sexuality. *Mental*: taking responsibility for what one is not responsible for. *Spiritual*: becoming bound to spirit so the soul may be free, submitting to the designs of spirit, choosing between good and evil.

Shadow. *Emotional*: addiction to emotions or relationships (emotional co-dependence), bewitchment, all things that interfere with free will. *Physical*: addiction to substances (drugs, money, food, clothes, sex). *Mental*: addiction to ideas and power (hierarchy or equality), political correctness. *Spiritual*: addiction to spirituality (fundamentalism, religious fanaticism), occult power, black magic, bondage, malevolence, evil.

Alchemy
The Bound Man as the Spirit of the Adult Spirit Shield uses the Mood of Spiritual Ruthlessness to Control the Physical Dream
Keeper of the Spirit of the Adult Spirit Shield. She wants an open and unlimited imagination.
Holder of the Mood of Spiritual Ruthlessness. She has the spiritual stability to remain bound to spirit and renounce (or accept) only those invitations (or temptations) that are faithful to her marriage to spirit.
Teacher of Controlling the Physical Dream. His relationship to spirit as partner means that he can manifest his desires from the dream into matter.
Awakened by the Balance. Her individual free will choice binds her to spirit.
Awakens the Sun _____

Dreamed by the Cactus _____

Dreams the Priestess. Her obedience to the laws of spirit allows her to see.
Completion of the Lovers. The spiritual marriage of the Bound Man completes the physical marriage of the Lovers.
Completed by the Ruler. Her obedience to the laws of spirit confers rulership in the world of substance.
Higher Alchemy. The Contractual Soul.

RELEASED MAN

Archetype
Energy. Masculine and feminine.
Number. Sixteen, All Enlightened Human Souls.
Type. Soul sensation.
Light. *Emotional*: egocentric ambitions are shattered, consequences of ambition, final shattering of the Mirror of Self-reflection. *Physical*: natural disaster, overthrow. *Mental*: disaster resulting in liberation, the old collapses to make way for the new. *Spiritual*: illumination, awakening, ascension, liberation, materialistic attitude dissolves.
Shadow. *Emotional*: disgrace, destruction, ruin, downfall. *Physical*: misfortune, sudden unexpected adversity, bankruptcy. *Mental*: loss of meaning. *Spiritual*: existential disorientation, nothing worth living for, suicide.

Alchemy
The Released Man as the Soul of the Adult Spirit Shield uses the Mood of Soul Ruthlessness to Assume Physical Authority
Keeper of the Soul of the Adult Spirit Shield. She/he gives to others unconditionally.
Holder of the Mood of Soul Ruthlessness. She/he is the soul catalyst that enables us to arrange our lives so that spirit can stalk us in each moment.
Teacher of Assuming Physical Authority. She/he is the final destruction of beliefs, theories, expectations and ways of seeing. This is the clearing away of what hides our inner authority from ourselves. We suffer from the violence done to us by the Self. If we are full of illusion then we experience collapse but if without illusion then we experience liberation from the designs of matter.
Awakened by the Hanged Man _____

_____

Awakens Planet Venus _____

_____

Dreamed by the Sage. The Sage dreams of his release from beliefs, wisdom, understanding and knowledge.
Dreams the Consort _____

_____

Completion of the Warrior. The Released Man is free because of the battles of the Warrior. The Warrior fought for what he believed in, the Released Man no longer has the need to believe.
Completed by the Priest _____

_____

Higher Alchemy. The Stream of Livingness Tower.

STAR

Archetype

Energy. Feminine, receptive, creative.

Number. Seventeen, the Sweet Dream Teachers.

Type. Emotional intuition.

Light. *Emotional*: faith, expectation, bright promises, inspiration, hope born from struggle. *Physical*: new direction, knowing your path. *Mental*: idealism, originality. *Spiritual*: vision, favourable omen, sees the light within the light, transpersonal will.

Shadow. *Emotional*: dispirited, unfulfilled hope, disappointment. *Physical*: disoriented, lack of direction. *Mental*: indifference, arrogance, stubbornness. *Spiritual*: loss of life purpose, no vision.

Alchemy

The Star as the Heart of the Child Spirit Shield uses the Mood of Emotional Patience to Erase Spiritual History

Keeper of the Heart of the Child Spirit Shield. She loves unconditionally, innocent yet wise, measured but unconditional.

Holder of the Mood of Emotional Patience. She walks her own Path with Heart guided by the light of her own star. She is the emotional expansiveness to be able to ride out emotional storms, to remain true to oneself in the face of inner or outer pressures, and to allowing the Self or spirit to determine.

Teacher of the spiritual aspect of Erasing Personal History. She sees the transpersonal meaning of her personal history.

Awakened by the Dead Man _____

Awakens Planet Earth. When she awakens to her true self all of Creation rejoices.

Dreamed by the Wheel _____

Dreams the Ruler. The individuated consciousness of the Star longs to become woven into collective consciousness.

Completion of the Cactus _____

Completed by the Lovers. She meets the incarnated image of her soulmate, the Beloved.

Higher Alchemy. The Sweet Dream Teachers.

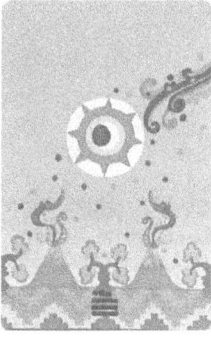

MOON

Archetype

Energy. Feminine, receptive, creative.

Number. Eighteen, Holder of the Book of Life.

Type. Physical intuition.

Light. *Emotional*: stillness, waiting, accepting, ripening, darkness, quiet, secrecy, muteness, hiddenness. *Physical*: all physical rhythms and cycles, sleep, hormones, growth, puberty, menstrual cycle, menopause, tides, death and rebirth. *Mental*: all fluids, dew, mist, rain, sea, blood, semen. *Spiritual*: the unseen world, the unconscious, the slower, natural cycles of life, powers of intuition.

Shadow. *Emotional*: deception, illusion, danger, plots, scandal, blackmail, gossip, hidden enemies, instability, variation, fluctuation. *Physical*: twilight, darkness, the unknown, instinctual terrors. *Mental*: indecision, uncertainty, mooniness, delusion, fantastic beliefs, lunacy, occult forces. *Spiritual*: chaos, regression, atavism, frenzy, madness, changeability, enchantment, magic, vampires, ghosts, werewolves.

Alchemy

The Moon as the Body of the Child Spirit Shield uses the Mood of Physical Patience to create Spiritual Death and Change

Keeper of the Body of the Child Spirit Shield. She heals others. She is close to the rhythms and patterns of the body, the Self and the cosmos. She is our body-knowing.

Holder of the Mood of the Mood of Physical Patience. She is the physical expansiveness that aligns us with the rhythms of nature. She allows the personal vision of the Star to emerge slowly into reality, and has the patience to wait for things come down from the dream and manifest in the physical world.

Teacher of Using Spiritual Death as an Advisor. She teaches about the Life-within-Death when we die and are reborn in each moment.

Awakened by the Temperate Man _____

Awakens the Priestess _____

Dreamed by the Balance _____

Dreams the Priest. The dream of the Moon is be the intermediary between the worlds of spirit and matter.

Completion of the Sage. The Sage's introspection into his own inner darkness enables him to see what is invisible.

Completed by the Warrior _____

Higher Alchemy. The Magical Mysterious Character Mirror of Self-reflection.

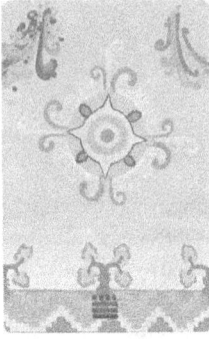

SUN

Archetype
Energy. Masculine, active, conceptive.
Number. Keeper of the Higher Self.
Type. Mental intuition.
Light. *Emotional*: happiness, contentment, joy, satisfaction, success, glory, honour. *Physical*: material fortune, energy, aliveness. *Mental*: enlightenment, clarity, revelation. *Spiritual*: life-force, inexhaustible spiritual energy for growth, divine fire, the will of the Creator.
Shadow. *Emotional*: anger, vanity, pride, delusions of grandeur, bluff, facade. *Physical*: delayed success or triumph. *Mental*: misunderstood. *Spiritual*: creative stagnation, uncertain future.

Alchemy
The Sun as the masculine, active, conceptive mind of the Child Spirit Shield uses the Mood of Mental Patience to Stop the Spiritual World
Keeper of the Mind of the Child Spirit Shield. He is the power of consciousness to dispel darkness and ignorance and bring meaning and illumination. He is the irrepressible search for meaning and he shares everything he knows.
Holder of the Mood of Mental Patience. He is the mental expansiveness to see past the outer form of things and see the inner light (the Shining) and see the outer light of nature (the *lumen naturae*). He reminds us of our connection all things.
Teacher of Stopping the Spiritual World. He brings spiritual order by bringing light into the darkness. He sees the light in matter and all things as a Design of Energy.
Awakened by the Bound Man. Being bound to the laws of spirit awakens illumination.
Awakens the Consort. The Sun awakens growth and movement.
Dreamed by the Hanged Man _____

_____
Dreams the Lovers. The limitless fire and passion of Grandfather Sun dreams of the passionate intimacy between the masculine and feminine.
Completion of the Wheel _____

_____
Completed by the Cactus _____

_____
Higher Alchemy. The Hokkshidehey.

PLANET VENUS

Archetype

Energy. Masculine, active, conceptive.

Number. Twenty, Great Spirit, God/Goddess, Creator.

Type. Spiritual intuition.

Light. *Emotional*: end of self-punishment and self-hatred, repentance, forgiveness. *Physical*: compassion and kinship with all things, higher and lower are joined, matter becomes spiritualised and spirit becomes materialised. *Mental*: deliverance from limitations. *Spiritual*: redemption, love and liberation, ego's reconciliation with the Self, soul reunites with the body, union of opposites, coming of peace, resurrection of new life, understanding the symbolic aspects of a concrete situation, seeing the meaning behind mundane daily events, bringing abstract realisations into everyday life.

Shadow. *Emotional*: trapped, situation one cannot escape from, impatience, hopelessness. *Physical*: confined for the time it takes to outgrow one's problems. *Mental*: harsh, wrathful judgement. *Spiritual*: despair of ever changing.

Alchemy

The Planet Venus as the Spirit of the Child Spirit Shield uses the Mood of Spiritual Patience to Control the Spiritual Dream

Keeper of the Spirit of the Child Spirit Shield. He finds and moves towards light and wholeness.

Holder of the Mood of Spiritual Patience. He is spiritual expansiveness, forgiveness, spiritual love, love of spirit, God's love and the love of God.

Teacher of the spiritual aspect of Controlling the Dream. He stands in the Crack-between-the-Worlds, the place of the marriage of spirit and substance.

Awakened by the Released Man _____

Awakens the Ruler. Kinship with all things awakens the capacities of rulership and stewardship.

Dreamed by the Dead Man. The Death-that-gives-life brought by the Dead Man gives the everlasting life of the Planet Venus.

Dreams the Warrior. The oneness of Planet Venus dreams the conflict of the Warrior.

Completion of the Balance _____

Completed by the Sage _____

Higher Alchemy. The Blessings of the Great Spirit.

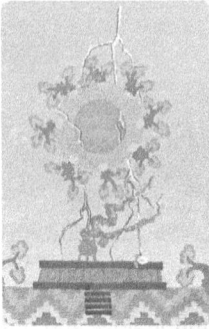

PLANET EARTH

Archetype

Energy. Feminine and masculine.

Number. All numbers and medicines in the Twenty Count.

Type. Soul intuition.

Light. *Emotional*: triumph, honour, recognition, success, achievement, satisfaction, joy, fulfilment, full participation in the dance of life. *Physical*: reward, promotion, cannot live by spirit alone and must have ordinary, earthly satisfactions. *Mental*: the end result, integration, all things live according to their own nature, seeing meaning and beauty in the most difficult events. *Spiritual*: perfection, seeing the luminosity of spirit in all matter, all things are "pure" and not contaminated by what they aren't, all things contain their opposite, all the opposites are joined, all things contain all other things, in the end is the beginning.

Shadow. *Emotional*: lack of closure, fear of change, self-sabotage, envy of success. *Physical*: inertia, fixity, stagnation. *Mental*: falling at the last hurdle, obstacles, failure, resistance. *Spiritual*: belittling of achievements, unfinished work, destruction, cataclysm.

Alchemy

Planet Earth as the Soul of the Child Spirit Shield uses the Mood of Soul Patience to Assume Spiritual Authority.

Keeper of the Soul of the Child Spirit Shield. She/he desires an open and unlimited circle of being. The joy, life, passion and beauty of the journey.

Holder of the Mood of Soul Patience. She/he is the soul expansiveness that loves the world in all its beauty and imperfections.

Teacher of Assuming Spiritual Authority. She/he is the totality that maintains its authority and does not permit too much dividedness or too much unity. She assumes the responsibility of the power, foolishness and beauty of being human.

Awakened by the Star. The spiritual vision of the Star awakens the wholeness of Planet Earth.

Awakens the Priest _____

Dreamed by the Temperate Man. The Temperate Man dreams Planet Earth where all things are in harmony and balance.

Dreams the Cactus _____

Completion of the Hanged Man _____

Completed by the Wheel. The Great Laws and Measure of the Universe become incarnated in the Wheel of Life on Planet Earth.

Higher Alchemy. The Marriage Basket of She Thoughts.

Credits

In the beginning this was never meant to be a book. Over the years after the dream of the five jaguars, I just gathered stuff that interested me. As a result, many of the ideas became migrants and nomads, diaspora'd from the land of their birth and their lineage, intermarrying, and producing children of many different colours. I have tried as best I can to reconstruct what came from where and to honour the mana of those who are the ancestors of this book and the Xultun Tarot. I acknowledge their contributions in the Preface and below. Every effort has been made to identify the sources used however I have been unable to identify some sources which were gathered many years before the idea of a book came over the horizon. I would welcome any further information.

Text

I have used Jung's Collected Works as the primary textual source with additional material from the more classical Jungians such as Edward Edinger, James Hillman and Marie-Louise von Franz. CW refers to C. G. Jung, *The Collected Works* (1953–1979). Herbert Read, Michael Fordham and Gerhard Adler (eds.) Princeton: Princeton University Press. I have quoted Jung extensively (or paraphrased where I have reached the limits of fair use) to remain close to the spirit of his words and not intervene between Jung and the reader. For Jungian commentary on the tarot (which is sparse) I have drawn from Irene Gad, Kenneth James and Sallie Nichols.

The medicine teachings are taken primarily from my personal notes and the books and privately published manuals of the Sweet Medicine Sundance Path (© Deer Tribe Metis Medicine Society, www.dtmms.org). I have omitted any of the advanced teachings about the cards. I have given only a basic outline of selected teachings sufficient to amplify the cards: Chapter 1, Twisted Hairs; Chapter 3, Medicine Wheel, Twenty Count, Children of Grandmother Earth; Chapter 4, Shields of Humans; Chapter 5, Moods of Stalking; Chapter 6, Movements of the Book of Life; Chapter 7, Mirror of Self-reflection; Chapter 9, Zero to Nine Law. As with Jung, I have attempted to stay close to the spirit of the teachings but this book does not claim to represent the work of SwiftDeer or the Deer Tribe and, as usual, any differences are the responsibility of the author. Additional material is from the writings of Carlos Castaneda and Hyemeyohsts Storm.

The alchemy of the major arcana (the patterns and inter-relationships between the cards) was given by the Xultun Tarot. The amplification of the cards using Jung and the medicine teachings was my own and that of the Xultun Tarot. The basic meanings of the individual cards are well-known in the standard tarot literature. The history, archaeology and epigraphy of Central America and the Maya, and the historical origins of some of the Xultun images, was sourced from a diverse range of books, websites and serendipity.

Illustrations

Front cover figure, the Major Arcana of the Xultun Tarot, and line drawings © Peter Balin. Reprinted by kind permission. Images from the Codex Nuttall are reprinted by kind permission of Dover Publications from Nuttall, Zelia (ed.) (1975) *The Codex Nuttall: A Picture Manuscript from Ancient Mexico, The Peabody Facsimile Edition*. Dover: New York. www.doverpublications.com. The images of the Marseilles Tarot are taken from *The Tarot of Marseilles, Maritxu de Guler*, www.wischik.com-/lu/tarot, not known to be copyrighted. Unless otherwise noted illustrations are by the author.

Figure 5. Maya priest star-gazing in a xultun, Madrid Codex.

Figure 6. Twisted Hair glyph of Tikal,
    en.wikipedia.org/wiki/File:Tikalemblem.jpg.

Figure 7. Historical Maya sites, en.wikipedia.org/wiki/File:Mayamap.png.

Figure 10. The Medicine Wheel, adapted from Reagan, 1994, p. 20.

Figure . Woodcut of triple-headed dragon, from Giovanni Battista, *Nazari Il metamorfosi metallico*, Brescia, 1564 Also frontispiece, CW 13.

Figure 13. The extraction of the spirit of Mercurius, The Figure of the Mirror of the Holy Trinity, from Reusner, *Pandora*, 1588.

Figure 16. The Moods of Stalking, adapted from Reagan, 1988, p. 61.

Figure 18. The Movements of the Book of Life, adapted from Reagan, 1988, p. 45.

Figure 27. Incised bone, Burial 116, Temple 1, Tikal. Source unknown.

Figure 28. Stormy Sky, Stela 31, Tikal, photo by Greg Willis, en.wikipedia.org-/wiki/File:Tikal_Stela_31.jpg.

Figure 29. Mount Taranaki, North Island, New Zealand, photo by nzsuster, out-doors.webshots.com/photo/2757547420049458519KMJfAI.

Figure 32. Starry night symbol. Source unknown.

Figure 33. Hasaw Chan K'awil, Temple 1, Lintel 3, Tikal. Source unknown. David Freidel, Anthropology 3312, Mesoamerican Archaeology, September 18, 2006, p. 33.

Figure 36. Stormy Sky, Stela 1, Tikal. Source unknown. Ref: David Freidel, Anthropology 3312, Mesoamerican Archaeology, September 25, 2006, p. 28.

Figure 39. Dark Sun, Lintel 2, Temple 3, Tikal. Source unknown.

Figure 40. Temple at Ek Balam, Yucatan. Photo: Dorothy Beals and Sarah Martin. en.wikipedia.org/wiki/File:Ekbalam-Jaguar-Altar-Right.png.

Figure 41. Conjuring House. Source unknown.

Figure 43. Maya mirror. Source unknown.

Figure 49. San Pedro cactus in flower. Source unknown.

Figure 50. The Alchemist in the Bath. Splendor Solis.

Figure 52. Maize God, stone sculpture, Copan. Source unknown.

Figure 60. Detail of right side, Stela 31, Tikal. Source unknown. David Freidel, Anthropology 3312, Mesoamerican Archaeology, September 25, 2006, p. 26.

Figure 62. Crystal skull. Photo: Michael Owen.

Figure 63. The British Museum crystal skull. Photo: Rafal Chalgasiewicz, en.wiki-pedia.org/wiki/File:Crystal_skull_british_museum_random9834672.jpg.

Figure 66. A ballcourt at Tikal. Source unknown.

Figure 67. The Umpire (figurine from Peten region). Source unknown.

Figure 70. Part of Lintel 2, Temple 3, Tikal. Source unknown.

Figure 71. The blood of Christ. From Edinger, *Ego and Archetype*.

Figure 75. The Mithraic god Aion, Museo Profano, Vatican. Source unknown.

Figure 76. Ox-Ha-Te Ixil Ahau, incised bone, Burial 116, Tikal. Source unknown.

Figure 77. Xipe Totec. Left: Xipe Totec Effigy Vessel. Right: Ceramic, Oaxaca Valles Centrales, c. 1100 CE. Source unknown.

Figure 78. Mixtec double-headed serpent, 15th century. Source unknown.

Figure 84. Temple 1, Tikal. Source unknown.

Figure 88. The Reunion of the Soul and the Body by William Blake. Source unknown.

Figure 89. Feathered Serpent. Source unknown.

Figure 90. Temple of the Feathered Serpent, Xochicalco. Source unknown.

Figure 91. Descent of Kukulkan, Chichen Itza. Source unknown.

Figure 92. Flammarion woodcut. En.wikipedia.org/wiki/File:Flammarion.jpg.

Figure 94. Tomb of Pacal, Palenque. Source unknown.

Figure 95. The arbor philosophica. Miscellanea d'Alchimia, Italy, 15th century.

Figure 96. Dream of the Virgin by Christoforo de Crocefissi c. 1350. Source unknown.

Figure 97. The Milky Way. Lund Observatory.

References

Chapter 1: Xultun

1. *The Tarot of Marseilles, Maritxu de Guler*. See www.wischik.com/lu/tarot.
2. Quoted in a book review by Valerie Harms of Nancy Ryley, *The Forsaken Garden: Four Conversations on the Deep Meaning of Environmental Illness*, Wheaton: IL, Quest, 1998, www.cgjungpage.org/articles/harmsview.html.
3. Rainer Maria Rilke, *Just as the Winged Energy of Delight*.
4. CW 9ii, *Aion*, § 78.
5. Peter Balin, *The Way of the Sorcerer*, pp. 2-5.
6. Barbara Fash, *Corpus of Maya Hieroglyphic Inscriptions*, Peabody Museum of Archaeology and Ethnology, http://140.247.102.177/CMHI/site.php?site=Xultun.
7. "Mural Found on Walls a First for a Maya Dwelling; Painted Numbers Reflect Calendar Reaching Well Beyond 2012." *ScienceDaily*. Accessed July 26, 2012. http://bit.ly/VpdhRv.
8. Peter Balin, *The Way of the Sorcerer*, p. 12.
9. Stuart Kaplan, *The Encyclopaedia of Tarot*, pp. 287-290.
10. In Maori, Aotearoa means "The Land of the Long White Cloud."
11. Ngati Kowhai o Waitaha, *Song of Waitaha: The Histories of a Nation*, p. 10.
12. Credo Mutwa, *Song of the Stars*, p. xiii.
13. Cornelius Van Dorp, *Crystal Mission*, p. 297.
14. Peter Matthews, *Maya Hieroglyph Dictionary*. Research.famsi.org/mdp/printall.php. David Stuart is Linda and David Schele Professor of Mesoamerican Art and Writing at the University of Texas, Austin.
15. Martha Macri, *Mutal, a possible Mixe-Zoque toponym*, Glyph Dwellers, 12, 2000, p. 1. http://nas.ucdavis.edu/NALC/R12.pdf
16. Hyemeyohsts Storm, *Lightningbolt*.
17. Michael Coe, *Breaking the Maya Code*.
18. Richardson Gill, *The Great Maya Droughts: Water, Life, and Death*.

Chapter 2: Jung

1. See Henri Ellenberger (1981) *The Discovery of the Unconscious: The History and Evolution of Dynamic Psychiatry*. New York: Basic Books.
2. See Meredith Sabini, *The Earth Has a Soul: The Nature Writings of C. G. Jung*.
3. I am indebted here to Lionel Corbett's excellent summary, *Basic Jung* (n.d.)
4. CW 17, *The Development of Personality*, § 169.
5. Joseph Campbell, *The Hero With a Thousand Faces*.
6. CW 8, § 382 and CW 7, § 103.
7. For a description of psychoid processes see Stanislav Grof, *Realms of the Human Unconscious*.
8. CW 10, *Civilization in Transition*, § 53.
9. CW 8, *The Structure and Dynamics of the Psyche*, § 342.
10. CW 9i, *The Archetypes and the Collective Unconscious*, § 87.
11. CW 10, *Civilization in Transition*, § 395.
12. CW 9i, *The Archetypes and the Collective Unconscious*, § 6.
13. Calvinist prayer, 18th century.
14. Harold Bayley, *The Lost Language of Symbolism*, 1912.
15. Anne Baring, *Cinderella: An Interpretation*.
16. CW 7, *Two Essays on Analytical Psychology*, § 305.

Chapter 2: Jung

17. CW 9i, *The Archetypes and the Collective Unconscious*, § 221.
18. CW 11, *Psychology and Religion: West and East*, § 140.
19. CW 14, *Mysterium Coniunctionis*, § 514.
20. Nick Hornby, *Fever Pitch.* p. 54.
21. CW 13, *Alchemical Studies*, § 335.
22. CW 14, *Mysterium Coniunctionis*, § 708.
23. CW 7, *Two Essays on Analytical Psychology*, § 334.
24. CW 9ii, *Aion*, § 33.
25. CW 6, *Psychological Types*, § 804.
26. CW 7, *Two Essays on Analytical Psychology*, § 336.
27. CW 16, *The Practice of Psychotherapy*, § 361.
28. CW 9i, *The Archetypes and the Collective Unconscious*, § 146f.
29. CW 7, *Two Essays on Analytical Psychology*, § 334.
30. James Hillman, *A Blue Fire*, p. 122.
31. Rodney Ravenswood, *The Symbolic Life*, www.hermes.net.au/ravens/symlife.htm
32. See CW 6, *Psychological Types*, and Mary Loomis, *Dancing the Wheel of Psychological Types*.
33. CW 16, *The Practice of Psychotherapy*, § 531.
34. CW 9i, *The Archetypes and the Collective Unconscious*, § 179.
35. CW 6, *Psychological Types*, § 725.
36. CW 6, *Psychological Types*, § 576.
37. CW 10, *Civilization in Transition*, § 317.
38. I shall use the capitalised Self to denote the organising centre of the psyche.

Chapter 3: Medicine

1. CW 9i, *The Archetypes and the Collective Unconscious*, § 291.
2. CW 9ii, *Aion: Researches into the Phenomenology of the Self*, § 126.
3. Marie-Louise von Franz, *The Interpretation of Fairytales*, p. 79.
4. CW 14, *Mysterium Coniunctionis*, § 365.
5. There are ten Twenty Counts in all. The count I use here is the east count, the Children's Count. See Harley Swiftdeer Reagan, *Shamanic Wheels and Keys*, pp. 91-114; Hyemeyohsts Storm, *Lightningbolt*, Thunder Strikes, *Song of the Deer*, and Roger Montgomery, *Twenty Count: Secret Mathematical System of the Aztec/Maya*.
6. CW 7, *Two Essays on Analytical Psychology*, § 32.
7. CW 14, *Mysterium Coniunctionis*, § 427.
8. CW 8, *The Structure and Dynamics of the Psyche*, § 414.
9. James Hillman, *Pan and the Nightmare*.
10. Hamlet, Act 3, Scene 1.
11. James Hillman, *Silver and the White Earth, Part Two*, pp. 56–57.
12. CW 12, *Psychology and Alchemy*, Fig. 232.

Chapter 4: Shields

1. Harley SwiftDeer Reagan, *Shamanic Wheels and Keys*, pp. 115-165 and Carlos Castaneda, *The Power of Silence*, p. 121.
2. Harley SwiftDeer Reagan, *Shamanic Wheels and Keys*, p. 142.
3. CW 17, *The Development of Personality*.

Chapter 5: Moods

1. C. G. Jung, *Letters 2*, p. 333.
2. Claudia van Corva & Thunder Strikes, *The Thirty Sacred Laws: The Universal and Cosmic Laws*.
3. CW 13, *Alchemical Studies*, § 17.

Chapter 5: Moods

4. Carlos Castaneda, *The Active Side of Infinity*, p. 246.
5. Michael Owen, *Jung and the Native American Moon Cycles*, pp. 12–13.

Chapter 6: Movements

1. See Carlos Castaneda, *Journey to Ixtlan*, Chapters 2–5 and Harley SwiftDeer Reagan, *The Mirror of Self-Reflection*.
2. Harley SwiftDeer Reagan, *Shamanic Wheels and Keys*, p. 31.
3. My thanks to Therese McLachlan for her insights about the give-aways of the Movements.
4. CW 12, *Psychology and Alchemy*, § 152.
5. W. B. Yeats, *Crazy Jane Talks with the Bishop*.
6. Queenie Rikihana Hyland, *Illustrated Maori Myths and Legends*, pp. 10–12.
7. For a detailed discussion see Michael Owen, *Jung and the Native American Moon Cycles*.
8. Carlos Castaneda, *Journey to Ixtlan*, pp. 33–35.
9. Liz Greene and Juliet Sharman-Burke, *The Mythic Tarot*.
10. Barbara Kingsolver, *The Poisonwood Bible*, p. 5.
11. Carlos Castaneda, *Tales of Power*, pp. 238, 240.
12. Carlos Castaneda, *Tales of Power*, p. vii.
13. Carlos Castaneda, *The Art of Dreaming*, pp. 19 & 67.
14. See Edward Edinger, *Ego and Archetype*.
15. CW 18, *The Symbolic Life*, § 630.
16. Carlos Castaneda, *The Eagle's Gift*, p. 209.
17. Carlos Castaneda, *Journey to Ixtlan*, pp. 39–40.
18. Joseph Henderson, *Thresholds of Initiation*, p. 202.
19. CW 10, *Civilization in Transition*, § 586.
20. James Hillman, *And Huge is Ugly*.
21. CW 11, *Psychology and Religion: West and East*, § 223.

Chapter 7: Mirror

1. See Kenneth James' discussion of the seven paths in *The Sevenfold Path to Wholeness* (audiotape) and Harley SwiftDeer Reagan, *The Mirror of Self-Reflection*.
2. C. G. Jung, *Memories, Dreams, Reflections*.
3. See James Hillman, *The Soul's Code: In Search of Character and Calling*.
4. CW 11, *Psychology and Religion: West and East*, § 904.
5. Carlos Castaneda, *Tales of Power*, pp. 155, 174.
6. See Michael Owen, *Jung and the Native American Moon Cycles*.

Chapter 8: DNA

1. See James Lovelock and Lynn Margulis, *Gaia: A New Look at Life on Earth*.
2. See Lynn Margulis, *Symbiotic Planet: A New Look at Evolution*.
3. www.erowid.org/culture/references/other/1997_krakowski_resproject_1.shtml.
4. C. G. Jung, *Memories, Dreams, Reflections*, p. 4.
5. Carlos Castaneda, *The Power of Silence*, p. 247.

Chapter 9: Loom of Time

1. See Claudia van Corva and Thunder Strikes, *The Thirty Sacred Laws: The Teachings of the Twisted Hairs Elders of Turtle Island, Volume II, Part 1, The Universal and Cosmic Laws*.
2. CW 9ii, *Aion*, § 17.
3. Alice Howell, *The Web in the Sea*. p. 11.
4. The ecliptic is the path taken by the sun, moon and planets across the Milky Way.

Chapter 10: Fool

1. Douglas Gillette, *The Shaman's Secret*, p. 137.
2. Sallie Nichols, *Jung and Tarot*, p. 34.
3. Marie-Louise von Franz, *Shadow and Evil in Fairytales*, p. 185.
4. Eleanora Woloy, *The Symbol of the Dog in the Human Psyche*, pp. 4-5.
5. Barbara Hannah, *The Archetypal Symbolism of Animals*, p. 58.
6. David Freidel, Linda Schele and Joy Parker, *Maya Cosmos*, p. 92.
7. Susan Milbrath, *Star Gods of the Maya*, p. 130.
8. Carlos Castaneda, *The Eagle's Gift*, p. 291.

Chapter 11: Sorcerer

1. David Freidel, *Mesoamerican Anthropology*, lecture, September 11, 2006
2. Linda Schele and David Freidel, *A Forest of Kings*, p. 156.
3. Peter Balin, *The Way of the Sorcerer*, p. 14.
4. C. G. Jung, *Memories, Dreams, Reflections*, p. 323.

Chapter 12: Priestess

1. CW 16, *The Practice of Psychotherapy*, § 375.
2. Nathan Schwartz-Salant, "Archetypal foundations of projective identification," in *The Borderline Personality*, pp. 97–130.
3. CW 14, *Mysterium Coniunctionis*, § 18.
4. CW 11, *Psychology and Religion: West and East*, § 180.
5. See for example, Louis Cozolino, *The Neuroscience of Human Relationships: Attachment and the Developing Social Brain*; Peter Fonagy, *Attachment Theory and Psychoanalysis*; Allan Schore, *Affect Regulation and the Origin of the Self: The Neurobiology of Emotional Development*
6. Michael Owen, *Jung and the Native American Moon Cycles*, pp. 222-227.
7. Hannah Segal, *Introduction to the Work of Melanie Klein*, p. 35.
8. See Mario Jacoby, *Jungian Psychotherapy and Contemporary Infant Research: Basic Patterns of Emotional Exchange*.
9. Otto Weininger, *Melanie Klein*, pp. 33, 37 & Otto Weininger, *View from the Cradle*, p. 98.
10. See Claudia van Corva and Thunder Strikes, *The Thirty Sacred Laws: The Teachings of the Twisted Hairs Elders of Turtle Island, Volume II, Part 3, The Ecological Balance Laws*.
11. Otto Weininger, *View from the Cradle*, pp. 93, 149.
12. Donald Kalsched, *The Inner World Of Trauma: Archetypal Defenses of the Personal Spirit*.
13. Carlos Castaneda, *The Power of Silence*. pp. 67, 164-165, 167, 170, 260.
14. G. W. F. Hegel, *Introduction to the Philosophy of History*.
15. Edward Edinger, *Ego and Self: The Old Testament Prophets*, p. 14.
16. For this description I am indebted to Martín Prechtel and his broad and deep knowledge of Maya culture and spirituality.
17. Laurie Layton Schapira, *The Cassandra Complex*.
18. Toni Wolff, *Structural Forms of the Feminine Psyche*.

Chapter 13: Consort

1. David Stuart, *The Arrival of Strangers: Teotihuacan and Tollan in Classic Maya History*, PARI Newsletter, 25, 1998, www.mesoweb.com/pari/publications/news_archive-/25/strangers/strangers.html
2. Verena Kast, *The Nature of Loving: Patterns of Human Relationship*, p. 44.
3. Irene Gad, *Tarot and Individuation*, p. 90.
4. See Hannah Rachel Bell, *Men's Business, Women's Business: The Spiritual Role of Gender in the World's Oldest Culture*.

Chapter 14: Ruler

1. Martin Brennan, *The Hidden Maya*, p. 214.
2. Susan Milbrath, *Star Gods of the Maya*, p. 263.
3. David Freidel, *Maya Cosmos*, pp. 101, 104.
4. www.telegraph.co.uk/news/obituaries/3795999/Sir-Lewis-Robertson.html
5. Douglas Gillette & Robert Moore, *The King: Accessing the King in the Male Psyche*.
6. Robert Bly, *Iron John*, p. 110.
7. John Weir Perry, *Lord of the Four Quarters*.
8. Jurgen Kremer and Fausto Flores (n.d.) *The Ritual Suicide of Maya Rulers*. Rheinische Friedrich-Wilhelms Universität, Bonn, winter semester 1991/92.
9. Linda Schele and David Freidel, *A Forest of Kings*, pp. 90, 415, 426.
10. Roger Cook, *The Tree of Life: Image for the Cosmos*.
11. See Jung's essay on the symbol of the tree, *The Philosophical Tree* in CW 13, *Alchemical Studies*, § 410.
12. Martin Brennan, *The Hidden Maya*, p. 130.
13. Susan Milbrath, *Star Gods of the Maya*, p. 286.
14. David Freidel, *Maya Cosmos*, p. 425.

Chapter 15: Priest

1. *Tikal's Dynastic Rulers*, www.tikalpark.com/dynasty.htm
2. John Major Jenkins, *Maya Cosmogenesis 2012*, p. 93.
3. Martin Brennan, *The Hidden Maya*, p. 26.
4. David Freidel, *Maya Cosmos*, p. 223.
5. Ibid., p. 222, and see Carlos Castaneda, *The Fire From Within*, pp. 78–96 for a description of an encounter with the other world through the portal of a mirror.
6. See Douglas Gillette, *The Shaman's Secret*.
7. See "Transformation Symbolism in the Mass" in CW 11, *Psychology and Religion*.
8. CW 7, *Two Essays on Analytical Psychology*, § 269.

Chapter 16: Lovers

1. Nicholas Saunders (2001) A dark light: reflections on obsidian in Mesoamerica, *World Archaeology*, 33(2), p. 221.
2. CW 6, *Psychological Types*, § 807.
3. C. G. Jung, *Letters 2*, p. 321.
4. CW 9ii, *Aion*, § 30–31.
5. CW 16, *The Practice of Psychotherapy*, § 422.
6. CW 9i, *The Archetypes and the Collective Unconscious*, § 61.
7. CW 7, *Two Essays on Analytical Psychology*, § 374.
8. CW 14, *Mysterium Coniunctionis*, § 99.
9. Marie-Louise von Franz, *Interpretation of Fairytales*, pp. 69 and 137.
10. CW 8, *The Structure and Dynamics of the Psyche*, § 189.

Chapter 17: Warrior

1. In this section I draw from Thomas Kirsch's *Initiation: The Living Reality of an Archetype*.
2. Carlos Castaneda, *Tales of Power*, p. 106.
3. CW 9i, *The Archetypes and the Collective Unconscious*, § 284.
4. CW 14, *Mysterium Coniunctionis*, § 756.
5. Marie-Louise von Franz, *Interpretation of Fairytales*, p. 45.
6. For much of this section I draw on James Hillman's study, *A Terrible Love of War*.
7. Barbara Ehrenreich, *Blood Rites*, p. 232.
8. Matthew 10:34.
9. Hillman, *A Terrible Love of War*, p. 215.
10. Quoted in Hillman, *A Terrible Love of War*, p. 78.

Chapter 17: Warrior

11. Ibid., pp. 210-211.
12. Christopher Marlowe, *Doctor Faustus*.
13. Helen Luke, *The Voice Within*, p. 83.
14. Its possible origin is "The rules of fair play do not apply in love and war," in *Euphues* (1578) by John Lyly, English poet and playwright.
15. For her superb essay on hatred see "Styx and stones: hatred and the art of cursing," in Lyn Cowan, *Tracking the White Rabbit*.
16. Carlos Driscoll (2009) *The Evolution of House Cats*, June 2009. www.scientificamerican.com/article.cfm?id=the-taming-of-the-cat.
17. Barbara Hannah, *The Archetypal Symbolism of Animals*, pp. 93-94.
18. Irene Gad, *Tarot and Individuation*, p. 78.
19. CW 14, *Mysterium Coniunctionis*, § 149.
20. Marie-Louise von Franz, *Interpretation of Fairytales*, p. 96.

Chapter 18: Cactus

1. Peter Balin, *The Flight of Feathered Serpent*, p. 98.
2. Richard Schultes and Albert Hoffman, *Plants of the Gods*, p. 156.
3. Linda Schele and David Freidel, *A Forest of Kings*, pp. 162-163.
4. CW 9i, *The Archetypes and the Collective Unconscious*, § 41.
5. CW 12, *Psychology and Alchemy*, § 277.
6. CW 14, *Mysterium Coniunctionis*, § 512n.
7. C. G. Jung, *Visions Seminars*, pp. 613-614.
8. Interview with Barbara Walters on ABC-TV, March 18, 1987.
9. Edward Edinger, *Anatomy of the Psyche*, p. 120.

Chapter 19: Sage

1. Stuart Kaplan, *The Encyclopaedia of Tarot*, p. 289.
2. Sarah Maitland, *The Book of Silence*.
3. CW 14, *Mysterium Coniunctionis*, § 258.
4. CW 14, *Mysterium Coniunctionis*, § 313.
5. See *The Phenomenology of the Spirit in Fairytales*, in CW 9i, § 384-455.
6. CW 9i, *The Archetypes and the Collective Unconscious*, § 402.
7. Here I have summarised James Hillman's chapter "On senex consciousness," in Patricia Berry (ed.), *Fathers and mothers*, pp. 18-36.
8. *Saturn Devouring His Son* (1819) by Francisco Goya (1746-1828), en.wikipedia.org/wiki/Saturn_Devouring_His_Son.
9. C. G. Jung, *Memories, Dreams, Reflections*, p. 326.
10. W. B. Yeats, *The Celtic Twilight*, p. 136.
11. Quoted in Joseph Cambray, *Synchronicity*, p. 69.
12. Carlos Castaneda, *Journey to Ixtlan*, p. 234.
13. Hunbatz Men, *Secrets of Mayan Science/Religion*, p. 84.
14. Michael Owen, *Jung and the Native American Moon Cycles*, p. 244.
15. CW 12, *Psychology and Alchemy*, § 111.
16. CW 8, *The Structure and Dynamics of the Psyche*, § 768-795.
17. CW 14, *Psychology and Alchemy*, § 312.

Chapter 20: Wheel

1. Tony Shearer, *Beneath the Moon and Under the Sun*, p. 102.
2. John Major Jenkins, *Maya Cosmogenesis 2012*, p. 97.
3. Henry V, Act 3 Scene VI.

Chapter 20: Wheel

4. C. G. Jung, *Letters 2*, p. 525, December 5, 1959.
5. Sallie Nichols, *Jung and Tarot*, p. 187.
6. C. G. Jung, *Memories, Dreams, Reflections*, p. 297.

Chapter 21: Balance

1. Linda Schele and David Freidel, *A Forest of Kings*, p. 161.
2. See www.maquahuitl.co.uk and en.wikipedia.org/wiki/macuahuitl
3. Linda Schele and Mary Ellen Miller, *The Blood of Kings*, pp. 66–73.
4. CW 10, *Civilization in Transition*, § 856.
5. I am indebted to David Whyte's poem *No one told me* for this image.
6. Marie-Louise von Franz and James Hillman, *Lectures on Jung's Typology*, p. 98.
7. Michael Owen, *Jung and the Native American Moon Cycles*, pp. 262–263.
8. Carlos Castaneda, *The Power of Silence*, p. 34.
9. C. G. Jung, *Letters 2*, p. 172.
10. Edward Edinger, *Anatomy of the Psyche*, p. 9.
11. CW 11, *Psychology and Religion: West and East*, § 396.
12. CW 17, *The Development of Personality*, § 207.
13. Douglas Gillette, *The Shaman's Secret*, pp. 67–70.
14. See Harley SwiftDeer Reagan, *Shamanic Wheels and Keys*; Hyemeyohsts Storm's story of the Twelve Worlds in *Song of Heyoehkah*, pp. 291–293; Nancy Red Star, *Star Ancestors*; and Chris Morton and Ceri Thomas, *The Mystery of the Crystal Skulls*.

Chapter 22: Hanged Man

1. en.wikipedia.org/wiki/Calvary, www.newadvent.org/cathen/03191a.htm.
2. CW 9ii, *Aion*, § 79.
3. CW 16, *The Practice of Psychotherapy*, § 470.
4. CW 9ii, *Aion*, § 126.
5. CW 7, *Two Essays on Analytical Psychology*, § 78.
6. Stefan Lovgren, *Lost Gospel Revealed; Says Jesus Asked Judas to Betray Him*, National Geographic News, April 6, 2006, http://news.nationalgeographic.com/news/2006/04-/0406_060406_judas.html.
7. CW 5, *Symbols of Transformation*, § 117-119. Italics in original.
8. CW 13, *Alchemical Studies*, § 20.
9. CW 11, *Psychology and Religion: West and East*, § 497.
10. C. G. Jung, *The Interpretation of Visions* (Spring, 1962), p. 154.
11. CW 5, *Symbols of Transformation*, § 461.
12. Edward Edinger, *Anatomy of the Psyche*, p. 101.
13. Edward Edinger, *Ego and Self: The Old Testament Prophets*, pp. 39, 63.
14. CW 11, *Psychology and Religion*, § 428.
15. Friedrich Holderlin (1770–1843), German poet.
16. CW 14, *Mysterium Coniunctionis*, § 307.
17. Marie-Louise von Franz, *Alchemy*, pp. 252–254.
18. CW 17, *The Development of Personality*, § 295–296.
19. Michelangelo, *The Sonnets of Michelangelo*, p. 32.

Chapter 23: Dead Man

1. See Marie-Louise von Franz, *On Dreams and Death*.
2. See www.ballgame.org
3. David Freidel, *Maya Cosmos*, p. 374; Douglas Gillette, *The Shaman's Secret*, p. 98.
4. Edward Edinger, *The Mystery of the Coniunctio*, p. 16.
5. CW 16, *The Practice of Psychotherapy*, § 537.
6. William Shakespeare, *A Midsummer Night's Dream*, Act V, Scene II, 12–17.

Chapter 23: Dead Man

7. Edward Edinger, *Anatomy of the Psyche*, pp. 85–87.
8. Stanton Marlan, *The Black Sun*, p. 22.
9. Marie-Louise von Franz, *Alchemy*, p. 254.
10. Stanton Marlan, *The Black Sun*, pp. 22–23.
11. Annemarie Schimmel, *The Mystery of Numbers*, p. 203.
12. Thomas Ogden, *The Primitive Edge of Experience*.
13. Aldo Carotenuto, *Eros and Pathos*, p. 81.
14. It's Alright, Ma (I'm Only Bleeding), *Bringing It All Back Home*, 1965.
15. CW 8, *The Structure and Dynamics of the Psyche*, § 800.
16. Douglas Gillette, *The Shaman's Secret*, pp. 80–84.
17. Carlos Castaneda, *Tales of Power*, p. 196.

Chapter 24: Temperate Man

1. CW 12, *Psychology and Alchemy*, § 148.
2. See Elemire Zolla, *The Androgyne*.
3. Carlos Castaneda, *The Fire from Within*, pp. 19, 53, 73.
4. Marie-Louise von Franz, *Alchemy*, p. 222.
5. R. Matthaei (ed.) *Goethe's Colour Theory*. New York: Van Nostrand Reinhold, p. 71. Original work published 1810.
6. Khunrath, quoted in Jung, CW 14, *Mysterium Coniunctionis*, § 392.
7. C. G. Jung, *C. G. Jung Speaking*, p. 228ff.
8. See Raymond Lee, *The Rainbow Bridge*.
9. CW 14, *Mysterium Coniunctionis*, § 388–401.
10. Genesis 9:12–13.
11. Edward Edinger, *The Bible and the Psyche*, pp. 22–23.
12. Edward Edinger, *Ego and Self: The Old Testament Prophets*, pp. 73–74.
13. CW 13, *Alchemical Studies*, § 359n.
14. In this section I draw from Chapter 9, "The Blood of Christ," in Edward Edinger, *Ego and Archetype*, pp. 225–259.
15. Exodus 24:4–8.
16. CW 7, § 76.
17. CW 14, *Mysterium Coniunctionis*, § 229.
18. Ibid., § 306.
19. Ibid., § 189.
20. Oriah Mountain Dreamer, *Confessions of a Spiritual Thrillseeker*, pp. 190-191.
21. D. H. Lawrence, "Tortoise Shout," in *Birds, Beasts and Flowers*.
22. See William Anderson, *Green Man*.
23. CW 14, *Mysterium Coniunctionis*, § 137.
24. John Hill, Amplification: Unveiling Emergent Patterns of Meaning, in Murray Stein (ed.) (2010) *Jungian Psychoanalysis: Working in the Spirit of Carl Jung*. Open Court: Chicago.
25. See CW 14, § 368–463.
26. C. G. Jung, *Letters 2*, p. xxxix. June 27, 1947.
27. C. G. Jung, *Letters 1*, p. 486.
28. As told to Natalie Curtis c. 1904, in Joseph Campbell, *The Power of Myth*, pp. 8, 18.
29. Annemarie Schimmel, *The Mystery of Numbers*, p. 209.
30. CW 8, *The Structure and Dynamics of the Psyche*, § 249.
31. C. G. Jung, *Psychological Reflections*.
32. See www.philemonfoundation.org
33. Louis Ginzberg, *Legends of the Bible*, p. 558.
34. Attributed to Saint Thomas Aquinas (1225–1274), Italian philosopher and Catholic theologian. Marie-Louise von Franz, *Aurora Consurgens*, p. 105.
35. Marie-Louise von Franz, *Alchemy*, pp. 264–265.
36. CW 11, *Psychology and Religion*, § 199–201, 272–274.

Chapter 24: Temperate Man

37. Marie-Louise von Franz, *Aurora Consurgens*, p. 166.
38. Gary Sparks, *At the Heart of Matter*, p. 153.
39. Alice Howell, *The Web in the Sea*, pp. 2-3.
40. CW 14, *Mysterium Coniunctionis*, § 247-249.
41. Edward Edinger, *The Bible and the Psyche*, p. 132.
42. CW 13, *Alchemical Studies*, § 54.
43. CW 9i, *The Archetypes and the Collective Unconscious*, § 64.
44. "Answer to Job," in CW 11, *Psychology and Religion*.
45. Edward Edinger, *The Bible and the Psyche*, p. 133.
46. Universal Declaration of Human Rights, General Assembly of the United Nations, 1948.
47. Marie-Louise von Franz, *C. G. Jung: His Myth in Our Time*, pp. 122, 136, 138.
48. Edward Edinger, *Anatomy of the Psyche*, p. 223.
49. Gilbert, in *The Critic as Artist*, part 1, published in *Intentions* (1891).
50. CW 14, *Mysterium Coniunctionis*, § 742.
51. Michael Owen, *Jung and the Native American Moon Cycles*, pp. 210–235.

Chapter 25: Bound Man

1. Quoted in Anne Maguire (2004) *Skin Disease: A Message from the Soul (A Treatise from a Jungian Perspective of Psychosomatic Dermatology)*. p. 38. From Louis Herbert Gray, (1920) *The Mythology of All Races*. Boston: Marshall Jones. p. 76.
2. Gerald May, *Addiction and Grace*, p. 14.
3. Anne Cameron, *Daughters of Copper Woman*, pp. 45–46.
4. Nathan Schwartz-Salant, *The Mystery of Human Relationship*, pp. 108, 120.
5. See "The Psychology of the Transference" in CW 16, *The Practice of Psychotherapy*, § 402–539.
6. Edward Edinger, *The Sacred Psyche*, p. 85.
7. Quoted in Adler, Gerhard (1975) Aspects of Jung's Personality and Work, in *Psychological Perspectives*, 6:1, 12.
8. CW 9ii, *Aion*, § 19.
9. Lynn Andrews, *Crystal Woman: Sisters of the Dreamtime*, p. 219.
10. C. G. Jung, *Nietzsche's Zarathustra*, p. 846.
11. Carlos Castaneda, *The Fire from Within*, pp. 33–34.
12. Marie-Louise von Franz, *C. G. Jung: His Myth in Our Time*, pp. 99, 137, 263.
13. Quoted in Edward Edinger, *The Sacred Psyche*, pp. 17–18.
14. Edward Edinger, *Ego and Self: The Old Testament Prophets*, pp. 43–44.
15. CW 14, *Mysterium Coniunctionis*, § 342.
16. C. G. Jung, *Visions Seminars*, pp. 624–625.
17. CW 14, *Mysterium Coniunctionis*, § 104.
18. John Layard, "The incest taboo and the virgin archetype," p. 149.
19. See Michael Stone, *Abnormalities of Personality: Within and Beyond the Realm of Treatment*.
20. CW 8, *The Structure and Dynamics of the Psyche*, § 107.
21. Perhaps misattributed to Saint Augustine (354–430 CE) and more likely from a homily by Saint Bernard of Clairvaux (1090–1153 CE).
22. Corinthians 7:8–9.
23. CW 16, *The Practice of Psychotherapy*, § 471.
24. Edward Edinger, *The Mysterium Lectures*, p. 187.
25. CW 14, *Mysterium Coniunctionis*, § 108.
26. John Layard, "The incest taboo and the virgin archetype," p. 157.
27. Jung discusses this in "The Psychology of the Transference," CW 16, § 425–449.
28. CW 16, *The Practice of Psychotherapy*, § 419.
29. John Layard, "The incest taboo and the virgin archetype," p. 167.
30. CW 16, *The Practice of Psychotherapy*, § 445.
31. Marie-Louise von Franz, *Alchemy*, p. 97.

Chapter 25: Bound Man

32. C. G. Jung, *Memories, Dreams, Reflections*, p. 325.
33. Helen Luke, *The Voice Within*, p. 20.
34. Carlos Castaneda, *The Art of Dreaming*, pp. 3-4.
35. CW 6, *Psychological Types*, § 761.
36. CW 18, *The Symbolic Life*, § 1095.
37. CW 9i, *The Archetypes and the Collective Unconscious*, § 278.
38. CW 8, *The Structure and Dynamics of the Psyche*, § 432.

Chapter 26: Released Man

1. David Freidel, Anthropology 3312, Mesoamerican Archaeology, Maya Civilization, Classic Maya States, September 18, 2006, p. 11.
2. Peter Balin, *The Way of the Sorcerer*, p. 28.
3. Edward Edinger, *Ego and Self: The Old Testament Prophets*, p. 92.
4. Marie-Louise von Franz, *Alchemy*, p. 218.
5. Michael Owen, *Jung and the Native American Moon Cycles*, pp. 206-207.
6. Diane Arbus (1923-1971), American photographer and writer.
7. Marie-Louise von Franz, *The Cat*, p. 119.

Chapter 27: Star

1. From Thomas Kirsch, *Initiation: The Living Reality of an Archetype*.
2. See Ronald Goodman, *Lakota Star Knowledge*.
3. http://news.bbc.co.uk/2/hi/science/nature/2679675.stm, 22-01-2003.
4. Hyemeyohsts Storm, *Song of Heyoehkah*, pp. 291-292.
5. Nancy Red Star, *Star Ancestors*.
6. Harald Meller, "Star Search," *National Geographic*, January 2004, pp. 77-86.
7. C. G. Jung, *Memories, Dreams, Reflections*, pp. 356-358.
8. CW 12, *Psychology and Alchemy*, § 32.
9. Hunbatz Men, *Secrets of Mayan Science/religion*, p. 57.
10. Annie Dillard, *Holy the Firm*, pp. 68-69.
11. CW 9i, *The Archetypes and the Collective Unconscious*, § 221.
12. CW 8, *The Structure and Dynamics of the Psyche*, § 771.
13. CW 9i, *The Archetypes and the Collective Unconscious*, § 638.
14. Marie-Louise von Franz, *C. G. Jung: His Myth in Our Time*, p. 74.
15. C. G. Jung, The Interpretation of Visions. *Spring*, 1969, p. 72.
16. Marie-Louise von Franz, *Alchemy*, pp. 263-264.
17. Ibid., p. 266.
18. Mary Ellen Miller, *The Gods and Symbols of Ancient Mexico and the Maya*, p. 140.
19. C. G. Jung, *Memories, Dreams, Reflections*, pp. 321-322.
20. CW 7, *Two Essays on Analytical Psychology*, § 275.
21. CW 9i, *The Archetypes and the Collective Unconscious*, § 343.

Chapter 28: Moon

1. Marie-Louise von Franz, *Alchemy*, p. 150.
2. Erich Neumann, "On the moon and matriarchal consciousness," pp. 61, 68.
3. Lisel Mueller (1996) *Alive Together: New and Selected Poems*, Lousiana State University Press. Also quoted in James Hillman, *The Azure Vault*.
4. Mircea Eliade, *Patterns in Comparative Religion*, pp. 154-187.
5. Edward Edinger, *The Mysterium Lectures*, pp. 106, 109.
6. Macrobius, *The Dream of Scipio*. In Edward Edinger, *Anatomy of the Psyche*, p. 134.
7. Michael Owen, *Jung and the Native American Moon Cycles*, p. 12.
8. Carlos Castaneda, *The Second Ring of Power*, p. 164.
9. Martin Brennan, *The Hidden Maya*, p. 34.

Chapter 28: Moon

10. David Freidel, *Maya Cosmos*, pp. 101–107, 425.
11. CW 16, *The Practice of Psychotherapy*, § 493.

Chapter 29: Sun

1. However Robert Johnson quotes this as, "There are many occasions for true happiness in human beings. The first is a surplus of energy. The second is the cessation of pain. The third is the absolute certainty that we are doing the will of God." See Robert Johnson, *Balancing Heaven and Earth*.
2. Ken Carey, *The Bird Tribes*, pp. 20, 45.
3. Marie-Louise von Franz, *Alchemy*, p. 172.
4. Verena Kast, *Joy, Inspiration and Hope*, p. 44.
5. CW 11, *Psychology and Religion*, § 151.
6. Ibid., § 276.
7. Quoted in CW 13, *Alchemical Studies*, § 104.
8. Annie Dillard, *Pilgrim at Tinker Creek*, p. 11.
9. James Hillman, *The Azure Vault*.
10. "Paracelsus as a Spiritual Phenomenon" in CW 13, *Alchemical Studies*, § 145–238.

Chapter 30: Planet Venus

1. Quoted in CW 14, *Mysterium Coniunctionis*, § 415n.
2. www.transitofvenus.co.nz/explorations/rs_cooks_1v.html
3. Edward Edinger, *Archetype of the Apocalypse*, p. 4.
4. See Stephen Hunt (2001) *Christian Millenarianism*. London: C. Hurst.
5. Tim LaHaye and Jerry Jenkins (1996) *Left Behind: A Novel of the Earth's Last Days*. Wheaton, IL: Tyndale House.
6. W. B. Yeats, *The Second Coming*.
7. Edward Edinger, *Archetype of the Apocalypse*, p. 169.
8. CW 11, *Psychology and Religion*.
9. Edward Edinger, *The Bible and the Psyche*, pp. 35, 40, 49.
10. CW 16, *The Practice of Psychotherapy*, § 513.
11. Alice Howell, *The Web in the Sea*, p. 44.
12. Edward Edinger, *Ego and Self: The Old Testament Prophets*, p. 28.
13. Dhyani Ywahoo, *Voices of Our Ancestors*.
14. Matthew Restall (2003) *Seven Myths of the Spanish Conquest*. Oxford: Oxford University Press. http://en.wikipedia.org/wiki/Quetzalcoatl.
15. Susan Milbrath, *Star Gods of the Maya*, p. 274.
16. Excerpt from Chapter 15, "The Written Hymns of Quetzalcoatl," in D. H. Lawrence, *The Plumed Serpent*.

Chapter 31: Planet Earth

1. CW 14, *Mysterium Coniunctionis*, § 351-352.
2. In this section I summarise Edward Edinger, *Ego and Archetype*, pp. 260–295.
3. For further examples of stones and their powers see Janet and Colin Bord, *The Secret Country*, pp. 31–64.
4. CW 14, *Mysterium Coniunctionis*, § 763.
5. Marie-Louise von Franz, *Divination and Synchronicity*, pp. 109-110.
6. Quoted in Stanton Marlan, *The Black Sun*, pp. 176-177.
7. Carlos Castaneda, *The Fire from Within*, p. 33.
8. C. G. Jung, *Letters 1*, pp. 449–50. December 18, 1946.
9. Juan Cirlot, *A Dictionary of Symbols*, p. 54.
10. C. G. Jung, *Memories, Dreams, Reflections*, p. 320.

Chapter 31: Planet Earth

11. James Hillman, *In Defense of Melancholia*. Symposium, Pacifica Graduate Institute, Santa Barbara, California, November 7, 1992.
12. James Hillman, *The Azure Vault*.
13. Quoted in CW 14, *Mysterium Coniunctionis*, § 11.
14. CW 14, *Mysterium Coniunctionis*, § 536.
15. CW 14, *Mysterium Coniunctionis*, § 691, 705, 763, 764, 774.
16. Martin Brennan, *The Hidden Maya*, p. 101.
17. For a more detailed explanation see David Freidel, *Maya Cosmos*, pp. 75–107.
18. CW 12, *Psychology and Alchemy*, § 357.
19. Munro Edmonson, *The Book of the Year*, p. 194.
20. Giorgio Santillana and Hertha von Dechend, *Hamlet's Mill*.
21. Barbara Tedlock, *Time and the Highland Maya*, pp. 89, 245.
22. John Major Jenkins, *Maya Cosmogenesis 2012*, p. 77.
23. Ibid., pp. 330, 332.
24. D. H. Lawrence, 1929. Unknown source.
25. James Hillman, *And Huge is Ugly*.
26. Edward Edinger, *Anatomy of the Psyche*, p. 130.
27. Carlos Castaneda, *Tales of Power*, pp. 292–293.

Bibliography

Abelar, Taisha (1993) *The Sorcerer's Crossing: A Woman's Journey*. New York: Penguin.

Andrews, Lynn (1984) *Flight of the Seventh Moon: The Teaching of the Shields*. San Francisco: Harper & Row.

_____ (2006) *Jaguar Woman*. New York: Jeremy Tarcher.

_____ (2007) *Medicine Woman*. New York: Jeremy Tarcher.

Bachelard, Gaston (2002) *Earth and Reveries of Will: An Essay on the Imagination of Matter*, trans. Kenneth Haltman. Dallas: Dallas Institute Publications.

Balin, Peter (1977) *The Way of the Sorcerer*. Venice, CA: Wisdom Garden Books.

_____ (1978) *The Flight of Feathered Serpent*. Venice, CA: Wisdom Garden Books.

_____ (2010) *The Xultun Tarot*. Tauranga: Kahurangi.

Barber, Elizabeth and Paul Barber (2004) *When They Severed Earth from Sky: How the Human Mind Shapes Myth*. Princeton: Princeton University Press.

Baring, Ann (1991) Cinderella: An Interpretation, in Murray Stein and Lionel Corbett (eds.) *Psyche's Stories: Modern Jungian Interpretations of Fairy Tales*. Wilmette, IL: Chiron.

Bayley, Harold (2006) *The Lost Language of Symbolism: An Inquiry into the Origin of Certain Letters, Words, Names, Fairy-Tales, Folklore, and Mythologies*. New York: Dover.

Bell, Hannah Rachel (1998) *Men's Business, Women's Business: The Spiritual Role of Gender in the World's Oldest Culture*. Rochester, VT: Inner Traditions.

Bly, Robert (1990) *Iron John: A Book About Men*. New York: Addison-Wesley.

Bord, Janet and Colin (1978) *The Secret Country*. London: Paladin.

Brennan, Martin (1998) *The Hidden Maya*. Santa Fe, NM: Bear & Co.

Cambray, Joseph (2009) *Synchronicity: Nature and Psyche in an Interconnected Universe*. College Station, TX: Texas A & M University Press.

Cameron, Anne (1981) *Daughters of Copper Woman*. Vancouver: Press Gang Publishers.

Campbell, Joseph (1988) *The Power of Myth*. New York: Doubleday, 1988.

Carey, Ken (1991) *The Bird Tribes*. San Francisco: HarperCollins, 1991.

Carotenuto, Aldo (1989) *Eros and Pathos: Shades of Love and Suffering*. Toronto: Inner City.

Castaneda, Carlos (1972) *Journey to Ixtlan: The Lessons of Don Juan*. New York: Simon & Schuster.

_____ (1974) *Tales of Power*. New York: Pocket Books.

_____ (1981) *The Eagle's Gift*. New York: Pocket Books.

_____ (1984) *The Fire From Within*. New York: Simon & Schuster.

_____ (1987) *The Power of Silence: Further Lessons of Don Juan*. New York: Simon & Schuster.

_____ (1993) *The Art of Dreaming*. New York: HarperCollins.

Cirlot, Juan (1971) *A Dictionary of Symbols (2nd ed.)*. London: Routledge.

Coe, Michael (2000) *Breaking the Maya Code*. London: Penguin.

Cook, Roger (1974) *The Tree of Life: Image for the Cosmos*. New York: Avon.

Corbett, Lionel (n.d.) *Basic Jung*. Lecture notes, www.pacifica.edu.

Cowan, Lyn (2002) *Tracking the White Rabbit: A Subversive View of Modern Culture*. London: Routledge.

Cozolino, Louis (2006) *The Neuroscience of Human Relationships: Attachment and the Developing Social Brain*. New York: W.W. Norton.

Dillard, Annie (1977) *Holy the Firm*. New York: Harper & Row.

_____ (1985) *Pilgrim at Tinker Creek*. New York: HarperPerennial.

Donner, Florinda (1992) *Being-in-Dreaming: An Initiation into the Sorcerer's World*. New York: HarperCollins.

Dorp, Cornelius Van (1992) *Crystal Mission*. Auckland: RSVP Publishing.

Driscoll, Carlos (2009) *The Evolution of House Cats*, June 2009, www.scientificamerican.com/article.cfm?id=the-taming-of-the-cat.

Edinger, Edward (1972) *Ego and Archetype: Individuation and the Religious Function of the Psyche*. New York: Putnam.

_____ (1985) *Anatomy of the Psyche: Alchemical Symbolism in Psychotherapy*. La Salle, IL: Open Court.

_____ (1986) *The Bible and the Psyche: Individuation Symbolism in the Old Testament*. Toronto: Inner City.

_____ (1994) *The Mystery of the Coniunctio: Alchemical Image of Individuation*. Toronto: Inner City.

_____ (1995) *The Mysterium Lectures: A Journey Through C. G. Jung's Mysterium Coniunctionis*. Toronto: Inner City.

_____ (1999) *Archetype of the Apocalypse: A Jungian Study of the Book of Revelation*. Chicago: Open Court.

_____ (2000) *Ego and Self: The Old Testament Prophets from Isaiah to Malachi*. Toronto: Inner City.

_____ (2004) *The Sacred Psyche: A Psychological Approach to the Psalms*. Toronto: Inner City.

Edmonson, Munro (1988) *The Book of the Year: Middle American Calendrical Systems*. Salt Lake City: University of Utah Press.

Ehrenreich, Barbara (1997) *Blood Rites: Origins and History of the Passions of War*. New York: Henry Holt.

Eliade, Mircea (1958) *Patterns in Comparative Religion*. Lincoln, NB: University of Nebraska Press.

Fonagy, Peter (2002) *Attachment Theory and Psychoanalysis*. New York: Other Press.

Freidel, David, Linda Schele and Joy Parker (1993) *Maya Cosmos: Three Thousand Years on the Shaman's Path*. New York: William Morrow.

Gad, Irene (1994) *Tarot and Individuation: Correspondences With Cabala and Alchemy*. York Beach, ME: Nicholas-Hays.

Giles, Cynthia (1996) *The Russian Tarot of St. Petersburg*. Stamford, CT: US Games.

Gill, Richardson (2001) *The Great Maya Droughts: Water, Life, and Death*. Albuquerque, NM: University of New Mexico Press.

Gillette, Douglas (1997) *The Shaman's Secret: The Lost Resurrection Teachings of the Ancient Maya*. New York: Bantam Books.

Gillette, Douglas and Robert Moore (1992) *The King: Accessing the King in the Male Psyche*. New York: William Morrow.

Ginzberg, Louis (1956) *Legends of the Bible*. New York: Simon & Schuster.

Goodman, Ronald (1992) *Lakota Star Knowledge: Studies in Lakota Stellar Theology*. Rosebud, SD: Sinte Gleska University.

Greene, Liz and Juliet Sharman-Burke (2001) *The Mythic Tarot*. New York: Fireside.

Greer, Mary (2002) *The Complete Book of Tarot Reversals*. Woodbury, MN: Llewellyn.

Grof, Stanislav (1975) *Realms of the Human Unconscious: Observations from LSD Research*. New York: Viking.

Hannah, Barbara (2006) *The Archetypal Symbolism of Animals*. Wilmette, IL: Chiron.

Hegel, G. W. F. (1988) *Introduction to the Philosophy of History*. Cambridge: Hackett.

Henderson, Joseph (1967) *Thresholds of Initiation*. Middletown: Wesleyan University Press.

Hillman, James (1972) *Pan and the Nightmare*. Zurich: Spring.

_____ (1980) Silver and White Earth, Part Two. *Spring*, 21–63.

_____ (1981) Alchemical Blue and the Unio Mentalis, in C. Eshleman (ed.) *Sulfur 1: A Literary Tri-Quarterly of the Whole Art*, Pasadena: California Institute of Technology Press, 1981. p. 37.

_____ (1988) *And Huge is Ugly*, Tenth Annual E. F. Schumacher Memorial Lecture, Bristol, England.

_____ (1990) On senex consciousness, in Patricia Berry (ed.), *Fathers and mothers* (Dallas, TX: Spring.

_____ (1991) *A Blue Fire: Selected Writings by James Hillman*. New York: HarperPerennial.

_____ (1997) *The Soul's Code: In Search of Character and Calling*. New York: Warner Books.

_____ (2004) *A Terrible Love of War*. New York: Penguin Press.

_____ (2006) The Azure Vault: the caelum as experience. In L. Cowan (ed.) *Barcelona 04, Edges of Experience: Memory and Emergence, Proceedings 16th International IAAP Congress of Analytical Psychology*. Einsedeln: Daimon Verlag.

Hornby, Nick (1996) *Fever Pitch*. London: Indigo.

Howell, Alice (1993) *The Web in the Sea: Jung, Sophia and Geometry of the Soul*. Wheaton, IL: Quest.

Hyland, Queenie Rikihana (2003) *Illustrated Maori Myths and Legends*. Wellington: Reed Books.

Jacoby, Mario (2001) *Jungian Psychotherapy and Contemporary Infant Research: Basic Patterns of Emotional Exchange*. London: Routledge.

James, Kenneth (1994) *The Tarot: Dynamic Map of the Psyche (4 Audiotapes)*. Evanston, IL: C. G. Jung Institute of Chicago.

_____ (1998) *The Sevenfold Path to Wholeness: Tarot Meditation and Divination Techniques (5 Audiotapes)*. Evanston, IL: C. G. Jung Institute of Chicago.

Jenkins, John Major (1998) *Maya Cosmogenesis 2012*. Santa Fe, NM: Bear & Co.

Johnson, Robert (1998) *Balancing Heaven and Earth*. New York: HarperOne.

Jung, Carl Gustav (1953–1979) *The Collected Works*. Herbert Read, Michael Fordham and Gerhard Adler, eds. Princeton: Princeton University Press.

_____ (1964) *Man and His Symbols*. London: Aldus.

_____ (1973) *Letters, Vol. 1, 1906–1950*. Gerhard Adler and Aniela Jaffe (eds.) Princeton: Princeton University Press.

_____ (1973) *Letters, Vol. 2, 1951–1961*. Gerhard Adler and Aniela Jaffe (eds.) Princeton: Princeton University Press.

_____ (1987) *C. G. Jung Speaking: Interviews and Encounters*. Princeton: Princeton University Press.

_____ (1989) *Memories, Dreams, Reflections.*. New York: Vintage Books.

_____ (1997) *Visions: Notes of the Seminar Given in 1930-1934, Vol. 1*. Claire Douglas (ed.) Princeton: Princeton University Press.

_____ (1998) *Nietzsche's Zarathustra*. Princeton: Princeton University Press.

Kaplan, Stuart (1978) *The Encyclopaedia of Tarot*. New York: US Games.

Kast, Verena (1984) *The Nature of Loving: Patterns of Human Relationship*. Wilmette, IL: Chiron.

_____ (1991) *Joy, Inspiration and Hope*. College Station, TX: Texas A & M University Press.

Keeney, Bradford (ed.) (2003) *Ropes to God: Experiencing the Bushman Spiritual Universe*. Philadelphia, PA: Ringing Rocks Press.

Kingsolver, Barbara (1998) *The Poisonwood Bible*. London: Faber & Faber.

Kirsch, Thomas (Ed.) (2007) *Initiation: The Living Reality of an Archetype*. London: Routledge.

Krakowski, Richard (1997) www.erowid.org/culture/references/other/1997_krakowski_resproject_1.shtml.

Kremer, Jurgen and Fausto Flores (n.d.) *The Ritual Suicide of Maya Rulers*. Rheinische Friedrich-Wilhelms Universität, Bonn, winter semester 1991/92.

LaHaye, Tim and Jerry Jenkins (1995) *Left Behind: A Novel of the Earth's Last Days*. Wheaton, IL: Tyndale House.

Lawrence, D. H. (1992) *The Plumed Serpent*. Vintage: New York.

Layard, John (1942) *Stone Men of Malekula*. Chatto and Windus, London.

_____ (1982) The incest taboo and the virgin archetype, in Joanne Stroud and Gail Thomas (eds.) *Images of the Untouched: Virginity in Psyche, Myth and Community*. Dallas, TX: Spring.

Lee, Raymond and Alistair Fraser (2001) *The Rainbow Bridge: Rainbows in Art, Myth, and Science*. University Park, PA: Penn State University Press.

Lovgren, Stefan (2006) *Lost Gospel Revealed; Says Jesus Asked Judas to Betray Him*, National Geographic News, April 6, 2006, http://news.nationalgeographic.com/news/2006/04/04-06_060406_judas.html.

Loomis, Mary (1991) *Dancing the Wheel of Psychological Types*. Wilmette, Ill: Chiron.

Lovelock, James and Lynn Margulis (1979) *Gaia: A New Look at Life on Earth*. Oxford: Oxford University Press.

Luke, Helen (1988) *The Voice Within: Love and Virtue in the Age of the Spirit*. New York: Crossroad.

Maitland, Sarah (2008) *The Book of Silence*. London: Granta.

Margulis, Lynn (2000) *Symbiotic Planet: A New Look at Evolution*. New York: Basic Books.

Marlan, Stanton (2005) *The Black Sun: The Alchemy and Art of Darkness*. College Station, TX: Texas A & M University Press.

May, Gerald (1991) *Addiction and Grace: Love and Spirituality in the Healing of Addictions*. New York: HarperOne.

Men, Hunbatz (1990) *Secrets of Mayan Science/Religion*. Santa Fe, NM: Bear & Co.

Menzies, Gavin (2005) *1421: The Year China Discovered America*. New York: Harper.

_____ (2009) *1434: The Year a Magnificent Chinese Fleet Sailed to Italy and Ignited the Renaissance*. New York: Harper.

Milbrath, Susan (1999) *Star Gods of the Maya: Astronomy in Art, Folklore, and Calendars*. Austin, TX: University of Texas Press.

Miller, Mary Ellen and Karl Taube (1993) *The Gods and Symbols of Ancient Mexico and the Maya: An Illustrated Dictionary of Mesoamerican Religion*. New York: Thames and Hudson.

Montgomery, John (2001) *Tikal: An Illustrated History of the Ancient Maya Capital*. New York: Hippocrene Books.

Montgomery, Roger (1995) *Twenty Count: Secret Mathematical System of the Aztec/Maya*. Santa Fe, NM: Bear & Company.

Morton, Chris and Ceri Thomas (2002) *The Mystery of the Crystal Skulls*. Rochester, VT: Bear & Co.

Mountain Dreamer, Oriah (1991) *Confessions of a Spiritual Thrillseeker: Medicine Teachings from the Grandmothers*. Toronto: Moonfox Press.

Mueller, Lisel (1996) *Alive Together: New and Selected Poems*, Lousiana State University Press.

Mutwa, Credo (1996) *Song of the Stars*. New York: Barrytown.

Neihardt, John (1932) *Black Elk Speaks: Being the Life Story of a Holy Man of the Ogalala Sioux*. Lincoln, NB: University of Nebraska Press.

Neumann, Erich (1956) On the moon and matriarchal consciousness, in *Dynamic Aspects of the Psyche*. New York: Analytical Psychology Club of New York.

Nichols, Sallie (1980) *Jung and Tarot*. York Beach, ME: Samuel Weiser.

Nuttall, Zelia (ed.) (1975) *The Codex Nuttall: A Picture Manuscript from Ancient Mexico, The Peabody Facsimile Edition*. Dover: New York.

Ogden, Thomas (1989) *The Primitive Edge of Experience*. Northvale, NJ: Jason Aronson.

Owen, Michael (2002) *Jung and the Native American Moon Cycles: Rhythms of Influence*. York Beach, ME: Nicolas-Hays.

Perry, John Weir (1991) *Lord of the Four Quarters: The Mythology of Kingship*. New York: Paulist Press.

Pollack, Rachael (2002) *The Forest of Souls: A Walk Through the Tarot*. St Paul, MN: Llewellyn.

Reagan, Harley SwiftDeer (1988) *The Mirror of Self-Reflection: The Inner Mirror Masks of the Mask of Self-Pity*. Privately published. Scottsdale, AZ: Deer Tribe Metis Medicine Society.

_____ (1994) *Shamanic Wheels and Keys: The Teachings of the Twisted Hairs Elders of Turtle Island, Volume 1*. Privately published. Scottsdale, AZ: Deer Tribe Metis Medicine Society.

_____ as Thunder Strikes (1999) Song *of the Deer: The Great SunDance Journey of the Soul*. Malibu, CA: Jaguar Books.

_____ as Thunder Strikes and Janneke Koole (2005) *Conscious Assembly Workbook*. Privately published. Scottsdale, AZ: Deer Tribe Metis Medicine Society.

Red Star, Nancy (2000) *Star Ancestors: Indian Wisdomkeepers Share the Teachings of the Extraterrestrials*. Rochester, VT: Destiny Books.

Restall, Matthew (2003) *Seven Myths of the Spanish Conquest*. Oxford: Oxford University Press. http://en.wikipedia.org/wiki/Quetzalcoatl.

Ribi, Alfred (1989) *Demons of the Inner World: Understanding Our Hidden Complexes*. Boston: Shambhala.

Sabini, Meredith (2002) *The Earth has a Soul: The Nature Writings of C.G. Jung*. Berkeley, CA: North Atlantic Books.

Sams, Jamie (1990) *Sacred Path Cards*. New York: HarperCollins.

____ (1994) *The Thirteen Original Clan Mothers*. New York: HarperCollins.

Sams, Jamie and David Carson (1988) *Medicine Cards*. New York: St Martin's Press.

Santillana, Giorgio and Hertha von Dechend (1969) *Hamlet's Mill: An Essay Investigating the Origins of Human Knowledge and its Transmission through Myth*. Cambridge, MA: Harvard.

Saunders, Nicholas (2001) A dark light: reflections on obsidian in Mesoamerica, *World Archaeology*, 33(2), p. 221.

Schapira, Laurie Layton (1988) *The Cassandra Complex: Living with Disbelief, a Modern Perspective on Hysteria*. Toronto: Inner City.

Schele, Linda and David Freidel (1990) *A Forest of Kings: The Untold Story of the Ancient Maya*. New York: William Morrow.

Schele, Linda and Mary Ellen Miller (1986) *The Blood of Kings: Dynasty and Ritual in Maya Art*. New York: George Braziller.

Schele, Linda and Peter Matthews (1998) *The Code of Kings: The Language of Seven Sacred Maya Temples and Tombs*. New York: Simon & Schuster.

Schimmel, Annemarie (1993) *The Mystery of Numbers*. New York: Oxford University Press.

Schore, Allan (1999) *Affect Regulation and the Origin of the Self: The Neurobiology of Emotional Development*. Hillsdale, NJ: Lawrence Erlbaum.

Schultes, Richard and Albert Hoffman (2001) *Plants of the Gods: Their Sacred Healing and Hallucinogenic Powers*. Rochester, VT: Inner Traditions.

Schwartz-Salant, Nathan (1989) *The Borderline Personality: Vision and Healing*. Wilmette, IL: Chiron.

Schwartz-Salant, Nathan (1998) *The Mystery of Human Relationship: Alchemy and the Transformation of the Self*. London: Routledge.

Segal, Hannah (1973) *Introduction to the Work of Melanie Klein*. London: Hogarth.

Shearer, Tony (1975) *Beneath the Moon and Under the Sun: A Re-appraisal of the Sacred Calendar and Prophecies of Ancient Mexico*. Santa Fe, NM: Sun Publishing.

Sparks, Gary (2007) *At the Heart of Matter: Synchronicity and Jung's Spiritual Testament*. Toronto: Inner City.

Steele, Edward (1998) *Lamarck's Signature: How Retrogenes are Changing Darwin's Natural Selection Paradigm*. Reading, MA: Perseus Books.

Stone, Michael (1993) *Abnormalities of Personality: Within and Beyond the Realm of Treatment*. New York: Norton.

Storm, Hyemeyohsts (1973) *Seven Arrows*. New York: Ballantine.

____ (1981) *Song of Heyoehkah*. New York: Ballantine.

____ (1994) *Lightningbolt*. London: HarperCollins.

Tedlock, Barbara (1992) *Time and the Highland Maya*. Albuquerque: Univ. of New Mexico Press.

van der Post, Laurens and Jane Taylor (1985) *Testament to the Bushman*. London: Penguin.

van Corva, Claudia and Thunder Strikes (2000) *The Thirty Sacred Laws: The Teachings of the Twisted Hairs Elders of Turtle Island, Volume II, Part 1, The Universal and Cosmic Laws*. Privately published. Scottsdale, AZ: Deer Tribe Metis Medicine Society.

____ (2002) *The Thirty Sacred Laws: The Teachings of the Twisted Hairs Elders of Turtle Island, Volume II, Part 2, The Magickal Laws*. Privately published. Scottsdale, AZ: Deer Tribe Metis Medicine Society.

____ (2009) *The Thirty Sacred Laws: The Teachings of the Twisted Hairs Elders of Turtle Island, Volume II, Part 3, The Ecological Balance Laws*. Privately published. Scottsdale, AZ: Deer Tribe Metis Medicine Society.

von Franz, Marie-Louise (1970) *Interpretation of Fairytales*. Dallas, TX: Spring.

____ (1975) *C. G. Jung: His Myth in Our Time*. London: Hodder & Stoughton.

____ (1980) *Alchemy: An Introduction to the Symbolism and the Psychology*. Toronto: Inner City.

____ (1980) *On Divination and Synchronicity: The Psychology of Meaningful Chance*. Toronto: Inner City.

____ (1986) *Shadow and Evil in Fairytales*. Dallas, TX: Spring.

____ (1998) *On Dreams & Death: A Jungian Interpretation*. Chicago: Open Court.

____ (1999) *The Cat: A Tale of Feminine Redemption*. Toronto: Inner City.

____ (2000) *Aurora Consurgens: A Document Attributed to Thomas Aquinas on the Problem of Opposites in Alchemy*. Toronto: Inner City.

von Franz, Marie-Louise and James Hillman (1986) *Lectures on Jung's Typology*. Dallas, TX: Spring.

Waitaha, Ngati Kowhai o (2003) *Song of Waitaha: The Histories of a Nation (2nd ed.)* Christchurch: Wharariki Press.

Weininger, Otto (1992) *Melanie Klein: From Theory to Reality*.London: Karnac.

____ (1993) *View from the Cradle: Children's Emotions in Everyday Life*. London: Karnac.

Whyte, David (1992) *Fire in the Earth*. Langley, WA: Many Rivers Press.

Wickes, Frances (1963) *The Inner World of Choice*. Englewood Cliffs, NJ: Prentice-Hall.

Wolff, Toni (1951) *Structural Forms of the Feminine Psyche*. Privately published, C. G. Jung Institute, Zurich.

Woloy, Eleanora (1990) *The Symbol of the Dog in the Human Psyche*. Wilmette, IL: Chiron.

Yeats, William Butler (2004) *The Celtic Twilight: Faerie and Folklore*. New York: Dover.

Ywahoo, Dhyani (1987) *Voices of Our Ancestors: Cherokee Teachings from the Wisdom Fire*. Boston: Shambhala.

Zolla, Elemire (1981) *The Androgyne: Reconciliation of Male and Female*. New York: Crossroads.

Index

CARD, AUTHOR AND NAME INDEX
and SUBJECT INDEX

Subject Index

Appendix

	Marseilles Tarot	Xultun Tarot
0	Fool	Fool
1	Magician	Sorcerer
2	Papess	Priestess
3	Empress	Consort
4	Emperor	Ruler
5	Pope	Priest
6	Lovers	Lovers
7	Chariot	Warrior
8	Strength	Cactus
9	Hermit	Sage
10	Wheel of Fortune	Wheel
11	Justice	Balance
12	Hanged Man	Hanged Man
13	Death	Dead Man
14	Temperance	Temperate Man
15	Devil	Bound Man
16	Tower	Released Man
17	Star	Star
18	Moon	Moon
19	Sun	Sun
20	Judgement	Planet Venus
21	World	Planet Earth

Figure 101. The Marseilles Tarot and the Xultun Tarot

Figure 102. The Marseilles Tarot
(Layout the same as the Xultun Tarot)

PRIESTESS	CONSORT	RULER	PRIEST	LOVERS
Emotional Feeling	Physical Feeling	Mental Feeling	Spiritual Feeling	Soul Feeling
Keeper of the Heart of the Child Substance Shield	Keeper of the Body of the Child Substance Shield	Keeper of the Mind of the Child Substance Shield	Keeper of the Spirit of the Child Substance Shield	Keeper of the Soul of the Child Substance Shield
Holder of Emotional Sweetness	Holder of Physical Sweetness	Holder of Mental Sweetness	Holder of Spiritual Sweetness	Holder of Soul Sweetness
Teacher of Erasing Emotional History	Teacher of Using Emotional Death as an Advisor	Teacher of Stopping the Emotional World	Teacher of Controlling the Emotional Dream	Teacher of Assuming Emotional Authority
Awakened by the Moon	Awakened by the Sun	Awakened by Planet Venus	Awakened by Planet Earth	Awakened by the Priestess
Awakens the Lovers	Awakens the Warrior	Awakens the Cactus	Awakens the Sage	Awakens the Wheel
Dreamed by the Bound Man	Dreamed by the Released Man	Dreamed by the Star	Dreamed by the Moon	Dreamed by the Sun
Dreams the Sage	Dreams the Wheel	Dreams the Balance	Dreams the Hanged Man	Dreams the Dead Man
Completion of the Dead Man	Completion of the Temperate Man	Completion of the Bound Man	Completion of the Released Man	Completion of the Star
Completed by the Balance	Completed by the Hanged Man	Completed by the Dead Man	Completed by the Temperate Man	Completed by the Bound Man

WARRIOR	CACTUS	SAGE	WHEEL	BALANCE
Emotional Thinking	Physical Thinking	Mental Thinking	Spiritual Thinking	Soul Thinking
Keeper of the Heart of the Adult Substance Shield	Keeper of the Body of the Adult Substance Shield	Keeper of the Mind of the Adult Substance Shield	Keeper of the Spirit of the Adult Substance Shield	Keeper of the Soul of the Adult Substance Shield
Holder of Emotional Cunning	Holder of Physical Cunning	Holder of Mental Cunning	Holder of Spiritual Cunning	Holder of Soul Cunning
Teacher of Erasing Mental History	Teacher of Using Mental Death as an Advisor	Teacher of Stopping the Mental World	Teacher of Controlling the Mental Dream	Teacher of Assuming Mental Authority
Awakened by the Consort	Awakened by the Ruler	Awakened by the Priest	Awakened by the Lovers	Awakened by the Warrior
Awakens the Balance	Awakens the Hanged Man	Awakens the Dead Man	Awakens the Temperate Man	Awakens the Bound Man
Dreamed by Planet Venus	Dreamed by Planet Earth	Dreamed by the Priestess	Dreamed by the Consort	Dreamed by the Ruler
Dreams the Temperate Man	Dreams the Bound Man	Dreams the Released Man	Dreams the Star	Dreams the Moon
Completion of the Moon	Completion of the Sun	Completion of Planet Venus	Completion of Planet Earth	Completion of the Priestess
Completed by the Released Man	Completed by the Star	Completed by the Moon	Completed by the Sun	Completed by Planet Venus

HANGED MAN	DEAD MAN	TEMPERATE MAN	BOUND MAN	RELEASED MAN
Emotional Sensation	Physical Sensation	Mental Sensation	Spiritual Sensation	Soul Sensation
Keeper of the Heart of the Adult Spirit Shield	Keeper of the Body of the Adult Spirit Shield	Keeper of the Mind of the Adult Spirit Shield	Keeper of the Spirit of the Adult Spirit Shield	Keeper of the Soul of the Adult Spirit Shield
Holder of Emotional Ruthlessness	Holder of Physical Ruthlessness	Holder of Mental Ruthlessness	Holder of Spiritual Ruthlessness	Holder of Soul Ruthlessness
Teacher of Erasing Physical History	Teacher of Using Physical Death as an Advisor	Teacher of Stopping the Physical World	Teacher of Controlling the Physical Dream	Teacher of Assuming Physical Authority
Awakened by the Cactus	Awakened by the Sage	Awakened by the Wheel	Awakened by the Balance	Awakened by the Hanged Man
Awakens the Released Man	Awakens the Star	Awakens the Moon	Awakens Sun	Awakens Planet Venus
Dreamed by the Priest	Dreamed by the Lovers	Dreamed by the Warrior	Dreamed by the Cactus	Dreamed by the Sage
Dreams the Sun	Dreams Planet Venus	Dreams Planet Earth	Dreams the Priestess	Dreams the Consort
Completion of the Consort	Completion of the Ruler	Completion of the Priest	Completion of the Lovers	Completion of the Warrior
Completed by Planet Earth	Completed by the Priestess	Completed by the Consort	Completed by the Ruler	Completed by the Priest

STAR	MOON	SUN	PLANET VENUS	PLANET EARTH
Emotional Intuition	Physical Intuition	Mental Intuition	Spiritual Intuition	Soul Intuition
Keeper of the Heart of the Child Spirit Shield	Keeper of the Body of the Child Spirit Shield	Keeper of the Mind of the Child Spirit Shield	Keeper of the Spirit of the Child Spirit Shield	Keeper of the Soul of the Child Spirit Shield
Holder of Emotional Patience	Holder of Physical Patience	Holder of Mental Patience	Holder of Spiritual Patience	Holder of Soul Patience
Teacher of Erasing Spiritual History	Teacher of Using Spiritual Death as an Advisor	Teacher of Stopping the Spiritual World	Teacher of Controlling the Spiritual Dream	Teacher of Assuming Spiritual Authority
Awakened by the Dead Man	Awakened by the Temperate Man	Awakened by the Bound Man	Awakened by the Released Man	Awakened by the Star
Awakens Planet Earth	Awakens the Priestess	Awakens the Consort	Awakens the Ruler	Awakens the Priest
Dreamed by the Wheel	Dreamed by the Balance	Dreamed by the Hanged Man	Dreamed by the Dead Man	Dreamed by the Temperate Man
Dreams the Ruler	Dreams the Priest	Dreams the Lovers	Dreams the Warrior	Dreams the Cactus
Completion of the Cactus	Completion of the Sage	Completion of the Wheel	Completion of the Balance	Completion of the Hanged Man
Completed by the Lovers	Completed by the Warrior	Completed by the Cactus	Completed by the Sage	Completed by the Wheel

Figure 103. The Types, Shields, Moods, Movements and Alchemy of the Xultun Tarot

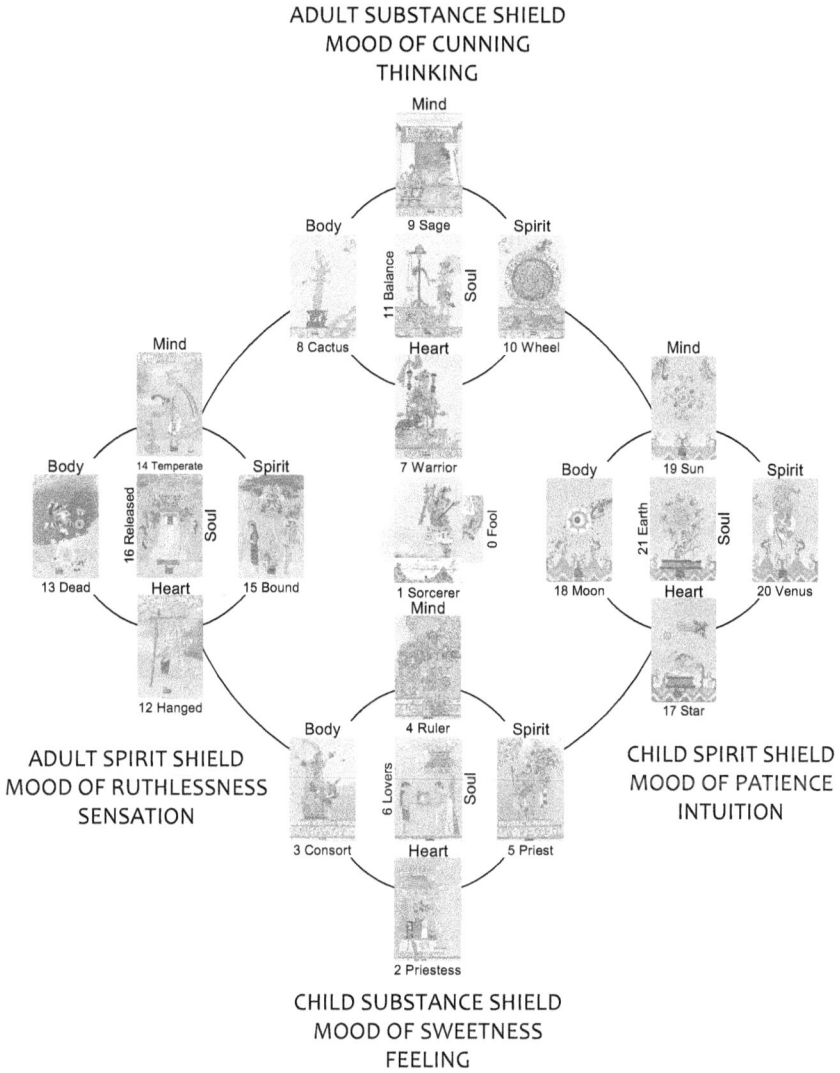

Figure 104. The Shields, Moods and Types of the Xultun Tarot
(Each wheel is a row of the Xultun Tarot and they move South–North–West–East.
To download a full colour .pdf go to www.xultun.com/page23.html)

STOPPING THE WORLD

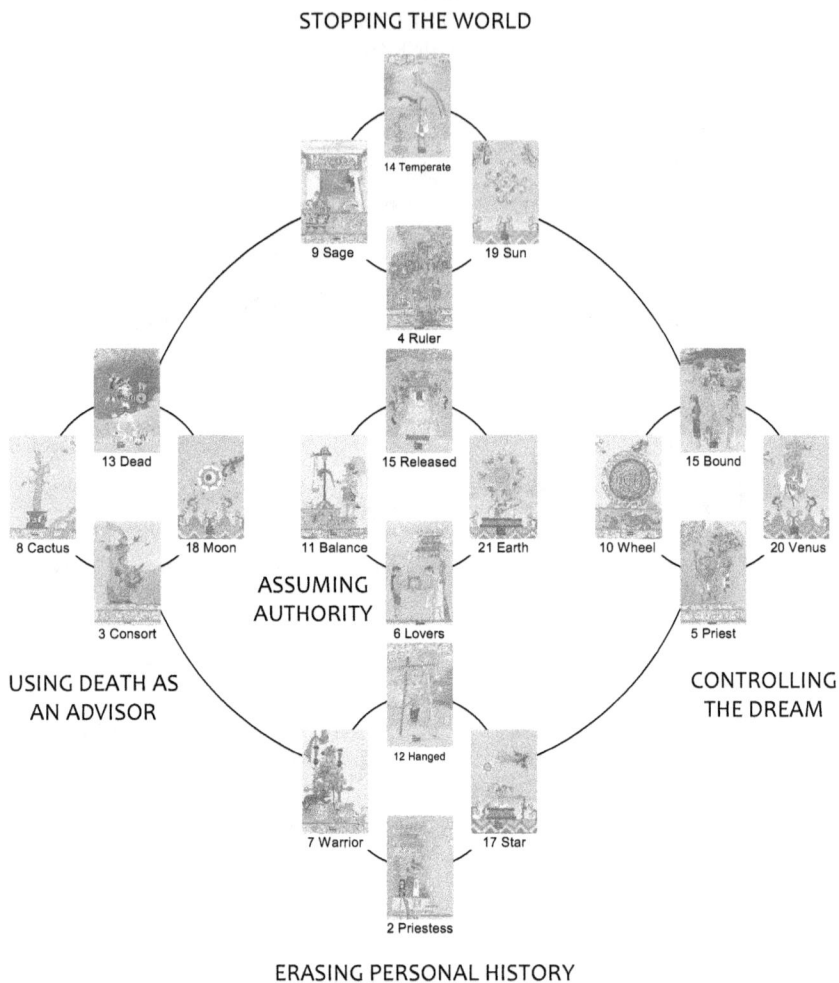

14 Temperate

9 Sage   19 Sun

4 Ruler

13 Dead   15 Released   15 Bound

8 Cactus   18 Moon   11 Balance   21 Earth   10 Wheel   20 Venus

3 Consort   6 Lovers   5 Priest

ASSUMING
AUTHORITY

USING DEATH AS   CONTROLLING
AN ADVISOR   THE DREAM

12 Hanged

7 Warrior   17 Star

2 Priestess

ERASING PERSONAL HISTORY

Figure 105. The Movements of the Xultun Tarot
(Each wheel is a column of the Xultun Tarot and they move South–West–North–East.
To download a full colour .pdf go to www.xultun.com/page23.html)

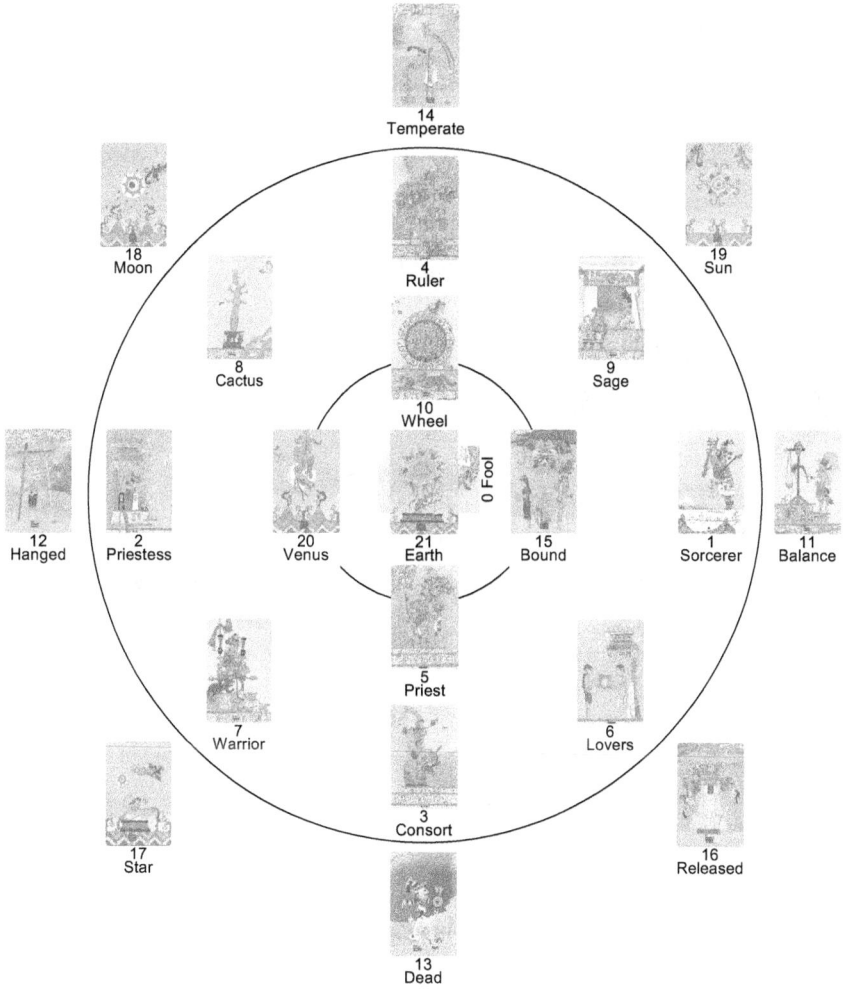

Figure 106. The Twenty Count and the Xultun Tarot
(To download a full colour .pdf go to www.xultun.com/page23.html)

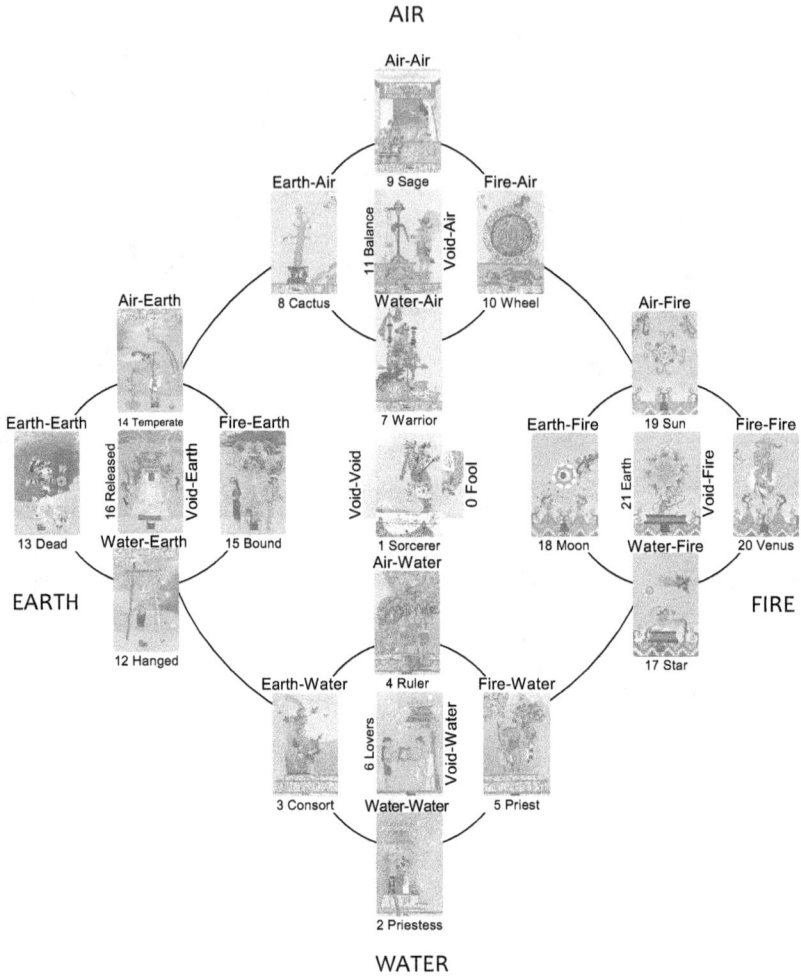

Figure 107. The Elements of the Xultun Tarot
(To download a full colour .pdf go to www.xultun.com/page23.html)

SOUTH
Heart
Erasing Personal History

WEST
Body
Using Death as an Advisor

NORTH
Mind
Stopping the World

EAST
Spirit
Controlling the Dream

CENTRE
Soul
Assuming Authority

SOUTH
Child Substance Shield
Sweetness without Foolishness
Water
Feeling

NORTH
Adult Substance Shield
Cunning without Cruelty
Air

WEST
Adult Spirit Shield
Ruthlessness without Harshness
Earth
Sensation

EAST
Child Spirit Shield
Patience without Negligence
Fire
Intuition

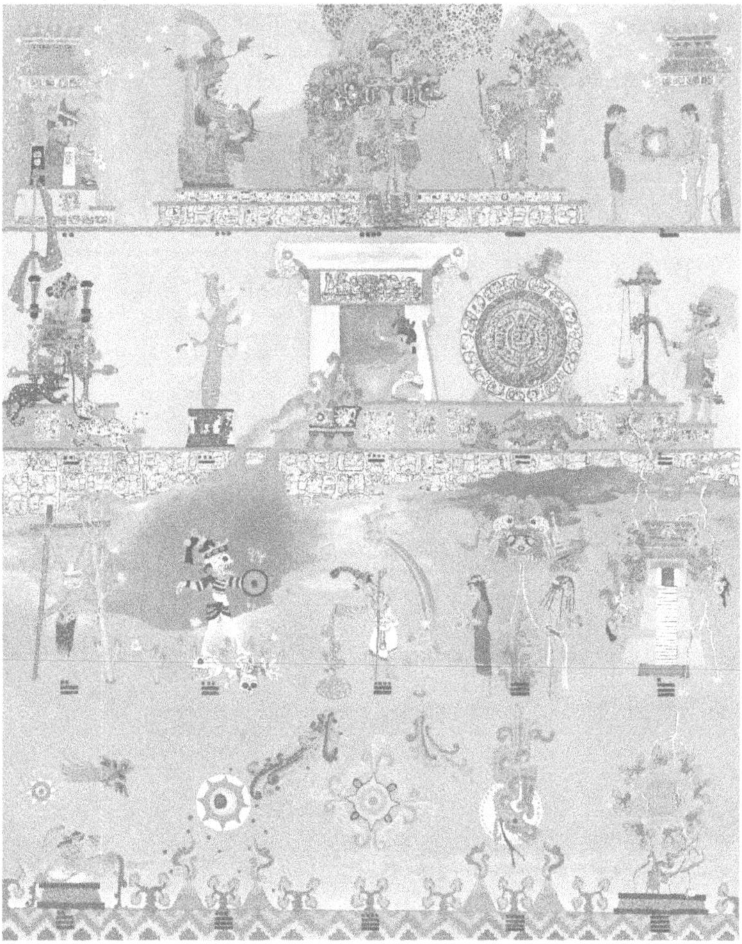

Figure 108. The Xultun Tarot
(The columns are the Aspects of Humans and the Movements.
The rows are the Shields, Moods, Elements and Types.
To download a full colour .pdf go to www.xultun.com/page23.html)

Figure 109. The Major Arcana of the Xultun Tarot
(To download a full colour .pdf go to www.xultun.com/page23.html)

MORE FROM KAHURANGI PRESS

XULTUN MAYA TAROT Classic Edition
by Peter Balin
The Xultun Tarot was created by Peter Balin in 1976. It was the first indigenous tarot deck and is based on images from Maya history and culture. Taken from a single painting, it is the only tarot where the major arcana form a complete picture. This picture tells the story of the marriage of spirit and matter and what C G Jung called the individuation process.
Original large size and vibrant colours, major and minor arcana, Kahurangi Press 2010, 80 cards, boxed, 136 x 89 mm, 5.3 x 3.5 ins
USD40.00 Amazon.com or Xultun.com (free shipping)

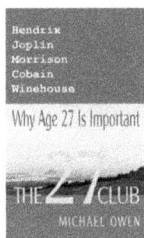

THE MAYA BOOK OF LIFE: Understanding the Xultun Tarot
by Michael Owen
The companion book to the Xultun Tarot explores the archetypes and alchemy of the major arcana through indigenous teachings and the analytical psychology of C G Jung.
Kahurangi Press 2010, ISBN 978-0-473-11989-8, 500 pages, 108 illustrations
USD40.00 Amazon.com or Xultun.com (free shipping)

THE 27 CLUB: Why Age 27 Is Important
by Michael Owen
Is the 27 club just a myth? (No). Is it a "curse?" (No). But The 27 Club is not what you think. It's more than the deaths of Jimi Hendrix, Amy Winehouse and others. Using the teachings of the Moon Cycles and C. G. Jung's notion of the puer (the creative person who is always young beyond his years and often dies an early death, physical or emotional) Michael Owen explains what happens to all of us in our mid- to late-twenties. Read about the other "Clubs" from 24 to 30. [for more visit www.27-club.net]
Kahurangi Press, 2012, 140 pages
USD9.99 Amazon.com or Xultun.com (free shipping)

JUNG AND THE NATIVE AMERICAN MOON CYCLES
by Michael Owen
The Moon Cycles teach us about the archetypal forces that affect throughout our lives. This book offers new insights into Jung's life and death and provides a fascinating perspective on some of Jung's important dreams. It also casts new light on Jung's fateful encounter with Freud as well as his relationships with women and his supposed anti-Semitism. See how to place the events of your own life on the Moon Cycles and gain a new perspective on the births and deaths (inner and outer) in your life. You will see what learning periods are ahead of you according to the 9 month, 3 year and 27 year cycles.
Nicolas-Hays, 2002, 288 pages
USD22.95 Amazon.com or **GBP16.99** Amazon.co.uk

KAHURANGI PRESS
www.kahurangi-press.com | www.xultun.com | www.27-club.net